# CRIMINAL LITIGATION PRACTICE AND PROCEDURE

Gary Atkinson

CLP

Published by

College of Law Publishing,
Braboeuf Manor, Portsmouth Road, St Catherines, Guildford GU3 1HA



British Library Cataloguing-in-Publication Data
A catalogue record for this book is available from the British Library.

ISBN 978 1 905391 36 3

Typeset by Style Photosetting Ltd, Mayfield, East Sussex
Printed in Great Britain by Ashford Colour Press Ltd, Gosport, Hampshire

# CRIMINAL LITIGATION PRACTICE AND PROCEDURE

# Preface

This book has been written principally for students studying criminal litigation as part of the Legal Practice Course (LPC). The book is designed so that it may be used both by students studying the basics of criminal litigation on the compulsory part of the LPC, and also students studying advanced criminal litigation as an elective subject. Although intended primarily as a student text, it is hoped that the level of detail in the book will also make it of use to trainee and newly qualified solicitors.

The book concentrates on the practice and procedure of criminal litigation, from the initial investigations carried out by the police through to appeals following conviction. Matters of substantive criminal law only arise where necessary to illustrate a point of practice or procedure, or in the context of the law of evidence.

The book employs a case study which has been integrated into the text to illustrate the most common documents that are created during the course of criminal proceedings, and how such documents should be drafted. In addition, worked examples are used to explain complex points of procedure and evidence. Flowcharts are provided, where appropriate, to demonstrate procedures. Each chapter concludes with a checklist, summarising the key points the chapter has covered. The appendix includes extracts from the Magistrates' Court Sentencing Guidelines.

I have endeavoured to state the law as at 30 June 2007.

In the interests of brevity, the masculine pronoun has been used throughout to include the feminine.

GARY ATKINSON
*York*

# Acknowledgements

Writing a textbook requires support from colleagues and others. I am fortunate to have enjoyed unstinting help and assistance from a number of people at the College of Law, but particular thanks must go to Sean Hutton for his valuable comments. Thanks must also go to David Stott for his ongoing editorial support and guidance, and to Alistair MacQueen for his enthusiasm and commitment to this project. More generally, I would like to thank all those colleagues who have taken an interest in the writing of this book, together with those students who have taken the trouble to provide constructive comments on the previous edition.

*For Jess*

# Contents

# Table of Cases

## S



## T



## W

# Table of Statutes

**International legislation**

# Table of Statutory Instruments

# Table of Abbreviations

| | |
|---|---|
| CJA | Criminal Justice Act [date] |
| CJPOA 1994 | Criminal Justice and Public Order Act 1994 |
| CPIA 1996 | Criminal Procedure and Investigations Act 1996 |
| CPO | community punishment order |
| CPS | Crown Prosecution Service |
| CrimPR | Criminal Procedure Rules 2005 |
| EAH | early administrative hearing |
| IPCC | Independent Police Complaints Commission |
| EFH | early first hearing |
| MCA 1980 | Magistrates' Courts Act 1980 |
| PACE 1984 | Police and Criminal Evidence Act 1984 |
| PCC(S)A 2000 | Powers of Criminal Courts (Sentencing) Act 2000 |
| PCMA | plea and case management hearing |
| PH | preparatory hearing |
| PTR | pre-trial review |
| RDCO | recovery of defence costs order |
| SOCA | Serious Organised Crime Agency |
| SOCPA 2005 | Serious Organised Crime and Police Act 2005 |
| TIC | (offences) taken into consideration |
| YJCEA 1999 | Youth Justice and Criminal Evidence Act 1999 |

# Part 1
# INTRODUCTION

# Chapter 1
# Introduction to Criminal Procedure



## 1.1 Introduction

If a member of the general public was asked to explain what he thought the job of a solicitor entailed, there is a very good chance that in his reply he would say that solicitors spend much of their time in court representing those who are accused of having committed criminal offences. Whilst it is not the case that every solicitor in practice spends his time representing clients charged with having committed a criminal offence, all solicitors need to have a thorough understanding of the criminal litigation process. At some stage in his professional life, a solicitor will be asked to advise a client (whether an individual or a limited company) on a matter of criminal law or procedure.

The purpose of this book is to provide an introduction to criminal procedure and evidence. Whilst the book is intended primarily for use by students studying the Legal Practice Course (LPC), it is hoped that it will also be of use to trainee and newly-qualified solicitors.

This introductory chapter (**Part 1**) covers a number of preliminary matters which are necessary for an understanding of how the criminal litigation process works. The chapter will begin by defining the role played by various persons or bodies within the criminal justice system. It will then go on to explain how criminal offences are classified and how this classification determines which type of court may deal with a particular offence. The chapter will also cover matters of professional conduct and human rights, together with an introduction to the Criminal Procedure Rules 2005.

Subsequent chapters will examine the functions and powers of the police in the criminal litigation process, and the role played by a solicitor who represents a client at the police station (**Part 2**). This will be followed by an explanation of the procedures that take place in both the magistrates' court and the Crown Court between a defendant being charged with an offence and his trial taking place (**Part 3**). The rules governing sentencing and the making of an appeal against conviction and/or sentence will then be examined (**Part 4**). Specific chapters are devoted to proceedings in the youth court and to the prosecution of road traffic offences (**Part 5**). The book will conclude with an introduction to the law of evidence and an explanation of the key evidential issues which commonly arise in the course of criminal proceedings (**Part 6**).

## 1.2 Key personnel

### 1.2.1 Defence solicitors

Although there is nothing to prevent a defendant in criminal proceedings from representing himself at court, most defendants will be represented by a solicitor. The defence solicitor will often become involved in a criminal case by providing advice and assistance to a suspect in the police station, before the suspect is charged. If the suspect is charged, the defence solicitor will then represent that person in proceedings before the magistrates' court and, if necessary, the Crown Court. If the case reaches the Crown Court, it is likely that the defence solicitor will instruct a barrister to be the client's advocate in court (although the solicitor will still have a significant role to play – see **Chapter 10**).

The majority of defence solicitors are solicitors in private practice, although in certain parts of the country a government-funded public defender service exists.

### 1.2.2 The police

The police are responsible for the investigation of suspected criminal offences and the apprehension of persons alleged to have committed those offences. The police possess a wide range of powers which they may exercise in the investigation of suspected criminal offences. These include powers to stop and search suspected offenders, powers to search premises and the power to arrest suspects. Following an arrest, the police have additional powers which they may exercise whilst a suspect is detained at the police station. The extent of the powers which the police may exercise in the investigation of a criminal offence is examined in **Chapters 2 and 3**. The role played by the solicitor who is representing a suspect in the police station will be explained in **Chapter 4**. **Chapter 5** will examine the various options open to an individual in the event that the police exercise their powers improperly or are otherwise guilty of misconduct.

Although the police will investigate the overwhelming majority of alleged criminal offences, other agencies exist to investigate particular types of crime (for example, HM Revenue & Customs, the Health and Safety Executive or the trading standards department of a local authority). The Serious Organised Crime and Police Act 2005 created a new body, the Serious Organised Crime Agency (SOCA). The rationale behind its creation was the establishment of a national agency able to combat criminal enterprises specialising in drugs and violence, together with tax evasion and serious fraud. Although the powers of agencies such as SOCA are beyond the scope of this book, it should be appreciated that they have extensive investigative powers which sometime exceed those which the police may exercise.

### 1.2.3 The Crown Prosecution Service

The Crown Prosecution Service (CPS) is responsible for prosecuting individuals (and companies) charged with having committed a criminal offence. The head of the CPS is the Director of Public Prosecutions (DPP).

Historically the police were responsible for deciding what charge a suspect should face. Once the police had charged the suspect, they would then pass the file to the CPS who would take over responsibility for the prosecution of the case before the criminal courts.

As a result of changes brought about by the Criminal Justice Act 2003, the CPS now plays a much fuller role at an earlier stage in the criminal process. For all but the most minor offences, responsibility for deciding the charge the suspect faces now rests with the CPS rather than the police. Representatives from the CPS are based in police stations, and once the police have completed their investigations, they will pass the file to the relevant CPS representative who will then decide if the suspect should be charged and, if so, what charge the suspect should face.

After a suspect has been charged, the CPS retains responsibility for the prosecution of the case. Solicitors from the CPS are responsible for collating the evidence on which the prosecution seek to rely and presenting this evidence to the court.

Although the CPS works closely with the police, it is an independent organisation. In deciding whether a prosecution should be brought, the CPS must apply the test set out in the Code for Crown Prosecutors. This provides that a prosecution should be brought only if there is enough evidence to provide a realistic prospect of conviction *and* it is in the public interest for a prosecution to be brought. Full details of the Code can be found on the CPS website (www.cps.gov.uk).

If the CPS declines to prosecute a case, an individual may bring a private prosecution. Such prosecutions are, however, rare and unlikely to succeed. Public funding is not available to finance a private prosecution, and the CPS has the power to take over the running of the prosecution and then to discontinue the proceedings.

In addition to the CPS, various other agencies (such as those noted at **1.2.2** above) may commence criminal proceedings against a defendant.

### 1.2.4 The magistrates' court

After a suspect has been charged with an offence, he will make his first appearance in court before the magistrates' court (unless he is aged 17 or under, in which case he will be normally be dealt with in the Youth Court – see **Chapter 14**). Depending on the type of offence with which the suspect has been charged, the case may either remain in the magistrates' court or be sent to the Crown Court for trial (see **1.3** below).

Approximately 95% of all criminal cases are dealt with by the magistrates' court. The functions of the magistrates' court include:

(a) issuing search and arrest warrants (see **Chapter 2**);
(b) issuing warrants for further detention under the Police and Criminal Evidence Act 1984 (see **Chapter 3**);
(c) trying summary offences and some either way offences (see **1.3** below);
(d) sending indictable only offences and committing some either way offences to the Crown Court for trial (see **1.3** below);
(e) dealing with applications for a representation order (see **Chapter 6**); and
(f) dealing with applications for bail (see **Chapter 7**).

Most magistrates are not legally qualified (although they do receive some training). They are members of the local community who have volunteered their services. It is usual for three magistrates to sit in court at any one time. The magistrates will be advised on matters of law, practice and procedure by a legal adviser (commonly referred to as the clerk to the justices). The legal adviser is responsible for the efficient running of the magistrates' court, and plays a significant role in proceedings. The legal adviser should not advise magistrates on questions of fact, only on matters of law.

In some magistrates' courts (particularly in large cities), a legally qualified magistrate known as a District Judge (Magistrates' Court) will sit alone to hear cases. This judge will be either a qualified solicitor, or a barrister.

### 1.2.5 The Crown Court

The Crown Court is the venue which deals with offenders charged with the most serious types of criminal offence. The main functions of the Crown Court are:

(a) to conduct the trial of and, following conviction, to sentence offenders convicted of all indictable only and some either way offences (see **1.3** below);
(b) to determine questions of bail and representation, particularly appeals by a defendant against the refusal of bail by the magistrates' court (see **Chapter 7**); and
(c) to hear appeals against conviction and/or sentence from the magistrates' court (see **Chapter 13**).

Proceedings in the Crown Court are before a judge and, if the case goes to trial, before a judge and jury. Judges of varying levels of seniority sit in the Crown Court. Most cases will be dealt with by a Circuit Judge. More serious cases (typically cases where the defendant is charged with murder, manslaughter or rape), and cases which are particularly high profile, will be heard before a High Court Judge. If the defendant pleads not guilty and the case goes to trial, the judge will decide matters of law and the jury matters of fact. If the Crown Court is hearing an appeal against sentence and/or conviction from the magistrates' court, no jury will be present but the judge will sit with between two and four magistrates.

Most advocacy in the Crown Court is performed by barristers (collectively referred to as counsel). Both the CPS and the solicitor representing the defendant will usually instruct a barrister to conduct their case in the Crown Court. Solicitors have very limited rights of audience in the Crown Court (see **Chapter 10**), although it is possible for solicitors achieve full rights of audience by passing a written and practical test.

### 1.2.6 The Probation Service

A representative from the Probation Service will always be present in court (whether the magistrates' court or the Crown Court) when a case is being heard. The Probation Service is responsible for compiling reports on defendants who have been convicted, should the court require a report before sentencing the defendant. Such reports are known as pre-sentence reports and focus on the defendant's background, previous convictions and likelihood of re-offending (see **Chapter 12**).

The Probation Service is also responsible for the administration of various types of community order which the court may impose as part of the sentence a defendant receives (see **Chapter 11**).

### 1.2.7 The Criminal Defence Service

The Criminal Defence Service (CDS) was created by the Access to Justice Act 1999. The purpose of the CDS is to provide funding for legal services for those suspected of having committed a criminal offence or facing criminal proceedings.

The CDS is funded by the Legal Services Commission. The CDS provides funding for defendants either by entering into a 'general criminal contract' with solicitors in private practice, or by providing salaried public defenders in certain parts of the country. All solicitors in private practice who wish to secure public funding for their clients must enter into a 'general criminal contract'.

Details of how a solicitor obtains public funding for a client charged with having committed a criminal offence are given in **Chapter 6**.

## 1.3 Classification of offences

### 1.3.1 Introduction

All criminal offences fall into one of three categories of offence: indictable only, either way or summary offences. It is necessary to know into which category a particular offence falls because the procedure at court for dealing with each type of offence is different.

### 1.3.2 Indictable-only offences

Indictable-only offences are the most serious form of criminal offence and must be dealt with by the Crown Court. Although a defendant charged with an indictable-only offence will make his first appearance before the magistrates' court, the magistrates will immediately send the case to the Crown Court for trial (see **Chapter 10**).

Examples of indictable-only offences include:

- murder;
- manslaughter;
- rape;
- robbery; and
- wounding/causing gbh with intent (s 18 of the Offences Against the Person Act 1861).

### 1.3.3 Either way offences

Either way offences can be dealt with either by the magistrates' court, or by the Crown Court. A defendant charged with an either way offence will make his first appearance before the magistrates' court, and the magistrates will then decide whether to keep the case before them or to commit the case to the Crown Court for trial because it is too serious for them to deal with. This is known as the mode of trial procedure. If the magistrates do decide to keep the case before them, the defendant has the right to elect trial by a judge and jury in the Crown Court (see **Chapter 6**).

Examples of either way offences include:

- theft;
- wounding/inflicting gbh (s 20 of the Offences Against the Person Act 1861);
- assault occasioning actual bodily harm (s 47 of the Offences Against the Person Act 1861);
- fraud; and
- most types of burglary.

Some of the powers which the police are granted by the Police and Criminal Evidence Act (PACE) 1984 may only be exercised in respect of offences which are termed 'indictable'. An indictable offence will be an indictable only offence *or* an either way offence.

### 1.3.4 Summary offences

Summary offences are the least serious form of criminal offence and may be dealt with only by the magistrates' court (see **Chapter 6**).

Examples of summary offences include:

- common assault (triable either way if racially or religiously aggravated);
- taking a conveyance without consent (TWOC); and
- various road traffic offences, such as driving whilst over the prescribed alcohol limit, speeding and careless driving.

Flowcharts giving an overview of the procedure for each type of offence are provided at **1.11** below.

## 1.4 The Criminal Procedure Rules 2005

### 1.4.1 Introduction

Prior to April 2005, the rules of procedure for both the magistrates' court and the Crown Court were found in a number of different statutes, statutory instruments and practice directions. The Criminal Procedure Rules (CrimPR), which came into effect in April 2005, placed these rules for the first time in one specific document. These rules are supplemented by the Consolidated Criminal Practice Direction. The Rules and Practice Direction can be found at www.dca.gov.uk.

### 1.4.2 The overriding objective (CrimPR, Part 1)

Rule 1.1(1) of the CrimPR states that the overriding objective of the Rules is 'that criminal cases be dealt with justly'. Under r 1.1(2), dealing with a criminal case 'justly' includes doing the following:

(a) acquitting the innocent and convicting the guilty;
(b) dealing with the prosecution and the defence fairly;
(c) recognising the rights of a defendant (particularly the right to a fair trial under Article 6 of the European Convention on Human Rights);
(d) respecting the interests of witnesses, victims and jurors, and keeping them informed of the progress of the case;
(e) dealing with the case efficiently and expeditiously;
(f) ensuring that appropriate information is available to the court when bail and sentence are considered;
(g) dealing with the case in ways that take into account the gravity of the offence alleged, the complexity of what is in issue, the severity of the consequences for the defendant and others affected, and the needs of other cases.

### 1.4.3 The duty of participants in a criminal case (CrimPR, Part 1)

Rule 1.2(2) of the CrimPR defines a participant as being 'anyone involved in any way with a criminal case'. This includes solicitors who are either prosecuting a case or representing the defendant. Each participant in a criminal case must prepare and conduct the case in accordance with the overriding objective and comply with the CrimPR. In particular, a participant must at once inform the court and all parties to the case of any significant failure to take any step required by the Rules (CrimPR, r 1.2(1)(c)).

### 1.4.4 The court's case management powers (CrimPR, Part 3)

Rule 1.3 of the CrimPR provides that the court must further the overriding objective. Under r 3.2(1), the court must do this by 'actively managing the case'. Active case management includes the following:

(a) the early identification of the real issues;
(b) the early identification of the needs of witnesses;
(c) achieving certainty as to what must be done, by whom, and when, in particular by the early setting of a timetable for the progress of the case;
(d) monitoring the progress of the case and compliance with directions;
(e) ensuring that evidence, whether disputed or not, is presented in the shortest and clearest way;
(f) discouraging delay, dealing with as many aspects of the case as possible on the same occasion, and avoiding unnecessary hearings;
(g) encouraging the participants to cooperate in the progression of the case;
(h) making use of technology.

Rule 3.3 provides that the parties in the case must assist the court in its duty actively to manage the case.

Under r 3.4(1), at the beginning of a case each party must nominate an individual responsible for the progress of the case, and must tell the other parties and the court who that individual is and how he may be contacted. Similarly, the court itself will nominate a court officer who is responsible for the progress of case (the 'case progression officer'). The case progression officer will ensure that the parties comply with any directions given by the court and keep the court informed about events which might affect the progress of the case.

Rule 3.5(1) provides the court with substantial case management powers to enable it actively to manage the case. The court is given the power to make any direction or take any step actively to manage a case, unless such a direction or step would contravene legislation. In particular the court may:

(a) nominate a judge, magistrate, justices' clerk or assistant to a justices' clerk to manage the case;
(b) give a direction on its own initiative or on application by a party;
(c) ask or allow a party to propose a direction;
(d) for the purpose of giving directions, receive applications and representations by letter, by telephone or by any other means of electronic communication, and conduct a hearing by such means;
(e) give a direction without a hearing;
(f) fix, postpone, bring forward, extend or cancel a hearing;
(g) shorten or extend a time limit fixed by a direction;
(h) require that issues in the case should be determined separately, and decide in what order they should be determined; and
(i) specify the consequences of failing to comply with a direction.

Integral to the court's active management of the case is r 3.8(1), which provides that whenever a case comes before the court, if the case cannot be concluded at that hearing, the court must give directions so that it can be concluded either at the next hearing or as soon as possible after that. Under r 3.8(2), at every hearing the court must, where relevant:

(a) if the defendant is absent – because he has failed to answer his bail – decide whether to proceed nonetheless (in *R v O'Hare* [2006] EWCA Crim 471, the Court of Appeal held that a trial could proceed in the absence of the defendant if he chose not to appear);
(b) ask the defendant to enter his plea of guilty or not guilty (unless he has already done so at an earlier hearing). If no plea can be taken, the court should ask what the defendant's plea is likely to be;
(c) set, follow or revise a timetable for the progress of the case;
(d) where a direction has not been complied with, find out why, identify who was responsible, and take appropriate action.

In a number of instances the Court of Appeal has stated that courts should take a robust view towards the progression of cases before them, and that judges should be less concerned with purely technical matters and more concerned with the overall interests of justice (see, for example, *R v Ashton* [2006] EWCA Crim 794 and *Malcolm v DPP* [2007] EWHC 363 (QB)).

## 1.5 The Criminal Justice Act 2003

In addition to the changes made to the management and organisation of the criminal litigation process by the CrimPR, huge changes to the substantive law of criminal procedure, evidence and sentencing have been made by the Criminal Justice Act 2003. The White Paper, *Justice for All* (2002), which preceded the Act, stated that the central purpose of the Act was to rebalance the criminal justice system in favour of victims and the community as a whole, whilst ensuring that suspects and offenders received fair treatment. The Act has made significant changes to most parts of the criminal litigation process, from the initial investigations carried out by the police through to the sentencing of offenders by the courts. Key sections of the Act will be analysed in subsequent chapters.

## 1.6 Professional conduct

### 1.6.1 Introduction

A solicitor involved in criminal litigation is likely to face issues of professional conduct on a regular basis. Set out below is a summary of the duties imposed on solicitors in criminal proceedings, and an overview of key areas of professional conduct of which a solicitor practising in this area should be aware.

### 1.6.2 Overriding duty not to mislead the court

Although one of the core duties owed to the client is that the solicitor must act in the client's best interests (Solicitors' Code of Conduct 2007, Rule 1), this duty does not extend to the solicitor deceiving or knowingly misleading the court. All solicitors involved in criminal proceedings have an overriding duty not to deceive or knowingly mislead the court (Solicitors' Code of Conduct 2007, Rule 11.01).

This duty is particularly important for a solicitor representing a defendant (see **1.6.4** below). The Code provides that the solicitor must treat the interests of the client as paramount, provided they do not conflict with the solicitor's obligations in professional conduct or the public interest in the administration of justice. In addition, Rule 1.06 states that a solicitor must not behave in a way which damages or is likely to damage the reputation or integrity of the profession.

If a client tells his solicitor that he intends to give evidence at court which is false (or that he intends to call a witness to give false evidence on his behalf), the solicitor must tell the client that he cannot be a party to this, and that he will need to withdraw from acting for the client unless the client agrees not to do this (see **1.6.4.11** below). To act for a client who places evidence before the court which the solicitor knows to be false is a clear breach of Rule 11.01 (the solicitor should also warn the client that to give false evidence may lead to the client, and any other witnesses who give false evidence on his behalf, being prosecuted for perjury or perverting the course of justice).

### 1.6.3 The prosecution

Prosecuting advocates are under a duty to ensure that all material evidence supporting the prosecution case is put before the court in a fair and dispassionate manner. In particular:

(a) when arguing a point of law, a prosecutor must inform the court of any relevant authority from statute or case law, even if that authority does not assist the prosecution case and favours the defendant;

(b) all relevant facts known to the prosecutor should be placed before the court including, if the defendant is convicted, any facts relevant to mitigation (see **Chapter 12**);

(c) if the prosecutor obtains evidence which may assist the defendant (for example, a witness who supports the defence case), the prosecutor must supply particulars of this evidence to the defence (see **Chapters 8 and 10**); and

(d) if a prosecution witness gives evidence at court which is inconsistent with any earlier statement made by that witness, the prosecuting solicitor should disclose this fact to the defence.

Prosecuting advocates are also under a duty to assist the court when the defendant is being sentenced by drawing attention to any statutory provisions that govern the court's sentencing powers (*R v Cain* [2006] All ER (D) 113 (Dec)).

### 1.6.4 The defence

#### 1.6.4.1 Accepting instructions from a third party

It is often the case that a solicitor will be asked by a relative or friend of a person who has been arrested to attend the police station to advise that person. Although there is nothing improper in this, the first step the solicitor should take in such circumstances is to telephone the police station and ask to speak to the arrested person, to determine if he wants the solicitor to attend the police station to act on his behalf. The solicitor should tell the arrested person that he is entitled to free legal advice from a solicitor of his choice, and he is not obliged to use him just because he has been contacted by his family or friends. Only if the arrested person decides to instruct the solicitor should that solicitor then attend the police station to represent the client.

#### 1.6.4.2 The client who admits his guilt

A client may admit his guilt to his solicitor during the course of the legal proceedings. Although it is still the client's decision as to what plea he should enter, the solicitor should advise the client that he would receive credit from the court when it comes to sentencing were he to enter an early guilty plea (see **Chapter 11**). If the client wishes to plead not guilty and insists on giving evidence in the witness box denying his guilt, the solicitor should decline to act. To act in such circumstances would involve misleading or deceiving the court (see **1.6.2** above). The solicitor may, however, properly continue to act on a not guilty plea if the defendant merely intends to put the prosecution to proof of its case without any evidence being given either by him or by any witnesses called on his behalf. Putting the prosecution to proof of its case means asking questions of prosecution witnesses in order to undermine or discredit their evidence. Such questioning should not, however, suggest facts to the court which the defence solicitor knows to be false. This important area of professional conduct is examined more fully in **Chapter 6**.

If a client admits his guilt to his solicitor at the end of a trial at which the client has been acquitted, the solicitor should not take any steps in response to this. As the court proceedings have concluded, there is no danger of the solicitor misleading the court. Nevertheless, the solicitor does owe a continuing duty of confidentiality to his client (see **1.6.4.5** below) which lasts beyond the end of the case, and so the solicitor should not disclose this admission to anyone else. A prudent solicitor will, however, make a note on the client's file of the admission that has been made, and will be cautious about representing the client in future.

A solicitor's personal opinion as to the truth of any defence his client intends to put forward is irrelevant. If a solicitor suspects that his client's defence is fabricated, but the client maintains the truthfulness of this defence, the solicitor will not risk breaching his overriding duty not to deceive or knowingly mislead the court by placing this defence before the court. Only if the client admits his guilt will the solicitor risk breaching this duty if he places before the court facts which he knows to be false.

If the client intends to enter a not guilty plea but the solicitor considers that the evidence against the client is such that the client will inevitably be convicted, the solicitor should advise the client of this fact and tell the client that he would receive a reduced sentence were he to enter an early guilty plea (see **Chapter 11**). The solicitor should not, however, insist that the client plead guilty.

### 1.6.4.3 The client with a defence who wants to plead guilty

Occasionally a client will wish to plead guilty despite the fact that his instructions indicate that he has a defence to the charge he faces. Typically this arises with clients who are apprehensive at the thought of having to take part in a trial. Such a client should be advised on the defence available to him. If he insists on pleading guilty, the solicitor may continue to act on his behalf. The client should be advised, however, that when delivering a plea of mitigation on the client's behalf, the solicitor will not be able to rely on the facts that may constitute a defence.

The solicitor should attempt to dissuade a client from pleading guilty to an offence the client denies having committed if the client wants to plead guilty as a matter of convenience or to get the case out of the way without the need for a trial to take place.

### 1.6.4.4 The client who gives inconsistent instructions

Defence solicitors regularly encounter clients who change their instructions. Typically a client will say one thing in the initial statement which he gives to his solicitor and will then change his story when he sees the evidence which the CPS seeks to rely upon. The mere fact that a client gives inconsistent instructions to his solicitor does not make it improper for the solicitor to continue to act on the client's behalf. If, however, it becomes clear to the solicitor that the client is changing his instructions with a view to putting forward false evidence to the court, the solicitor should refuse to act.

#### 1.6.4.5 Disclosure of the defence case

A solicitor owes a duty of confidentiality to his client (Solicitors' Code of Conduct 2007, Rule 4.01). A solicitor should not, therefore, without the express consent of his client, disclose details of his client's case to any other party. A typical example of when a request for disclosure may arise is when the client is jointly charged with another person, and the solicitors representing the co-defendant ask for disclosure of the client's case. Such a request should be treated with caution and the client's instructions taken. Only rarely will it be in the client's interests for his defence to be disclosed. If the solicitor does consider it to be in the client's interests to disclose information, the solicitor will need to explain to the client why he considers this to be the case.

Ideally, the solicitor should obtain his client's written consent before disclosing details of the client's defence.

#### 1.6.4.6 Arguing a point of law

A solicitor representing a defendant has no duty to inform the prosecution or the court of any evidence or witnesses that would prejudice the defendant's case. The solicitor's only duty in such circumstances is a negative one, namely, not to mislead the court by allowing evidence to be given by the defendant (or on his behalf) which the solicitor knows to be untrue. If a point of law is in dispute, however, the defendant's solicitor is under a positive duty to assist the court by supplying any relevant authority from statute or case law, even if such authority is harmful to the defendant's case.

#### 1.6.4.7 The client who gives a false name to the court

A solicitor should not act for a client who, to the knowledge of the solicitor, provides the court with a false name, address or date of birth. If faced with this problem, the solicitor should try to persuade the client to change his mind. If the client refuses to do so, the solicitor should cease to act on the client's behalf.

#### 1.6.4.8 Knowledge of previous convictions

On occasions, and particularly before the defendant is sentenced, the prosecution will provide to the court a list of the defendant's previous convictions. Sometimes this list may be inaccurate or incomplete because not all the defendant's convictions have been recorded. If asked to confirm the accuracy of the list, the defence solicitor should decline to comment. To confirm the list as accurate would amount to a positive deception of the court. On the other hand, disclosing previous convictions without the client's express consent would be a breach of the duty of confidentiality owed to the client. To avoid such difficulties, the solicitor should always attempt to obtain from the CPS a list of his client's previous convictions prior to going to court so that the solicitor may discuss any problems with his client. The client should be warned of the dangers of misleading the court. If the client indicates that, if asked, he will pretend the list is accurate, the solicitor must cease to act.

#### 1.6.4.9 Conflicts of interest

A solicitor must not act for two (or more) defendants where there is a conflict of interest between them (Solicitors' Code of Conduct 2007, Rule 3.01). The most obvious example of a conflict of interest is when two defendants are jointly accused of having committed an offence and each defendant blames his co-defendant for the commission of that offence. The solicitor should decline to act for one of the defendants and suggest that this defendant obtain separate legal advice. Even if there is no obvious conflict of interest between defendants, a solicitor must be alert to the possibility that a conflict may arise. This is particularly the case where two defendants charged with the same offence both enter guilty pleas. Although both defendants admit the offence, one defendant may wish to say in mitigation that he played a very small role in the commission of the offence and the larger role was played by his co-defendant. If a solicitor considers that a conflict of interest may arise, he should decline to act for one of the defendants and suggest that this defendant obtain separate legal advice.

If a conflict of interest arises *after* the solicitor has begun to act for both defendants, the solicitor should normally withdraw from the case entirely. To continue to act for both clients would be a breach of Rule 3.01 above. The only circumstance in which the solicitor may continue to act for one of the defendants is if this would not put at risk the duty of confidentiality owed to the defendant he was no longer representing (Solicitors' Code of Conduct 2007, Rule 3.03). This is unlikely ever to be the case in the context of a criminal matter because, were the solicitor to continue to act for only one of the defendants, he would almost certainly have in his possession information about the other defendant which could be used to assist the defendant for whom he was continuing to act.

The Law Society has provided specific advice to defence solicitors who may be asked to represent more than one defendant in criminal proceedings. This advice forms part of the guidance notes to Rule 3 (conflict of interests) in the Solicitors' Code of Conduct 2007.

Further details about how a solicitor should deal with potential or actual conflicts of interest between clients are provided in **Chapter 4**.

#### 1.6.4.10 Interviewing prosecution witnesses

Although there is a general rule that there is 'no property in a witness', defence solicitors should always proceed with caution if they intend to interview a prosecution witness. The usual course of action would be to notify the prosecution of the fact that a witness is to be interviewed and to invite a representative from the CPS to attend the interview as an observer. Such a step will avoid suspicion that the solicitor is attempting to pervert the course of justice. It should also prevent a later allegation that a witness has been pressured in some way to change his evidence.

#### 1.6.4.11 Withdrawing from the case

If circumstances arise which require a solicitor to withdraw from a case (where, for example, the defendant intends to give evidence which the solicitor knows to be false), the reason for withdrawal should not normally be given to the court. To do so would breach the duty of confidentiality owed to the client (see **1.6.4.5** above). The solicitor should simply explain that a matter has arisen which makes it impossible for him to continue to act in the case. A common euphemism that solicitors often employ is to tell the court that they must withdraw from the case 'for professional reasons'.

The duty of confidentiality which the solicitor owes to the client continues after the retainer has been terminated (Solicitors' Code of Conduct 2007, Rule 4.01). The solicitor must therefore not disclose details of the instructions he received whilst still acting for the client after he has ceased to act for the client.

## 1.7 Legal professional privilege

Communications between a client and his solicitor are privileged if the purpose of the communication is the giving or receiving of legal advice. This will include all letters, records of telephone calls, witness statements and other documents prepared by the defence solicitor. The defence cannot be compelled to reveal the contents of such communications to any other party, and the defendant cannot be asked about their contents when being cross-examined.

This privilege extends to communications between the defendant or his solicitor and a third party, provided such communications are made in contemplation of pending or anticipated proceedings and the purpose, or dominant purpose, was to prepare for the litigation. Common examples of such communications include statements taken from witnesses who will give evidence on the defendant's behalf and letters of instruction to experts. The defence cannot be compelled to reveal the contents of such communications to any other party.

When giving evidence at trial, a defendant may waive privilege. For example, a defendant may say that he remained silent when interviewed at the police station after receiving advice from his solicitor that he was not in a fit state to be interviewed. This area is examined more fully in **Chapter 4**.

## 1.8 Human rights

### 1.8.1 Introduction

Human rights issues sometimes arise during the course of criminal proceedings and, where appropriate, have been highlighted in subsequent chapters. This chapter will provide a general introduction to the subject of human rights by discussing the key sections of the Human Rights Act 1998 and the significant parts of the European Convention for the Protection of Human Rights and Fundamental Freedoms 1950.

### 1.8.2 The Human Rights Act 1998

The Human Rights Act (HRA) 1998 came into force on 2 October 2000. The Act gives effect in domestic law to the rights and freedoms guaranteed by the European Convention for the Protection of Human Rights and Fundamental Freedoms 1950 (ECHR), to which the UK is a signatory.

Section 3 of the HRA 1998 provides that courts must, so far as it is possible to do so, interpret and give effect to legislation in a way which is compatible with the ECHR. If it is not possible to interpret legislation so as to be compatible with the ECHR, courts do not have the power to 'strike down' that legislation. However s 4 of the HRA 1998 enables the High Court, the Court of Appeal and the House of Lords to declare such legislation to be incompatible with the ECHR ('a declaration of incompatibility'). Such a declaration operates as a clear signal to Parliament and the Government that an incompatibility has been found. Section 10 of the 1998 Act allows Government Ministers to make a remedial order to amend the relevant legislation to make it compatible with the ECHR.

Section 6 of the HRA 1998 provides that it is 'unlawful for a public authority to act in a way which is incompatible with a convention right'. The term 'public authority' is widely defined and will include a criminal court. An individual who claims that a public authority has contravened s 6 may rely on the rights granted to him by the ECHR as a defence in civil and criminal proceedings, or as the basis of an appeal. Alternatively, an individual may seek judicial review of a decision or action taken by a public authority, or bring civil proceedings for damages against that authority.

Section 8(1) of the HRA 1998 provides that

> in relation to any act (or proposed act) of a public authority which the court finds is (or would be) unlawful, it may grant such relief or remedy, or make such order, within its powers as it considers just and appropriate.

This means that criminal courts will have the power to stay proceedings as an abuse of process (ie, stop a case where the police or the prosecution have abused their powers – see **Chapter 21**), quash a charge which a defendant faces, make a ruling that evidence is inadmissible or quash a conviction. A considerable body of case law has built up concerning human rights issues within the criminal litigation process, and a defence solicitor should always be alert to such issues arising when he is representing a client in the police station or at court.

### 1.8.3 The European Convention for the Protection of Human Rights and Fundamental Freedoms 1950

Since the HRA 1998 came into force, defence solicitors have been able to rely on the ECHR in criminal proceedings. Defence solicitors are now able to test domestic law and practice for compliance with the ECHR, and in particular the following articles:

(a) Article 3 – the prohibition of torture;
(b) Article 5 – the right to liberty and security;
(c) Article 6 – the right to a fair trial;
(d) Article 7 – no punishment without law;
(e) Article 8 – the right to respect for private and family life.

Extracts from each article are set out below.

*Article 3*

*Prohibition of torture*

No one shall be subjected to torture or to inhuman or degrading treatment or punishment.

*Article 5*

*Right to liberty and security*

1. Everyone has the right to liberty and security of person. No one shall be deprived of his liberty save in the following cases and in accordance with a procedure prescribed by law:
   (a) the lawful detention of a person after conviction by a competent court;
   (b) the lawful arrest or detention of a person for non-compliance with the lawful order of a court or in order to secure the fulfilment of any obligation prescribed by law;
   (c) the lawful arrest or detention of a person effected for the purpose of bringing him before the competent legal authority on reasonable suspicion of having committed an offence or when it is reasonably considered necessary to prevent his committing an offence or fleeing after having done so;
   (d) the detention of a minor by lawful order for the purpose of educational supervision or his lawful detention for the purpose of bringing him before the competent legal authority;
   (e) the lawful detention of persons for the prevention of the spreading of infectious diseases, of persons of unsound mind, alcoholics or drug addicts or vagrants;

(f) the lawful arrest or detention of a person to prevent his effecting an unauthorised entry into the country or of a person against whom action is being taken with a view to deportation or extradition.

2. Everyone who is arrested shall be informed promptly, in a language which he understands, of the reasons for his arrest and of any charge against him.
3. Everyone arrested or detained in accordance with the provisions of paragraph 1(c) of this article shall be brought promptly before a judge or other officer authorised by law to exercise judicial power and shall be entitled to trial within a reasonable time or to release pending trial. Release may be conditioned by guarantees to appear for trial.
4. Everyone who is deprived of his liberty by arrest or detention shall be entitled to take proceedings by which the lawfulness of his detention shall be decided speedily by a court and his release ordered if the detention is not lawful.
5. Everyone who has been the victim of arrest or detention in contravention of the provisions of this article shall have an enforceable right to compensation.

*Article 6*

*Right to a fair trial*

1. In the determination of his civil rights and obligations or of any criminal charge against him, everyone is entitled to a fair and public hearing within a reasonable time by an independent and impartial tribunal established by law. Judgment shall be pronounced publicly but the press and public may be excluded from all or part of the trial in the interest of morals, public order or national security in a democratic society, where the interests of juveniles or the protection of the private life of the parties so require, or to the extent strictly necessary in the opinion of the court in special circumstances where publicity would prejudice the interests of justice.
2. Everyone charged with a criminal offence shall be presumed innocent until proved guilty according to law.
3. Everyone charged with a criminal offence has the following minimum rights:
   (a) to be informed promptly, in a language which he understands and in detail, of the nature and cause of the accusation against him;
   (b) to have adequate time and facilities for the preparation of his defence;
   (c) to defend himself in person or through legal assistance of his own choosing or, if he has not sufficient means to pay for legal assistance, to be given it free when the interests of justice so require;
   (d) to examine or have examined witnesses against him and to obtain the attendance and examination of witnesses on his behalf under the same conditions as witnesses against him;
   (e) to have the free assistance of an interpreter if he cannot understand or speak the language used in court

*Article 7*

*No punishment without law*

1. No one shall be held guilty of any criminal offence on account of any act or omission which did not constitute a criminal offence under national or international law at the time when it was committed. Nor shall a heavier penalty be imposed than the one that was applicable at the time the criminal offence was committed.
2. This article shall not prejudice the trial and punishment of any person for any act or omission which, at the time when it was committed, was criminal according to the general principles of law recognised by civilised nations.

*Article 8*

*Right to respect for private and family life*

1. Everyone has the right to respect for his private and family life, his home and his correspondence.

2. There shall be no interference by a public authority with the exercise of this right except such as is in accordance with the law and is necessary in a democratic society in the interests of national security, public safety or the economic well-being of the country, for the prevention of disorder or crime, for the protection of health or morals, or for the protection of the rights and freedoms of others.

## 1.9 Key skills, documents and forms

### 1.9.1 Introduction

All the examples of key skills and documents in this textbook are based on a fictitious case study. The documents forming this case study are for illustrative purposes only, and are *not* meant to be read together as a single case study.

### 1.9.2 Key skills

The following key skills are demonstrated in the book:

(a) Completing a police station attendance pro forma – **Chapter 4**.
(b) Drafting a written statement for a client at the police station – **Chapter 4**.
(c) Intervening in an audibly-recorded interview at the police station – **Chapter 4**.
(d) Completing an application for a representation order – **Chapter 6**.
(e) Drafting a statement from a client – **Chapter 6**.
(f) Making an application for bail – **Chapter 7**.
(g) Drafting a bail appeal notice – **Chapter 7**.
(h) Conducting an examination-in-chief – **Chapter 9**.
(i) Conducting a cross-examination – **Chapter 9**.
(j) Drafting a brief to counsel – **Chapter 10**.
(k) Drafting a defence case statement – **Chapter 10**.
(l) Making a plea in mitigation – **Chapter 12**.

### 1.9.3 Key documents

The following key documents are illustrated in the book:

(a) Custody record – **Chapter 3**.
(b) Charge sheet – **Chapter 3**.
(c) Disclosure statement prepared by the police – **Chapter 4**.
(d) Representation order – **Chapter 6**.
(e) Advance disclosure – **Chapter 6**.
(f) Bail notice/full argument certificate – **Chapter 7**.
(g) Disclosure letter from CPS and police schedule of non-sensitive unused material – **Chapter 8**.
(h) Indictment – **Chapter 10**.
(i) Pre-sentence report – **Chapter 12**.

### 1.9.4 Key forms

The following key forms are reproduced in this book:

(a) Magistrates' Court case progression – **Chapter 8**.
(b) Magistrates' Court – Directions for case sent to the Crown – **Chapter 10**.

(c) Magistrates' Court - Directions for case committed to the Crown Court - **Chapter 10**.
(d) Notice of intention to introduce hearsay evidence - **Chapter 19**.
(e) Notice of opposition to the introduction of hearsay evidence - **Chapter 19**.
(f) Notice of intention to adduce evidence of the defendant's bad character - **Chapter 22**.
(g) Application to exclude evidence of the defendant's bad character - **Chapter 22**.
(h) Application for leave to adduce non-defendant's bad character - **Chapter 22**.

## 1.10 Additional sources of information

### 1.10.1 Practitioner texts

This book is designed to provide an introduction to criminal procedure and the law of evidence. There are several practitioner texts which can be consulted to check more detailed points of practice or procedure:

*Blackstone's Criminal Practice* (2007) - this is an authoritative guide to practice and procedure in both the magistrates' court and the Crown Court. It also has very full sections dealing with substantive criminal offences, the investigative powers of the police and the law of evidence. (See also the companion website at www.oup.co.uk.)

*Archbold: Criminal Pleading, Evidence and Practice* (2007) - this is very similar in its scope and format to the *Blackstone's* text, and is used mainly by practitioners in the Crown Court.

*Archbold: Magistrates' Courts Criminal Practice* (2007) - this book is intended for the solicitor in the magistrates' court. It contains a section dealing with the substantive law, with other helpful sections dealing with procedural and evidential matters.

*Stone's Justices' Manual* (2007) - a comprehensive guide to all matters of practice and procedure in the magistrates' court.

*Anthony and Berryman's Magistrates' Courts Guide* (2007) - this provides useful information about all the offences that are likely to arise in the magistrates' court, including a particularly helpful section on road traffic offences.

*Wilkinson's Road Traffic Offences* (22nd edn, 2005) - this is the standard reference work on all matters of law, practice and procedure concerning road traffic offences.

There are also a number of weekly journals which provide useful articles and up-to-date case reports:

- *The Gazette*, published by The Law Society (www.lawgazette.co.uk);
- *The Solicitors Journal*, published by Waterlow (www.solicitorsjournal.com);
- *The New Law Journal*, published by LexisNexis Butterworths (www.new-law-journal.co.uk);
- *Criminal Law Week* (www.criminal-law.co.uk).

### 1.10.2 Websites

There are a number of websites that are useful sources of information for the busy criminal litigation solicitor:

*www.justice.gov.uk* – the website of the Ministry of Justice. This gives access to the Criminal Procedure Rules 2005 and amendments that have been made to the Rules.

*www.courtservice.gov.uk* – the website of the Court Service. This gives access to various court forms and also key judgments.

*www.sentencing-guidelines.gov.uk* – the website of the Sentencing Guidelines Council, which contains sentencing guidelines issued by the Council (see **Chapter 11**).

*www.cps.gov.uk* – the website of the CPS, which contains the Code for Crown Prosecutors and a useful summary of various evidential matters.

*www.homeoffice.gov.uk* – the website of the Home Office. This gives access to the Codes of Practice for police conduct issued under PACE 1984, and also details of proposed further reforms to the criminal justice system.

*www.jsboard.co.uk* – the website of the Judicial Studies Board (JSB). The JSB is responsible for training members of the judiciary. The website contains specimen directions for judges to give in criminal cases, and is particularly useful for specimen directions about evidential matters. It also provides access to the Magistrates' Court Sentencing Guidelines (see **Chapter 11**).

*www.legalservices.gov.uk* – the website of the Legal Services Commission, which contains details of the various forms of public funding available in criminal litigation matters, together with the payment rates solicitors may claim and the forms which must be completed in order to obtain payment.

## 1.11 Procedural flowcharts

### 1.11.1 Introduction

In **1.3** above, the classification of offences into the categories of indictable only, either way or summary offences was explained. Set out below are three flowcharts which provide a general overview of the procedural steps that are followed for each type of offence. The details of each stage in the process will be explained in subsequent chapters.

### 1.11.2 Indictable only offences

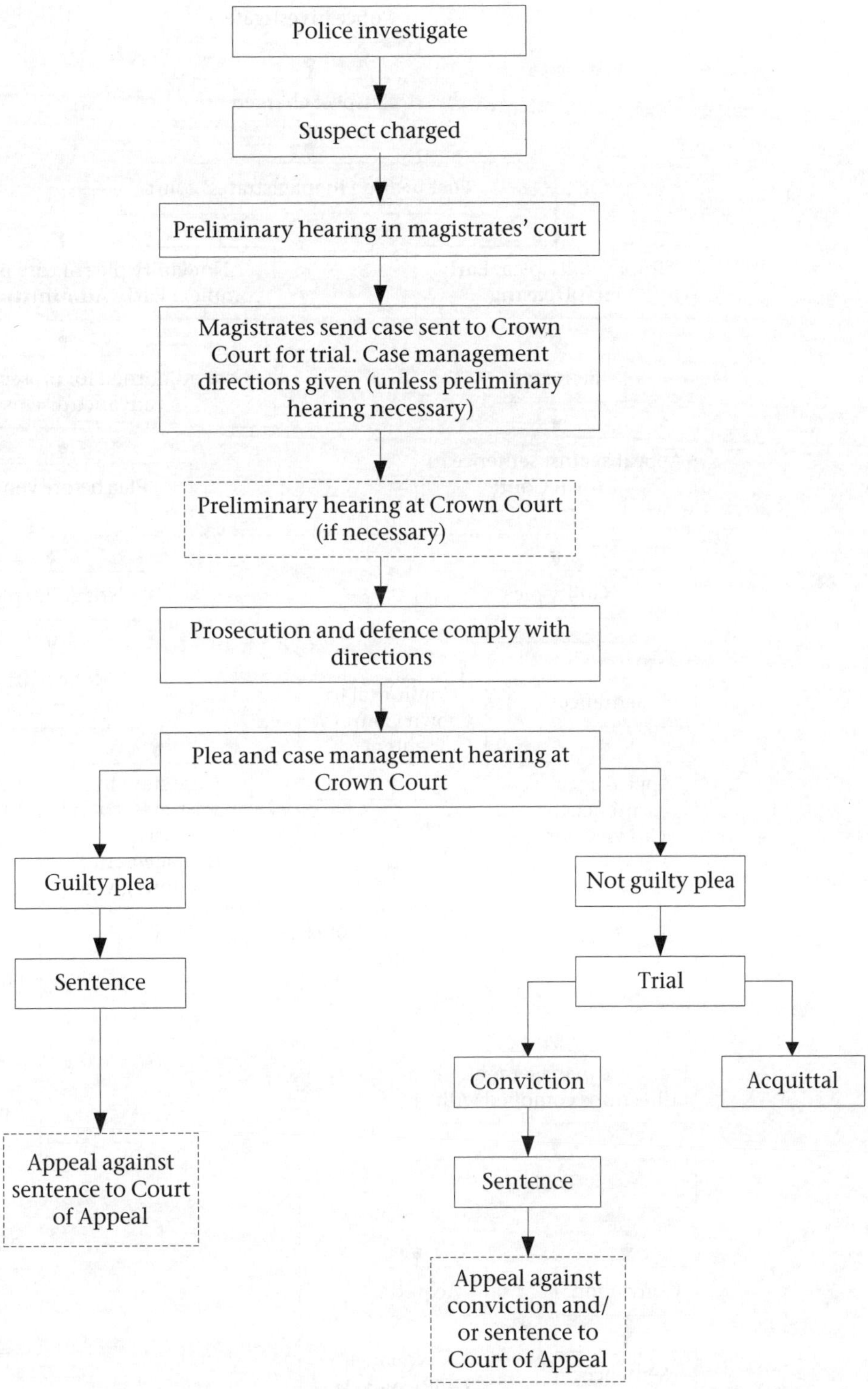

### 1.11.3 Either way offences

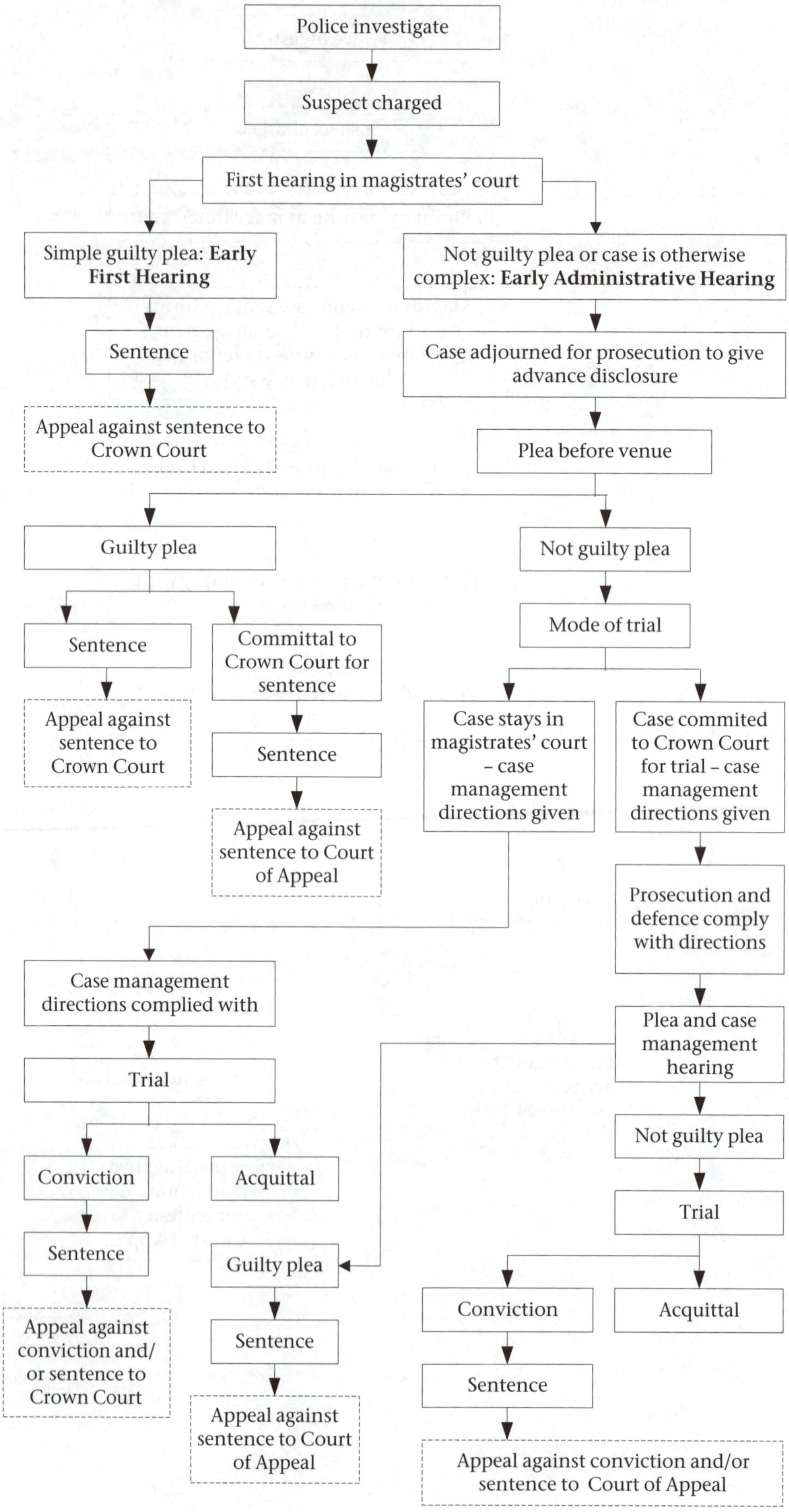

### 1.11.4 Summary offences

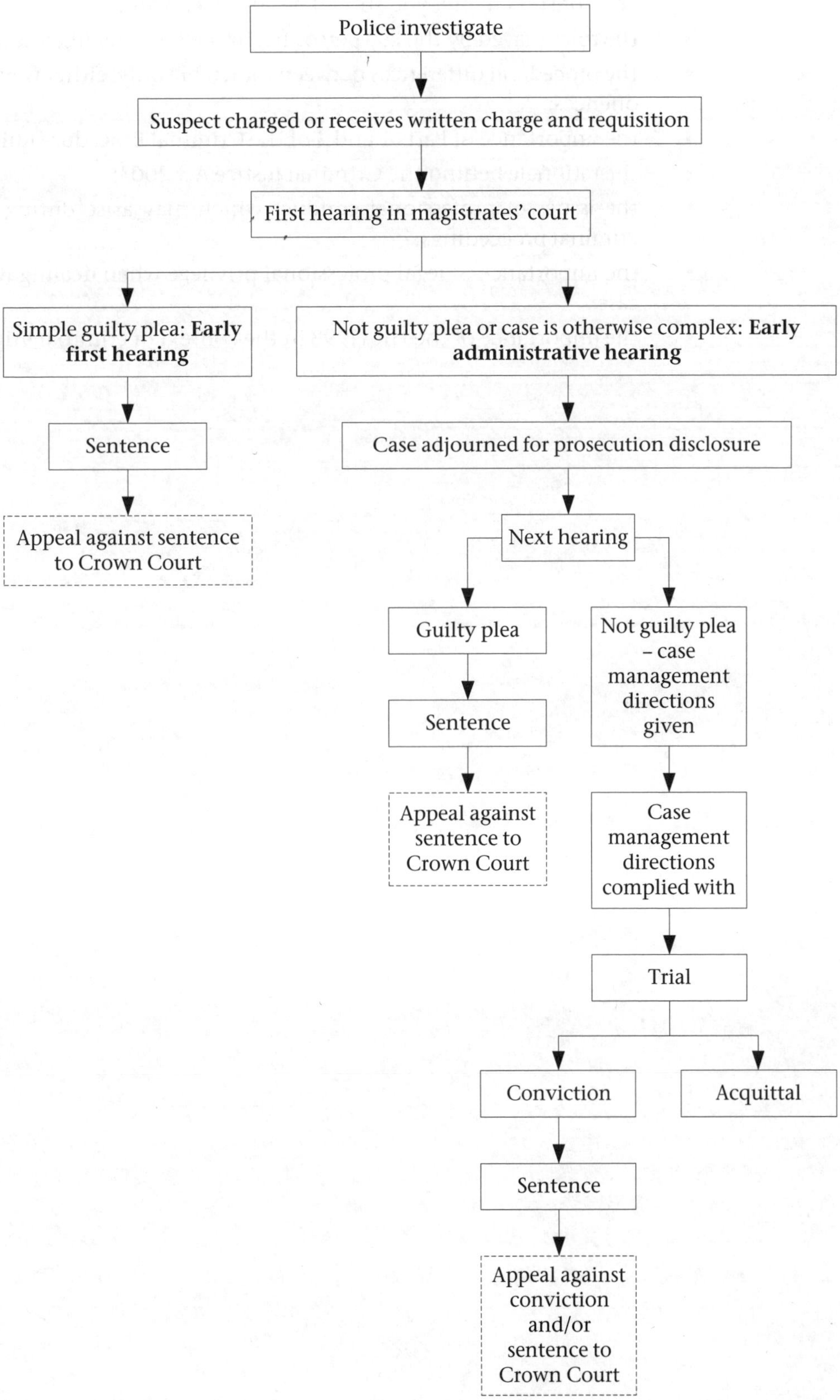

## 1.12 Checklist

At the end of this chapter you should be able to explain:

- the roles played by the key personnel in the criminal litigation process;
- the procedural differences between indictable only, either way and summary offences;
- the importance of Parts 1 and 3 of the Criminal Procedure Rules 2005;
- the rationale behind the Criminal Justice Act 2003;
- the issues of professional conduct which may arise during the course of criminal proceedings;
- the importance of legal professional privilege when dealing with a criminal case;
- the importance of the HRA1998 in the context of criminal litigation.

# Part 2
# THE CLIENT AND THE POLICE

# Chapter 2

# The Investigative Powers of the Police (1) – Outside the Police Station



## 2.1 Introduction

The criminal litigation process begins before a solicitor is asked to represent a suspect in the police station or a defendant at court. The first stage in the process involves the police carrying out investigations after a criminal offence has been committed. Only when the police have investigated an offence and arrested a suspect is a solicitor likely to become involved.

This chapter will look at the powers the police exercise *outside* the police station when investigating an offence. The powers that will be described are:

(a) the power to stop and search persons and vehicles;

(b) the power of arrest; and

(c) the power to enter and search premises (and to seize and retain items found on premises).

Most powers exercised by the police are granted to them by the Police and Criminal Evidence Act (PACE) 1984. The Act is supplemented by eight Codes of Practice (A to H) which provide police officers with detailed guidance as to how to exercise these powers. References to section numbers in this chapter are, unless otherwise stated, to PACE 1984. References to Code A are to the Code of Practice on the Exercise by Police Officers of Statutory Powers of Stop and Search. References to Code B are to the Code of Practice for Searches of Property and the Seizure of Property. References to Code C are to the Code of Practice for the Detention, Treatment and Questioning of Persons by Police Officers. References to Code G are to the Code of Practice for the Statutory Power of Arrest by Police Officers.

## 2.2 Stop and search

### 2.2.1 What can the police search for?

This section will examine the powers of stop and search the police may exercise under PACE 1984. Brief details of the main additional powers of stop and search which the police may exercise are set out at **2.2.7** below.

Under s 1(2), a police officer is given the power to search any person or vehicle (or anything which is in or on a vehicle) for stolen or prohibited articles, or any articles to which s 1(8A) applies. The officer can detain a person or vehicle for the purpose of carrying out such a search.

Stolen articles have their ordinary meaning. Prohibited articles are articles which are offensive weapons (see below), or which are either:

(a) made or adapted for use in the course of or in connection with the offences set out in s 1(8); or
(b) intended by the person having that article for such use by him or by some other person.

The offences listed in s 1(8) are:

(a) burglary;
(b) theft;
(c) taking a motor vehicle or other conveyance without authority;
(d) fraud;
(e) destroying or damaging property (Criminal Damage Act 1971, s 1).

Examples of articles which could fall into this category are a crowbar, wrench or jemmy.

Offensive weapons are defined in s 1(9) as being any article which is either:

(a) made or adapted for use for causing injury to persons (such as a cosh or a gun); or
(b) intended by the person having it with him for such use by him or by some other person (such as a baseball bat which is not manufactured for use as an offensive weapon).

Articles to which s 1(8A) applies are any articles which would contravene the offence of having an article with a blade or a point in a public place contrary to s 139(1) of the Criminal Justice Act 1988. This covers most types of knife, except a folding pocket knife.

A police officer may seize any article discovered during a search if he has reasonable grounds for suspecting the article to be a stolen or prohibited article, or an article to which s 1(8A) applies (s 1(6)).

### 2.2.2 Where can the power to stop and search be exercised?

Section 1(1)(a) allows a police officer to carry out a stop and search:

(a) in any place to which at the time of the search the public, or any part of the public, have access, whether by payment or otherwise, and whether the access is as of right or by virtue of express or implied permission; or
(b) in any other place (other than a dwelling) to which people have ready access at the time the officer intends to carry out the search.

Examples of locations which would fall into the first category above are shopping centres, public houses, parks and bus stations, as well as the public highway. The second category could include the garden or yard attached to a house (but not the house itself), as these are places to which the public have ready access.

### 2.2.3 When can the power of stop and search be exercised?

Before exercising the power of stop and search conferred by s 1(2), a police officer must have 'reasonable grounds for suspecting that he will find stolen or prohibited articles or any article to which [s 1(8A)] applies' (s 1(3)). Paragraph 2.2 of Code A provides that:

> Reasonable grounds for suspicion depend on the circumstances in each case. There must be an objective basis for that suspicion based on facts, information, and/or intelligence which are relevant to finding an article of a certain kind ...

The police cannot use a person's age, appearance or race, or the knowledge that a person has a previous conviction as valid grounds for searching that person. Reasonable suspicion should be based on accurate and current intelligence or information. This could, for example, be information about an article a person is carrying, about a suspected offender, or about a person seen carrying a type of item that is known to have been stolen recently from local premises. The police do not have the power to stop or detain a person in order to find grounds for a search (Code A, para 2.11).

Paragraph 1.4 of Code A stresses that the main function of stop and search powers is 'to enable officers to allay or confirm suspicions about individuals without exercising their power of arrest'. If an officer who has reasonable grounds for suspicion detains a person in order to carry out a search, the officer may ask questions about the person's behaviour or presence in circumstances which gave rise to the suspicion. Any response to such questions might confirm the reasonable grounds for suspicion required to detain the person, or might remove those grounds (if, for example, the detained person gives a satisfactory explanation).

If the person is in the garden or yard of a dwelling, a police officer can exercise his power of stop and search only if he has reasonable grounds for believing that the person does not live in the dwelling and does not have the express or implied permission of the owner of the dwelling to be there (s 1(4)).

Similarly, if a vehicle is in the garden or yard of a dwelling, a police officer can exercise his power of stop and search only if he has reasonable grounds for believing that the person in charge of the vehicle does not live in the dwelling and the vehicle is not in the garden or yard with the express or implied permission of the owner of the dwelling.

### 2.2.4 What steps need to be taken prior to search?

If a police officer intends to search a person or a vehicle which is attended by a person, the officer must first take reasonable steps, if he is not in uniform, to bring to the attention of the person to be searched or in charge of the vehicle documentary evidence that he is a police officer (by producing his warrant card).

The officer, whether or not he is in uniform, must then take reasonable steps to bring to the attention of that person the following information:

(a) the fact that the person is being detained for the purposes of a search;

(b) the officer's name and the name of the police station to which he is attached;

(c) the object of the proposed search (ie, details of the article(s) for which there is a power to search); and

(d) the officer's grounds for proposing to carry out the search (s 2(2)).

### 2.2.5 How should the search be conducted?

Paragraph 3.1 of Code A provides that all stops and searches 'must be carried out with courtesy, consideration and respect for the person concerned'.

Under s 117, a police officer is allowed to use 'reasonable force' in the exercise of any other powers contained within PACE 1984. Force may be used for a stop and search only if the person is unwilling to cooperate or resists. The exercise of reasonable force is a 'last resort' (Code A, para 3.2).

The period of time during which a person or vehicle is detained must be kept to a minimum, and the thoroughness and extent of the search depends on what is suspected of being carried, and by whom (Code A, para 3.3). The search must be carried out 'at or near the place where the person or vehicle was first detained' (Code A, para 3.4).

The only items of clothing a detained person can be required to remove in public are an outer coat, jacket and gloves (Code A, para 3.5). A search in public of a detained person's clothing which has not been removed can be only a 'superficial examination of outer garments' (Code A, para 3.5). If a police officer has reasonable grounds for considering it necessary that a more thorough search be conducted (for example, by requiring a detained person to remove a shirt), this must be done out of public view, such as in a police van (Code A, para 3.6).

### 2.2.6 What must be done after the search?

The police officer who carried out the search must make a record of it at the time, unless there are exceptional circumstances making this wholly impracticable (such as in a public disorder situation, or if the officer's presence is urgently required elsewhere). If a record is not made at the time, it must be made as soon as practicable afterwards (Code A, para 4.1).

A copy of a record made at the time must be given immediately to the person who has been searched (Code A, para 4.2).

### 2.2.7 What other powers of stop and search may the police exercise?

Annex A to Code A summarises the main stop and search powers enjoyed by the police. The other significant powers of stop and search the police may exercise in addition to those powers granted by PACE 1984 are:

(a) powers to search persons and vehicles for controlled drugs (and to seize and detain anything found which appears to be evidence of an offence) under s 23(2) of the Misuse of Drugs Act 1971;

(b) powers to search persons and vehicles for offensive weapons or dangerous instruments to prevent incidents of serious violence, or to deal with the carrying of such items under s 60 of the Criminal Justice and Public Order Act 1994; and

(c) powers of search of persons and vehicles under anti-terrorist legislation (particularly ss 44–47 of the Terrorism Act 2000).

Unless they are exercising statutory powers of stop and search, the police have no general right to detain a person for the purpose of making enquiries, or to require a person to give his name and address (*Rice v Connolly* [1966] 2 All ER 649). There are, however, some exceptions to this. For example, provisions in the Road Traffic Act 1988 permit the police to stop a motorist and require him to undergo a breath alcohol test if the police suspect the motorist of driving whilst over the prescribed alcohol limit.

## 2.3 Arrest

### 2.3.1 Introduction

A police officer's decision to arrest a suspect is a pivotal stage in the criminal process. In *Christie v Leachinsky* [1974] AC 573, Lord Simonds characterised arrest as being the beginning of imprisonment. Arrest will be the first occasion when a suspect has been deprived of his liberty, and must have a clear legal justification and be necessary. Arresting or detaining someone who it is reasonably suspected has committed a criminal offence is one of the exceptions to an individual's right to liberty and security under Article 5 of the ECHR (see **Chapter 1**). However, such action is justified only if the arrest is 'lawful'.

Paragraphs 1.2 and 1.3 of Code G state:

> 1.2 The right to liberty is a key principle of the Human Rights Act 1998. The exercise of the power of arrest represents an obvious and significant interference with that right.
>
> 1.3 The use of the power must be fully justified and officers exercising the power should consider if the necessary objectives can be met by other, less intrusive means.

Failure by the police to observe PACE 1984 and the Codes of Practice when exercising the statutory power of arrest may prejudice both the legality of the arrest and the conduct of any subsequent investigation into the offence (Code G, para 1.4).

### 2.3.2 What is an arrest?

An arrest is a restraint on the liberty of the person under due process of law. There are two requirements for an arrest to be valid:

(a) there must be a *power* of arrest (see **2.3.4** below); and

(b) the arrest must be carried out in the proper *manner* (see **2.3.5** below).

If either of these requirements is not fulfilled, an arrest will be invalid and the detention of any person following such an arrest will be unlawful and in breach of his right to liberty under Article 5 of the ECHR. The person wrongfully detained would be entitled to claim damages in such circumstances (see **Chapter 5**).

### 2.3.3 Interviews prior to arrest

#### 2.3.3.1 Introduction

Most interviews which the police carry out with suspects will take place at the police station after the suspect has been arrested. Such interviews will be audibly recorded, and the recording can be played at any subsequent trial if there is a dispute as to what was said during the interview. It will, however, often be the case that, outside of the police station and prior to that person's arrest, the police will want to ask questions of a person whom they suspect of having committed an offence to ascertain if their suspicions are justified and to enable them to establish the necessary grounds for then arresting that person.

Prior to arresting a suspect, the police are permitted to question that person about his suspected involvement in a criminal offence, although the suspect is under no legal obligation to answer such questions. The police may not detain a suspect to ask such questions prior to arrest (*Kenlin v Gardiner* [1967] 2 QB 510). The only exception to this is if the police are exercising their powers of stop and search under s 1 (see **2.2** above).

If the police do interview a suspect prior to arrest and the suspect makes an admission or a confession, requirements are set out in Code C to ensure both that any such comment is properly recorded and that the suspect is given the opportunity to comment on any remarks that he is alleged to have made. These provisions are commonly referred to as the 'anti-verballing rules' and are designed as safeguards to prevent the police from later misrepresenting.

### 2.3.3.2 What constitutes an interview?

Paragraph 11.1A of Code C states that:

> An interview is the questioning of a person regarding their involvement or suspected involvement in a criminal offence or offences which, under paragraph 10.1, must be carried out under caution. . . .

This means that if the police question a suspect in the street *before* that suspect has actually been arrested, this may count as an interview. Questioning a suspect prior to arrest will count as an interview only if the police have 'some reasonable, objective grounds for suspicion, based on known facts or information which are relevant to the likelihood the offence has been committed and the person to be questioned committed it' (Code C, Notes for Guidance, para 10A).

The significance of such questioning being an interview is contained in para 10.1 of Code C, which provides that:

> A person whom there are grounds to suspect of an offence, see *Note 10A*, must be cautioned before any questions about an offence, or further questions if the answers provide the grounds for suspicion, are put to them if either the suspect's answers or silence, (ie failure or refusal to answer or answer satisfactorily) may be given in evidence to a court in a prosecution. . . .

In other words, a police officer must caution a suspect before carrying out an interview as defined by para 11.1A above. The wording of the caution is as follows:

> You do not have to say anything. But it may harm your defence if you do not mention when questioned something which you later rely on in court. Anything you do say may be given in evidence. (Code C, para 10.5)

#### Example

PC Singh is called to a public house where one of the customers has been assaulted. The customer did not recognise his assailant but is able to provide PC Singh with an accurate description of this person. PC Singh leaves the public house and sees Oliver nearby. Oliver closely matches the description of the assailant given by the customer. PC Singh asks Oliver where he has just come from. Oliver tells him that he has come from the same public house where the assault occurred. This gives PC Singh reasonable grounds to suspect that Oliver may have committed the assault. PC Singh should therefore caution Oliver before asking him any further questions about the assault.

Should a police officer fail to caution a suspect before conducting an interview in these circumstances, this may result in any subsequent admission or confession made by the suspect being ruled inadmissible at trial under s 78 of PACE 1984 (see **Chapters 20** and **21**).

### 2.3.3.3 Recording interviews outside the police station

Paragraph 11.7(a) of Code C states that 'an accurate record must be made of each interview, whether or not the interview takes place at a police station'. If the record is not made at the time of the interview, it must be made as soon as practicable after the completion of the interview (Code C, para 11.7(c)). Paragraph 11.11 of Code C provides that a person who has been interviewed shall, unless it is impracticable, be given the opportunity to read the interview record and sign it as correct, or to indicate how they consider it inaccurate. To comply with these paragraphs, if the interview takes place outside the police station, the police officer will usually make a note of the interview in his pocket book, and then invite the suspect to read the note and sign this as being correct.

The police must also make a written record of any comments made by a suspect (including any unsolicited comments) which are outside the context of an interview but which might be relevant to the offence (Code C, para 11.13). As with the record of an interview, if practicable the suspect should be given the opportunity to read the record and either to sign it as correct, or to indicate how he considers it inaccurate.

Once a suspect has been arrested, any further interview(s) with that suspect should generally take place only at the police station, where they can be audibly recorded (see **2.3.7** below). At the start of such an interview at the police station, the police will put to the suspect any significant statement made by the suspect either prior to his arrest, or after his arrest but prior to the start of the interview (Code C, para 11.4; see **Chapter 3**).

## 2.3.4 The sources of the police powers of arrest

### 2.3.4.1 Introduction

Arrests that are made by the police will be carried out either after a warrant for the arrest of the relevant person has been issued, or without a warrant.

Arrests under a warrant are rare and usually arise when a defendant fails to attend court and the court issues a warrant for the defendant's arrest.

> **Example**
>
> Malcolm is charged with theft and is bailed to appear before the magistrates' court. Malcolm fails to attend court at the required time so the magistrates issue a warrant for Malcolm's arrest. The warrant gives the police the power to arrest Malcolm, whom they will then bring before the court as soon as possible after his arrest.

The powers of the police to arrest without a warrant derive from two sources:

(a) powers of arrest in PACE 1984;
(b) the common law power to arrest for a breach of the peace.

Each of these powers will be examined in turn.

### 2.3.4.2 Powers of arrest in PACE 1984

**Powers of arrest granted only to the police**

The statutory powers of arrest which the police may exercise are contained in s 24 of PACE 1984. Section 24 gives police officers a power of arrest in respect of any criminal offence (no matter how minor that offence may be), provided that certain conditions are satisfied. These conditions are explained in Code G, which states that a lawful arrest made under s 24 requires two elements:

(a) a person's involvement, or suspected involvement or attempted involvement in the commission of a criminal offence; *and*
(b) reasonable grounds for believing that the arrest is necessary (Code G, para 2.1).

The wording of s 24 is as follows:

> **24 Arrest without warrant: constables**

(1) A constable may arrest without a warrant—
  (a) anyone who is about to commit an offence;
  (b) anyone who is in the act of committing an offence;
  (c) anyone whom he has reasonable grounds for suspecting to be about to commit an offence;
  (d) anyone whom he has reasonable grounds for suspecting to be committing an offence.

(2) If a constable has reasonable grounds for suspecting that an offence has been committed, he may arrest without a warrant anyone whom he has reasonable grounds to suspect of being guilty of it.

(3) If an offence has been committed, a constable may arrest without a warrant—
  (a) anyone who is guilty of the offence;
  (b) anyone whom he has reasonable grounds for suspecting to be guilty of it.

(4) But the power of summary arrest conferred by subsection (1), (2) or (3) is exercisable only if the constable has reasonable grounds for believing that for any of the reasons mentioned in subsection (5) it is necessary to arrest the person in question.

(5) The reasons are—
  (a) to enable the name of the person in question to be ascertained (in the case where the constable does not know, and cannot readily ascertain, the person's name, or has reasonable grounds for doubting whether a name given by the person as his name is his real name);
  (b) correspondingly as regards the person's address;
  (c) to prevent the person in question—
    (i) causing physical injury to himself or any other person,
    (ii) suffering physical injury,
    (iii) causing loss of or damage to property,
    (iv) committing an offence against public decency (subject to subsection (6)), or
    (v) causing an unlawful obstruction of the highway;
  (d) to protect a child or other vulnerable person from the person in question;
  (e) to allow the prompt and effective investigation of the offence or of the conduct of the person in question;
  (f) to prevent any prosecution for the offence from being hindered by the disappearance of the person in question.

(6) Subsection (5)(c)(iv) applies only where members of the public going about their normal business cannot reasonably be expected to avoid the person in question.

Section 24 therefore enables a police officer to arrest anyone who is, or whom he reasonably suspects is:

(a) about to commit an offence; or
(b) in the act of committing an offence; or
(c) guilty of having committed an offence,

provided that the officer has reasonable grounds for believing that it is necessary to arrest the suspect for one or more of the reasons set out in s 24(5).

### Example 1

PC Smith sees Tony break a window to gain access to a house. PC Smith arrests Tony on suspicion of burglary. It transpires that the house belongs to Tony and he broke the window to get in because he had lost his key. PC Smith had valid grounds for arresting Tony under s 24(1)(d) if he reasonably suspected that Tony was committing a burglary and one or more of the conditions in s 24(5) was satisfied.

### Example 2

Abdul is the victim of an assault which results in his sustaining a broken nose. Abdul gives a detailed description of his assailant to PC Smith. Shortly after the assault, PC Smith sees Brian near the scene of the assault. Brian matches the description of the assailant given by Abdul and Brian's shirt is covered in blood. PC Smith arrests Brian on suspicion of assault occasioning actual bodily harm. It later transpires that Brian was not the assailant. Brian merely resembled the assailant and his shirt was covered in blood following a nosebleed. PC Smith had valid grounds for the arrest under s 24(3)(b) if he reasonably suspected that Brian was guilty of the assault and one or more of the conditions in s 24(5) was satisfied.

### Example 3

From a distance PC Smith sees Martin punch Patrick in the face, causing Patrick's nose to break. PC Smith runs after Martin and arrests him on suspicion of assault occasioning actual bodily harm. At his trial, Martin is acquitted on the basis that (unknown to PC Smith) Patrick had attacked him first and Martin was acting in reasonable self-defence. Even though Martin had therefore not committed an offence, PC Smith had valid grounds for the arrest under s 24(2) if he reasonably suspected an offence had been committed by Martin and one or more of the conditions in s 24(5) was satisfied.

### Example 4

There has been a spate of robberies in a particular park. Rachel knows that her friend Alison will be walking through the park late one evening. She decides to play a trick on Alison by hiding in some bushes and jumping out in front of her as she walks by. PC Smith sees Rachel hiding in the bushes. Thinking that she may be about to commit a robbery, PC Smith arrests Rachel as she is waiting for Alison to walk past. PC Smith had valid grounds for the arrest under s 24(1)(c) if he reasonably believed that Rachel was about to commit a robbery, as long as one or more of the conditions in s 24(5) was satisfied.

The conditions in s 24(5) (referred to in Code G as the 'necessity criteria') are deliberately drawn widely, and a police officer should have little difficulty in persuading a court that one or more of these conditions was satisfied at the time he decided to make the arrest. Even if none of the other conditions in s 24(5) is satisfied, a police officer will normally be able to justify an arrest under s 24(5)(e) on the basis that he has reasonable grounds for believing that the arrest was necessary for the 'prompt and effective investigation of the offence or of the conduct of the person in question'. Paragraph 2.9 of Code G gives several examples of when the condition in s 24(5)(e) will be satisfied:

(a) where there are grounds to believe that:
  (i) the person has made false statements,
  (ii) the person has made statements which cannot be readily verified,
  (iii) the person has presented false evidence,
  (iv) the person may steal or destroy evidence,
  (v) the person may make contact with co-suspects or conspirators,

(vi) the person may intimidate, or threaten or make contact with witnesses,

(vii) it is necessary to obtain evidence by questioning; or

(b) when the offence is indictable, there is a need to:

(i) enter and search any premises occupied or controlled by a person,

(ii) search the person,

(iii) prevent contact with others,

(iv) take fingerprints, footwear impressions, samples or photographs of the suspect.

When applying the necessary criteria, the officer must 'take into account the situation of the victim, the nature of the offence, the circumstances of the suspect and the needs of the investigation process' (Code G, para 2.8).

In *R (C) v Chief Constable of A* [2006] EWHC 2352 (Admin), the Administrative Court held that the police should be afforded a wide discretion as to when an arrest was 'necessary' under s 24(4). An arrest would be unnecessary only if it satisfied the *Wednesbury* test for unreasonableness (ie, if the reasons relied upon for the arrest being necessary were so unreasonable that no reasonable police officer would ever have sought to rely upon them).

**Powers of arrest granted to other persons**

In addition to the powers of arrest given to the police under s 24, persons other than police officers (ie, members of the public) are given a more limited power of arrest under s 24A of PACE 1984. The detailed provisions of s 24A are beyond the scope of this book.

#### 2.3.4.3 Arrest to prevent a breach of the peace

The only remaining power of arrest at common law is the power to arrest to prevent a breach of the peace. The Court of Appeal defined what is meant by the term 'breach of the peace' in *R v Howell* [1982] QB 416:

> ... there is a breach of the peace whenever harm is actually done or is likely to be done to a person or in his presence to his property or a person is in fear of being so harmed through an assault, an affray, a riot or other disturbance.

Any person (not just a police officer) may arrest for a breach of the peace:

(a) committed in his presence;

(b) when he has reasonable cause to believe that a breach of the peace will be committed by a person in the immediate future; or

(c) when a breach of the peace has been committed and he has reasonable grounds to believe that it will be renewed if the person is not arrested.

### 2.3.5 How should the police conduct an arrest?

#### 2.3.5.1 Use of force

An arrested person must understand that he is under physical restraint. Words alone can suffice to make a suspect understand this, but if the suspect does not submit to words alone the police officer may be required to use physical restraint (such as handcuffs).

The police are permitted to use force in carrying out an arrest. Section 117 permits the police to use 'reasonable force' in exercising any other power conferred by PACE 1984. In addition, s 3 of the Criminal Law Act 1967 provides that any person may use such force as is reasonable in the circumstances for effecting or assisting in the lawful arrest of offenders or suspected offenders.

#### 2.3.5.2 Information to be given to the suspect

A police officer making an arrest must tell the suspect:

(a) that he is under arrest, even if the fact of the arrest is obvious. If it is not possible to give this information immediately (for example, because the suspect has passed out drunk), the suspect must be told that he is under arrest as soon as practicable after his arrest (s 28(1)); and

(b) the ground(s) for the arrest, even if the ground(s) are obvious. If it is not possible to give this information immediately (for example, because the suspect is acting violently), the suspect must be told of the ground(s) for his arrest as soon as is practicable after the arrest (s 28(3)).

Paragraph 2.2 of Code G confirms this by providing that an arresting officer must inform the suspect that:

(a) he is being arrested (even if this is obvious);

(b) he is being arrested as a result of his involvement, or suspected involvement or attempted involvement in the commission of a criminal offence; and

(c) there are reasonable grounds for believing that his arrest is necessary.

The arresting officer must also inform the custody officer of this information when the suspect arrives at the police station and is brought before the custody officer in order for the suspect's ongoing detention at the police station to be authorised (Code C, para 2.2) – see **Chapter 3**.

A suspect must also be cautioned on being arrested (Code C, para 10.5; see **2.3.3.2** above). The giving of the caution may be delayed if it is impracticable to caution the suspect immediately because of the suspect's condition or behaviour (Code G, para 3.4 (a)).

Under para 4.1 of Code G, a police officer carrying out an arrest must record the following information (normally in his pocket book):

(a) the nature and circumstances of the offence leading to the arrest;

(b) the reason or reasons why the arrest was necessary;

(c) the giving of the caution; and

(d) anything said by the person at the time of the arrest.

Such information should be recorded at the time of the arrest unless it is impracticable to do so, in which case the record should be made as soon as possible thereafter (Code G, para 4.2). This information must also be recorded in the custody record when the suspect arrives at the police station (Code G, para 4.3; see **3.2.2.2**).

### 2.3.6 Searches following arrest

Section 32(1) permits a police officer to search a person who is arrested anywhere other than at a police station, if the officer has reasonable grounds for believing that the person may present a danger to himself or to others.

Under s 32(2)(a), a police officer may also search an arrested person for anything which he might use to assist him to escape from custody, or which might be evidence relating to an offence. A search for items under s 32(2)(a) may be carried out only if the police officer has reasonable grounds to believe that the person to be searched may have concealed on his person anything for which a search is permitted under that subsection (s 32(5)).

Under s 32(2)(b), a police officer is permitted to enter and search any premises in which the arrested person was when he was arrested or immediately before he was arrested, for evidence relating to the offence for which he has been arrested. This power of search applies only to offences which can be tried on indictment (ie indictable-only or either way offences).

A police officer may search premises under s 32(2)(b) only if he has reasonable grounds for believing that there is evidence for which a search is permitted on the premises (s 32(6)).

**Example**

Basil uses a pistol to commit an armed robbery (an indictable offence). PC Morgan chases Basil and follows him into a warehouse. As Basil attempts to leave the warehouse he is arrested by PC Jones. When arrested Basil does not have the pistol on his person. PCs Morgan and Jones may search the warehouse to see if Basil has deposited the pistol there, because Basil was in the warehouse immediately before he was arrested and there are reasonable grounds for believing the pistol may be there.

The power of search in s 32(2) is only a power to search to the extent that is reasonably required for the purpose of discovering any such item or evidence (s 32(3)).

The powers of search in s 32 do not permit a police officer to require a person to remove any item of clothing in public other than an outer coat, a jacket or gloves. The powers do, however, authorise a search of a person's mouth (s 32(4)).

### 2.3.7 Interviews after arrest

When a police officer has made a decision to arrest a suspect, that suspect should not be interviewed about the relevant offence except at a police station or other authorised place of detention. The only exceptions to this are if the delay caused by having to take the suspect to the police station to be interviewed would be likely to:

(a) lead to interference with, or harm to, evidence connected with an offence; or
(b) lead to interference with, or physical harm to, other people; or
(c) lead to serious loss of, or damage to, property; or
(d) lead to alerting other people suspected of committing an offence but not yet arrested for it; or
(e) hinder the recovery of property obtained in consequence of the commission of an offence (Code C, para 11.1).

The rules concerning the conduct of interviews at the police station are described in **Chapter 3**.

### 2.3.8 What happens after arrest?

A person arrested at any place other than a police station must be taken to a police station 'as soon as practicable after the arrest' (s 30(1A)). There is an exception to this in s 30A, which permits a police officer to release an arrested person on bail at any time before he arrives at the police station. This exception was created by s 4 of the Criminal Justice Act 2003 and has attracted the label 'street bail'. The rationale behind this is that, at the time of the arrest, the police officer may still be investigating the offence and, rather than wanting to interview the arrested person at the police station immediately, may prefer to delay interviewing the arrested person until the investigations are complete. If the police officer does grant the suspect 'street bail', he must give the arrested person a notice informing him when he should attend for interview and at which police station. The police have the power to arrest without warrant a suspect who fails to answer street bail.

A police officer may impose conditions on street bail if such conditions are necessary:

(a) to secure that the person surrenders to custody;
(b) to secure that the person does not commit an offence while on bail;
(c) to secure that the person does not interfere with witnesses or otherwise obstruct the course of justice, whether in relation to himself or any other person; or
(d) for the person's own protection, or, if aged under 17, for the person's own welfare or in the person's own interests.

A police officer may impose any conditions other than requiring the arrested person to provide a security or surety, or to reside in a bail hostel (see **Chapter 7**). The arrested person may ask the police or the magistrates' court to vary the conditions imposed on street bail. The police have the power to arrest without warrant a suspect who breaches conditions attached to street bail.

## 2.4 Entry, search and seizure

### 2.4.1 Introduction

This chapter has already looked at:

(a) the power to carry out a stop and search of persons and vehicles under s 1 of PACE 1984 (see **2.2** above); and
(b) the power to search an arrested person, or the premises where that person was arrested or where that person was immediately prior to arrest, under s 32 of PACE 1984 (see **2.3** above).

The rest of the chapter will look at the other powers to enter and search premises conferred on police officers by the 1984 Act.

When exercising any powers of search, entry and seizure, police officers must comply with the requirements of Code B. Paragraph 1.3 of Code B states:

> The right to privacy and respect for personal property are key principles of the Human Rights Act 1998. Powers of entry, search and seizure should be fully and clearly justified before use because they may significantly interfere with the occupier's privacy. Officers should consider if the necessary objectives can be met by less intrusive means.

A search of premises which is carried out unlawfully will contravene a suspect's right to respect for his private and family life under Article 8 of the ECHR (see **1.8.3**), and may entitle the suspect to claim damages for trespass in civil proceedings (see, eg, *Keegan v United Kingdom* (2006) 21 BHRC 189).

Any powers of search should be exercised courteously and with respect, and any force used in carrying out a search should be both reasonable and necessary and proportionate in the circumstances (Code B, para 1.4).

## 2.4.2 Section 8

### 2.4.2.1 When may a search warrant be issued under s 8?

Section 8(1) permits a police officer to apply to a magistrate for a warrant to enter and search premises. A magistrate may issue such a warrant if he is satisfied that there are reasonable grounds for believing:

(a) that an indictable offence has been committed;

(b) that there is material on the premises specified in the application which is likely to be of substantial value (whether by itself or together with other material) to the investigation of the offence;

(c) that the material is likely to be relevant evidence;

(d) that it does not consist of or include items subject to legal privilege, excluded material or special procedure material (such as health records or journalistic material); and

(e) that *any* of the conditions specified in s 8(3) apply.

The conditions in s 8(3) are:

(a) that it is not practicable to communicate with any person entitled to grant entry to the premises;

(b) that it is practicable to communicate with a person entitled to grant entry to the premises but it is not practicable to communicate with any person entitled to grant access to the evidence;

(c) that entry to the premises will not be granted unless a warrant is produced; or

(d) that the purpose of a search may be frustrated or seriously prejudiced unless a police officer arriving at the premises can secure immediate entry to them.

Under s 8(2), a police officer may seize and retain anything for which a search has been authorised by the magistrate.

In the light of the very wide powers of search granted by other sections of PACE 1984 (and particularly s 18, which is explained at **2.4.4** below), search warrants are usually confined to premises other than those controlled by an arrested person.

> **Example**
>
> Sanjay is arrested on suspicion of smuggling stolen paintings into the country for onward sale. The police believe that documents confirming the sale of these paintings are located in an office controlled by Richard, Sanjay's business partner. The police can apply to a magistrate under s 8 to obtain a warrant to search Richard's office if the requirements of s 8(1) are satisfied.

### 2.4.2.2 Procedural safeguards

A number of safeguards are provided by ss 15 and 16, and any entry on or search of premises by a police officer under a warrant is unlawful unless these safeguards are complied with.

Under s 15(2), a police officer applying for a warrant must:

(a) state the ground on which he makes the application and the statute under which the warrant would be issued;

(b) specify the premises which the officer wants to enter and search (there may be more than one set of premises specified but, if so, the details of each set of premises must be set out);

(c) identify, so far as is practicable, the articles or persons to be sought.

Paragraph 3.1 of Code B states that the officer must take reasonable steps to check that the information on which an application for a search warrant is based is 'accurate, recent and not provided maliciously or irresponsibly'.

An application for a warrant under s 8 will be made in writing to a magistrate, but without notice of the application being given to the owner or occupier of the premises which are the subject matter of the warrant. The police officer making the application is required to answer on oath any question that the magistrate may put to him about the application. The application must be supported by a signed written authority from an officer of at least the rank of inspector (Code B, para 3.4(a)).

If the police are unable to specify all the premises which a person occupies or controls, they may ask the court to issue an 'all premises warrant', as opposed to the usual warrant to search a specific set or sets of premises (s 8(1A)(a) and (b)). Such a warrant will enable the police to search both the specific premises noted in the warrant and, in addition, any further premises which are occupied or controlled by the person, even though the details of such premises are currently unknown (and will become known only when the police have carried out further investigations). All premises warrants are likely to be issued in cases of high-level fraud or organised crime.

### 2.4.2.3 Contents of the warrant

Any warrant that is issued will normally authorise entry on one occasion only (s 15(5)) and the warrant itself will specify:

(a) the name of the person who applied for it;

(b) the date on which it was issued;

(c) the statute under which it was issued; and

(d) the premises to be searched.

Additionally the warrant must identify, as far as practicable, the articles or persons to be sought (s 15(6)).

Section 15(5) does permits the court to issue a search warrant authorising entry and search of premises on more than one occasion, but *only* if it is necessary to carry out multiple searches to achieve the objective of the search.

### 2.4.2.4 Execution of the warrant

The warrant to enter and search premises must be executed within three months from the date of its issue (s 16(3)). The warrant must be executed at a reasonable hour, unless the police officer executing the warrant believes that the purpose of the search may be frustrated by entry at a reasonable hour (s 16(4)).

If the occupier of the premises to be entered and searched is present when the police officer executes the warrant, the officer must:

(a) identify himself to the occupier (and show him his warrant card to prove he is a police officer if he is not in uniform);

(b) show the warrant to the occupier; and

(c) supply the occupier with a copy of the warrant.

If the occupier of the premises is not present when the police officer executes the warrant, but some other person is present who appears to be in charge of the premises, the above steps must be taken in relation to that person. If nobody is present who appears to be in charge of the premises when the police officer executes the warrant, a copy of the warrant must be left in a prominent place on the premises.

Section 16(8) provides that any search under a warrant 'may only be a search to the extent required for the purpose for which the warrant was issued'.

### 2.4.3 Section 17

Section 17 allows a police officer to enter and search any premises for the purpose of:

(a) executing a warrant of arrest;

(b) arresting a person for an indictable offence;

(c) arresting a person for any one of a specified list of non-indictable offences, including an offence under s 4 of the Public Order Act 1986 (fear or provocation of violence) and the offence of driving whilst under the influence of drink or drugs (Road Traffic Act 1988, s 4);

(d) recapturing any person who is unlawfully at large and whom he is pursuing; or

(e) saving life or limb, or preventing serious damage to property.

The powers of entry and search for all but the last of the above purposes may be exercised only if the police officer has reasonable grounds for believing that the person he is seeking is on the premises (s 17(2)(b)).

**Example**

Mark commits a burglary of shop premises (an indictable offence) and his image is captured on a CCTV camera. The police investigate and are informed by Mark's parents that Mark is hiding in a flat belonging to Carol, his girlfriend. The police may enter and search Carol's flat to arrest Mark for the offence of burglary, as they will have reasonable grounds for believing that he is there.

The power of search in s 17 is only a power to search to the extent that is reasonably required for the purpose for which the power of entry is exercised (s 17(4)).

Section 17(6) expressly preserves the common law power the police have to enter premises to deal with or prevent a breach of the peace.

### 2.4.4 Section 18

Section 18(1) allows a constable to enter and search any premises *occupied or controlled* by a person who has been arrested for an indictable offence. This section allows the police to search a suspect's home address (since these will be premises occupied by the suspect) and also other premises over which the suspect has some form of control (eg business premises). In order to carry out such a search and entry, the police officer must have reasonable grounds for suspecting that there is on the premises evidence (other than items subject to legal privilege) that relates:

(a) to that offence; or

(b) to some other indictable offence which is connected with or similar to that offence.

**Example**

Frank, a bank manager, is arrested on suspicion of obtaining a pecuniary advantage by deception (an indictable offence). The police are informed by one of Frank's colleagues that documents relating to the offence are located in Frank's office at the branch of the bank where he works. The police will be able to search Frank's office under s 18 because these are premises controlled by Frank and the police have reasonable grounds for suspecting that evidence relating to the offence is on the premises.

Under s 18(2), a police officer may seize and retain any items for which he is permitted to search under s 18(1). The power to search in s 18(1) is only a power to search to the extent that is reasonably required for the purpose of discovering such evidence (s 18(3)).

The power of search under s 18 may be exercised only if it has been authorised in writing by an officer with the rank of inspector or above (s 18(4)). The only exception to this is s 18(5), which permits an officer to search premises before obtaining such authorisation (and before taking the arrested person to the police station or releasing him on 'street bail') if the police officer considers that the presence of the arrested person at the premises is necessary for the effective investigation of the offence. This situation is likely to arise only when there is evidence at the premises which is about to be destroyed and taking the person to the police station would facilitate its destruction.

### 2.4.5 Powers of seizure

Section 19 provides the police with a general power to seize items when an officer is 'lawfully on any premises'. A police officer will be lawfully on any premises if he is there:

(a) with the consent of the occupier (since there is nothing to prevent a police officer asking an occupier if he may enter and search premises when he has no other authority to enter);
(b) to execute a search warrant under s 8; or
(c) pursuant to any of the powers granted by ss 17, 18 or 32.

Under s 19(2), a police officer may seize *anything* which is on the premises if he has reasonable grounds for believing that:

(a) it has been obtained in consequence of the commission of an offence (not necessarily the offence he is currently investigating); and
(b) it is necessary to seize it in order to prevent it being concealed, lost, damaged, altered or destroyed.

**Example**

Julian is arrested on suspicion of handling stolen bank notes following the robbery of a local bank. PC Briggs enters Julian's house to carry out a search under s 18 for evidence relating to that offence. Whilst carrying out the search, PC Briggs finds a suitcase full of items of jewellery, recently reported as stolen following a burglary at a local hotel. PC Briggs will be able to seize the jewellery if he considers that it has been obtained by Julian as a result of the commission of an offence and it is necessary to seize the jewellery to prevent it being concealed, lost, damaged, altered or destroyed.

Under s 19(3), a police officer may seize *anything* which is on the premises if he has reasonable grounds for believing that:

(a) it is evidence in relation to an offence which he is investigating or any other offence; and
(b) it is necessary to seize it in order to prevent the evidence being concealed, lost, altered or destroyed.

**Example**

Reginald is arrested on suspicion of having taken part in a robbery at a local bank. PC Briggs enters Reginald's house to carry out a search under s 18 for the missing bank notes. Whilst carrying out the search, PC Briggs finds a set of scales, a quantity of plastic bags and some weights. PC Briggs suspects that these items are evidence that Julian is concerned in the cultivation and/or supply of controlled drugs. PC Briggs will be able to seize these items if he considers that such items are evidence in relation to an offence and it is necessary to seize the items to prevent them from being concealed, lost, altered or destroyed.

The power of seizure in s 19 is wider than the power of seizure granted by s 18, because under s 19 a police officer may seize any item found on the premises. Under s 18 a police officer can seize only items relating to the specific offence he is investigating, or some other indictable offence which is connected with or similar to that offence.

The only limitation on the power of seizure in s 19 is that a police officer cannot seize any item that he has reasonable grounds for believing is subject to legal privilege.

### 2.4.6 Powers of retention

Under s 22, anything which a police officer has seized by virtue of s 19 may be retained by the police 'so long as is necessary in all the circumstances' (s 22(1)).

Section 22(2) provides that anything seized for the purposes of a criminal investigation may be retained:

(a) for use as evidence at a criminal trial; or

(b) for forensic examination, or for investigation in connection with an offence.

### 2.4.7 Other powers of search, seizure and retention

In addition to the powers contained in PACE 1984, the police enjoy additional statutory powers of search, seizure and retention in respect of certain specific offences. An example is s 23(3) of the Misuse of Drugs Act 1971, which permits the police to enter any premises (by force if necessary) to search both the premises and anyone found on the premises either for controlled drugs, or for documents related to the production of such drugs. The police may seize and retain any drugs or documents found. Before exercising this power the police must obtain a warrant from a magistrate authorising them to enter the premises.

The police also enjoy more extensive powers of search, seizure and retention when investigating terrorist offences.

## 2.5 Checklist

At the end of this chapter you should be able to explain:

- the powers which the police may exercise to stop and search persons and vehicles (PACE 1984, s 1);
- the safeguards which are in place should the police wish to interview a person prior to arrest and to record any comments made during that interview (the 'anti-verballing rules');
- the powers of arrest which the police may exercise (PACE 1984, s 24);
- how an arrest should lawfully be carried out by the police (PACE 1984, s 28);

- the powers which the police may exercise to search a person following arrest (PACE 1984, s 32);
- the powers which the police may exercise to enter and search premises (PACE 1984, ss 8, 17 and 18);
- the powers which the police may exercise to seize and retain items found during a search (PACE 1984, ss 19 and 22).
- the importance of the police complying with the requirements of the Codes of Practice when exercising their investigative powers outside the police station.

# Chapter 3

# The Investigative Powers of the Police (2) – Inside the Police Station



## 3.1 Introduction

This chapter examines the powers the police may exercise when a suspect has been arrested and is detained at the police station. What occurs at the police station can be of great significance when a case gets to trial, particularly if the defendant's solicitor attempts to argue that prosecution evidence obtained whilst his client was detained at the police station is inadmissible because the police breached the provisions of PACE 1984 or the Codes of Practice.

References to section numbers in this chapter are, unless otherwise stated, to PACE 1984. References to Code C are to the Code of Practice for the Detention, Treatment and Questioning of Persons by Police Officers. References to Code D are to the Code of Practice for the Identification of Persons by Police Officers. References to Code E are to the Code of Practice on Audio Recording Interviews with Suspects, and references to Code F are to the Code of Practice on Visual Recording with Sound of Interviews with Suspects.

## 3.2 Procedure on arrival at the police station

### 3.2.1 Introduction

A suspect who has been arrested other than at a police station must be taken to the police station 'as soon as is practicable after the arrest' (s 30(1A)), unless the arresting officer decides to grant 'street bail' (see **Chapter 2**).

Occasionally a suspect may be arrested at the police station. If the police do not have sufficient evidence to arrest a suspect, they may ask that person to attend voluntarily at the police station to answer questions. There is no obligation to do this and a 'volunteer' who attends a police station is free to leave at any time. He can be prevented from leaving only if the police decide to place him under arrest before he leaves the police station (s 29). The police will often arrest a 'volunteer' if, when interviewed, the volunteer makes admissions which then give the police sufficient grounds to arrest him (see **Chapter 2**).

Paragraph 1.1 of Code C provides that 'all persons in custody must be dealt with expeditiously, and be released as soon as the need for detention no longer arises'.

### 3.2.2 The custody officer

#### 3.2.2.1 Who will the custody officer be?

A suspect who has been arrested must be brought before a custody officer in the custody suite on his arrival at the police station (or after his arrest if he was arrested at the police station). The custody officer is responsible for authorising the detention of the suspect and supervising his welfare whilst in police custody. The custody officer will normally be a police officer holding at least the rank of sergeant, who should not be involved in the investigation of the offence for which the suspect has been arrested.

Paragraph 2.1A of Code C confirms that a suspect who has been arrested (or who is attending the police station to answer bail) should be brought before the custody officer as 'soon as practicable'.

When the arresting officer brings the suspect before the custody officer, he must tell the custody officer:

(a) that the suspect was arrested as a result of his involvement, or suspected involvement or attempted involvement in the commission of a criminal offence; and

(b) why he considered it was necessary to arrest the suspect (Code G, para 2.2).

#### 3.2.2.2 What initial steps must the custody officer take?

The custody officer is responsible for opening and then maintaining a custody record for each suspect who has been arrested and brought to the police station. This is a written document which records certain key information:

(a) the suspect's name, address, telephone number, date of birth and occupation;

(b) the offence for which the suspect has been arrested and why the arresting officer considered it necessary to arrest the suspect;

(c) the time of the suspect's arrest and the time of his arrival at the police station;

(d) the reason why the suspect's ongoing detention at the police station has been authorised by the custody officer (see **3.3.2** below);

(e) the time such detention was authorised;

(f) confirmation that the suspect has been given details of the rights he may exercise whilst detained at the police station (see below), and whether he has requested legal advice from a solicitor; and

(g) details of the items of property the suspect has on his person, and details of any medical condition he suffers from.

The custody record will also have attached to it a detention log. This is a record of all the significant events that occur whilst the suspect is in police custody.

The custody officer must also inform the suspect about his ongoing rights which may be exercised at any time whilst the suspect is in custody:

(a) the right to have someone informed of the suspect's arrest (s 56);

(b) the right for the suspect to consult privately with a solicitor (the suspect must be told that free independent legal advice is available; s 58); and

(c) the right to consult the Codes of Practice.

### 3.2.2.3 Search of the detained person

The custody officer must also find out what items of property a suspect has on his person, and he may make a record of these items (s 54(1) and (2)). The custody officer may either search the suspect himself, or may authorise a search of the suspect, to the extent he considers necessary to ascertain what items the suspect has on his person. Detailed rules are set out in Annex A to Code C if the custody officer wants to search intimate parts of the suspect's body, or if the custody officer requires a suspect to remove more than his outer clothing during the conduct of the search.

Section 54(3) permits the custody officer to seize and retain any items the suspect has on his person. Items of clothing and personal effects may be seized only if the custody officer has reasonable grounds for believing that they may be evidence (for example, a blood-soaked shirt), or if the custody officer believes that the suspect may use them:

(a) to cause physical injury to himself or others;
(b) to cause damage to property;
(c) to interfere with evidence; or
(d) to assist him to escape.

Examples of such items are a penknife, a key, a sharpened comb or a razor blade.

## Key Document – The Custody Record

# Cheshire Police

## Custody Record

Custody number: 000687/07

**Detained Person**

| | | |
|---|---|---|
| Name: | DICKSON, GARY PAUL | |
| Date of birth: | 28/10/80 | Place of birth: York |
| Address: | 17 Marsh Street, Chester CH3 7LW United Kingdom | |
| Height: | 180cm Weight: 14 stones | Build: Well-built Gender: Male |
| Hair Colour: | Dark brown | Eye colour: Blue |
| Officer defined ethnicity: | 1. White Euro | Self defined ethnicity: W1. White British |

**Arrest details/Offences**

| | |
|---|---|
| Arrest time: | 18/12/07 11.40 |
| Arrest reason: | Assault occasioning actual bodily harm |
| Place of arrest: | 17 Marsh Street Chester CH3 7LW United Kingdom |
| Arresting Officer: | 911 Chambers, G |
| Investigating Officer: | 911 Chambers, G |
| Delivering Officer: | |
| Occurrence #: | Crime: ABH @ 18/12/07 03.15 (O/S Connelley's nightclub, Central Street, Chester) |

| **Offence date** | **Status** | **Offence/Charge Summary** |
|---|---|---|
| 18/12/07 | Pending | A.B.H |

**Offence disposals**

**Detentions**

| | |
|---|---|
| Station: | CUSTODY CHESTER (Police Station, North Park Road, Chester, United Kingdom, CH1 9RP) |
| Circumstances of Arrest: | DP arrives in custody. Handcuffed but compliant. Circs given by 911 in the presence of the DP. Police attended outside Connelley's nightclub following report of assault. On arrival spoke to victim and a witness who noted the vehicle registration number of the vehicle used by the assailant. Vehicle was found to be owned by DP. DP arrested by 911 Chambers at his home address at 17 Marsh Street, Chester. |
| Time of arrival: | 18/12/07 12.00 |
| Time of authorised det: | 18/12/07 12.30 Authorising det. Officer: 568 Dunn, S |
| Time of release: | N/A |
| Total det. Time: | |

---

**Medical**

| Type | D/P/Other | Signature fac. | Officer Name | Signed time |
|---|---|---|---|---|
| Medical | Dickson, G.P. | *G.P. Dickson* | 568 Dunn, S | 18/12/07 12.40 |

Do you have any illness or injury: NO If so, what and when:
Have you seen a doctor for this illness or injury:
Are you taking any medication: NO If so, what and when:
Are you suffering from any mental health problems, nervous disorder or depression: NO
If yes, give details:
Have you ever tried to harm yourself: NO If so when and why:
Have you consumed alcohol recently: NO If so, when:
Do you have any special dietary needs: NO If so, what:

I confirm that the above details relating to my health are correct.

*G P Dickson*

---

**Property**

| Type | D/P/Other | Signature fac. | Officer Name | Signed time |
|---|---|---|---|---|
| Property recorded | Dickson, G.P. | *G.P. Dickson* | 568 Dunn, S | 18/12/07 12.45 |

Added item: Mobile phone, quant: 1 police prevent damage/injury Motorola
Added item: Wallet and misc cards & papers, quant: 1 police prevent damage/injury
Added item: bank card, quant: 1 police no need to refer Alliance and Leicester card
Added 4 £1 coin(s) (cash)
Added 1 £5 coin(s)/note(s) (cash)

Added 2 £20 note(s) (cash)
Added £.05 of copper coin (cash)
Added £.90 of silver coin (cash)

Sealed in bags ME 89540 and LA 9994

---

**Rights**

| Type | D/P/Other | Signature fac. | Officer Name | Signed time |
|---|---|---|---|---|
| Rights given | Dickson, G.P. | G.P. Dickson | 568 Dunn, S | 18/12/07 12.50 |
| | A notice setting out my rights has been read to me and I have also been provided with a written notice setting out my entitlements whilst in police custody. | | | |
| Rights given | Dickson, G.P. | G.P.Dickson | 568 Dunn, S | 18/12/07 12.52 |
| | I have been informed of my right to speak to a solicitor in person on the telephone at any time during my custody. I do not want to speak to a solicitor. | | | |

---

**Detention Log**

| Type | D/P/Other | Signature fac. | Officer Name | Signed time |
|---|---|---|---|---|
| General detention | Dickson, G.P. | G.P. Dickson | 568 Dunn, S | 18/12/07 12.30 |
| | The officer has advised me that the reason for the arrest is: ALLOW THE PROMPT AND EFFECTIVE INVESTIGATION (INTERVIEW) AND TO PREVENT PHYSICAL INJURY TO OTHERS | | | |

---

| | | |
|---|---|---|
| Detention Authorisation | 568 Dunn, S | 18/12/07 12.30 |

Detention Authorised for the following reasons:

(Evidence) Detention is authorised as there are reasonable grounds for believing that detention without charge is necessary to obtain evidence by questioning.

---

| | | |
|---|---|---|
| General detention | 568 Dunn, S | 18/12/07 13.00 |

D P placed in cell 4

---

| | | |
|---|---|---|
| General detention | 568 Dunn, S | 18/12/07 14.00 |

Checked, standing in cell, in order. Cup of tea provided

---

| | | |
|---|---|---|
| Meal/drink | 568 Dunn, S | 18/12/07 15.00 |
| Checked, sitting in cell, in order. Cup of tea refused | | |
| Meal/drink | 568 Dunn, S | 18/12/07 16.00 |
| Meal offered - refused | | |
| General detention | 568 Dunn, S | 18/12/07 17.00 |
| Welfare check – in order – dp pacing up and down cell | | |
| Detention review | 568 Dunn, S | 18/12/07 18.00 |
| Review of detention by Insp. 420 HUDSON. Continued detention authorised to obtain evidence by questioning | | |
| General detention | 568 Dunn, S | 18/12/07 18.20 |
| DP transferred into custody of PC 911 CHAMBERS. Taken to interview room. Interviewed by PC 911 CHAMBERS. | | |
| General detention | 568 Dunn, S | 18/12/07 18.45 |
| DP returned to custody of PS 568 DUNN. | | |
| General detention | 568 Dunn, S | 18/12/07 19.00 |
| DP charged with assault occasioning actual bodily harm. No reply on charge. | | |
| General detention | 568 Dunn, S | 18/12/07 19.05 |
| DP refused bail by PS 568 DUNN. Reasonable grounds to believe DP will fail to appear in court and will commit further offences if bail granted. | | |

## 3.3 Detention at the police station

### 3.3.1 Is there sufficient evidence to charge the suspect?

After opening the custody record and informing the suspect of his rights, the custody officer must determine whether there is already 'sufficient evidence' to charge the suspect with the offence for which he has been arrested (s 37(1)). To do this, the custody officer will ask the investigating officer – usually in the presence of the suspect – for details of the evidence that already exists against the suspect and what steps the officer proposes to take if the further detention of the suspect is authorised (this will normally be some form of investigative procedure such as an audibly recorded interview with the suspect or the holding of an identification procedure – see **3.5** below). The custody officer should note in the custody record any comments made by the suspect in relation to the account given by the arresting officer of the reasons for the arrest (Code C, para 3.4). The custody officer should not himself put any questions to the arrested person about his involvement in any offence (Code C, para 3.4).

The custody officer may detain the suspect at the police station for as long as it is necessary for him to determine if sufficient evidence exists to charge the suspect. If there is such evidence, the suspect should be charged straight away, and either released on bail to appear before the magistrates' court or remanded in police custody until he can be brought before the magistrates.

### 3.3.2 Grounds for detention

If there is not sufficient evidence to charge a suspect immediately, the suspect should be released either on bail or without bail, unless:

(a) the custody officer has reasonable grounds for believing that detaining the suspect without charge is necessary to *secure* or *preserve* evidence relating to an offence for which he is under arrest; or
(b) it is necessary to obtain such evidence by *questioning* (s 37(2)).

If either of these grounds is satisfied, the custody officer may authorise the suspect to be kept in police detention (s 37(3)).

The usual ground upon which a custody officer will authorise detention is to enable the officer investigating the offence to obtain evidence by questioning the suspect about his involvement in the offence under investigation.

The first ground above may be useful in situations where the police want to carry out a search of the suspect's premises under s 18 (see **Chapter 2**), or where they are still looking for evidence of the offence. In such cases the police may want to detain the suspect in the police station so that he has no opportunity to hide or destroy the evidence before it can be found. This ground can also be used where the police want to obtain some form of identification evidence and can do so only whilst the suspect is in the police station.

#### Example 1

Jackie is arrested on suspicion of theft of a necklace from a jewellery shop. The police believe that Jackie has hidden the necklace somewhere in her flat and want to carry out a search of the flat under s 18. The custody officer may authorise Jackie's detention at the police station if he has reasonable grounds for believing that, if released, Jackie may remove or destroy the necklace before the officer conducting the search is able to find it.

#### Example 2

Anthony is arrested on suspicion of the burglary of a factory. The police have found fingerprints on the frame of the window which was smashed by the burglar to gain entry to the property. The custody officer may authorise Anthony's detention at the police station if he has reasonable grounds for believing that Anthony's detention will be necessary in order for Anthony's fingerprints to be taken to see if they match those found at the factory.

If the custody officer becomes aware at any time that the grounds on which a suspect's detention was authorised have ceased to apply (and that no other grounds to justify his continued detention exist), the suspect must be released immediately (s 39).

### 3.3.3 Conditions of detention

The cell in which a suspect is held must be adequately heated, cleaned and ventilated, and also adequately lit (Code C, para 8.2). Any bedding supplied to a suspect must be of a reasonable standard and in a clean and sanitary condition (Code C, para 8.3). A suspect must be provided with access to toilet and washing facilities (Code C, para 8.4).

A suspect must be offered at least two light meals and one main meal in any 24-hour period, and drinks should be provided at meal times and upon reasonable request between meals (Code C, para 8.6). A suspect should be offered brief outdoor exercise daily if this is practicable (Code C, para 8.7).

Suspects should be visited in their cells at least every hour (Code C, para 9.3).

If the custody officer considers that a suspect is injured, appears to be suffering from physical illness or mental disorder, or appears to need clinical attention, the custody officer must make arrangements to ensure that the suspect receives appropriate clinical attention as soon as reasonably practicable (Code C, para 9.5). Normally in such cases the custody officer will arrange for the suspect to be seen by the police surgeon.

### 3.3.4 Periods of detention

#### 3.3.4.1 The initial maximum period

Section 41 provides that a person 'shall not be kept in police detention for more than 24 hours without being charged'. This 24-hour period begins from the 'relevant time'. The relevant time is determined as follows:

(a) in the case of a person attending voluntarily at the police station who is then arrested at the police station, *the time of his arrest* (s 41(2)(c));

(b) in the case of a person who attends a police station to answer 'street bail' granted under s 30A, *the time when he arrives at the police station* (s 41(2)(ca));

(c) in any other case, the relevant time is *the time when the suspect arrested arrives at the first police station to which he is taken after his arrest* (s 41(1)(d)).

**Example 1**

Stuart is attending the police station as a volunteer to answer questions about his suspected involvement in an assault. Stuart arrives at the police station at 11 am. His interview begins at 11.15 am and ends at 12.00 pm. Stuart is arrested at 12.10 pm. The 'detention clock' will start running from 12.10 pm, the time of Stuart's arrest. The police will be able to detain Stuart for a maximum period of 24 hours from this time.

**Example 2**

Eric is arrested by PC Long on suspicion of theft. There are witnesses to the theft from whom PC Long wants to take statements before interviewing Eric. He therefore grants Eric street bail, requiring him to attend at the police station at 1 pm the following day. Eric complies with the terms of his street bail, and attends the police station at 1 pm the following day. The 'detention clock' will start running from this time. The police will be able to detain Eric for a maximum period of 24 hours from this time.

**Example 3**

Hussein is arrested at home at 3.30 pm on suspicion of theft. He is taken to the police station and arrives there at 3.45 pm. His detention is authorised by the custody officer at 4.00 pm. The 'detention clock' will start running from 3.45 pm, the time of Hussein's arrival at the police station. The police will be able to detain Hussein for a maximum period of 24 hours from this time.

#### 3.3.4.2 Can the police extend the maximum period of detention?

Under s 42, the police have the power to extend the period of a suspect's detention in the police station up to a period of 36 hours from the 'relevant time' if certain conditions are met.

Such an authorisation must be given by an officer of the rank of superintendent or above, and may only be given if the superintendent has reasonable grounds for believing that:

(a) the detention of the suspect without charge is necessary to secure or preserve evidence relating to an offence for which the suspect is under arrest, or to obtain such evidence by questioning him;

(b) the offence is an indictable offence (ie, an either way or an indictable only offence); and

(c) the investigation is being carried out diligently and expeditiously.

**Example**

Victor is arrested on suspicion of the murder of Margaret. He arrives at the police station at 9.00 am and is questioned about the offence. Victor refuses to answer any questions, but at 8.00 am the following day, during the course of searching Victor's house, the police find a bloodstained knife that they believe Victor used as the murder weapon. The investigating officer wants to question Victor about this new piece of evidence, and asks the superintendent to authorise Victor's continued detention to enable him to do this.

The superintendent is likely to authorise the extension of the initial detention period. Murder is an indictable offence and the investigating officer wants to question Victor to find out what Victor has to say about the knife which has only just been found. As long as the superintendent believes that the investigating officer is carrying out the investigation diligently and expeditiously, the officer's request will be granted. If the request is granted, Victor may be detained at the police station until 9 pm that day.

#### 3.3.4.3 Are any further extensions possible?

The police are able to obtain a warrant of further detention from a magistrates' court if the conditions set out below are satisfied (s 43). If the magistrates are persuaded to grant a warrant of further detention, this can be for such period of time as the magistrates think fit, but up to a maximum period of 36 hours. This is on top of the police superintendent's power to extend the basic detention period up to a maximum of 36 hours from the 'relevant time'. Therefore, if the magistrates grant a warrant of further detention, this may result in the suspect being detained in the police station for a total of 72 hours (ie, three days).

The police may apply for a warrant of further detention only if the offence under investigation is an indictable offence (s 43(4)(b)). The application to the magistrates' court must be made on oath by a police officer and must be supported by a written application (called an 'information'). A copy of the information must be supplied to the suspect, and the suspect must be brought to court for the hearing. The suspect is entitled to legal representation at the hearing.

The magistrates will grant a warrant of further detention only if they consider that there are 'reasonable grounds for believing that the further detention of the person to whom the application relates is justified' (s 43(1)). Such detention can be justified only if:

(a) the suspect's detention without charge is necessary to secure or preserve evidence relating to an offence for which he is under arrest, or to obtain such evidence by questioning him; and

(b) the investigation is being conducted diligently and expeditiously (s 43(4)).

**Example**

Clare is arrested at 4 pm on 15 March on suspicion of robbery and is taken to the police station, arriving there at 4.30 pm. This is the relevant time for detention purposes. Clare can be detained initially for a maximum period of 24 hours, and so must be released or charged no later than 4.30 pm on 16 March. If, before 4.30 pm on 16 March, a superintendent authorises Clare's continued detention under s 42, Clare can be detained until 4.30 am on 17 March, at which point she must be released or charged. But if, before this time, the police apply to the magistrates' court for a warrant of further detention and a warrant is granted for a 36-hour period, the police will be able to detain Clare until 4.30 pm on 18 March, at which point she must be released or charged.

In exceptional cases, the police can make an additional application to a magistrates' court under s 44 for an extension of the warrant of further detention granted under s 43. The same procedural requirements as are required for an application under s 43 must be complied with, and the magistrates will grant an extension only if the grounds under s 43 above are satisfied and there are reasonable grounds for believing that the further detention is justified (s 44(1)).

An extension granted under s 44 'shall be for any period as the court thinks fit' but cannot:

(a) be longer than 36 hours; or

(b) end later than 96 hours after the 'relevant time'.

This means that the police can detain a suspect in police custody for a maximum period of *four days* before that suspect must be either released or charged (the only exception to this is the powers of detention in respect of certain terrorist offences, which are beyond the scope of this book).

**Example**

Continuing with the example of Clare above, the police may apply for an extension of the warrant of further detention at any time before the warrant granted under s 43 expires. This extension can be for a maximum of 36 hours but cannot end later than 96 hours after the 'relevant time'. The relevant time in this case is 4.30 pm on 15 March. Therefore the extension cannot go beyond 4.30 pm on 19 March. At this point Clare must be released or charged with an offence.

#### 3.3.4.4 Detention reviews

In addition to the time limits for detention set out in **3.3.4.3** above, the police are obliged to carry out periodic reviews of the suspect's detention to ensure that the grounds on which the detention was initially authorised by the custody officer are still applicable (s 40). This is a mandatory requirement and, if such reviews are not carried out, any detention after this time will be unlawful and will amount to the tort of false imprisonment (*Roberts v Chief Constable of the Cheshire Constabulary* [1999] 1 WLR 662).

Reviews of detention that take place before a suspect is charged are carried out by an officer of at least the rank of inspector who is not directly involved in the investigation (s 40(2)(b)). This officer is usually referred to as the 'review officer'.

The first review must take place no later than six hours after the custody officer first authorised the detention of the suspect (*not* six hours after the suspect first arrived at the police station). The second review must take place no later than nine hours after the first review. Subsequent reviews must take place at intervals of not more than nine hours.

**Example**

Simeon is arrested at 10 am. He arrives at the police station at 10.15 am (the 'relevant time' for the purpose of calculating the maximum period of detention). The custody officer authorises his detention at 10.30 am. The first custody review must be carried out no later than 4.30 pm. If that review takes place at, for example, 4.15 pm, the next review would need to take place no later than 1.15 am the following day (ie, no more than nine hours after the first review). Further reviews after that would then need to take place at intervals of no more than nine hours.

## 3.4 Rights of the suspect

### 3.4.1 Right to have someone informed of the arrest

Section 56(1) states:

> Where a person has been arrested and is being held in custody in a police station or other premises, he shall be entitled, if he so requests, to have one friend or relative or other person who is known to him or who is likely to take an interest in his welfare told, as soon as practicable ... that he has been arrested and is being detained there.

In certain situations the police may delay the exercise of this right. Any delay must be authorised by an officer of at least the rank of inspector and can only be authorised when the suspect has been detained for an indictable offence (s 56(2)(a) and (b)). The length of any delay can be for a maximum of 36 hours from the 'relevant time' (s 56(3)). Authorisation may be given orally but, if it is, must be confirmed in writing as soon as is practicable (s 56(4)).

The police officer who authorises the delay may do so only if he has reasonable grounds for believing that telling the named person of the arrest *will*:

(a) lead to interference with or harm to evidence connected with an indictable offence, or interference with or physical injury to other persons;

(b) lead to the alerting of other persons suspected of having committed such an offence but not yet arrested for it; or

(c) hinder the recovery of any property obtained as a result of such an offence (s 56(5)).

The right not to be held incommunicado in the police station is a fundamental right, and the police cannot delay the exercise of this right if they have merely have reasonable grounds for believing that telling the named person of the arrest *might* lead to any of the above consequences. The police need to have reasonable grounds for believing that telling the named person *will* lead to any one or more of these consequences.

**Example**

Fred is a member of a notorious criminal gang whose members all have previous convictions for armed robbery. Fred is arrested on suspicion of having taken part in an armed robbery at a bank, after an image of his face was captured on the bank's CCTV system. A number of other people took part in the robbery, but they have not yet been identified. Several thousand pounds were stolen in the robbery.

Fred wants to notify Vince, his brother, that he has been arrested. Vince is known to be a member of the gang. The police believe that, if notified that Fred has been arrested, Vince will alert the other gang members who participated in the robbery and these people will then take steps to dispose of the money that was stolen. The police will be able to take advantage of the provisions in s 56 to delay Vince being notified of Fred's arrest for up to 36 hours. Armed robbery is an indictable offence, and the police appear to have reasonable grounds for believing that notifying Vince of Fred's arrest will lead to the alerting of other suspects and will hinder the recovery of property obtained as a result of the offence.

## 3.4.2 Right to legal advice

### 3.4.2.1 The basic right to legal advice

A suspect who has been arrested and detained at the police station has the right to receive free and independent legal advice.

Section 58(1) states:

> A person arrested and held in custody in a police station or other premises shall be entitled, if he so requests, to consult a solicitor privately at any time.

If a suspect makes such a request, he must be permitted to consult a solicitor 'as soon as practicable' (s 58(4)).

Paragraph 6.1 of Code C reinforces this by providing that:

> ... all detainees must be informed that they may at any time consult and communicate privately with a solicitor, whether in person, in writing or by telephone, and that free independent legal advice is available from the duty solicitor.

If a solicitor attends the police station to see a particular suspect, that suspect must be informed of the solicitor's arrival at the police station (whether or not he is being interviewed at the time of the solicitor's arrival). The suspect must then be asked if he would like to see the solicitor, even if he has previously declined legal advice (Code C, para 6.15). The solicitor's attendance and the suspect's decision must be noted in the custody record.

Code C also states that at no time should a police officer do or say anything with the intention of dissuading a person from obtaining legal advice (Code C, para 6.4).

### 3.4.2.2 When can the right to legal advice be delayed?

The police have a very limited right to delay the exercise of this right. Any delay must be authorised by an officer with at least the rank of superintendent, and can be authorised only when a suspect has been arrested for an indictable offence (s 58(6)). The length of any delay can be for a maximum of 36 hours from the relevant time (s 58(5)). Authorisation for delaying a suspect's access to legal advice can be given orally but, if it is, must be confirmed in writing as soon as is practicable (s 58(7)).

A police officer may authorise a delay in the suspect receiving access to legal advice only if he has reasonable grounds for believing that the exercise of this right, at the time when the suspect wishes to exercise it, *will*:

(a) lead to interference with or harm to evidence connected with an indictable offence, or interference with or physical injury to other persons;
(b) lead to the alerting of other persons suspected of having committed such an offence but not yet arrested for it; or
(c) hinder the recovery of any property obtained as a result of such an offence (s 58(8)).

Access to legal advice is a fundamental right, and the police cannot delay the exercise of this right if they think merely that allowing the suspect to exercise his right to obtain legal advice *might* lead to one or more of the above consequences. The police must reasonably believe that allowing the suspect to exercise this right *will* lead to one or more of these consequences. This is a very difficult test for the police to satisfy. Guidelines which the police must follow when determining whether to delay a suspect's access to legal advice are contained in Annex B to Code C.

Occasionally the police will attempt to use their powers under s 58 if they consider that the particular solicitor a suspect has asked to consult may himself be involved or implicated in criminal activity. It will of course be very rare for a police officer to believe that a solicitor would knowingly pass on information in breach of s 58, and any grounds put forward by the police to justify delaying the right would need to be specific to the solicitor concerned.

If the police have reasonable grounds for such a belief in respect of the particular solicitor a suspect has asked to consult, the suspect should still be offered the opportunity to consult the duty solicitor. The duty solicitor will be a solicitor chosen from a list of local solicitors who have agree to be members of the 'Duty Solicitor Scheme' for the relevant police station, and who are available to attend the police station on a rota basis to represent those suspects who do not have a solicitor of their own (or whose solicitor is unavailable). The identity of the particular duty solicitor who attends the police station will depend on which solicitor on the rota is 'on call' at the time the suspect requests access to legal advice. This means that the duty solicitor could be any one of a number of individuals, and in these circumstances it will be very difficult for the police to establish the necessary grounds for delaying access to legal advice.

Alternatively, the police may think that a solicitor will be an unwitting dupe and may inadvertently pass on information to other suspects still at liberty. This point was considered in *R v Samuel* [1988] QB 115. The Court of Appeal held that the police officer must have a reasonable belief that one of the statutory grounds for exclusion applies and that the consequence will very probably happen. The Court went on to say that it would be a rare occurrence for a solicitor to be an unwitting dupe, and any suspicion that a suspect will try to use the solicitor in this role would have to be specific to the suspect, such as where the suspect is known or suspected to be a member of a criminal gang.

Although ss 56 and 58 enable the police to keep a suspect incommunicado and to deny the suspect access to legal advice for up to 36 hours, the exercise of this power by the police can be for a period of less than 36 hours, and a suspect must be told as soon as the grounds on which delay was authorised no longer apply.

#### Example

George is arrested on suspicion of murder. It is alleged that George committed the murder together with Jeremy. At the time of George's arrest Jeremy has not been apprehended, and the police delay the exercise of George's rights under s 56 and s 58 on the basis that exercising these rights will lead to the alerting of Jeremy. Ten hours after George arrives at the police station, the police arrest Jeremy. The only ground on which the exercise of George's rights under s 56 and s 58 was delayed has now been removed. The police should now inform George of his right to have someone informed of his arrest and his right to obtain free and independent legal advice.

### 3.4.3 Right to consult the Codes of Practice

A suspect who has been arrested is also entitled to ask to consult the Codes of Practice (A–H) which supplement the provisions of PACE 1984.

## 3.5 Interviews and identification evidence

### 3.5.1 Introduction

Once the custody officer has authorised the detention of a suspect at the police station, the officer investigating the offence will then take steps to further his investigation. The steps that an investigating officer can take to secure, preserve or obtain evidence whilst the suspect is detained at the police station will involve one or more of the following:

(a) carrying out an audibly recorded interview with the suspect about the suspect's alleged involvement in the offence(s);

(b) carrying out a form of identification procedure to see if a witness to, or a victim of, the offence is able to recognise the suspect;

(c) taking fingerprints from the suspect to see if these match fingerprints found at the scene of the crime, or on any relevant objects or articles which the police have recovered;

(d) taking samples from the suspect to see if these match any samples obtained during the course of the police investigation; and

(e) taking photographs of the suspect.

These investigative powers will be examined further below.

### 3.5.2 Interviews with the suspect

#### 3.5.2.1 Introduction

Interviews that take place in the police station must comply with the requirements of Codes C and E. Such interviews are recorded (usually on a tape) and are referred to in the Codes of Practice as 'audibly recorded' interviews. Code E provides detailed guidance as to the procedure that need to be followed in such interviews.

Paragraph 2.1 of Code E states: 'Recording of interviews shall be carried out openly to instil confidence in its reliability as an impartial and accurate record of the interview.'

The interview will normally be recorded on two tapes. One of the tapes, the master tape, is sealed in the presence of the suspect at the end of the interview. This seal will be broken and the tape opened at trial only if there is any dispute about what was said. The other tape is called the working copy and will be used by the police to prepare a written summary or transcript of the interview if the suspect is subsequently charged with an offence. Some police forces will use three tapes, with the third tape being given to the suspect if he is subsequently charged so that he may pass this on to his solicitor for the solicitor to listen to (see **Chapter 6**).

### 3.5.2.2 Should the suspect be interviewed at all?

Paragraph 11.18 of Code C provides that suspects who, at the time of the interview, appear unable to:

(a) appreciate the significance of questions or their answers; or

(b) understand what is happening because of the effects of drink, drugs, or any illness, ailment or condition,

should not generally be interviewed (although there are some limited exceptions to this in cases where an interview needs to be held as a matter of urgency).

Paragraph 2(b) of Annex G to Code C states that a suspect might be 'at risk' in an interview if '... anything the [suspect] says in the interview ... *might* be considered unreliable in subsequent court proceedings because of their physical or mental state'.

If a suspect is deemed to be at risk, the custody officer will normally ask a health care professional to see the suspect, and then ask that professional to advise on whether the suspect is fit to be interviewed

### 3.5.2.3 Start of the interview

**The caution**

At the start of the interview, the police officer conducting the interview will caution the suspect. The wording of the caution is as follows:

> You do not have to say anything. However it may harm your defence if you do not mention when questioned something which you later rely on in court. Anything you do say may be given in evidence. (Code C, para 10.5)

The caution is worded in this way because, although the suspect has a right to remain silent and cannot be compelled to answer questions in the interview, if the suspect exercises this right but then at his trial raises facts as part of his defence which he could have mentioned during the interview, the court may draw an 'adverse inference' from his silence under s 34 of the Criminal Justice and Public Order Act 1994 (see **Chapter 18**).

If, however, the interviewing officer wants the suspect to account for an object, substance or mark found on his person, in or on his clothing or footwear, otherwise in his possession or in the place where he was arrested, a 'special caution' must be given. Such a caution will also be required if the suspect was arrested at the place where the offence was committed at or about the time of the offence, and the officer wants the suspect to account for his presence. If the special caution is given and the suspect then fails to answer the question (or to answer the question satisfactorily), the court at trial will be able to draw an adverse inference from this pursuant to ss 36–37 of the Criminal Justice and Public Order Act 1994 (see **Chapter 18**). If the officer fails to administer the special caution, no such inference may be drawn at trial.

The special caution requires the suspect to be informed of the following matters (in ordinary language):

(a) what offence is being investigated;

(b) what fact the suspect is being asked to account for;

(c) this fact may be due to the suspect taking part in the commission of the offence;

(d) a court may draw a proper inference if the suspect fails or refuses to account for this fact; and

(e) a record is being made of the interview and it may be given in evidence if the suspect is brought to trial (Code C, para 10.11).

After cautioning the suspect, the officer must also remind the suspect that he is entitled to free and independent legal advice, even if the suspect has his solicitor present at the interview (Code C, para 11.2). The caution and the reminder that the suspect is entitled to free and independent advice must be given at the start of each interview the police have with the suspect.

### Significant statements and silences

After complying with the above, the interviewing officer must then put to the suspect 'any significant statement or silence which occurred in the presence and hearing of a police officer ... before the start of the interview' (Code C, para 11.4). The interviewing officer must ask the suspect whether he confirms or denies that earlier statement or silence, and if he wants to add anything to it. The terms 'significant statement' and 'significant silence' are defined in Code C, para 11.4A. A 'significant statement' is a statement which appears capable of being used in evidence against the suspect at trial, in particular a direct admission of guilt. A 'significant silence' is a failure or refusal to answer a question, or which might allow the court to draw adverse inferences from that silence at trial (see **Chapter 18**).

#### Example 1

PC Singh is called to a public house where one of the customers has been assaulted. The customer did not recognise his assailant but is able to provide PC Singh with an accurate description of this person. PC Singh leaves the public house and sees Oliver nearby. Oliver closely matches the description of the assailant given by the customer. PC Singh asks Oliver where he has just come from. Oliver tells him that he has come from the same public house where the assault occurred. This gives PC Singh reasonable grounds to suspect that Oliver may have committed the assault. PC Singh should therefore caution Oliver before asking him any further questions about the assault.

If, on being asked where he had come from when being questioned in the street by PC Singh, Oliver told PC Singh 'I came from the pub but it wasn't me that hit him', this would be a significant statement. Oliver has not been told by PC Singh that an assault took place at the pub, and the only explanation for Oliver's comments is that he was at the pub and knows something about the assault. This is an admission by Oliver, and should be put to him at the start of the interview.

#### Example 2

PC Rogers is called to a jewellery shop in connection with the suspected theft of a gold bracelet by Alex. Following PC Roger's arrival at the shop, and in his hearing, the owner of the shop says to Alex: 'I saw you pick the bracelet up and put it in your pocket when you thought I wasn't looking. Why did you try to steal it?' Alex doesn't reply to this. This is a significant silence. Although Alex has not admitted his guilt, had he not done what the owner of the shop accused him if doing, it would have been reasonable to expect him to have denied the shop owner's version of events. The significant silence should be put to Alex at the start of his interview at the police station.

Should the police officer fail to put to a suspect at the start of the interview a significant statement or silence made outside the police station, this may result in the contents of that statement or the nature of that silence being ruled inadmissible at trial under s 78 of PACE 1984 (see **Chapter 21**).

### 3.5.2.4 Conduct of the interview

The way in which the interviewing officer may conduct the interview is subject to limitations imposed by Code C. Paragraph 11.5 provides:'No interviewer may try to obtain answers or elicit a statement by the use of oppression.'

'Oppression' might occur if the interviewing officer:

(a) raises his voice or shouts at the suspect;
(b) makes threatening gestures towards the suspect;
(c) leans towards the suspect so that he is 'in the suspect's face';
(d) stands over or behind the suspect; or
(e) threatens to detain the suspect indefinitely unless he makes a confession.

Paragraph 11.5 also states that: '... no interviewer shall indicate, except to answer a direct question, what action will be taken by the police if the person being questioned answers questions, makes a statement or refuses to do either.' This means that an interviewing officer should not offer any inducements to a suspect to admit his guilt. This may occur if the interviewing officer indicates to the suspect that he will be released from police detention much more quickly if he admits to having committed the offence under investigation.

The interview must cease when

> the officer in charge of the investigation is satisfied all the questions they consider relevant to obtaining accurate and reliable information about the offence have been put to the suspect, this includes allowing the suspect an opportunity to give an innocent explanation and asking questions to test if the explanation is accurate and reliable, eg to clear up ambiguities or clarify what the suspect said. (Code C, para 11.6)

If interviews with a suspect take place over more than one day, in any period of 24 hours the suspect must be given a continuous period of at least eight hours for rest. This period will usually be at night and must be free from questioning or any other interruption in connection with the offence (Code C, para 12.2).

Similarly, breaks from interviews should take place at recognised meal times, and short refreshment breaks should be taken at approximately two-hour intervals (Code C, para 12.8).

If the conduct of an interview breaches any of the above provisions of Code C, at any subsequent trial the court may rule inadmissible any admission or confession made by the defendant in that interview (see **Chapter 20**).

### 3.5.2.5 Can a suspect be interviewed before receiving legal advice?

**The general position**

In general, a suspect who requires legal advice should not be interviewed (or continue to be interviewed) until such advice has been received (Code C, para 6.6). This means that the police should not seek to interview a suspect who has indicated that he requires legal advice. Similarly, where a suspect has indicated that he does not require legal advice, is then interviewed and indicates at some point during the interview that he has changed his mind and now requires legal advice, the police should stop the interview to allow the suspect to obtain such advice.

**Exceptions to the general position**

The police may interview a suspect before that suspect has obtained independent legal advice in the following situations:

(a) As noted at **3.4.2.2** above, s 58 allows the police to delay a suspect receiving any legal advice for up to 36 hours. If the police exercise their powers under s 58 to delay a suspect's access to legal advice, the police may (and usually will) want to interview the suspect prior to allowing him access to legal advice.

(b) Even if the police do not exercise their powers under s 58 to delay the suspect having access to legal advice, they are still permitted to interview a suspect before that suspect has received legal advice if an officer of at least the rank of superintendent reasonably believes that the delay which would be caused by the time taken to obtain such advice might:
   (i) lead to interference with, or harm to, evidence connected with an offence;
   (ii) lead to interference with, or physical harm to, other people;
   (iii) lead to serious loss of, or damage to, property;
   (iv) lead to alerting other people suspected of having committed an offence but not yet arrested for it; or
   (v) hinder the recovery of property obtained in consequence of the commission of an offence (Code C, para 6.6(b)(i)).

(c) The police are also permitted to interview a suspect before that suspect has received legal advice if the relevant solicitor has agreed to attend the police station, but awaiting his arrival would 'cause unreasonable delay to the process of investigation' (Code C, para 6.6(b)(ii)).

(d) The police may interview a suspect before the suspect has received legal advice if the solicitor the suspect has asked to speak to either cannot be contacted or has declined to attend the police station, and the suspect has then declined the opportunity to consult the duty solicitor (Code C, para 6.6(c)).

(e) If a suspect asks for legal advice but then changes his mind about this, the police may interview the suspect provided the suspect agrees to this (either in writing or during the interview) and an officer with at least the rank of inspector has given authority for the interview to proceed (Code C, para 6.6(d)).

In the situations at (a), (b) and (c) above, the caution given to the suspect at the start of the interview will be as follows: 'You do not have to say anything, but anything you do say may be given in evidence.' The reason for this wording is that no adverse inferences may be drawn at trial from the suspect's silence in interview if the suspect had not at the time of the interview been allowed access to legal advice (Youth Justice and Criminal Evidence Act 1999, s 58). This will not apply to the situations at (d) and (e) above, because in these cases the suspect is allowed to speak to the duty solicitor (situation (d)) or a solicitor of his own choice (situation (e)). The caution in these cases will be the normal caution given at the start of the interview (see **3.5.2.3** above).

### 3.5.3 Identification procedures

#### 3.5.3.1 Introduction

In addition to wanting to interview an arrested person about his suspected involvement in a criminal offence, the other main reason for the police to arrest a suspect is to enable them to obtain additional evidence which points to that suspect's guilt. The most common method which the police use to obtain such evidence is to see if the victim of and/or witnesses to the offence are able visually to identify the suspect.

The procedures which the police need to follow when obtaining identification evidence are contained in Code D. Paragraph 1.2 of Code D provides:

> Identification by witnesses arises, eg if the offender is seen committing the crime and a witness is given an opportunity to identify the suspect in a video identification, identification parade or similar procedure. The procedures are designed to:
>
> - test the witness' ability to identify the person they saw on a previous occasion
> - provide safeguards against mistaken identification.

If the police do not know the identity of the suspect, they are permitted to take a witness to a particular neighbourhood or place to see if that witness is able to identify the person he saw.

If the identity of the suspect is known to the police and the suspect has been arrested, the police may then use a form of identification procedure to see if the witness can identify the suspect. There are four different types of identification procedure:

(a) video identification;

(b) an identification parade;

(c) a group identification; and

(d) confrontation by a witness.

The police must keep a record of the suspect's description as *first* given to them by a potential witness (Code D, para 3.1). Before any form of identification procedure takes place, a copy of this record should be given to the suspect or his solicitor. This may prove useful at trial if there are discrepancies between this description and the appearance of the suspect.

#### 3.5.3.2 Video identification (Code D, Annex A)

A video identification occurs when the witness is shown moving images of a known suspect, together with similar images of others who resemble the suspect.

The images must include the suspect and 'at least eight other people who, so far as possible, resemble the suspect in age, height, general appearance and position in life' (Code D, Annex A, para 2). The images that are shown to the witness show the suspect and the other people in the same positions, or carrying out the same sequence of movements (Code D, Annex A, para 3).

The suspect or his solicitor must be given a reasonable opportunity to see the full set of images (normally referred to as 'foils') before they are shown to any witness. If there is a 'reasonable objection' to the images or to any of the other participants (such as one of the other participants not resembling the suspect), the police must take steps, if practicable, to remove the grounds for objection (Code D, Annex A, para 7). Such steps may include not using the image of a participant who does not resemble the suspect, and instead replacing this with an image of someone who does resemble the suspect.

If a suspect has any unusual features (such as a facial scar, a tattoo, or distinctive hair style or colour) which do not appear on the images of the other people, the police may take steps to conceal those features on the video or to replicate those features on the images of the other people (Code D, Annex A, para 2A). Such concealment or replication may be done electronically. If a witness, having seen video images where concealment or replication has been used, wants to see an image without the concealment or replication of the unusual feature, the witness may be allowed to do so (Code D, Annex A, para 2C).

A suspect will not be present at the video identification, although the suspect will have attended the police station on an earlier date to be video-taped for the purpose of the video identification. The suspect's solicitor should be given reasonable notice of the time and place of the video identification so that he may attend to ensure that it is carried out properly (Code D, Annex A, para 9).

Only one witness may see the video at a time. The playback of the video may be frozen and there is no limit on the number of times the suspect may see the video (Code D, Annex A, para 11). Before they see the set of images, witnesses must not be able to:

(a) communicate with each other about the case;
(b) see any of the images which are to be shown;
(c) see, or be reminded of, any photograph or description of the suspect, or be given any other indication as to the suspect's identity; or
(d) overhear a witness who has already seen the material (Code D, Annex A, para 10).

The police must not discuss with the witness the composition of the set of images, and a witness must not be told whether a previous witness has made an identification.

If a suspect refuses to consent to take part in a video identification, the police are permitted to proceed with a covert video identification.

#### 3.5.3.3 Identification parades (Code D, Annex B)

An identification parade occurs when a witness sees the suspect in a line of other persons who resemble the suspect.

The identification parade will consist of at least eight people (in addition to the suspect) who, so far as possible, resemble the suspect in age, height, general appearance and position in life (Code D, Annex B, para 9).

If a suspect has any unusual features (such as a facial scar, tattoo or distinctive hair style or colour) which it is not possible to replicate on the other participants in the parade, the police may take steps to conceal those features. For example, a plaster may be used to hide a facial scar, or a hat may be used to hide distinctive hair colour (Code D, Annex B, para 10).

Paragraph 14 of Code D, Annex B provides that the police must make appropriate arrangements to ensure that, before attending the parade, witnesses are not able to:

(a) communicate with each other about the case, or overhear a witness who has already seen the identification parade;

(b) see any member of the identification parade;

(c) see, or be reminded of, any photograph or description of the suspect, or be given any other indication as to the suspect's identity; or

(d) see the suspect before or after the identification parade.

The suspect is allowed to choose his own position in the line (and may change positions between witnesses if more than one witness is to attend the parade), but cannot otherwise alter the order of people forming the line. Paragraph 16 of Code D, Annex B states:

> Witnesses shall be brought in one at a time. Immediately before the witness inspects the identification parade, they shall be told the person they saw on a specified earlier occasion may, or may not, be present and if they cannot make a positive identification, they should say so. The witness must also be told they should not make any decision about whether the person they saw is on the identification parade until they have looked at each member twice.

Sometimes a witness will ask to have a parade member speak, move or adopt a particular posture. If a witness makes such a request, he should first be asked whether he can identify any person on the parade on the basis of appearance only. A witness who asks a parade member to speak must be reminded that the participants in the parade have been chosen on the basis of physical appearance only. Only when the police have done that may a member of the parade then be asked to comply with the request to hear him speak, move or adopt a particular posture. (If a suspect is picked out after he has been asked to speak, whilst this evidence will be admissible at trial, the judge will give a very strong warning to the jury to treat such evidence with the utmost caution.)

A colour photograph or video recording of the identification parade should always be taken (Code D, Annex B, para 23).

The police cannot compel a suspect to take part in an identification parade should the suspect refuse to consent to taking part.

### 3.5.3.4 Group identification (Code D, Annex C)

A group identification occurs when the witness sees the suspect in an informal group of people.

Group identifications may take place either with the consent and cooperation of the suspect, or covertly if the suspect does not consent (Code D, Annex C, para 2).

The place where a group identification should be held is a place where other people are passing by or waiting around informally (such as on an escalator, or in a shopping centre or bus station). The suspect should be able to join these people and be capable of being seen by the witness at the same time as others in the group (Code D, Annex C, para 4).

In selecting the location for the holding of a group identification, the police must reasonably expect that the witness will see some people whose appearance is broadly similar to that of the suspect (Code D, Annex C, para 6). Beyond that, however, there is no requirement that the other persons whom the witness sees in addition to the suspect have any particular likeness to the suspect.

If a suspect refuses to consent to a group identification and such an identification is held covertly, the police will be required to take the witness to a place where the suspect is likely to be at a given time. If, for example, the suspect is in employment, the group identification could take place outside the suspect's place of work at the time when the suspect is known to start or finish work, since it is likely that the suspect would then be in a group of fellow workers arriving or leaving work at the same time.

#### 3.5.3.5 Confrontation (Code D, Annex D)

A confrontation occurs when a witness is brought face to face with a suspect in the police station. Confrontations are extremely rare.

Prior to a confrontation taking place, the witness must be told that the person he saw may, or may not, be the person he is to confront and that if he is not that person, the witness should say so (Code D, Annex D, para 1).

Confrontations will usually take place in the presence of the suspect's solicitor.

#### 3.5.3.6 Who arranges the identification procedure?

**The identification officer**

Identification procedures are the responsibility of an officer not below the rank of inspector who is not involved with the investigation. This officer is known as the 'identification officer' (Code D, para 3.11). The identification officer will be in charge of the identification procedure and must ensure that it complies with the requirements of Code D. The identification officer will be present throughout the procedure and must be in uniform. When an identification procedure needs to be held, para 3.11 of Code D provides that 'it must be held as soon as practicable'. If the police decide to hold an identification procedure, the suspect will normally be released on police bail (see **3.7.3** below) with a requirement to re-attend the police station at a later date when the identification procedure will take place. This will then enable the police to arrange for witnesses to attend the police station (in the case of an identification parade) or to obtain the necessary images (in the case of a video identification).

The investigating officer will have no involvement in the conduct of the identification procedure. Paragraph 3.11 of Code D states: 'No officer ... involved with the investigation of the case against the suspect ... may take part in [identification] procedures or act as the identification officer.' This ensures that there is no risk of the investigating officer seeking to influence in any way the witnesses who are to take part in the identification procedure.

**Steps to be taken by the identification officer**

Before a video identification, identification parade or group identification is arranged, the identification officer must explain the following matters to the suspect:

(a) the purpose of the identification procedure to be used;

(b) the suspect's entitlement to free legal advice;

(c) the procedure to be followed, including the suspect's right to have a solicitor or friend present;

(d) that if the suspect refuses to consent to the identification procedure taking place, such refusal may be given in evidence at trial, or the police may proceed covertly without the suspect's consent (ie, by holding a covert video or group identification), or make other arrangements to test whether a witness can identify the suspect (ie, by arranging a confrontation);

(e) that if the suspect has significantly altered his appearance between being offered an identification procedure and the time of the procedure, this may be given in evidence at trial and the identification officer may consider other forms of identification;

(f) whether, before the suspect's identity became known, the witness was shown photographs, or a computerised or artist's composite likeness or image by the police; and

(g) that the suspect or his solicitor will be provided with details of the description of the suspect as first given by any witnesses who are to attend the identification procedure *before* the procedure takes place (Code D, para 3.17).

### 3.5.3.7 When must an identification procedure be held?

If:

(a) a witness has identified or purported to have identified a suspect; or

(b) a witness thinks he can identify the suspect, or there is a reasonable chance that the witness can identify the suspect,

*and* the suspect disputes being the person the witness claims to have seen, para 3.12 of Code D states that an identification procedure *shall* be held unless it is not practicable or would serve no purpose in proving or disproving whether the suspect was involved in committing the offence. Code D goes on to give an example of when it would not be necessary to hold an identification procedure, namely when it is not disputed that the suspect is already *well known* to the witness. In such a case, an identification procedure would serve no purpose because the witness would inevitably pick out the suspect.

An identification procedure should be held if a witness to a crime has purported to identify the suspect in the street some time after the crime was committed, since the purpose of an identification procedure is to test the reliability of the eye-witness's identification.

#### Example 1

Tom is arrested on suspicion of assault. A witness, Barbara, saw the assault. She does not know Tom, but thinks she can identify the person she saw commit the assault. Tom disputes being the person Barbara claims to have seen. An identification procedure should be held to see if Barbara can pick out Tom as the person she saw committing the assault.

#### Example 2

Tom is arrested on suspicion of assault. A witness, Barbara, saw the assault. She recognised Tom as the person who committed the assault because he was at school with her some years previously. Tom disputes being the person Barbara claims to have seen. He also says that he vaguely recalls Barbara from school, but didn't know her very well. He also comments that it is several years since he left school and Barbara was two years ahead of him. An identification procedure should be held to see if Barbara can pick out Tom, since Tom is disputing the fact that he is well known to Barbara.

#### Example 3

Tom is arrested on suspicion of assault. A witness, Barbara, saw the assault. She identifies Tom as the person who committed the assault. Tom disputes being the person Barbara claims to have seen. Barbara has known Tom for several years as they are both members of the same gym. Tom does not dispute that he is *well known* to Barbara. There would be no useful purpose in holding an identification procedure since Barbara would clearly pick out Tom were a procedure to be held.

**Example 4**

An assault takes place outside a pub and is witnessed by Barbara. The assailant runs away before he can be apprehended. Barbara does not know the identity of the person who carried out the assault, but thinks she will be able to identify this person if she sees him again. PC Smith later takes Barbara to the area where the assault occurred. Barbara sees Tom and recognises him as the person who committed the assault. An identification procedure should be held to test the reliability of Barbara's street identification of Tom.

An identification procedure may also be held if the officer in charge of the investigation considers it would be useful (Code D, para 3.13).

### 3.5.3.8 Which type of identification procedure should be used?

Paragraph 3.14 of Code D provides that a suspect should initially be offered a video identification unless:

(a) a video identification is not practicable;

(b) an identification parade is both practicable and more suitable than a video identification; or

(c) the officer in charge of the investigation considers that a group identification is more suitable than a video identification or identification parade, and the identification officer considers it practicable to arrange a group identification.

The decision on which type of procedure is offered to the suspect will be made by the investigating officer in conjunction with the identification officer. A video identification is now the most common form of identification procedure used by the police. Identification parades are held only rarely. A video identification is normally preferred to an identification parade, if it can be arranged and completed sooner than an identification parade. Paragraph 3.14 states:

> An identification parade may not be practicable because of factors relating to the witnesses, such as their number, state of health, availability and travelling requirements. A video identification would normally be more suitable if it could be arranged and completed sooner than an identification parade.

A group identification may be offered if the officer in charge of the investigation considers it to be more suitable than a video identification or identification parade, and the identification officer considers it practicable to arrange (Code D, para 3.16).

Confrontations are very much a last resort.

### 3.5.3.9 Can an identification procedure be used if a witness has recognised a suspect from a photograph?

The police will keep photographs of individuals with previous convictions, and may show these photographs to a witness when they are trying to identify the person responsible for a crime (see **3.5.7** below).

Before a witness is shown any photographs, that witness's first description of the suspect must have been recorded (Code D, Annex E, para 2).

The witness must be shown at least 12 photographs at a time (Code D, Annex E, para 4). As soon as a witness makes a positive identification from photographs, no other witnesses should be shown the photographs. The witness who made the identification and any other witnesses should then be asked to take part in one of the identification procedures outlined above (Code D, Annex E, para 6).

The suspect or his solicitor must be notified if a witness attending an identification procedure has previously been shown photographs, or a computerised or artist's composite (Code D, Annex E, para 9).

If the case subsequently comes to trial, when giving evidence the witness will not be permitted to say that he originally identified the suspect from photographs shown to him by the police.

## 3.5.4 Fingerprints and impressions of footwear

### 3.5.4.1 Fingerprints

Fingerprints are a form of identification evidence. The police may want to take a suspect's fingerprints to see if they match fingerprints found at the scene of a crime, or fingerprints found on an object or article which the police have recovered during their investigation (such as a weapon, or an item which it is alleged the suspect has stolen).

A suspect's fingerprints may be taken either with or without his consent under s 61 (Code D, para 4.2). Consent must be given in writing if the suspect is at the police station. Section 61 allows the police to take fingerprints from a person who has been detained at the police station for a recordable offence, or charged with or convicted of such an offence. Fingerprints may also be taken from a person who had been given a caution, reprimand or warning for a recordable offence. The term 'recordable offence' relates to those offences for which convictions, cautions, reprimands and warnings may be recorded in national police records. At present, a recordable offence is any offence which carries a possible sentence of imprisonment upon conviction.

The police may also take a person's fingerprints away from the police station if the officer reasonably suspects that the person is committing or attempting to commit an offence, or has committed or attempted to commit an offence, and either the name of the person is unknown or cannot reasonably be ascertained by the officer, or the officer has reasonable grounds for doubting whether the name given by the person is his real name (s 61). These provisions will enable 'street bail' (see **Chapter 2**) to work effectively.

The police may use reasonable force if necessary to take a person's fingerprints without his consent (Code D, para 4.6).
Before fingerprints are taken, the suspect must be informed:

(a) why the fingerprints are being taken;

(b) of the grounds relied on if the fingerprints are not taken with consent; and

(c) that the fingerprints may be retained and made the subject of a speculative search (Code D, para 4.7).

### 3.5.4.2 Impressions of footwear

Section 61A of PACE 1984 allows the police to take impressions of a suspect's footwear. A suspect can either give written consent to having such an impression taken, or the police may take an impression without consent. An impression can be taken without consent if:

(a) the suspect is arrested, charged or told that he will be reported for a recordable offence (see **3.5.4.1** above); and

(b) he has not already had such an impression taken in the course of the investigation (s 61A(3)).

Reasonable force may be used to take an impression of footwear (Code D, para 4.18).

Before an impression of footwear is taken, the suspect must be informed:

(a) of the reason for the taking of the impression;
(b) that the impression may be retained and made the subject of a speculative search (s 61A(5) and (6)).

## 3.5.5 Samples

### 3.5.5.1 Types of sample

Samples are a form of identification evidence which the police may use to link a suspect to a crime or crime scene. For example:

(a) in a burglary investigation, the police may use paint samples from underneath a suspect's fingernails to match with paint on the window frame of the property that was burgled;
(b) in a case of assault by biting, the police may use a dental impression from a suspect to match with the bite mark left on the victim;
(c) in a rape investigation, the police may use a sample of semen from a suspect to match with semen recovered from the victim.

Samples are divided into two types, intimate and non-intimate (s 65).

An *intimate sample* is:

(a) a dental impression;
(b) a sample of blood, semen or any other tissue fluid;
(c) a sample of urine;
(d) a sample of pubic hair;
(e) a swab taken from a person's body orifice other than the mouth; or
(f) a swab taken from any part of a person's genitals (including pubic hair).

A *non-intimate* sample is:

(a) a sample of hair other than pubic hair;
(b) a sample taken from a nail or from under a nail;
(c) any swab taken from a person's body, unless the swab would satisfy the definition of an intimate sample;
(d) saliva; or
(e) a skin impression other than a fingerprint.

### 3.5.5.2 When can intimate samples be taken?

Under s 62, intimate samples may be taken only on the authority of a police officer with at least the rank of inspector *and* with the 'appropriate consent' (this means the consent in writing of the suspect if over 17, the suspect's parent or guardian if he is under 14, or the consent of both the suspect and his parent or guardian if he is aged between 14 and 17 inclusive).

The officer who authorises the taking of the sample must have reasonable grounds for suspecting the suspect's involvement in a recordable offence (see **3.5.4.1** above). He must also believe that the sample will tend to confirm or disprove the suspect's involvement in that offence.

**Example**

Trevor is arrested on suspicion of murdering his girlfriend, Carol. Carol was struck on the head with a hammer. The police have recovered the hammer which was covered in blood. Forensic examination has revealed that there are two distinct blood types on the hammer. One of the blood types is Carol's blood. The police believe the other blood type to be Trevor's. The police would be able to take a sample of Trevor's blood to confirm or disprove this if the necessary authority is obtained from an officer with at least the rank of inspector and the appropriate consent is obtained from Trevor.

### 3.5.5.3 Why should a suspect consent to an intimate sample being taken?

A court is entitled to 'draw such inferences as appear proper' if a suspect refuses, without good cause, to consent to the taking of an intimate sample (s 62(10)). If, for example, a suspect charged with rape refused to provide a sample of semen to the police, the court may draw from this refusal an inference that the suspect does not want to give such a sample because the sample would match semen recovered from the victim of the alleged rape.

Paragraph 6.3 of Code D states: 'Before a suspect is asked to provide an intimate sample, they must be warned that if they refuse without good cause, their refusal may harm their case if it comes to trial ...'

### 3.5.5.4 When may non-intimate samples be taken?

A non-intimate sample may be taken with the written consent of the suspect. In addition, s 63 allows for non-intimate samples to be taken from persons in police custody without their consent in the following circumstances:

(a) if the person is in police detention following his arrest for a recordable offence (see **3.5.4.1**) and he has not had a non-intimate sample of the same type and from the same part of his body taken in the course of the investigation, or such a sample has been taken but it has proved to be insufficient (s 63(2A)–(2C));

(b) if the person is being held in custody by the police on the authority of the court and an officer of at least the rank of inspector authorises such a sample to be taken (s 63(3)); or

(c) if a person has been charged with a recordable offence or told that he will be reported for such an offence, and either that person has not had a non-intimate sample taken from him during the course of the investigation or, if such a sample has been taken, it has proved to be unsuitable or insufficient (s 63(3A));

(d) if the person has been convicted of a recordable offence (s 63(3B)).

The police are permitted to use reasonable force to take a non-intimate sample from a person without that person's consent (Code D, para 6.7).

### 3.5.5.5 Conclusion

Intimate and non-intimate samples may be used for speculative searches (see **3.5.6** below).

Before the police take from a suspect any intimate sample with consent or a non-intimate sample with or without consent, the person from whom the sample is to be taken must be told:

(a) the reason for taking the sample;

(b) the grounds on which the relevant authority has been given; and

(c) that the sample may be retained and be made the subject of a speculative search (Code D, para 6.8).

### 3.5.6 Speculative searches

Fingerprints, impressions of footwear or DNA samples taken by the police may be the subject of a 'speculative search'. This means that the fingerprints, impressions of footwear or DNA sample may be checked against other fingerprints, impressions of footwear and DNA samples which the police have obtained during the course of previous investigations, to see if the suspect may be linked to other crimes under investigation (s 63A).

Section 64 of PACE 1984 allows the police to retain fingerprints, impressions of footwear and samples taken during the course of an investigation. The police are permitted to do this only in certain circumstances, the most common being if the suspect from whom the sample is taken is subsequently convicted of the offence. Fingerprints, impressions of footwear and samples which the police are not permitted to retain must be destroyed.

### 3.5.7 Taking photographs of the suspect

Section 64A permits a police officer to photograph a person detained at a police station either with his consent, or without his consent if it is withheld or it is not possible to obtain it. Section 64A also permits the police to take photographs of a suspect with or without his consent when that suspect is away from the police station if the suspect falls within one of the categories set out in s 64(1B). The most important category is suspects who have been arrested.

Section 64A also permits the police to retain and use or disclose any photographs of the suspect which they have taken for the following purposes:

(a) the prevention or detection of offences;
(b) the investigation of offences; or
(c) the conduct of prosecutions.

Example

Sam is arrested on suspicion of theft. His photograph is taken whilst he is at the police station. Sam is subsequently charged and convicted of theft. The police may retain the photograph. When a further theft takes place and a witness sees (but does not recognise) the thief, the police may show the witness Sam's photograph, together with at least 11 others, to see if the witness recognises Sam or one of the other people as the thief (see **3.5.3.9** above). This would be using the photograph for the purpose of investigating an offence.

If a suspect refuses to consent to having his photograph taken, the police may use reasonable force to take the photograph if the photograph cannot be taken covertly (Code D, para 5.14).

When the police take a photograph of a suspect, the suspect must be told the purposes for which the photograph may be used, disclosed or retained (Code D, para 5.16).

## 3.6 Juveniles

### 3.6.1 Introduction

A solicitor will often be called to the police station to represent an individual who falls within one of several special categories of suspect, and to whom specific rules apply. These categories are:

(a) juveniles – suspects who are aged between 10 and 16 inclusive (although para 1.5 of Code C provides that the police should treat anyone who *appears* to be under 17 as a juvenile in the absence of clear evidence to the contrary);
(b) suspects who suffer from a mental disability or otherwise appear to be mentally vulnerable;
(c) suspects who are deaf, dumb or blind; and
(d) suspects who cannot speak or understand English.

This section of the book will concentrate on the specific rules which apply to juveniles.

## 3.6.2 Initial steps the custody officer must take

### 3.6.2.1 Informing the person responsible for the juvenile's welfare

A juvenile who has been arrested and detained at the police station has the right to have a person informed of his arrest under s 56 (see **3.4.1** above) and the right to receive free and independent legal advice from a solicitor under s 58 (see **3.4.2** above), in just the same way as an adult suspect.

In addition, however, if a juvenile has been arrested, the custody officer must, if practicable, find out the person responsible for his welfare (Code C, para 3.13). That person may be:

(a) the juvenile's parent or guardian;
(b) if the juvenile is in local authority or voluntary organisation care, the person appointed by that authority or organisation to have responsibility for the juvenile's welfare (Children and Young Persons Act 1933, s 34(8)); or
(c) any other person who has, for the time being, assumed responsibility for the juvenile's welfare.

That person must be informed as soon as practicable that the juvenile has been arrested, why he has been arrested and where he is being detained. This right is in addition to the juvenile's right under s 56 to have a person informed of his arrest (see **3.4.1** above).

If a juvenile is known to be the subject of a court order under which a person or organisation is given any statutory responsibility to supervise or monitor him (for example, a supervision order), reasonable steps must also be taken to notify that person or organisation. The person notified is known as the 'responsible officer' and will usually be a member of a Youth Offending Team (Code C, para 3.14).

### 3.6.2.2 Informing the appropriate adult

Under para 3.15 of Code C, the custody officer must, as soon as practicable:

(a) inform the 'appropriate adult' (who is likely to be the same person who is responsible for the juvenile's welfare) of the grounds of the juvenile's detention and his whereabouts; and
(b) request that the adult comes to the police station to see the detainee.

## 3.6.3 The appropriate adult

### 3.6.3.1 Who may be an appropriate adult?

The 'appropriate adult' is a person who attends the police station to provide support and assistance to the juvenile. There is a hierarchical order the police should follow when contacting an appropriate adult for a juvenile, as follows:

(a) The police should initially attempt to contact the juvenile's parent or guardian (or a representative from the local authority where the juvenile is in local authority care) to act as an appropriate adult.

(b) If no one in (a) is available, the police should then ask a social worker from the local authority to act as an appropriate adult.

(c) If a social worker is not available, the police should finally contact another responsible adult who is aged 18 or over and not connected to the police (Code C, para 1.7). This may, for example, be an aunt or uncle, or a grandparent. Although the adult must be aged 18 or over, the police may consider that an adult who is only just 18 or over may not be sufficiently responsible to fulfil the role.

A solicitor should never be an appropriate adult, because support and assistance from an appropriate adult is in addition to any legal advice a suspect receives from his solicitor at the police station. Other persons who should not fulfil the role of appropriate adult include:

(a) police officers or persons employed by the police;

(b) an interested party such as the victim of the offence, another suspect, a potential witness or anyone else involved in the investigation (this would, for example, prevent a juvenile's mother acting as appropriate adult if the juvenile has been arrested on suspicion of assaulting her, as she would be the victim);

(c) a person, such as a parent or social worker, to whom the juvenile has made admissions *prior* to that person being asked to attend the police station to fulfil the role of an appropriate adult; and

(d) an estranged parent (but only when the juvenile expressly and specifically objects to the presence of such a person).

### 3.6.3.2 What is the role of the appropriate adult?

The Home Office has produced a document entitled 'Guidance for Appropriate Adults' that will be issued to an appropriate adult upon his arrival at the police station. The guidance can be found on the Home Office website (www.homeoffice.gov.uk).

The guidance provides that the appropriate adult has 'a positive and important role', and that the appropriate adult is not at the police station simply to act as an observer but rather to ensure that the suspect 'understands what is happening to them and why'. The key roles and responsibilities of an appropriate adult are:

(a) to support, advise and assist the suspect, particularly when the suspect is being questioned;

(b) to ensure that the suspect understands his rights whilst at the police station, and the role played by the appropriate adult in protecting those rights;

(c) to observe whether the police are acting properly, fairly and with respect for the rights of the suspect; and

(d) to assist with communication between the suspect and the police.

The guidance makes it clear that it is not the role of the appropriate adult to provide the suspect with legal advice, and any conversations the appropriate adult has with the suspect are not covered by legal privilege (see **Chapter 4**).

The defendant's solicitor needs to ensure that the appropriate adult is aware of his role, and must ensure that the appropriate adult understands that it is not his role to help the police. The solicitor should also make it clear to the appropriate adult that, whilst he is there to help the suspect understand what the police are doing, he should not answer questions on behalf of the suspect, particularly in an interview situation. The appropriate adult should, however, intervene in an interview if he considers that the juvenile has not understood a question which has been asked and that clarification of the question is necessary.

The custody officer should explain his rights whilst at the police station to a juvenile in the presence of the appropriate adult, or repeat those rights in the presence of the appropriate adult if he had already explained these rights to the juvenile before the appropriate adult arrived at the police station (Code C, para 3.17). The custody officer should also advise the juvenile that:

(a) the duties of the appropriate adult include giving advice and assistance; and
(b) the juvenile may consult privately with the appropriate adult at any time (Code C, para 3.18).

### 3.6.4 Interviewing juveniles

Paragraph 10.12 of Code C provides that if a juvenile is cautioned in the absence of the appropriate adult, this caution must be repeated in the appropriate adult's presence.

Similarly, a juvenile must not normally be interviewed, or asked to provide or sign a written statement under caution or record of interview, in the absence of the appropriate adult (Code C, para 11.15).

When an appropriate adult is present in an interview, he must be informed by the police that he is not there simply to act as an observer, and that the purpose of his presence in the interview is to:

(a) advise the person being interviewed;
(b) observe whether the interview is being conducted properly and fairly; and
(c) facilitate communication with the person being interviewed (Code C, para 11.17).

The appropriate adult's presence at the police station (and particularly during the interview) is necessary to help the juvenile cope with the demands of custody and questioning, and to appreciate the seriousness of the situation. The appropriate adult should help the juvenile gain a degree of understanding of what is taking place so that he can make a sensible decision as to the course of action he should take. The appropriate adult should not, however, attempt to answer questions on behalf of the juvenile during the interview.

The 'Notes for guidance' to Code C clarify the role an appropriate adult should play in an interview. Paragraph 11C states that:

> Although juveniles . . . are often capable of providing reliable evidence, they may, without knowing or wishing to do so, be particularly prone in certain circumstances to provide information that may be unreliable, misleading or self-incriminating. Special care should always be taken when questioning such a person, and the appropriate adult should be involved if there is any doubt about a person's age, mental state or capacity. Because of the risk of unreliable evidence it is also important to obtain corroboration of any facts admitted whenever possible.

### 3.6.5 Identification procedures

In addition to the requirements imposed by Code C, if the police require a juvenile to take part in an identification procedure, to provide a sample, or to give his fingerprints or an impression of his footwear, they must comply with additional provisions in Code D.

Paragraph 2.12 of Code D provides that where any procedure in Code D requires a person's consent (for example, if a suspect is asked to consent to taking part in an identification parade or video identification), the following conditions apply:

(a) if the suspect is a juvenile aged 14 or over, consent must be obtained both from the juvenile *and* from the juvenile's parent or guardian;

(b) if the suspect is a juvenile aged under 14, consent must be obtained from the juvenile's parent or guardian (rather than from the juvenile).

## 3.7 Charging the suspect

### 3.7.1 Introduction

Once the police have exercised their investigative powers whilst the suspect is detained in the police station, they will then need to determine what step to take next in the case. The decision on what to do next will be made by the custody officer. He has four options:

(a) release the suspect without charge and without bail;

(b) release the suspect without charge but on bail whilst the police make further enquiries;

(c) release the suspect without charge but on bail (or keep the suspect in police detention) for the purpose of enabling the CPS to make a decision on charges; or

(d) charge the suspect (or offer the suspect an alternative to charge – see **3.9** below).

Each option will be examined in turn.

### 3.7.2 Release without charge and without bail

If, having investigated the offence, the police determine that the suspect did not in fact commit the crime under investigation (or there is insufficient evidence against the suspect and it is unlikely that any further evidence will be obtained), the custody officer should release the suspect without charge and without any requirement that the suspect return to the police station at a later date. This means that, from the suspect's point of view, the matter is closed, although there is nothing to prevent the police from re-arresting the suspect at a later date should any further evidence come to light which implicates the suspect.

**Example**

Aftab is arrested on suspicion of assault. Aftab is interviewed and denies the assault. The only witness to the assault is the victim, Louise. A video identification is arranged but Louise fails to pick out Aftab as the person who assaulted her. The police have no additional evidence against Aftab. He should be released without charge and should not be required to return to the police station at a later date.

### 3.7.3 Release on bail whilst the police make further enquiries

It is often the case that, after exercising their investigative powers in the police station, the police will need to make further enquiries before deciding whether to charge a suspect or to pass their file to the CPS to determine if there is sufficient evidence to charge the suspect. In such circumstances the police will release the suspect on bail under s 47(3)(b).

**Example**

Richard is arrested on suspicion of assaulting Wayne in a nightclub. Wayne has given a statement saying that this was an unprovoked attack. In an audibly recorded interview at the police station, Richard states that he was initially attacked by Wayne, and that any violence he used was only in self-defence. Richard also gives the interviewing officer the names of two of his friends who witnessed the incident and who will confirm his version of events. The police did not take statements from these people when carrying out their initial investigations. The police will need to speak to these witnesses to see if they back up Richard's version of events, and also speak to Wayne again to put to him what Richard has said. The police should therefore release Richard without charge but on bail, with a requirement that Richard attend the police station again at a future date when the police have determined what course of action they are going to take after carrying out their further investigations.

Details of the time and date when the suspect needs to re-attend the police station will be contained in a written notice which will be given to him by the police.

When the suspect answers his bail, the police may:

(a) release him without charge (if, after making further enquiries, the police have insufficient evidence to charge);

(b) exercise further investigative powers (such as re-interviewing the suspect);

(c) release the suspect again on bail if their further enquiries are incomplete or, having completed their enquiries, they wish to pass their file to the CPS for advice (see **3.7.4** below);or

(d) charge the suspect (if, after making further enquiries, the police have sufficient evidence to charge).

If the suspect fails to answer his bail at the police station, he may be arrested without warrant (s 46A). Although failing to answer bail at the police station is technically a criminal offence, it is very rare in practice for the police to charge a suspect with this offence.

The police may impose conditions on bail granted to a suspect whilst the police make further enquiries into the alleged offence (s 47(1A)). The police may, for example, impose a condition of residence or a condition preventing a suspect from entering a certain area. The police may arrest without warrant a suspect who breaches such conditions. A suspect who wishes to vary any conditions which are imposed may ask the police to vary such conditions or make an application to the magistrates' court for this to be done (see **3.8.2** below).

### 3.7.4 Release on bail (or detain in custody) whilst the file is passed to the CPS

The Criminal Justice Act 2003 has made significant changes to the procedure for deciding when a suspect should be charged and what offence that suspect should be charged with. The Act creates a new s 37B of PACE 1984, which provides that it is for the CPS to determine whether the suspect should be charged and, if so, with what offence.

It will therefore usually be the case that once the police believe there is sufficient evidence to charge a suspect, the police will need to send the case papers to the CPS for it to determine the exact charge. Lawyers from the CPS are often present at the police station to advise on charging and so, in a straightforward case, a decision on the appropriate charge can be made there and then. In such a case, the custody officer will authorise the suspect's continued detention in police custody whilst the CPS lawyer present at the police station reviews the case papers. If a CPS lawyer is not present at the police station and the matter is relatively straightforward, the police may telephone a CPS lawyer to obtain advice on the appropriate charge. The custody officer may detain the suspect in custody whilst this is done.

In more complex cases, the CPS may be unable to make an immediate decision on charge. In such cases, the police will send their file to the CPS so that the CPS may review the case.

The CPS will apply a two-part test to determine whether or not the suspect should be charged:

(a) there must be sufficient evidence to provide a 'realistic prospect of conviction'; and

(a) if there is sufficient evidence, the CPS will then need to determine if it is in the public interest to charge the suspect, or whether the matter should be dealt with other than by way of charge (see **3.9** below).

It will take several weeks for the CPS to review a file, and the police will therefore need to release the suspect on bail under s 47(3)(b) whilst this is done. As with releasing the suspect on bail whilst the police make further enquiries, the suspect will be required to re-attend the police station at a future time and date, and will be given a notice to this effect. When the suspect answers his bail, the police may:

(a) charge the suspect (if the CPS found there was sufficient evidence to charge and a charge was in the public interest);

(b) exercise further investigative powers if the CPS considered that further evidence was needed (eg, re-interviewing the suspect);

(c) release the suspect without charge (if the CPS found there was insufficient evidence to charge); or

(d) deal with the matter other than by way of a charge if the CPS found there was sufficient evidence to charge the suspect but a charge was not in the public interest (see **3.9** below).

The police may impose conditions on a suspect who is released on bail pending consultations with the CPS (s 47(1A). For example, conditions may be imposed requiring a suspect to reside at a particular address, not to enter a specified area or not to contact specified persons.

#### Example

Francis is arrested on suspicion of assaulting his wife, Laura. The police refer the file to the CPS to determine what charge Francis should face. Francis is released on bail whilst the CPS reviews the papers. Francis tells the police that he will be staying at his brother's house rather than returning to the matrimonial home. The police impose conditions on the bail granted to Francis, requiring him to live at his brother's address and not to speak to, or try to communicate with, Laura.

If the suspect fails to answer his bail at the police station, or the police reasonably suspect that the suspect has broken any conditions attached to his bail, he may be arrested without warrant (s 46A). Failing to answer bail at the police station is a criminal offence, although it is rare in practice for the police to charge a suspect with this offence.

### 3.7.5 Charging the suspect

#### 3.7.5.1 Procedure

If the police consider that they have sufficient evidence to charge the suspect, they will either charge him themselves or pass the case papers to the CPS for it to determine what the appropriate charge should be.

The usual practice will be for the police to refer the case to the CPS for it to determine the appropriate charge. However, the police will still decide on the appropriate charge themselves in minor cases, particularly if the offence is summary only and it is expected that the suspect will enter a guilty plea.

When a decision has been made to charge a suspect, the suspect will be formally charged at the police station. In accordance with para 16.2 of Code C, the suspect must be cautioned on charge and anything the suspect says in response to the charge should be written down. The wording of the caution is the same as that used at both the time of the suspect's arrest the start of the interview in the police station (see **3.5.2**).

The suspect should also be given a written notice (the 'charge sheet') which gives the particulars of the offence. Paragraph 16.3 of Code C states: ' ... As far as possible the particulars of the charge shall be stated in simple terms, but they shall also show the precise offence in law with which the detainee is charged ...'

If the suspect is a juvenile, the written notice should be given to the appropriate adult (Code C, para 16.3).

In certain circumstances, a suspect against whom there is sufficient evidence to bring a charge may be offered an alternative means of having the matter disposed of. These alternatives are described at **3.9** below.

#### 3.7.5.2 Further interviews after charge

A suspect who has been charged cannot be interviewed further by the police about the offence for which he has been charged, unless the interview is necessary:

(a) to prevent or minimise harm or loss to some other persons, or the public;

(b) to clear up an ambiguity in a previous answer or statement; or

(c) in the interests of justice for the suspect to have put to him, and to have an opportunity to comment on, information concerning the offence which has come to light since he was charged (Code C, para 16.5).

If the police do interview a suspect after he has been charged, the suspect must be cautioned before any interview takes place. The wording of the caution is the 'old' caution which was used prior to the court being given the power under the Criminal Justice and Public Order Act 1994 to draw an adverse inference from a suspect's silence at the police station. The wording of the caution will be: 'You do not have to say anything, but anything you do say may be given in evidence.' This means that the suspect may remain silent in the interview and not have any adverse inference drawn from that silence at his trial.

## Key Document – Charge Sheet

**CHESHIRE POLICE**
**CHARGE(S)**

| | | | | | | |
|---|---|---|---|---|---|---|
| Surname: | Dickson | Custody No. | CH | 000687 | 07 | |
| Forename: | Gary Paul | Arrest Date: | 18.12.07 | | | |
| Address | 17 Marsh Street<br>Chester | YO• PYO• | Station: | Chester | | |
| | | M✓ F• | Date of Birth: | 28 | 10 | 1980 |
| | Postcode:<br>CH3 7LW | PO:• | Ethnicity: | | Self Class: | |
| | | Name of interpreter: | | | | |

You are charged with the offence(s) shown below. You do not have to say anything. But it may harm your defence if you do not mention now something which you may later rely on in court. Anything you do say may be given in evidence.

| | |
|---|---|
| Consec. No.<br>1<br>RT24317 | Charge(s) ☐<br>673023<br><br>That you on Tuesday 18th December 2007 assaulted Vincent Lamb causing him actual bodily harm<br><br>CONTRARY TO SECTION 47 OF THE OFFENCES AGAINST THE PERSON ACT 1861<br><br>(End of offences)<br><br>Continuation charges: Yes• No ✓ |

| | | | | | | | | | | |
|---|---|---|---|---|---|---|---|---|---|---|
| Reply (if any) | *No reply* | | | | | | | | | |
| Signed (person charging) | | G Chambers | | Signed (appropriate adult) | | | | | | |
| Officer charging | Surname: | G Chambers | Rank: | PC | No: | 911 | Station: | Chester | | |
| Investigating officer | Surname: | G Chambers | Rank: | PC | No: | 911 | Station: | Chester | | |
| Charge accepted | Surname: | Dunn | Rank: | PS | No: | 568 | Time: | 19.00 hrs | Date: | 18.12.07 |

Not bailed – Appearing at Chester Magistrates' Court at 09.45 on 19th December 2007

File copy• Court copy• Custody copy• Person charged ☑

## 3.8 Bail after charge

### 3.8.1 When may the police deny bail to a suspect?

When a suspect is charged at the police station, the custody officer must then decide:

(a) whether to keep him in police custody until he can be brought before a magistrates' court, or to release him; and

(b) if the latter, whether to release him on bail with conditions or without conditions (s 38(1)).

Section 38(1)(a) provides that only if one or more of certain circumstances are satisfied may bail be denied to a suspect who has been charged with an offence:

(1) Where a person arrested for an offence . . . is charged with an offence, the custody officer shall, subject to section 25 of the Criminal Justice and Public Order Act 1994, order his release from police detention, either on bail or without bail, unless

(a) . . .

(i) his name or address cannot be ascertained or the custody officer has reasonable grounds for doubting whether a name or address furnished by him as his name or address is his real name or address;

(ii) the custody officer has reasonable grounds for believing that the person arrested will fail to appear in court to answer to bail;

(iii) in the case of a person arrested for an imprisonable offence, the custody officer has reasonable grounds for believing that the detention of the person arrested is necessary to prevent him from committing an offence;

(iiia) in a case where a sample may be taken from the person under section 63B below, the custody officer has reasonable grounds for believing that the detention of the person is necessary to enable the sample to be taken from him;

(iv) in the case of a person arrested for an offence which is not an imprisonable offence, the custody officer has reasonable grounds for believing that the detention of the person arrested is necessary to prevent him from causing physical injury to any other person or from causing loss of or damage to property;

(v) the custody officer has reasonable grounds for believing that the detention of the person arrested is necessary to prevent him from interfering with the administration of justice or with the investigation of offences or of a particular offence; or

(vi) the custody officer has reasonable grounds for believing that the detention of the person arrested is necessary for his own protection . . .

Example 1

Rashid is charged with burglary. He has several previous convictions for failing to attend court to answer bail. The custody officer may refuse bail as he would have reasonable grounds for believing that Rashid would fail to appear in court if he was granted bail.

Example 2

Melanie is charged with theft. She has numerous previous convictions for theft and related offences, including several offences that were committed whilst she was on bail in the course of previous proceedings. The custody officer may refuse bail as he would have reasonable grounds for believing that Melanie would commit further offences whilst on bail.

If the suspect is a juvenile, the custody officer may also deny the suspect bail if he has reasonable grounds for believing that it is in the suspect's 'own interests' to be detained (s 38(1)(b)).

### 3.8.2 Conditional bail

If the custody officer decides to grant bail to a suspect who has been charged, he must then decide whether it is necessary to impose conditions on that bail (Bail Act 1976, s 47(1A)). Conditions may be imposed only if they are necessary:

(a) to prevent the suspect from failing to surrender to custody;

(b) to prevent the suspect from committing an offence whilst on bail;

(c) to prevent the suspect from interfering with witnesses or otherwise obstructing the course of justice (whether in relation to himself or another person); or

(d) for the suspect's own protection or, if the suspect is a child or young person (ie 17 or under), for his own welfare or in his own interests (Bail Act 1976, s 3A(5)).

The custody officer may impose most of the same types of condition which a magistrates' court could impose on bail granted to a defendant (see **Chapter 7**), although he cannot impose a condition that a suspect reside at a bail hostel, undergo medical examination or see his legal adviser. The custody officer may, for example, impose conditions requiring the suspect:

(a) to reside at a particular address;
(b) not to speak to or contact any witnesses;
(c) not to enter a particular area or set of premises; or
(d) to observe a curfew at night between specified hours.

A suspect who wishes to vary conditions imposed on bail which the police have granted may either:

(a) ask the custody officer who imposed the conditions (or another custody officer at the same police station) to vary the conditions (Bail Act 1976, s 3A(4)); or

(b) make an application to the magistrates' court for the conditions to be varied (Magistrates' Courts Act 1980, s 43(B)(1) and CrimPR, r 19.1).

### 3.8.3 When will the suspect make his first appearance at court?

#### 3.8.3.1 Suspects granted bail by the police

If a suspect is granted bail by the police after being charged, the date of his first appearance in the magistrates' court will be the first sitting of the court after he is charged with the offence (s 47(3A)), unless his appearance cannot be accommodated by the court until a later date. This means that a suspect is likely to make his first appearance in court within at most one to two weeks of being charged.

#### 3.8.3.2 Suspects denied bail by the police

If the police refuse to grant bail to a suspect after he has been charged, the suspect will be kept in police custody (unless he is a juvenile – see **3.8.3.3** below) and must be brought before the magistrates' court as soon as is practicable, and in any event not later than the first sitting of the court after he is charged with the offence (s 46(2)). In practice this means that the suspect will normally appear before the court within 24 hours of being charged.

#### 3.8.3.3 Juveniles refused bail after charge

If the custody officer denies bail after charge to a juvenile, the suspect will normally be kept in local authority accommodation rather than at the police station pending his first appearance before the Youth Court. The only two situations when a juvenile may be kept in police custody after charge are:

(a) if it is impracticable to move the suspect to local authority accommodation; or

(b) if the juvenile is aged at least 12, there is no *secure* local authority accommodation available and keeping him in other local authority accommodation would not be adequate to protect the public from serious harm from him (s 38(6)). 'Secure accommodation' is accommodation provided for the purpose of restricting liberty (Children Act 1989, s 25(1)).

If either of these criteria is satisfied and the juvenile is detained at the police station, para 8.8 of Code C provides that the juvenile must be kept separate from adult suspects and must not be detained in a cell unless it is not practicable to supervise the juvenile other than in a cell. The suspect will normally be kept in a juvenile detention room.

The guidance notes to Code C provide that, unless one of the conditions in s 38(6) is satisfied, neither a juvenile's behaviour nor the nature of the offence provides grounds for the custody officer to decide that it is impracticable to arrange the juvenile's transfer to local authority care (Code C, Notes for Guidance, para 16D). This paragraph also states that the lack of secure local authority accommodation does not make it impracticable to transfer the juvenile unless the juvenile is aged 12 or over *and* the local authority accommodation would not be adequate to protect the public from serious harm by the juvenile.

### 3.8.4 Breaching police bail (after charge)

If a suspect has been bailed to attend court following charge, s 7(3) of the Bail Act 1976 gives a police officer the power to arrest that person where he reasonably believes either that the person is unlikely to surrender to custody, or that the person has breached, or is likely to breach, his bail conditions. A person who is arrested under s 7 must be brought before a magistrates' court within 24 hours. The magistrates will determine if there has been a breach of bail conditions (usually by hearing evidence from the arresting officer and the defendant) and, if so, whether they should grant bail to the defendant or remand him in custody. Breach of bail conditions is *not* in itself a criminal offence, although a defendant who has breached police bail may experience difficulties in persuading the magistrates to grant him bail subsequently.

## 3.9 Alternatives to charging

### 3.9.1 Adult offenders

#### 3.9.1.1 Introduction

It is not inevitable that a suspect against whom there is sufficient evidence to bring a charge will always be charged with an offence. Where the suspect is aged over 17, rather than charging him, it may be possible to deal with the matter in one of the following ways:

(a) an informal warning;

(b) a penalty notice;

(c) a formal caution;

(d) a conditional caution.

Each of these is examined further below.

#### 3.9.1.2 Informal warnings

In minor cases the police have always had discretion to release a suspect without charge but to give him an informal warning about his future conduct. Such informal warnings are often given to individuals arrested for minor public order offences. An informal warning will not appear on a defendant's list of previous convictions if he is later charged with another offence.

#### 3.9.1.3 Penalty notices

The police may issue a penalty notice to dispose of minor offences without the need for the offender to go to court. Fixed penalty notices (FPNs) are used for minor road traffic offences, and for offences such as littering and dog fouling. Penalty notices for disorder (PNDs) may be used for anti-social behaviour, such as being drunk and disorderly. The notice will require the offender to pay a fine. An offender who disputes the notice may contest this before the magistrates' court. The receipt of a FPN is not a criminal conviction. The use of FPNs has recently been expanded to cover a wider range of offences (for example, first time offenders who have committed a minor shoplifting offence).

#### 3.9.1.4 Formal cautions

Instead of giving an informal warning, the police (in conjunction with the CPS) may instead decide to issue a formal caution. The giving of formal cautions was originally developed for cases involving juveniles, but can now be used only for adult offenders.

Although records are kept of cautions that are given, a formal caution is not the same as a conviction. If a defendant who has received a caution is later convicted of a separate offence, the caution may be mentioned to the court when the court is considering what sentence to pass. In reality this rarely happens, although a caution given for the same kind of offence as the offence to be sentenced will normally be cited.

Cautions are usually given in the police station by a police officer with at least the rank of inspector. The offender must sign a form acknowledging that he agrees to the caution and that he admits the offence for which the caution is being given. Before a caution is given, three conditions must be satisfied:

(a) sufficient evidence must have been collected to have justified a prosecution;
(b) there must be clear and reliable evidence of a voluntary admission by the offender that he has committed the offence;
(c) the offender must agree to being cautioned, having been made aware that the caution might be raised in court were he to be convicted of a later offence.

Any defendant who has no previous convictions or cautions for similar offences will be eligible to receive a caution, although cautions are particularly common for the following types of offender:

(a) the elderly;
(b) the infirm;
(c) those suffering from severe physical illness;
(d) those suffering from some form of mental illness or impairment, particularly if the strain of the proceedings would cause this to worsen; and
(e) those showing signs of severe emotional distress.

Offenders are unlikely to receive more than one caution. Usually an offender with a caution on his record will be charged if he commits a further offence.

#### 3.9.1.5 Conditional cautions

One of the principal goals of the Criminal Justice Act 2003 is to achieve 'restorative justice'. This is best described as bringing offenders and their victims into some form of contact, with a view to an agreement being reached as to what the offender should do to make reparation for the crime he has committed. The intention is to make an offender appreciate the effect his crime has had upon his victim, and to improve victim satisfaction with the criminal justice process. Conditional cautions must be seen against this backdrop.

Conditional cautions do not replace the system of police cautioning detailed at 3.9.1.4 above. However, in contrast to formal cautions, they have a statutory basis and may be given only with the approval of the CPS.

Under s 22 of the Criminal Justice Act 2003, a conditional caution can be given to a person aged 18 or over, provided that the five requirements set out in s 22(3) of the Act (see below) are satisfied. The conditions that are imposed must have as their objective any or all of the following:

(a) facilitating the rehabilitation of the offender;
(b) ensuring that the offender makes reparation for the offence;
(c) punishing the offender.

The five requirements that must be satisfied before a conditional caution may be given are:

(a) there must be evidence that the offender has committed an offence;
(b) the CPS must decide that there is sufficient evidence to charge the offender with the offence, and that a conditional caution should be given to the offender in respect of that offence;
(c) the offender must admit that he committed the offence;
(d) the effect of the conditional caution must be explained to the offender, and he must be warned that any failure to comply with any of the conditions attached to the caution may result in his being prosecuted for the offence itself; and
(e) the offender must sign a document containing the details of the offence, an admission that he committed the offence, his consent to a conditional caution and the conditions attached to the caution (Criminal Justice Act 2003, s 22(3)).

Section 25 of the Criminal Justice Act 2003 provides that if an offender fails 'without reasonable excuse' to comply with any conditions attached to the caution, he may be arrested and prosecuted for the original offence and the document he has signed may be used in evidence against him (ie, as evidence that he has admits having committed the offence).

The conditions that are likely to be attached to cautions will be geared either towards *rehabilitating* the offender, or towards the offender making *reparation* to his victim. The former may include, for example, a condition that the offender takes part in an anger management course, receives treatment for drug or alcohol dependency (such as joining Alcoholics Anonymous), or attends driver rectification classes. The latter may include making an apology to the victim, paying financial compensation to the victim or some other financial penalty, restoring to the victim stolen goods, making good damage caused to property (such as cleaning off graffiti), or doing other unpaid work.

### 3.9.1.6 Disadvantages of accepting a (conditional) caution

A client who accepts a caution will not be prosecuted for the offence. He must, however, be told about the following disadvantages in accepting a caution:

(a) a caution is a formal recorded admission of guilt which will form part of an offender's record and may affect how he is sentenced should he re-offend in future;
(b) the client will almost certainly lose the opportunity of receiving a caution on a subsequent occasion;
(c) the existence of the caution will be disclosable should the client apply for certain for certain types of employment (particularly entry to a profession);
(d) if the offence is sexual, the client will be placed on the sex offenders register (see **11.3.2.9**); and
(e) the police may retain fingerprints and other identification data taken from the client (a record of cautions is usually kept for minimum of five years).

A client should accept a caution only if he accepts his guilt and there is sufficient evidence against him. If there is insufficient evidence, the CPS may choose not to prosecute. A solicitor should not advise a client to accept a caution as matter of convenience, simply to dispose of the case.

## 3.9.2 Suspects aged 17 and under

### 3.9.2.1 Reprimands and final warnings

Before a defendant aged 17 or under ever comes before a Youth Court (see **Chapter 14**), it is likely that he will have been through the formal system of reprimands and warnings created by ss 65 and 66 of the Crime and Disorder Act 1998. Reprimands and final warnings are the equivalent of police cautions for adult offenders (see **3.9.1.4** above). They may be given both to juveniles (ie, offenders aged 16 and under) and to offenders aged 17.

Reprimands and final warnings are not court orders and can be given only by the police. They can, however, be referred to in court when the court is being given details of a defendant's antecedents.

An offender is likely to receive a reprimand or final warning from the police when the following conditions are satisfied:

(a) there is sufficient evidence against the offender to provide a realistic prospect of conviction;
(b) the offender admits to having committed the offence;
(c) the offender has no previous convictions; and
(d) it would not be in the public interest to prosecute the offender.

The police must also take into account the seriousness of the offence when deciding whether to administer a reprimand or final warning, or whether to charge the offender. In determining the seriousness of the offence, the police will use a guidance document prepared by the Association of Chief Police Officers (ACPO), entitled 'Final Warning Scheme: Guidance for the Police and Youth Offending Teams'. The guidance operates by giving each criminal offence a 'gravity score' and then suggesting what the most appropriate course of action is for the police depending on the score for the offence(s) the offender has committed. The gravity score may be raised or lowered depending on the presence of any aggravating or mitigating factors. The guidance can be found on the Home Office website (www.homeoffice.gov.uk).

If an offence is suitable for a reprimand or final warning, the police will start by administering a reprimand to the offender. A reprimand may be given only if the offender has not previously been reprimanded or given a final warning. If an offender has received a reprimand and then offends again, he may be likely to receive a final warning instead of being charged with the offence. An offender who has received a final warning cannot receive another final warning in respect of any further offence unless more than two years have elapsed since the previous warning *and* the further offence is not sufficiently serious as to require a charge to be brought. Such an offender must be charged with the offence.

Reprimands and final warnings can be given by the police only when an offender admits his guilt. A Youth Court may take them into account when deciding whether to grant bail to a defendant, or when sentencing a defendant (see **Chapter 14**). A defendant who is convicted of a further offence within two years of receiving a final warning cannot be given a conditional discharge by the Youth Court unless exceptional circumstances exist.

#### 3.9.2.2 What is the effect of a final warning or reprimand?

A solicitor advising a client at the police station needs to identify the circumstances when the client may be eligible to receive a reprimand or final warning, and to be able to advise the client on the consequences of accepting a reprimand or a final warning. The solicitor must also ensure that he does not persuade the client to agree to a reprimand or a final warning when the client is adamant that he did not commit the offence. A client should not be permitted to admit to something he has not done simply because this may appear to be the easiest short-term option.

The advantages of a client accepting a reprimand or final warning are that:

(a) this avoids the client being charged with the offence and having to appear before the Youth Court; and

(b) a reprimand or final warning is not a criminal conviction (which may be important when the client is completing a future job application).

There are, however, consequences of accepting a reprimand or final warning which must be pointed out to the client:

(a) A record of the reprimand or final warning will be retained until the offender is 18 or for a period of five years, whichever is the longer (this includes fingerprints, photographs and any DNA samples taken).

(b) If a final warning is given, the police must refer the client to the Youth Offending Team, who will then assess him and probably require him to take part in some form of programme (this is very similar to a 'referral order' – see **Chapter 14**).

(c) Although a reprimand or final warning will not generally need to be disclosed when making a future job application, it may need to be disclosed if the client wishes to enter a profession (eg, law, teaching or medicine).

(d) A client who accepts a reprimand or final warning will lose the option of having a further offence dealt with in this way should he reoffend (unless he does not reoffend for at least two years *and* the further offence is not sufficiently serious as to require a charge to be brought – see **3.9.2.1** above).

(e) if the offence is sexual, the client will be placed on the sex offenders register.

## 3.10 Commencing a case other than by charge (CrimPR Parts 4 and 7)

For some summary only offences (particularly relatively minor road traffic offences such as careless driving), a suspect may not have been arrested by the police and may not even have needed to attend the police station. An alternative method of commencing criminal proceedings exists for such offences.

Prior to the enactment of the Criminal Justice Act 2003, in such cases the police would 'lay an information' (ie, supply written details of the case) before the magistrates' court, and the court would then issue a summons requiring the defendant to attend court at a particular time on a particular day. The 2003 Act has put in place new arrangements for commencing prosecutions in this type of case. Under these arrangements, a prosecutor (ie, the police or the CPS) will send to the person a document called a 'written charge', which charges that person with the offence (Criminal Justice Act 2003, s 29(1)). The prosecutor must also send the person charged a document called a 'requisition', requiring that person to appear before a magistrates' court at a given time and place to answer the charge (Criminal Justice Act 2003, s 29(2)).

## 3.11 Flowchart – procedure at the police station

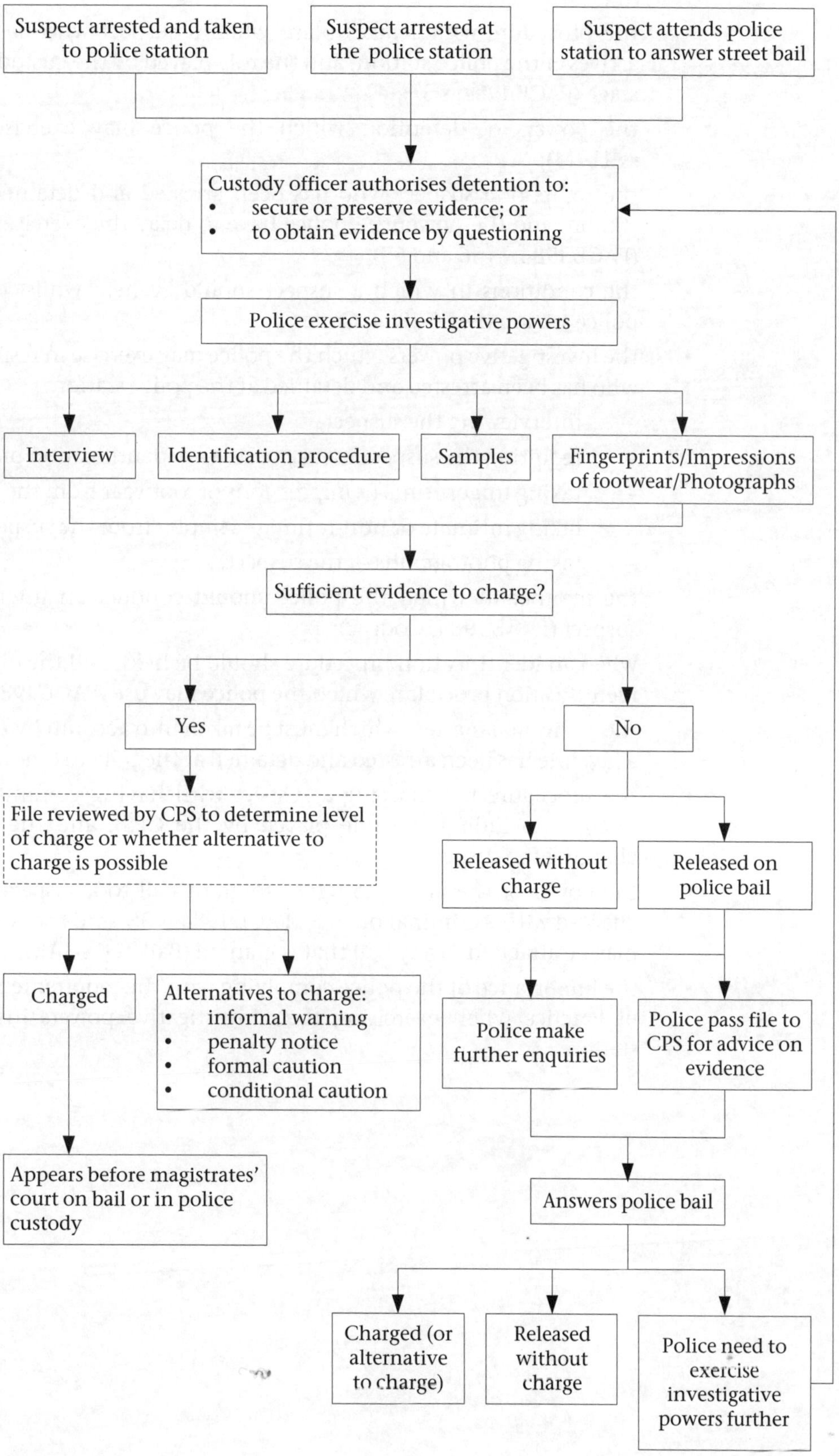

## 3.12 Checklist

At the end of this chapter you should be able to explain:

- the procedure which takes place when a suspect who has been arrested arrives at the police station, and the role played by the custody officer at this stage (PACE 1984, s 37);
- the powers of detention which the police may exercise (PACE 1984, ss 41–44);
- the rights of a suspect who has been arrested and detained at the police station, and the power the police have to delay the exercise of those rights (PACE 1984, ss 56 and 58);
- the conditions in which a suspect should be held whilst detained at the police station (PACE 1984, Code C);
- the investigative powers which the police may exercise in respect of a suspect who has been arrested and detained at the police station:
  - — interviewing the suspect,
  - — requiring the suspect to take part in an identification procedure,
  - — taking fingerprints or impressions of footwear from the suspect,
  - — taking intimate or non-intimate samples from the suspect,
  - — taking photographs of the suspect.
- the manner in which the police should conduct an interview with the suspect (PACE 1984, Code C);
- when an identification procedure should be held, and the different types of identification procedure which the police may use (PACE 1984, Code D);
- the additional matters which must be taken into account by the police when a juvenile has been arrested and detained at the police station;
- the procedure for charging a suspect with having committed a criminal offence (including the role played by the CPS), and the alternatives to charging the suspect;
- the power of the police to refuse to grant bail to a suspect who has been charged with a criminal offence (PACE 1984, s 38) and the conditions which may be attached to any bail that is granted (Bail Act, s 3A);
- the importance of the police complying with the requirements of the Codes of Practice when exercising their investigative powers inside the police station.

# Chapter 4
# The Role of the Solicitor at the Police Station



## 4.1 Introduction

A suspect who has been arrested and detained at the police station is entitled to free legal advice and to be represented by a solicitor (PACE 1984, s 58).

The role which a solicitor plays at the police station is set out in para 6D of the Notes for Guidance to Code C (the Code of Practice for the Detention, Treatment and Questioning of Persons by Police Officers). This states:

> The solicitor's *only* role in the police station is to *protect and advance* the legal rights of their client. On occasions this may require the solicitor to give advice which has the effect of the client avoiding giving evidence which strengthens the prosecution case. . . . (emphasis added)

Protecting and advancing the legal rights of clients may bring a solicitor into conflict with the police, who are likely to view the solicitor's attendance at the police station as at best a nuisance which gets in the way of their investigation.

This chapter *must* be read in conjunction with **Chapter 18**, which deals with the evidential implications of a client exercising his right to remain silent when interviewed at the police station.

## 4.2 Preparation for attending the police station

### 4.2.1 The initial telephone contact

#### 4.2.1.1 To whom will the solicitor speak?

A solicitor may be required to attend the police station at any time of the day or night (particularly if the solicitor is a member of the duty solicitor scheme – see **Chapter 3**). The solicitor will usually be telephoned by the custody officer at the police station to say that a suspect who has been arrested wants the solicitor to attend the police station to represent him. The custody officer is unlikely to provide any details of the case against the client at this stage, other than to confirm the client's name and the offence he is alleged to have committed.

After speaking to the custody officer, the solicitor should speak to the client. The solicitor will need to identify himself (if he has not represented the client on a previous occasion), ask the client to confirm that he wants the solicitor to come to the police station to represent him, and remind the client that any advice given will be free. The solicitor will also need to give some brief initial advice to the client. Although the telephone conversation should be private, the solicitor should not assume that the conversation will be completely confidential, and the client should therefore be advised to confine himself to 'Yes/No' answers in response to any questions from the solicitor. The solicitor should not allow the client to give his detailed version of events in case the client can be overheard by the police. The solicitor will need to tell client:

(a) when he will attend the police station and what he will do when he does attend;

(b) not to talk to anyone about the case; and

(c) in the solicitor's absence, not to agree to be interviewed, not to sign anything, not to give any samples and not to take part in an identification procedure.

#### 4.2.1.2 The attendance kit

Solicitors who attend the police station on a regular basis will have a standard 'kit' of materials which they take with them whenever required to attend the police station. This kit will normally include a pro forma on which to record the client's instructions, together with an up-to-date copy of PACE 1984 and the Codes of Practice. What happens at the police station can have major repercussions later in the case, and it is therefore vital that the solicitor records everything of significance that happens whilst he is at police station. An example of a standard, completed police station attendance pro forma is set out below.

## Key skill – completing a police station attendance pro forma

| PERSONAL DETAILS | |
|---|---|
| Name: | *Gary Paul Dickson* |
| Date of birth: | *28/10/80* |
| Address: | *17 Marsh Street*<br>*Chester*<br>*CH3 7LW* |
| Telephone number: | *Chester 431809* |
| National Insurance Number: | *NS 61 52 43 D* |
| Employer: | *Self-employed scaffolder/steeplejack*<br>*Also works part time as bouncer at Connelley's Night club* |
| Health Problems:<br>If yes, details: | ~~YES~~/NO |
| Outstanding criminal cases/on bail:<br>If yes details: | ~~YES~~/NO |

| | |
|---|---|
| Previous Convictions:<br>If yes, details: | YES/~~NO~~<br>*Theft x 2 (2001)*<br>*Threatening behaviour x 2 (2005/6)*<br>*ABH (2006)*<br>*Failure to surrender (2006)* |
| **INFORMATION FROM CUSTODY RECORD** | |
| Date and time of arrest: | *18/12/07 - 11.40* |
| Date and time of arrival at police station: | *18/12/07 - 12.00* |
| Date and time detention authorised: | *18/12/07 - 12.30* |
| Offence: | *ABH outside Connelley's night club* |
| Grounds for Detention: | *To obtain evidence by questioning* |
| Rights given: | YES/~~NO~~ |
| Searches carried out<br>If yes, details: | YES/~~NO~~<br>*Search after detention authorised - various items retained by police* |
| Injuries/Police Surgeon required:<br>If yes, details: | ~~YES~~/NO |
| Samples taken:<br>If yes, details: | ~~YES~~/NO |
| Appropriate Adult required:<br>If yes, details: | ~~YES~~/NO |
| **INFORMATION FROM INVESTIGATING OFFICER** | |
| Name and rank: | *PC Chambers* |
| Details of disclosure: | *Handed disclosure statement by PC Chambers. Dickson alleged to have attacked Vincent Lamb outside Connelley's night club at 03.15 today. Lamb was DJ at night club where Dickson works as bouncer. Earlier incident between Lamb and Dickson during course of evening when Dickson alleged to have threatened Lamb. Witness saw Dickson strike Lamb in face several times and then drive away. Disclosure sufficient to enable me to give proper advice to Mr Dickson (although identity of witness not revealed despite request to do so)* |
| Co-accused:<br>If yes, details: | ~~YES~~/NO |

| | |
|---|---|
| What Steps does IO take? | *Interview Dickson to put allegations to him and to obtain his response.* |
| **CONSULTATION WITH CLIENT** | |
| Client's case: | *Denies allegation. Says he was in bed at home at time of assault and partner will confirm this. Has no knowledge of incident and thinks someone at the night club has it in for him. Doesn't know Vincent Lamb and no knowledge of Lamb being DJ at night club that night. Denies that there was any incident earlier in the evening. Never went inside night club and spent all his time on pavement outside front.* |
| Advice to client: | *Advised client on possible options in interview and explained possible adverse inferences from silence under ss 34, 36 and 37. Told him that disclosure was sufficient to run risk of adverse inference if he stayed silent and he should get his version of events out. Client did however appear fatigued and emotional. Concerned client would come across badly in interview. Advised client to hand in written statement and give no comment interview.* |
| **OUTCOME** | |
| No further action: | ~~YES~~/NO |
| Bail back to Police Station<br>If yes, details: | ~~YES~~/NO |
| Caution/Warning/Reprimand:<br>If yes, details: | ~~YES~~/NO |
| Charge<br>If yes, details: | YES/~~NO~~<br>*Client charged with assaulting Vincent Lamb on 18/12/07 causing him actual bodily harm* |
| Bail Granted:<br>Details: | ~~YES~~/NO<br>*Bail refused on grounds that Dickson would fail to appear and would commit further offences.* |

| Details of First Hearing: | *Chester Magistrates' Court - 10.00 am on 19/12/07.* |
|---|---|

**TELEPHONE LOG**

| Date and time | Person spoken to | Details |
|---|---|---|
| *18/12/07 - 12.40* | *PS Dunn* | *Gary Dickson arrested on suspicion of ABH and has asked that we represent him.* |
| *18/12/07 - 12.45* | *Gary Dickson* | *Mr Dickson confirmed he wants me to represent him at the police station. Confirmed he was entitled to free legal advice and that I would attend the police station immediately. Told Mr Dickson not to talk to anyone about allegation until I arrived, and not to take part in interview/ ID procedure or to give samples.* |

**CASE NARRATIVE**

| Date and times | Details |
|---|---|
| *18/12/07: 12.50-13.00* | *Travel from office to Chester police station.* |
| *18/12/07: 13.00-13.10* | *Waiting in front office at police station.* |
| *18/12/07: 13.10-13.20* | *Reading custody record and speaking to investigating officer. No problem highlighted by custody record and disclosure given was sufficient for me to advise Mr Dickson properly. Made representations about identity of witness alleged to have seen incident, but police refused to disclose this information.* |
| *18/12/07: 13.20-13.50* | *Consultation with Mr Dickson and advice given (see comments above)* |
| *18/12/07: 13.50-14.20* | *Attending audibly-recorded interview. No comment interview and written statement handed to interviewing officer.* |
| *18/12/07: 14.20-14.40* | *Further consultation with Mr Dickson. Advised him on options open to police following interview* |

| | |
|---|---|
| 18/12/07: 14.40-14.50 | Attending whilst Mr Dickson charged with ABH. Made representation for bail but bail declined and Mr Dickson kept in custody pending first appearance before Chester MC on 19th December. |
| 18/12/07: 14.50-15.00 | Return travel to office. |

### 4.2.2 When must the solicitor attend the police station?

A solicitor is not obliged to attend the police station immediately after the initial telephone contact, even if the client has insisted that the solicitor attends straight away. If, for example, the client is drunk and the custody officer tells the solicitor that the investigating officer is not proposing to take any further steps until the client has sobered up and is ready for interview, the solicitor need not usually attend until the police notify him that they are ready to interview the client. The solicitor must attend the police station straight away, however, in the following situations:

(a) the offence is a serious one;

(b) the police intend to carry out an interview or other investigative procedure (such as taking samples or conducting an identification procedure) straight away;

(c) the client is vulnerable (eg, a juvenile or a client with mental problems);

(d) the client complains that he has been mistreated by the police;

(e) the solicitor needs to make representations about the client's detention and he cannot do this effectively over the telephone; or

(f) the client needs to speak to the solicitor in confidence.

In deciding whether it is necessary to attend the police station straight away, the solicitor should *not* take into account the fact that:

(a) the client insists the solicitor attends (unless any of the above factors is present);

(b) this may be inconvenient for the solicitor;

(c) the client has experience of police detention or questioning, or the client reassures the solicitor that he can cope on his own.

### 4.2.3 Other steps the solicitor needs to take

If the solicitor does not need to attend the police station immediately, there are two other steps which he may usefully take in preparation for his later attendance, as noted below.

#### 4.2.3.1 Check the law

The solicitor will know the offence(s) which the client has been arrested on suspicion of having committed from his conversation with the custody officer. The solicitor should check the legal elements of each offence so that he is aware of what will need to be proved to secure a conviction against the client. This may be relevant when the solicitor is assessing the strength of the police case and advising the client on his strategy in interview.

#### 4.2.3.2 Check old files

If the firm has represented the client in previous criminal proceedings, the solicitor should check the outcome of such proceedings to see if the client has any previous convictions and, if so, whether these are for the same type of offence that the police are currently investigating. This may be relevant if the police choose to question the client about such convictions. The old files may also reveal whether the client is under any form of disability or mental impairment which makes him 'vulnerable' and which may in turn affect the advice the solicitor will give as to whether the client should answer questions in interview.

## 4.3 Information gathering on arrival at the police station

### 4.3.1 The custody officer

On arrival at the police station the first person the solicitor is likely to speak to is the custody officer. Although the custody officer is not involved in the investigation of the offence, he will be able to supply the solicitor with basic information about the circumstances of the client's detention in police custody. In particular, the custody officer should allow the solicitor to view the custody record and detention log (Code C, para 2.4) in which the custody officer will have recorded all the significant events which have occurred since the client arrived at the police station (see **Chapter 3**). The solicitor should use the custody record to obtain (or confirm) his client's basic details (name, address, date of birth, etc), unless he already has this information. The solicitor then needs to obtain (or confirm) the following additional details from the custody officer and/or the custody record:

(a) the alleged offence(s) for which the client has been arrested;

(b) the time at which the custody officer authorised the client's detention and the reason such authorisation was given (ie, was detention authorised to obtain or preserve evidence, or to obtain such evidence by questioning?);

(c) any significant comments made by the client whilst at the police station (for example, an admission of guilt);

(d) any samples, fingerprints or impressions of footwear which may already have been taken from the client (see **3.5.4** and **3.5.5**);

(e) any identification procedure which may already have taken place (see **3.5.3**);

(f) any interview which may already have taken place at the police station (if, for example, the client has decided to obtain legal advice only after already having been interviewed by the police);

(g) whether the client is under any form of physical or mental disability, or requires the attendance of an appropriate adult (see **3.6**);

(h) any illness which the client may be suffering from, or any indication that the client is in any way vulnerable or requires medical treatment (or details of any medical treatment which the client has already received whilst at the police station). Similarly, the solicitor should find out if the client is suffering from the effects of drink and/or drugs;

(i) any significant items found as a result of a search either of the client's person, or of any premises owned, used or occupied by the client or premises where the client was arrested (for example, items it is alleged the client has stolen or used in the commission of the offence); and

(j) if the client has already been at the police station for six hours or more, details of any detention reviews which have been carried out and the reason why the client's continued detention has been authorised (see **3.3.4.4**).

### 4.3.2 The investigating officer

Once the solicitor has obtained some basic details about the circumstances of the client's detention, he will then need to speak to the officer who is dealing with the case. The purpose of speaking to the investigating officer is to obtain the following information:

(a) the facts of the offence;
(b) disclosure;
(c) significant statements; and
(d) the next steps the investigation officer proposes to take.

#### 4.3.2.1 The facts of the offence

The solicitor needs to know what his client is alleged to have done which constitutes a criminal offence.

#### 4.3.2.2 Disclosure

Although the police are not obliged to provide the solicitor with any details of the case against the client, they will normally provide the solicitor with some (if not all) of the evidence they have. The investigating officer will summarise orally the contents of the witness statements which he has obtained, allow the solicitor to view copies of such statements or supply the solicitor with a typed disclosure statement summarising the evidence which the police have. The last form of disclosure is the more common method now used by the police. The solicitor should push the investigating officer to disclose as much information as possible about the case against his client. He should try to find out if the police have any other evidence in addition to statements from witnesses. The police may, for example, have obtained samples or fingerprints, the suspect may have been caught committing the offence on CCTV, or there may be an item of documentary or real evidence (such as a weapon it is alleged the suspect used, or drugs found on the suspect's person). If the investigating officer refuses to make any disclosure, or discloses only a very limited amount of information, the solicitor should point out to him that in those circumstances the solicitor cannot properly advise his client as to the nature of the case against him and will only be able to advise his client to give a 'no comment' interview (see **4.4.3** below). In such a situation the solicitor could usefully employ the 'DEAL' technique to persuade the officer to give proper disclosure by:

(a) Describing the 'offending' behaviour – telling the officer that he is making insufficient disclosure of the case against the client;
(b) Explaining why it offends – insufficient disclosure means that the solicitor will be unable properly to advise his client;
(c) Asking the officer to refrain from the offending behaviour – asking the officer to make proper disclosure;
(d) Letting the officer know what will happen if he refuses to refrain from such behaviour – the solicitor will advise the client to give a 'no comment' interview, state the reason for this during the interview and request that the officer's refusal to disclose details of the case against the client be noted in the custody record. The solicitor will also tell the officer that he will make a record of the officer's refusal to give disclosure of the case against his client in the solicitor's police station attendance log.

**Example**

Vincent is arrested on suspicion of burglary and is detained at the police station for questioning. Vincent's solicitor attends the police station and seeks disclosure of the police case from PC Thomas, the investigating officer. PC Thomas refuses to disclose any details of the police case, telling the solicitor that the police case will be put in full to Vincent in interview. The solicitor would respond as follows:

> 'Officer, whilst I appreciate that you are under no legal obligation to disclose to me the evidence you have obtained against my client, if I am to advise my client properly I need to know what the case against my client is. I would ask you to reconsider your decision. If you are unwilling to provide me with such details, I will have no alternative other than to advise my client to give a "no comment" interview and not to answer any questions you might put to him. I will also state during the interview the reasons I have given this advice, and insist that your refusal to provide me with any details of the case against my client is recorded in the custody record. I will also make a written record of your refusal to supply these details.'

An example of a police disclosure statement is set out below.

## Key document – police disclosure statement

### Disclosure Statement

The complainant, Mr Vincent Lamb, had been working as a guest disc jockey at Connelley's night club in Chester city centre on the evening of 17th December 2007. Gary Dickson works at the same night club as a bouncer.

During the evening of 17th December Gary Dickson had threatened Mr Lamb when Mr Lamb had been talking to a girl called Jill who was at the night club.

Mr Lamb left the night club at approximately 3 am on 18th December and was returning to his car which was parked in a nearby car park. At approximately 3.15 am, as Mr Lamb was walking to his car, a vehicle pulled up beside Mr Lamb. The driver got out and struck Mr Lamb in the face several times with his fist, causing Mr Lamb to fall to the ground and lose consciousness. Mr Lamb was unable to see his assailant because he was dazzled by the headlights on the assailant's vehicle.

The incident was seen by an independent witness who made a note of the registration number of the vehicle driven by the assailant. The number was L251 CVM. The owner and registered keeper of this vehicle is Gary Dickson.

Gary Dickson has been arrested on suspicion of assault occasioning actual bodily harm. The purpose of the interview is to obtain an account of Gary Dickson's whereabouts at or about 3.15 am on 18th December, and to obtain Mr Dickson's account of the incident which is alleged to have occurred when Dickson threatened Mr Lamb earlier that evening.

Statement prepared by PC 911 Chambers on 18/12/07

#### 4.3.2.3 Significant statements

The solicitor needs to find out if, prior to his arrival at the police station, the client has made any significant statement (or if there has been a significant silence) that is likely to be put to the client in interview (see **3.5.2.3**). The client may, for example, have made an admission on arrest which the police will wish to put to him at the start of the interview.

#### 4.3.2.4 The next steps which the investigating officer proposes to take

The solicitor needs to find out from the investigating officer what his intentions are. For example, is the client going to be interviewed straight away, or will the police require the client to take part in an identification procedure, or to provide fingerprints or samples?

### 4.3.3 The client

The solicitor should speak to his client only once he has obtained as much information as he can about the case from the custody officer and the investigating officer. The solicitor needs to discuss the following matters with his client:

(a) *The solicitor's identity and role.* Unless the solicitor has represented the client previously, this is likely to be the first meeting between the solicitor and the client. Although the solicitor may have already spoken to the client on the telephone (see **4.2.1** above), this is likely to have been several hours earlier and the client is unlikely to recall much of what the solicitor said. Furthermore, the client may be in a vulnerable emotional state and may not fully understand who the solicitor is and what his role is at the police station. The solicitor needs to make it clear to the client that he is there to provide the client with free independent legal advice and that he has no connection with the police. The solicitor should point out to the client that his only role at the police station will be to protect and advance the client's legal rights. The solicitor must also tell the client that anything he is told by the client will remain confidential (even after the solicitor has stopped acting for him), although the solicitor is bound by certain rules of professional conduct which in certain circumstances may limit what he is able to do or say on the client's behalf (see **4.3.4** below).

(b) *Details of the alleged offence.* The solicitor should give the client details of what he has been told by the investigating officer about the offence the client is alleged to have committed. The level of information the solicitor can give to the client will depend upon the level of disclosure given by the police (see **4.3.2.2** above), but it is important that the client has a clear picture of what the solicitor has been told. As part of telling the client about the police case, the solicitor should also advise the client about the relevant substantive law. In particular, the solicitor should advise the client as to what the police will need to prove in order to obtain a conviction for the offence for which the client has been arrested.

(c) *The client's instructions.* Once the client knows what the police case against him is, the solicitor should then get the client's version of events. Given the pressures of time that exist at the police station, it may not be possible for the solicitor to obtain a full proof of evidence from the client. The solicitor should, however, try to take detailed instructions from the client. Any advice which the solicitor subsequently gives to the client will be based on this information, and it is therefore important that the solicitor takes as full instructions as time permits.

(d) *The next step in the police investigation.* The client may already have been detained at the police station for several hours and be anxious to know what the police intend to do. The solicitor needs to advise the client as to what the next step in the police investigation will be. In the majority of cases, the next step will be for the police to require the client to take part in an audibly recorded interview.

(e) *Prepare the client for interview.* This involves:

    (i) advising the client on whether or not to answer questions put to him in the interview (ie, advising the client what is the 'safest option' in the interview – see **4.4.6** below);

    (ii) preparing a written statement on the client's behalf if the client is to give a 'no comment' interview, but hand the statement to the police so that his defence is put 'on record' (see **4.4.5** below);

(iii) advising the client how the interview will be conducted by the police (see **4.5.1** below); and

(iv) advising the client what role the solicitor will play in the interview (see **4.5.2.2** below).

## 4.3.4 Conduct issues

### 4.3.4.1 The client who admits his guilt

A solicitor may take instructions from a client who confirms that he has in fact committed the offence for which he has been arrested, but who wants to deny the offence when interviewed by the police. If the client admits his guilt to his solicitor, the solicitor must advise the client that he cannot then attend an interview to represent the client if the client intends to deny having committed the offence. The solicitor cannot be a party to the client giving information to the police which the solicitor knows to be false since this would amount to a breach of the solicitor's duty not to deceive or knowingly mislead the court under Rule 11.01 of the Solicitors' Code of Conduct 2007. The solicitor could attend an interview where the client intends to give a 'no comment' response to police questions, since this would not involve the giving of false information.

If the client insists on giving false information in interview, the solicitor should decline to act any further on the client's behalf. As the solicitor owes an ongoing duty of confidentiality to the client (Solicitors' Code of Conduct 2007, Rule 4.01), the police should not be told why the solicitor is no longer acting on the client's behalf. It is usual in such a case for a solicitor to say that he is withdrawing from the case for 'professional reasons'.

A solicitor representing a client who intends to lie to the police in interview should attempt to dissuade the client from doing so. It is appropriate for the solicitor to advise the client that, if he admits his guilt in the interview, he will receive credit from the court for cooperating with the police when he is later sentenced.

### 4.3.4.2 Conflicts of interest

**When may a conflict arise?**

A solicitor will often be asked to advise two (or more) individuals at the police station who are jointly suspected of having committed an offence. Although a solicitor is permitted to act for two or more suspects where there is no conflict of interest, the difficulty faced by a solicitor at the police station is spotting when a potential conflict of interest may arise. On arrival at the police station the solicitor will know little more than the names of the clients and the offence for which they have been arrested. Until the solicitor knows what the police version of events is (and what version of events his potential clients are giving), he is not going to know whether there is an actual or potential conflict of interest. It is the responsibility of the solicitor to determine whether a conflict of interest exists. If the custody officer suggests to the solicitor that there is a conflict, the solicitor should ask the officer to clarify why he considers this to be the case, but stress to the officer that ultimately it is the decision of the solicitor alone as to whether a conflict exists and not that of the police (Code C, Notes for Guidance, para 6G).

**Steps the solicitor should take**

Once he has spoken to the investigating officer, the solicitor should speak to one of the suspects (usually the first suspect to have requested the solicitor's attendance at the police station). If that suspect's account suggests a clear conflict of interest (if, for example, the suspect denies guilt and accuses the other suspect of having committed the offence), the solicitor should decline to act for the second suspect and inform the police that he should receive separate legal advice. To act for both suspects would be a breach of Rule 3.01 of the Solicitors' Code of Conduct 2007, whereby a solicitor must not act where there is a conflict of interest between two or more clients. Even if there is no obvious conflict of interest, the solicitor should be alert to a potential conflict of interest arising later in the case. This could occur, for example, if both suspects admit the offence but, when the case comes to court, the mitigation for one of the suspects is going to be that he played only a minor role in the commission of the offence and that the larger role was played by the other suspect.

If, after speaking to the first suspect, the solicitor considers there is any risk of a conflict of interest developing, he should decline to see the second suspect and tell the police that this suspect must get legal advice elsewhere. If a conflict of interest emerges only after the solicitor has seen both suspects, the appropriate course of action is for the solicitor to withdraw from the case completely. To continue acting for both suspects would be a clear conflict of interest, and it would be inappropriate to continue to act for only one of the suspects because the solicitor would be in possession of confidential information about the other suspect. which he would be unable to pass on to the suspect whom he was continuing to represent. Only if the solicitor is able to act for one suspect without putting at risk his duty of confidentiality to the other suspect may he continue to represent that first suspect (Solicitors' Code of Conduct 2007, Rule 3.03). This is unlikely to be the case, because the confidential information received from the suspect the solicitor no longer acts for is likely to assist the case of the suspect the solicitor is continuing to represent and so confidentiality will be put at risk.

Detailed advice for solicitors asked to represent more than one client at the police station is contained in the Solicitors' Code of Conduct 2007 in the guidance notes to Rule 3 (conflict of interests).

**Should a solicitor disclose to one client information he has been given by another client?**

If a solicitor decides that there is no conflict of interest and he is able to represent both suspects, he must still not disclose to one client anything he has been told by the other (in order to comply with his duty of confidentiality), unless:

(a) he has obtained the other client's consent (preferably in writing) to disclose this information;

(b) both clients are putting forward the same defence; and

(c) he considers it in his client's best interests for the information to be disclosed.

If the client is a juvenile, the client would need to provide written authority for the solicitor to disclose any information, and such authority must be given in the presence of the appropriate adult.

Even if the above considerations are satisfied, the solicitor must also have regard to his overriding duty not to mislead the court. Co-accused who are represented by the same solicitor may attempt to use that solicitor to pass information between each other so that they can jointly fabricate a defence and give the police a consistent 'story'. To guard against this, the solicitor should ensure that before telling the second client what he has been told by the first client, he obtains an account of the second client's version of events. If this is consistent with the account given by the first client, the solicitor will be able to pass on the relevant information. If, however, the stories are inconsistent, the solicitor will need to withdraw from the case. It would be inappropriate for the solicitor to continue to act for just one of the clients because he would be in possession of confidential information about the other.

#### 4.3.4.3 Disclosing the client's case to a third party

A solicitor representing a client at the police station may be asked for details of his client's defence by another solicitor representing a co-accused who has been arrested in connection with the same matter. Such a request should be treated with caution. The solicitor owes a duty of confidentiality to his client and should therefore not respond to such a request by releasing any such information. The only exception to this is if the solicitor considers it is in the client's best interests for such information to be disclosed. This will only very rarely be the case. If the solicitor does consider that it would be in the client's interests to disclose this information, the solicitor should explain his reasoning to the client and obtain the client's express instructions (ideally in writing) to disclose the information.

#### 4.3.4.4 The appropriate adult

If an appropriate adult is required, the solicitor must ensure that the appropriate adult understands what his role is, that he is not present simply as an observer and that he is *not* at the police station to assist the police.

Issues of professional conduct may arise when an appropriate adult attends the police station to assist a juvenile. Some common issues which may arise are as follows.

**A conflict in instructions between the appropriate adult and the juvenile**

It will often be the case that a juvenile wishes to pursue one course of action whilst the appropriate adult wants him to do something else.

> Example
>
> Jacob is aged 15 and has been arrested on suspicion of theft. He asks for legal advice from a solicitor and his father is also called to the police station as the appropriate adult. Jacob admits to his solicitor that he committed the theft, but the solicitor considers that the police have insufficient evidence to prove the allegation. The solicitor therefore advises Jacob to remain silent in interview. Jacob's father is unhappy about this and instructs the solicitor that Jacob must tell the truth.

In this situation the solicitor's client is the juvenile, not the appropriate adult. The solicitor's duty is to act in the client's best interests. The solicitor would attempt to explain to the appropriate adult why it would be in the best interests of the juvenile to follow his advice.

**The duty of confidentiality**

Appropriate adults do not owe the juvenile a duty of confidentiality. In the example given above, Jacob's father could therefore tell the police what Jacob had said. He would also be able to give evidence for the prosecution at Jacob's trial, repeating what Jacob had said. The solicitor could ask the appropriate adult, prior to the solicitor giving advice, if the appropriate adult is willing to be bound by confidentiality during the consultation (and to confirm this in writing). If the appropriate adult agrees to this, there is nothing to prevent the appropriate adult changing his mind and disclosing such information to the police. If the appropriate adult refuses to be bound by confidentiality, the solicitor should tell the police that he objects to that person continuing to act as the appropriate adult.

**Legal professional privilege**

Even if the appropriate adult agrees to treat the consultation as being confidential, since legal professional privilege does not apply to appropriate adults, there is nothing to prevent the prosecution from calling the appropriate adult to give evidence at trial as to what was said during the consultation.

To circumvent these potential problems, para 1E of the Notes for Guidance to Code C provides that a juvenile should always be given the opportunity to consult privately with a solicitor in the absence of the appropriate adult (if the appropriate adult is a social worker, it is standard practice for social workers not to sit in on the consultation, so such problems do not arise). A solicitor attending the police station will usually ask the juvenile whether he wants the appropriate adult to attend any consultation prior to the consultation starting. If the juvenile indicates that he does want the appropriate adult to be present, the solicitor will then ask the appropriate adult if he is prepared to treat the consultation as confidential. If the appropriate adult is not prepared to agree to this, the solicitor should suggest to the juvenile that he reconsider his decision to have the appropriate adult present at the consultation. If the appropriate adult is prepared to treat the consultation as confidential, the solicitor should ask him to sign something to this effect. Ultimately, it is the decision of the juvenile as to whether he wants the appropriate adult to attend the consultation with his solicitor.

#### 4.3.4.5 Withdrawing from acting

If, for reasons of professional conduct, a solicitor is unable to continue acting for a client (or clients) at the police station, the solicitor needs to do the following:

(a) explain to the client why he is no longer able to represent him;

(b) tell the client that he is entitled to free legal advice from another solicitor of his choice or the duty solicitor;

(c) tell the client that, although he is no longer able to represent him, the solicitor owes to the client an ongoing duty of confidentiality and will not therefore tell the police why he is unable to act; and

(d) tell the custody officer that he is no longer able to act, but not disclose the reason why. If the solicitor told the custody officer why he was no longer able to act, this would be a breach of the ongoing duty of confidentiality owed to his client under Rules 1.04 and 4.01 of the Solicitors' Code of Conduct 2007.

## 4.4 Should the suspect answer questions in interview?

### 4.4.1 Introduction

The usual ground upon which the custody officer will authorise the detention of a suspect at the police station is to enable the investigating officer to obtain evidence by questioning the suspect in an audibly recorded interview. The reason for the police wanting to interview a suspect is their hope that the suspect will 'crack' and say something incriminating when put under the pressure of an interview situation. Most suspects who are interviewed by the police end up either making an admission of guilt or contradicting themselves, so that their account of the case is shown to lack credibility when the interview is either played or read out to the court at trial (see **Chapter 9**). The most important role the solicitor has at the police station is to advise his client whether or not to answer questions in police interview. A client whom the police wish to interview has four options:

(a) to answer all the questions put to him;
(b) to give a 'no comment interview';
(c) to give a 'mixed interview', where he answers some questions but not others;
(d) to give a 'no comment interview', but either during the interview or before being charged hand a written statement to the police setting out facts he will rely upon in his defence at trial.

Each of these options will be examined in turn below. Whilst the final decision as to which option to take is that of the client, the client is likely to follow the advice received from his solicitor. It is therefore vital that the solicitor makes an accurate note of the advice given to the client, and the reasons for giving such advice.

## 4.4.2 Answer all questions

### 4.4.2.1 Advantages

The advantage of a client answering all questions in interview is that this allows the client to put his version of events on record straight away. This can be particularly important if the client is raising a specific defence which imposes an evidential burden on him, such as self-defence or the defence of alibi (see **Chapter 16**). If the client's defence is particularly strong and the client comes across well when interviewed, answering questions in full may even result in the police deciding not to pursue the case any further if they accept the truth of the client's version of events. Even if the client is subsequently charged by the police, the credibility of his evidence at trial will be boosted if he can show that he placed his defence on record at the earliest opportunity, and has told a consistent 'story' throughout.

Answering all the questions put by the police is also likely to ensure that at trial the court or jury will not be permitted to draw adverse inferences against the client under ss 34, 36 or 37 of the Criminal Justice and Public Order Act (CJPOA) 1994 (see **Chapter 18** and **4.4.3** below).

If the client is admitting his guilt, it may also be sensible to answer questions in interview to confirm this. If the client has no previous convictions and has never previously been cautioned by the police, the police may decide to deal with the matter by way of a caution rather than charging the client with the offence if, when interviewed, the client admits his guilt (see **3.9**). Even if the police decide to charge the client with having committed the offence, an admission of guilt during the interview at the police station is a matter that may be raised when the client's solicitor is giving his plea in mitigation to the court prior to the client being sentenced (see **12.7.4.3**). The solicitor will be able to tell the court that his client co-operated with the police from the first opportunity and that, by making a prompt admission of guilt, the client saved the police spending additional time and resources investigating the offence. Guidelines produced by the Sentencing Guidelines Council suggest that, when determining the reduction in sentence a defendant will receive for entering an early guilty plea, the court may consider that the defendant should have indicated a willingness to plead guilty when interviewed at the police station (see **11.4.2.5**).

#### 4.4.2.2 Disadvantages

The disadvantage in answering questions put by the police in interview is that many suspects will either say something incriminating or make comments which undermine their credibility. Police officers are particularly adept at 'tripping up' suspects in interview, and it is very easy for a suspect to become flustered, confused or angry, particularly if he is in an emotional condition. Suspects in such a state may be led into admitting their involvement in the offence, or into asserting facts which are contradictory or which the police can show to be untrue.

If the suspect is subsequently charged with the offence and pleads not guilty, a transcript of the interview record will be read out at court (or the recording of the interview may be played). A suspect who comes across as being confused or angry, who makes admissions, or who gives a contradictory or implausible account of events is likely to have his credibility severely damaged in the eyes of the jury or magistrates.

Even clients who are able to give their solicitor a clear version of events may be vulnerable to confusion in an interview situation. This is particularly the case with young or immature clients, clients who have not previously been in trouble with the police or clients who the solicitor believes may be emotionally vulnerable.

The solicitor also needs to consider whether the police have provided sufficient disclosure of the evidence which they have obtained in the course of their investigations in order to enable the client to answer all the questions which the police put. A common tactic employed by the police is to hold back from the suspect's solicitor a particular piece of information which is then put to the suspect in interview, hoping to catch him off-guard. If the solicitor does not consider that the police have made a full disclosure of their case, it is a hazardous step for the solicitor then to advise the client to answer questions in police interview. The client is likely to be caught out when the police raise a matter which was not disclosed to his solicitor.

An additional potential problem in the client answering questions is that the line of questioning pursued by the police may lead the client to make an attack on the character of another person. If the client is subsequently prosecuted for the offence, such an attack may enable the CPS to raise in evidence at trial any previous convictions the client may have (see **Chapter 22** and **4.5.3.3** below).

### 4.4.3 Give a 'no comment' interview

#### 4.4.3.1 Advantages

The advantage of a client declining to answer questions in interview (other than to say 'no comment' in reply to each question) is that there is no danger of the client incriminating himself by making any admissions, or inadvertently giving the police a piece of evidence which they would not otherwise have had. If the case against the client is weak and the police are hoping to bolster it by getting the client to say something damaging in interview, giving a 'no comment' interview may mean that the police will not then have sufficient evidence to enable them to charge the client with the offence, and the client is likely to be released without charge.

#### 4.4.3.2 Disadvantages

The disadvantage of a client giving a 'no comment' interview is that, if the client is subsequently charged and pleads not guilty, the magistrates or jury may in certain circumstances draw an adverse inference under ss 34, 36 or 37 of the CJPOA 1994 from the client's silence in interview. The circumstances in which an adverse inference may be drawn are examined fully in **Chapter 18**. In summary, however, if the client fails to answer questions in police interview and then at trial raises a defence the details of which could have been given to the police in interview, the court or jury are entitled to conclude that the defence is a sham and was fabricated by the defendant after he had left the police station, when he had the opportunity to 'get his story straight'.

#### 4.4.3.3 When is a solicitor likely to advise the client to give a 'no comment' interview?

A solicitor is permitted to advise a client who admits his guilt to the solicitor to give a 'no comment' interview. This will be important if the solicitor considers that the case against the client is weak and the police do not currently have sufficient evidence to prove the allegation. A client who answers questions in such a situation may make a damaging admission which will give the police sufficient evidence to charge him. This course of action would not involve the solicitor being a party to the client lying to or misleading the police, and the police may decide not to pursue the case if they are unable to obtain any admissions from the client in interview.

The other occasions on which a solicitor may advise his client to give a 'no comment' interview are if:

(a) he considers that the police have not provided him with full disclosure of the evidence they have obtained against his client (so that the solicitor is unable properly to advise his client on the strength police case against him). Lack of full disclosure from the police creates a real risk that the client may implicate himself if he answers questions in interview. This is a particularly important consideration if a co-accused has also been arrested and interviewed by the police, especially if the police are not prepared to disclose what they consider the role of the co-accused to have been, or if the police are not prepared to disclose what the co-accused has said in interview;

(b) linked to (a), the solicitor considers that the police may attempt to 'ambush' the client during the interview by revealing a piece of evidence which they had not disclosed to the solicitor in advance of the interview (in the hope that, when confronted with this evidence, the client will say something incriminating or be lost for words);

(c) the client denies involvement in the offence and the police do not currently have sufficient evidence to charge the client (since if the client agrees to answer questions in interview he runs the risk of giving the police the additional evidence they need to enable them to charge him);

(d) the client is physically or mentally unfit to be interviewed (if, for example, the client is suffering from the effects of drink or drugs), or the solicitor considers that the client would fail to give a good account of his case in interview because the client is distressed, emotional or fatigued. This is likely to be the case if the interview is to take place late at night, the client has been at the police station for a number of hours before the interview takes place, or the client has been involved in an upsetting incident (often in connection with the alleged offence);

(e) the client is likely to perform badly in interview due to his:

(i) age,
(ii) lack of maturity,
(iii) psychological vulnerability, or
(iv) previous inexperience of police detention and questioning.

If the client is particularly young, he may lack the maturity to answer questions properly or may become aggressive during the interview. Older clients often become easily confused or 'lost' during interviews at the police station. If the client appears particularly agitated or ill at ease, the solicitor may consider that the client is psychologically vulnerable to the questioning techniques the police may employ during the interview. Similar considerations will apply if this is the first time the client has been arrested and he has no previous experience of custody or questioning by the police. A solicitor may also have suspicions that the client could be suffering from some form of mental impairment if the client is behaving strangely, or if the client is unable to give the solicitor coherent instructions;

(f) the facts of the case are so complex, or relate to matters occurring so long ago, that the client cannot reasonably be expected to provide an immediate response to the allegations made against him, or that any immediate response he is able to give will not be accurate. This may be a particular consideration in a fraud case in which the police want to ask the client about complex financial matters, or in a case involving allegations of physical or sexual abuse carried out many years previously;

(g) although the client says he did not commit the offence, the client does not have a viable case or defence. If the solicitor considers that the client has no case that will, at that time, stand up to police questioning, the best course of action may be to give a 'no comment' interview, since the client will only come across badly in interview if he attempts to answer questions to which he has no real response; or

(h) the client has any other good personal reasons for staying silent. A common situation when a client may have a good personal reason for staying silent is if the client would suffer extreme embarrassment if he were to tell the police what actually happened.

### Example

Gerry is arrested on suspicion of the burglary of a shop in the early hours of the morning. Gerry instructs his solicitor that he did not commit the burglary and has an alibi. The alibi is that, at the time the burglary is alleged to have occurred, Gerry was at the home of Anthea, with whom he is having an affair. Gerry is married and doesn't want his wife to find out about the affair. If, when interviewed, Gerry tells the police details of his alibi, the police will check it and it is likely that Gerry's wife will find out about the affair. Gerry will have a good personal reason for wanting to remain silent. (In this situation the solicitor would advise Gerry that he would need to balance the risk that his wife might find out about the affair against the greater likelihood of his being convicted if he fails to put forward a defence to the allegation made against him.)

If a client decides to give a 'no comment' interview on the basis of the legal advice he has received, the solicitor must explain to the client that this will not necessarily prevent a court from drawing adverse inferences from this silence at any subsequent trial (see **Chapter 18**). If the solicitor has advised a client to remain silent, he should ensure that he makes a full written note of the reasons for his advising this. Such a record may have important evidential value at trial (see **Chapter 18**).

### 4.4.4 Give a 'mixed interview'

A solicitor should *not* advise a client to answer some of the questions put by the police but not others. Doing this comes across very badly at trial when the interview transcript is read out or the recording of the interview is played to the court. By answering some questions but not others, it will appear to the magistrates or the jury that the defendant has something to hide and is refusing to reply to those difficult questions for which he has no satisfactory answer.

### 4.4.5 Hand in a written statement

#### 4.4.5.1 When might a written statement be used?

Handing in a written statement to the police is a useful strategy to employ if the solicitor considers that his client needs to place his version of events on record to avoid an adverse inference being drawn at trial (if, for example, the client has a positive defence such as self-defence or alibi), but the solicitor is concerned that the client may perform badly if he answers questions in interview. This is likely to be the case if the client is young, emotional, or has never previously been arrested and detained at the police station. If the client is to hand in a written statement to the police, the solicitor will advise him to answer 'no comment' to questions put by the police in interview. The written statement will be handed to the police either during the interview, or after the interview but prior to the client being charged.

#### 4.4.5.2 What should the statement contain?

A written statement will be drafted by the solicitor and will allow the client to set out his defence in a clear and logical way. As long as the written statement sets out all the facts which the client later relies upon in his defence at trial, handing in a written statement should avoid the risk of any inferences being drawn at trial under s 34 of the CJPOA 1994 (see **4.4.3.2**), even if the client answers 'no comment' to the questions put to him by the police in interview. In drafting the statement, the solicitor should also take care to cover those matters about which the police might ask the client in interview and which may at trial be the subject of an adverse inference under s 36 or s 37 of the CJPOA 1994 (see **Chapter 18**).

The statement should say no more than is necessary to prevent the drawing of adverse inferences at trial, although the statement may need updating if the police make further disclosure of their case. An example of a written statement drafted by the solicitor and to be handed in to the police is set out below.

## Key skill – drafting a written statement for a client at the police station

**Statement of Gary Paul Dickson**

I have been arrested on suspicion of assaulting Vincent Lamb at approximately 3.15 am on 18th December 2007.

On the evening of 17th December 2007 I was working as a bouncer at Connelley's night club in Chester city centre. I understand that Vincent Lamb was the guest DJ at Connelley's that evening. I was not aware of this because I spent the evening stood on the pavement at the front of the night club. I do not know Mr Lamb and there was no altercation between Mr Lamb and myself during the evening.

My shift finished at 1.30 am and at this time I drove home to 17 Marsh Street, Chester. I arrived home at approximately 1.45 am and went straight to bed. At 3.15 am I was asleep in bed with my partner Jill Marsh.

I do own a vehicle with the registration number L251 CVM. At the time Mr Lamb is alleged to have been assaulted, this vehicle was parked on the road outside 17 March Street, Chester. The person who claims to have identified this vehicle as the vehicle used by Mr Lamb's attacker is mistaken.

I did not assault Vincent Lamb and I know nothing about this incident.

Signed: *Gary Paul Dickson*

Dated: *18th December 2007*

### 4.4.5.3 When should the statement be handed in to the police?

The written statement can be handed in to the police either during the interview, or just prior to charge. It is normal practice for the statement to be handed in at the start of the interview and for the suspect then to answer 'no comment' to questions put by the police during the interview. If, however, the defence solicitor feels that the police case is particularly weak, it may be better to hold back the handing in of the defence statement until the police have actually decided to charge the client (but before the client is formally charged). Handing in the statement earlier may give the police some additional information, which might lead them to decide to charge the client when otherwise they might not have done so. For example, in the statement the client may make a partial admission which gives the police sufficient evidence to enable them to charge him with the offence.

**Example**

Julia is arrested on suspicion of burglary of shop premises and is to be interviewed at the police station. Before the interview takes place, Julia's solicitor obtains disclosure of the case against Julia from the investigating officer. The solicitor considers that the police case against Julia is weak and that Julia is unlikely to be charged if she gives a 'no comment' interview. In particular, the police do not have any direct evidence placing Julia at the shop premises at the time of the burglary.

When the solicitor takes instructions from Julia, she tells him that she did not commit the burglary but was outside the shop premises when the burglary took place. Julia's solicitor advises her that if she discloses this fact to the police, this will strengthen the case against her and make it more likely that she will be charged. Julia accepts her solicitor's advice and gives a 'no comment' interview. However, Julia's solicitor also prepares a written statement in Julia's name setting out her defence. The solicitor will not hand this statement in to the police during the interview. If the police do decide to charge Julia, however, the solicitor will hand in the statement before Julia is charged. If the statement contains the facts Julia will later raise in her defence at trial, this will prevent any adverse inferences being drawn.

Very occasionally a solicitor will take a written statement from his client but, rather than hand the statement to the police whilst the client is at the police station, retain the statement on the client's file. This may occur when the solicitor has doubts as to the accuracy of the instructions he has received from his client and is reluctant to disclose the client's defence to the police because he suspects that the facts put forward by the client either will not stand up to scrutiny, or may 'change' later in the case. In such circumstances, the solicitor will retain the statement on his file and produce it at a later stage in the case, if necessary, to prevent the court drawing an inference that the client's defence was fabricated after he had left the police station. Adopting such a tactic will not, however, prevent other adverse inferences being drawn by the court at trial. This could include an inference that the defendant was not sufficiently confident in his defence to expose it to police scrutiny or investigation, or that he had not thought up all the details of his defence at the time of the interview.

**Example**

Paul is arrested on suspicion of assault and is to be interviewed at the police station. Paul tells his solicitor that it is a case of mistaken identity and that he was elsewhere at the time of the assault (although he cannot recall exactly where he was). The identification evidence against Paul is extremely strong and Paul's solicitor doubts that Paul's account will stand up to police scrutiny. The solicitor takes a written statement from Paul who then gives a 'no comment' interview. The solicitor does not hand a copy of the statement to the police but retains the statement on his file.

*Scenario 1* – Paul is subsequently charged with assault. Paul's defence at trial is the same as the account he gave to his solicitor at the police station. Paul's solicitor can produce the statement to the court to prevent the court drawing an inference of recent fabrication (that Paul thought up his defence only after he had left the police station). The court will, however, be able to draw the adverse inference that Paul was not sufficiently confident in his defence to expose it to police questioning at the police station.

*Scenario 2* – Paul is subsequently charged with assault. Paul changes his version of events and now tells his solicitor that he was present at the time of the assault but claims to have been acting only in self-defence. The solicitor will not use Paul's statement obtained at the police station because the basis of Paul's defence has changed. The court will be able to draw an inference of recent fabrication. However, by not handing in Paul's statement when Paul was originally detained at the police station, Paul's solicitor has avoided the far more damaging situation of Paul saying one thing at the police station and then saying something totally different when his case comes to trial.

### 4.4.6 Conclusion

Giving the correct advice to a client on whether or not to answer questions in an interview at the police station is one of the hardest tasks a defence solicitor will face, because there are a number of considerations that need to be taken into account. To help solicitors who advise clients at the police station to give the correct advice, The Law Society has produced a 'Safest defence: decision-making template' for solicitors to use at the police station when deciding what advice to give to their clients. A copy of the template is reproduced below. It lists a number of factors which the solicitor should take into account when advising a client on whether to answer questions, and the matters the solicitor should consider when assessing the importance of each factor. The factors are:

(a) the degree of disclosure given by the police;
(b) the strength of the prosecution case;
(c) the age and maturity of the client;
(d) the degree of experience of police questioning and custody which the client has;
(e) the psychological vulnerability of the client;
(f) the strength of the client's case; and
(g) whether the client has any personal reasons for staying silent.

The template also sets out the most appropriate advice the solicitor should give to his client, dependent on the solicitor's assessment of the risks involved in the client answering questions.

## 4.5 Role of the solicitor in the interview

### 4.5.1 Preparing the client for interview

The solicitor needs to explain to his client the procedure to be followed in the audibly recorded interview, and to warn the client about the tactics the police are likely to adopt in an attempt to get him to answer questions if he gives a 'no comment' interview. The following points need to be explained to the client:

(a) The interview will be audibly recorded and all parties (including the client and the solicitor) will be asked to identify themselves on the recording.

(b) The interview can be stopped at any time if the client requires further legal advice from the solicitor. The client should be told that he can ask for the interview to be stopped for this purpose, or the solicitor may intervene of his own volition to suggest that the interview be stopped so he can give further advice to the client.

(c) The solicitor will be present in the interview to protect the client's interests, and will intervene in the interview when necessary if the solicitor considers that the police questioning is in any way inappropriate, or if he considers that the client would benefit from further legal advice in private.

(d) If the client is to remain silent in the interview, he should be advised to use the stock phrase of 'no comment' in answer to all the questions which are put to him. It is easier for clients to answer questions in this way rather than to remain totally silent.

(e) A client who is to remain silent should be advised that the police will often employ certain tactics to get him to talk. In particular the police may:

  (i) try to get him to talk by asking apparently innocuous questions that have nothing to do with the offence under investigation;

  (ii) try to alienate him from the solicitor by suggesting that the legal advice he has received from his solicitor is incorrect; or

  (iii) warn him that certain consequences may arise (for example, he may be detained at the police station indefinitely) unless he answers questions.

  The client should be advised to ignore such tactics and to maintain his silence.

(f) If the client is to answer questions in the interview, the solicitor should remind him not to 'lose his cool' during the interview, and not to become hostile or abusive in his comments towards the interviewing officer. If the recording of the interview is subsequently played out at his trial, the client is likely to lose credibility in the eyes of the jury or magistrates if he acts in this way. The client should also be warned against making personal attacks on others during the interview. An attack on the character of another person made during the course of an interview may enable to prosecution to adduce evidence of the suspect's previous convictions at his trial.

### 4.5.2 The interview

#### 4.5.2.1 Seating arrangements

The solicitor should ensure that he is permitted to sit beside his client during the interview and must never allow the police to prevent him from being able to make eye contact with his client. The police will occasionally try to 'distance' the client from his solicitor by asking the solicitor to sit behind him, so that he is unable to make proper eye contact with the client, thereby isolating the client and making

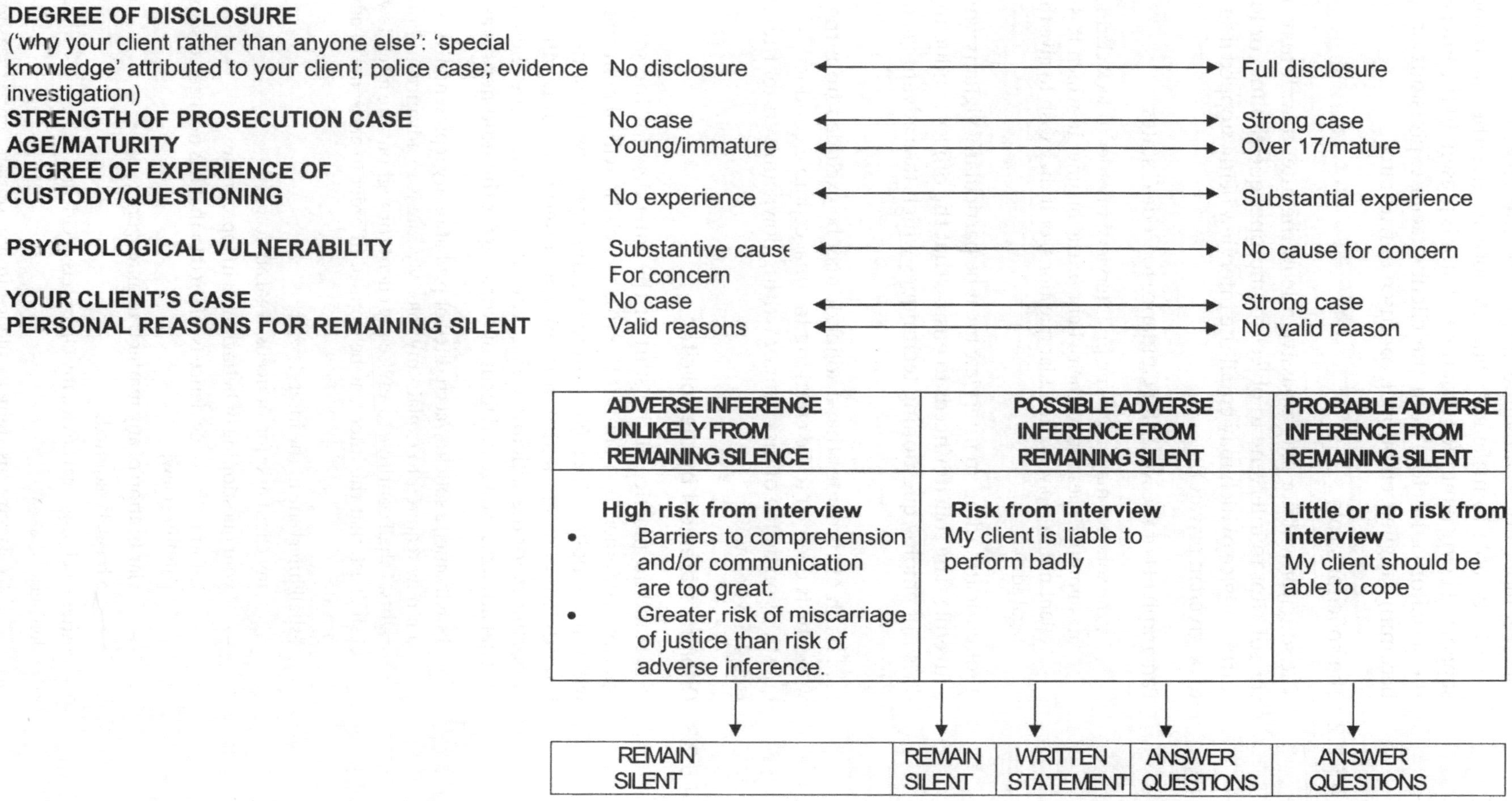


Safest defence: decision-making template

him feel more alone and vulnerable in the interview. The client and the solicitor need to be able to make eye contact, both to give the client the psychological support of being reminded that the solicitor is present in the interview and so that the solicitor can detect from the client's facial expressions or gestures if he is becoming fatigued, emotional, confused or frustrated.

#### 4.5.2.2 The solicitor's role

The solicitor will not play a passive role in the interview. It may be necessary for the solicitor to intervene to object to improper questioning, or to give the client further advice (which may entail the interview being stopped if such advice needs to be given in private).

Paragraph 6D of the Notes for Guidance to Code C states:

> ... the solicitor may intervene [in interview] in order to seek clarification, challenge an improper question to their client or the manner in which it is put, advise their client not to reply to particular questions, or if they wish to give their client further legal advice.

A solicitor attending an interview must be particularly vigilant when representing a juvenile. The solicitor needs to ensure that the officer conducting the interview does not employ questioning techniques which take advantage of the juvenile's age.

Paragraph 6D provides that a solicitor may be excluded from the interview only when he is deemed to be engaging in 'unacceptable conduct', such as answering questions on behalf of his client or writing down answers for the client to read out (see **4.5.5** below).

#### 4.5.2.3 Opening statement by the solicitor

It is standard practice at the start of the interview for the solicitor to make an opening statement explaining the role which he will play in the interview. This will put the police officer(s) conducting the interview on notice that the solicitor intends to play an active role in the interview, and will also provide an opportunity for the solicitor to state the advice given to the client and the reasons for that advice. A suggested form of wording for the statement is as follows:

> I am [name], a solicitor/accredited or probationary representative with [firm name]. I am now required to explain my role. My role is to advance and protect my client's rights. I shall continue to advise my client throughout the interview and if necessary I shall ask that the interview be stopped in order to allow me to advise my client in private.
>
> I shall intervene in the interview if:
>
> — my client asks for, or needs, legal advice;
>
> — your questioning or behaviour is inappropriate;
>
> — information or evidence is referred to that has not been disclosed to me before this interview;
>
> — clarification of any matter is required; or
>
> — a break is required.
>
> After receiving legal advice my client has decided:
>
> [either]
>
> — to exercise his right to silence [if appropriate, give a reason for this advice] because [reason]. Please respect that decision. [My client is however prepared to hand to you a written statement about this matter.]
>
> [or]

— to answer questions which you may raise which are relevant to my client's arrest/voluntary attendance.

It is important that a solicitor makes an opening statement, both to make it clear to the police that the solicitor knows his role (and if the solicitor does need to intervene, to justify such intervention in advance) and to give the client confidence in the solicitor's ability, which in turn will give the client important psychological support.

## 4.5.3 When should a solicitor intervene during the interview?

### 4.5.3.1 Examples of when a solicitor should intervene

A solicitor should intervene during the course of the interview if he considers that:

(a) the questioning techniques employed by the police are inappropriate or improper;
(b) the police are behaving in an inappropriate manner; or
(c) his client would benefit from further (private) legal advice.

Set out below is a non-exhaustive list of the types of situation which may occur during an interview when it would be appropriate for the solicitor to intervene.

**The solicitor is unhappy about the seating arrangements for the interview**

Even before the interview has commenced, the solicitor should intervene if the police have arranged the seats so that he cannot properly advise his client (for example, by seating the solicitor behind the client so that the solicitor cannot make eye contact with the client), or if the solicitor considers the seating to be oppressive (if, for example, the interviewing officer places his chair right next to the client's chair). See **4.5.2.1** above.

**The police are acting in an oppressive manner**

This would encompass situations in which, for example, the interviewing officer raises his voice or shouts at the client, uses threatening gestures towards the client, or if he leans towards or stands over the client. The interviewing officer will also be acting oppressively if he insists that the client makes eye contact with him (there is no requirement for the client to do this), or insists that the client answer questions. Oppressive behaviour further includes long silences during the interview when the police hope the client will 'crack' and start to answer questions. Continued repetitive questioning of a suspect in the face of a suspect's sustained denial of guilt may also amount to oppressive conduct.

**Multiple/unclear questions**

This covers the situation where the interviewing officer asks the client several questions at once without giving the client a proper opportunity to reply, or if the officer interrupts a reply the client is making. The solicitor will also intervene if the questions being asked are unclear and require clarification by the officer, or if the questions are too wide or so lengthy that the client is unable to understand what he is actually being asked about (or to know which question to answer).

**Irrelevant questions**

The solicitor should intervene if the interviewing officer asks questions that have nothing to do with the allegations against the client or the reasons for the client's arrest (if, for example, the officer asks the client about his involvement in another offence for which the client has not been arrested, or if the officer asks the client personal questions that are not related to the offence under investigation). A common police tactic is to ask such questions in the hope of 'wearing down' the suspect.

**Making a statement/asserting facts**

This refers to the situation where the interviewing officer makes a statement to the client as opposed to putting a question to him, particularly if that statement is an allegation of guilt that is not supported by any evidence (if, for example, the officer states to the client: 'I think you are guilty of this offence. You're just making up a story as you go along').

**Misrepresenting the law**

If the interviewing officer gives an incorrect explanation of the law concerning the offence(s) the client has been arrested for, the solicitor should intervene, particularly if this is done to suggest to the client that the police case is stronger than it actually is.

**Misrepresenting the strength of the case against the client**

Again, the solicitor should intervene if the interviewing officer suggests that the case against the client is stronger than it actually is (this is sometimes done by the police in the hope that the client will think there is no point in denying his involvement in the offence).

**'Upgrading' a response from the client/putting words in the client's mouth/ making assumptions**

The interviewing officer will sometimes ask a question based on an earlier reply from the client which the officer has upgraded. For example, if a client says that he is unable to remember being in a particular pub, it would be an upgrading of this response for the officer then to say: 'So you admit being in the pub ...' The solicitor should also intervene if, when asking further questions, the interviewing officer makes false or inaccurate assumptions based on answers given by the client, or if the officer asks leading questions which assume the existence of a fact which has not yet been established. If the officer asks such a question, the solicitor should ask the officer to disclose any additional evidence which the officer has to justify his assertion that a particular fact exists.

**Threats/consequences of silence**

The solicitor should intervene if, for example, the interviewing officer threatens to keep the client at the police station indefinitely, or until the client answers questions or makes an admission. Alternatively, the interviewing officer may tell the client that he will come across badly at court if he doesn't answer questions, or that he will get a heavier sentence if he doesn't admit his guilt. The solicitor should intervene immediately if the interviewing officer questions the client's decision to exercise his right of silence. He should also intervene if the police attempt to undermine the advice he has given to his client by, for example, telling the client that advice he has received to stay silent is bad advice or will get him into trouble at court.

**Inducements**

If, for example, the interviewing officer tells the client that he will get a lighter sentence if he admits his guilt, or that he will be able to leave the police station immediately if he confesses, the solicitor should intervene at once. A common tactic adopted by the police is to tell a suspect that he will get bail only if he answers questions and admits his guilt.

**Previous convictions**

The purpose of the interview is to enable the police to obtain evidence about the current offence, not to discuss a suspect's previous convictions. Although a defendant's previous convictions may be admissible in evidence at trial (see below and also **Chapter 22**), such convictions should not need to be discussed in the interview about the offence the police are currently investigating, and the solicitor should object if these convictions are raised by the officer conducting the interview (but see **4.5.3.2** below).

**New information**

The solicitor should intervene if the interviewing officer asks questions based on evidence which has not previously been disclosed to the solicitor and which the police have kept back. The solicitor should ask the officer to disclose this evidence to him so that he can then take his client's instructions upon it before the interview proceeds any further.

**Hypothetical/speculative questions**

An interviewing officer may sometimes say to a suspect: 'How do you think this would look to somebody else? If you were in my place, wouldn't you think that this evidence is pretty strong?' The client is not in the interview to answer hypothetical questions but rather to answer factual questions about the alleged offence. The officer should be asked to refrain from asking such questions. Similarly, the police should not ask questions requiring the client to give his opinion or to give a speculative answer. The solicitor should be particularly on his guard to prevent the client being asked to give his opinion about the character of another person. Any critical comments made by the client could lead to his own bad character or previous convictions being used in evidence against him at trial (see further below).

**'This is your chance to tell your story'**

Interviewing officers will sometimes suggest to a client that the purpose of the interview is for the client to put his account on record. This is not the case; the purpose is for the police to obtain evidence, not for the police to invite the client to give his story. The solicitor should intervene in such a situation.

**The officer asks the client if he would be prepared to take part in further investigative procedures**

The interviewing officer may, during the course of the interview, ask the client if he is prepared to take part in an identification procedure, or to provide fingerprints or samples. Such matters should not be raised in interview because the client is entitled to receive legal advice from his solicitor in private before agreeing to take part in any such procedure.

**The solicitor is concerned about the client's behaviour or conduct**

The solicitor should intervene to suggest to the client that further confidential advice is required if the client:

(a) shows signs of stress, confusion or emotion;

(b) begins to tell lies, or starts to answer questions having agreed that he would give a 'no comment' interview; or

(c) becomes abusive or hostile towards the interviewing officer.

**The client is making comments that may have adverse consequences later in the case**

If the client makes derogatory or critical comments about any other person (such as a prosecution witness or a co-accused), this may result in any previous convictions the client has becoming admissible at his later trial (see **Chapter 22**). The solicitor should intervene immediately if he considers that the client is in danger of putting his own bad character in issue by attacking the character of another person. The solicitor should also intervene if the client makes comments that might cause the police to refuse the client bail if he is charged or if he would otherwise be released on bail pending further enquiries or consultations with the CPS (if, for example, the client makes a threat of physical violence against a potential prosecution witness).

**Inaccurate summary**

If, at the end of the interview, the officer summarises the interview in an inaccurate way (by suggesting that the client has admitted more than he has actually said) and then asks the client to confirm that the summary is accurate, the solicitor should intervene.

**Sufficient evidence to charge**

The solicitor should intervene at any point during the interview if the police say anything to suggest that they think there is sufficient evidence to charge the client (if, for example, the police say to the client: 'The judge is going to come down heavily on you when you're sentenced'). The interview should not be prolonged if the client has given any explanation he wishes to give and the police consider there is sufficient evidence to charge (Code C, para 11.6 – see **3.3.1**).

#### 4.5.3.2 Previous convictions

There is some issue as to whether the police are permitted to question a suspect about his previous convictions on the basis that such convictions will have some evidential value at trial as they might show that the suspect either has a propensity to commit offences of the same kind as the offence about which he is being questioned, or a propensity to be untruthful. However, even if the police are permitted to ask such questions, it should be accepted practice for them to ask them in a separate interview, rather than in the interview when the suspect is being questioned about the alleged offence for which he has been arrested. This will ensure that if such previous convictions are ruled at trial to be inadmissible, the record of the interview will not need to be edited but rather the separate interview will simply not be used as part of the prosecution case.

### 4.5.4 How to intervene

A solicitor who intervenes in police interview needs to ensure that his intervention follows a proper structure, so that the police can understand why he has intervened and what he is asking the police to do. A useful structure for interventions is the 'DEAL' technique described at **4.3.2.2** above.

## Key skill – intervening in the police interview

Set out below is a transcript of the record of the audibly recorded interview carried out by the police in the Gary Dickson case study. Mr Dickson did not have a solicitor present in the interview. Had a solicitor been present, he should have intervened on several occasions.

**CHESHIRE POLICE**

**RECORD OF AUDIBLY RECORDED INTERVIEW**

**INTERVIEW OF:** Gary Dickson DATE OF BIRTH: 28.10.80

**ADDRESS:** 17 Marsh Street, Chester DATE: 18.12.2007

**INTERVIEW AT:** Chester Police Station

**TIME COMENCED:** 6.30 pm **TIME CONCLUDED:** 6.40 pm

**DURATION OF INTERVIEW:** 10 mins **TAPE REFERENCE NO:** SG01/WPC/1232000

**INTERVIEWING OFFICER:** PC G Chambers **OTHER PERSONS PRESENT** None

Signature of officer preparing record: *Gareth Chambers* PC911

| Tape times | PARTICULARS OF INTERVIEW |
|---|---|
| 0.00 | Introductions.<br>Caution. Reminded of right to free legal advice. |
| 0.50 | PC911: Right Mr Dickson, I think you know why you're here, don't you? You have been arrested for assaulting Vincent Lamb near to Connolley's Nightclub. |
| 1.12 | GD: I've been here most of the day and I haven't had much sleep, so do you think you could let me go now or what?<br>PC911: Just answer the question Mr Dickson and we can both go home.<br>GD: Look, just because I work at the club that doesn't mean you can pin any kind of trouble on me. I'm saying nothing. |
| 2.42 | PC911: Mr Dickson, why don't we just get this over with? Look I'm going off duty soon and if we don't deal with this interview now I won't be back on duty until tomorrow afternoon. You don't want to have to wait until then, do you?<br>GD: No I don't. My girlfriend will be worried about me – she will think that I'm in some sort of trouble. Could I at least telephone her? |
| 3.20 | PC911: Don't worry, this will be over sooner than you think. Let's make a start then. Where were you at 3.15 am this morning? |

| Tape times | PARTICULARS OF INTERVIEW |
|---|---|
| 3.56 | GD: I would have finished work by then so I'd be at home.<br><br>PC911: Are you sure about that, because I have reason to believe you were still near to the club and you assaulted Mr Lamb there?<br><br>GD: No. That's not true. I had been at the club earlier but I left much earlier than 3.15 am.<br><br>PC911 Oh come on Mr Dickson, don't play the innocent with me or we'll be here all night. |
| 4.20 | GD: Look I don't know where you are getting the idea in your head that I've been assaulting someone. It's just rubbish. |
| 4.50 | PC911: Come on Mr Dickson, let's be serious, shall we? You were angry with Lamb because he'd tried to chat up your girlfriend earlier in the evening. You chased him in your car didn't you? And you got out of the car and then you beat him?<br><br>GD: No, I did not.<br><br>PC911: You were seen Mr Dickson. Driving your own car at the time wasn't very clever was it?<br><br>GD: No, you are seriously barking up the wrong tree here. The person who saw me is obviously confused. I was at the club and I did drive it to work and home again. But I didn't stop to beat anyone up and I wasn't on the road at 3.15 am. I would have got home much earlier than that. |
| 5.20 | PC911: That's rubbish isn't it? We have a witness who says that he saw you go over to Mr Lamb, hit him in the face several times and then drive away back in the direction towards Marsh Street.<br><br>GD: He's making it up. |
| 6.40 | PC911: Why would the witness lie? You must realise this is a very serious charge, Mr Dickson. We're not going to get anywhere if you're going to play these stupid games with me. Perhaps you'd like to stop being clever or I'll take you back to the cells. Don't you want to get out of here tonight? What's it to be?<br><br>GD: I've told you already what happened.<br><br>PC911: Oh come on.<br><br>GD: You lot have really got it in for me haven't you? |
| 7.20 | PC911: We both know you've been in trouble before – so it's likely you did exactly what our witness says.<br><br>GD: Why don't you get off my back and go and find the person that really did it? |

| Tape times | PARTICULARS OF INTERVIEW |
|---|---|
| 7.50 | PC911: Come on, Dickson that isn't very helpful is it? We both know it was you so it seems futile to deny it.<br><br>GD: Well if it makes you happy, so what if it was me? You should know that I always get even with people who get on the wrong side of me. |
| 8.20 | PC911: I think you're getting carried away again. Why don't we just finish this interview and then you can go and get some sleep? I think we both know that it's going to be better for you if you just tell me what really happened. The courts tend to come down heavy on repeat offenders you know. All I need is for you to accept that you assaulted Vincent Lamb. Do you admit you did that?<br><br>GD: Yes, I suppose so.<br><br>PC911: You don't mean you suppose so, do you? You mean you did it. |
| 9.10 | GD: Yes.<br><br>PC911: Do you have anything further you wish to say before I terminate this interview? |
| 9.50 | GD: No. |
| 10.00 | INTERVIEW TERMINATED AT 6.40 PM |

Some examples of when a solicitor might have intervened in this interview using the DEAL technique follow:

### Example 1

At 2.42 on the interview tape PC Chambers states:

'Look I am going off duty soon and if we don't deal with this interview now I won't be back on duty until tomorrow afternoon. You don't want to have to wait until then, do you?'

The solicitor's intervention would have been as follows:

'Officer I object to this line of questioning. You are threatening to keep my client in the police station unless my client makes an admission of guilt. You are not permitted to make such threats to my client. I would ask you to refrain from making such threats. If you continue to make such threats I will ask you to terminate the interview so that I may make representations to your superior officers. I will record the reason for the termination of the interview in my attendance record, and also ask that a note of the reason for the termination of the interview be made in the custody record.'

### Example 2

At 4.50 on the interview tape PC Chambers states:

'Come on Mr Dickson, let's be serious, shall we? You were angry with Lamb because he'd tried to chat up your girlfriend earlier in the evening. You chased him in your car didn't you? And you got out of the car and then you beat him?'

The solicitor's intervention would have been as follows:

'Officer you are asking my client multiple questions. You have asked my client three questions without giving my client a proper opportunity to reply. I would ask you to refrain from this behaviour. Please ask my client one question at a time and allow my client to reply fully before asking a further question. If you continue to ask my client multiple questions I will advise my client not to answer such questions.'

#### Example 3

At 6.40 on the interview tape PC Chambers states:

'Why would the witness lie? You must realise this is a very serious charge, Mr Dickson. We're not going to get anywhere if you're going to play these stupid games with me. Perhaps you'd like to stop being clever or I'll take you back to the cells. Don't you want to get out of here tonight? What's it to be?'

The solicitor's intervention would have been as follows:

'Officer my client has not been charged with an offence. If you consider that you already have sufficient evidence to charge my client, please terminate the interview immediately. If you do not have sufficient evidence to charge my client, I would remind you that the purpose of the interview is to ask my client factual questions, not for you to make threats against my client. You are putting pressure on my client to admit his guilt by threatening to keep him here indefinitely. I also consider that the language you have used is oppressive. I would ask you to refrain from using such language and stop threatening my client. If you are not prepared to do this, I ask that you end the interview so that I may make representations to your senior officer. I shall make a note of the reason for the termination of the interview in my attendance record, and I will ask the custody officer to record the reason for the termination of the interview in the custody record.'

#### Example 4

At 8.20 on the interview tape PC Chambers states:

'I think we both know it is going to be better for you if you just tell me what really happened. The courts tend to come down heavy on repeat offenders you know. All I need is for you to accept that you assaulted Vince Lamb. Do you admit you did that?'

The solicitor's intervention would have been as follows:

'Officer you are offering an inducement to my client in the hope that he will make an admission. You are also making reference to previous convictions which my client has. My client's previous convictions are not relevant to your enquiry and you should not attempt to persuade my client to admit his guilt in the hope that he will receive a lesser sentence. I would ask you to refrain from doing this. If you make any further reference to my client's previous convictions, or offer any further inducements to my client to admit guilt, I will ask you to stop the interview. I will record the reason for the termination of the interview in my attendance record, and also ask that a note of the reason for the termination of the interview be made in the custody record.'

### 4.5.5 Can a solicitor be removed from the interview?

Paragraph 6.9 of Code C states that a solicitor may be required to leave the interview only 'if their conduct is such that the interviewer is unable properly to put questions to the suspect'. Paragraph 6D of the Notes for Guidance to Code C provides that para 6.9 will apply only if the solicitor's approach or conduct prevents or unreasonably obstructs proper questions being put to the suspect, or the suspect's response being recorded. Examples of such unacceptable conduct would include answering questions on a suspect's behalf, or providing written replies for the suspect to quote. A solicitor should not be removed from the interview simply because he tells his client not to answer questions, or because he intervenes when he considers that the police are asking questions in an inappropriate manner.

If the officer conducting the interview considers that the conduct of the solicitor is preventing him from properly putting questions to the suspect, the interviewer must stop the interview and consult an officer of at least the rank of superintendent (Code C, para 6.10). This officer must then speak to the solicitor and decide if the interview should continue in the presence of the solicitor or not. If it is decided that the solicitor should be excluded from the interview, the suspect must be given the opportunity to consult another solicitor before the interview continues, and that other solicitor must be given an opportunity to be present at the interview.

## 4.6 Identification procedures

### 4.6.1 Initial advice to the client

If the police do not want to interview a suspect immediately, it is likely that they will require the suspect to take part in an identification procedure (probably a video identification or possibly an identification parade). In such circumstances, there are several matters which the solicitor will need to explain to his client, and various checks which the solicitor will need to carry out prior to the identification procedure taking place. On the assumption that the police will want to hold a video identification or identification parade, the solicitor should advise the client to agree to such a procedure being carried out. If the witness attending the procedure cannot identify the client, the police may release the client without charge.

If the client is not prepared to take part in a video identification or identification parade, the solicitor should warn the client that the police may hold a less satisfactory form of identification procedure, such as group identification or even a confrontation (see **Chapter 3**). These procedures are less satisfactory than a video identification or an identification parade because it is more likely that the suspect will be identified by the witness, as the suspect will not be seen in a group of people who resemble him in appearance. The police may also choose to video the suspect covertly for a video identification.

Even if the police do not decide to organise a form of identification procedure that does not require the consent of the suspect, refusal to take part in an identification procedure is admissible at trial, and the court may therefore draw an adverse inference from the refusal of a suspect to take part in a video identification or an identification procedure. The adverse inference will be that the suspect refused to take part in the procedure because he thought he would be recognised by the witness(es) who would have attended the procedure.

Occasionally the police will decide not to organise an identification procedure, even if the suspect disputes the identification made by the witness and is not well known to the witness. For the police not to hold an identification procedure in such circumstances is a breach of Code C, para 3.12 (see **3.5.3.7**). If the solicitor considers that the police should carry out an identification procedure in order to comply with Code C, he should make representations to this effect to the investigating officer.

### 4.6.2 Identification parades

Before the parade takes place, the solicitor should ensure that the police provide him with details of the first description of the suspect given by the potential witness (Code D, para 3.1). The solicitor should explain to the client what will happen at the parade (see **3.5.3.3**). The solicitor should tell the client that he may choose where to stand on the parade and that whilst the parade is taking place he should not speak or do anything to draw attention to himself.

The solicitor needs to check that the other participants in the parade resemble the client in age, height, general appearance and position in life. If they do not, the solicitor should make representations to the identification officer and ask either for the parade to be postponed, or for some form of disguise to be used to overcome any disparity in the appearance of the other participants. If, for example, the other participants in the parade are taller than the suspect, the solicitor may ask that all the people taking part in the parade be seated. Alternatively, if the suspect has a distinctive style or colour of hair, the solicitor could ask that all participants in the parade wear hats.

The solicitor should check that the witnesses are properly segregated before the parade and that there is no opportunity for the witnesses to see either the client or the other participants in the parade before the parade takes place. This may involve the solicitor checking the route which the witnesses will take to get to the parade and ensuring that the witnesses who are waiting to take part in the procedure are kept in separate rooms. The solicitor should ensure that there is no opportunity for a witness who has already attended the parade to speak to another witness before that witness has attended the parade. The solicitor should ensure that the investigating officer is to play no part in the identification parade.

If the solicitor considers that the parade has been contaminated in any way, he should ask the witness if he has discussed the description of the offender with anyone, either before attending or whilst at the police station. He should also ask that a note of his concerns be made by the identification officer in the written record of the parade.

### 4.6.3 Video identification

If the police intend to hold a video identification, the solicitor will be entitled to attend this procedure (see **3.5.3.2**). The solicitor needs to obtain from the police details of the first description of the suspect given by the potential witness (Code D, para 3.1). The solicitor needs to check in advance that the images which are to be used (referred to as the 'foils') resemble the suspect in age, height, general appearance and position in life. Again, the solicitor will need to object if the images do not comply with this requirement, and ensure that the police obtain further images. If the suspect has a distinctive feature (such as a prominent tattoo) the solicitor should ensure that this is covered up both on the image of the client and on the other foils.

The solicitor should attend the video identification to ensure that the witnesses attending the procedure are segregated from each other and that no unauthorised persons (such as the investigating officer) are present. The solicitor should check the number of witnesses who are to attend, where the witnesses will be kept before and after the procedure (making sure that a witness who has attended the procedure has no opportunity to speak to a witness who has not yet taken part), and the route the witnesses will take both to view and then to leave the procedure.

If the solicitor considers that the video identification has been contaminated in any way, he should ask the witness if he has discussed the description of the offender with anyone, either before attending or whilst at the police station. He should also ask that a note of his concerns be made by the identification officer in the written record of the video identification procedure.

### 4.6.4 Written records

Whichever form of identification procedure is used, the solicitor needs to keep a detailed record of what happens. The solicitor must ensure that the identification officer complies with the procedural requirements of Code D, Annex A (in the case of a video identification), or Code D, Annex B (in the case of an identification parade) when conducting the procedure. The solicitor should also make sure that that any objections he makes to the conduct of the procedure (if, for example, the solicitor considers that the witnesses have not been properly segregated before an identification parade takes place) are recorded in full by the identification officer. Any comments made during the procedure (whether by the witness, the identification officer or anyone else) should also be recorded.

## 4.7 Fingerprints and samples

The solicitor should advise his client to cooperate in the giving of fingerprints, impressions of footwear or non-intimate samples. If the client refuses to consent to such samples being taken, the police are entitled to obtain such samples using reasonable force (see **3.5.4.1**).

Although a client is not obliged to provide the police with an intimate sample, the solicitor should warn his client that if he refuses to provide such a sample, an adverse inference may be drawn from this by the magistrates or jury at trial under s 62(10) of PACE 1984 (see **3.5.5.3**). The inference that will be drawn by the court is that the client has something to hide. Such a refusal is also capable of amounting to corroboration of other evidence that may exist against the client.

#### Example

Norman is being questioned about a rape. He denies having intercourse with the victim but refuses to give a sample of semen. This refusal is capable of corroborating evidence from the victim that non-consensual sexual intercourse between her and Norman took place.

## 4.8 Charge and bail after charge

When the police have completed their investigations, the solicitor may consider that the evidence the police have compiled indicates either that his client is not guilty, or that there is insufficient evidence to justify his client being charged. The solicitor should draw this to the attention of both the investigating and the custody officer, and make appropriate representations to persuade the custody officer to release the client without charge.

If the police decide that there is sufficient evidence to charge the client, the solicitor should (in cases where the client admits his guilt and the evidence against him is strong) consider making representations to the police that the client should be dealt with other than by way of charge. For an adult offender this would mean persuading the police to deal with the offender by way of an informal warning, a penalty notice, a formal caution or a conditional caution. For an offender aged 17 or under, this would mean persuading the police to consider a reprimand or final warning. A solicitor should only ever advise a client to accept such a disposal if the client admits his guilt and the solicitor considers that the evidence against the client is such that the client would be convicted were he to be charged. A client who denies his guilt should not be advised to accept a caution, penalty notice, reprimand or final warning merely to get the matter out of the way. The client also needs to be advised about the potential consequences of accepting one of these options (see **Chapter 3**).

If the police decide to charge a suspect, the custody officer will then need to consider if the suspect should be granted bail pending his first appearance before the magistrates' court, or whether he should instead be remanded in police custody. If the custody officer indicates that he is minded to refuse bail, the suspect's solicitor should consider making representations in support of bail being granted. This will often involve the solicitor suggesting that the custody officer should consider granting bail with appropriate conditions, rather than the suspect being denied bail altogether (see **3.8** above).

**Example**

Trevor is interviewed at the police station about his suspected involvement in several night-time burglaries of commercial premises on a particular industrial estate. Trevor is subsequently charged with these burglaries. The custody officer informs Trevor's solicitor that he is reluctant to grant bail to Trevor as he believes that, if released on bail, Trevor will commit further offences. Trevor's solicitor should suggest to the custody officer that he consider imposing bail with conditions (to prevent Trevor committing further offences), rather than refusing bail. Such conditions might involve the imposition of a curfew, or a restriction on Trevor entering the area where the industrial estate is located.

## 4.9 The Police Station Representative Accreditation Scheme

A suspect who is detained at the police station may receive legal advice from a solicitor or an accredited police station representative. An accredited police station representative will be an individual who is accredited by the Legal Services Commission (LSC) to provide advice to suspects in the police station. The aim of the Police Station Representative Accreditation Scheme is to certify non-solicitors to advise and assist suspects being held at a police station, and to allow them to claim payment from the LSC for having provided such assistance.

If a trainee solicitor wishes to represent suspects at the police station, he must become an accredited representative. In order to do this, the trainee solicitor must first register as a probationary police station representative with the LSC. This will enable him to claim payment from the LSC for any police station work he does before he gains full accreditation. In order to gain full accreditation, the trainee then has one year from registering as a probationary representative to complete two forms of assessment:

(a) The trainee will be required to attend the police station on a specified number of occasions to represent suspects. The trainee will be expected to produce a 'portfolio' of these attendances, detailing what each case involved, the issues that arose, how the trainee responded to these issues and how the trainee feels he could have performed more effectively.

(b) The trainee will be required to take a 'critical incidents' test. This simulates police station situations on audio cassette and tests the trainee's proficiency in such situations by recording his response or the advice he gives.

Those other than trainee solicitors who wish to gain accreditation (such as ex-police officers employed by a firm of solicitors) must also pass a written test on matters of criminal law, evidence and procedure. Trainee solicitors who have successfully completed the Legal Practice Course are exempt from this requirement.

## 4.10 Checklist

At the end of this chapter you should be able to explain:

- the role played by a solicitor when representing a client at the police station;
- the steps the solicitor should take prior to attending the police station to represent a client;
- the steps the solicitor should take, and the information he should seek to obtain, upon arrival at the police station;
- the advantages and disadvantages of the solicitor advising the suspect to adopt the following courses of action in a police interview:
  - answer all the questions put by the police,
  - give a 'no comment interview',
  - give a 'no comment' interview but also hand in to the police a written statement;
- the relationship between the advice a solicitor may give to a suspect at the police station and the ability of the court under ss 34, 36 and 37 of the CJPOA 1994 to draw adverse inferences at trial from the defendant's refusal to answer questions in a police station interview;
- the role played by the solicitor in an audibly recorded interview at the police station, including when a solicitor should intervene during the course of an interview and how an intervention should be made;
- the role played by the solicitor, and the advice that should be given to the suspect, should the police decide to hold an identification procedure;
- the advice the solicitor should give to a suspect from whom the police wish to obtain fingerprints, impressions of footwear or samples (intimate and non-intimate);
- the representations the solicitor should make to the police (in an appropriate case) to deal with the matter other than by charging the suspect;
- the representations the solicitor should make to the custody officer to obtain police bail for the suspect in the event that the suspect is charged with an offence.

# Chapter 5

# Remedies for Police Misconduct



## 5.1 Introduction

A solicitor who has represented a suspect at the police station may be required to advise the suspect on the remedies available to him if the police have behaved improperly or illegally during the course of their investigations. The two remedies which a victim of police misconduct may pursue are:

(a) to make a complaint against the police (see **5.2** below); or

(b) to pursue a claim for damages against the police in civil proceedings (see **5.3** below).

## 5.2 The Independent Police Complaints Commission

### 5.2.1 Introduction

The Independent Police Complaints Commission (IPCC) is an independent body that oversees and investigates complaints against the police. Any decisions it makes may be overturned only by the courts. The IPCC is run by 18 commissioners. Acting under the commissioners are investigation teams which investigate incidents of alleged police misconduct independently of the police. These investigators may exercise the full powers of the police whilst carrying out their investigations, and can demand access to police records and premises.

### 5.2.2 Making a complaint

Any individual may make a complaint alleging misconduct by the police. Complaints should in the first instance be made directly to the police force concerned. Complaints must be made within one year of the incident complained of, and must be about a particular officer or officers (as opposed to general police practice and policy). Complaints made outside this one-year period will not be considered unless good reason for the delay can be shown or injustice would otherwise be caused.

### 5.2.3 Local resolution

Most of the less serious complaints that are made against the police are dealt with through a procedure called local resolution, whereby the complaint is resolved through dialogue between the relevant police force and the person who has made the complaint. Local resolution is particularly appropriate where it is alleged that a police officer has spoken to a member of the public in a rude or an aggressive manner. The complaint will be resolved through an explanation or an apology. If a complainant does not want his complaint resolved through local resolution, he may ask the IPCC to progress directly to an investigation.

### 5.2.4 Investigations

Certain complaints that are made against the police must be referred to the IPCC by the police. These categories of complaint are:

(a) allegations of assault;
(b) allegations of hate crime;
(c) allegations of corruption;
(d) allegations of serious offences;
(e) cases involving deaths in police custody; and
(f) when the police have used firearms.

In cases not falling within the above categories, the police have the option of referring a complaint to the IPCC. If the IPCC does investigate a complaint, it may deal with the complaint in one of three ways:

(a) in the most serious cases the IPCC will carry out an independent investigation that will not have any police involvement;
(b) in less serious cases the IPCC will arrange for the police themselves to carry out an investigation which the IPCC will manage (a 'managed investigation');
(c) in most cases the police will deal with the complaint and the IPCC will either have a supervisory role (a 'supervised investigation'), or have no formal role at all (a 'local investigation'). A local investigation should not be confused with the local resolution procedure.

### 5.2.5 Powers of the IPCC

If an investigation has been carried out either by the police or by the police under the management of the IPCC, a report will be prepared. If the complaint is serious and the complaint is upheld, this may result in disciplinary proceedings being taken against individual police officers. In appropriate cases, the IPCC may recommend to the CPS that criminal proceedings be commenced against the relevant officer(s). The IPCC does not have the power to award the payment of compensation to individuals. An individual seeking compensation from the police must bring a claim in civil proceedings (see **5.3** below).

If the CPS decides not to bring a prosecution, it is possible for an individual to bring a private prosecution against the relevant police officer. Such prosecutions are extremely rare and, if the CPS has determined that there is insufficient evidence to charge the officer, have little chance of success. Public funding will not be available to finance such a prosecution, and the DPP may take over the conduct of any private prosecution and then discontinue proceedings.

## 5.3 Civil proceedings

A victim of police misconduct may be entitled to compensation if the misconduct amounts to a tort. Some of the most common types of claim are:

(a) *battery* – if the police use an excessive amount of force in carrying out an arrest or during the course of a suspect's detention;
(b) *trespass* – if the police enter and search property without the necessary authority to do so;
(c) *false imprisonment* – if the police detain a suspect without justification, or if a suspect is held in police detention beyond detention time limits or without proper reviews of detention being carried out;

(d) *malicious prosecution* – if the police bring a prosecution from malicious motives and without reasonable or probable cause;

(e) *claims for unlawful killing or personal injury* – where there is an allegation of death or injury at the hands of the police (usually whilst a suspect is in custody);

(f) *damage to goods* – if, for example, items of property are damaged during a search.

An individual may also seek damages under the Human Rights Act 1998. Under Article 5(5) of the ECHR (see **1.8.3**), an individual who has been the victim of arrest or detention in contravention of any other provision in Article 5 has an enforceable right to compensation. This would provide an individual who is unlawfully arrested by the police, or unlawfully detained at the police station, with a right to damages.

Guidance on the level of damages that the courts should award in claims against the police was given by the Court of Appeal in *Thompson v The Commissioner of Police for the Metropolis* [1997] 2 All ER 762. Any civil claim against the police will be against the Chief Constable of the relevant force, as he is vicariously liable for any torts committed by his officers. Public funding from the Community Legal Service is available for civil claims against the police, depending on the merits of the case and the individual's financial means.

## 5.4 Checklist

By the end of this chapter you should be able to explain:

- the role played by the IPCC and the powers which the IPCC may exercise;
- the types of civil claim which may be made against the police.

# Part 2 Summary – The Suspect and the Police

| *Topic* | *Summary* | *References* |
|---|---|---|
| Investigative powers the police exercise outside the police station | The police may stop and search any person or vehicle for stolen or prohibited articles. | PACE 1984, s 1(2) |
| | The police have wide powers of arrest. | s 24(1)–(3) |
| | The arrest must, however, be 'necessary'. | s 24(4), (5) |
| | The police also have a common law power of arrest to prevent a breach of the peace. | |
| | A person who has been arrested may be searched. | ss 32(1) and 32(2)(a) |
| | The police also have extensive powers to enter and search premises. | ss 8, 17, 18 and 32(2)(b) |
| | Items found during a search may be retained. | ss 19 and 22 |
| Detention of the suspect at the police station | A suspect who has been arrested must be taken to the police station 'as soon as practicable after the arrest'. | PACE 1984, s 30(1A) |
| | On arrival, he must be brought before the custody officer, who must determine if there is sufficient evidence to charge the suspect. | s 37(1) |
| | If such evidence does not exist, the suspect must be released unless his detention is necessary either to secure or preserve evidence, or to obtain such evidence by questioning. | s 37(2) |
| Rights of the suspect whilst detained at the police station | The suspect is permitted access to legal advice and to have someone told of his arrest. The exercise of these rights may be delayed in certain circumstances. | PACE 1984, ss 58 and 56 |
| | The suspect may initially be detained for a maximum period of 24 hours. | s 41 |
| | A superintendent may extend this period by up to 12 hours. | s 42 |
| | Further extensions may be obtained from the magistrates' court, up to a maximum total detention time of 96 hours. | ss 43 and 44 |
| | Whilst the suspect is detained at the police station, the custody officer must ensure that the conditions in which the suspect is held comply with the requirements of Code C of the Codes of Practice. | |

| *Topic* | *Summary* | *References* |
|---|---|---|
| Interviews under caution | Most suspects who are detained at the police station will be interviewed under caution by the police. The suspect is not obliged to answer questions in interview, and the solicitor who is representing the suspect will need to advise him as to whether he should answer questions or not. The solicitor will need to consider:<br>• the level of disclosure given by the police;<br>• the strength of the case against the suspect;<br>• whether the suspect is fit for interview; and<br>• how well the suspect is likely to perform in interview.<br>A suspect who answers questions should avoid the drawing of adverse inferences at trial under ss 34, 36 and 37 of the CJPOA 1994, and may enhance his credibility in the eyes of the jury or magistrates. He may be released if he can persuade the police that he is innocent. The suspect may say something incriminating if he answers questions, however, and may come across badly to the court. The safest option is often to hand to the police a written statement but then give a 'no comment' interview.<br>The solicitor will attend the interview with the suspect, and will need to intervene during the course of the interview if the suspect requires further legal advice or if the police are conducting the interview in an inappropriate manner. | |
| Identification procedures | The police may employ a number of steps to obtain identification evidence, including holding a formal identification procedure and taking fingerprints, impressions of footwear and samples from the suspect.<br>If the police choose to hold an identification procedure, this will normally be a video identification or an identification parade. The suspect's solicitor must ensure that such procedures are carried out in accordance with the requirements of Code D of the Codes of Practice. | Code D |

| *Topic* | *Summary* | *References* |
|---|---|---|
| Options the police may exercise after interview | The police may:<br>• release the suspect (if there is no evidence against him);<br>• release the suspect on bail (whilst further enquiries are made);<br>• release the suspect on bail (whilst the CPS reviews the papers); or<br>• charge the suspect (after consulting with the CPS) | |
| | If the suspect is charged, he will either be bailed to appear before the magistrates' court or be remanded in police custody pending his appearance before the magistrates' court. | PACE 1984, s 38. |
| | If the offence is relatively minor, the matter may be dealt with other than by way of the suspect being charged. The police may give the suspect an informal warning, a penalty notice, a formal caution or a conditional caution. | |
| Juveniles | A juvenile is any suspect who appears to be under 17 years of age. | Code C, para 1.5 |
| | The police must notify the person responsible for the juvenile's welfare that the juvenile has been arrested. | Code C, para 3.13 |
| | The police must also inform the 'appropriate adult', and ask that the 'appropriate adult' attend the police station. | Code C, para 3.15 |
| | The role of the 'appropriate adult' is to provide support to the suspect, to check that the suspect understands what is happening and to ensure that the police treat the suspect in the correct manner. | |

# Part 3

# PROCEDURE FROM CHARGE TO TRIAL

# Chapter 6

# Initial Hearings in the Magistrates' Court



## 6.1 Introduction

All defendants aged 18 or over who are charged with a criminal offence will make their first appearance at court before the magistrates' court. If the defendant is charged with an indictable only offence, the magistrates will immediately send the case to the Crown Court for trial under s 51 of the Crime and Disorder Act 1998. The procedure for doing this is described in **Chapter 10**. Defendants aged 17 and under will usually be dealt with in the Youth Court (see **Chapter 14**).

This chapter will concentrate on adult defendants who are charged with an either way offence or a summary offence. It will describe what happens when the defendant makes his initial appearance at court and the role played by the defence solicitor at this stage in obtaining funding for the case, finding out details of the prosecution case against his client and advising the client as to his plea. It will also examine the procedure which takes place to determine whether an either way offence will ultimately be dealt with by the magistrates' court or by the Crown Court.

## 6.2 The first hearing

### 6.2.1 Defendants on bail

If the defendant was charged by the police he will either:

(a) come to court in custody if the police refused to grant him bail; or

(b) attend court to 'answer' his bail if he was granted bail by the police.

A defendant who has received a written charge and requisition (see **3.10**) will come to court on the date and at the time specified in the requisition.

If the defendant is attending court having been granted bail by the police, the first hearing will be either an Early First Hearing (EFH) or an Early Administrative Hearing (EAH). Which type of hearing takes place will depend on the complexity of the case and the plea which the defendant is expected to enter.

### 6.2.2 Early First Hearing

#### 6.2.2.1 Introduction

If a defendant is going to enter a 'simple guilty plea' to the offence, his first appearance before the court will be an EFH. A 'simple guilty plea' is when the defendant admits all the elements of the offence and there are no complex issues involved.

#### 6.2.2.2 Summary offences

If the offence is a summary matter which can be dealt with only by the magistrates, the defendant will appear before a full bench of three magistrates. The charge will be read out to the defendant and he will enter a guilty plea. A representative from the CPS will then tell the magistrates the facts of the case and the defendant's solicitor will give a plea in mitigation on the defendant's behalf. The magistrates will then either sentence the defendant straight away, or adjourn the case to a later date if they want to obtain any reports (such as a report from the Probation Service) before sentencing the defendant. If the case is adjourned, the magistrates will consider whether the defendant should be granted bail or remanded in custody prior to the next hearing (see **Chapter 7**).

**Example**

Bhupinder is charged with careless driving (a summary only offence) after he drove his car into the rear of another vehicle at a set of traffic lights. Bhupinder intends to plead guilty to the offence. At the EFH, Bhupinder enters a guilty plea. The CPS representative outlines the facts of the case to the magistrates, and Bhupinder's solicitor then gives a plea in mitigation on Bhupinder's behalf. The magistrates decide that they do not require a pre-sentence report from the Probation Service before deciding on their sentence. Bhupinder is sentenced straight away.

#### 6.2.2.3 Either way offences

If the offence is an either way matter, the defendant will again appear before a full bench of magistrates. The charge will be put to him and he will enter a guilty plea. After the defendant enters his guilty plea, the magistrates will then need to determine whether they should sentence the defendant, or whether the defendant should be committed to the Crown Court for sentence because, given the seriousness of the case, their sentencing powers will be insufficient (see **6.9** below).

As with summary offences, if the case is adjourned the magistrates will go on to consider whether the defendant should be granted bail or remanded in custody prior to the next hearing (see **Chapter 7**). The case may need to be adjourned either for the magistrates to obtain a pre-sentence report from the Probation Service before sentencing the defendant, or, if the magistrates have decided to commit the defendant to Crown Court to be sentenced, for the sentencing hearing at the Crown Court to take place.

**Example**

Carol is charged with the theft (an either way offence) of an iPod from an electrical shop. Carol intends to plead guilty to the offence. At the EFH, Carol enters a guilty plea. The CPS representative outlines the facts of the case to the magistrates, and Carol's solicitor gives a plea in mitigation on Carol's behalf. The magistrates decide that they will sentence Carol (rather than her being committed to the Crown Court for sentence). However, the magistrates decide that, before sentencing Carol, they require a pre-sentence report from the Probation Service. Carol's case is adjourned for three weeks to enable the report to be prepared. The magistrates grant bail to Carol prior to the sentencing hearing.

### 6.2.3 Early Administrative Hearing

An EAH is essentially an organisational or administrative hearing, and will follow the same format whether the defendant is charged with a summary only or an either way offence. The magistrates will check if the defendant has legal representation, and the case may be adjourned to enable the defendant to see a solicitor and to obtain public funding for his case (see **6.4** below). Even if the defendant has already secured legal representation, the case is likely to be adjourned so that the solicitor instructed by the defendant may advise the defendant on the strength of the prosecution case and the plea he should enter. In order to do this, the solicitor will need to obtain disclosure of the prosecution case (see **6.6** below). The solicitor may have received some details of the prosecution case (such as copy witness statements) at court, but will need time to read these fully and to take his client's instructions on their contents. The solicitor will also need to listen to the tape(s) of his client's interview in the police station, and to view any CCTV recordings which may form part of the prosecution case.

When the case is adjourned the magistrates will consider whether the defendant should be granted bail or remanded in custody prior to the next hearing (see **Chapter 7**). The case will typically be adjourned for two to three weeks. When the defendant appears before the court again, the magistrates will expect him to be in a position to enter his plea (see **6.8** below). There are several steps the defendant's solicitor needs to take prior to this next hearing. These are outlined at **6.3** below.

As an EAH normally deals with purely administrative matters, it can be conducted by the magistrate's clerk/legal adviser rather than before a bench of magistrates. However, if there is any prosecution objection to the defendant being granted bail, the hearing should take place before a bench of magistrates so that an application for bail can be made by the defendant's solicitor.

Example

Vikram is charged with affray following a fight outside a nightclub. He intends to enter a not guilty plea. At the EAH, the magistrates check that Vikram has obtained legal representation. Vikram has instructed a solicitor to represent him. Vikram's solicitor has been handed a bundle of witness statements from the CPS, but has not yet had the opportunity to read these or to obtain Vikram's instructions on their contents. He has also received a tape showing CCTV footage of the alleged affray, which he will need to view. At the EAH, Vikram's solicitor explains to the magistrates that Vikram will not be in a position to enter a plea until the solicitor has taken the above steps. The magistrates therefore adjourn the case for three weeks to enable the solicitor to take these steps. The magistrates grant bail to Vikram prior to the next hearing.

### 6.2.4 Defendants refused police bail

If the police refused to grant the defendant bail after he was charged, the defendant will be kept in police custody until he can be brought before a magistrates' court. This will normally be either later on the day on which the defendant was charged, or on the following day.

Defendants who make their first appearance before the court in custody appear at what are termed 'remand hearings'. What happens at a remand hearing will be similar to either an EFH or an EAH, depending on whether the defendant is pleading guilty or not. Unless the defendant is pleading guilty to the charge and can be sentenced there and then, the most significant part of the remand hearing will be when the court considers whether to grant the defendant bail prior to the next hearing. If the police refused bail it is likely that the CPS will oppose bail being granted to the defendant, and a full bail hearing will be necessary to determine whether the defendant should be granted bail or remanded in custody prior to the next hearing (see **Chapter 7**).

## 6.3 Role of the defence solicitor

Unless the case involves a straightforward summary only offence, few defendants will enter their plea (whether guilty or not guilty) at their first appearance before the magistrates' court. Usually their cases will be adjourned for them to take advice from their solicitors.

The solicitor's role at this stage involves taking the following steps:

(a) obtaining funding from the LSC to pay for the work he will do on his client's behalf (unless the client is paying his solicitor privately);

(b) taking a statement from the client;

(c) obtaining details of the prosecution case from the CPS;

(d) advising the client on the strength of the prosecution evidence and the plea the client should enter; and

(e) in the case of an either way offence, informing the client that his case may be dealt with either by the magistrates' court or by the Crown Court, and advising the client about the advantages and disadvantages of each court.

Each of these matters is considered in greater detail below.

## 6.4 Funding the case

### 6.4.1 Introduction

Most defendants in criminal proceedings do not pay their solicitors on a private basis for the legal work done on their behalf. Rather, defence solicitors will normally make applications on behalf of their clients for the clients' cases to receive public funding from the LSC. The public funding of a defendant's legal representation in a criminal case is specifically provided for by Article 6(3) of the ECHR (see **1.8.3**), which states that defendants who do not have sufficient means to pay for legal assistance should receive this free from charge when this is in the interests of justice. The relevant domestic legislation is the Access to Justice Act 1999, supplemented by the Criminal Defence Service (General) (No 2) (Amendment) Regulations 2006 (SI 2006/2490).

The public funding of criminal defence work is administered by the Criminal Defence Service, which is itself part of the LSC. Full details of the different types of public funding that are available in criminal litigation matters can be found on the LSC website (www.legalservices.gov.uk), together with details of the rates of payment that solicitors receive and the various forms which must be completed to obtain payment. In order to obtain public funding for their clients, a firm of solicitors must have a contract with the LSC to represent defendants in criminal proceedings. This is known as a 'general criminal contract'. To be eligible for such a contract, a firm must first pass a preliminary audit to obtain a 'Specialist Quality Mark'. Firms awarded a contract will be subject to an annual audit by the LSC to ensure that their files are being run properly and that the firm's case management systems are working correctly. A firm which fails to pass the audit may have its contract removed, in which case it will no longer be able to obtain public funding for its clients.

### 6.4.2 Work done before the client is charged

#### 6.4.2.1 Work done at the police station

The first advice solicitors normally provide to their clients will be at the police station. All persons attending at the police station (whether under arrest, or attending voluntarily - see **3.2.1**) are entitled to free legal advice, regardless of their means. Work done by a solicitor at the police station will be claimed as a fixed fee under the Police Station Advice and Assistance Scheme. Non-solicitors (such as trainees) can attend the police station and charge for this work as long as they are either accredited or probationary police station representatives (see **4.9** above).

Some solicitors are members of duty solicitor schemes for a given police station. These solicitors have their names entered on a rota, and they may be called out to attend the police station if they are 'on duty' and the person who has been arrested does not have his own solicitor. The duty solicitor scheme has separate arrangements for payment. The LSC is also piloting a scheme called 'CDS Direct' in which suspects accused of minor offences receive legal advice from a solicitor by telephone, rather than the solicitor attending the police station.

#### 6.4.2.2 Work done outside the police station

If a client is of limited means (ie, in receipt of income support or income-based jobseeker's allowance), the solicitor will be able to fund any preliminary work he carries out on the client's behalf outside the police station under the Advice and Assistance Scheme. This scheme covers work done before the client is charged. It may, for example, cover taking initial instructions from a client who has been released on police bail and is due to return to the police station at a later date. The scheme does not cover any work done for a client after the client has been charged. In such cases it will be necessary for the client to apply for a representation order (see **6.4.3.2** below). Any work done under the Advice and Assistance Scheme can be claimed for by the solicitor under fixed hourly rates.

### 6.4.3 Work done after the client is charged

#### 6.4.3.1 The duty solicitor scheme

The duty solicitor scheme operates in the magistrates' court in a similar way to at the police station (see **6.4.2.1** above). Solicitors who are members of a court duty scheme will again have their names on a rota. On the day when it is his turn to attend court as the duty solicitor, the particular solicitor will be available to advise any defendants who do not have their own solicitors but who require legal representation. The duty solicitor will claim his costs in attending court from the LSC under the Advocacy Assistance (Court Duty Solicitor) Scheme.

In recent years the duty solicitor scheme has been extended to allow solicitors who are members of the scheme to represent defendants at preliminary hearings in their capacity as duty solicitors, even though they are not on the rota to attend court as the duty solicitor that day. A solicitor who is on a particular court's duty solicitor panel may represent a client as that client's 'duty solicitor of choice' at an EFH or EAH, and at one further hearing. The solicitor will claim his costs in attending court from the LSC under the Advocacy Assistance Scheme.

**Example**

Roger is charged with theft. He has admitted his guilt in police interview and is bailed to appear at the magistrates' court. Roger asks his solicitor, Charles, to represent him before the magistrates. Charles is a member of the duty solicitor scheme but is not on the rota to attend court that day as the duty solicitor. Charles can attend court to represent Roger as Roger's 'duty solicitor of choice'.

As Roger is pleading guilty, his first appearance is an EFH. After Roger enters his guilty plea the magistrates decide to adjourn sentencing because they want to obtain a pre-sentence report on Roger from the Probation Service. Charles will be able to represent Roger at this further hearing as Roger's 'duty solicitor of choice'.

The 'duty solicitor of choice' scheme will cover straightforward cases where a defendant pleads guilty and is sentenced either immediately or after one further hearing. For any other type of case (and particularly cases where the defendant is pleading not guilty) it will be necessary for the defendant to apply for a representation order, discussed below.

#### 6.4.3.2 Applying for a representation order

A defendant who wishes to apply for criminal legal aid must satisfy two tests:

(a) the *interests of justice test* – the defendant must show that it is in the interests of justice that he receive public funding to cover the cost of his legal representation; and

(b) the *means test* – the defendant must demonstrate that his finances are such that he is unable to pay for the cost of his legal representation. The means test currently applies only to cases in the magistrates' court, although it is anticipated that this will be extended to cover Crown Court cases as well by the end of 2007. A defendant who is charged with an indictable-only offence that is sent to the Crown Court for trial will not be required to satisfy the means test, since his case will automatically be sent to the Crown Court for trial following an initial hearing in the magistrates' court (see **10.4.1**). A defendant who is charged with an either way offence where either the magistrates decline jurisdiction or the defendant elects trial in the Crown Court (see **6.10** below), or a defendant who pleads guilty to an either way offence before the magistrates' court and is then committed to the Crown Court for sentence (see **6.9** below), will still need to satisfy the means test for that part of his case which is dealt with in the magistrates' court. As soon as his case is sent to the Crown Court, however, the defendant will be entitled to legal aid if he satisfies the interests of justice test alone.

The interests of justice test and the means test are discussed further in **6.4.3.3** and **6.4.3.4** below.

In order to apply for legal aid in the magistrates' court, the defendant must submit to the court an application form (Form CDS 14 – Application for Legal Aid in Criminal Proceedings). Unless the defendant automatically satisfies the means test (see **6.4.3.4**), he must also submit a financial statement (Form CDS 15), together with any supporting paperwork. If the defendant is remanded in custody and therefore unable to supply the necessary supporting documentation, unless he automatically satisfies the means test, he must complete a statement of truth (Form CDS 17) declaring that the means information he has given is accurate and that, due to being in custody, he is unable to provide written evidence of his income.

Although criminal legal aid is administered by the Criminal Defence Service on behalf of the LSC, the day-to-day running of the system is administered by the magistrates' court, and the relevant application forms must be sent to the magistrates' court that is dealing with the defendant's case rather than to the LSC. The court will then determine whether the defendant satisfies the eligibility criteria or not. The relevant forms may be obtained from the LSC website (www.legalservices.gov.uk).

### 6.4.3.3 The interests of justice test

Legal aid will be granted by the magistrates' court only if it is in the interests of justice for the defendant to have his legal costs paid from public funds. This ensures compliance with Article 6(3)(a) of the ECHR, which provides that a defendant who does not have sufficient means to pay for legal assistance should receive this free 'when the interests of justice' so require.

The factors that are taken into account in deciding whether a defendant can satisfy the interests of justice test are set out in Sch 3, para 5(2) to the Access to Justice Act 1999:

> In deciding what the interests of justice consist of in relation to any individual, the following factors must be taken into account—
>
> (a) whether the individual would, if any matter arising in the proceedings is decided against him, be likely to lose his liberty or livelihood or suffer serious damage to his reputation,
>
> (b) whether the determination of any matter arising in the proceedings may involve consideration of a substantial question of law,
>
> (c) whether the individual may be unable to understand the proceedings or to state his own case,
>
> (d) whether the proceedings may involve the tracing, interviewing or expert cross-examination of witnesses on behalf of the individual, and
>
> (e) whether it is in the interests of another person that the individual be represented.

These factors are repeated in para 4a of Form CDS 14. A solicitor completing Form CDS 14 must discuss each factor with his client and, if that factor is relevant to the client's case, tick the appropriate box. Full details in support must then be inserted in para 4b. Further guidance on what might be said about each factor is set out below.

**'It is likely that I will lose my liberty if any matter in the proceedings is decided against me'**

This is relevant if the defendant is charged with a serious offence which is likely to result in a prison sentence if he is convicted. A solicitor can find out the likely sentence for a particular offence by consulting the Magistrates' Courts Sentencing Guidelines or, for cases which are likely to be tried in the Crown Court, guidelines set by the Court of Appeal or the Sentencing Guidance Council (see **Chapter 11**). The solicitor will effectively be presenting the prosecution case against his client 'taken at its most serious' in order to justify why his client should receive public funding for his case. The solicitor will need to refer to any factual allegations made by the prosecution which aggravate the seriousness of the offence (see below), and will also need to make reference to any previous convictions the defendant may have for the same or similar types of offence. Such previous convictions will be taken into account by a sentencing court, and are likely to lead to the court imposing a more severe sentence than if the defendant had no previous convictions.

This factor is also relevant if, regardless of the sentence which the court is likely to impose if the defendant is convicted, it is likely that the defendant will be refused bail in the proceedings and will be remanded in custody whilst the case is ongoing (see **Chapter 7**). A defendant who has a poor bail record (for example, a defendant who has failed to answer his bail in previous criminal proceedings, or a defendant who has offended previously whilst on bail), or against whom the CPS is likely to oppose bail, should state this.

*Magistrates' court*

If the offence with which the defendant is charged would normally be dealt with by way of a custodial sentence following conviction, this factor will always be relevant. Extracts from the Magistrates' Courts Sentencing Guidelines are contained in the **Appendix**. For each offence (summary or either way) that is or may be dealt with by the magistrates' court, the guidelines set out the maximum penalty for the offence and then a guideline or 'entry point' sentence. The guideline sentence is the usual sentence the magistrates would pass on a first-time offender who has entered a guilty plea but been convicted following a trial. By way of example, the guideline sentence for assault occasioning actual bodily harm is a custodial sentence.

Even if the sentencing guidelines do not indicate that the magistrates would normally impose a custodial sentence for that offence, the solicitor should consider if there are any *aggravating* factors which make the offence more serious than it otherwise would be, and which may in turn lead the magistrates to impose a custodial sentence. The sentencing guidelines set out a list of potentially aggravating factors for each offence. For example, the guideline sentence for theft is a community penalty, but if aggravating factors are present, the magistrates might consider custody. Aggravating factors in a theft case will include if the theft was of an item of high value, if it was planned (as opposed to being opportunistic) or if the victim of the theft was vulnerable (such as an elderly person). Aggravating factors in an assault case would include the use of a weapon, premeditation, kicking or biting, or if the victim was vulnerable or serving the public (such as a bus driver).

Similarly, even if the offence is not particularly serious in itself and would not usually result in the imposition of a custodial sentence, if the client has a number of serious convictions for the same or similar types of offence, this could result in the client receiving a prison sentence if convicted of the current offence, because the court will treat such convictions as aggravating factors which make the offence more serious (Criminal Justice Act 2003, s 143(2)).

*Crown Court*

If the client is charged with an indictable-only offence, there should be no difficulty in arguing that a custodial sentence is likely upon conviction. Defendants convicted of such offences will almost certainly receive a custodial sentence if convicted. Similarly, if the client is charged with an either way offence which the solicitor considers will be dealt with by the Crown Court (because the specific facts of the offence mean that magistrates are likely to decide that it is too serious for them to deal with – see **6.10.2.1** below), completing this section should be straightforward. To find out the sentence his client is likely to receive if sentenced in the Crown Court, the solicitor will need to access the case compendium which can be found on the Sentencing Guidance Council website (www.sentencing-guidelines.gov.uk). The compendium contains details of the significant cases in which the Court of Appeal has set out sentencing guidelines for all the types of case likely to come before the Crown Court. The Sentencing Guidelines Council is has also provided its own definitive sentencing guidelines for certain offences (such as robbery). Such guidelines may also be found on the website.

**'I have been given a sentence that is suspended or non-custodial. If I break this, the court may be able to deal with me for the original offence'**

This will be relevant if the defendant is subject to a suspended prison sentence in respect of a previous offence (see **Chapter 11**) and commits a further offence during the period of the suspension. There is a statutory presumption that a defendant who is convicted of a further offence during the period of suspension will have his sentence activated and so will go to prison (Criminal Justice Act 2003, Sch 8, para 12).

Similarly, this will be relevant if, at the time of his offence, the defendant was subject to a conditional discharge imposed following a previous offence. A defendant who commits a further offence during the period of a conditional discharge may have his discharge revoked and be sentenced for his original offence (see **Chapter 11**).

This will also be relevant if the defendant is currently the subject of a generic community order (see **Chapter 11**) imposed on a previous occasion when the defendant was before the court for another offence. If the defendant is convicted of the current offence, the court has the power to revoke the order and re-sentence the defendant. The likely 'new' sentence will be a term of imprisonment.

**'It is likely that I will lose my livelihood'**

This will be relevant if the defendant is in employment and a conviction is likely to lead to the loss of that employment (it may also be relevant to a defendant who is genuinely unemployed for a short period between jobs). It will apply to any defendant in employment who is likely to face a prison sentence if convicted, but can also be relevant for other defendants who are unlikely to receive a prison sentence but have particular types of job which may be lost in the event of conviction. For example, the defendant may be a bus driver charged with a road traffic offence (such as dangerous driving), which will result in his disqualification from driving if he is convicted. Alternatively the defendant may be a teacher charged with common assault (since a conviction for an offence of violence will preclude a defendant from working with children in the future). This is also relevant for a defendant who is in a position of trust at work and who may lose his job if convicted of an offence involving dishonesty (such as a bank manager accused of a minor theft).

A defendant who intends to enter a guilty plea may raise arguments using this factor, although he will need to show how legal representation might help him avoid losing his livelihood. A good example of this is a defendant who drives in the course of his employment and who intends to plead guilty to a minor motoring offence that will result in him having 12 or more penalty points on his licence. Such a defendant will face an automatic disqualification from driving for at least six months unless he can put forward 'mitigating circumstances' to avoid such a disqualification. 'Mitigating circumstances' have a very precise definition (see **Chapter 15**), and the defendant will need legal representation to help him place such circumstances before the court.

**'It is likely that I will suffer serious damage to my reputation'**

'Serious' damage will occur when the disgrace of a conviction is more than the direct effect of the penalty, and will result in the defendant losing his reputation for honesty or trustworthiness. This will *only* apply to defendants with either no previous convictions or convictions for very minor offences (usually minor road traffic offence such as speeding). If the defendant has no previous convictions and has a position of standing or respect in the community (such as a vicar, local councillor or school governor), a conviction for any criminal offence, even if the offence is relatively minor, may cause serious damage to his reputation.

**'A substantial question of law may be involved (whether arising from an act, judicial authority or other source)'**

This is relevant when a piece of prosecution evidence is in dispute and it will be necessary to challenge the admissibility of this evidence at trial, or if the defendant wishes to adduce evidence which the CPS may argue is inadmissible Examples of when this may arise are:

(a) if there is disputed identification evidence and the court needs to apply the *Turnbull* guidelines to assess the credibility of such evidence (see **Chapter 17**);

(b) if there is a possibility that the court may draw adverse inferences under ss 34, 36 or 37 of the CJPOA 1994 from the defendant's refusal to answer questions at the police station (see **Chapter 18**);

(c) if either the prosecution or the defence are seeking to persuade the court to admit hearsay evidence under s 114 of the Criminal Justice Act 2003 (see **Chapter 19**);

(d) if the defence are seeking to use ss 76 or 78 of PACE 1984 to argue that a confession made (or allegedly made) by the defendant should be excluded (see **Chapter 20**);

(e) if the prosecution are wanting to adduce at trial evidence of the defendant's previous convictions under s 101 of the Criminal Justice Act 2003, or either party is seeking to adduce the previous convictions of any other person under s 100 of the same Act (see **Chapter 22**).

**'I may not be able to understand the court proceedings or present my own case'**

This will be relevant either if the defendant is unable to understand court proceedings without the benefit of legal representation, or if the defendant requires such representation in order to present his case properly to the court. Reasons which may prevent the defendant being able to understand the court proceedings or present his case include:

(a) mental or physical disability;

(b) poor knowledge of English (particularly relevant for defendants from overseas);

(c) age (a defendant who is particularly young or old); and

(d) vulnerability (a defendant who is emotionally immature or otherwise vulnerable).

When the court assesses whether the defendant requires legal representation here, it will take into account the complexity of the case.

### 'Witnesses may need to be traced or interviewed on my behalf'

This will be relevant when a defendant wishes to call a witness in support of his case, such as a witness who can support a defence of alibi or, for a defendant charged with assault, a witness who will say that the defendant was acting in reasonable self-defence. Such witnesses will need to be traced and a statement taken from them. This may also be important if the defendant needs to call expert evidence in support of his defence (for example, a forensic scientist in a murder case). The defendant will need to explain why he requires legal representation to trace or interview witnesses.

A defendant who intends to enter a guilty plea may raise this factor if a witness needs to be traced or interviewed with a view to that witness either giving a written statement or giving oral evidence at court to assist in the plea in mitigation that will be given on the defendant's behalf (see **Chapter 12**).

### 'The case involves expert cross-examination of a prosecution witness (whether an expert or not)'

This will be relevant if a witness needs to be cross-examined to determine a question of law or to decide on the admissibility of a particular piece of evidence, or if the evidence given by the witness is complex or technical. For example, if the defendant's solicitor is attempting to persuade the court to exclude a confession his client made when interviewed at the police station (on the basis that the confession was made only as a result of improper conduct by the police), it will be necessary to cross-examine any police officers who are giving evidence for the prosecution to establish that the Codes of Practice issued under PACE 1984 were breached. Only a person with legal expertise could properly conduct such a cross-examination. Similarly, only someone with a detailed knowledge of the law concerning disputed identification evidence could properly conduct a cross-examination of a prosecution witness who claims to have identified the defendant as the person who committed an offence when the defendant disputes this identification.

This factor will also be relevant if the prosecution seek to rely on any expert evidence, such as evidence from a forensic scientist. If the contents of the evidence to be given by the forensic scientist are disputed, this will require expert cross-examination to cast doubt upon the expert's conclusions.

### 'It is in someone else's interests that I am represented'

This factor will apply when it would be inappropriate for a defendant to represent himself because he would then need to cross-examine prosecution witnesses in person. For example, were the defendant charged with a sexual or violent offence, it would be inappropriate for the defendant to cross-examine in person the complainant in such a case (in certain situations the law prevents the defendant from conducting a cross-examination in person in cases involving alleged sexual offences). It would also be inappropriate for a defendant to cross examine a child witness in person (particularly if the defendant was charged with having abused the child). This factor should *not* be used to argue that legal representation is in the general interests of the defendant's family or the court.

### Any other reasons

This is designed to cover any matters not falling under the other headings. The guidance notes suggest that further details should be given here if the defendant is likely to receive a 'demanding' community sentence (see **Chapter 11**) if convicted.

To determine if this is likely, the solicitor will need to consult the relevant section of the Magistrates' Court Sentencing Guidelines (see above). Details should also be provided under this heading if a defence witness requires skilful examination-in-chief in order to bring out his evidence in a way which is most favourable to the defendant.

Unless there is something specific to the particular case that needs to be raised, if the defendant is pleading not guilty it is common practice to state that the defendant intends to enter a not guilty plea, since a defendant who is pleading not guilty is likely to need much more in the way of legal advice than a defendant who intends to plead guilty, particularly if the charge is a serious one and the case is likely to be tried in the Crown Court.

#### 6.4.3.4 The Means Test

The following will receive criminal legal aid automatically without needing to satisfy the means test:

(a) applicants who receive income support, income-based jobseeker's allowance or a guaranteed state pension credit;
(b) applicants who are under the age of 16;
(c) applicants who are aged 16 or 17 with no income and living with their parents/guardian; and
(d) applicants who are under 18 and in full-time education.

Applicants who fall into any of the above categories will indicate this on Form CDS 14. Such applicants will not be required to fill in Form CDS 15.

Those applicants who do not automatically satisfy the means test must complete Form CDS 15. They will also be required to supply to the court the necessary paperwork to substantiate their financial details as given on Form CDS 15. This will include items such as pay slips, tax returns (if the applicant runs his own business or is a company director), bank statements, other tax forms, mortgage statements or rental/tenancy agreements, and proof of childcare costs.

Upon receipt of Form CDS 15, the court will apply a simple means test to determine whether the applicant is financially eligible for legal aid. The means test considers the applicant's income and expenses, but not the applicant's capital. The court will first calculate the applicant's *adjusted income* by taking the applicant's gross annual income and then dividing this. The figure by which the gross annual income is divided is weighted, and depends on whether the applicant has a partner or children. If the applicant's *adjusted income* is under £12,007, the applicant will qualify for legal aid. If the applicant's *adjusted income* exceeds £21,487, the applicant will not qualify for legal aid. If the applicant's *adjusted income* is between £12,007 and £21,487, the court will then need to carry out a full means test.

The purpose of the full means test is to calculate the applicant's *disposable income*. The court calculates this by deducting the following items from the applicant's gross annual income:

(a) tax and national insurance;
(b) annual housing costs;
(c) annual childcare costs;
(d) annual maintenance to former partners and any children; and
(e) an adjusted annual living allowance.

To qualify for criminal legal aid, the applicant's *annual disposable income* must not exceed £3,720.

An applicant does not have the right to appeal against a refusal of legal aid because of a failure to satisfy the means test. If, however, an applicant does not satisfy the means test but can demonstrate that he genuinely cannot fund his own defence, the applicant may ask that his entitlement to criminal legal aid be reviewed on the grounds of hardship by completing an application for review on the grounds of hardship (Form CDS 16).

### 6.4.3.5 The scope of a representation order

If a defendant satisfies both the interests of justice test and the means test, the magistrates' court will grant a criminal defence representation order (CDRO) and the order will be sent to his solicitor.

The representation order granted to a defendant for a summary only matter, or an either way matter which is dealt by the magistrates (see **6.9** below), will cover all the work done by the solicitor in connection with those proceedings in the magistrates' court, and may be extended to cover an appeal to the Crown Court against conviction and/or sentence (see **Chapter 13**). If, for an either way matter, the magistrates decline jurisdiction or the defendant elects trial in the Crown Court (see **6.10** below), the representation order will extend automatically to cover the proceedings in the Crown Court (see **10.4.2.1**). A representation order granted in respect of an offence that is triable only on indictment will cover proceedings in both the magistrates' court and the Crown Court (see **10.4.1.2**).

A defendant whose application for legal aid is refused under the interests of justice test may appeal against this decision to the magistrates either by adding further details to his original Form CDS 14 and resubmitting this to the court, or by writing to the court requesting an appeal. There is no right of appeal against the refusal of legal aid as a result of a failure to satisfy the means test (although the defendant may ask that his application be reviewed on the grounds of hardship – see **6.4.3.4** above).

At the conclusion of the case the defence solicitor will claim back any costs incurred under the representation order from the LSC (see **6.4.4** below). A magistrates' court has no power to order at the end of the case that a defendant who has received a representation order and who has been convicted should make any payment towards the cost of his publicly-funded legal representation. A defendant who is convicted before the Crown Court may be ordered to make such a contribution (see **6.11.3** below).

An example of a completed Form CDS 14 is set out below, together with an example of a representation order.

## Key skill– applying for a representation order

*Please note that this form is also available in Welsh.

Form CDS14

Official use: Priority case: Custody ☐ Vulnerable ☐ Youth ☐

Official use: MAAT Ref:

legal services COMMISSION

*Before completing this form, please refer to the guidance notes at the back.

# Application for Legal Aid in Criminal Proceedings

## Part A - About you

### Your details

1 Your first name: Gary

2 Your surname: Dickson

See Note 1

3 Date of birth: 28 / 10 / 80

4 National Insurance No (Letters / Numbers / Letter): N A 6 4 3 8 2 1 P

5 Single ☐ Married ☐ Married, but separated ☐ Divorced ☐
Widowed ☐ Living with a partner ☒ Civil Partner ☐

6 Home phone number 01244 431809
Mobile phone number 05573 372537
Work phone number 01244 531289

7 Usual home address 17 Marsh Street Chester CH3 7LW

8 Postal address (if different from home address)

### Your age

See Note 2

9 Are you:

under the age of 18 and in full time education? No ☒ Yes ☐ Go to page 3

aged 16 or 17 with no income and living with your parents/guardian? No ☐ Yes ☐ Go to page 3

under the age of 16? No ☐ Yes ☐ Go to page 3

Form CDS14

legal services COMMISSION

Part A - About you

### Your relationship status

'Partner' refers to a person you are married to or a person you normally live with as a couple. If you have a partner, you must fill in the details below, and throughout the rest of the form where necessary.

10 Are you married or living with your partner? No ☐ Yes ☒

### Your benefit status

See Note 2

11 Do you or your partner receive any of the following benefits?

| | You | *Your partner* |
|---|---|---|
| Income Support | No ☒ Yes ☐ | *No* ☒ *Yes* ☐ |
| Income-based Jobseeker's Allowance | No ☒ Yes ☐ | *No* ☒ *Yes* ☐ |
| Guarantee State Pension Credit | No ☒ Yes ☐ | *No* ☒ *Yes* ☐ |

### Your partner's details - if you don't have a partner, go to page 3.

See Note 3

12 Is your partner involved in the case as: a victim, a Prosecution witness or a co-defendant with a conflict (whose interests may conflict with yours)? No ☒ Yes ☐ Go to page 3

13 Your partner's first name: Jill

14 Your partner's surname: Summers

15 Your partner's date of birth: 11 / 03 / 1981

16 Your partner's NI No: (Letters) N S (Numbers) 6 4 5 7 4 2 (Letter) D

17 Partner's address if different from your own: Same address

See Note 4

18 Your partner's current contact details if they are unable to sign the declaration on this form:

Place and address where they are staying e.g. the name of the hospital and ward: Not applicable

Please give reasons why your partner is unable to sign:

CDS14

2

Form CDS14

Part A - About you

legal services COMMISSION

**Further information.**

See Note 5

See Note 6

You do not have to fill in this section. This will be treated in the strictest confidence and will be used purely for statistical monitoring and research.

Are you male or female?

Male [X] Female [ ]

**Disability Monitoring**

The Disability Discrimination Act defines disability as 'a physical or mental impairment with a substantial and long-term adverse effect on a person's ability to carry out day-to-day activities'.

Do you consider yourself to have a disability?

No [X] Yes [ ]

**Equal Opportunities Monitoring**

Tick all the boxes which apply.

**Ethnic Monitoring**

| White | Mixed | Asian or Asian British | Black or Black British | Chinese | Other Ethnic Group |
|---|---|---|---|---|---|
| British [X] | White and Black Caribbean [ ] | Indian [ ] | Black Caribbean [ ] | Chinese [ ] | Other [ ] |
| Irish [ ] | White and Black African [ ] | Pakistani [ ] | Black African [ ] | | |
| White other [ ] | White & Asian [ ] | Bangladeshi [ ] | Black other [ ] | | |
| | Mixed other [ ] | Asian other [ ] | | | |

Form CDS14

legal services COMMISSION

## Part B - Interests of Justice

I apply for the right to representation for the purposes of criminal proceedings under the Access to Justice Act 1999 and the Criminal Defence Service (General) (No. 2) Regulations 2001 (as amended).

### 1 Case details

See Note 7

1a What charges have been brought against you? Describe briefly what you have been accused of. E.g. theft of £1000 from your employer or assault on a neighbour.

Assault occasioning actual bodily contrary to s 47 of the Offences Against The Person Act (1861)

1b Are there any co-defendants in this matter? [X] No. Go to question 2 [ ] Yes

If 'yes', please give their names.

1c Give reasons why you and your co-defendants cannot be represented by the same solicitor.

### 2 The court proceedings

2a I am due to appear before the Chester court

On 19 / 12 / 2007 at 10am

Or

2b I appeared before the court

On / / at

**And (tick whichever applies)**

| | |
|---|---|
| My case has been sent to the Crown Court for trial under section 51 of the Crime and Disorder Act 1998. | [ ] |
| My case has been transferred to the Crown Court for trial. | [ ] |
| I was committed for trial to the Crown Court because I elected Crown Court trial. | [ ] |
| I was committed for trial to the Crown Court because the court of prosecution elected Crown Court trial. | [ ] |
| I was convicted and/or sentenced and I want to appeal against the conviction or sentence. | [ ] |
| I was convicted and committed for sentence to the Crown Court. | [ ] |
| A retrial has been ordered under section 7 of the Criminal Appeal Act 1968. | [ ] |
| Other (please give the nature of the hearing) | [ ] |

CDS14 4

Form CDS14

legal services COMMISSION

**Part B - Interests of Justice**

## 3 Outstanding matters

If there are any other outstanding criminal charges or cases against you, give details, including the court where you are due to appear.

Not applicable

## 4 Reasons for wanting legal aid

See Note 8

**4a. Please tick the reason or reasons below which apply to your case.**

| | |
|---|---|
| (i) It is likely that I will lose my liberty if any matter in the proceedings is decided against me. | ☒ |
| (ii) I have been given a sentence that is suspended or non-custodial. If I break this, the court may be able to deal with me for the original offence. | ☐ |
| (iii) It is likely that I will lose my livelihood. | ☒ |
| (iv) It is likely that I will suffer serious damage to my reputation. | ☐ |
| (v) A substantial question of law may be involved (whether arising from an act, judicial authority or other source of law). | ☒ |
| (vi) I may not be able to understand the court proceedings or present my own case. | ☐ |
| (vii) Witnesses may need to be traced or interviewed on my behalf. | ☒ |
| (viii) The proceedings may involve expert cross-examination of a prosecution witness (whether an expert or not). | ☒ |
| (ix) It is in the interests of another person (such as the person making a complaint or other witness) that I am represented. | ☒ |
| (x) Any other reasons. | ☒ |

Form CDS14

Part B - Interests of Justice

legal services COMMISSION

......question 4 continued

See Note 8

**4b Please give the details of the reason or reasons you selected in question 4a.**

**Using the same numbering as box 4a above:**

**(i) I am charged with ABH. The guideline sentence for this offence in the Magistrates' Courts Sentencing Guidelines is custody. The prosecution will also allege there are aggravating factors - an unprovoked assault with multiple blows to the head. Also I have one previous conviction for the same offence and other convictions for assault/threatening behaviour, all of which will aggravate the seriousness of the offence if I am convicted. The CPS oppose bail so I may be remanded in custody during the case.**

**(iii) I work as a scaffolder/steeplejack and a nightclub doorman. I have been told that I will lose these jobs if I am sent to prison. A prison sentence would also prevent future employment as a doorman.**

**(v) I will challenge the identification evidence to be given by John Barnard - R v Turnbull (1977).**
**I will challenge the admissibility of a police station confession under ss 76 and 78 of PACE (1984).**
**I will dispute the admissibility of my previous convictions which the prosecution will want to use to suggest I have a propensity to commit acts of violence (CJA 2003, s 101(d)). I will apply to exclude any evidence of my bad character (CJA 2003, s 101(3) and s103(3); R v Hanson & others (2005)).**

**(vii) I will be calling my partner as a witness to support my alibi defence. She will need to be interviewed and a witness statement taken from her.**

**(viii) The 'Turnbull witness' (John Barnard) requires expert cross examination to undermine the credibility of his evidence.**
**The police officer who interviewed me at the police station (PC Chambers) requires expert cross examination to establish that there were multiple breaches of PACE/Codes of Practice during the interview.**

**(ix) I am charged with a violent offence and it would be inappropriate for me to cross examine the complainant in person.**

**(x) I am pleading not guilty and the case is likely to be tried in the Crown Court.**

## 5 Legal Representation

a If you do not choose a solicitor, the court will choose one for you

b You must tell the solicitor that you have named him or her

c If you have been charged with another person or people, the court may appoint a solicitor other than the solicitor of your choice

The solicitor I want to act for me is:
Mr Matthew Simpson

Give the firm's name and address if known:
Collaws Solicitors
129 Westgate
Chester CH1 4TD

Form CDS14

legal services COMMISSION

## Part C - Declaration

You must complete declarations which apply to your application.

### Authority by your partner

See Note 9

If you have a partner whose details have been completed on this form, they must sign the authority below, unless your partner is abroad, in hospital or otherwise unable to sign.

This is a true statement of my financial circumstances, *as supported by the information detailed on the CDS15 (*delete if not applicable).

I agree to the Legal Services Commission and HM Courts Service checking these facts with others such as the Department for Work and Pensions and HM Revenue & Customs. I authorise those people or organisations to provide the information that we may request.

Signature............................................................ Date....................../....................../...................

Full name (in BLOCK CAPITALS).................................................................................................................

### Your declaration

This is a true statement of my financial circumstances, and that of my partner, *as supported by the information detailed on the CDS15 (*delete if not applicable).

I understand that if I tell you anything untrue on this form, or the documents I send with it, or leave anything out:

a I may be taken to court; or
b the Legal Services Commission may take away my legal aid so I have to pay all my legal fees.

I understand that if I have made a statement which is false; or I knowingly withhold information, I may be prosecuted, which may result in a prison sentence or a fine.

I agree to the Legal Services Commission and HM Courts Service checking these facts with others such as the Department for Work and Pensions and HM Revenue & Customs. I authorise those people or organisations to provide the information that we may request.

I agree to the Legal Services Commission contacting my partner to check the information I have given about their means.

I will:
a provide more evidence if the Legal Services Commission or HM Courts Service ask; and
b tell the Legal Services Commission or HM Courts Service if anything I have said here changes.

I understand that if my case goes to the Crown Court or any higher court, the court may order that I pay some or all of the costs of the proceedings through a Recovery of Defence Costs Order. I understand the information given in this form will be provided to that court so that it can consider whether a Recovery of Defence Costs Order should be made and I may be required to give details of my means to the court or LSC.

I understand that if my case goes to the Crown Court or any higher court, I will have to tell the Legal Services Commission or HM Courts Service (or both) details of my financial circumstances.

Signature............................................................ Date....................../....................../...................

Full name (in BLOCK CAPITALS).................................................................................................................

### Declaration to be completed by the legal representative

I,……………………………………, representing the applicant, confirm that I am authorised to provide representation under a contract issued by the Legal Services Commission (e.g. a general criminal contract or an individual case contract).

I understand that only firms with a contract issued by the Commission (e.g. a general criminal contract or an individual case contract) may provide representation in the Magistrates' Court.

Or

I,……………………………………, representing the applicant, confirm that I have been instructed to provide representation by either:

- a firm who holds a contract issued by the Legal Services Commission (e.g. a general criminal contract or individual case contract), or;
- a solicitor employed by the Legal Services Commission in a Public Defender Office who is authorised to provide representation.

Signature ......................................................... Date ....................../....................../...................

Legal Service Provider LSC account number | | | | | | | |

Form CDS14

legal services COMMISSION

**Data Protection Act - Access to personal information**

We will use the information you provide in this form, and any other information we may receive, to process your application for legal aid. We will keep it in line with the principles of the Data Protection Act 1998 and any relevant confidentiality arrangements.

The Legal Services Commission is the data controller. If necessary, we may check or share the information you provide with other organisations, such as:

- the Department for Work and Pensions;
- HM Revenue & Customs;
- the Land Registry;
- Companies House;
- credit reference agencies

We will only share the information if it is necessary to protect the public funds or where we have to do so by law.

We or HM Courts Service may also process your information to produce management or research information. The results of our research will only be published in a statistical or anonymous form.

We will keep information for as long as is necessary to fulfil our duties under the Access to Justice Act 1999. You have the right to look at the personal information held about you, to inspect it, and have it corrected if it is wrong.

## For official use only

List any other factors considered when deciding the application, including any information given orally.

Decision on the Interests of Justice Test Passed ☐ Refused ☐

I have considered all the available details of all the charges and against the Interests of Justice criteria. I give the following reasons.

Decision on financial eligibility:

Signature............................................. Name of appropriate officer .................................................

Date......................./......................./...................

Case number: ☐

Representation order number: ☐

To be completed where right to representation extends to Crown Court:

Statement of means Form B given to defendant on ____/____/____

Indicate type of case:

- Sent case under S51 Crime and Disorder Act 1988 ☐
- Transferred for trial ☐
- Committal for trial/sentence ☐
- Retrial under S7 of the Criminal Appeal Act 1988 ☐
- Other (specify) ________________________________________

First date of hearing at Crown Court ____/____/____

legal services COMMISSION

# Notes on how to fill in the form
# CDS14: Application for Legal Aid in Criminal Proceedings

## General

You must answer all questions on the form and provide evidence where necessary. If you do not, it may delay your legal aid and you may not receive free legal help from your solicitor.

We can only grant legal aid if you pass both the Interests of Justice and financial eligibility tests.

You must fill in the form in BLOCK CAPITALS and black or blue ink. If we can't read your application, we will return it. You should ask a solicitor for advice if you are not sure how to answer any questions on the form.

If your case will be heard in the Crown Court, you must fill in this form and court Form B only.

More detailed guidance can be found in 'Criminal Legal Aid Application Guide' at www.hmcourts-service.gov.uk

## Part A - About you

**Note 1** **Do I need to provide my National Insurance number (in question 4 on page 1)?**

The question is only compulsory if you receive a benefit named in question 11. If you or your partner cannot provide your National Insurance number and you receive a benefit in question 11 you must provide recent evidence instead, which must not be more than 3 months old e.g. a benefit book or notice of entitlement or a letter from Job Centre Plus setting out the benefits you receive.

**Note 2** **Why do you need to know my age (question 9) and benefit status (question 11)?**

If you tick 'yes' to either question 9 or question 11, you are automatically financially eligible for legal aid. But if you tick 'no', you must also fill in form CDS15 and submit it with this form.

**Note 3** **What happens if I tick 'yes' to question 12 about my partner's involvement in the case?**

If you tick 'yes', you do not need to fill in any partner details throughout the form.

**Note 4** **What should I do if my partner is unable to sign the declaration?**

If your partner is abroad or in hospital or otherwise unable to sign, for your application to be accepted you must set out the reasons why they are unable to sign and their current contact details in question 18 in Part A.

**Note 5** **What is the Further Information section for?**

You may give us any additional information in support of your claim.

**Note 6** **What is the Disability and Equal Opportunities Monitoring part for?**

You may fill in this part, but it isn't compulsory. Your personal information will be held confidentially and would help us with our statistical monitoring and research

legal services COMMISSION

## Part B - Interests of Justice

**Note 7** **How do I fill in this section?**

If you can, you should get help from a solicitor to fill in PART B. This is because they can provide you with the proper legal reasons why you should be granted legal aid.

Your solicitor may wish to consult the guidance by the Justices' Clerks' Society on the interests of justice test, which is available at www.legalservices.gov.uk.

**Note 8** **I don't understand the reasons for wanting representation given in question 4a.**

i) It is likely that I will lose my liberty if any matter in the proceedings is decided against me:

Loss of liberty does not include non-custodial sentences but does include remands in custody and prison sentences (including hospital orders). If the entry point for this offence in the Magistrates' guidelines is not custody, please explain why you think custody is likely in this case (for example, relevant previous convictions). Please give dates of relevant convictions, if known.

ii) I have been given a sentence that is suspended or non-custodial. If I break this, the court may be able to deal with me for the original offence:

You should give details of your sentence and its conditions.

iii) It is likely that I will lose my livelihood:

The loss of livelihood should be a direct result of the conviction or sentence - please provide supporting evidence where possible. This would normally refer to your current livelihood, although it can apply if someone is genuinely unemployed for a short period between jobs. If you plan to plead guilty, please explain how legal representation might help you avoid losing your livelihood.

iv) It is likely that I will suffer serious damage to my reputation:

Reputation refers to good character, including honesty and trustworthiness, and is not related to social class or position. 'Serious' damage is judged to happen in cases where the disgrace of a conviction is more than the direct effect of the penalty. If you plan to plead guilty, please explain how legal representation might help you avoid serious damage to your reputation.

v) A substantial question of law may be involved (whether arising from an act, judicial authority or other source of law):

This applies where any matter in relation to the proceedings raises a point of law which you cannot be expected to deal with unaided. Please explain why the question of law is relevant to the case. Questions of fact alone are not relevant. Where possible, please list the cases or laws which give rise to the question of law.

vi) I may not be able to understand the court proceedings or present my own case:

There may be a number of reasons why you may not be able to understand court proceedings or to present your own case. These may include (but are not limited to) mental or physical disability, poor knowledge of English, age or vulnerability. The ability to understand proceedings or to present your own case is also likely to depend on how complicated the case is.

legal services COMMISSION

vii) Witnesses may need to be traced or interviewed on my behalf:

You may need witnesses to be traced or interviewed to see whether they can support your case if pleading not guilty or to help with a plea of mitigation (an explanation for the offence given on behalf of a guilty party in order to excuse or partly excuse the offence committed in an attempt to minimise the sentence) if pleading guilty. You should explain why you need legal representation to trace or interview witnesses.

viii) The proceedings may involve expert cross-examination of a prosecution witness (whether an expert or not):

Expert cross-examination is likely to be needed where you are pleading not guilty and you expect the prosecution to call witnesses whose evidence you want to challenge. You are likely to need a lawyer to carry out expert cross-examination on your behalf if the evidence to be given by the prosecution witness is complicated or technical.

ix) It is in the interests of another person (such as the person making a complaint or other witness) that I am represented:

If you are charged with a sexual or violent offence, or where the person making a complaint is a child, it would not be appropriate for you to cross-examine in person. This criterion should not be used to argue that legal representation is in the general interests of your family or of the court.

x) Any other reasons

Please provide full details of any other reasons (which you have not mentioned elsewhere on the form) why you think it would be in the interests of justice that you are represented. For example, legal representation might be justified if you are likely to receive a demanding community sentence if convicted or if defence witnesses need skilful examination.

## Part C - Declaration

**Note 9** **My partner is unable to sign the declaration.**

If your partner is unable to sign, please refer to note 4 and question 18 in Part A, please also note, by signing your declaration on this form you are giving the Legal Services Commission your consent to approach and check the information where your partner is contactable.

## Key document – Representation Order

Royal
coat of
arms

Chester Magistrates' Court
The Square
Chester
CH1 1PF

**BOARD COPY**

Mr Gary Paul Dickson
17 Marsh Street
Chester
Ch3 7LW

Date: 19.12.2007
Order Number: LO 45756567 Board Number: LA/474575/05/07
Date of Grant: 19.12.2007

Date of Hearing: 19.12.2007

In accordance with the provisions of Section 12(2) of the Access to Justice Act 1999 the court now grants representation to Gary Paul Dickson for proceedings before a Magistrates Court in connection with:-

Assault occasioning actual bodily harm, contrary to Section 47 of the Offences Against the Person Act 1861.

The representation granted shall consist of the following:-

Solicitor
including advice on the preparation of the case for the proceedings and advice on appeal against conviction and/or sentence.

The solicitor assigned is:-

Mr M. Simpson
Collaws
129 Westgate
Chester

Clerk to the Justices

*White Copy* – Legal Aid Board *Pink Copy* – Solicitor *Blue Copy* – Court *Green Copy* – Defendant *Yellow* - C.P.S.

#### 6.4.3.6 Rates of payment under a representation order

In most cases where the client has the benefit of a representation order, the solicitor will claim a 'standard fee' for the work done on the client's behalf. This is a fixed payment, the level of which is determined by the way in which the case was dealt with. For example, a case where the client pleads not guilty and the matter goes to trial attracts a higher standard fee than a case in which the client enters an immediate plea, because of the extra work involved in representing a client on a not guilty plea. If the amount of work done by the solicitor is in excess of the level of the standard fee, the solicitor may claim payment for the work done on the basis of set hourly charging rates prescribed by the LSC.

If a solicitor submits an application for a representation order on behalf of a client which passes the interests of justice test but then fails the means test, the solicitor is entitled to claim a fixed fee payment if it was necessary to represent the client at his first court hearing before the means test part of the application had been determined by the court (the 'early cover' scheme). Similarly, if a solicitor represents a client at a first hearing and the client's application for a representation order is subsequently refused because it fails the interests of justice test, the solicitor may claim payment for the work carried out at the hearing under a pre-order cover scheme. If the solicitor carries out work for a client prior to a representation order being granted, the work done prior to the grant of the representation order will fall within the standard fee that the solicitor will claim at the end of the case.

### 6.4.4 Claiming payment

When a solicitor has attended the police station to represent a client, he will complete a Claim Costs Summary Sheet (Form CDS 11) which details the work he has done for the client, the times involved and the fees claimed. If the client is charged and the solicitor then obtains a representation order in respect of the court proceedings, a separate CDS 11 will be completed to record the work done by the solicitor at court. Any CDS 11 forms that are completed will be retained on the client's file and not sent to the LSC. At the end of each month, the solicitor's firm will send a Contract Work Report Form (Form CDS 6) to the LSC to claim payment for all the police station attendances and court work the firm has carried out during that month. This form will contain a summary of all the individual CDS 11 forms which the firm has completed for that month. When the LSC carries out its annual audit of the firm, the LSC will check a sample of the CDS 11 forms retained on the solicitor's files to ensure that these have been completed correctly.

### 6.4.5 The Carter Report

The Carter Report was published on 13 July 2006. The purpose of the report was to make proposals for the future development of the public funding of legal services. The main proposals made in the report were:

(a) the introduction of fixed fees for police station work (this has already taken effect – see **6.4.2.1** above);

(b) the revision of the current standard fees system in the magistrates' court (with fixed fees rather than payment by reference to hourly rates); and

(c) a move towards 'best value tendering' for criminal contracts (ie, ultimately firms will compete for publicly-funded work).

## 6.5 Taking a statement from the client

A defence solicitor will usually meet his client for the first time either at the police station, or when the client makes his first appearance at court. On neither occasion is the solicitor likely to have sufficient time to take a detailed statement from the client.

A full and accurate statement needs to be taken from the client as soon as possible.

The statement will not be disclosed to the court or the prosecution and can be written using the type of language which the client would normally use. It is good practice to get the statement checked and signed by the client so that there are no misunderstandings as to what the client's 'story' is later in the case. The matters that should be included in a statement are as follows:

(a) the client's personal details – name, address date of birth, contact telephone number, National Insurance number, etc;
(b) details of the charge and the court where the client's case is being heard;
(c) the client's education and employment history;
(d) details of the client's family circumstances;
(e) any health problems the client may have;
(f) any previous convictions the client has;
(g) what the client has to say about the current offence;
(h) any factors that might be relevant to mitigation (particularly if the client intends to plead guilty);
(i) any factors that might be relevant to a bail application, such as a potential surety (see **7.5.1**);
(j) the client's comments on the prosecution evidence – these can be added to the statement when details of the prosecution case are received.

An example of a completed client's statement is set out below. The prosecution witness statements referred to in the latter half of the client's statement are included in the advance disclosure package set out at **Key Document – Advance Disclosure** at p 172 below.

## Key skill – drafting the client's statement

STATEMENT OF GARY PAUL DICKSON

Statement of Gary Paul Dickson will say as follows:

**Personal Details**

My full name is Gary Paul Dickson and I reside at 17 Marsh Street, Chester CH3 7LW with my girlfriend Jill Summers. The property is owned by Jill's parents and we share a flat on the top floor.

I am 27 years old, having been born on 28th October 1980. I have two jobs. My main occupation is as a scaffolder/steeplejack. I do contract work throughout the country. Basically I am sent wherever there is work. I also do some part-time work as a doorman/bouncer on a weekend and the odd night during the week at Connolley's Nightclub in Chester.

My contact telephone numbers are:

HOME – Chester 431809

MOBILE – 05573 372537

**Charge**

I am charged with a s 47 assault on Vincent Lamb in the early hours of the morning of 18th December 2007. I know nothing about any assault on Mr Lamb and it is my intention to enter a not guilty plea to this charge.

**Education and Employment History**

I was born and brought up in York. I attended Burnholme Community College until I was 16. I left school with GCSEs in English Language, Maths, Woodwork and Art.

After leaving school I joined the army. I served as a private and latterly as a corporal with the Green Howards regiment. I left the army in 2002 and moved to Chester to live with some former school friends.

I started doing some scaffolding work for a firm based in Chester on a part-time basis and found that I liked the work. I was never an employee of the firm, but just did contract work as and when it became available. I started doing similar work for a couple of other firms and was soon doing this work all the time. I can earn good money doing the scaffolding. The work takes me to all parts of the country and occasionally I go abroad to work.

I've been doing the work as a doorman for about three years. I'm quite a big lad and when I was having a drink in Connolley's one day, the manager asked if I'd like to do some door work. I jumped at the chance because I thought it was a way to earn some easy money.

**Family Circumstances**

I've been with my girlfriend Jill Summers for about 18 months. Our relationship is serious and we hope to get married at some point in the future. We are saving up money to get our own place together. Sharing a flat is fine for the moment but we'd like to start a family and need the extra space.

**Health**

As far as I am aware I don't have any health problems. The army gets you fairly fit and I need to stay in good physical shape to do the work as a doorman.

**Previous Convictions**

I have 2 convictions for threatening behaviour, one conviction for assault occasioning actual bodily harm and one conviction for common assault. I also have a conviction for failing to answer bail in a previous case.

My recent convictions for violence are all as a result of customers at the nightclub getting aggressive or drunk and needing to be ejected from the premises. Sometimes customers get a bit lippy or even try to punch you when they are being thrown out. I was only ever doing my job, but the customers occasionally complain to the police that they have been assaulted. The police don't like professional doormen and so always press charges if they can. I pleaded guilty to these offences because it was my word against the customers and a lot of their mates.

My last conviction was on 13th December 2006 for ABH. I gave a lad a thump when he wouldn't leave the nightclub when we were closing. I pleaded guilty and got 200 hours' unpaid work. I completed this work about six months ago.

The conviction for common assault happened whilst I was still in the army. I was having a drink at a pub in York when a lad accused me of knocking his drink over. He got abusive so I pushed him away and he fell over, banging his head on a table. I pleaded guilty.

**Current Offence**

At about 11.00 am on Monday 18th December 2007 I was asleep in bed with Jill at 17 Marsh Street. I had been working at the nightclub until the early hours and Jill had been out the previous evening as well. As far as I was concerned it had been a normal evening at the nightclub. I had to deal with a couple of drunks but nothing other than that. I stayed on the door all night and didn't go into the area where the stage was.

A policeman woke me up by banging on the door. I answered the door and he asked me if I was the owner of a dark blue VW Golf registration number L251 CVM. I told him I was, but as it was parked outside the house I thought this was obvious. He then asked me to confirm my whereabouts at 3.15 am that morning. I told him I was in bed with Jill. I asked him what was going on, and he told me that there had been a complaint of an assault by a man driving a car which matched the description and registration number of my car. I told him I didn't know what he was talking about.

He asked me if I would accompany him to the police station to answer some questions. I refused to go so he arrested me. When we got to the police station I was put in a cell for several hours. I hadn't had anything to eat or drink since the previous night, but the police wouldn't give me a drink or a meal. They didn't tell me why I had been stuck in a cell.

At about 6.00 pm I was told that I was going to be interviewed. I asked to speak to a solicitor before I was taken to the interview room. They said that I had to be interviewed there and then, or wait until the following morning. I didn't want to stay there any longer than necessary and so agreed to be interviewed without a solicitor. By the time the interview started I was totally pissed off with the way I had been treated. I said some stupid things which weren't true and which I now regret. They kept asking me the same questions over and over again, and it was clear that they weren't going to believe a word I said when I told them that I knew nothing about the assault. I eventually said it was me just to get out of there.

**Mitigation**

I have nothing to say in mitigation because I am not guilty of this offence and I will be pleading not guilty when the charge is put to me at court. I know nothing about the attack on Mr Lamb. At the time of the attack I was asleep at home.

**Matters Relevant to Bail**

I intend to continue working at Connolley's because the money is good. I suppose there is always the chance of more trouble with the public, but this is an occupational hazard. All the other doormen have previous convictions. We are an easy target for the police because there is no shortage of lads who want to try it on with us and then go squealing to the police when they get a smack.

The conviction I have for failing to answer my bail was just a mix up over court dates. I thought my trial was going to be dealt with in the afternoon, and didn't appreciate that I needed to be at court for 10.00 am regardless. I did turn up at court in the afternoon, but a warrant for my arrest had already been issued. I was arrested at court. This was a genuine oversight on my part but the magistrates convicted me anyway.

I am due to go away to Kerry in the Republic of Ireland in six months' time to do some scaffolding work. Until then I will be working on a contract in the Chester area, so I will be working locally.

I understand that any bail the court grants me may be subject to conditions. Until I am due to go away with work I would be able to abide by a condition that I report to the police station daily or that I live at 17 Marsh Street.

I could afford to pay a security if required.

Signed: *Gary Dickson*

Dated: 19th December 2007

**Comments on Prosecution Witness Statements**

**PC Gareth Chambers**

This is pretty much correct. I have been arrested by PC Chambers before and he obviously has it in for me. He knows about my previous convictions. He obviously wasn't going to let me out of the interview until I said I was guilty, even though I didn't do it.

**John Barnard**

He must be mistaken. If he had been drinking all night as he claims, his recollection can't be reliable. He says I have short hair and a white tight-fitting T-shirt. This is the uniform worn by all the staff at Connolley's so that description could apply to any of the door staff or many of the customers as well.

He isn't very sure of the car registration number. He has either not remembered it properly or the police have told him the number. He did pick me out at the video identification, but he got that wrong as well. Perhaps the police told him who to pick.

**Vincent Lamb**

I don't know and have never heard of Vincent Lamb. He may have been the guest disc jockey that night. I don't really know what is going on inside the nightclub unless there is any trouble. I spend all my time at the entrance and on the street outside. I am adamant that I have never met Vincent Lamb. I'm sorry if he got his face smashed in, but I had nothing to do with it. Mr Lamb says that at one point during the evening I went over to the stage, shook my fist in his face and told him to lay off a clubber called Jill. This is untrue. I did no such thing. I spent the entire evening at the front of the nightclub. If this is meant to be a reference to my girlfriends Jill it is incorrect. Jill did not go to Connolley's that evening. Perhaps Mr Lamb has got me mixed up with another bouncer. There is another bouncer who looks a bit like me.

**Peter Hansen**

There is nothing I can say about this. There must be loads of dark VW Golfs on the road.

**Record of audibly recorded interview**

This seems to be right in terms of what was said, but the confession I made is just not true. I only said I assaulted Vincent Lamb because this was the only way I could think of to get out of the police station. Even though PC Chambers said I would be allowed to leave the police station on bail if I admitted my guilt, after I was charged the custody officer wouldn't let me have bail and I was kept in the cells overnight until court the next day.

**Record of previous convictions**

This is correct. As I said in my statement, you get plenty of grief on the door of the club. I sometimes gave the odd customer a smack if I thought they deserved it, but I never attacked anyone in the way I am supposed to have hit Lamb.

## 6.6 Obtaining disclosure from the prosecution

### 6.6.1 Introduction

If the solicitor has represented the client at the police station, he may have some knowledge as to what the prosecution case against his client is and what evidence the CPS has to support this case. He is unlikely, however, to have seen copies of the witness statements which the police have obtained. It is vital for the defendant's solicitor to see all the prosecution evidence as soon as possible after the defendant has been charged so he may advise the defendant as to the strength of the case against him and take his instructions on what the prosecution witnesses are saying.

What the CPS must disclose to the defendant's solicitor varies depending on whether the offence the defendant has been charged with is a summary offence or an either way offence.

### 6.6.2 Summary offences

If the offence is summary only, there is no statutory obligation on the CPS to disclose details of the prosecution case to the defendant's solicitor. As a matter of good practice, however, the CPS will provide the defendant's solicitor with at least a summary of the case against his client, and more usually with copies of the statements of the witnesses upon whose evidence the prosecution are going to rely at trial. The Attorney-General has issued guidelines stating that the CPS should disclose to the defence all the evidence upon which the prosecution will seek to rely at trial (*Attorney-General's Guidelines on Disclosure of Information in Criminal Proceedings 2005*).

### 6.6.3 Either way offences

A defendant charged with an either way offence in entitled to receive 'advance disclosure' of the prosecution case (CrimPR, r 21.3). The CPS will serve on the defendant's solicitor an advance disclosure package containing:

(a) copies of the written statements given by prosecution witnesses;

(b) a transcript of any audibly recorded interviews with the defendant in the police station (together with a copy of the interview tape, unless the suspect was given a copy of the tape on charge – see **3.5.2.1**); and

(c) details of any previous convictions which the defendant may have.

An example of an advance disclosure package is set out below.

## Key Document – Advance Disclosure

**CHESHIRE POLICE**

Station or Section: Chester Division: G

Statement of (name of witness): VINCENT LAMB Date: 20 December 2007
(in full – Block letters)

Date and place of birth: Over 18 England

Occupation: Entertainer

---

This statement (consisting of 1 page signed by me) is true to the best of my knowledge and belief and I make it knowing that if it is tendered in evidence I shall be liable to prosecution if I have wilfully stated in it anything which I know to be false or do not believe to be true.

Dated: 20th December 2007 Signed: *Vincent Lamb*

---

I am employed as a freelance disc jockey.

At about 3.15 am on 18th December 2007, I was walking away from Connolley's Nightclub intending to go to the nearby multi-storey car park to get my van and then return to the club to pack away all my equipment. I was in a really good mood as I had finished an evening as the guest disc jockey at the club and I thought it had gone extremely well.

It was very dark as I walked along. I heard a car approach from behind me at speed. I turned and was dazzled by the headlights so I couldn't see very much at all. The car screeched to a halt and the driver's side door opened. Someone got out and I was aware of the shadow of a large man silhouetted against the headlights of the car. I could not see what the man looked like or what he was wearing. He walked straight up to me and struck me in the face with his fist. I was struck several times in the face and was knocked to the ground. I must have lost consciousness because the next thing I remember was coming around on the pavement after my attacker had gone.

A passer-by called an ambulance and I was taken to Chester Hospital where I received treatment. As a result of the attack I have a broken nose and a deep cut above my left eyebrow. A splint was put on my nose and some stitches were put in my eyebrow. I have to go back to hospital next week to have the stitches removed.

I can't think why anyone would want to attack me. My wallet was still in my pocket and nothing was missing. The only untoward thing that happened during the evening was when one of the bouncers told me to lay off one of the clubbers. The bouncer was Gary Dickson. I was chatting to a girl called Jill when Dickson came across, shook his fist in my face, and told me I would get a smack if I didn't leave her alone. I think she might have been his girlfriend.

Signed: *Vincent Lamb* Signature witnessed by: *PC Chambers*

**CHESHIRE POLICE**

Station or Section: Chester Division: G

Statement of (name of witness): JOHN BARNARD Date: 20th December 2007

(in full – Block letters)

Date and place of birth: Over 18 England

Occupation: Engineer

---

This statement (consisting of 1 page signed by me) is true to the best of my knowledge and belief and I make it knowing that if it is tendered in evidence I shall be liable to prosecution if I have wilfully stated in it anything which I know to be false or do not believe to be true.

Dated: 20th December 2007 Signed: *John Barnard*

---

I am a mechanical engineer employed by Imperial Chemicals at Bootle Merseyside and live at 10 Tower Court, Bellevue Road, Liverpool.

On 17th December 2007 I had been out for the evening in Chester. I had been to a club called Connolley's and had quite a bit to drink; about seven pints over the course of the evening.

At approximately 3.15 am on Tuesday 18th December I was walking back to a friend's house where I had agreed to stay the night. I noticed a dark coloured VW Golf zoom past me at speed and pull up sharply next to a young man who was walking about 50 metres in front of me. A well-built man got out of the driver's seat and proceeded to hit the other man in the face several times. There didn't seem to be any provocation for the attack. The man who was hit didn't put up any real resistance, as he was quite a lot smaller than the well-built man. The big man then got back in his car and sped back the way he had just come, so that he passed me again. He must have been travelling at about 40 mph by the time he passed me so I only managed to glimpse him as he passed. He was white, clean shaven with short dark hair and a tight-fitting white T-shirt. As the car disappeared I tried to remember the registration. I used to be in the army and I have done checkpoint duty in Northern Ireland so I have had some training in vehicle recognition. I made a mental note at the time and told a police officer later that evening that I thought the registration number was either C251 CVM or L251 CVM. It was a dark blue Golf. It did not appear to have any body damage on the side I saw. I am not sure of the numbers as I had quite a bit to drink that night but I'm quite certain it was 'CVM' at the end.

I was subsequently asked to see if I could pick out the man in the car at a video identification. I picked out foil number four in the video identification.

**[Gary Dickson was foil number four]**

Signed: *John Barnard* Signature witnessed by: *PC Chambers*

**CHESHIRE POLICE**

Station or Section: Chester Division: G

Statement of (name of witness): GARETH CHAMBERS Date: 18 December 2007
(in full – Block letters)

Date and place of birth: Over 18 England

Occupation: Policeman

---

This statement (consisting of 1 page signed by me) is true to the best of my knowledge and belief and I make it knowing that if it is tendered in evidence I shall be liable to prosecution if I have wilfully stated in it anything which I know to be false or do not believe to be true.

Dated: 18th December 2007 Signed: *Gareth Chambers*

---

I am Police Constable 911 of Cheshire Police based at Chester.

On Tuesday 18th December 2007 I was on mobile patrol in Chester town centre. Acting on information received I attended at 17 Marsh Street at 11.10 am. I knocked on the door of 17 Marsh Street and a man known to me as Gary Dickson answered. I asked Mr Dickson if he was the owner of a dark blue VW Golf registration number L251 CVM. He said that he was. I then asked Mr Dickson to confirm his whereabouts in the early hours of 18th December at approximately 3.15 am. I explained that if he would accompany me to the station then I could take a statement and it may be that he would be eliminated from our enquiries.

Mr Dickson refused to accompany me so I returned to my vehicle and called for back up. Once further police officers attended following my request I again asked Mr Dickson to accompany me to the station. He refused so I arrested him on suspicion of having committed an assault on Vince Lamb the previous evening. He made no reply.

I conveyed Gary Dickson and myself to Chester Police Station. At the police station the custody officer authorised the detention of Gary Dickson for questioning. I later interviewed Mr Dickson in Interview Room 2 at Chester Police Station in accordance with the Codes of Practice. Two tapes were used and the sealed master tape is available as exhibit 'GC1'.

At 18.30 hours the interview was commenced and it was concluded at 18.40 hours.

I have prepared a copy of the salient points of the interview, which I produce as exhibit 'GC1'.

At 19.45 hours, after Mr Dickson had taken part in a video identification, I took Mr Dickson before the custody officer who charged him with assault occasioning actual bodily harm. He made no reply.

Signed: *Gareth Chambers*

Taken by: PC 244 Hansen

**CHESHIRE POLICE**

Station or Section: Chester Division: G

Statement of (name of witness): PETER HANSEN Date: 29th December 2007
(in full – Block letters)

Date and place of birth: Over 18 England

Occupation: Police Constable

---

This statement (consisting of 1 page signed by me) is true to the best of my knowledge and belief and I make it knowing that if it is tendered in evidence I shall be liable to prosecution if I have wilfully stated in it anything which I know to be false or do not believe to be true.

Dated: 29th December 2007 Signed: *Peter Hansen*

---

I am Police Constable 244 of Cheshire Police based at Chester.

On 18th December 2007 I made a request to the Vehicle Licensing Authority at Swansea for confirmation of the details of the registered keeper and registered address of the vehicles with the registration number C251 CVM and L251 CVM. C251 CVM is a silver BMW and L251 CVM is a dark blue VW Golf. The registered keeper of the latter vehicle is Gary Paul Dickson.

Signed: *P Hansen*

Taken by: PC244 Hansen

**CHESHIRE POLICE**

Station or Section: Chester Division: G

Statement of (name of witness): HARBHAJAN SINGH Date: 29th December 2007
(in full – Block letters)

Date and place of birth: Over 18 England

Occupation: Doctor

---

This statement (consisting of 1 page signed by me) is true to the best of my knowledge and belief and I make it knowing that if it is tendered in evidence I shall be liable to prosecution if I have wilfully stated in it anything which I know to be false or do not believe to be true.

Dated: 29th December 2007 Signed: *Harbhajan Singh*

---

I am a Senior House Officer employed by Chester Hospital in the Accident and Emergency Department.

This statement is taken from the notes which I made at the time of my examination of Vincent Lamb.

Mr Lamb was seen in the Accident and Emergency Department on 18th December 2007 at about 3.45 am. Mr Lamb alleged that he had been assaulted and had sustained facial injuries. He had lost consciousness following the assault, but had not vomited or suffered any visual disturbance.

When examined Mr Lamb was slightly groggy and had a laceration over his left eyebrow and swelling over the bridge of his nose. An X-ray of his facial bones was organised and this showed a fracture in the bone over the bridge of the nose.

Four stitches were put into the laceration over the left eyebrow and a splint was provided for the broken nose. Mr Lamb was advised about possible problems following a head injury, and was allowed home.

Mr Lamb was seen again 7 days later when the stitches and the splint were removed.

Signed: *Harbhajan Singh* Signature witnessed by: *PC Chambers*

**CHESHIRE POLICE**

**RECORD OF AUDIBLY RECORDED INTERVIEW**

| | |
|---|---|
| **INTERVIEW OF:** Gary Dickson | DATE OF BIRTH: 28.10.80 |
| **ADDRESS:** 17 Marsh Street, Chester | DATE: 18.12.2007 |
| **INTERVIEW AT:** Chester Police Station | |
| **TIME COMMENCED:** 6.30 pm | **TIME CONCLUDED:** 6.40 pm |
| **DURATION OF INTERVIEW:** 10 mins | **TAPE REFERENCE NO:** SG01/WPC/1232000 |
| **INTERVIEWING OFFICER:** PC G Chambers | **OTHER PERSONS PRESENT** None |

Signature of officer preparing record: *Gareth Chambers* PC911

| Tape times | PARTICULARS OF INTERVIEW |
|---|---|
| 0.00 | Introductions.<br><br>Caution. Reminded of right to free legal advice. |
| 0.50 | PC911: Right Mr Dickson, I think you know why you're here, don't you? You have been arrested for assaulting Vincent Lamb near to Connolley's Nightclub. |
| 1.12 | GD: I've been here most of the day and I haven't had much sleep, so do you think you could let me go now or what?<br><br>PC911: Just answer the question Mr Dickson and we can both go home.<br><br>GD: Look, just because I work at the club that doesn't mean you can pin any kind of trouble on me. I'm saying nothing. |
| 2.42 | PC911: Mr Dickson, why don't we just get this over with? Look I'm going off duty soon and if we don't deal with this interview now I won't be back on duty until tomorrow afternoon. You don't want to have to wait until then, do you?<br><br>GD: No I don't. My girlfriend will be worried about me – she will think that I'm in some sort of trouble. Could I at least telephone her? |
| 3.20 | PC911: Don't worry, this will be over sooner than you think. Let's make a start then. Where were you at 3.15 am this morning? |
| 3.56 | GD: I would have finished work by then so I'd be at home.<br><br>PC911: Are you sure about that, because I have reason to believe you were still near to the club and you assaulted Mr Lamb there?<br><br>GD: No. That's not true. I had been at the club earlier but I left much earlier than 3.15 am.<br><br>PC911 Oh come on Mr Dickson, don't play the innocent with me or we'll be here all night. |
| 4.20 | GD: Look I don't know where you are getting the idea in your head that I've been assaulting someone. It's just rubbish. |

| Tape times | PARTICULARS OF INTERVIEW |
|---|---|
| 4.50 | PC911: Come on Mr Dickson, let's be serious, shall we? You were angry with Lamb because he'd tried to chat up your girlfriend earlier in the evening. You chased him in your car didn't you? And you got out of the car and then you beat him?<br><br>GD: No, I did not.<br><br>PC911: You were seen Mr Dickson. Driving your own car at the time wasn't very clever was it?<br><br>GD: No, you are seriously barking up the wrong tree here. The person who saw me is obviously confused. I was at the club and I did drive it to work and home again. But I didn't stop to beat anyone up and I wasn't on the road at 3.15 am. I would have got home much earlier than that. |
| 5.20 | PC911: That's rubbish isn't it? We have a witness who says that he saw you go over to Mr Lamb, hit him in the face several times and then drive away back in the direction towards Marsh Street.<br><br>GD: He's making it up. |
| 6.40 | PC911: Why would the witness lie? You must realise this is a very serious charge, Mr Dickson. We're not going to get anywhere if you're going to play these stupid games with me. Perhaps you'd like to stop being clever or I'll take you back to the cells. Don't you want to get out of here tonight? What's it to be?<br><br>GD: I've told you already what happened.<br><br>PC911: Oh come on.<br><br>GD: You lot have really got it in for me haven't you? |
| 7.20 | PC911: We both know you've been in trouble before – so it's likely you did exactly what our witness says.<br><br>GD: Why don't you get off my back and go and find the person that really did it. |
| 7.50 | PC911: Come on, Dickson that isn't very helpful is it? We both know it was you so it seems futile to deny it.<br><br>GD: Well if it makes you happy, so what if it was me? You should know that I always get even with people who get on the wrong side of me. |

| Tape times | PARTICULARS OF INTERVIEW |
|---|---|
| 8.20 | PC911: I think you're getting carried away again. Why don't we just finish this interview and then you can go and get some sleep? I think we both know that it's going to be better for you if you just tell me what really happened. The courts tend to come down heavy on repeat offenders you know. All I need is for you to accept that you assaulted Vincent Lamb. Do you admit you did that? |
| | GD: Yes, I suppose so. |
| | PC911: You don't mean you suppose so, do you? You mean you did it. |
| 9.10 | GD: Yes. |
| | PC911: Do you have anything further you wish to say before I terminate this interview? |
| 9.50 | GD: No. |
| 10.00 | INTERVIEW TERMINATED AT 6.40 PM |

**CHESHIRE POLICE**

**RECORD OF PREVIOUS CONVICTIONS**

THIS PRINTOUT IS PRODUCED FOR THE USE OF THE COURT, DEFENCE AND PROBATION SERVICE ONLY AND MUST NOT BE DISCLOSED TO ANY OTHER PARTY

DATA PROTECTION LEGISLATION

THESE PERSONAL DATA ARE PROVIDED TO YOU FOR THE AGREED SPECIFICATION PURPOSE(S). KEEP THE DATA SECURE AND PROTECT THEM AGAINST LOSS OR UNAUTHORISED ACCESS

COURT/DEFENCE/PROBATION PRINT

PRINT OF PNC RECORD

PRINT FOR: DEFENDANT PRINT

TOTAL NUMBER OF PAGES ATTACHED 3

PLEASE NOTE THAT IN THE ABSENCE OF FINGERPRINTS, IDENTITY CANNOT BE POSITIVELY CONFIRMED WITH THE SUBJECT OF YOUR ENQUIRY AND YOU SHOULD CONFIRM THE INFORMATION WITH THE PERSON

YOUR ATTENTION IS DRAWN TO THE PROVISIONS OF THE REHABILITATION OF OFFENDERS ACT 1974

THIS PRINTOUT IS PRODUCED FOR THE USE OF THE COURT, DEFENCE AND PROBATION SERVICE ONLY AND MUST NOT BE DISCLOSED TO ANY OTHER PARTY

YOUR ATTENTION IS DRAWN TO THE PROVISIONS OF THE REHABILITATION OF OFFENDERS ACT 1974

DATA PROTECTION LEGISLATION

THESE PERSONAL DATA ARE PROVIDED TO YOU FOR THE AGREED SPECIFICATION PURPOSE(S). KEEP THE DATA SECURE AND PROTECT THEM AGAINST LOSS OR UNAUTHORISED ACCESS

---

SURNAME : DICKSON
FORENAME(S) : GARY PAUL
BORN : 28/10/80
ADDRESS : 17 MARSH STREET
CHESTER
CH3 7LW

---

SUMMARY OF CONVICTIONS AND REPRIMANDS/WARNINGS/CAUTIONS

---

CONVICTION(S) : OFFENCE(S): 4

DATE FIRST CONVICTED: 29/11/01 DATE LAST CONVICTED: 13/12/06

2 OFFENCES AGAINST THE PERSON (2001-2006)

2 PUBLIC ORDER ACT OFFENCES (2005-2006)

1 MISCELLANEOUS OFFENCE (2006)

---

SUMMARY OF REPRIMANDS/WARNINGS/CAUTIONS

NONE

---

END OF SUMMARY OF CONVICTIONS AND REPRIMANDS/WARNINGS/CAUTIONS

---

```
                    CONVICTIONS
                    -----------

1.  29/11/01 YORK MAGISTRATES COURT

    1. COMMON ASSAULT        CONDITIONAL DISCHARGE (12 MONTHS)
       CRIMINAL JUSTICE                      COSTS £25
       ACT 1988 S 39

---------------------------------------------------------------

1.  10/09/05  CHESTER MAGISTRATES COURT

    1.  THREATENING BEHAVIOUR                     FINE £150
        PUBLIC ORDER ACT 1986 s 4                 COSTS £25

---------------------------------------------------------------

2.  17/03/06 CHESTER MAGISTRATES COURT

    1.  THREATENING BEHAVIOUR                     FINE £250
        PUBLIC ORDER ACT 1986 s 4                 COSTS £25

---------------------------------------------------------------

3.  13/12/06 CHESTER MAGISTRATES COURT

    1.   ABH                          GENERIC COMMUNITY ORDER-
         OFFENCES AGAINST THE         200 HOURS UNPAID WORK
         PERSON ACT 1861 s 47            COMPENSATION £100
                                         COSTS £50

    2.    FAILURE TO SURRENDER                    FINE £300

---------------------------------------------------------------

---------------------------------------------------------------

END OF CONVICTION REPORTS
```

## 6.7 Advising the client on plea

### 6.7.1 Matters to discuss with the client

After he has obtained details of the prosecution case, the defendant's solicitor will then need to take further instructions from his client. The following matters will have to be discussed:

(a) the client's response to the prosecution case – each prosecution witness statement needs to be discussed with the client and an accurate note taken of any points of dispute. This note should then be added to the client's statement. The solicitor should also listen to the interview tape to check that the transcript with which he has been provided is accurate. If the client made any admissions when interviewed, the solicitor needs to take instructions from his client – are the admissions correct, or did the client make admissions because of the manner in which the interview was conducted or just to get out of the police station as quickly as possible? Does the client come across well on tape (in which case, should the solicitor ask for the interview to be played out at trial rather than the transcript being read out)? Are there grounds on which an application may be made to the court to exclude the interview record from being used in evidence at trial? (See **Chapters 20** and **21**.);

(b) the strength of the prosecution case – whilst it is the client's decision as to the plea he will enter, if the prosecution case is overwhelming the solicitor should inform the client of this, and remind the client that he will be given credit for entering an early guilty plea when he is subsequently sentenced (see **Chapter 11**);

(c) whether it is necessary to obtain any further evidence in support of the defendant's case – for example, in the light of the prosecution evidence which has been disclosed, the client may recall the identity of other witnesses who could give evidence on his behalf;

(d) if the defendant has been charged with an either way offence and is pleading not guilty, whether he should elect to be tried in the magistrates' court, or before a judge and jury in the Crown Court (see **6.11** below).

The ultimate decision the client will need to take once the CPS has disclosed details of its case is what plea to enter. This is the client's decision, not the solicitor's. As mentioned in (b) above, as part of his duty to act in the best interests of his client, the solicitor should give the client his view of the strength of the evidence against him. It is also appropriate for the solicitor to advise the client that, when it comes to sentencing, the client will receive a reduced sentence for entering an early guilty plea.

### 6.7.2 Professional conduct

Occasionally a client will tell his solicitor that he is guilty of the offence but nevertheless intends to enter a not guilty plea at court. This will raise issues of professional conduct for the solicitor who, whilst under a duty to act in his client's best interests, is under an overriding duty not to mislead the court (Solicitors' Code of Conduct 2007, Rule 11.01). In such circumstances the client has two options – to plead guilty, or to plead not guilty. To comply with his duty to act in his client's best interests, the solicitor will need to advise the client of the benefits were the client to enter a guilty plea, and of the limitations on the solicitor's ability to continue representing the client were he to enter a plea of not guilty.

#### 6.7.2.1 Benefits of pleading guilty

The solicitor should advise the client that, were he to plead guilty, the client would receive credit from the court for entering an early guilty plea when the court was deciding what sentence to impose (see **Chapter 11**). Similarly, if the client enters a guilty plea, the solicitor will be able to give a plea in mitigation on the client's behalf before the client is sentenced (see **Chapter 12**).

#### 6.7.2.2 Limitations if the client pleads not guilty

If the client insists on maintaining a not guilty plea, he must be advised that the solicitor may still represent him at his trial but that the solicitor is limited in what he can do on the client's behalf because of his overriding duty not to mislead the court. At trial, the solicitor would be able to cross-examine prosecution witnesses and put the prosecution to proof of their case, since this would not involve misleading the court (although, in cross-examining the prosecution witnesses, the solicitor would need to be careful not to assert any positive defence that he knew to be false). Similarly, the solicitor would be able to make a submission of no case to answer at the end of the prosecution case and to ask the magistrates to dismiss the case, as again this would not involve misleading the court. Such a submission could be made if the prosecution failed to discharge their evidential burden to show that the defendant had a case to answer (see **9.5**).

The defendant's solicitor would, however, be unable to continue acting for the defendant if the submission of no case to answer was unsuccessful and the defendant then insisted on entering the witness box to give evidence which the solicitor knew to be false. In this situation, the defendant's solicitor could not be a party to misleading the court and would need to withdraw from the case. The solicitor would nevertheless still owe a duty of confidentiality to his client and so could not indicate to the court the reason for his withdrawal from the case (Solicitors' Code of Conduct 2007, Rules 1.04 and 4.01). A common euphemism that defence solicitors use in such situations is to tell the court that they are withdrawing from the case 'for professional reasons'.

Example

Shane is charged with theft from a shop. The evidence against him consists only of identification evidence from the owner of the shop. Shane admits his guilt to his solicitor but enters a not guilty plea, believing that he may be acquitted if the evidence given by the shop owner at court is unconvincing. Shane's solicitor is entitled to cross-examine the owner of the shop at trial to cast doubt on the credibility of the evidence he gives. For example, the shop owner may have caught only a fleeting glimpse of Shane from a long distance away, and may admit under cross-examination that he cannot be certain of the identification he has made. If the evidence given by the shop owner is unconvincing, Shane's solicitor will then be able to make a submission of no case to answer at the conclusion of the prosecution case and ask the magistrates to dismiss the case. If, however, the magistrates decline to dismiss the case and Shane then insisted on giving evidence in his own defence, his solicitor would need to withdraw from the case so as not to be a party to the court being misled. The solicitor would tell the court that he could not continue to act in the case for 'professional reasons' so as not to breach his duty of confidentiality to Shane.

## 6.8 The next hearing – entering a plea

### 6.8.1 Introduction

Once the defendant's solicitor has had the opportunity to obtain details of the prosecution case and to discuss these with his client, the court will expect the defendant to be in a position to enter his plea at the next hearing following the EAH.

### 6.8.2 Summary offences

If the offence is a summary one, the defendant will enter a plea of guilty or not guilty. If the defendant pleads guilty, the magistrates will then either sentence the defendant immediately, or adjourn the case for the preparation of reports (usually from the Probation Service) before sentencing the defendant. The magistrates may also need to adjourn the case if the defendant pleads guilty but disputes the specific factual allegations made by the CPS. In such a situation a separate hearing (called a '*Newton* hearing' – see **12.4**) will be necessary to determine the factual basis upon which the defendant will be sentenced. The sentencing procedure in the magistrates' court is described in **Chapter 12**.

If the defendant is pleading not guilty, the court will fix a date for the defendant's trial to take place and issue case management directions which both prosecution and defence must comply with before trial. Details of the directions the court will make are given in **Chapter 8**.

Whether the defendant is pleading guilty or not guilty, if the case is adjourned the magistrates will need to determine whether the defendant should be released on bail or remanded in custody prior to the next hearing (see **Chapter 7**).

### 6.8.3 Either way offences

If the offence is an either way matter, the defendant may still enter his plea as for a summary only offence. However, before going any further, the magistrates must then determine whether the defendant is to be sentenced (if he is pleading guilty) or tried (if he is pleading not guilty) in the magistrates' court, or in the Crown Court. This is known as the plea before venue and mode of trial procedure.

## 6.9 Plea before venue

The procedure that will take place when the defendant appears before the magistrates is as follows:

(a) The charge will be read out to the defendant by the court clerk/legal adviser, who will also check that the defendant's solicitor has received advance disclosure of the prosecution case.

(b) The clerk will then tell the defendant that he may indicate to the court how he would plead if the matter were to proceed to trial (the defendant is under no obligation to indicate his plea). The clerk will also tell the defendant that, if he indicates a guilty plea, he will then be treated as having pleaded guilty before the magistrates, who may then either sentence him or commit him to the Crown Court to be sentenced if they consider their own sentencing powers to be inadequate.

(c) The clerk will then ask the defendant to give his plea.

(d) If the defendant indicates a guilty plea, the CPS representative will then outline the facts of the case to the magistrates and tell the magistrates about any previous convictions the defendant may have. The defendant's solicitor will then give a plea in mitigation on the defendant's behalf. At this point the magistrates will need to determine if their sentencing powers are sufficient to deal with the case, or if the defendant should be sentenced by a Crown Court judge who has greater sentencing powers. The maximum sentence a magistrates' court may pass is six months' imprisonment for a defendant who is convicted of one either way offence, rising to a maximum of 12 months where a defendant is convicted of two or more either way offences. The magistrates will determine whether their sentencing powers are sufficient by assessing the overall seriousness of the offence, looking at the guideline sentence in the Magistrates' Court Sentencing Guidelines (see **11.4.3.2** and the **Appendix**) and considering whether there are any aggravating or mitigating factors present which make the offence either more or less serious.

(e) If the magistrates decide that their sentencing powers are sufficient, they will then either sentence the defendant straight away, or adjourn the case for reports before sentencing the defendant (the magistrates will also need to adjourn the case if they consider that a '*Newton* hearing' is necessary – see **6.8.2** above). If the case is adjourned for sentence, the defendant will be released on bail or remanded in custody prior to the sentencing hearing.

Example

Hamish is charged with theft of a necklace. At the plea before venue hearing he enters a guilty plea. The CPS representative then outlines the facts of the case to the magistrates. The magistrates hear that the necklace was worth £100 and that Hamish has returned the necklace to the police. They also hear that Hamish has no previous convictions for any kind of offence. The magistrates decide that their sentencing powers are sufficient. They will either sentence Hamish immediately, or adjourn the case for reports before sentencing Hamish.

(f) If the magistrates decide that their sentencing powers are insufficient, they will commit the defendant to Crown Court for sentence pursuant to the Powers of Criminal Courts (Sentencing) Act 2000, s 3. This section allows the magistrates to commit the defendant to Crown Court for sentence if they consider that the offence (or, if there is more than one offence, the combination of the offences) is so serious that the Crown Court should have the power to deal with the defendant as if he had been convicted at a Crown Court trial. The procedural rules which must be complied with when a defendant is committed to the Crown Court for sentence are set out in Part 43 of the Criminal Procedure Rules 2005.

Example

Danny is charged with theft of a necklace. At the plea before venue hearing he enters a guilty plea. The CPS representative then outline the facts of the case to the magistrates. The magistrates hear that the necklace was worth £10,000 and has not been recovered. They are also told that Danny has numerous previous convictions for theft. In the light of this information the magistrates decide that their sentencing powers are insufficient, and they to commit Danny to the Crown Court for sentence.

If the defendant is committed to the Crown Court for sentence, he will be remanded either in custody, or on bail. In most cases where a defendant pleads guilty at the plea before venue hearing and is committed to Crown Court for sentence, the magistrates will not alter the position as regards bail or custody. Thus when a defendant who has been on bail enters a guilty plea, the magistrates are likely to grant him bail, even if they anticipate that the defendant will receive a custodial sentence at the Crown Court. If a defendant who has been in custody enters a guilty plea at the plea before venue hearing, he is likely to remain in custody prior to the sentencing hearing at the Crown Court (*R v Rafferty* [1999] 1 Cr App R 235).

(g) If the defendant either refuses to enter a plea (as he is entitled to do) or enters a not guilty plea, a procedure called 'mode of trial' will then occur. This will conclude with the case either staying in the magistrates' court for trial, or being sent to the Crown Court for trial.

## 6.10 Mode of trial

### 6.10.1 Introduction

The mode of trial process has two stages. At the first stage, the magistrates will determine in which type of court it is more appropriate for the defendant to be tried. If the magistrates decide that the case is more suitable for a summary trial before them, the second stage will then take place. At this stage, the defendant has the option either of agreeing to his trial taking place in the magistrates' court, or of electing trial before a judge and jury at the Crown Court.

### 6.10.2 The first stage

#### 6.10.2.1 Procedure

In the first stage, the magistrates must decide whether the offence is more suitable for summary trial or committal for trial on indictment in the Crown Court.

The prosecutor will outline the facts of the case to the magistrates and indicate in which court he considers the case should be tried. The defendant's solicitor will then address the court to indicate where he considers the trial should take place. After hearing representations, the magistrates will then decide whether the case is more suitable for summary or Crown Court trial. In reaching their decision, they must take into account:

(a) the nature of the offence;

(b) whether the circumstances make the offence one of serious character;

(c) whether the punishment which the magistrates' court would have power to inflict for the offence would be adequate; and

(d) any other circumstances which appear to the court to make it more suitable for the offence to be tried at one venue rather than the other (Magistrates' Courts Act 1980, s 19(3)).

The magistrates must *not* take into account any previous convictions the defendant may have when making their decision.

#### 6.10.2.2 The mode of trial guidelines

In reaching their decision, the magistrates must consider guidelines issued in *Practice Direction (Criminal Proceedings: Consolidation)* [2002] 3 All ER 904, para 51, Mode of trial. The purpose of the guidelines is to assist magistrates to determine whether or not to commit an either way offence for trial in the Crown Court.

The guidelines make some general points and then identify certain features of specific offences which may make them unsuitable for trial by magistrates.

**General points**

The following general observations are made in the guidelines:

(a) the magistrates should assume the prosecution version of events to be correct;

(b) where cases involve complex points of law or questions of fact, committal to the Crown Court for trial should be considered;

(c) where two or more defendants are charged jointly with an offence, each has an individual right to elect his mode of trial; and

(d) the magistrates should presume that the case will be tried summarily unless one of the relevant circumstances listed below is relevant *and* the sentencing powers of the magistrates are considered to be insufficient.

**Specific offences**

The guidelines identify certain features of specific offences which may make them unsuitable for trial by the magistrates. The guidelines for some common either way offences are set out below.

*Burglary of a dwelling house*

Cases should be tried summarily unless the court considers that one or more of the following features is present in the case *and* that its sentencing powers are insufficient:

(a) entry in the daytime when the occupier (or another) is present;

(b) entry at night of a house which is normally occupied, whether or not the occupier (or another) is present;

(c) the offence is alleged to be one of a series of similar offences;

(d) when soiling, ransacking, damage or vandalism occurs;

(e) the offence has professional hallmarks;

(f) the unrecovered property is of high value (ie, over £10,000);

(g) the offence is racially motivated.

*Theft and fraud*

Cases should be tried summarily unless the court considers that one or more of the following features is present in the case *and* that its sentencing powers are insufficient:

(a) breach of trust by a person in a position of substantial authority, or in whom a high degree of trust is placed;

(b) theft or fraud which has been committed or disguised in a sophisticated manner;

(c) theft or fraud committed by an organised gang;

(d) the victim is particularly vulnerable to theft or fraud, eg the elderly or infirm;

(e) the unrecovered property is of high value (ie, over £10,000).

Guidelines

*Handling*

Cases should be tried summarily unless the court considers that one or more of the following features is present in the case *and* that its sentencing powers are insufficient:

(a) dishonest handling of stolen property by a receiver who has commissioned the theft;

(b) the offence has professional hallmarks;

(c) the property is of high value (ie, over £10,000).

*Violence (ss 20 and 47 of the Offences against the Person Act 1861)*

Cases should be tried summarily unless the court considers that one or more of the following features is present in the case *and* that its sentencing powers are insufficient:

(a) the use of a weapon of a kind likely to cause serious injury;
(b) a weapon is used and serious injury is caused;
(c) more than minor injury is caused by kicking or head-butting;
(d) serious violence is caused to those whose work has to be done in contact with the public or are likely to face violence in the course of their work;
(e) violence to vulnerable people, eg the elderly and infirm;
(f) the offence has clear racial motivation.

#### 6.10.2.3 The magistrates' decision

If the magistrates decide that the case is more suitable for trial in the Crown Court, the case will be adjourned to a later date so that a committal hearing can take place. This is the formal hearing at which the defendant is committed to stand trial at the Crown Court (see **Chapter 10**).

Example

Veronica is charged with assault occasioning actual bodily harm. At the plea before venue hearing she indicates a not guilty plea. The prosecuting solicitor and Veronica's solicitor then address the magistrates as to the more appropriate venue for trial. The magistrates hear from the prosecuting solicitor that the alleged assault was racially motivated and involved kicking to the head. The magistrates decide that their sentencing powers would be insufficient were Veronica to be convicted. Veronica's case will be adjourned to a committal hearing.

If the magistrates decide that the case is suitable for summary trial, the second stage then takes place.

### 6.10.3 The second stage

The magistrates' clerk/legal adviser will tell the defendant that has the right to elect trial in the Crown Court. The clerk will also tell the defendant that if he consents to trial before the magistrates' court and is convicted, the magistrates have the power to commit him to the Crown Court for sentence if they consider their sentencing powers to be inadequate (see **6.11.3.1** below).

The defendant will make his decision. If he consents to a summary trial, the magistrates will then fix a date for the trial to take place and issue case management directions for the parties to comply with prior to trial (see **Chapter 8**). If the defendant elects trial in the Crown Court, the case will be adjourned for a committal hearing to take place (see **6.10.2.3** above).

Example 1

Shona is charged with theft. She indicates a not guilty plea at the plea before venue hearing and, after hearing representations from the prosecuting solicitor and Shona's solicitor, the magistrates accept jurisdiction. The magistrates then explain to Shona that she may consent to summary trial, or elect trial before the Crown Court. Shona consents to summary trial. The magistrates then fix a date for Shona's trial to take place and issue case management directions for the parties to comply with prior to trial.

Example 2

Shona is charged with theft. She indicates a not guilty plea at the plea before venue hearing and, after hearing representations from the prosecuting solicitor and Shona's solicitor, the magistrates accept jurisdiction. The magistrates then explain to Shona that she may consent to summary trial, or elect trial before the Crown Court. Shona elects trial at the Crown Court. The magistrates then adjourn Shona's case so that a committal hearing can take place.

A flowchart summarising the plea before venue and mode of trial procedure is set out at **6.12** below.

### 6.10.4 Different pleas at the plea before venue hearing

Occasionally a defendant who is charged with more than one either way offence will indicate different pleas at the plea before venue hearing. He may indicate a plea of guilty to one offence, but a plea of not guilty to the other. In such circumstances the magistrates will proceed with the mode of trial hearing in respect of the offence to which the defendant has indicated a not guilty plea.

If, at the mode of trial hearing, the magistrates accept jurisdiction (and the defendant does not elect trial at the Crown Court), the magistrates will either sentence the defendant immediately for the offence to which he has pleaded guilty, or adjourn sentence until the end of the trial of the offence to which he has entered a not guilty plea.

If, at the mode of trial hearing, the magistrates decline jurisdiction (or the defendant elects trial at the Crown Court), the magistrates will commit the offence to which the defendant has entered a not guilty plea to the Crown Court for trial. In this situation, the magistrates will then have a choice as to what to do with the offence to which the defendant has pleaded guilty. They may either sentence the defendant themselves, or commit the defendant to the Crown Court for sentence.

The defendant may be committed to the Crown Court for sentence in one of two situations:

(a) if the magistrates consider that their sentencing powers in respect of the offence to which the defendant has pleaded guilty are inadequate, they will commit the defendant to Crown Court for sentence under s 3 of the Powers of Criminal Courts (Sentencing) Act 2000 (see **6.9** above); or

(b) if the magistrates consider their sentencing powers in respect of the offence to which the defendant has pleaded guilty to be adequate, the magistrates may still commit the defendant to the Crown Court for sentence if the offence is 'related' to the offence for which the defendant has been sent for trial (Powers of Criminal Courts (Sentencing) Act 2000, s 4). 'Related' offences are offences which can be tried on the same indictment (see **10.5.5**). It is common practice for the magistrates to commit 'related' offences to the Crown Court for sentence, so that all the offences the defendant is convicted of can be dealt with at the same time.

Example

Jackie is charged with theft and assault occasioning actual bodily harm. She is alleged to have stolen a watch from a market stall and then assaulted the stallholder when he attempted to chase after her. At the plea before venue hearing, Jackie pleads guilty to the theft but not guilty to the assault. The magistrates accept jurisdiction in respect of the assault charge, but Jackie elects trial at the Crown Court. The magistrates may:

- sentence Jackie themselves for the theft; or

- commit Jackie to the Crown Court to be sentenced for the theft if they consider their sentencing powers to be inadequate; or
- if they consider their sentencing powers in respect of the theft charge to be adequate, commit Jackie to the Crown Court to be sentenced for the theft because this is 'related' to the assault (as both offences arose out of the same set of factual circumstances).

## 6.11 Advising the client on trial venue

### 6.11.1 Introduction

If the magistrates consider that an either way case is suitable for summary trial, the defendant will then have a choice as to whether he wants his trial to take place in the magistrates' court or the Crown Court. The defendant's solicitor must advise him about the factors in favour of each venue.

### 6.11.2 Factors in favour of the Crown Court

#### 6.11.2.1 Greater chance of acquittal

Statistically, more defendants are acquitted following a jury trial in the Crown Court than are acquitted following a trial before a bench of magistrates or a district judges in the magistrates' court. Juries are perceived to be more sympathetic to defendants than 'case-hardened' magistrates. In particular, if the prosecution case includes evidence from police officers who often give evidence before the same magistrates' court, it is felt that a defendant will get a fairer hearing in the Crown Court where the jurors are hearing from each of the witnesses for the first time. Magistrates may be pre-disposed to favour the evidence of police officers from whom they may have heard evidence in previous cases, whereas jurors are perhaps more likely to question the testimony of police officers whose evidence is disputed by the defendant. Similarly, if the defendant has several previous convictions before the same magistrates' court, the magistrates before whom he is tried may be aware of such convictions and may be prejudiced against him.

#### 6.11.2.2 Better procedure for challenging admissibility of prosecution evidence

The procedure for deciding the admissibility of disputed prosecution evidence is better for the defendant in the Crown Court than in the magistrates' court.

In the Crown Court, when a dispute over the admissibility of a piece of prosecution evidence (such as a confession) arises, the jury will be asked to leave the courtroom and the judge will conduct a mini-trial to decide whether or not the evidence should be admitted. This mini-hearing is known as a voire dire (or a 'trial within a trial'). Only if the judge decides that the evidence is admissible will the jury ever hear about it. If the judge rules the evidence to be inadmissible, the evidence will not be placed before the jury.

Were such a situation to arise in the magistrates' court, because the magistrates are responsible for determining both matters of law and matters of fact, the magistrates themselves would need to determine whether the evidence was admissible. If the magistrates decided that a piece of prosecution evidence was inadmissible, when considering their verdict the magistrates would need to set to one side their knowledge of the existence of that piece of evidence. There is a risk that such knowledge would remain in the back of their minds and affect their decision as to the defendant's guilt or innocence.

(Although the Crown Court remains the better venue for determining the admissibility of disputed items of prosecution evidence, most magistrates' courts do now attempt to determine issues of admissibility of evidence at pre-trial hearings rather than at the hearing itself. Such hearings will take place before a different bench of magistrates from the bench who hear the trial, so there is no risk that the defendant will be prejudiced at trial by the magistrates being aware of any item of prosecution evidence which has been found to be inadmissible. Such hearings regularly take place in relation to applications to adduce bad character or hearsay evidence (see **Chapters 19** and **22**).)

#### 6.11.2.3 More time to prepare the case for trial

If the case against the defendant is complex, as the case will take longer to get to trial in the Crown Court, there will be more time to prepare the defence case. This is also relevant if there are a large number of potential witnesses for the defence who need to be interviewed.

### 6.11.3 Factors in favour of magistrates' court

#### 6.11.3.1 Limited sentencing powers

The biggest advantage in electing summary trial is the limited sentencing powers magistrates have. The maximum sentence which the magistrates may impose is six months' imprisonment (rising to 12 months when the defendant is convicted of two or more either way offences). The sentencing powers available to a Crown Court judge are much greater.

However, even if the defendant is tried before the magistrates' court, the magistrates retain the power to commit the defendant to the Crown Court for sentence if, during or after the trial, facts emerge that make the offence more serious than it appeared at the mode of trial hearing and so render the magistrates' sentencing powers inadequate (if, for example, the defendant is convicted at trial and the magistrates then find that he has numerous previous convictions for the same offence).

#### 6.11.3.2 Speed and stress

A trial in the magistrates' court takes place much sooner than a trial in the Crown Court. Cases in the magistrates' court generally get to trial within a matter of weeks, whilst in the Crown Court it can often take several months for a case to come to trial. This may be significant for a defendant who needs his case to be concluded relatively quickly, such as a defendant who has been offered employment in another part of the country or overseas. This will also be a very important consideration for a defendant who has been denied bail and is remanded in custody prior to trial.

Cases in the magistrates' court are also less stressful for defendants. The procedure in the magistrates' court is less formal than and not as intimidating as the Crown Court (for example, the judge and the barristers in the Crown Court wear wigs and gowns, whereas the magistrates and the advocates in the magistrates' court do not). This may be significant for a defendant who has never previously been charged with an offence, and who is likely to be intimidated by the greater formality of the Crown Court. This is, however, unlikely to be a significant consideration for a defendant with numerous previous convictions who is no stranger to the criminal courts.

#### 6.11.3.3 Prosecution costs

If a defendant is convicted in either the magistrates' court or the Crown Court, he is likely to be ordered to make a contribution towards the costs incurred by the CPS in bringing the case against him. Such costs are likely to be higher in the Crown Court because of the greater amount of work that goes into preparing a case for trial in the Crown Court (such as the need to instruct counsel).

#### 6.11.3.4 Defence costs

A defendant who is convicted in the Crown Court may be ordered to pay a contribution towards his solicitor's costs if his case was publicly funded. The order is called a recovery of defence costs order (RDCO). The procedure for making an RDCO is set out in Part 77 of the Criminal Procedure Rules. In making such an order, the judge must have regard to the defendant's means. This is an important consideration if a solicitor represents a defendant with substantial means. An RDCO cannot be made by a magistrates' court.

If the defendant funds his case privately, proceedings before the magistrates' court will be significantly cheaper than the Crown Court.

#### 6.11.3.5 No obligation to serve defence statement

A defendant pleading not guilty in the Crown Court is effectively obliged to serve on both the Crown Court and the prosecution a defence statement under ss 5, 6 and 6A of the Criminal Procedure and Investigations Act 1996 (see **10.8.2**). Such a statement must set out the nature of the defence, indicate any factual matters on which the defendant takes issue with the prosecution, and indicate any points of law the defendant will rely on at trial. The giving of a defence statement will put the prosecution on notice about the defence which the defendant is going to raise well in advance of the trial, and will allow the CPS time to prepare to rebut such a defence. The defendant will therefore lose any element of surprise at trial.

In the magistrates' court there is no obligation on the defendant to provide a defence statement either to the court or to the CPS. The giving of such a statement in the magistrates' court is entirely optional, and in practice is very rarely done.

## 6.12 Flowchart – plea before venue and mode of trial

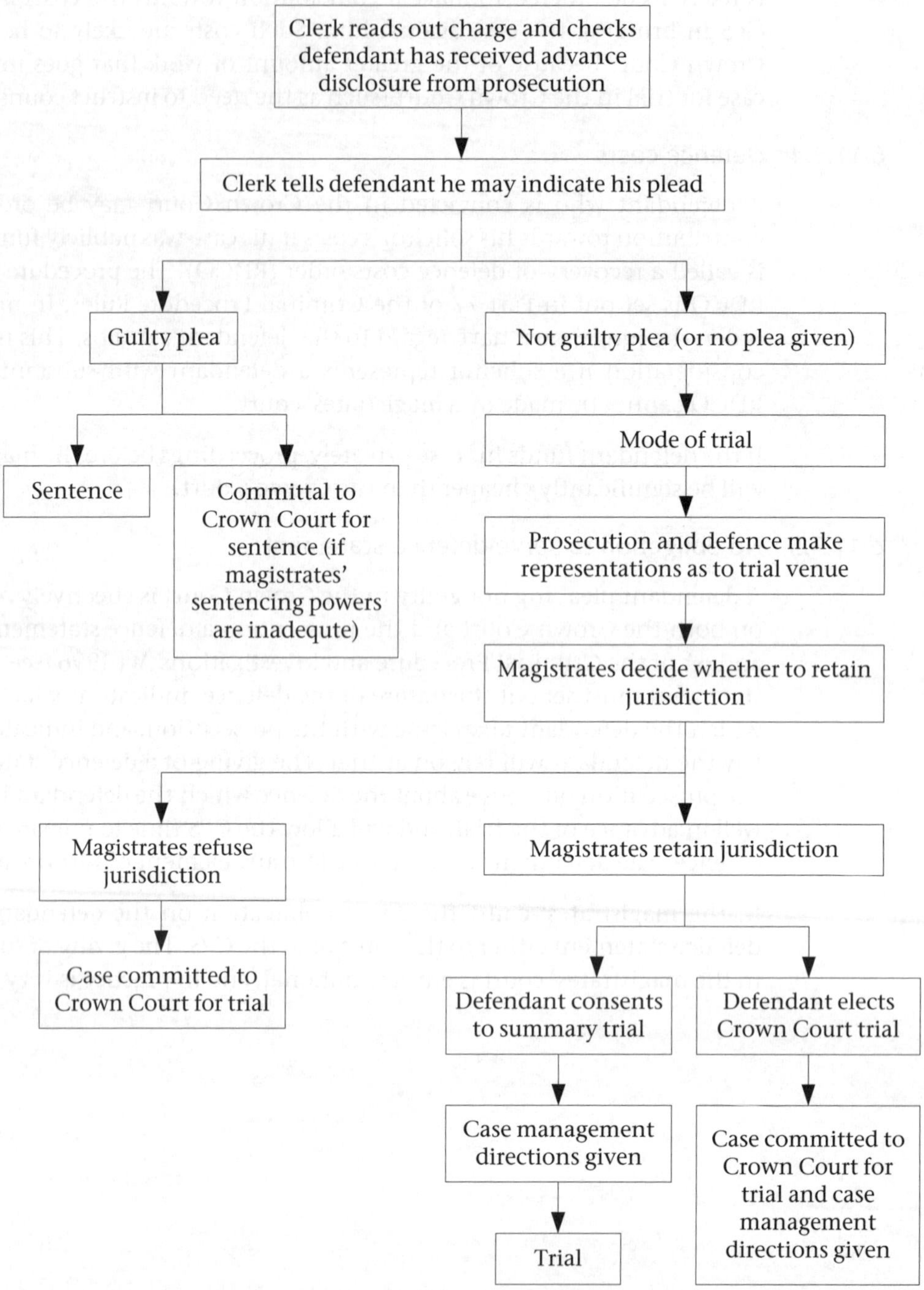

## 6.13 Checklist

At the end of this chapter you should be able to explain:

- the matters which will be dealt with at an EFH, an EAH and a remand hearing;
- the role played by the defendant's solicitor at the above hearings;
- the forms of public funding available to a defendant in a criminal case;
- how to complete an application for a representation order;
- how to take a statement from a client;
- the obligations on the CPS to make disclosure to the defendant's solicitor of the details of the case against a defendant charged with a summary or either way offence;
- the matters to be taken into account when the defendant's solicitor advises his client on the plea to be entered;
- the procedure which is followed at the plea before venue and mode of trial hearings;
- the matters to be taken into account by the defendant's solicitor when advising his client whether to elect trial in the Crown Court.

# Chapter 7

# Bail



## 7.1 Introduction

It is rare for a criminal case to be completed on the first occasion on which the defendant appears before the magistrates' court. This is likely to happen only in the case of a straightforward summary offence where the defendant pleads guilty at the early first hearing and the magistrates sentence him immediately (see **6.2.2.2**). In any other type of case there will need to be one or more adjournments before the case is concluded. Common reasons for cases needing to be adjourned are:

(a) for the CPS to provide the defendant's solicitor with details of the case against the defendant prior to the defendant entering his plea (see **Chapter 6**);

(b) for the CPS and the defendant's solicitor to comply with case management directions given by the court after the defendant has entered a not guilty plea and prior to the defendant's trial taking place (see **Chapter 8**);

(c) for a hearing date to take place at the Crown Court if the magistrates have declined jurisdiction in an either way matter, or have sent an indictable only case to the Crown Court for trial (see **Chapter 10**); and

(d) for the court to obtain reports on the defendant before passing sentence (see **Chapter 12**).

This chapter will look at the ways in which a magistrates' court may adjourn a case and the time limits that apply when a case is adjourned. It will then go on to examine a defendant's right to be granted bail when his case is adjourned and the grounds on which the court may refuse bail. The chapter will explain the types of condition which the magistrates may impose on a bail which has been granted to a defendant, and will consider the options open to a defendant who is refused bail by the magistrates. It will also examine the consequences for a defendant who either breaches conditions imposed on his bail, or fails to attend court to answer bail.

## 7.2 Remand periods

### 7.2.1 What is a remand?

When a case is adjourned by the magistrates (or by a judge in the Crown Court) the defendant will be remanded. A 'remand' is an adjournment where the court attempts to ensure the defendant will attend the next hearing. A defendant may be remanded in one of three ways:

(a) a remand in custody;

(b) a remand on bail with conditions attached to that bail; or

(c) a remand on unconditional bail.

### 7.2.2 Remands prior to conviction

#### 7.2.2.1 Remands in custody

**The basic rule**

The basic rule is that a defendant may not be remanded in custody for more than eight clear days at a time. However, where there are successive remands in custody, the defendant need be brought before the court only on every fourth remand, provided he has consented to this and has legal representation. In addition, the court may remand a defendant in custody for up to 28 days if:

(a) it has previously remanded him in custody for the same offence; and

(b) he is before the court; and

(c) it can set a date to remand him to on which it expects the next stage of the proceedings to take place.

Example

Abdul is charged with theft. He is refused bail by the police and appears before the magistrates' court in custody on 2 April. Abdul's solicitor makes an application for bail which is refused. Abdul is remanded in custody by the magistrates for seven days and so appears before the court again on 9 April. At the hearing on 9 April the prosecution confirm that they will shortly be in a position to serve advance disclosure on Abdul's solicitor. The magistrates refuse bail again and remand Abdul in custody for 28 days until 7 May when the plea before venue hearing will take place. The magistrates are able to do this because Abdul is before the court, he has previously been remanded in custody, and the next stage of proceedings (plea before venue) can take place at the next hearing. (In practice, the hearing on 9 April will usually be conducted by live video link with the prison or remand centre where Abdul is being held, rather than Abdul being brought to court.)

**Custody time limits**

Time limits exist to ensure that defendants who are remanded in custody have their cases brought promptly to trial (the Prosecution of Offences (Custody Time Limits) Regulations 1987 (SI 1987/299)). The overall maximum period of remand in custody (normally referred to as the custody time limit) in the magistrates' court is 70 days before trial for an either way offence and 56 days before trial for a summary only offence. However, if the case involves an either way offence and the mode of trial hearing takes place within 56 days, the custody time limit for the either way offence is reduced to 56 days.

The prosecution may apply to the court to extend the custody time limit, although for an application to be successful the prosecution will need to show on the balance of probabilities that there is good and sufficient cause to do this and that it has acted with due diligence and expedition (Prosecution of Offences Act 1985, s 22). The application may be made orally, although a written notice of intention must be served on the defendant not less than two days before the hearing. Unless the prosecution make a successful application to extend the custody time limit, once the time limit has expired the defendant must be released on bail until his trial. If the magistrates grant a prosecution application to extend the custody time limit, the defendant has a right of appeal to the Crown Court. Similarly, the prosecution may appeal to the Crown Court against the magistrates' refusal to extend the custody time limit. The relevant procedural rules that must be complied with when an appeal is made are contained in Part 20 of the Criminal Procedure Rules 2005. The custody time limits which apply to cases in the Crown Court are detailed in **Chapter 10**.

**Where will the defendant be kept whilst in custody?**

Defendants who are remanded in custody will normally be kept at a prison or remand centre. However, s 128(7) of the Magistrates' Courts Act 1980 allows a magistrates' court to remand a defendant to police custody for up to three days if this is necessary for the purposes of making enquiries in relation to offences other than the offence for which the defendant had been charged. The CPS is likely to apply for such a remand when a defendant has been arrested and charged for one offence but the police suspect his involvement in other matters about which they wish to interview him. A defendant made subject to such a remand must be brought back before the magistrates as soon as the need to make enquiries has ceased. Whilst he is at the police station, the defendant is entitled to the same rights as if he had been arrested and detained prior to charge (for example, the right to free legal advice; see **3.4** above).

#### 7.2.2.2 Remands on bail

A defendant who is on bail can be remanded prior to conviction for any period of time, subject to his consent.

### 7.2.3 Remands after conviction

Following conviction a defendant may be remanded in custody prior to sentence (usually for the preparation of pre-sentence reports) for successive periods of not more than three weeks. If the defendant is remanded on bail this may be for successive periods of not more than four weeks.

### 7.2.4 Remands after case committed or sent to Crown Court

A defendant who is committed to the Crown Court for sentence (see **6.9**), or whose case is sent or committed to the Crown Court for trial (see **Chapter 10**), may be remanded in custody or on bail until the case comes before the Crown Court.

## 7.3 The right to bail

Whenever a case is adjourned the magistrates (or judge) must then consider whether to remand the defendant in custody, or to remand the defendant on bail (with or without conditions).

The substantive law concerning the grant or refusal of bail is contained predominantly in the Bail Act 1976. The procedural rules which are relevant to the issue of bail are found in Parts 18 to 21 of the Criminal Procedure Rules 2005.

Under s 4 of the Bail Act 1976, there is a presumption that bail will be granted to the following types of defendants (unless one or more exceptions apply):

(a) all defendants prior to conviction;
(b) defendants who have been convicted if their case has been adjourned for the court to obtain reports before sentencing (see **Chapter 12**); and
(c) defendants who are appearing before the court for breach of a community sentence (see **Chapter 11**).

The presumption in favour of bail does not apply to defendants:

(a) who have been committed to the Crown Court for sentence by the magistrates (see **6.9** above); or
(b) who are appealing against conviction or sentence (see **Chapter 13**).

The only other limitation on the presumption that bail will be granted is in respect of defendants charged with the most serious types of offence. Under s 25 of the Criminal Justice and Public Order Act 1994, if the defendant is charged with one of a number of specified offences and has previously been convicted of any of these offences (not necessarily the same offence as he is currently charged with), a court can grant bail to that defendant only if exceptional circumstances exist. The specified offences are:

(a) murder;
(b) attempted murder;
(c) manslaughter;
(d) rape;
(e) attempted rape;
(f) a number of other serious sexual offences.

## 7.4 Exceptions to the right to bail

### 7.4.1 Imprisonable offences

The exceptions to the presumption in favour of bail for defendants who are charged with imprisonable offences are set out in paras 2 to 7 of Sch 1, Pt 1 to the Bail Act 1976:

> 2.—(1) The defendant need not be granted bail if the court is satisfied that there are substantial grounds for believing that the defendant, if released on bail (whether subject to conditions or not) would—
> (a) fail to surrender to custody, or
> (b) commit an offence while on bail, or
> (c) interfere with witnesses or otherwise obstruct the course of justice, whether in relation to himself or any other person.
>
> 2A.—(1) If the defendant falls within this paragraph he may not be granted bail unless the court is satisfied that there is no significant risk of his committing an offence while on bail (whether subject to conditions or not).
> (2) The defendant falls within this paragraph if—
> (a) he is aged 18 or over, and
> (b) it appears to the court that he was on bail in criminal proceedings on the date of the offence.
>
> 3. The defendant need not be granted bail if the court is satisfied that the defendant should be kept in custody for his own protection or, if he is a child or young person, for his own welfare.

4. The defendant need not be granted bail if he is in custody in pursuance of the sentence of a court or of any authority acting under any of the Service Acts.

5. The defendant need not be granted bail where the court is satisfied that it has not been practicable to obtain sufficient information for the purpose of taking the decisions required by this Part of the Schedule for want of time since the institution of proceedings against him.

6.—(1) If the defendant falls within this paragraph, he may not be granted bail unless the court is satisfied that there is no significant risk that, if released on bail (whether subject to conditions or not), he would fail to surrender to custody.

(2) Subject to sub-paragraph (3) below, the defendant falls within this paragraph if—

(a) he is aged 18 or over, and

(b) it appears to the court that, having been released on bail or in connection with the proceedings for the offence, he failed to surrender to custody.

(3) Where it appears to the court that the defendant has reasonable cause for his failure to surrender to custody, he does not fall within this paragraph unless it also appears to the court that he failed to surrender to custody at the appointed place as soon as reasonably practicable after the appointed time.

(4) For the purpose of sub-paragraph (3) above, a failure to give to the defendant a copy of the record of the decision to grant him bail shall not constitute a reasonable cause for his failure to surrender to custody.

7. Where his case is adjourned for inquiries or a report, the defendant need not be granted bail if it appears to the court that it would be impracticable to complete the inquiries or make the report without keeping the defendant in custody.

[Paragraphs 2A and 6 above apply only when the defendant is charged with an offence that carries a possible sentence of life imprisonment.]

The most common ground upon which the CPS normally objects to bail being granted to a defendant is that set out in para 2 above, namely that there are *substantial grounds* for believing that the defendant will, if released on bail:

(a) fail to surrender to custody;

(b) commit an offence whilst on bail; or

(c) interfere with a witness in the case (or otherwise obstruct the course of justice).

In deciding whether any of these *grounds* are satisfied, the court must take into account the following *factors*:

(a) the nature and seriousness of the offence (and the probable sentence the defendant will receive for it);

(b) the character, antecedents, associations and community ties of the defendant;

(c) the defendant's record in respect of previous grants of bail in criminal proceedings; and

(d) the strength of the evidence against the defendant (Bail Act 1976, Sch 1, Pt 1, para 9).

Each of these factors will be examined in turn.

#### 7.4.1.1 The nature and seriousness of the offence and the probable method of dealing with the defendant for it

This factor is most likely to be relevant to a prosecution argument that there are substantial grounds for believing that the defendant would fail to surrender to custody if he were to be granted bail. If the defendant has been charged with a serious offence that is likely to result in a prison sentence if he is convicted, the CPS may argue that the defendant will fail to surrender to custody (usually referred to as absconding – see **7.9** below) to avoid such a fate.

**Example**

Neil pleads not guilty to a charge of wounding with intent. The prosecution allege that Neil attacked his victim with a hammer in an unprovoked assault, causing the victim to suffer head injuries from which he will never fully recover. This is a serious offence and, if convicted, Neil will receive a lengthy prison sentence. The prosecution will argue that Neil should be denied bail as there are substantial grounds for believing that, if granted bail, Neil will fail to surrender to custody. The factor they will rely on to support this is that if Neil is convicted, the court will deal with the matter by way of a custodial sentence, and Neil will abscond to avoid being sent to prison.

This can be a difficult argument for the defence to counter. If the defendant's solicitor considers that the offence is not as serious as the prosecution suggest (and so will not inevitably result in a custodial sentence were the defendant to be convicted), this should be pointed out to the court. To assess whether the defendant is likely to receive a custodial sentence if convicted, the defendant's solicitor will need to check the guideline sentence in the Magistrates' Court Sentencing Guidelines (see **11.4.2.2**) or, for more serious offences, either any definitive sentencing guidelines issued by the Sentencing Guidelines Council (SGC) or the case compendium of guideline sentences given by the Court of Appeal, both of which may be found at www.sentencing-guidelines.gov.uk (although a defendant charged with an indictable-only offence will almost certainly receive a custodial sentence if convicted). He will also need to consider whether the guideline sentence is likely to be affected by the presence of any aggravating or mitigating factors.

**Example**

Nicola is charged with theft of a bracelet (worth £50) from a shop. The allegation is that, after paying for some other goods which she had purchased, as she was leaving the shop Nicola grabbed the bracelet and ran. Nicola denies the charge. She has several previous convictions for shoplifting offences. The prosecution oppose bail on the ground that there are substantial grounds for believing that Nicola will abscond if granted bail. The prosecution argue that, because of her previous convictions, Nicola is likely to receive a custodial sentence if convicted and so will abscond to avoid this possibility. Nicola's solicitor will argue that the offence will not merit a custodial sentence. The item stolen was not of high value, the offence does not appear to have been planned and is not in any way sophisticated, and the alleged victim is not 'vulnerable'.

Often, however, the best response to an argument concerning the seriousness of the offence is to acknowledge that the offence is serious but to go on to say that the defendant is pleading not guilty and is anxious to attend court to ensure that he is acquitted and his name cleared. The defendant's solicitor may also say that the very seriousness of the offence will make it more likely that his client will answer his bail, because the defendant will not want to make matters any worse for himself by not turning up at court.

A defendant who has been convicted but whose case is adjourned for reports has a prima facie right to bail (see **7.3** above). A defendant who is convicted of a serious offence and whose case is adjourned for reports is likely to be refused bail, however, if the court considers that there are substantial grounds to believe that the defendant will abscond to avoid a probable custodial sentence.

#### 7.4.1.2 The defendant's character, antecedents, associations and community ties

**Character and antecedents**

The reference to a defendant's character and antecedents is a reference to the defendant's previous convictions. A defendant's criminal record may be raised by the CPS when bail is being considered, to suggest that there are substantial grounds for believing that the defendant will commit further offences if he is released on bail. This is likely to be relevant if the defendant has a history of committing the same (or similar) types of offence as that with which he has been charged. It will also be an argument raised by the prosecution if the reason for the defendant's previous offending is ongoing (such as a serial shoplifter who steals to fund a drug addiction), or if the defendant has previously committed offences whilst on bail for other matters.

Example 1

Dawn pleads not guilty to a charge of shoplifting. Dawn has 10 previous convictions for the same type of offence within the preceding three years. Dawn's previous offences were committed to obtain money to support her heroin addiction (which is ongoing). The CPS will argue that Dawn should be denied bail as there are substantial grounds for believing that, if granted bail, Dawn will commit further offences. The factor it will rely to support this is that Dawn's character and antecedents indicate that she commits this type of offence on a regular basis to support her ongoing drug addiction.

Example 2

Adam pleads not guilty to a charge of theft. Adam's list of previous convictions reveals that he has twice been convicted of other property-related offences which were committed whilst he was on bail for other matters. The CPS will argue that Adam should be denied bail as there are substantial grounds for believing that, if released on bail, Adam will commit further offences. The factor it will rely on to support this is that Adam's previous convictions show a history of offending whilst on bail.

If a defendant has several previous convictions for the type of offence with which he is currently charged, unless the last of these convictions was relatively recent, his solicitor may suggest to the court that there are not 'substantial grounds' for believing that the defendant will commit further offences if released on bail. Similarly, if the CPS suggests that the defendant offends for a particular reason, his solicitor may argue that there is no longer any need for such offending because the defendant's circumstances have changed (if, for example, the defendant stole previously to fund a drug addiction, but that addiction has been successfully treated, or if the defendant stole to raise money because he was unemployed but has now gained employment). Another argument which the defendant's solicitor can raise is that, although the defendant may have extensive previous convictions, the defendant is pleading not guilty to the current offence and so does not accept that he has offended on this occasion. If a defendant has several previous convictions but has never previously been convicted of committing an offence whilst on bail, this may be used to suggest that 'substantial grounds' do not exist for believing that the defendant will commit further offences if released on bail.

The prosecution may also rely on this factor to support an allegation that there are substantial grounds for believing that the defendant will fail to surrender to custody if released on bail, particularly if the evidence against the defendant is strong. If the defendant is convicted of the offence with which he is currently charged, when he comes to be sentenced the court will treat any previous convictions he has as aggravating factors, particularly if the previous convictions are for offences committed recently or are for similar types of offence (Criminal Justice Act 2003, s 143(2)). The presence of any aggravating factors will result in a defendant receiving a greater sentence. This may be particularly significant if the defendant's previous convictions might lead a court to consider imposing a custodial sentence when otherwise it would not have done so. The CPS will argue that in such a case the defendant may abscond rather than run the risk of imprisonment. This will also be a strong argument if the defendant is currently subject to a suspended sentence of imprisonment which is likely to be 'activated' if the defendant is convicted of the current offence (see **11.5.6.4**). It will also be an argument the prosecution will raise if the defendant is currently subject to a conditional discharge. If he is convicted of the current offence, the court may revoke the conditional discharge and impose a sentence for the original offence (see **11.8**).

Example

Morgan pleads not guilty to a charge of assault occasioning actual bodily harm. Six months previously, Morgan was convicted of unlawful wounding and received a sentence of 12 months' imprisonment, suspended for two years. The evidence against Morgan in respect of the current charge is strong, consisting of good quality identification evidence and a confession Morgan is alleged to have made when first arrested. The CPS will argue that Morgan should be denied bail as there are substantial grounds for believing that, if released on bail, Morgan would fail to surrender to custody. The factor it will rely on to support this is that Morgan's antecedents show he is subject to a suspended sentence of imprisonment which is likely to be activated if Morgan is convicted of the current offence. Morgan is likely to be convicted because of the strength of the evidence against him.

If a defendant's antecedents show that he has a history of failing to respond to court orders (for example, a defendant who has previously breached the requirements of a community order), the CPS may use this to argue that there are substantial grounds for believing that, if released on bail, the defendant will fail to surrender. The CPS will argue that if the defendant has failed to respond to court orders in the past, he will fail to answer to a court order granting him bail until the next hearing for the current offence.

### Associations

The reference to the defendant's associations may be relevant to a prosecution argument that, if released on bail, there are substantial grounds for believing that the defendant will commit further offences, abscond or interfere with witnesses.

If a defendant is known to associate with other criminals, or is alleged to be a member of a criminal gang, the CPS may use this to suggest there are 'substantial grounds' to believe that he may commit further offences if released on bail. Similarly, if the defendant is known to have criminal connections either abroad or in other parts of the country, the CPS may suggest that the defendant will use these connections to enable him to leave the area and will thus fail to surrender to custody.

The CPS may also suggest that a defendant's associations are relevant if a witness is known to the defendant and there is a fear that the defendant may attempt to interfere with the witness. This often arises in the case of domestic assaults when the victim is a relative of the defendant and there is a fear that the defendant may put pressure on the victim to 'change his story'. To counter this argument, the defence will normally suggest that appropriate conditions be imposed on any bail granted to the defendant to prevent the defendant from contacting the witness or victim (see 7.5 below).

**Example 1**

James pleads not guilty to a charge of armed robbery of a bank. The CPS alleges that James is a member of criminal gang responsible for several similar armed robberies. None of the other members of the gang has as yet been identified or arrested by the police, and none of the proceeds from the bank robberies have been recovered. The CPS will argue that James should be denied bail as there are substantial grounds for believing that, if released on bail, James would commit further offences. The factor it will rely on is that James's associations include membership of a gang responsible for a series of armed robberies, the other members of which are still at large.

**Example 2**

Nigel pleads not guilty to a charge of indecent assault. The CPS alleges that Nigel indecently assaulted his 11-year-old daughter (who lives at the same address as Nigel). In her statement to the police, Nigel's daughter has said that Nigel has threatened to 'shut her up' unless she changes her story. The CPS will argue that Nigel should be denied bail on the basis that there are substantial grounds for believing that, if granted bail, Nigel will attempt to interfere with a witness. The factor it will rely on to support this is that Nigel is closely associated with his alleged victim. Nigel and his victim share the same home, and the victim has already indicated that he has attempted to persuade her to change her story.

### Community ties

The strength or otherwise of a defendant's community ties will be relevant to an argument that there are substantial grounds for believing that the defendant will fail to surrender to custody if released on bail. If, for example, the defendant is unemployed, has no relatives in the local area, has lived in area only for a short time or is of no fixed abode, the CPS may argue that there is nothing to keep him in the area and nothing to prevent him from absconding. From the opposite point of view, if the defendant is in employment (or at least has a written offer of employment), has family in the area, has lived in the area for a long time or owns a property in the locality, the defendant's solicitor may argue that the defendant has every reason to stay in the area and so will not abscond.

**Example**

Naveed pleads not guilty to a charge of possession of Class A drugs. Naveed is unemployed and lives alone in bedsit accommodation. Naveed has no family or known friends in the local area, and most of his relatives are known to live some 200 miles away. Naveed moved to the area only some three months ago. The CPS will argue that Naveed should be denied bail as there are substantial grounds for believing that, if granted bail, Naveed will fail to surrender to custody. The factor it will rely on to support this is Naveed's lack of community ties, because Naveed appears to have nothing to tie him to the local area.

#### 7.4.1.3 The defendant's record in relation to previous grants of bail

If a defendant has previous convictions, it is almost certain that at some stage he will have been granted bail by the court whilst being dealt with for these previous offences. If his criminal record discloses that he has a conviction for the offence of absconding (ie, failing to answer his bail – see **7.9** below), the CPS is likely to raise this to suggest there are substantial grounds for believing that the defendant will fail to surrender if he is granted bail in the current proceedings. If such an argument is raised by the CPS, the circumstances of the absconding need to be investigated further by the defendant's solicitor to see if there is some explanation for the absconding: Did the defendant purposely fail to attend court, or was there simply a mix up over the date of the hearing? Was the defendant arrested for breaching his bail, or did he voluntarily surrender himself to custody? If the defendant has been convicted of absconding, the way in which the court sentenced him for this offence may be relevant. If, for example, the court imposed no separate penalty for the offence, or if the defendant received a further grant of bail in the substantive proceedings, this would suggest that the court did not view the absconding as being particularly serious.

A defendant with an extensive criminal record who has no convictions for absconding is in a strong position to argue that there are not substantial grounds for believing that he will fail to answer his bail. Such a defendant will have been granted bail many times previously, and the absence of any convictions for absconding will show that the defendant has always answered his bail in the past. This is a particularly strong argument for a defendant who has previously answered bail for an offence for which he was subsequently imprisoned.

**Example 1**

Jack pleads not guilty to a charge of affray. Jack has three previous convictions for failing to answer bail in relation to other public order offences with which he was charged. The CPS will argue that Jack should be denied bail as there are substantial grounds for believing that, if granted bail, Jack will fail to surrender to custody. The factor it will rely upon to support this is that Jack's record in relation to previous grants of bail shows that he has a history of failing to answer his bail.

**Example 2**

Janine pleads not guilty to a charge of theft. Janine has numerous previous convictions for theft and other property-related offences. Janine has no previous convictions for absconding. The CPS is unlikely to be able to establish that there are substantial grounds for believing that, if granted bail, Janine would fail to surrender to custody. The fact that Janine has appeared before the courts (and presumably been granted bail) on a regular basis, but has no previous convictions for absconding, shows that Janine always answers her bail.

#### 7.4.1.4 The strength of the evidence

If the CPS considers the evidence against the defendant to be strong (for example, good quality identification evidence from an eye-witness, or a confession made by the defendant when interviewed by the police), it may use this to argue that if released on bail there are substantial grounds for believing that the defendant would fail to surrender to custody. Such an argument is often combined with an argument that the offence is serious and will result in a custodial sentence if the defendant is convicted.

#### Example

Vivian pleads not guilty to a charge of unlawful wounding. The CPS alleges that he struck his victim in the face with a broken bottle, causing the victim to suffer a severe laceration needing 15 stitches. There were numerous witnesses to the incident who will say that Vivian launched an unprovoked attack, and when interviewed at the police station, Vivian made several admissions. The CPS will argue that Vivian should be denied bail as there are substantial grounds for believing that, if granted bail, Vivian will fail to surrender to custody. The factors it will rely to support this are that the seriousness of the offence means that Vivian will receive a prison sentence if convicted and, given the strength of the evidence against Vivian, a conviction is likely.

The defendant's solicitor will often try to counter this by arguing that the evidence is not as strong as the prosecution have suggested. He may, for example, argue that identification evidence on which the prosecution are relying is disputed (and that the quality of such evidence is poor), or that there will be a challenge to the admissibility of the confession evidence on which the CPS seeks to rely. The defendant's solicitor may also say that the defendant has an innocent explanation for a piece of evidence on which the CPS seeks to rely (such as the defendant's fingerprints being found on an item of stolen property).

#### Example

Sharon is charged with theft of items of clothing from a shop. She denies the charge, claiming that she was elsewhere at the time of the theft. Sharon has extensive previous convictions and the CPS opposes bail, arguing that there are substantial grounds for believing that Sharon will abscond because, if convicted, she is likely to face a custodial sentence as a result of her previous record. The CPS argues that Sharon is likely to be convicted because the evidence against her is strong. The evidence against Sharon consists of identification evidence from a store detective, who claims to recognise Sharon as the person he saw running from the shop after committing the theft. Sharon's solicitor will challenge the alleged strength of such evidence by suggesting that it is weak and unlikely to result in a conviction. He will argue that that the store detective got only a brief glimpse of the thief, that the store detective did not see the thief's face, and that his description of the thief does not match Sharon's appearance. He will argue that Sharon is unlikely to be convicted on the basis of such evidence.

### 7.4.2 Non-imprisonable offences

It is extremely rare for a defendant charged with a non-imprisonable offence not to be granted bail, as there are only very limited circumstances in which the CPS would ever oppose the grant of bail to such a defendant. Under Sch 1, Pt 2 to the Bail Act 1976, the court may refuse bail to a defendant charged with a non-imprisonable offence only if:

(a) the defendant was granted bail in previous criminal proceedings but failed to answer this bail and the court believes that, if granted bail in the current proceedings, the defendant would again fail to surrender to custody;

(b) the defendant needs to be kept in custody for his own protection or, in the case of a defendant under 18 years of age, for his own welfare;

(c) the defendant is currently serving a custodial sentence in respect of a separate offence; or

(d) the defendant was granted bail at an earlier hearing in the same proceedings, but has been arrested either for failing to answer his bail or for breaking any conditions of his bail, and the court is satisfied that there are substantial grounds for believing that, if released on bail, the defendant would fail to surrender to custody, commit an offence or interfere with witnesses or otherwise obstruct the course of justice

## 7.5 Conditional bail

A court has the power to grant bail to a defendant subject to the defendant complying with one or more conditions that the court attaches to that bail. The conditions must be necessary to:

(a) prevent the defendant from absconding;

(b) prevent the defendant committing a further offence whilst on bail;

(c) prevent the defendant interfering with witnesses or obstructing the course of justice;

(d) ensure that the defendant makes himself available for the purpose of obtaining medical or other reports;

(e) ensure that the defendant keeps an appointment with his solicitor; or

(f) ensure the defendant's own protection or, in the case of a defendant aged under 18, for his own welfare or in his own interests (Bail Act 1976, s 3(6)).

When he is making an application for bail on behalf of his client, the defendant's solicitor will normally invite the magistrates to consider granting conditional bail to his client if the magistrates are not minded to grant bail on an unconditional basis. The most common conditions that the court may impose are described at **7.5.1 to 7.5.8** below.

### 7.5.1 Sureties

A surety may be used to ensure that a defendant answers his bail. A surety is a person who enters into what is termed a 'recognisance' of money and is under an obligation to use every reasonable effort to ensure that the defendant attends court. The surety will be required to appear before the court at the bail hearing to confirm his willingness to be a surety, although he will not be required to pay over any money at this stage.

If the defendant fails to answer his bail at the next hearing, the court must declare the immediate and automatic forfeiture of the recognisance. The court will order the surety to appear before the court to explain why he should not pay over the sum. The court will then determine whether some or all of the surety should be paid.

Before accepting a proposed surety, the court will want to ensure that the person who is proposed as the surety is suitable. The surety will be required to give evidence to the court about his financial resources, his character and any previous convictions he has, and his relationship to the defendant. As the surety is meant to ensure that the defendant attends the next hearing, the court will also want to find out how close the surety lives to the defendant and how regularly the surety sees the defendant.

A court is unlikely to accept as a surety a person who has a criminal record, who lives a long distance from the defendant or who has no financial means. As a matter of professional conduct, a solicitor should never stand surety for a defendant.

### 7.5.2 Security

A security may be required by the court to ensure that the defendant answers his bail. If the court orders a security, the defendant will be required to deposit a sum of money (or goods) with the court. If the defendant fails to attend court to answer his bail, he will forfeit the security he has given. A security can be used only for defendants of substantial financial means.

### 7.5.3 Reporting to a police station

This is another condition which may be used to ensure that the defendant will not abscond. The court may order the defendant to report to his local police station on a regular basis (often once each day at a specified time) so that the police may ensure that the defendant remains in the local area.

### 7.5.4 Residence

This is a common condition which the courts use to ensure that defendants will not abscond. If such a condition is imposed, the court will require the defendant to reside at a specified address. The police will often check that such a condition is being complied with by visiting the address late at night or early in the morning to check that the defendant is there.

If a defendant does not have a permanent address, the court may impose a condition of residence in a bail hostel run by the Probation Service (if a place is available). This can also be useful if the circumstances of the case mean that a defendant cannot reside at his normal home address. The most common example of this is when there is an allegation of a domestic assault where the defendant and his alleged victim reside in the same property.

To support a condition of residence, the court may order that the defendant be electronically monitored (commonly referred to as 'tagging').

### 7.5.5 Curfew

This condition may be used to prevent a defendant committing further offences whilst on bail. The court can require a defendant to remain at his place of residence between certain specified hours (for example, between 8 pm and 7 am). As with a condition of residence, the police may visit the residence during these hours to check that the defendant is there. A curfew is often used for a defendant with a history of night-time offending. To support a curfew, the court may order that the defendant be electronically monitored.

### 7.5.6 Non-communication with prosecution witnesses

This condition may be used to prevent a defendant interfering with prosecution witnesses if the court is concerned that the defendant may try to intimidate a witness. The condition can cover not only face-to-face contact with the witnesses, but also contacting the witnesses by telephone or in writing. If a witness resides in the same property as the defendant, the defendant will need to secure alternative accommodation (see **7.5.4** above). This condition may also be used when the defendant is charged with a violence offence and the court is concerned he may commit further offences of violence against the complainant.

### 7.5.7 Restriction on entering specified areas

This condition can be use either to prevent the defendant interfering with prosecution witnesses, or to prevent the defendant committing further offences whilst on bail. A condition may be imposed preventing the defendant from entering the geographical area or town where a prosecution witness resides. Such a condition may also be used where the defendant habitually commits offences in the same place or type of place. For example, a defendant with a history of committing thefts at a certain shopping centre may be prohibited from entering that shopping centre or a defendant with a history of committing serious assaults in a city centre may be prohibited from entering that city centre.

### 7.5.8 Attending appointments with his solicitor or the Probation Service

A common condition which magistrates impose is to require a defendant to keep in regular touch with his solicitor and to attend meetings with his solicitor as and when required. The purpose behind such a condition is to ensure that the case is not delayed because the defendant has failed to provide his solicitor with prompt instructions.

Similarly, if following conviction the magistrates want to obtain a pre-sentence report from the Probation Service or a medical report on the defendant before passing sentence, a condition will be imposed requiring the defendant to attend such meetings or appointments as are necessary for the preparation of such reports. This is designed to ensure that cases are not delayed because a defendant has failed to keep an appointment.

### 7.5.9 Surrender of passport

If the court is concerned that the defendant may attempt to abscond, a condition may be imposed requiring the defendant to surrender his passport. This condition is only likely to be appropriate in serious cases where the defendant is known to have substantial financial assets or criminal contacts outside the UK.

## 7.6 Procedure for applying for bail

If the CPS objects to bail being granted, the following procedure will take place at court:

(a) The CPS representative will apply to the magistrates for the defendant to be remanded in custody. He will give the magistrates a list of the defendant's previous convictions and then outline the *grounds* on which the prosecution object to bail being granted. He will support these grounds by citing the relevant details of the case and applying the *factors* referred to at 7.4.1 above. (If the defendant is applying for bail *after* he has been convicted but prior to sentence, the prosecution plays no part in the bail procedure, other than to answer any questions asked by the magistrates. The CPS representative will therefore not make any representations as to the grant or refusal of bail.)

(b) The defendant's solicitor will then make an application for bail on his client's behalf. He will take each of the prosecution *grounds* for objecting to bail in turn and respond to these, applying, where appropriate, the same *factors*. The defendant's solicitor should ask the magistrates to grant his client unconditional bail, but should also suggest appropriate conditions, which the magistrates may impose if they are not prepared to grant unconditional bail.

(c) The magistrates may hear evidence from other persons in support of the defendant's application for bail, such as a prospective employer if the defendant has recently been offered employment, or a person who is prepared to provide the defendant with accommodation if the defendant is currently of no fixed abode.

(d) The magistrates will then decide whether to remand the defendant in custody or on bail. If the magistrates grant bail to the defendant, they will specify any conditions on that bail which they consider necessary. If bail is granted subject to a surety, the court will hear evidence on oath from the surety to ensure that he is suitable to act in that capacity.

A flowchart showing the procedure at a contested bail application is set out at **7.11.2** below.

A record of the magistrates' decision will be made and a copy of this given to the defendant. If the magistrates refuse bail or grants bail subject to conditions, reasons for the refusal or reasons for the conditions which have been imposed must also be recorded and a copy given to the defendant. If the CPS opposed bail but bail is granted by the magistrates, a record must be made of the reasons for granting bail and a copy given to the CPS upon request.

A court which has granted conditional bail to a defendant may, at a later hearing, vary these conditions on the application either of the CPS, or of the defendant's solicitor. A common situation that arises regularly in the magistrates' court is for the defendant to ask the magistrates to vary a condition that he does not enter a specified area, because he has just gained employment and his place of work is in that area. In such a case, the magistrates will vary the condition to permit the defendant to enter the specified area solely for the purposes of employment.

If the magistrates grant unconditional bail to the defendant, they may subsequently impose conditions on such bail if they consider that conditions have become necessary for one or more of the reasons specified at **7.5** above.

## Key skill – making an application for bail

### PROSECUTION SUBMISSION

Sir, the prosecution wish to raise objections to bail being granted to the defendant under Schedule 1, Part 1 of the Bail Act 1976. In particular the prosecution consider that, if released on bail, there are substantial grounds for believing that the defendant either will fail to surrender to custody, or will commit further offences whilst on bail. I will deal with each of these grounds in turn.

Starting with the risk that the defendant will fail to surrender to custody, the evidence against the defendant is such that a conviction is very likely. The defendant was picked out by an eye-witness to the assault at an identification parade and, when questioned by the police, the defendant confessed to having committed the assault. The defendant is accused of having committed a prolonged and unprovoked attack on his victim, punching the victim in the face several times and causing the victim to suffer a fractured nose and split eyebrow. If convicted, the defendant is likely to receive a custodial sentence. The defendant also has a number of convictions for similar offences, which will aggravate the seriousness of the current offence in the event that he is convicted. In these circumstances, the defendant may very well fail to surrender to custody so as to avoid this significant risk of imprisonment.

Another factor which may lead the defendant to fail to surrender to custody is the defendant's lack of community ties. The prosecution understand that the defendant has no close friends or family in the Chester area and does not own his own property in the area. The prosecution also understand that the defendant works as a scaffolder and regularly works away from the Chester area, including some work that is done out of the country.

As can be seen from the defendant's list of previous convictions, the defendant already has one recent previous conviction for failing to surrender to bail. This was also in respect of an assault charge which the defendant faced. When seen in the context of the current offence, this must raise substantial doubts that the defendant will surrender to custody.

The second objection to bail being granted is that the defendant may commit further offences if released on bail. Sir, this is a defendant with a history of violent offending. The defendant has been convicted of three offences involving violence within the last two and a half years. He also has a conviction for common assault from six years ago. On 13th December 2006 the defendant was convicted of the same offence with which he is currently charged. Furthermore, all these offences appear to be connected to the defendant's employment as a nightclub bouncer. Given that the defendant is likely to continue in this employment, the prosecution would say that it is only a matter of time before the defendant offends again.

Sir, for the reasons I have outlined, I oppose bail being granted to the defendant and ask that the defendant be remanded in custody until this matter next comes before the court.

**DEFENCE SUBMISSION**

Sir, I wish to apply for unconditional bail on behalf of Mr Dickson. I will take the prosecution objections to bail being granted in turn, but before doing so I would like to remind you that under section 4(1) of the Bail Act 1976 there is a presumption that bail will be granted to Mr Dickson. Bail can be refused only if you consider that there are substantial grounds for believing that Mr Dickson would either fail to surrender to custody, or would commit further offences were he to be released on bail. This is a very high test for the prosecution to satisfy and, in my submission, the prosecution have failed to do this.

I will deal first with the allegation that Mr Dickson will fail to surrender to custody if released on bail. Whilst I concede that the charge Mr Dickson faces is a serious one, this makes it all the more likely that Mr Dickson will in fact attend the next hearing. Mr Dickson will be pleading not guilty in this matter. He is anxious to clear his name and does not wish to worsen the situation by failing to answer his bail.

The prosecution suggest that Mr Dickson is unlikely to come to court of his own volition because the evidence against him is strong. I would dispute the supposed strength of the prosecution evidence. A challenge to the admissibility of Mr Dickson's confession will be made at trial under sections 76 and 78 of PACE 1984. In addition, the credibility of the identification evidence of the eye-witness will be challenged, and an alibi witness will be called on Mr Dickson's behalf. Mr Dickson has a good defence to this charge and wants nothing more than to come to court to clear his name.

The prosecution also seek to place reliance upon Mr Dickson's previous conviction for failing to surrender to bail. This must be placed in context. Mr Dickson did not actively abscond. Rather, there was a misunderstanding over the time Mr Dickson's case was due to start. Mr Dickson thought his case was due to start in the afternoon, and did not appreciate that he needed to be at court at 10.00 am. Mr Dickson did turn up at court in the afternoon at the time he thought he was supposed to attend. This is not the same thing as purposely seeking to avoid coming to court and I would urge you to give little significance to the prosecution's arguments on this point.

The prosecution suggest that Mr Dickson's lack of community ties mean that he is likely to abscond. Mr Dickson does in fact have strong ties to his local community. He is living with his partner in a property owned by his partner's parents, and has employment in the local area from the evening and weekend work he does as a bouncer. I am also instructed that, contrary to the assertion made by the prosecution, Mr Dickson's main employment as a scaffolder will not be taking him away from the Chester area for the next six months, as Mr Dickson will be working on a job in the local area.

The second ground raised by the prosecution is that Mr Dickson will commit further offences if released on bail. I would submit that this is not the case. First I would reiterate that Mr Dickson will be pleading not guilty to this offence. In addition, Mr Dickson does not have a lengthy list of previous convictions. Whilst he has four previous convictions for relevant offences, these convictions are spread over a six-year period and do not create substantial grounds for believing that Mr Dickson will offend again.

Mr Dickson's conviction for common assault occurred six years ago, and Mr Dickson did not then re-offend for four years. All of Mr Dickson's recent convictions for offences of violence relate to incidents when he was working as a nightclub bouncer. The allegation in this case is that the assault occurred away from the nightclub where Mr Dickson was working, and there is no suggestion that the assault had anything to do with the circumstances of Mr Dickson's employment as a bouncer, save that the victim of the assault had been working at the nightclub as a disc jockey.

Sir, for the reasons I have set out I would ask that you grant unconditional bail to Mr Dickson. Should you feel unable to grant bail on an unconditional basis, there are a number of conditions which I would invite you to consider imposing to remove any concerns you might have as to Mr Dickson's willingness to attend court on the next occasion. If you deem conditions to be appropriate, you might wish to consider imposing a condition that Mr Dickson report to his local police station on a regular basis, or a condition that he resides at 17 Marsh Street. Mr Dickson would also be able to provide a security to the court should one be required. I would submit that the imposition of such conditions would remove any substantial grounds for believing that Mr Dickson would fail to come to court on the next occasion.

For the reasons I have outlined, I do not consider that the prosecution have established substantial grounds for believing that Mr Dickson will commit further offences if released on bail. However, should you have any concerns with regard to this, I would submit that any such concerns may be addressed by imposing a condition that Mr Dickson must not enter Chester city centre, other than for the purposes of his employment, or a condition that Mr Dickson have no contact with any witnesses for the prosecution.

Sir, unless I can be of any further assistance, those are my submissions.

## 7.7 Further applications for bail

If bail is refused, the magistrates are under a duty to consider the question of bail at any subsequent hearing if the defendant is still in custody and the presumption in favour of bail (see **7.3** above) still applies. However, this does not mean that the defendant's solicitor is permitted to make a full bail application at each subsequent hearing.

At the first hearing after the hearing at which the court refused to grant bail, the defendant's solicitor is permitted to make a full application for bail using *any* argument as to fact or law, even if he used the same arguments in his first unsuccessful application. At any subsequent hearing, the court need not hear arguments as to fact or law which it has heard previously (Bail Act 1976, Sch 1, Pt IIA).

Thus, a defendant who is refused bail is entitled to have his solicitor make one further full bail application, but if this is refused his solicitor may make a further bail application only if he is able to raise a *new* legal or factual argument as to why bail should be granted.

#### Example

Amir makes his first appearance before the magistrates on 14 May. His solicitor makes a full application for bail, but this is refused and Amir is remanded in custody for seven days. When Amir appears before the court again on 21 May, his solicitor may make a further full application for bail using any argument as to fact or law, whether or not this argument was used in the bail application made on 14 May. If the magistrates refuse bail on 21 May, Amir's solicitor can make a further application for bail only if he can raise a new argument that he has not used previously. For example, a potential surety might have become available (who can ensure Amir's attendance at subsequent hearings), or Amir might have been offered employment (in which case he will be less likely to abscond).

In applying the above rule, the magistrates will ignore a hearing at which bail was refused on the basis that it had not been practicable to obtain sufficient information about the defendant to determine whether bail should be granted (see **7.4.1** above).

If the magistrates' court remands a defendant in custody after hearing a fully argued bail application, it must issue a certificate confirming that it has heard such an application. This is known as a 'full argument certificate' and will be handed to the defendant's solicitor.

An example of a full argument certificate is set out below.

## Key document – full argument certificate

Chester Magistrates' Court
The Square
Chester
CH1 1PF
Tel 01244 431809

**Bail Notice**

| | | |
|---|---|---|
| Date **26 December 2007** | Name **Gary Paul Dickson** | Unique no **CH000687/07** |
| Address: **17 Marsh Street Chester CH3 7LW** | | D.O.B. **18.10.80** |
| Alleged Offence(s): **Assault occasioning actual bodily harm (s 47)** | | |

[✓] This Court today has remanded the defendant to appear at ~~9.30am~~/10.00am/~~11.00am/11.30am/2.00pm~~ before the Magistrates'/~~Youth~~ Court at **Chester** on **15th January 2008**

[ ] This Court has committed/released the defendant to appear before the Crown Court on

[ ] and has granted bail without conditions

[ ] granted bail with the conditions set out below

[✓] committed the defendant to custody/~~Local Authority accommodation~~ having found the following exceptions to the right to unconditional bail on the following grounds

| Grounds | Factors |
|---|---|
| [✓] substantial grounds would fail to surrender | [✓] defendant has previously failed to answer bail and/or committed offences on bail |
| [✓] substantial grounds would commit offence on bail | [✓] nature and gravity of offence and/or probable sentence |
| [ ] substantial grounds would interfere with witnesses and/or obstruct the course of justice | [✓] defendant's character/breakdown/associations lack of community ties |
| [ ] arrested under s.7 Bail Act 1976 for failing to answer/breaking bail conditions impracticable to obtain sufficient information for bail decisions for want of time | [ ] recent arrest and details not verified |
| [ ] impracticable to obtain sufficient information for bail decision for want of time | [✓] strength of evidence against defendant |
| [ ] serving custodial sentence imposed on | [ ] no likelihood of defendant's co-operation for purposes of obtaining reports |
| [ ] impracticable to obtain report or complete enquiries for sentencing purposes | [ ] evidence of self injury/attempted suicide/inability to look after him/her self |
| [ ] defendant needs protection and/or welfare | [ ] behaviour towards and/or proximity to prosecution witnesses |
| [ ] this offence has been committed on bail in other proceedings | [ ] as found by the Crown Court |
| [ ] as found by the Crown Court | |

CONDITIONS OF BAIL

[ ] live and sleep at
[ ] to remain indoors at the address between pm and am each day
[ ] to report at police station each day/Mon/Tues/Wed/Thurs/Fri/Sat/Sun/day betweer
[ ] not to approach or interfere or communicate with
[ ] to provide surety/sureties in the sum of £ (each)
[ ] to abide by the rules of the Hostel
to live and sleep at an address as directed by the Local Authority which is currently

CERTIFICATE OF FULL ARGUMENT FOR BAIL

[✓] I certify that a full argument on an application for bail was heard by this Court today

[ ] at a previous hearing and that this Court today had the following new considerations or change of circumstances placed before it

Failure to surrender to bail or comply with bail conditions can result in your arrest. Failure to surrender to bail is an offence punishable by a maximum of 12 months imprisonment and/or limited fine. You must report to the Court Usher, at the Court in which your name is listed, no later than the time shown above. You are then in the custody of the Court and must not leave without permission.

By Order of the Court *F. Smithson* Clerk of the Court present in the proceedings

## 7.8 Appeals against decisions on bail

### 7.8.1 Appeals by the defendant (CrimPR, r 19.18)

A defendant who is refused bail by the magistrates' court may appeal against this decision to the Crown Court provided the magistrates have issued the 'full argument certificate' referred to in 7.7 above. Although a defendant may make an appeal to the Crown Court after the magistrates have made an initial refusal of bail, for tactical reasons most defence solicitors will delay making an appeal to the Crown Court until they have made two full applications for bail before the magistrates' court. Delaying an appeal until after the second full application before the magistrates maximises the number of potentially successful applications for bail which the defendant will be able to make.

To appeal to the Crown Court against a refusal of bail by the magistrates, the defendant's solicitor must complete a notice of application, which needs to be sent to the Crown Court and served on the CPS (at least 24 hours before the hearing). The notice of application will contain details of the defendant's previous applications for bail, details of the stage the case has reached before the magistrates, the nature and grounds of the defendant's appeal, and details of any proposed sureties.

The appeal will be heard before a Crown Court judge in chambers and will normally take place within a matter of days of the notice of application being sent to the Crown Court (it is normal practice to obtain a date for the hearing from the Crown Court at the same time as completing the application). The judge will need to have the following documents before him when considering the application:

(a) the notice of application;

(b) the 'full argument certificate'; and

(c) a record of the defendant's previous convictions.

The defendant's solicitor should ensure that he sends the 'full argument certificate' and details of the defendant's previous convictions to the court prior to the appeal being heard. Failure to do so may mean that the judge refuses to consider the appeal.

At the hearing in chambers, the judge will hear representations from the CPS and the defendant's solicitor. The judge may refuse the defendant's application or grant bail to the defendant, with or without conditions. If the judge grants bail, a copy of the judge's order will need to be sent to the prison or remand centre where the defendant is being held so that the defendant may be released from custody.

## Key skill – drafting a bail appeal notice

**Form of notice of application relating to bail in the Crown Court**

*(Criminal Procedure Rules, r 19.18(4))*

Take notice that an application relating to bail will be made to the Crown Court

at CHESTER

on 3rd January 2008 at 10am

on behalf of the defendant.

**Name of defendant/appellant:** Gary Paul Dickson

**Crown Court No** CH08001

**Solicitor for the Applicant**: Collaws

**Address:**129 Westgate, Chester

*If defendant/appellant is in custody state place of detention and give Prison No if applicable*

**State particulars of proceedings during which defendant was committed to custody or bailed (un)conditionally:**

Defendant charged with assault occasioning actual bodily harm, contrary to s 47 of the Offences Against the Person Act 1861. Remand hearing on 19/12/07 and further remand hearing on 26/12/07. Case adjourned for prosecution to give advance disclosure. Plea before venue/mode of trial to take place on 15/01/08.

Defendant currently remanded in custody at Chester Remand Centre.
Prison No: CRC04378

**Enter details of any relevant previous applications for bail or variation of conditions of bail:**

19/12/07 – first full application for bail

26/12/07 – second full bail application

**Nature and grounds of application:** *(State fully facts relied on and list previous convictions (if any). Give details of any proposed sureties and answer any objections raised previously):*

The following arguments will be raised to counter the prosecution objections to bail:

Fail to surrender to custody:

Mr Dickson has one previous conviction for failure to surrender to custody. This failure was due to a genuine misunderstanding as to the time that Mr

Dickson's case was due to start. Mr Dickson did attend court of his own volition later in the day.

Mr Dickson is pleading not guilty to the one charge he faces and will come to court to clear his name. Mr Dickson has a strong defence to this charge and the evidence against him will be challenged. It will be alleged that the eye witness who purports to identify Mr Dickson as the assailant is mistaken. The admissibility of the confession evidence obtained by the police will be challenged under ss 76 & 78 of PACE 1984. An alibi witness will be called on Mr Dickson's behalf.

Mr Dickson has strong community ties. Mr Dickson resides in the Chester area with his partner. He and his partner reside in a property owned by his partner's parents. Mr Dickson has some part-time employment in the Chester area from his employment as a nightclub doorman. Mr Dickson's full-time employment as a scaffolder will require him to work on a local contract in the Chester area for the next six months.

Commit offences on bail

Mr Dickson is pleading not guilty to the current charge. He has never previously committed an offence whilst on bail, and he does not have a lengthy list of previously convictions. Mr Dickson's last conviction was over one year ago. All of Mr Dickson's recent convictions relate to incidents when Mr Dickson was working as a nightclub doorman and was dealing with customers. The current charge relates to an alleged incident which occurred after Mr Dickson left his place of employment. There is no reason to believe that Mr Dickson will offend again whilst on bail. Mr Dickson's only other conviction was for common assault some six years ago. Mr Dickson did not re-offend for some four years after this.

Bail Conditions

The following bail conditions will be put forward:

i) residence at 17 Marsh Street, Chester
ii) reporting to Chester Police Station on regular basis
iii) security
iv) not to enter Chester city centre other than for the purposes of his employment
v) not to contact an witnesses for the prosecution.

Notes

The appropriate officer of the Crown Court should be consulted about the time and place of the hearing before this notice is sent to the other party to the application. A copy of this notice should be sent to the Crown Court.

### 7.8.2 Appeals by the prosecution (CrimPR, rr 19.16 and 19.17)

If the magistrates grant bail to a defendant who has been charged with an imprisonable offence, s 1 of the Bail (Amendment) Act 1993 gives the CPS the right to appeal against this decision to a Crown Court judge in chambers. The CPS must have initially objected to the grant of bail before the magistrates' court, and oral notice of the appeal must be given by the CPS representative at the conclusion of the hearing in the magistrates court at which bail was granted *before* the defendant is released from custody. This oral notice must be confirmed in writing and served on the defendant within two hours of the hearing in the magistrates' court concluding. The appeal must be heard at the Crown Court within 48 hours of the magistrates' decision to grant bail. The defendant will be remanded in custody by the magistrates until the appeal is heard.

The CPS will not appeal against the grant of bail to a defendant in every case where it initially opposed the grant of bail. The Code for Crown Prosecutors provides that appeals should be made only in cases of 'grave concern', and should not be made merely because the Crown prosecutor disagrees with the magistrates' decision.

## 7.9 Failing to surrender (absconding)

### 7.9.1 What steps will the court take if the defendant fails to surrender?

A defendant who is granted bail (either by the police after he has been charged, or by the court following a hearing) is under a duty to surrender to the court at the time and place appointed for the next hearing. If the defendant fails to attend court to answer his bail at the appointed time and date, the magistrates will issue a warrant for his arrest (Bail Act 1976, s 7(1)). The warrant will either be backed with bail (which means that the police, having arrested the defendant, will then release him again pending his next court appearance), or, as is much more common, not backed with bail. If the warrant is not backed with bail, the police will arrest the defendant and then keep him in police custody until he can be brought before the court. The defendant will be brought before the magistrates' court at the next hearing (which will usually be on the day following his arrest).

### 7.9.2 What will happen when the defendant appears before the court?

What happens when the defendant is brought before the court will depend on whether the defendant has breached bail which has been granted by the police or bail granted by the court.

A defendant who has been charged by the police and bailed to appear before the magistrates' court will be in breach of *police* bail if he fails to attend court at the appointed date and time. When that defendant is arrested and brought before the court, whether he is charged with failing to surrender to custody under s 6(1) or (2) of the Bail Act 1976 (see **7.9.3** below) is a matter for the CPS. If the defendant's solicitor can persuade the CPS representative that there is a reasonable explanation for the defendant failing to attend court (if, for example, the defendant made a genuine mistake as to the date of his first appearance at court), the CPS representative may decide not to take proceedings against the client for failing to surrender.

If, however, the defendant has already made an appearance before the court, was been granted bail by the court and then failed to surrender at the next hearing, the decision to commence proceedings against him for failing to surrender will be made by the court rather than the CPS because the defendant will be in breach of *court* bail.

### 7.9.3 Offences with which the defendant may be charged

The Bail Act 1976 creates two offences with which a defendant who fails to surrender to custody at the appointed time and date may be charged:

(a) if the defendant fails without reasonable cause to surrender to custody, he will be guilty of the offence of absconding under s 6(1);

(b) if the defendant did have a reasonable cause for failing to surrender, he will still be guilty of an offence under s 6(2) unless he surrendered to custody as soon as it was reasonably practicable for him to do so. For example, a defendant who is unable to answer his bail because he is injured in a road traffic accident and has to go to hospital will still be guilty of an offence under s 6(2) unless he answers his bail as soon as reasonably practicable after his release from hospital.

### 7.9.4 Procedure at court

If the defendant has failed to answer *police* bail (see **7.9.2** above) and the CPS wishes to pursue the matter, the CPS representative will ask that a charge under either s 6(1) or s 6(2) be put to the defendant. The defendant may then plead either guilty or not guilty to the charge.

If the defendant has failed to answer *court* bail, when the defendant is brought before the court he will be asked informally by the court clerk the reason for his failure to surrender. If the defendant puts forward a reasonable excuse, it is unlikely that the court will take the matter any further. If the defendant is unable to put forward a reasonable excuse, however, the charge of absconding will then be put to him and he will plead guilty or not guilty.

If the defendant pleads guilty to a charge of absconding (whether in respect of police bail or court bail), the court may either sentence him immediately or adjourn sentence until the conclusion of the substantive proceedings. If the defendant pleads not guilty, the court will deal with the matter straight away, with the defendant giving evidence and being cross-examined on the reasons for his failing to attend. The burden of proof will be on the defendant to show, on a balance of probabilities, that he had reasonable cause for his failure to surrender.

### 7.9.5 The sentence

The maximum sentence for a defendant convicted of absconding is a prison sentence and/or a fine. The Magistrates' Courts Sentencing Guidelines (see **Chapter 11**) recommend a community penalty as the 'guideline' sentence for a defendant convicted of absconding after pleading not guilty to such a charge. Even if the magistrates decide not to impose a separate penalty for the absconding offence, they may decide to refuse the defendant bail in the substantive proceedings, or grant bail but with a much more stringent package of conditions.

A defendant convicted of absconding may be sentenced immediately or at the end of the trial in respect of the substantive offence. How the court sentences a defendant who is convicted of absconding will depend on the factual circumstances of the offence, with the court considering any aggravating or mitigating factors. Aggravating factors will include:

(a) wilful absconding by the defendant;

(b) absconding over a long period of time;

(c) previous convictions for absconding;

(d) a defendant who left the jurisdiction; and

(e) absconding which causes a trial date to be postponed (although the court does have the power to conduct a trial in the absence of a defendant who has absconded).

Mitigating factors will include:

(a) a genuine misunderstanding (for example, a defendant who made a genuine mistake as to the time he was due to appear at court);

(b) a defendant who, having realised his mistake, attends court later that day; and

(c) a defendant who wilfully absconded but then surrendered voluntarily to custody.

### 7.9.6 Will the defendant receive a further grant of bail in the substantive proceedings?

Although a defendant who has absconded may still receive a further grant of bail in the substantive proceedings, much will depend on the actual circumstances of the failure to surrender. The CPS is likely to object to a further grant of bail being made on the basis that there are substantial grounds to believe that, if released on bail, the defendant will fail to surrender.

The court may be persuaded to make a further grant of bail to the defendant if his failure to surrender was the result of a genuine misunderstanding, or if the defendant voluntarily surrendered. In such a case, the court may grant bail on the same conditions as previously, or bail subject to more stringent conditions. The defendant is unlikely to be granted bail again, however, if he wilfully failed to surrender and had to be arrested by the police.

#### Example

Michaela is charged with theft and makes her first appearance before the magistrates' court on unconditional bail. Her case is adjourned so that the CPS can make advance disclosure of its case to her solicitor. Michaela fails to attend the next hearing and a warrant for her arrest is issued. Michaela then arrives at court the day after the hearing was due to take place. She explains that her failure to attend was a genuine oversight on her part after she got the dates mixed up. When Michaela is brought before the magistrates, the magistrates accept that she made a mistake and they also take into account the fact that she surrendered voluntarily. The magistrates make a further grant of bail to Michaela, although this is now subject to a condition of residence and a condition that she report daily to the police station.

If a defendant absconds prior to his trial, the court may proceed with the trial in his absence (*R v O'Hare* [2006] EWCA Crim 471).

## 7.10 Breaches of bail

A defendant who breaches any bail conditions other than a condition to attend the next court hearing (for example, a defendant who fails to comply with a curfew, a condition of residence or a condition not to contact a prosecution witness) does *not* commit a criminal offence by breaching such conditions. However, a defendant who breaches his bail conditions is likely to have his bail reviewed by the magistrates, who may decide that his failure to comply with the conditions necessitates a remand in custody.

Section 7(3) of the Bail Act 1976 empowers a police officer to arrest a person who has been bailed to attend court (either by the police following charge, or by the court at a previous hearing) if the officer reasonably believes that the person:

(a) is not likely to surrender to bail; or
(b) has broken, or is likely to break, his bail conditions.

A defendant who is arrested will be detained in police custody and must then be brought before the magistrates' court within 24 hours. The magistrates will then decide whether to remand the defendant in custody, or whether to grant bail with or without conditions pending the next substantive hearing in the case. The magistrates will adopt a two-stage approach:

(a) The magistrates will determine if there has been a breach of the bail conditions previously imposed. Unless the defendant admits to breaching his bail conditions, the magistrates are likely to hear oral evidence from both the police officer who arrested the defendant and the defendant himself to determine whether a breach has occurred.
(b) If the magistrates determine that there has been a breach of bail conditions, they will decide whether the defendant should be remanded in custody or on bail pending the next hearing (unless the case can be disposed of at that hearing). The magistrates will assess the seriousness of the breach and the reasons for the breach. The magistrates will hear representations from the CPS (the CPS is likely to be opposing the further grant of bail) and the defendant's solicitor before coming to a decision. A defendant who has breached his bail conditions without good reason is likely to be remanded in custody, although the magistrates may be persuaded to make a further grant of bail but with more stringent conditions attached to it.

#### Example 1

The police charge Qasim with theft and release him on conditional bail pending his first appearance before the magistrates' court one week later. The condition is that Qasim does not contact any prosecution witnesses. Two days after being charged, Qasim is arrested for breaching this condition. Manaz, an eye-witness to the theft, alleges that Qasim approached her and asked her to change her story. The police arrest Qasim and bring him before the magistrates' court within 24 hours of his arrest. Qasim denies contacting Manaz but, after a hearing at which both Qasim and the police officer who arrested him for breaching his bail condition give evidence, the magistrates decide that Qasim did breach his bail conditions. Qasim's solicitor makes an application for Qasim to be granted bail prior to the next hearing. This is opposed by the CPS, and the magistrates refuse bail on the basis that there are substantial grounds for believing that, if released on bail, Qasim will interfere with witnesses. Qasim is remanded in custody until the next hearing.

#### Example 2

The police charge Nick with affray following an incident at a city centre pub, and release him on conditional bail pending his first appearance before the magistrates' court one week later. The condition is that Nick does not enter a defined area in the city centre. The following day Nick attends the birthday party of a friend at another pub. This pub is within the area Nick is not supposed to enter, although Nick genuinely thought that it was outside this area. Nick is arrested for breaching his bail condition and is brought before the magistrates' court within 24 hours. Nick accepts that he breached his bail condition, but explains that he made an honest mistake. Nick makes a further application for bail and this is opposed by the CPS. The magistrates nevertheless decide to make a further grant of bail to Nick, although this is made subject to more onerous conditions. In addition to keeping out of the city centre, the magistrates impose an additional condition that Nick is not to enter any public house.

## 7.11 Procedural flowcharts

### 7.11.1 Will the defendant be granted bail?

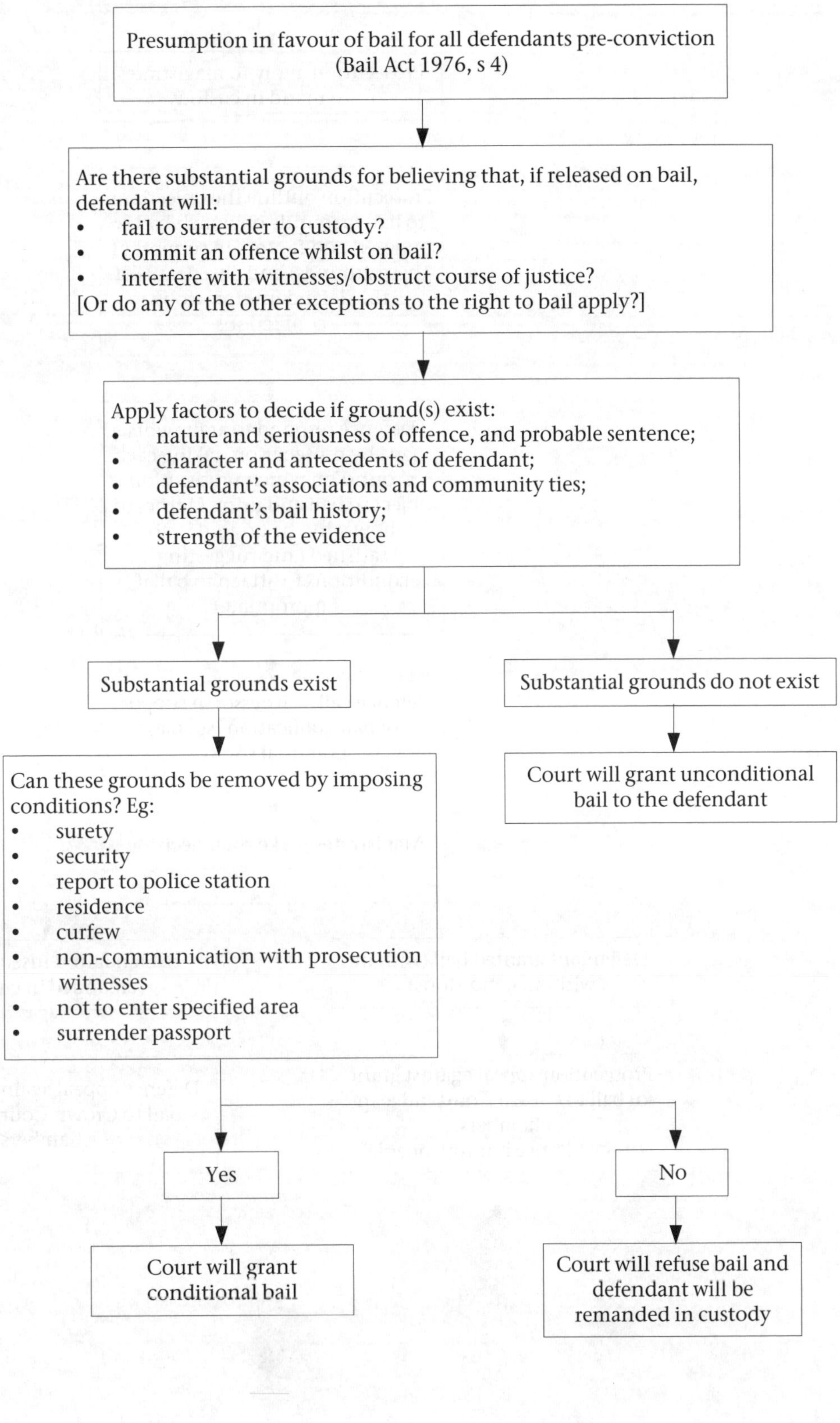

### 7.11.2 Procedure at contested bail application

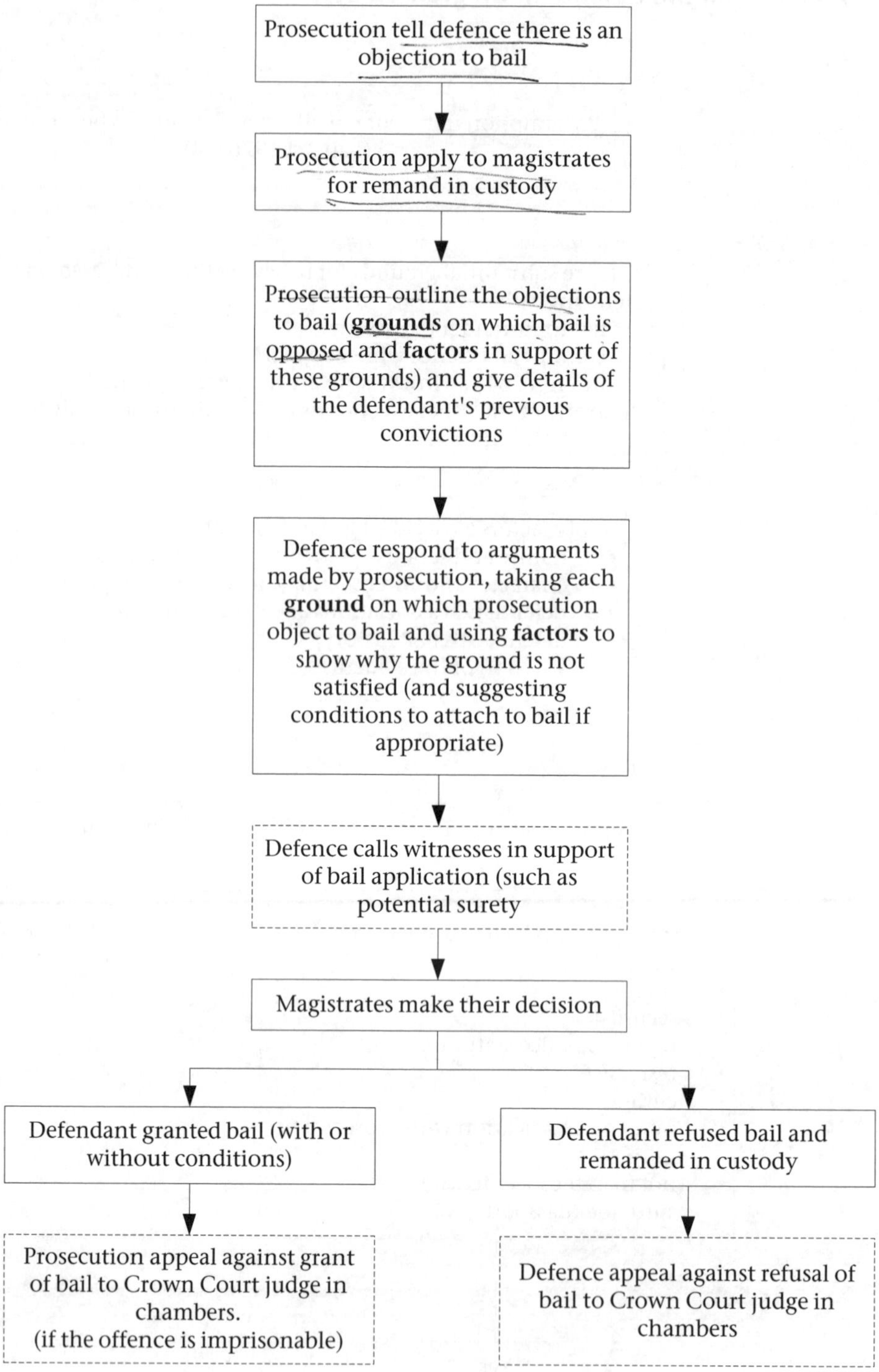

## 7.12 Checklist

At the end of this chapter you should be able to explain:

- the remand periods and custody time limits which apply in the magistrates' court;
- the presumption in favour of bail which applies to most types of defendant under s 4 of the Bail Act 1976;
- the exceptions to the right to bail set out in Sch 1, Pt 1 to the Bail Act 1976;
- the difference between the *grounds* on which bail may be refused by the court and the *factors* to be taken into account in deciding whether those grounds are satisfied;
- the conditions which may be attached to a grant of bail;
- the procedure for making an application for bail;
- the further applications for bail which may be made to the magistrates' court if the initial application is unsuccessful;
- the procedure for appealing to the Crown Court against a refusal of bail by the magistrates' court;
- the consequences for a defendant who fails to answer his bail, or who breaches any conditions attached to his bail.

# Chapter 8
# Preparation for Trial in the Magistrates' Court



## 8.1 Introduction

After a defendant has entered a not guilty plea to a summary offence, or has pleaded not guilty to an either way offence and has consented to a trial in the magistrates' court (see **Chapter 6**), the magistrates will fix the date when the defendant's trial is take place. The magistrates will also give a series of directions that the CPS and the defendant's solicitor must comply with prior to the trial. This chapter will look at the steps which the defendant's solicitor needs to take in order to prepare his client's case for trial. These steps include obtaining evidence from witnesses other than the defendant and obtaining details of any 'unused' material the CPS has which may assist the defence case.

## 8.2 Directions

### 8.2.1 Introduction

Prior to the Criminal Procedure Rules 2005 coming into effect, there were no standard case management directions that the magistrates' court would give in order to ensure that the CPS and the defendant's solicitor were properly prepared for trial. Once a defendant had entered his not guilty plea, the court would either fix a trial date immediately (if the case was straightforward) or would arrange for a hearing called a pre-trial review to take place. The purpose of the pre-trial review was to make arrangements for the trial in a more complex case and to ensure that the parties were ready for trial. The Criminal Procedure Rules 2005 have replaced this system with a formal set of case management directions with which the parties must comply.

### 8.2.2 Case management hearing

The court will give case management directions either at the same hearing at which the defendant enters his plea of not guilty (and, for an either way offence, after the plea before venue/mode of trial hearing), or at a subsequent hearing. The hearing at which case management directions are given is referred to in the Criminal Procedure Rules as a case management hearing, although some courts call this a pre-trial review.

The case management directions are standard directions, although the court may vary them if necessary. The directions allow the parties eight weeks to prepare the case for trial (or 14 weeks when expert evidence is required). The form used to record the directions is reproduced at **8.6** below.

The directions will specify time limits within which the parties must comply with certain requirements, for example:

(a) the service of the prosecution case papers;

(b) the disclosure by the prosecution of any unused material in its possession (see **8.4.6** below);

(c) the service of any notices relating to hearsay or bad character evidence (see **Chapters 19** and **22**);

(d) the service of any notices relating to the use of special measures at trial (see **Chapter 16**); and

(e) the service of any reports from expert witnesses upon which a party seeks to rely.

## 8.3 Case analysis

To provide his client with a properly argued defence at trial, the defendant's solicitor must carry out an analysis of the case against his client to determine what the issues in the case are and what evidence can be placed before the court to ensure that those issues are resolved in the defendant's favour and that the defendant is ultimately acquitted.

Set out below is a six-point template which should be followed by the defendant's solicitor when analysing the prosecution case against his client:

(a) *What are the legal elements of the offence charged?* The first step in analysing a case is to determine what it is that the CPS will need to prove in order to secure a conviction. To do this the defendant's solicitor must find out what the *actus reus* and *mens rea* are for the offence with which his client is charged.

(b) *What is the prosecution account of the case?* What story does the CPS want the court to believe? To discover this the defendant's solicitor should prepare a brief narrative account of the prosecution case. If the prosecutor could tell the magistrates what it is alleged the defendant did when the offence was committed, what would he say?

(c) *What is the defendant's account of the case?* This is the same procedure as in (b) above, but from the defendant's point of view. If the defendant was telling the court his 'story', what would he say?

(d) *What are the facts in issue?* If steps (b) and (c) have been properly completed, the defendant's solicitor should now have two accounts or versions of what the court is going to be asked to believe happened. Wherever the accounts diverge there is a fact in issue. The defendant's solicitor needs to make a list detailing each fact in issue in the case.

(e) *How is each party going to prove its version of the facts in issue?* Once the defendant's solicitor has a list of the factual issues that the court needs to resolve, he must then analyse the evidence which exists. For each fact in issue he needs to determine what evidence the CPS has to support its version of events and what evidence his client has to rebut this.

(f) *Is any further evidence required?* The final stage in the case analysis model is for the defendant's solicitor to assess the adequacy of the evidence that currently exists to support the defendant's case. Will this evidence be sufficient to result in an acquittal, or is further evidence necessary? If there are weaknesses in the defendant's case, where is the further evidence going to come from to strengthen this case?

## 8.4 Obtaining additional evidence

### 8.4.1 Introduction

If the case analysis described in **8.3** above shows that additional evidence in support of the defendant's case is necessary, the defendant's solicitor should consider with his client where such evidence may be obtained. Additional evidence may come from witnesses as to fact, from expert witnesses, or it may be in the form of documentary evidence. Such documentary evidence is likely to be 'unused material' which the CPS has compiled but does not wish to rely on as part of its case against the defendant. The defendant's solicitor must ensure that he obtains from the CPS any 'unused material' which may assist the defence case (see **8.4.6** below).

### 8.4.2 Witnesses as to fact

#### 8.4.2.1 Introduction

The defendant's solicitor needs to find out from his client if he is aware of any witnesses who might be prepared to give evidence on his behalf. For example, a defendant charged with assault who is pleading not guilty on the basis that he acted in self-defence, may have been with a friend at the time of the assault who will support the defendant's account of what happened.

Any witnesses who are located need to be interviewed and a signed statement taken from them. The defendant's solicitor needs to take a view on how helpful a particular witness will be to his client's case, and how credible that witness will be if he gives evidence at court. Careful consideration needs to be given before calling a defence witness who has previous convictions, since the CPS may attempt to raise such convictions when the witness is being cross-examined in order to undermine the credibility of his evidence (see **Chapter 22**).

#### 8.4.2.2 Securing the attendance of the witness at trial

Witnesses who are prepared to give a written statement are often reluctant to attend court to give oral evidence at trial, and a prudent solicitor will secure their attendance by obtaining a witness summons from the magistrates' court. The procedural rules which apply when an application for a witness summons is necessary are contained in Part 28 of the Criminal Procedure Rules 2005.

The court will issue a witness summons if it is satisfied that the witness can give material evidence in the proceedings and it is in the interests of justice for a summons to be issued (Magistrates' Courts Act 1980, s 97). The defendant's solicitor will usually ask a potential defence witness to confirm in writing that he will attend court. If a negative response is received, or if, as is much more likely, no response is received, the solicitor should then write to the court requesting that it issue a witness summons. The court will issue a witness summons requiring the witness to attend the trial.

#### 8.4.2.3 Disclosure obligations

Under s 6C of the Criminal Procedure and Investigations Act (CPIA) 1996, a defendant must serve on the CPS a notice setting out the names, addresses and dates of birth of any witnesses he intends to call to give evidence. This rule was introduced to enable the CPS to check whether any defence witnesses have previous convictions, although there is nothing to stop the CPS, via the police, interviewing these witnesses (since there is no property in a witness). Should the police wish to interview a defence witness, a code of practice exists which governs the conduct of the interview (CPIA 1996, s 21A).

Unlike civil proceedings, there is no requirement for a defendant in a criminal case to serve on the CPS copies of the statements taken from the witnesses whom he intends to call to give evidence at trial. The only exception to this are reports from any expert witnesses whom the defendant wishes to call to give evidence at trial. These must be served on the CPS (see **8.4.3** below). A defendant may, however, serve a more general defence statement on the prosecution (see **8.4.7** below).

## 8.4.3 Expert witnesses

### 8.4.3.1 When may an expert be required?

Expert evidence may be required at trial in respect of any technical matter which is outside the competence of the magistrates. Evidence may, for example, be required from a forensic scientist or a medical expert, particularly if the CPS has already obtained expert evidence which the defendant disputes. Expert evidence should be obtained as soon as possible, although if the defendant's case is funded by way of a representation order, the defendant's solicitor should obtain prior authority from the Legal Services Commission (LSC) to instruct the expert.

### 8.4.3.2 Disclosure obligations

If the defendant's solicitor wishes to call an expert to give evidence at trial, he must serve a copy of the expert's report on the CPS in advance of trial (there is no obligation to serve the statements of any other defence witnesses on the CPS – see **8.4.2.3** above). An expert witness is unlikely to require a witness summons, although the defendant's solicitor must check the expert's availability to attend trial so that the trial can be fixed on a date when the expert is available to attend court.

Under s 6D of the CPIA 1996, the defendant is obliged to serve on the CPS a notice giving the name and address of any expert witness who has been *consulted* (in addition to serving a copy of the report from an expert who will actually give evidence at trial). This means that if the defendant's solicitor has obtained a report from an expert but does not intend to call that expert to give evidence at trial (because the expert's opinion does not assist the defendant's case), it will be open to the CPS to approach that expert and possibly call him to give evidence *against* the defendant (since there is no property in a witness).

## 8.4.4 Do all witnesses need to attend the trial?

Some witnesses may give evidence that is not in dispute. For example, in an assault case the CPS may obtain a statement from a doctor who treated the victim for his injuries. If the defendant accepts that he caused these injuries but claims that he was acting in self-defence, there is little point in the CPS having to call the doctor to give evidence if the nature of the injuries is accepted and the doctor's evidence will go unchallenged by the defendant.

Section 9 of the Criminal Justice Act 1967 provides that a written statement from a witness will be admissible at trial (as opposed to the witness having to come to court to give evidence) provided that:

(a) it is signed and dated;

(b) it contains the following declaration:

This statement (consisting of [1] page signed by me) is true to the best of my knowledge and belief and I make it knowing that if it is tendered in evidence I shall be liable to prosecution if I have wilfully stated in it anything which I know to be false or do not believe to be true.

(c) a copy has been served before the hearing on the other parties in the case; and

(d) none of the other parties has objected within seven days.

The statement may only contain matters which would have been admissible if the witness had given oral evidence at court.

'Section 9' witness statements should be used only for evidence which is not in dispute (although the CPS routinely serves the statements of all prosecution witnesses in the form of a s 9 statement). If the party receiving a statement which is served in this form wishes to challenge the admissibility of anything said in the statement, or to cross-examine the maker of the statement, it should object in writing within seven days.

Example

Nosheen is charged with theft of a bracelet from a shop. Nosheen denies the theft on the basis of mistaken identity and will state that she was elsewhere at the time of the theft. The CPS serves on Nosheen's solicitor statements it has obtained from the owner of the shop and a customer who claims to identify Nosheen as the person who took the bracelet. Both statements are served under s 9 of the Criminal Justice Act 1967. The statement from the shop owner merely confirms that the bracelet is missing and the value of the bracelet. The shop owner states that he did not witness the theft because he was elsewhere at the time. Nosheen's solicitor will write to the CPS within seven days of receiving the statements, confirming that he objects to the customer's statement being used at trial without the customer being called to give oral evidence. The customer will need to be cross-examined at trial as the identification evidence he gives is disputed. Nosheen's solicitor will not object to the statement from the shop owner being used at trial without the shop owner needing to attend court. The shop owner did not see the alleged theft and says nothing that Nosheen will dispute. He merely confirms the fact of the theft, which Nosheen is not disputing.

### 8.4.5 Documentary evidence

Documentary evidence which may be used at trial will often take the form of plans or photographs of the place where the alleged crime occurred. Any plans or photographs should be verified by a witness statement from the person who prepared the plan or took the photographs.

### 8.4.6 Obtaining unused material from the CPS

#### 8.4.6.1 Introduction

When the police investigate an alleged offence they will compile a large amount of documentary evidence (for example, witness statements, business records, CCTV footage, etc). In the case of an either way offence, any evidence obtained which will subsequently be relied upon as part of the prosecution case at trial will be supplied to the defendant's solicitor as part of the 'advance disclosure' package (see **6.6.3** above). In a summary only matter, the CPS has no such duty of disclosure but will, in accordance with guidelines given by the Attorney-General (see **6.6.2**), supply the defence with details of the evidence the prosecution seek to rely on.

The remaining material which the CPS has in its possession but which it does not propose to rely upon at trial is referred to as 'unused material'. A common example of unused material is statements taken from witnesses who the police initially think may help the prosecution case, but who in fact do not say anything which assists the case against the defendant.

#### 8.4.6.2 The prosecution's duty to disclose unused material

The CPS is under an obligation to retain any unused material which it receives from the police. If the defendant subsequently enters a not guilty plea, the CPS is obliged to disclose this material to the defendant's solicitor if certain conditions are satisfied. Those conditions are set out in s 3 of the CPIA 1996, which provides that the CPS must disclose:

> ... any prosecution material which has not previously been disclosed to the accused and which might reasonably be considered capable of *undermining the case for the prosecution against the accused*, or of *assisting the case for the accused.* (emphasis added)

Unused material which may need to be disclosed by the CPS under the above test includes:

(a) records of the first description of a suspect given to the police by a potential eye-witness if that description differs from that of the defendant;

(b) any information provided by the defendant which indicates an innocent explanation for the offence for which he has been charged;

(c) any material casting doubt on the reliability of a witness, such as any previous convictions the witness may have;

(d) any material casting doubt on the reliability of a confession;

(e) any statement taken from a witness which appears to support the defendant's version of events.

**Example 1**

Adam is charged with theft from a shop. Adam denies the offence on the basis of mistaken identity. As part of its advance disclosure obligations, the CPS serves on Adam's solicitors statements from two witnesses who saw the theft and who give a description of the thief which matches Adam's description. Adam is 5 feet 8 inches tall, of slim build and with short brown hair. The CPS has also obtained a statement from another witness to the theft, who describes the thief as being 6 feet tall, of medium build and with long brown hair. The CPS does not intend to call this witness to give evidence at trial, but it is under an obligation to serve a copy of the statement on Adam's solicitors. The statement undermines the prosecution case that Adam was the thief and supports Adam's defence of mistaken identity.

**Example 2**

Gregory is charged with assaulting Trevor. Gregory denies the offence and claims that Trevor threw the first punch, and that he was acting only in self-defence. The CPS serves on Gregory's solicitor several statements from eye-witnesses who state that Gregory threw the first punch. The CPS also has a statement from another witness who says that Trevor threw the first punch. The CPS does not intend to rely on evidence from this witness at trial, but it is under an obligation to serve a copy of the statement on Gregory's solicitor. The statement undermines the prosecution case that Gregory threw the first punch and assists Gregory's case that he was acting in self-defence after being attacked.

**Example 3**

Paul is charged with assaulting Sunil. Paul's defence is that Sunil attacked him first and that he was acting in self-defence. Sunil has several previous convictions for offence of violence. The CPS is under a duty to disclose this information to Paul's solicitor. This information casts doubt on the reliability of Sunil's evidence (that Paul attacked him) and so will undermine the prosecution case (the CPS Disclosure Manual provides that all previous convictions of prosecution witnesses be disclosed to the defence, regardless of their likely relevance to the case).

This duty of disclosure is a continuing duty and so the CPS must keep under review the question of whether there is any material that meets the above test (CPIA 1996, s 7A).

If the CPS does disclose any unused material which satisfies the test in s 3 above to the defendant's solicitor, the solicitor must consider how best to make use of such material. He should, for example, seek to interview a witness who appears to assist the defendant's case, and ask that witness if he would be prepared to give evidence at trial on behalf of the defendant. Alternatively, if the CPS discloses the fact that a prosecution witness has previous convictions, the defendant's solicitor should consider making an application for permission to raise such convictions at trial when cross-examining that witness (see **Chapter 22**).

### 8.4.6.3 Procedure for disclosure of unused material

When the CPS makes disclosure of any unused material in its possession which satisfies the test in s 3, the defendant's solicitor will be sent a standard disclosure letter by the CPS which will have attached to it a document headed 'Police Schedule of Non-sensitive Unused Material'. This is a list which records all the non-sensitive items of unused material the CPS has. It will also record whether such documents are to be supplied to the defence (because they satisfy the test set out at **8.4.6.2** above), or whether such documents should not be supplied to the defence because they do not appear either to undermine the case for the prosecution or to assist the case for the defence. Any documents which are to be supplied to the defence will normally be provided at the same time as the list is sent to the defendant's solicitor.

When he receives this list from the CPS, the defendant's solicitor may ask for clarification of any items on the list (if, for example, the items are described in such a vague manner that the defendant's solicitor is unable to determine what they actually are). He may also ask the CPS to supply a copy of an item from the list (which the CPS has not already supplied) if he considers that the item may satisfy the test at **8.4.6.2** above. If the list does not include items which the defendant's solicitor suspects the CPS may have, he may challenge the contents of the list, and ask the CPS to confirm that the list is a full schedule of all the unused material it has.

#### Example 1

Scott is charged with handling stolen DVDs which the police seized following a search of his flat. When Scott's solicitor receives the list of unused material from the CPS, one of the items listed reads: 'Various receipts found at the accused's flat.'

These documents are not supplied to Scott's solicitor because the CPS states that they do not satisfy the test for disclosure under s 3. Scott's defence is that he bought the DVDs from a market stall and that one of the documents the police removed from his flat (which is not being relied upon as part of the prosecution case) is a receipt for these items. Scott's solicitor will ask the CPS to clarify the contents of the list by giving a proper description for each receipt. If the receipt for the DVDs is found to be among these receipts, Scott's solicitor will then ask the CPS to supply a copy of this document since it would satisfy the test under s 3.

Example 2

Guy is charged with assault following an altercation outside a nightclub. Guy's defence is that he was attacked first and was acting only in self-defence. Guy tells his solicitor that he recalls several witnesses to the incident giving statements to the police at the time of the incident. The only eye-witness evidence the CPS seeks to rely on at Guy's trial is from the alleged victim. When the CPS serves the list of unused material, there in no reference to statements being obtained from any other witnesses. Guy's solicitor suspects that such statements were obtained by the police and that these may support Guy's defence. Guy's solicitor will write to the CPS to challenge the extent of the disclosure of unused material that has been made.

An example of a standard disclosure letter from the CPS and a schedule of non-sensitive unused material is set out below (see **Key document – Disclosure Letter and Police Schedule of Non-sensitive unused material**).

## Key Document – Disclosure Letter and Police Schedule of Non-sensitive Unused Material

CPS

Chester Office
East Chambers
Saville Street
Chester
CH1 4NJ

Switchboard:
Facsimile: 01245 123423
DX No: 61616 Chester

Collaws Solicitor
Chester

Direct Line: 01245 423123

Our Ref:
Your Ref:
Date: 25th February 2008

Dear Sirs

**DISCLOSURE OF PROSECUTION MATERIAL UNDER SECTION 3 CRIMINAL PROCEDURE AND INVESTIGATIONS ACT 1996**

**R v Gary Paul Dickson**

**URN CH/000/687/08**

**COURT CHESTER CROWN COURT**

I am required by section 3 Criminal Procedure and Investigations Act 1996 (CPIA) to disclose to you any prosecution material which has not previously been disclosed, and which in my opinion might undermine the case for the prosecution against your client or which might reasonably be expected to assist the case for your client.

Attached to this letter is a copy of a schedule of non-sensitive unused material prepared by the police in compliance with their duty under Part II CPIA and the provisions of the Code of Practice. The schedule has been prepared by the police Disclosure Officer, who in this case is PC 911 Chambers.

Unless the word 'evidence' appears alongside any item, all the items listed on the schedule are not intended to be used as part of the prosecution case. You will receive a written notice should the position change.

At this stage, it is my opinion that there is no prosecution material which requires disclosure to you, other than items 2 and 4 on the schedule. Copies of these items are enclosed with this letter.

If you supply a written defence statement to me and to the court within 14 days, the material will be further reviewed in the light of that statement.

A defence statement is required by section 5 CPIA in Crown Court cases. In magistrates' court cases, section 6 CPIA makes a defence statement optional. Please bear in mind that we will rely upon the information you provide in the statement to identify any remaining material which has not already been disclosed but which might reasonably assist the defence case as you have described it. The statement will also be relied on by the court if you later make an application under section 8 CPIA.

If you do not make a defence statement where one is required, or provide one late, the court may permit comment and/or draw an adverse inference.

If you have a query in connection with this letter, please contact the writer.

Yours faithfully

*CPS*

Crown Prosecution Service.

**CHESHIRE POLICE**
**POLICE SCHEDULE OF NON-SENSITIVE UNUSED MATERIAL**

Page No ….1….of….2……

URN: | CH | 000 | 687 | 08 |

R v Gary Paul Dickson…….

Is there any material in this case which has not been examined by either the investigating or disclosure officer? Yes No If 'yes' please attach MG11 (refer to para. 7.9.11 of the Manual of Guidance)

The Disclosure Officer believes that the following material which does not form part of the prosecution case is NOT SENSITIVE

**FOR CPS USE:** *Enter D = Disclosure to Defence
1 = Defence may inspect

| Item No. | DESCRIPTION AND RELEVANCE (Give sufficient details for CPS to decide if material should be disclosed or requires more detailed examination) | LOCATION | * | COMMENT |
|---|---|---|---|---|
| 1. | Computer entry of general incident 10067579 | Force records | | Does not appear to undermine case/assist defence – do not disclose |
| 2. | Full copy file of Gary Paul Dickson including all MG forms and previous convictions of Dickson | Force records | | Disclose – Common Law |
| 3. | Pocket book entry for PC Chambers (details arrest) | Officer's possession | | Does not appear to undermine case/assist defence – do not disclose |
| 4. | Record of previous convictions of Vincent Lamb | Force records | | Disclose – appears to undermine case |
| 5. | Rough notes of Gary Paul Dickson interview | Force records | | Does not appear to undermine case/assist defence - do not disclose |
| 6. | Input documents – description of Gary Paul Dickson held on PNC | Force records | | Does not appear to undermine case/assist defence - do not disclose |

Signature: *G Chambers* Name : G Chambers PC 911
Date: 12.02.2008

Reviewing lawyer signature: *P Jones*
Print name: P JONES
Date: 25.02.08

**CHESHIRE POLICE**
**POLICE SCHEDULE OF NON-SENSITIVE UNUSED MATERIAL**

Page No ….2….of….2……

URN:

| CH | 000 | 687 | 08 |
|---|---|---|---|

R v ..Gary Paul Dickson……

Is there any material in this case which has not been examined by either the investigating or disclosure officer? Yes No If 'yes' please attach MG11 (refer to para. 7.9.11 of the Manual of Guidance)

The Disclosure Officer believes that the following material which does not form part of the prosecution case is NOT SENSITIVE

| Item No. | DESCRIPTION AND RELEVANCE (Give sufficient details for CPS to decide if material should be disclosed or requires more detailed examination) | LOCATION |
|---|---|---|
| 7. | Pocket note book entry for PC Chambers (details presence during interview) | Officer's possession |
| 8. | Charge set of fingerprints of Gary Paul Dickson | Force records |
| 9. | Video identification record of Inspector Greene | Officer's possession Secure Store |

Signature: *G Chambers* Name : G Chambers PC 911
Date: 12.02.2008

**FOR CPS USE:** *Enter D = Disclosure to Defence
1 = Defence may inspect

| * | COMMENT |
|---|---|
| | Does not appear to undermine case/assist defence – do not disclose |
| | Does not appear to undermine case/assist defence – do not disclose |
| | Does not appear to undermine case/assist defence – do not disclose |

Reviewing lawyer signature: *P Jones*

Print name: P JONES
Date: 25.02.2008

In certain circumstances the CPS may withhold disclosure of items of unused material which are 'sensitive' (see **Chapter 10**).

### 8.4.7 Serving a defence statement on the prosecution

A defendant in the magistrates' court may serve on the CPS a defence statement under ss 5, 5A and 6 of the CPIA 1996. Defence statements are dealt with only very briefly in this chapter because it is unusual for a defence statement to be given in the magistrates' court (for reasons which are set out below). The giving of a defence statement is examined in much more detail in **Chapter 10**, which describes procedures in the Crown Court where defence statements are much more common.

The defence statement is a document which sets out the nature of the defence, the factual issues in the case where the defendant takes issue with the prosecution version of events, and any points of law the defendant will seek to rely on in the case. The giving of such a statement is discretionary in the magistrates' court. If the defendant does give a defence statement, he will do this after the CPS has made disclosure of any unused material in its possession (see **8.4.6** above).

For a case in the magistrates' court, the defendant's solicitor should consider serving a defence statement on the CPS only if he thinks that the CPS will, in the light of the information disclosed in the statement, be in a position to disclose to him additional unused material that may assist the defence case. Such a situation is likely to arise only if the defence statement contains additional details about the defence of which the CPS was previously unaware. An example of when such a situation may arise is provided at **10.8.7**.

In reality it is extremely rare for a defence statement to be served on the prosecution in the magistrates' court. The possible advantage of gaining additional disclosure from the CPS is heavily outweighed by the disadvantage of giving away details of the defence case to the CPS prior to the trial when there is no obligation to do so. The giving of a defence statement is normally confined to the Crown Court, where the service of such a statement on the CPS is effectively obligatory (see **10.8.2**).

A flowchart summarising the disclosure obligations imposed on the CPS and the defendant in both the magistrates' court and the Crown Court is provided at **10.11.1**.

## 8.5 Checklist

At the end of this chapter you should be able to explain:

- the case management directions with which the CPS and the defendant's solicitor must comply prior to a trial in the magistrates' court, and the time limits for compliance with these directions;
- how to carry out an effective case analysis and to identify any additional evidence that needs to be obtained in support of the defendant's case;
- the forms of additional evidence which may assist the defendant's case and how such additional evidence should be obtained;
- the disclosure obligations imposed on the CPS in respect of any unused material in its possession;
- when the defendant's solicitor may challenge the extent of the disclosure of unused material given by the CPS, and how this should be done;
- the circumstances in which a defence statement may be given in the magistrates' court and the reason why such statements are given only rarely.

## 8.6 Magistrates' court case progression form

**MAGISTRATES' COURT**

**CASE PROGRESSION**

**............................................Magistrates' Court**
**Date of hearing:..............................................**

| Name of defendant | Case no | Remand status | Youth jointly charged with adult? | Represented by: |
|---|---|---|---|---|
| D1 | | Bail/cust/COM | | |
| D2 | | Bail/cust/COM | | |
| D3 | | Bail/cust/COM | | |
| D4 | | Bail/cust/COM | | |

**COM= in custody on other matters**

Defence telephone numbers:
D1..........................(home)..............................(mobile) D1 solicitor ..................................(office)
D2..........................(home)..............................(mobile) D2 solicitor ..................................(office)
D3..........................(home)..............................(mobile) D3 solicitor ..................................(office)
D4..........................(home)..............................(mobile) D4 solicitor ..................................(office)

Prosecution telephone number....................................................

**CASE DETAILS**

**Date of trial:...............................................**

**Estimated length of trial:..........................**

Has the defendant been advised that the case may proceed in his or her absence?

D1: Y ☐ N ☐ D2: Y ☐ N ☐

D3: Y ☐ N ☐ D4: Y ☐ N ☐

Has the defendant been advised about credit for pleading guilty?

D1: Y ☐ N ☐ D2: Y ☐ N ☐

D3: Y ☐ N ☐ D4: Y ☐ N ☐

| Trial issues (e.g. identification – please give details) |
|---|
| |

| Applications to be made (e.g. special measures, bad character, hearsay) |
|---|
| |

**Defence witnesses**

| Defendant | Likely no of witnesses | Type of witness* (e.g. 2 x civ; 1 x child) |
|---|---|---|
| D1 | | |
| D2 | | |
| D3 | | |
| D4 | | |

**Prosecution witnesses**

| Name of witness | Type of witness* | Required by which defendant | To be read s.9? |
|---|---|---|---|
| | | | |
| | | | |
| | | | |
| | | | |
| | | | |
| | | | |
| | | | |
| | | | |
| | | | |
| | | | |

***P = police; Civ = civilian; Ex = expert; Child = child; VA = vulnerable adult**

**Note: parties must notify the court and the other party immediately if there is any change in witness availability or requirement to attend.**

Give details of any special arrangements (e.g. interpreter, intermediary, wheelchair access, hearing loop system) for anyone attending the trial:

**STANDARD DIRECTIONS APPLY UNLESS THE COURT DIRECTS OTHERWISE**

**A COPY OF THE STANDARD DIRECTIONS IS AVAILABLE FROM THE COURT**

Please record any further directions here (e.g. in relation to bad character, hearsay, special measures, disclosure, expert evidence):

# Chapter 9

# Summary Trial and Advocacy Techniques



## 9.1 Introduction

This chapter will begin by giving an outline of the sequence of events at a summary trial in the magistrates' court. It will then examine particular aspects of the trial process in more depth, before concluding with an introduction to some basic advocacy skills. Although the chapter will focus on a trial in the magistrates' court, the advocacy techniques described will be just as applicable to a trial in the Crown Court. The trial process in the Crown Court is described in **Chapter 10**.

## 9.2 Order of events at trial (CrimPR, Part 37)

The normal order of events at a trial in the magistrates' court is as follows:

(a) Opening speech by the solicitor from the CPS.

(b) The prosecution witnesses will then be called in turn to give evidence. Each witness will be examined in chief by the prosecuting solicitor and then cross-examined by the defendant's solicitor. The prosecuting solicitor may then choose to re-examine the witness.

(c) (Possible submission of no case to answer by defendant's solicitor.)

(d) The defence witnesses will then be called in turn to give evidence (with the defendant being called first). Each witness will be examined in chief by the defendant's solicitor and will then be cross-examined by the prosecuting solicitor. The defendant's solicitor may then choose to re-examine the witness.

(e) Closing speech by the defendant's solicitor (the prosecuting solicitor is not entitled to make a closing speech).

(f) The magistrates retire to consider their verdict.

(g) The magistrates deliver their verdict.

(h) If the defendant is found guilty, the magistrates will then either sentence the defendant immediately, or adjourn sentence until a later date if they wish to obtain pre-sentence reports on the defendant. If the defendant is acquitted, he will be formally discharged by the magistrates and told that he is free to go.

A flowchart summarising the above procedure is provided at **9.9.1** below.

## 9.3 Professional conduct

### 9.3.1 Duties of the defendant's solicitor

A solicitor representing a defendant in a trial before the magistrates is under a duty to say on behalf of his client what that client would properly say for himself were he to have the necessary skills and knowledge to do this. In other words, it is the duty of the defence solicitor to act in his client's best interests and to ensure that the CPS discharges the onus placed upon it to prove the client's guilt. Therefore, even if a client admits his guilt to his solicitor, it would still be appropriate for the solicitor to put the prosecution to proof of its case if the solicitor considered that case to be weak (see **Chapter 6**).

The defendant's solicitor nevertheless remains under an overriding duty not to mislead the court (Solicitors' Code of Conduct 2007, Rule 11.01). He cannot therefore say anything in his client's defence which he knows to be untrue. Although the defendant's solicitor is not under a duty to inform the CPS or the court of any facts which may have been overlooked, he is under a duty to tell the court what the relevant law is, even if this proves detrimental to the client's case.

The defendant's solicitor also owes a duty of confidentiality to his client. This means that if the defendant's solicitor has to cease to act for his client (if, for example, the client insists on the solicitor putting false or misleading information before the court), the defence solicitor should not tell the court why he is ceasing to act for his client. A defence solicitor who withdraws from acting in such circumstances will tell the court that he is no longer able to act for his client for 'professional reasons'.

The professional duties imposed on a solicitor when acting as the advocate for the prosecution are summarised at **1.6.3**.

The detailed rules of professional conduct with which a solicitor must comply when acting as an advocate (whether for the prosecution or the defence) are contained in Rule 11 ('Litigation and Advocacy') of the Solicitors' Code of Conduct 2007.

### 9.3.2 Preparing the defendant to give evidence

Prior to the trial, the defendant's solicitor must tell his client what is likely to happen at the trial. If the client is to give evidence in his own defence, it is a sensible step to supply the client with a copy of his witness statement, so that he can read it before the trial commences. The client will not be able to refer to his witness statement when giving evidence, but it is useful for him to be able to refresh his memory as to what he first told his solicitor about the offence.

The defendant's solicitor should be careful, however, not to 'coach' his client (or indeed any other defence witness). Advocates in the magistrates' court (whether representing the prosecution or the defence) should not rehearse or coach witnesses in relation to their evidence, or in the way in which that evidence should be given.

### 9.3.3 Modes of address

A trial in the magistrates' court will normally be conducted before a bench of three magistrates. Traditionally magistrates were addressed collectively as 'Your Worships', although it is now more common for remarks to be addressed to the chairperson of the bench of magistrates, using 'Sir' or 'Madam' as appropriate. If the trial takes place before a District Judge, 'Sir' or 'Madam' should be used as appropriate.

## 9.4 The prosecution case

### 9.4.1 Opening speech

A trial in the magistrates' court will begin with the solicitor from the CPS giving an opening speech. This does not form part of the evidence on which the magistrates will decide the case and is more a matter of 'setting the scene'. The opening speech will normally begin with the prosecuting solicitor telling the magistrates the factual details about the charge which the defendant faces. He will then explain to the magistrates the relevant substantive law and will tell them what the prosecution will need to prove in order to secure a conviction. The prosecuting solicitor should remind the magistrates that the prosecution have the burden of proving beyond a reasonable doubt that the defendant is guilty, and that the defendant is entitled to an acquittal unless the magistrates are sure that he is guilty (see **16.2**). The prosecuting solicitor will outline what the prosecution case consists of, tell the court which witnesses he intends to call to give evidence for the prosecution, and summarise briefly the evidence that is to be given by these witnesses. He may also refer the magistrates to any points of law which he anticipates may arise during the trial (for example, the *Turnbull* guidelines if the case consists of disputed identification evidence (see **17.2**), or ss 76 or 78 of PACE 1984 if there is disputed confession evidence (see **20.4** and **20.5**).

### 9.4.2 Prosecution evidence

After completing his opening speech, the prosecuting solicitor will call his first witness to give evidence. It is customary for the first prosecution witness to be the 'victim' of the alleged crime. For example, in an assault case the first prosecution witness is likely to be the person who was injured in the assault. In a theft case the first prosecution witness is likely to be the person whose property has been stolen. After the victim has given evidence, other prosecution witnesses (including any expert witnesses) will be called to give evidence.

Each prosecution witness who is called to give evidence will initially be asked questions by the prosecuting solicitor. This is called examination in chief and is designed to allow the witness to place his account before the court (see **9.8.1** below). The defendant's solicitor will then have the opportunity to cross-examine the witness (see **9.8.2** below). At the end of the cross-examination, the prosecuting solicitor may, if he chooses, briefly re-examine the witness (see **9.8.3** below).

Any prosecution witnesses who are not being called to give evidence (for example, witnesses who have given a statement under s 9 of the Criminal Justice Act 1967 to which the defence have not objected – see **8.4.4** – or witnesses whose statements are to be read out as hearsay evidence – see **Chapter 19**), will have their statements read out to the court by the prosecuting solicitor.

If the defendant was interviewed at the police station, either a summary or the full transcript of the interview will be read out to the court, unless the defendant's solicitor objects to this. If the defence solicitor does object (if, for example, the summary does not include points made by the defendant in support of his defence, or if the solicitor considers that the defendant came across well in the interview), the audio recording of the interview will be played to the court.

### 9.4.3 Arguments on points of law

During the presentation of his case, the prosecuting solicitor may seek to place evidence before the court which the defendant's solicitor considers to be inadmissible. A common example of this is when the prosecution seek to adduce evidence that the defendant made a confession, and the defendant's solicitor seeks to challenge the admissibility of this confession under s 76 of PACE 1984 on the basis that the confession was obtained in circumstances rendering it unreliable (see **20.4.3**). Another example is if the prosecution seek to adduce evidence that the defendant was visually identified by a witness following an identification procedure, and the defendant's solicitor seeks to challenge the admissibility of this evidence under s 78 of PACE 1984 on the basis that the identification procedure was not carried out in accordance with the requirements of Code D (see **3.5.3** and **17.5**).

If such a situation arises, the magistrates will normally hold a hearing called a voire dire to determine the admissibility of the particular piece of evidence in dispute. Such hearings are also often referred to as 'a trial within a trial'.

A voire dire will involve witnesses giving evidence on matters relevant to the admissibility of the evidence (for example, in the case of a disputed confession made in the context of an interview at the police station, both the police officer who conducted the interview and the defendant are likely to give evidence). After the witnesses have given evidence, the prosecuting solicitor and the defendant's solicitor will make legal submissions as to the admissibility of the disputed evidence.

If the magistrates decide that the evidence is inadmissible, the prosecuting solicitor will not be permitted to make any further reference to such evidence during the course of the trial. If the evidence is ruled to be admissible, it may then be produced by the prosecuting solicitor as part of the prosecution case (although the defendant's solicitor will still be entitled to attempt to undermine the reliability or cogency of such evidence during the trial).

#### Example 1

Robert is charged with theft. In an audibly recorded interview at the police station he confessed to the theft, and the CPS wishes to adduce evidence of this at Robert's trial. Robert's solicitor challenges the admissibility of the confession, arguing that it was obtained in circumstances which make it unreliable. The basis of this argument is that Robert claims that he confessed only after being told by the interviewing officer that he was going to be kept at the police station until he made a confession. At the voire dire the magistrates are likely to hear evidence from Robert and the interviewing officer, and they will also read a transcript of the interview or have the recording of the interview played out. Submissions will also be made by the prosecuting solicitor and Robert's solicitor. At the conclusion of the voire dire, the magistrates decide that the confession is inadmissible. This means that the prosecuting solicitor cannot use the confession as part of his case against Robert.

#### Example 2

Fiona is charged with common assault. In an audibly recorded interview at the police station, Fiona confessed to having committed the assault. Fiona's solicitor argues that the magistrates should rule the confession to be inadmissible because in the police interview the interviewing officer told Fiona that if she confessed to the offence she would receive a lighter sentence. Fiona's solicitor argues that this renders the confession unreliable. At the voire dire the magistrates will hear evidence from both the interviewing officer and Fiona, and will also either read a transcript of the interview or have the recording of the interview played out. The magistrates will also hear legal submissions from the prosecuting solicitor and from Fiona's solicitor. At the conclusion of the voire dire, the magistrates decide that the confession is admissible. The prosecuting solicitor will therefore be able to place evidence of the confession before the magistrates as part of his case against Fiona. Fiona's solicitor will still be permitted to attempt to undermine the reliability or cogency of this evidence during the trial (both when cross-examining the interviewing officer and when Fiona is giving evidence in chief), and will be able to make reference to this in his closing speech.

The difficulty faced by the defendant's solicitor when conducting a voire dire in the magistrates' court is that the magistrates decide matters of both law and fact. This means that even if the magistrates decide that a piece of prosecution evidence is inadmissible, the magistrates will still be aware of the existence of that item of evidence. Thus, when deciding their verdict, the magistrates will need to perform 'mental gymnastics' so as to set aside their knowledge of the inadmissible evidence. This situation will not arise in a Crown Court trial where the judge will conduct a voire dire in the absence of the jury, who will therefore never hear about any prosecution evidence which the judge rules to be inadmissible. The absence of a satisfactory procedure for dealing with the question of the admissibility of disputed prosecution evidence in a magistrates' court trial is one of the reasons why a defendant may elect trial in the Crown Court when charged with an either way matter (see **6.11.2.2**).

As an alternative to holding a separate 'trial within a trial', the magistrates may sometimes hear the disputed evidence as part of the trial itself, and then consider the question of the admissibility of such evidence either when the defendant's solicitor makes a submission of no case to answer at the conclusion of the prosecution case (see **9.5** below), or when he makes his closing submissions at the end of the trial.

To overcome problems at trial with magistrates being aware of the existence of an item of prosecution evidence even if they have decided that such evidence is admissible, many magistrates' courts now hold pre-trial hearings to determine the admissibility of disputed evidence. Pre-trial hearings will be held before a different bench of magistrates to the bench which ultimately conducts the trial, thus ensuring that the magistrates who actually decide the case need never be aware of items of evidence which are inadmissible.

## 9.5 Submission of no case to answer

When presenting his case to the magistrates, the prosecuting solicitor bears an evidential burden. This burden is to present sufficient evidence to the court to justify a finding of guilt (see **16.2.2.1**). If the prosecuting solicitor fails to satisfy this burden, the defendant's solicitor should make a submission of no case to answer at the conclusion of the prosecution case, asking the magistrates to dismiss the case.

A submission of no case to answer will be made by the defendant's solicitor if either:

(a) the prosecution have failed to put forward evidence to prove an essential element of the alleged offence; or

(b) the evidence produced by the prosecution has been so discredited as a result of cross-examination, or is so manifestly unreliable, that no reasonable tribunal could safely convict on it.

Example 1

Harvinder is charged with the theft of a bicycle. In presenting his case, the prosecuting solicitor fails to produce evidence that the bicycle belonged to another person. Proving that the item stolen belonged to another person is an essential element in the offence of theft. Harvinder's solicitor should therefore make a submission of no case to answer and request that the magistrates dismiss the case.

Example 2

Matthew is charged with assault occasioning actual bodily harm following an incident outside a night club. The victim of the alleged assault was attacked from behind and never saw his attacker. The prosecution case is based solely on evidence from a passer-by who witnessed the assault. This witness has identified Matthew, but in cross-examination by Matthews's solicitor this evidence is shown to be unreliable. The witness confirms in cross-examination that it was dark at the time of the assault, he was standing some distance away, he got only a fleeting glimpse of the assault and he didn't see the attacker's face. At the conclusion of the prosecution case, Matthew's solicitor will make a submission of no case to answer on the basis that the prosecution evidence is so manifestly unreliable that the court cannot safely convict on it.

If the magistrates accept a submission of no case to answer, the charge against the defendant will be dismissed. If the magistrates reject the submission of no case to answer, the defendant may then present his case and call witnesses. The fact that the prosecution have satisfied the evidential burden does not mean that the prosecution are entitled to a conviction at that stage. This is because the court will not yet have heard either from the defendant, or from any witnesses the defendant wishes to call in support of his defence.

## 9.6 The defence case

### 9.6.1 Should the defendant give evidence?

#### 9.6.1.1 Competence and compellability of the defendant

A defendant is a competent witness for the defence but is not compellable. This means that a defendant can give evidence on his own behalf but he is not obliged to do so (Criminal Evidence Act 1898, s 1(1)). Prior to the trial taking place the defendant's solicitor should always discuss with the defendant whether or not he should give evidence in his own defence. A defendant may be reluctant to give evidence, particularly if he is young or nervous, or if he fears that his 'story' will not stand up to cross-examination by the prosecuting solicitor.

In the normal course of events it will be necessary for the defendant to give evidence (assuming there has not been a successful submission of no case to answer by his solicitor). For example, a defendant who is raising a defence such as self-defence or alibi has the evidential burden of placing some evidence of this defence before the court (see **16.2.2.2**). The simplest way to discharge this burden is for the defendant himself to give evidence. Similarly, if the prosecution have adduced evidence of a confession made by the defendant, and the defendant disputes the truth of this confession, the defendant will need to give evidence to explain why he made a false confession.

A defendant who answered questions (or provided a written statement) at the police station will have the credibility of this evidence enhanced if he goes into the witness box at trial and repeats what he said at the police station. A defendant who does this will enable his solicitor, when giving his closing speech, to say that the defendant has put forward a consistent defence since first being arrested and questioned.

### 9.6.1.2 Criminal Justice and Public Order Act 1994, s 35

In addition to the above, as a result of s 35 of the CJPOA 1994, a defendant who fails to give evidence on his own behalf at trial is likely to find that the court will draw an adverse inference from such failure. Section 35(2) provides that:

> ... the court shall, at the conclusion of the evidence for the prosecution, satisfy itself ... that the accused is aware that the stage has been reached at which evidence can be given for the defence and that he can, if he wishes, give evidence and that, if he chooses not to give evidence, or having been sworn, without good cause refuses to answer any question, it will be permissible for the court or jury to draw such inferences as appear proper from his failure to give evidence or his refusal, without good cause, to answer any question.

The effect of s 35 is that, if the prosecution have raised issues which call for an explanation from the defendant, should the defendant then fail to give evidence the court will be entitled to infer from that failure that the defendant has either no explanation, or no explanation that will stand up to cross-examination.

**Example**

Marcus is charged with common assault. Marcus pleads not guilty on the basis that he was acting in self-defence. At the end of the prosecution case, Marcus declines to enter the witness box to give evidence on his own behalf. The court is entitled to infer from this that Marcus has no defence to the charge, or no defence that will stand up to cross-examination (in other words, an inference that Marcus is guilty of the offence).

A defendant may not be convicted of an offence if the only evidence against him is an adverse inference from his failure to give evidence in his defence at trial (CJPOA 1994, s 38(3)).

In the cases of *R v Cowan; R v Gayle; R v Ricciardy* [1995] 4 All ER 939, the Court of Appeal stated that the court had to take into account the following matters when considering the application of s 35:

(a) the burden of proof remains on the prosecution throughout;
(b) the defendant is entitled to remain silent;
(c) *before* drawing an adverse inference from the defendant's silence, the court had to be satisfied that there was a case to answer on the prosecution evidence;
(d) an adverse inference from the defendant's failure to give evidence cannot on its own prove guilt; and
(e) no adverse inference could be drawn unless the only sensible explanation for the defendant's silence was that he had no answer to the case against him, or none that could have stood up to cross-examination.

In *R v Whitehead* [2006] EWCA Crim 1486, the Court of Appeal stated that the jury or magistrates should start by considering the prosecution evidence rather than the defendant's silence. They had to conclude that this evidence was sufficiently cogent to call for an explanation before considering the implications of the defendant's silence. Once that threshold had been crossed, the jury or magistrates were then entitled to consider the defendant's silence as a further evidential factor and in the context of the evidence as a whole.

#### 9.6.1.3 Advice to the defendant

In light of s 35, it will be very rare for a defendant's solicitor to advise his client not to give evidence. The only potential advantage to not giving evidence is that this will prevent a defendant either incriminating himself, or coming across as lacking credibility in the witness box; but this is heavily outweighed by the risk that an adverse inference will be drawn from such silence. A defendant who is raising a specific defence (such as alibi or self-defence) will need to enter the witness box to discharge his evidential burden and to substantiate that defence. Similarly, there may be a need for the defendant to give evidence if it is necessary to 'explain' away a piece of evidence on which the CPS seeks to rely. For example, a defendant may have an explanation for having made an admission or confession upon which the CPS seeks to rely, or there may be a need to explain why an adverse inference should not be drawn under s 36 or s 37 of the CJPOA 1994 if, when interviewed by the police, the defendant failed to account for the presence of a mark, object or substance, or he failed to account for his presence at a particular location.

A flowchart summarising whether the defendant will be required to give evidence and the consequences of a defendant not giving evidence is set out at **9.9.2** below.

### 9.6.2 Order of defence witnesses

If a defendant is to give evidence on his own behalf, he must be called prior to any other witnesses for the defence unless the court 'otherwise directs' (PACE 1984, s 79). The rationale behind this is that the defendant will be in court throughout the proceedings. Therefore, if other defence witnesses were to give evidence before the defendant, the defendant would have the opportunity to hear what they said and could then tailor his own testimony to take account of the comments made by the other defence witnesses.

Defence witnesses will give evidence in the same way as prosecution witnesses. Each defence witness will be examined in chief by the defendant's solicitor and will then be cross-examined by the prosecuting solicitor. The defendant's solicitor will then have the opportunity to re-examine the witness.

### 9.6.3 The closing speech

The defendant's solicitor has a choice in the magistrates' court as to whether to make an opening or a closing speech. In practice, solicitors representing the defendant will nearly always choose to make a closing speech, given the tactical importance of having the last word after all the evidence has been presented to the court. Like the prosecution opening speech (see **9.4.1** above), the defence closing speech is not itself evidence. It does, however, allow the defendant's solicitor to sum up the case from the defence point of view, to point out all the weaknesses in the prosecution case and to remind the court of all the points in favour of the defendant.

Although there is no set format for making a closing speech, the following points should be borne in mind:

(a) The closing speech should be kept short and to the point. Closing speeches that are too long often have little impact on the magistrates.

(b) The defendant's solicitor must always remind the magistrates that the CPS bears the burden of proving beyond a reasonable doubt that the defendant is guilty of the offence with which he is charged. The magistrates should be told that the defendant is entitled to an acquittal unless they are sure that the defendant is guilty (see **16.2.1**). The defendant does not need to prove that he is innocent. All he need do to secure an acquittal is to demonstrate that the CPS has failed to prove its case beyond a reasonable doubt.

(c) The defendant's solicitor should refer back to the opening speech made by the prosecuting solicitor, in which the prosecuting solicitor set out what he was going to prove. The defendant's solicitor should point out each and every area where the prosecution case has 'come up short'. The defendant's solicitor should place particular emphasis on the factual weaknesses or discrepancies in the prosecution case.

(d) The defendant's solicitor may also need to cover evidential issues during the closing speech. If, for example, the prosecution have relied upon disputed identification evidence, the defendant's solicitor will need to give a *Turnbull* warning (see **17.4**) to the magistrates. Alternatively, if the CPS has have been permitted to rely on disputed confession evidence, the defendant's solicitor should seek to undermine the credibility of such evidence. If the evidence of the defendant's bad character has emerged at trial (see **Chapter 22**), the defendant's solicitor will need to downplay the significance of such evidence. If, on the other hand, the defendant is of good character, it should be pointed out to the magistrates that this is of relevance both to the defendant's propensity to commit the offence with which he has been charged, and also as to his credibility as a witness (see **22.8**).

(e) The closing speech is all about persuasion. In other words, the defendant's solicitor should 'show' the magistrates how to find the defendant not guilty. It is often a sensible tactic to conclude the closing speech by listing all the weaknesses of the prosecution case (and the strengths of the defence case), and then invite the magistrates to conclude that the only possible verdict is one of not guilty.

## 9.7 The verdict

The magistrates will normally retire to consider their verdict. Most trials in the magistrates' court will be before a bench of three magistrates. The magistrates may make their decision by majority. There does not need to be unanimous agreement on the verdict. When the magistrates return to court after deciding upon the verdict, the defendant will be asked to stand and will be told by the chairperson of the bench that he has been found either not guilty or guilty.

If the defendant is found guilty, the magistrates will move on to consider the sentence to be imposed. The magistrates will either sentence the defendant immediately, or adjourn the case for a number of weeks if they wish to obtain medical or other reports before passing sentence. If the defendant is sentenced immediately, his solicitor will deliver a plea in mitigation to the magistrates prior to sentence (see **12.7**). If the magistrates adjourn the case before passing sentence, they will need to consider whether the defendant should be granted bail or remanded in custody prior to the sentencing hearing (see **7.3**). A defendant who has been found guilty following a trial in the magistrates' court has the right to appeal against his conviction and/or sentence to the Crown Court. The procedure for doing this is described in **Chapter 13**.

If the defendant is acquitted by the magistrates, he will be formally discharged and told that he is free to go. In such a case, if the defendant's case was not funded by way of a representation order, the magistrates will usually direct that his legal costs be paid for from central funds (ie, by the State).

## 9.8 Advocacy techniques

### 9.8.1 Introduction

Although this chapter is principally concerned with the procedure at a summary trial in the magistrates' court, the advocacy techniques suggested below are equally applicable to a trial in the Crown Court.

The evidence which a bench of magistrates (or a jury in the Crown Court) will consider when deciding the defendant's guilt or innocence will be the oral evidence they have heard from witnesses at the trial, together with any statements which have been read out at trial and any documentary or real evidence (such as the audio-recording of the defendant's interview at the police station, any CCTV footage that exists, or any items produced as exhibits such as a weapon used in an assault or allegedly stolen goods). The evidence which the court hears from each witness who is called to give evidence at trial falls into three parts:

(a) examination-in-chief;

(b) cross-examination;

(c) re-examination.

### 9.8.2 Examination in chief

#### 9.8.2.1 Purpose

The purpose of examination-in-chief is to allow a witness to 'tell his story'. The advocate conducting the examination-in-chief should ask questions which enable the witness to repeat the version of events which that witness has provided in his witness statement.

The difficulty in conducting an examination-in-chief is that the advocate is not allowed to ask leading questions. Leading questions are questions which are suggestive of the answer.

**Example**

Murray is called as a prosecution witness. He is to testify to the fact that at 2 pm on 5 June he saw Grant steal a tin of baked beans from Sainsbury's.

The prosecuting solicitor cannot say to Murray: 'Did you see Grant steal a tin of baked beans from Sainsbury's at 2 pm on 5 June?' This is a leading question.

#### 9.8.2.2 Techniques

Instead of asking leading questions, an advocate conducting an examination-in-chief should use 'open' questions to elicit the information from the witness.

**Example**

Continuing with the example at **9.8.2.1** above, the prosecutor could elicit the information from Murray in the following way:

Q Where were you on 5 June at about 2 pm?

A In Sainsbury's.

Q Did anything unusual happen whilst you were in Sainsbury's?

A Yes, I saw Grant pick up a tin of baked beans and put this in his pocket.

Q What happened next?

A I saw Grant walk out of the shop without paying for the tin of baked beans.

Inexperienced advocates sometimes find that their conduct of an examination-in-chief involves repeating the same question to the witness ('And what happened next?') time after time. A far better technique to adopt is 'piggy-backing', where each question builds on the answer to the last question.

**Example**

Q Are you in employment, Mr Brown?

A Yes, I am the manager at Barclays Bank in Bishopthorpe.

Q Were you at work at the bank on 15 November?

A Yes.

Q What time did you get to work?

A About 8.30 am.

Q What did you after you got to work?

A I opened up the bank and made myself a cup of coffee. Whilst I was waiting for other members of staff to arrive, I opened that morning's post.

Q What did you do after you had opened the post?

A I went to open the front door of the bank to let in the other members of staff.

Q Did anything unusual happen as you went to open the front door?

A Yes, I was confronted by a man wearing a balaclava and brandishing a sawn-off shotgun.

### 9.8.2.3 Witnesses who don't 'come up to proof'

A witness who is called to give evidence for either the prosecution or the defence will usually have provided a written statement (sometimes referred to as a 'proof of evidence') to the party for whom he is going to give evidence. The questions asked in examination-in-chief will be designed to allow the witness to state orally for the court what he has already said on paper in his witness statement.

A witness who is called to give evidence may not give the evidence expected of him. This is known colloquially as a witness 'not coming up to proof'. If the failure to 'come up to proof' is not deliberate (and occurs only because the witness is nervous, forgetful or ignorant), the party calling the witness is not allowed to contradict or to try to discredit the witness. If, however, the witness appears to be unwilling (rather than unable) to tell the truth on behalf of the party calling him, that party may then apply to the magistrates (or the judge in the Crown Court) to declare the witness to be 'hostile'. If the witness is declared hostile, he may:

(a) be cross-examined by the party calling him (this will allow that party to put leading questions to the witness to show that he is being untruthful); and

(b) have any previous inconsistent statement put to him by the party calling him (see **9.8.3.2** below).

In practice, witnesses are commonly shown to be hostile by proving that they have made an earlier out-of-court statement from which they appear to be deliberately and dishonestly departing.

**Example**

Michael is a member of a criminal gang. A fellow gang member, Robby, is on trial for theft, and Michael is due to give evidence for the prosecution confirming that Robby committed the theft. Michael has given a written statement to the police confirming this. However at Robby's trial, Michael denies that Robby had anything to do with the theft. The prosecution can apply to the court to declare Michael to be 'hostile'. If Michael is declared hostile, he can be asked leading questions by the prosecution to show that he is being untruthful, and his previous inconsistent statement (in which he said that Robby committed the theft) may be put to him.

#### 9.8.2.4 May a witness refresh his memory in the witness box?

A witness who attends court to give oral evidence is not allowed to have a copy of his statement in front of him when giving evidence. However, the party calling that witness may apply to the court for the witness to refresh his memory in the witness box from a document which was made or verified by him at an earlier time. Section 139(1) of the Criminal Justice Act 2003 allows a witness to do this if the witness confirms to the court that the document records his recollection of the matters at that earlier time, and his recollection of the matters is likely to have been significantly better at the earlier time than it is at the time of his giving evidence.

**Example**

Roderick is charged with theft from a shop. On leaving the shop he was apprehended by PC White, who will say that Roderick immediately confessed to having committed the theft as soon as he had been stopped. PC White then made a note of the exact words used by Roderick. When giving evidence in the witness box, PC White will be permitted to refer to his note book to refresh his memory as to exactly what Roderick said, as long as the court is satisfied that the entry in the note book records PC White's recollection of the confession made by Roderick at the earlier time, and that PC White's recollection of the confession is likely to have been significantly better at the time he made the record in his note book than at the time of giving evidence at trial.

In *R v McAfee* [2006] EWCA Crim 2914, it was held that there was no requirement the document used to refresh memory must have been made contemporaneously.

**Example**

Joanne witnesses a burglary taking place at factory premises. She sees the burglars drive away in a vehicle and makes a mental note of the registration number. Several hours later Joanne makes a note of the registration number in her pocket diary. When giving evidence for the prosecution, Joanne will be permitted to refer to her pocket diary to refresh her memory as to the details of the registration number, as long as the court is satisfied that the entry made by Joanne in her diary records the details of the registration number, and that Joanne's recollection of the registration number is likely to have been significantly better at the time she made the note than at the time of her giving the evidence. The fact that Joanne made the note in her diary several hours after seeing the registration number will not prevent Joanne from being able to use the diary entry to refresh her memory.

If a witness is permitted to use a document to refresh his memory whilst in the witness box and is cross-examined on the contents of the document, the document will itself become an item of evidence in the proceedings, and will be admissible as evidence of any matter of which oral evidence by the witness would have been admissible (Criminal Justice Act 2003, s 120(3)). Thus, in the example above, Joanne's entry in her pocket diary will itself be admissible as evidence to show that the burglars drove away in a vehicle with the relevant registration number.

#### 9.8.2.5 Previous consistent statements

**The common law position**

Prior to the Criminal Justice Act 2003 coming into force, there was a common law rule against previous consistent or self-serving statements, which prevented a witness from being asked about a previous oral or written statement made by him and consistent with his evidence. For example, in *R v Roberts* [1942] 1 All ER 187, the defendant was convicted of murdering his girlfriend by shooting her. The Court of Appeal held that the trial judge had correctly excluded evidence from the defendant that, two days after the shooting, he had told his father that the gun had gone off accidentally. The Court held that this type of evidence had no evidential value, because the fact that a defendant said something to another person on a previous occasion did not confirm his evidence at court.

This common law rule was subject to an exception in cases involving a sexual offence. If the victim of an alleged sexual offence made a voluntary complaint shortly after the offence had been committed, the prosecution were permitted to call to give evidence the person to whom the complaint was made. Evidence from this person was not admissible to prove that the offence had actually taken place, but was admissible to show that the victim had acted in a consistent way and was therefore a credible witness.

### Criminal Justice Act 2003

Section 120(4) of the Criminal Justice Act 2003 has extended the above common law exception to *all* types of offence (not just sexual offences), by providing that a previous statement made by a witness is admissible as evidence of any matter stated of which oral evidence by the witness would be admissible, provided one or more of certain conditions is satisfied.

Section 120(4) states:

> (4) A previous statement by the witness is admissible as evidence of any matter stated of which oral evidence by him would be admissible if—
> (a) any of the following three conditions is satisfied, and
> (b) while giving evidence the witness indicates that to the best of his belief he made the statement, and that to the best of his belief it states the truth.

The first condition is that the statement identifies or describes a person, place or object (s 120(5)).

The second condition is that the statement was made by the witness when the matters stated were fresh in his memory, but he does not remember them, and cannot reasonably be expected to remember them, well enough to give oral evidence of them in the proceedings (s 120(6)).

The third condition is set out in s 120(7), which provides:

(a) the witness claims to be a person against whom an offence has been committed;

(b) the offence is one to which the current criminal proceedings relate;

(c) the statement consists of a complaint made by a witness about conduct which would, if proved, constitute the offence;

(d) the complaint was made as soon as could reasonably be expected after the alleged conduct;

(e) the complaint was not made as a result of a threat or promise; and

(f) before the statement is adduced, the witness gives oral evidence in connection with its subject matter.

#### Example

Derrick, a student, is charged with raping Samantha at an end-of-term party held at Derrick's house. Derrick denies the charge, claiming that Samantha consented to sexual intercourse. The rape is alleged to have occurred at approximately 11.00 pm. Samantha left the house 15 minutes after the alleged rape occurred, in the company of a friend, Rachel. On their way home, Samantha broke down in tears and told Rachel what had happened. A few days later Samantha made a complaint to the police, claiming that she had been raped by Derrick. Rachel also gave a statement to the police, detailing what she had been told by Samantha on their way home from Derrick's house. At Derrick's trial, Samantha will give evidence as to what she told Rachel, and Rachel will be permitted to give evidence confirming what she was told by Samantha, provided the above conditions in s 120(4) and (7) are satisfied. (The evidence will be admissible both to show that the rape occurred and also that Samantha has acted consistently (ie, by making an immediate allegation of rape to Rachel and subsequently reporting this to the police) – see below.

In *R v O* [2006] EWCA Crim 556, the defendant was convicted of various sexual offences committed against his step-daughter, who had given evidence against him. The trial judge had permitted the prosecution to adduce a complaint the step-daughter had made to her mother about the defendant's behaviour, and a further complaint the step-daughter had made to her brother some four months later. This evidence was admitted under s 120(4) and (7). The defendant challenged the admissibility of the evidence, arguing that the condition in s 120(7) that the complaint be made as soon as could reasonably be expected after the alleged conduct was not met. This argument was rejected by the Court of Appeal.

A statement which is repeated in evidence at trial by virtue of s 120(4) and (7) is admissible both to prove the truth of the matters contained in the statement and also to show the credibility of the witness by demonstrating that the witness has given a consistent version of events throughout. Thus in *R v O*, evidence of the complaints made by the step-daughter was admissible both to prove that the defendant had committed the offences and also to support the step-daughter's credibility as a witness.

A statement to which s 120(4) applies will constitute hearsay evidence, but will be admissible in evidence at trial by virtue of s 114(1)(a) of the Criminal Justice Act 2003 (see **Chapter 19**).

### Rebutting a suggestion of recent fabrication

Subject to s 120(4) of the Criminal Justice Act 2003 (see above), the common law rule against the admissibility of previous self-serving statements remains. However, if in cross-examination it is put to the witness that his evidence has recently been fabricated, in re-examination the witness may be asked about evidence of a previous consistent statement to negative the suggestion of recent fabrication and to confirm his credibility.

#### Example 1

Fergus is on trial for theft and raises an alibi defence. When interviewed about the theft at the police station following his arrest, Fergus gave a 'no comment' interview. Whilst at the police station Fergus did give a statement to his solicitor setting out his defence of alibi, but the solicitor did not hand the statement to the police. In cross-examination at trial, it is put to Fergus that his alibi defence was made up after he left the police station. In re-examination, Fergus will be permitted to give evidence that he gave a statement to his solicitor at the police station setting out his defence.

Example 2

In *R v Oyesiku* (1971) 56 Cr App R 240, the defendant was convicted of assaulting a police officer. His wife gave evidence that the police officer had been the aggressor. It was put to her in cross-examination that she had fabricated this account. The Court of Appeal held that the trial judge had properly allowed it to be put to her in re-examination that she had in fact made a prior statement to her husband's solicitor confirming the police officer as being the aggressor. This statement had been made just after her husband's arrest but before she had been able to speak to him. The Court of Appeal held that the trial judge should also have permitted the jury to inspect the statement itself to enable them to judge the extent to which the statement refuted the suggestion that the wife's evidence had been fabricated.

If a previous statement made by a witness is admitted in evidence to rebut a suggestion that the evidence given by the witness has been fabricated, the previous statement is admissible both to show that the witness has given a consistent account throughout and also to show that the account given by the witness in true (Criminal Justice Act 2003, s 120(2)). Thus, in **Example 1** above, the statement given by Fergus to his solicitor will be admissible both to show that Fergus has given a consistent version of events throughout (rather than fabricating his defence after he left the police station), and also as evidence of the truth of the alibi defence which Fergus is putting forward at trial.

As with s 120(4), a statement to which s 120(2) applies will constitute hearsay evidence, but will be admissible in evidence at trial by virtue of s 114(1)(a) of the Criminal Justice Act 2003 (see **Chapter 19**).

### 9.8.2.6 Anticipating cross-examination

In addition to letting the witness tell his story, an advocate conducting an examination-in-chief should also anticipate any matters which are likely to arise in cross-examination. If the advocate considers that there are any damaging matters which are likely to come out in cross-examination, he may minimise such damage by raising these matters in examination-in-chief. This is particularly relevant for a defendant's solicitor who is carrying out an examination-in-chief of a client who has a number of previous convictions which are likely to be raised in cross-examination by the prosecuting solicitor (see **Chapter 22**). If the defendant's solicitor knows that evidence of his client's previous convictions is going to emerge in cross-examination, it is better for him to raise such convictions himself in examination-in-chief. Doing this will take the 'sting' out of a prosecution attack on the defendant's character and enable the defendant to give a proper explanation for his previous conduct.

## Key skill – conducting an examination-in-chief

Q Mr Barnard, do you recall 17 December 2007?
A Yes, I was at work during the day and then I went out that evening.
Q When you went out for the evening, where did you go?
A I went out to a club called Connolley's in Chester city centre at about 10.30 pm.
Q How long were you in Connolley's?
A Four or five hours. I left at approximately 3 am the following morning.
Q What did you do when you left the club?
A I set off to walk to a friend's house where I was going to spend the night.
Q Did anything happen as you walked to your friend's house?

A About 15 minutes after I set off I saw a dark coloured VW Golf zoom past me then stop sharply next to a young man who was walking ahead of me.
Q Did anything happen after the car stopped?
A The driver of the car got out.
Q Did the driver of the car do anything after he got out of the car?
A Yes, he hit the other man in the face several times.
Q Did the other man do anything to provoke the attack?
A No.
Q What happened after the attack had finished?
A The man got back in his car and drove away, passing me again.
Q Can you describe the man who carried out the attack?
A Yes, he was a well-built man with short dark hair and a tight-fitting white t-shirt. He was white and clean shaven.
Q Do you recall any further details about the car?
A It was a dark blue Golf. The registration number was either C251 CVM or L251 CVM.
Q How can you be sure of this?
A I used to be in the army and have had training in vehicle recognition. I made a mental note of the registration number at the time and told a police officer later on in the evening.
Q Mr Barnard did you subsequently attend at a video identification at Chester police station?
A Yes.
Q At the video identification were you able to pick out the person you had seen on 18 December?
A Yes.
Q Do you see that person in court today?
A Yes, it's Mr Dickson, the defendant.

## 9.8.3 Cross-examination

### 9.8.3.1 Purpose

The cross-examination of a witness called by the other party in the case has two purposes:

(a) to enable the party conducting the cross-examination to put his case to the witness; and

(b) to undermine the credibility of the evidence which that witness has just given in examination-in-chief.

In some circumstances, a defendant is not permitted to cross-examine in person certain categories of prosecution witness (Youth Justice and Criminal Evidence Act (YJCEA) 1999, ss 34–36 and CrimPR, Part 31). The detailed provisions of this are beyond the scope of this book, but in summary a defendant may not cross-examine in person a complainant in a case involving an alleged sexual offence (YJCEA 1999, s 34). For some offences, restrictions also exist on a defendant being able to cross-examine in person a complainant who is a child, or any other child witness (YJCEA 1999, s 35). Where the witness is neither a child nor the victim of alleged sexual offence, the court may make an order preventing the defendant from personally cross-examining that witness if:

(a) the quality of evidence given by the witness on cross-examination:

(i) is likely to be diminished if the cross-examination is conducted by the defendant in person, and

(ii) the quality of such evidence would be likely to be improved if the witness were not cross-examined by the defendant in person; and

(b) it would not be contrary to the interests of justice to prevent the defendant from cross-examining the witness in person (YJCEA 1999, s 36).

#### 9.8.3.2 'Putting your case'

'Putting your case' means suggesting to a witness that the version of events which that witness has just put forward in examination-in-chief is incorrect, and suggesting an alternative version of events. It is always necessary for an advocate to put his client's version of events to a witness in cross-examination. For example, in an assault case where the defendant is claiming he acted only in self-defence, the defendant's solicitor must, when cross-examining the alleged victim of the assault, put to the victim that he (the victim) attacked the defendant first and that the defendant was acting only in self-defence. If the defendant's solicitor fails to put to the witness that the defendant was acting in self-defence, the defendant will then not be entitled to enter the witness box and say that he was acting in self-defence.

Putting your case often means asking a witness a series of questions which elicit a negative response. This is something which can be disconcerting for inexperienced advocates but is still something which needs to be done.

**Example**

Q Mr Green, you have told the court that my client attacked you without provocation?

A Yes.

Q That's not correct is it Mr Green?

A Yes it is correct.

Q Mr Green, isn't it the case that you attacked my client first?

A No.

Q Mr Green, I put it to you that you punched my client in the face and my client was only defending himself?

A No.

Q Mr Green, my client was only acting in self-defence wasn't he?

A No.

#### 9.8.3.3 Discrediting the witness

Discrediting the testimony which the witness has just given in examination-in-chief involves undermining the credibility of the witness and exposing any weaknesses in his evidence. For example, if the court gives leave, the witness should be cross-examined about any previous convictions he has for offences involving untruthfulness (such as perjury or fraud), or offences where the witness was convicted by the court after he had entered a not guilty plea, to suggest that he is not a credible witness and his testimony should not be relied upon (see **Chapter 22**). Alternatively, if the defendant is charged with assault and raises the defence of self-defence, the victim of the alleged assault should be cross-examined about any previous convictions he has for offences involving violence. (See **Chapter 22**.) If the witness is unsure or uncertain about any point, this should be exploited to suggest that the witness's recollection of events is incomplete and unreliable. If possible, advocates should avoid suggesting to a witness that his evidence has been intentionally fabricated, or that the witness is intentionally lying. Most witnesses in criminal cases do attempt to tell the truth, and witnesses are far more liable to give contradictory evidence as a result of being confused or unsure, rather than from any malicious motive. A direct attack on the character of a prosecution witness in cross-examination is likely to lead to the court permitting the prosecuting solicitor to adduce evidence of the defendant's previous convictions (see **Chapter 22**).

#### 9.8.3.4 Restrictions on questions to undermine the credibility of the witness

There are no general restrictions on the type of questions that may be asked of a witness to undermine the credibility of the evidence given by him. However, in cases where the defendant has been charged with a sexual offence, s 41 of the Youth Justice and Criminal Evidence Act 1999 imposes restrictions on the defendant adducing evidence about the complainant's previous sexual behaviour, or the complainant being cross-examined about such behaviour. A defendant is not permitted to adduce evidence or ask questions in cross-examination about the previous sexual conduct of the complainant unless leave of the court is obtained. In the leading case of *R v A (Complainant's Sexual History)* [2001] 3 All ER 1, the House of Lords considered when leave should be given in the context of a case where the defendant raised the defence of consent (or a reasonable belief that the complainant consented) and wanted to adduce evidence of his previous sexual relationship with the complainant. Their Lordships held that leave should be given in such a case when the evidence and the questioning in relation to it was so relevant to the issue of consent that to exclude it would endanger the fairness of the trial under Article 6 of the ECHR (see **1.8.3**). The procedural steps which must be followed by a defendant seeking leave to adduce evidence at trial of a complainant's previous sexual history are contained in Part 36 of the Criminal Procedure Rules.

In *R v V* [2006] EWCA Crim 1901, the Court of Appeal held that any cross-examination genuinely directed towards establishing that the complainant had made a previous false complaint about a sexual matter falls outside s 41 as long as it relates to the alleged lies rather than to the sexual behaviour itself. This decision was upheld in *R v Stephenson* [2006] All ER (D) 120 (Aug). The defendant was convicted of various sexual offences. The trial judge had refused the defendant leave under s 41 to cross-examine the complainant on her sexual history. The defendant had wanted to cross-examine the complainant about the fact that she had made similar allegations (of rape and sexual assault) against every other male she had ever come into contact with, allegations which had subsequently proved to be false. The Court of Appeal held that the purpose of such cross-examination was to undermine the credibility of the complainant, rather than to question her sexual history.

There is a general rule that the answer given by a witness to a question designed to undermine the credibility of that witness shall be final and no further questions may be put to the witness on the same point. This rule is subject to a number of exceptions which permit further questions if the witness responds negatively to such a question. These exceptions are:

(a) a question asked to prove that the witness is *biased* (if the witness responds by denying that he is biased, further questions may be asked of the witness to establish that bias exists);

(b) a question asked to prove that the witness has made a *previous inconsistent statement* (see **9.8.3.5** below); and

(c) a question asked to prove that the witness has a relevant *previous conviction* (if the witness denies having such a conviction, further questions may be asked to establish this and a memorandum of conviction may be placed before the court – see **22.7.6**).

### 9.8.3.5 Previous inconsistent statements

A previous inconsistent statement may be put to a witness in cross-examination (or to a witness during examination-in-chief if the court has declared the witness to be 'hostile') in order to undermine the credibility of the oral evidence given by the witness. In addition, s 119(1) of the Criminal Justice Act 2003 provides that if a person giving oral evidence at trial admits that he made a previous inconsistent statement, or it is proved that such a statement was made, that previous statement will itself be admissible in evidence to show that the contents of this statement are in fact correct. The previous inconsistent statement will be hearsay evidence, but will be admissible by virtue of s 114(1)(a) of the Criminal Justice Act 2003.

#### Example 1

Graham is charged with theft and raises the defence of alibi, claiming that he was at home with his wife Gillian at the time of the theft. While Graham is being questioned at the police station, the police take a statement from Gillian. Gillian states that, at the time the theft is alleged to have taken place, Graham was not with her but had gone out shopping. Gillian subsequently refuses to give evidence for the prosecution at Graham's trial (as Graham's spouse she cannot be compelled to give evidence for the prosecution – see **Chapter 16**). Gillian is then called as a defence witness at Graham's trial. She gives evidence that, at the time Graham is alleged to have committed the theft, Graham was at home with her. In cross-examination the prosecuting solicitor will be able to put to Gillian the previous inconsistent statement to the police, in order to undermine the credibility of the evidence Gillian has given in support of Graham's alibi. Gillian's statement to the police will itself also be admissible in evidence to show that the contents of the statement are correct, and that Graham was not in fact at home with her at the time of the theft.

#### Example 2

*R v Joyce and Joyce* [2005] EWCA Crim 1785 – the defendants were convicted of various firearms offences in connection with a shooting. A number of witnesses for the prosecution had provided statements to the police identifying the defendants (who were personally known to them) as the persons who had carried out the shooting. At trial these witnesses retracted their statements, and claimed that their earlier identifications of the defendants were incorrect. Despite this retraction, the jury convicted the defendants, having clearly decided that the initial account given to the police by the witnesses was correct. The conviction was upheld by the Court of Appeal, which held that the jury were entitled to view the previous inconsistent statements not only as something to undermine the credibility of the evidence given by the witnesses at trial, but also as evidence that the contents of the previous inconsistent statements were in fact true, and that the defendants were responsible for the shooting.

### 9.8.3.6 Techniques of cross-examination

Carrying out an effective cross-examination requires an advocate to 'control' the answers which the witness gives. This is done by asking 'closed' questions. 'Closed' questions are questions which require a Yes/No answer. 'Open' questions, which allow the witness to expand upon the evidence he has given when examined in chief, should never be asked in cross-examination.

Example

Q Mr Green, you had been out drinking on the night in question hadn't you?
A Yes.
Q You'd been in the pub for several hours hadn't you?
A Yes.
Q And you drank six pints of lager and a couple of whisky chasers?
A Yes.
Q So you would agree with me that you had a lot to drink?
A Yes.
Q Having a lot to drink will impair your judgement, won't it Mr Green?
A Not necessarily.
Q Would you drink six pints of lager and a couple of whisky chasers before driving your car?
A No.
Q Because it would impair your judgement wouldn't it?
A Yes.

## Key skill – conducting a cross-examination

Q Mr Barnard, you told the court that you spent the evening of 17 December at a club?
A That's correct.
Q You had quite a bit to drink, didn't you Mr Barnard?
A I wouldn't say I had that much.
Q Well according to your statement you had seven pints to drink. Is that correct?
A Yes.
Q That's quite a lot isn't it Mr Barnard?
A I suppose so.
Q You have said that as you were walking to your friend's house a car zoomed past you and pulled up 50 metres away?
A Yes.
Q 50 metres is just a guess?
A Yes.
Q It could have been further couldn't it?
A Yes.
Q And this was at 3.15 am in the middle of December wasn't it?
A Yes.
Q So it must have been very dark?
A Yes.
Q You say that a well-built man got out of the car and attacked a pedestrian?
A Yes.
Q That's not a very full description is it?
A I suppose not, but I saw the man again when he drove past me after he had done the assault.
Q When the man drove past you after committing the assault you have said he was travelling at about 40 mph?
A Yes, but I got a fair look at him.
Q That's not what you said in your statement Mr Barnard. In your statement you said you only managed to glimpse him. That's correct isn't it?
A Yes.

Q Mr Barnard, are you familiar with Connelley's nightclub?
A Yes
Q Mr Barnard do the staff at Connelley's wear a uniform?
A Yes.
Q What is that uniform?
A They all wear tight-fitting white t-shirts.
Q And the driver of the car was wearing a tight-fitting white t-shirt wasn't he Mr Barnard?
A Yes.
Q So you saw an incident from a long distance away, it was dark at the time, you'd had a lot to drink and the only description you can give could apply to numerous other people. That's correct isn't it?
A Yes.

### 9.8.4 Re-examination

Following cross-examination, the advocate who originally called the witness to give evidence in chief may carry out a brief re-examination of the witness. Re-examinations are rare and should be carried out only where a case has been damaged in cross-examination *and* the advocate considers that some of that damage can be repaired by way of re-examination. An advocate should seek to avoid carrying out a re-examination if at all possible, because this is a clear indication to the court that the advocate's case has been damaged. Re-examination can only ever cover matters which have been raised in cross-examination. An advocate who has forgotten to raise a matter with witness in examination-in-chief cannot raise that matter in re-examination, unless the matter has been brought up in cross-examination by the opposing advocate.

## 9.9 Procedural flowcharts

### 9.9.1 Trial procedure in the magistrates' court

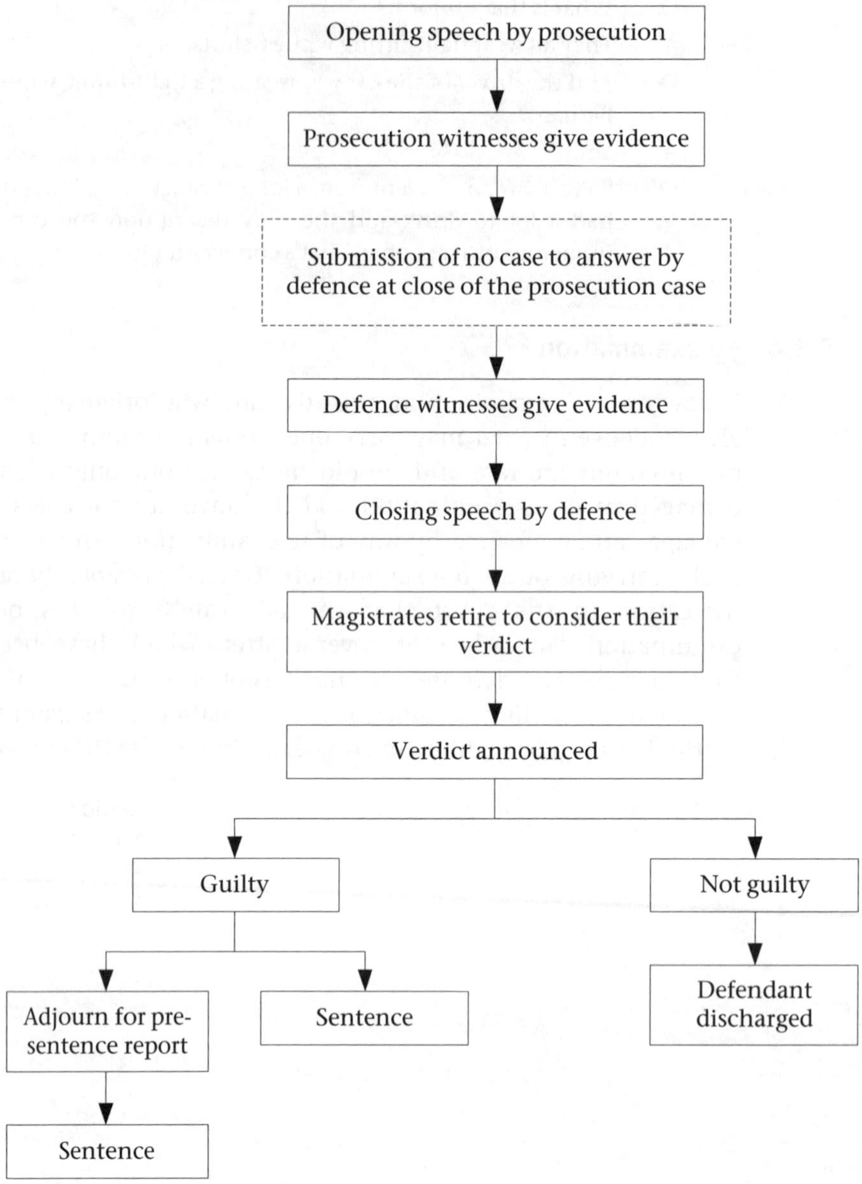

### 9.9.2 Will the defendant need to give evidence?

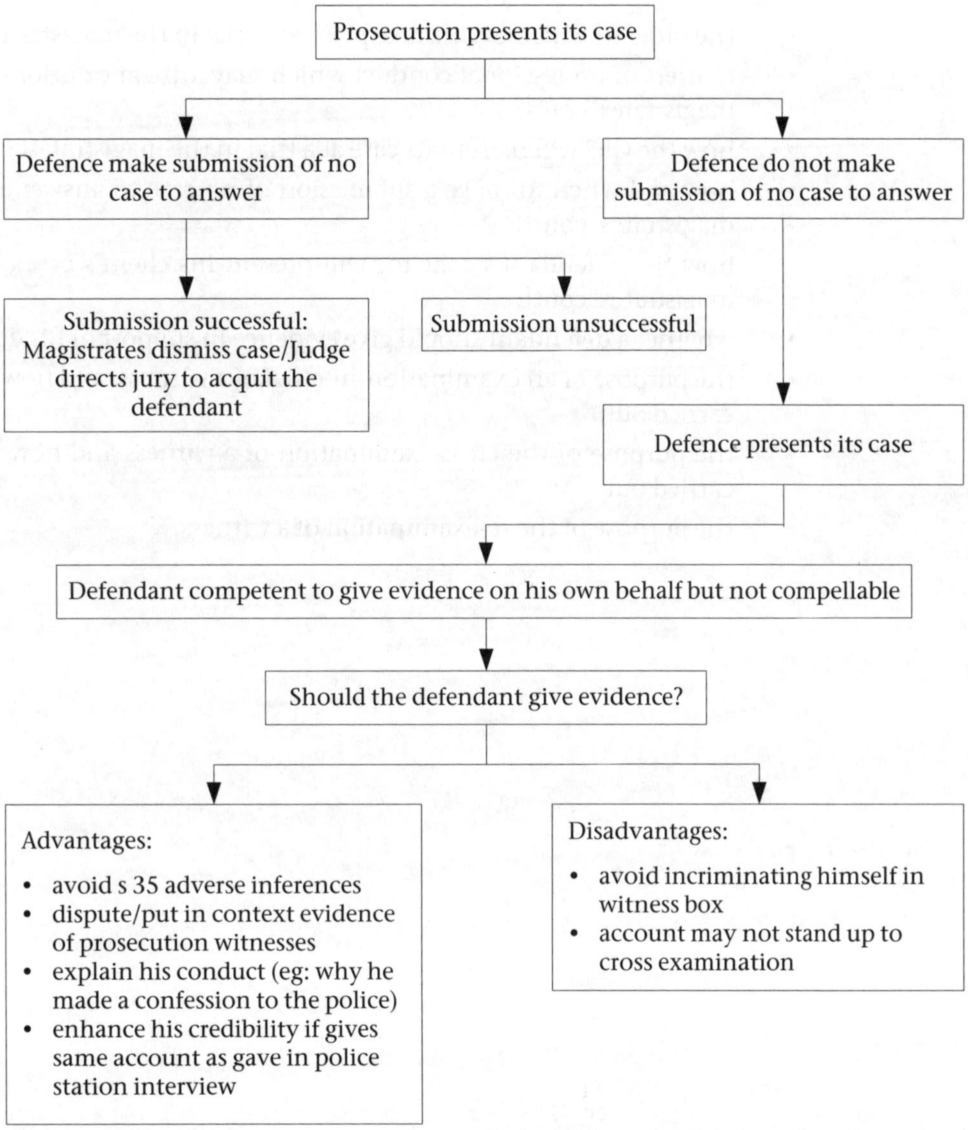

## 9.10 Checklist

At the end of this chapter you should be able to explain:

- the order in which events take place at a trial in the magistrates' court;
- matters of professional conduct which may arise at or prior to a trial in the magistrates' court;
- how the CPS will present its case at a trial in the magistrates' court;
- how and when to make a submission of no case to answer at a trial in the magistrates' court;
- how the defendant's solicitor will present his client's case at a trial in the magistrates' court;
- whether a defendant should give evidence in support of his defence at trial;
- the purpose of an examination-in-chief of a witness, and how this should be carried out;
- the purpose of the cross-examination of a witness and how this should be carried out;
- the purpose of the re-examination of a witness.

# Chapter 10

# The Crown Court



## 10.1 Introduction

This chapter will begin by describing the types of case which may be dealt with by the Crown Court and will then go on to examine the procedure by which an indictable-only offence or an either way offence (where the magistrates have declined jurisdiction or the defendant has elected Crown Court trial) gets to the Crown Court for trial. The standard case management directions which apply in Crown Court cases will be explained, as will the significance of the plea and case management hearing. The chapter will describe the role played by the defendant's solicitor in a Crown Court case, with particular emphasis placed on how to 'brief' counsel and the drafting of the defence statement. The chapter will conclude with a description of the procedure which takes place at a trial in the Crown Court.

## 10.2 Cases dealt with in the Crown Court

The Crown Court has jurisdiction to deal with the following types of case:

(a) *Indictable-only offences* – these offences must be dealt with before the Crown Court. The procedure by which these cases reach the Crown Court is described at **10.4** below.

(b) *Either way offences where the defendant pleads not guilty* – these offences will be committed to the Crown Court for trial if either the magistrates refuse jurisdiction, or if the magistrates accept jurisdiction but the defendant elects Crown Court trial (see **6.10** above).

(c) *Either way offences where the defendant pleads guilty* – if the magistrates consider their sentencing powers to be inadequate, a defendant who has appeared before them and entered a guilty plea to an either way offence at the plea before venue hearing will be committed to the Crown Court for sentence (see **6.9** above).

(d) *Appeals from the magistrates' court* – a defendant who wishes to appeal against his conviction and/or sentence imposed by the magistrates' court for an either way or summary only offence has a right of appeal to the Crown Court (see **13.2.1**).

Defence appeals against the refusal of bail by the magistrates' court, or appeals by the CPS against a decision by the magistrates to grant bail to a defendant, will also be heard before the Crown Court. Such appeals will take place before a Crown Court judge in chambers (see 7.8).

This chapter will focus on the procedure to be followed in respect of:

(a) indictable-only offences; and

(b) either way offences where the defendant pleads not guilty and either the magistrates decline jurisdiction or the defendant elects Crown Court trial.

## 10.3 Trial by judge and jury

In the magistrates' court, the magistrates decide matters of both fact and law. In a Crown Court trial these functions are split between the judge and the jury. The jury (which is made up of 12 members of the public) will decide any matters of fact which are in dispute, and will ultimately decide upon the defendant's guilt or innocence. The judge will resolve any disputes that arise over points of law during the course of a trial, and will direct the jury as to the relevant law which they must apply to the facts of the case when they retire to consider their verdict. Although the judge will also sum up for the jury the evidence which they have heard before the jury retire to consider their verdict, the jury are solely responsible for deciding what the true facts of the case are. The judge will also be responsible for sentencing the defendant in the event that he is found guilty.

There are some limited situations in which trials may take place without a jury being present, so-called 'judge-alone' trials. The detailed rules as to when such a trial can take place are outside the scope of this book.

## 10.4 Getting to the Crown Court

### 10.4.1 Indictable-only offences (CrimPR, Part 12)

#### 10.4.1.1 Which offences qualify?

Where an adult appears before a magistrates' court charged with an indictable-only offence, the court must send him to the Crown Court for trial pursuant to s 51(1) of the Crime and Disorder Act 1998:

(a) for that offence; and

(b) for any either way offence or summary offence with which he is charged which fulfils the 'requisite conditions'.

The 'requisite conditions' are that:

(a) the either way or summary offence appears to the court to be related to the indictable-only offence; and

(b) in the case of a summary only offence, it is punishable with imprisonment, or involves obligatory or discretionary disqualification from driving (Crime and Disorder Act 1998, s 51(11)).

##### Example

Tony is charged with robbery and assault occasioning actual bodily harm. The CPS alleges that Tony attacked his victim to steal the victim's mobile phone and in the process struck the victim in the face, causing the victim to sustain a fractured nose. Robbery is an indictable-only offence and so must be sent to the Crown Court for trial. Assault occasioning actual bodily harm is an either way offence. It fulfils the 'requisite conditions' because it is related to the indictable-only offence.

If Tony had been charged with common assault (a summary only offence) instead of assault occasioning actual bodily harm, the 'requisite conditions' would still be satisfied. The common assault charge is related to the indictable-only offence, and common assault is punishable by imprisonment.

#### 10.4.1.2 The preliminary hearing in the magistrates' court

An adult defendant charged with an indictable-only offence will be sent straight to the Crown Court for trial following a preliminary hearing in the magistrates' court, pursuant to s 51(1) of the Crime and Disorder Act 1998. This preliminary hearing will usually take place at the first available court sitting after the defendant has been charged by the police. The purpose of the preliminary hearing is to determine whether an indictable-only offence is charged and whether there are related offences which should also be sent to the Crown Court (see **10.4.1.1** above).

When the magistrates have determined that the defendant is charged with an indictable-only offence, they will set a date for the plea and case management hearing at the Crown Court (see **10.6** below) – or a date for a preliminary hearing in the Crown Court if such a hearing is necessary (see **10.5.2** below) – and will remand the defendant either on bail or in custody to appear at the Crown Court. Unless a preliminary hearing is to take place at the Crown Court, the magistrates will also give a set of standard case management directions for the CPS and the defendant's solicitor to comply with prior to the plea and case management hearing taking place. The form used to give these directions is reproduced at **10.13.1** below. The magistrates will give the defendant a notice specifying the offence(s) for which he has been sent for trial and the Crown Court at which he is to be tried. A copy of the notice will also be sent to the relevant Crown Court (Crime and Disorder Act 1998, s 51D).

The magistrates also have the power at the preliminary hearing to make a representation order to cover the defendant's legal representation in both the magistrates' court and the Crown Court (see **6.4.3.2** above).

### 10.4.2 Either way offences

#### 10.4.2.1 Procedure

A defendant charged with an either way offence who pleads not guilty at the plea before venue hearing will be tried in the Crown Court if either the magistrates decline jurisdiction, or the defendant elected Crown Court trial (see **6.10**). In such a case a final hearing (the committal) takes place before the magistrates' court. Its purpose is to ensure that there is a case for the defendant to answer before the Crown Court. There are two types of committal proceedings:

(a) committal without consideration of the evidence (Magistrates' Courts Act 1980, s 6(2)); and

(b) committal with consideration of the evidence (Magistrates' Courts Act 1980, s 6(1)).

**Committals without consideration of the evidence**

In advance of the hearing the CPS will serve on the defendant's solicitor the evidence which makes up its case and offer the defendant a committal without consideration of the evidence. If the evidence disclosed clearly shows a case to answer, the defendant's solicitor will normally agree to a committal without consideration of the evidence.

At the hearing, the defendant's solicitor will concede that there is a case to answer on the basis of the evidence submitted and the magistrates (without reading the evidence) will commit the defendant to stand trial at the Crown Court.

**Committals with consideration of the evidence**

The defendant will ask for this form of committal only if he wishes to make a submission of no case to answer (because the prosecution case is very weak).

At the hearing, the CPS solicitor will either read out or orally summarise the prosecution evidence. No witnesses will be called. The defendant's solicitor will then make a submission of no case to answer to the magistrates. The test to be applied by the magistrates was set out in *R v Galbraith* [1981] 2 All ER 1060. The magistrates must ask themselves whether the prosecution case, taken at its highest, is such that a jury properly directed could not properly convict on it. To succeed, the defendant will need to show either that the CPS has failed to adduce evidence in support of an essential element of the offence, or that the case against the defendant is so unreliable that a jury could not convict upon it.

If the submission succeeds, the defendant will be discharged. If the submission fails, the magistrates will commit the defendant to stand trial at the Crown Court.

#### 10.4.2.2 Ancillary matters following committal

If the defendant is committed for trial, the magistrates will set a date for the plea and case management hearing at the Crown Court (see **10.6** below) and will remand the defendant either on bail or in custody to appear before the Crown Court. The magistrates will also give case management directions for the CPS and the defendant's solicitor to comply with prior to the plea and case management hearing taking place. The form used to give these directions is reproduced at **10.13.2** below. The defendant's representation order will be extended to cover the Crown Court proceedings.

#### 10.4.2.3 Linked summary offences

Just as with indictable-only offences, a defendant who is committed for trial in respect of an either way offence may also be charged with another offence that is summary only.

If the summary only offence is common assault, taking a conveyance without consent, driving whilst disqualified or criminal damage, the defendant may be tried for these offences at the Crown Court if the offence is founded on the same facts as the either way offence, or is part of a series of offences of the same or a similar character (CJA 1988, s 40(1)).

**Example**

Jarvis is charged with theft of goods from a motor vehicle and taking a conveyance without consent. The CPS alleges that Jarvis took a vehicle without the owner's consent and stole some CDs from the vehicle whilst it was in his possession. Jarvis is committed to the Crown Court for trial on the theft charge after he enters a not guilty plea at the plea before venue hearing and elects Crown Court trial. The summary only offence of taking a conveyance without consent can also be tried in the Crown Court as it is founded on the same facts as the either way offence.

In addition to the above, if the magistrates commit a defendant for trial for one or more either way offences, they may also send him for trial of any summary only offence with which he is also charged if the summary only offence:

(a) is punishable with imprisonment or disqualification from driving; and
(b) arises out of circumstances which are the same as or connected to the circumstances of the either way offence (CJA1988, s 41(1)).

If the defendant, on conviction for the either way offence, pleads guilty to the summary only offence, the Crown Court can sentence for the summary offence, although its sentencing powers are limited to those of the magistrates. If the defendant is acquitted of the either way offence, or pleads not guilty to the summary only offence, this offence must be remitted back to the magistrates' court for trial.

**Example**

Len is committed for trial to the Crown Court on a charge of assault occasioning actual bodily harm. He also faces a charge for the summary only public order offence of using threatening behaviour. Both charges arise out of the same incident. If Len is convicted of the assault charge at the Crown Court, he can also be sentenced for the public order offence if he pleads guilty to it. If Len is acquitted of the assault charge or pleads not guilty to the public order offence, however, the Crown Court must remit the public order offence back to the magistrates' court for trial.

## 10.5 Standard case management directions and other preliminary matters

### 10.5.1 Standard case management directions

The Criminal Procedure Rules contain standard case management directions that will apply when a case is sent or committed for trial. In some limited circumstances, however, when an indictable-only case is sent for trial, a preliminary hearing may take place at the Crown Court. If such a preliminary hearing is needed, any directions necessary will be given by the judge at this hearing.

### 10.5.2 Preliminary hearings

A preliminary hearing will take place in the case of an indictable-only offence if:

(a) there are case management issues which the Crown Court needs to resolve;
(b) the trial is likely to exceed four weeks;
(c) it is desirable to set an early trial date;
(d) the defendant is under 18 years of age; or
(e) there is likely to be a guilty plea and the defendant could be sentenced at the preliminary hearing.

A preliminary hearing must take place within 14 days of the date on which the magistrates send the case to the Crown Court.

### 10.5.3 Challenging a case sent for trial under s 51 (CrimPR, Part 13)

A defendant whose case is sent to the Crown Court for trial may apply to a Crown Court judge for the charge(s) against him to be dismissed prior to his trial taking place if the evidence against him is particularly weak. Section 6(1) of the CJA 1987 provides that a judge 'shall dismiss a charge ... if it appears to him that the evidence against the [defendant] would not be sufficient for a jury to properly convict him'.

The procedure which must be followed when a defendant seeks to challenge a case sent for trial is set out in Part 13 of the Criminal Procedure Rules. To make an application to challenge a case sent for trial, the defendant must give written notice both to the CPS and the court within 14 days of the CPS disclosing its case to the defendant (see **10.5.2** above). This notice may include an application for leave to call witnesses to give oral evidence at the hearing. The CPS then has seven days to file a reply to the application. The court will list the matter for a hearing, at which the judge will either dismiss the charge against the defendant or refuse the application to dismiss the charge.

### 10.5.4 Custody time limits

Time limits exist for the maximum period during which a defendant may be remanded in custody prior to the start of his trial in the Crown Court.

If the defendant is charged with an indictable-only offence, the maximum period of time he may be remanded in custody prior to his trial starting is 182 days from the date on which the magistrates sent his case for trial, *less* any time during which the defendant was remanded in custody by the magistrates' court prior to being sent for trial (Prosecution of Offences (Custody Time Limits) Regulations 1987 (SI 1987/299)).

If the defendant is charged with an either way offence, the maximum period of time he may be remanded in custody whilst his case is before the magistrates' court is 70 days (this is reduced to 56 days if the mode of trial hearing takes place within 56 days). After the defendant has been committed to the Crown Court for trial, the maximum period of time he may be remanded in custody prior to his trial starting is 112 days from the date of the committal (Prosecution of Offences (Custody Time Limits) Regulations 1987 (SI 1987/299)).

The CPS may apply to the Crown Court to extend the custody time limit at any time before its expiry. The application may be made orally, although a written notice of intention must be served on the defendant not less than five days before the hearing. In order to obtain an extension, the CPS will need to persuade the court that (on the balance of probabilities):

(a) there is good and sufficient cause for extending the custody time limit; and
(b) the CPS has acted with due diligence and expedition throughout (Prosecution of Offences Act 1985, s 22).

Reasons that do *not* come within (a) or (b) above include the seriousness of the charge the defendant faces, the fact that a refusal of the court to extend the custody time limit would lead to an automatic right to bail, and police delays in obtaining evidence due to understaffing or sickness.

If the initial custody time limit has expired and the Crown Court has not extended this period, the defendant must be released on bail until the start of his trial.

### 10.5.5 The indictment (CrimPR, Part 14)

The indictment is the formal document which sets out the charge(s) upon which the defendant is to be tried in the Crown Court. The indictment will be drafted by the CPS. The CPS will send a draft indictment to the Crown Court within an extendable 28-day time limit (which runs from the date of service of the prosecution case papers on a defendant in a case sent for trial or, in the case of an either way offence, the date on which the defendant was committed for trial). A court officer will then sign the draft (at which point it becomes the indictment) and serve a copy on both the prosecution and defence (CrimPR, r 14.1).

The indictment must contain a paragraph called a count. A count must contain:

(a) a statement of the offence charged, which describes the offence in ordinary language and identifies any legislation which creates it; and

(b) particulars of the conduct constituting the commission of the offence so as to make clear what the prosecution is alleging (CrimPR, r 14.2(1)).

Rule 14.2(2) provides that a single count may include more than one incident of the offence alleged if those incidents amount to a course of conduct in time, place or purpose. The indictment may contain more than one count if the offences charged are founded on the same facts, or form or are part of a series of offences of the same or similar character (CrimPR, r 14.2(3)).

An example of an indictment is set out below.

## Key Document – Indictment

No CH 080248

**INDICTMENT**

**IN THE CROWN COURT AT CHESTER**

**THE QUEEN – v – GARY PAUL DICKSON**

**GARY PAUL DICKSON is charged as follows:**

**STATEMENT OF OFFENCE**

Assault occasioning actual bodily harm, contrary to section 47 of the Offences Against the Person Act 1861

**PARTICULARS OF OFFENCE**

Gary Paul Dickson on or about the 18th day of December 2007 assaulted Vincent Lamb causing him actual bodily harm

*Michael Richards*
Date *15 February 2008* Crown Court Officer

## 10.6 Plea and case management hearing

### 10.6.1 Introduction

The purpose of the plea and case management hearing (PCMH) is to enable the defendant to enter his plea and, if the defendant is pleading not guilty, to enable the judge to give further case management directions for the CPS and the defendant's solicitor to comply with prior to trial.

Where a case has been sent for trial and no preliminary hearing is held, the PCMH should take place 14 weeks after sending if the defendant is in custody, or 17 weeks if the defendant is on bail. If a case has been committed for trial, the PCMH will be held within 7 weeks of committal.

### 10.6.2 The arraignment

At the start of the PCMH the defendant will be arraigned. This means that the count(s) on the indictment will be put to the defendant and he will either plead guilty or not guilty. If the defendant pleads guilty to some counts but not guilty to others, the jury at the defendant's trial in respect of the counts to which he pleaded not guilty will not be told about the counts to which he has pleaded guilty (so they are not in any way prejudiced against the defendant).

It will sometimes be the case that a defendant charged with several counts will agree with the CPS that he will plead guilty to certain counts if the CPS does not proceed with other counts. If this happens, at the arraignment the CPS will offer no evidence in respect of these other counts and the judge will order that a verdict of not guilty be entered. The CPS will also offer no evidence at the arraignment if, since the case was sent for trial, further evidence has become available which leads it to conclude that there is no longer a reasonable prospect of securing a conviction. In this case, the judge will again order that a not guilty verdict be entered and the defendant will be formally discharged.

As an alternative to offering no evidence, the CPS may ask that a count 'lie on the court file'. This may happen when there are several counts on the indictment and the CPS evidence in respect of each count is strong. If the defendant is prepared to plead guilty to the more serious counts, the CPS may agree to lesser counts being left on the file. In such a case a not guilty verdict will not be entered and (in theory) with the leave of the court the CPS may be permitted to re-open the case at a later date.

### 10.6.3 Guilty pleas

If the defendant pleads guilty at the PCMH, the judge will either sentence him immediately or, if necessary, adjourn sentence for the preparation of pre-sentence reports, such as medical reports or reports from the Probation Service (see **12.2**). The judge may also need to adjourn the case if the defendant pleads guilty but disputes the specific factual allegations made against him by the prosecution witnesses. In such a situation a separate hearing (called a '*Newton* hearing' – see **12.4**) will be necessary to determine the factual basis on which the defendant will be sentenced. If the case is adjourned, the defendant will either be released on bail or remanded in custody pending either the sentencing hearing or the '*Newton* hearing'.

### 10.6.4 Indication of sentence

Following the judgment of the Court of Appeal in *R v Goodyear* [2005] EWCA Crim 888, a judge is now permitted at the PCMH to give a defendant an advance indication of the likely sentence he would receive were he to enter a guilty plea at that stage. The defendant must specifically ask for such an indication. If the judge gives an indication and the defendant then enters a guilty plea, the indication given by the judge will be binding.

### 10.6.5 Not guilty pleas

If the defendant pleads not guilty at the PCMH, the judge will then consider if any further directions are necessary to prepare the case for trial. To determine whether further directions may be necessary, the judge will require the prosecution and defence advocates present at the PCMH to be in a position to supply him with the following information:

(a) a summary of the issues in the case;

(b) details of the number of witnesses who will be giving oral evidence at trial and the estimated length of the trial;

(c) whether the transcript(s) of the defendant's police station interview(s) require(s) editing;

(d) whether a defence statement has been served and, if so, whether there is there any issue as to the adequacy of the statement;

(e) whether the prosecution will be serving any additional evidence;

(f) whether there is any dispute as to the adequacy of disclosure of unused material by the prosecution;

(g) whether any expert evidence is to be called and, if so, whether any additional directions are needed in respect of this;

(h) whether any further directions are necessary concerning hearsay or bad character evidence;

(i) whether special measures are required for any witnesses;

(j) any facts which can be formally admitted;

(k) any points of law or issues concerning the admissibility of evidence which are likely to arise at trial;

(l) dates of availability to attend trial of the witnesses and the advocates.

### 10.6.6 Listing the case for trial

At the PCMH, the judge will give any further case management directions that are necessary in the light of the information disclosed by the parties (see **10.6.5** above), and then either fix a date for the defendant's trial or place the case in the 'warned list'. The warned list is a list of cases awaiting trial that have not been given a fixed date for the trial to start. If a case is placed in the warned list, the Crown Court will contact the defendant's solicitor to let him know that the case has been listed for trial shortly before the date when the trial is due to start.

At the conclusion of the PCMH, the defendant will either be released on bail, or remanded in custody pending his trial.

### 10.6.7 Change of plea

A defendant who initially enters a not guilty plea may, at the discretion of the judge, change this to a guilty plea at any time before the jury return their verdict. This is likely to happen if a defendant admitted his guilt but pleaded not guilty in the hope that a successful submission of no case to answer could be made at the end of the prosecution case but before the defendant needed to give evidence. If the submission is unsuccessful, the defendant will change his plea to guilty. A defendant may also change his plea to guilty during the trial if the judge makes a ruling on a point of law or the admissibility of a piece of evidence which deprives the defendant of a defence he wanted to rely on.

## 10.7 Role of the defence solicitor

### 10.7.1 Rights of audience

Most advocacy in the Crown Court is carried out by barristers (collectively referred to as counsel), whom the solicitor will 'brief' to represent the defendant in the Crown Court proceedings. Similarly the CPS will brief counsel to conduct the prosecution case in the Crown Court.

Solicitors generally have rights of audience in the Crown Court which are limited to:

(a) appeals against the refusal of bail by the magistrates (see **7.8**);

(b) appeals against conviction and/or sentence from a magistrates' court, provided a member of the solicitor's firm conducted the hearing in the magistrates' court (see **13.2.1**);

(c) representing a defendant who has been committed by the magistrates' court to the Crown Court for sentence following a guilty plea at the plea before venue hearing in the magistrates' court, provided a member of the solicitor's firm conducted the hearing in the magistrates' court (see **6.9**); and

(d) preliminary hearings in the Crown Court where the defendant has been sent for trial (see **10.5.2** above).

A solicitor is therefore unable to represent his client at a trial in the Crown Court, unless the solicitor has obtained an additional qualification giving him rights of audience in the higher courts.

### 10.7.2 Briefing counsel

If counsel is to be instructed, a brief to counsel should be prepared and sent to counsel's clerk as soon as the case has been sent or committed for trial by the magistrates' court. The brief should be as full as possible and should be broken down into sections, as follows:

(a) *Enclosures* – this will list all the documents that are being sent to counsel along with the brief (such as prosecution witness statements, correspondence with the prosecution, the draft indictment, police station interview transcripts, a copy of the representation order, the defendant's witness statement, copies of any hearsay or bad character notices given or received, etc).

(b) *Introduction* – this deals with basic personal information about the defendant, the charge, the history of the case, bail arrangements and the prosecution witnesses who are to attend trial.

(c) *Prosecution case* – this contains a summary of the evidence to be given by each prosecution witness (and may also contain an analysis of the strengths and weaknesses of the prosecution case).

(d) *Defence case* – this contains a summary of the defence evidence, including details of the defendant's version of events and any supporting evidence, such as a witness who supports the defendant's alibi (the solicitor may also attempt to assess the strengths and weaknesses of the defendant's case).

(e) *Evidence and related procedural issues* – any significant points of evidence likely to arise at trial should be highlighted for the benefit of counsel. This may include, for example, issues relating to the admissibility of a confession, hearsay evidence or bad character evidence, whether adverse inferences may be drawn from the defendant's silence at the police station, or whether the case involves evidence from a '*Turnbull* witness'. Any related procedural issues should be covered as well, such as the preparation of the defence statement, and the giving or receiving of notices or applications under Parts 34 and 35 of the Criminal Procedure Rules in relation to hearsay evidence or bad character evidence (see **Chapters 19** and **22**).

(f) *Mitigation* – any facts relevant to mitigation in the event of the defendant being convicted should be mentioned. If the defendant has any previous convictions, these should (if possible) be distinguished from the facts of the current offence. In the case of a defendant who is pleading not guilty, this section of the brief will focus on 'offender' rather than 'offence' mitigation, since the defendant is denying having committed the offence (see **12.7.4**).

(g) *Conclusion* – counsel will normally be asked in the conclusion to advise the defendant in conference, to attend the PCMH, to represent the defendant at trial and, if necessary, to make a plea in mitigation on the defendant's behalf following conviction. If the defendant is convicted, counsel should also be asked to provide written advice on whether there is any merit in an appeal against conviction and/or sentence being made.

An example of a completed brief to counsel is set out below.

## Key skill – preparing a brief to counsel

**BRIEF TO COUNSEL**

IN THE CROWN COURT — Case No CH 060248

AT CHESTER

R

–v–

GARY PAUL DICKSON

BRIEF TO COUNSEL ON BEHALF OF THE DEFENDANT TO APPEAR AT THE PLEA AND CASE MANAGEMENT HEARING ON WEDNESDAY 2ND APRIL 2008 AT 10.30AM AND AT THE TRIAL ON A DATE TO BE FIXED

Counsel has copies of the following documents:

1. Representation order
2. Custody record
3. Charge sheet
4. Indictment
5. Prosecution case papers comprising:
   - statement of PC Gareth Chambers
   - statement of John Barnard
   - statement of Vincent Lamb
   - statement of Peter Hansen
   - statement of Dr Harbhajan Singh
   - record of audibly recorded interview at police station
6. Record of previous convictions of Gary Paul Dickson

7. Statement of Gary Paul Dickson
8. Dickson's comments on the prosecution witness statements
9. Statement of Jill Summers
10. Directions given by magistrates (for case committed for trial)
11. Prosecution schedule of non-sensitive unused material
12. Defence statement
13. John Barnard's first description of the individual who assaulted Vincent Lamb
14. Video identification record
15. Prosecution notice of intention to adduce evidence of Dickson's bad character at trial
16. Defence application to exclude evidence of Dickson's bad character at trial.
17. Correspondence received from the CPS.

**INTRODUCTION**

Counsel is instructed on behalf of Gary Paul Dickson of 17 Marsh Street, Chester CH3 7LW. The defendant is on conditional bail, the condition being that he reside at this address and report to his local police station every second day. The defendant is charged with assaulting one Vincent Lamb on 18th December 2007, causing Mr Lamb actual bodily harm, contrary to s 47 of the Offences Against the Person Act 1861. The defendant will plead not guilty. At a plea before venue before Chester Magistrates' Court on 15th January 2008, the magistrates declined jurisdiction and the defendant was subsequently committed for trial at a committal hearing on 5th February 2008. The magistrates gave directions for the parties to prepare for the plea and case management hearing on 2nd April 2008.

In accordance with these directions, the prosecution have served the evidence on which they seek to rely at trial. The defence have confirmed that all prosecution witnesses will be required to attend the trial to give oral evidence, with the exception of PC Peter Hansen and Dr Singh. A schedule of non-sensitive unused material has been served by the prosecution, together with details of the previous convictions of the complainant, Vincent Lamb, referred to at item 4 in the schedule. The prosecution have confirmed in writing that, other than Lamb's previous convictions, they have no other unused material in their possession which might reasonably be considered capable of undermining the case for the prosecution or assisting the case for the defence. A defence statement has been served. The prosecution have reviewed their position in respect of the disclosure of unused material following the service of the defence statement, and have served a copy of the first description of the individual who committed the assault on Vincent Lamb given to the police by the prosecution witness, John Barnard, together with the video identification record referred to at item 9 in the schedule of non-sensitive unused prosecution material. The prosecution have served notice that they intend to introduce evidence of the defendant's bad character at trial. An application to exclude such evidence from being used at trial has been made by the defence.

**THE PROSECUTION CASE**

The prosecution case is that on the evening of Tuesday 18th December 2007 the defendant was working as a bouncer at Connolley's nightclub in Chester. The defendant left work at just prior to 3.15 am the following morning, driving a dark blue VW Golf registration number L251 CVM. On his way home, the defendant stopped his car, got out and assaulted Vincent Lamb, who had been a guest disc jockey at Connolley's nightclub that evening. The defendant then got back in his car and drove away. At the time of the assault, Mr Lamb was walking back to the multi-storey car park where his own car was parked. The allegation is that the defendant punched Mr Lamb several times in the face. The assault was witnessed by John Barnard, who later picked out the defendant in a video identification at Chester police station. Mr Lamb sustained a fractured nose and a split left eyebrow. When interviewed about the assault at the police station, the defendant confessed to having committed the offence. The prosecution suggest that the defendant attacked Mr Lamb because Mr Lamb had been chatting up the defendant's girlfriend earlier in the evening. Mr Lamb alleges that the defendant had shaken his fist in Mr Lamb's face earlier in the evening and told Mr Lamb to lay off a clubber called Jill who Mr Lamb had been speaking to.

**THE DEFENCE CASE**

The defendant accepts that he was working as a bouncer at Connolley's that evening and that he does own a VW Golf registration number L251 CVM. The defendant does not know Vincent Lamb. Whilst Mr Lamb may have been a guest disc jockey at Connolley's that evening, the defendant was not aware of this because he was standing at the entrance to the nightclub rather than inside the nightclub premises. The defendant left work at 1.30 am and drove straight home to 17 Marsh Street, Chester. At the time of the alleged assault on Mr Lamb, the defendant was asleep in bed with his partner, Ms Jill Summers. John Barnard has made a mistake in identifying the defendant as the person who committed the assault. The defendant accepts that he made a confession at the police station, but says he made the confession only as a result of the conduct of the police both before and during the interview. The defendant will say that the confession is untrue. The defendant also states that the incident which is alleged to have occurred earlier in the evening (when he is supposed to have threatened Mr Lamb) did not occur and Mr Lamb is mistaken.

**EVIDENCE**

Counsel's attention is particularly drawn to the following points of evidence:

(i) The identification evidence given by John Barnard – there do not appear to be any grounds on which the admissibility of the identification evidence given by John Barnard may be challenged under s 78 of PACE 1984. The record of the video identification suggests that the video identification procedure was carried out in accordance with the requirements of PACE Code D. The credibility of Mr Barnard's identification evidence may, however, be challenged in cross-examination. Mr Barnard is not known to the defendant and there is no suggestion that Mr Barnard's evidence has been intentionally fabricated. The defendant will say that Mr Barnard is simply mistaken. The credibility of the evidence given by Mr Barnard will need to be challenged at trial under the *Turnbull* guidelines. In particular it appears that Mr Barnard saw the assault from a distance of some 50 metres away, at a time when it was dark and after he had consumed a substantial amount of alcohol. Further, the initial description of the attacker which Mr Barnard gave to the police differs in several respects from the actual appearance of Mr Dickson.

(ii) The confession – the admissibility of the confession made by the defendant when interviewed under caution at Chester Police Station will need to be challenged at trial under s 76(2) and s 78 of the Police and Criminal Evidence Act 1984. The police appear to have actively dissuaded the defendant from obtaining legal advice prior to being interviewed, and the conduct of the interview could be said to be oppressive or, at the very least, such as to render the defendant's confession unreliable. The interviewing officer gives a clear impression to the defendant that he will be detained at the police station until he makes a confession. There are several breaches of Code C (the Code of Practice dealing with the detention, treatment and questioning of suspects).

(iii) The defendant's previous convictions – the defendant has one previous conviction for s 47 assault in December 2006, two convictions for threatening behaviour in September 2005 and March 2006, and one conviction for common assault in November 2001. The prosecution have given notice that they intend to adduce evidence of these convictions at trial under s 101(1)(d) of the Criminal Justice Act 2003 in order to demonstrate that the defendant has a propensity to commit offences of the kind with which he is charged. An application has been made to exclude this evidence under s 101(3) because there is no factual similarity between these offences and the current offence, and these convictions do not demonstrate a propensity to commit offences of the kind charged (*R v Hanson and Others* [2005] Crim LR 787. Other than the conviction for common assault, the previous offences were all committed in the course of the defendant's employment as a bouncer, whereas the current offence is alleged to have occurred after the defendant left his place of employment.

An application has been made to exclude evidence of the conviction for common assault under s 103(3) of the Criminal Justice Act 2003. This conviction was in 2001, and it is submitted that as a result of the time which has passed since the conviction it would be unjust for the prosecution to be allowed to rely upon it.

The admission of all of the defendant's previous convictions under s 101(d) is also challenged under s 101(3) of the Criminal Justice Act 2003 on the basis that to raise such convictions would be unfair to the defendant, in the eyes of the jury such convictions would be more prejudicial to his case than probative of his guilt.

(iv) The alibi defence – this defence has been confirmed in the defence statement which has been served on the prosecution. Ms Summers has provided a statement confirming details of the alibi, and has confirmed that she will attend trial to give evidence on the defendant's behalf.

**MITIGATION**

Instructing solicitors have considered the question of a plea in mitigation if the defendant is convicted. The defendant is aged 27 and resides with Ms Summers in a property owned by Ms Summer's parents. In addition to working on a part-time basis as a bouncer, the defendant works on a contract basis as a scaffolder and steeplejack. The defendant left school at 16 and joined the army. The defendant left the army in 2002 when he moved to the Chester area.

**CONFERENCE**

Counsel is requested to advise in conference, to attend the plea and case management hearing, to represent the defendant at trial on a plea of not guilty and, if necessary, to make a plea in mitigation on behalf of the defendant. In the event of the defendant being convicted, counsel is asked to advise in writing on the prospects of a successful appeal being made to the Court of Appeal against conviction and/or sentence.

Dated this 10th day of March 2008

Collaws Solicitors

### 10.7.3 Conference with counsel

Counsel will usually be instructed immediately after the hearing at which the magistrates send or commit the case to Crown Court for trial. Unless a preliminary hearing is necessary, any conference with counsel is likely to take place prior to the PCMH. Although a conference will not take place in every case, it is sensible for a conference to be arranged, if for no other reason than to introduce counsel to the client before the PCMH.

A conference with counsel should always be held when:

(a) the defendant is to enter a not guilty plea (counsel will need to make an assessment as to how the defendant will perform as a witness and to 'test' the defendant on the strength of his case);

(b) the defendant requires advice from counsel as to the plea he should enter;

(c) there are any particular complications in the case, or if the case may involve serious consequences (such as a custodial sentence being likely in the event that the defendant is convicted); or

(d) there is a need to consider with the defendant any tactical or evidential matters (for example, whether the defendant should give evidence at trial, or whether the defendant's previous convictions are likely to emerge in evidence at trial).

### 10.7.4 Preparation for trial

Although the barrister will present the defendant's case at trial, the defendant's solicitor still has an important role to play in preparing the case for trial. For example, at the conference with counsel, counsel may indicate that he requires a statement to be obtained from a particular witness, or that the CPS should be asked to divulge some additional information or document. It will be the solicitor's job to contact the relevant witness, or to write to the CPS in such circumstances.

Similarly, the defendant's solicitor will need ensure that a representative from his office attends the trial to assist counsel and, in particular, to take a detailed note of what each witness says when giving evidence. Such a note will often be used by counsel when preparing his closing argument for the jury (see **10.10** below). A note of the evidence and the judge's summing up may also be helpful when drafting grounds of appeal against sentence and/or conviction (see **Chapter 13**).

## 10.8 Disclosure

### 10.8.1 Introduction

The disclosure obligations with which both the CPS and the defendant must comply in a case before the Crown Court are contained in the Criminal Procedure and Investigations Act (CPIA) 1996. In addition, parties in a Crown Court case must comply with a Disclosure Protocol published in February 2006, 'Disclosure: A Protocol for the Control and Management of Unused Material in the Crown Court'. The Protocol provides that, when a party is obliged to provide disclosure, such disclosure should be given promptly. When checking and recording the existence of any unused material (see **10.8.2** below), the police must act 'thoroughly, scrupulously and fairly'. The CPS must then make full and prompt disclosure of unused material to the defendant's solicitor to ensure that 'justice is not delayed, denied or frustrated'. Defence statements (see **10.8.6** below) must be sufficiently detailed to comply with the requirements of the CPIA 1996 and must be served by the due date.

### 10.8.2 Prosecution duty of disclosure

Just as in the magistrates' court, the CPS is obliged to serve on the defendant all the evidence on which it wishes to rely at trial to prove the defendant's guilt.

In addition to this evidence, the prosecution will also have a quantity of 'unused material', such as statements from witnesses whom the CPS does not intend to call to give evidence at trial. The CPS is obliged to retain this material; and in the event of the defendant entering a not guilty plea, the CPS must disclose any such material to the defendant if the material satisfies the test set out in s 3 of the CPIA 1996. Section 3 provides that such material must be disclosed if it 'might reasonably be considered capable of undermining the case for the prosecution ... or of assisting the case for the accused'. Examples of the types of material that require disclosure include:

(a) records of the first description of a suspect given to the police by a potential eye-witness if that description differs from that of the defendant;

(b) any information provided by the defendant which indicates an innocent explanation for the offence;

(c) material casting doubt on the reliability of a witness (eg, previous convictions);

(d) material casting doubt on the reliability of a confession;

(e) any statements from witnesses which appear to support the defendant's account.

The case management directions referred to at **10.5.1** above give time limits as to when the prosecution must make initial disclosure of any unused material in their possession which satisfies the test in s 3 of the CPIA 1996. The CPS usually sends to the defendant's solicitor a schedule of all the non-sensitive unused material in its possession, together with copies of any items on the schedule which satisfy the test in s 3.

The duty of disclosure on the CPS is ongoing, and so the CPS must apply this test to any further material it receives after making initial disclosure (CPIA 1996, s 7A). The CPS must also consider the need to make further disclosure in the light of any information received from the defence about the nature of the defence case (see **10.8.5** below).

If the defendant's solicitor considers that the disclosure made by the CPS is incomplete, he will request disclosure of any 'missing' items when drafting the defence statement (see **10.8.6** below). The disclosure given by the CPS may be incomplete if:

(a) the CPS has failed to supply a copy of a document listed on the schedule of unused material because it erroneously considers that document does not satisfy the above disclosure test; or

(b) the CPS has failed to include on the list a document which the defendant's solicitor believes it may have in its possession (for example, a statement from a witness whose evidence may assist the defendant's case).

Should the CPS refuse to supply to the defendant's solicitor items which the solicitor has requested, the solicitor may apply to the court to request the specific disclosure of such items under s 8(2) of the CPIA 1996. Such an application may be made only if the defendant has provided a defence statement (see **10.8.8** below).

### 10.8.3 Can the prosecution withhold disclosure of unused material?

In addition to having non-sensitive items of unused material, the CPS may also have 'sensitive' items which it does not wish to disclose. Examples include:

(a) material relating to matters of national security or intelligence;

(b) material relating to the identity of police informants or under-cover police officers;

(c) material revealing techniques and methods relied upon by the police (eg, covert surveillance techniques used); and

(d) material relating to a child witness (such as material generated by a local authority social services department).

If such material satisfies the test in s 3 of the CPIA 1996 (see **8.4.6.2** above), the CPS can withhold the material only if it is protected by 'public interest immunity'. It is the decision of the court as to whether disclosure can be avoided on the grounds of public interest immunity (*R v Ward* [1993] 1 WLR 619). The CPS must therefore make an application to the court for a finding that it is not obliged to disclose the relevant material. The relevant procedural rules which must be followed when a public interest immunity application is made to the court are set out in Part 25 of the Criminal Procedure Rules.

It is usual, when drafting a defence statement (see **10.8.6** below), to ask the CPS if a schedule of sensitive materials has been prepared and, if so, whether the CPS has made any application to the court for an order that it is not obliged to disclose the existence of such material.

### 10.8.4 Confidential medical records

A defendant's solicitor may need access to the medical records of a complainant if those records cast doubt on the credibility of the evidence he gives. To obtain access to such records, the defendant's solicitor must apply to the court for a witness summons under Part 28 of the Criminal Procedure Rules (see **10.10.2** below). If the summons is granted, it will be served on the NHS Trust which is in possession of the records, and will require the Trust to produce the records.

### 10.8.5 Defence disclosure

Once the CPS has made its initial disclosure of unused material, the onus switches to the defendant's solicitor. If the defendant is to enter a not guilty plea, within 14 days of the CPS making initial disclosure of any unused material it has, the defendant should serve a defence statement (sometimes referred to as a 'Defence Case Statement' or DCS) on the CPS and send a copy of the statement to the Crown Court. If the case is particularly complex and 14 days will be insufficient, the defendant may apply to the court for a longer period within which to serve the defence statement. In a case involving two or more co-accused, s 5A of the CPIA 1996 permits the court to make an order that a copy of the defence statement made by each defendant is to be served on the other defendants in the case. The requirements for the contents of a defence statement are set out at **10.8.6** below.

Although the giving of a defence statement is not strictly a mandatory requirement, in practice a defence statement will always be given in the Crown Court if the defendant is to plead not guilty. This is because the court is permitted to draw an adverse inference against the defendant if a defence statement is not provided (see **10.8.8** below).

### 10.8.6 Contents of the defence statement

The contents of the defence statement are prescribed by s 6A of the CPIA 1996. The defence statement must be a written statement which:

(a) sets out the nature of the defence, including any particular defences on which the defendant intends to rely (for example, alibi or self-defence);

(b) indicates the matters of fact on which the defendant takes issue with the prosecution and why he takes such issue;

(c) indicates any points of law (including any point as to the admissibility of evidence) that the defendant wishes to take at trial, and any legal authority on which the defendant intends to rely for this purpose; and

(d) in the case of an alibi defence, provides the name, address and date of birth of any alibi witness, or as many of these details as are known to the defendant.

It is normal practice when drafting a defence statement also to include a paragraph asking if a schedule of sensitive material has been prepared and, if so, if the prosecution have made an application to court for an order that they are not obliged to disclose any such material. The types of document that might fall under this heading are described at **10.8.2**.

The defence are under a continuing duty to update the defence statement if the details to be given under any of the above points should change before trial (if, for example, an witness comes forward who is able to support an alibi given by the defendant and whose existence was unknown at the time the initial defence statement was prepared) (CPIA 1996, s 6B(3)).

An example of a completed defence statement is set out below.

## Key skill – drafting the defence statement

**DEFENCE STATEMENT**

(Criminal Procedure and Investigations Act 1996, sections 5 & 6)

Crown Court Case No CH 060248

To the prosecutor: **Crown Prosecution Service (Cheshire)**

To the Court: **Chester Crown Court**

Name of accused: **Gary Paul Dickson**

Charge: **Assault Occasioning Actual Bodily Harm (Offences Against the Person Act 1861, section 47)**

Name and address of solicitors for the accused: **Collaws Solicitors, 129 Priory Street, Chester CH1 5RJ**

Date: 8th March 2008

If called upon to establish a defence at trial, the following statement is served in accordance with the provisions of the Criminal Procedure and Investigations Act 1996.

1. **The nature of the accused's defence is:** alibi.

2. **The accused takes issue with the prosecution in relation to the following matters of fact:**
   (i) the allegation that the accused threatened the complainant Vincent Lamb and shook his fist in the complainant's face at Connolley's Nightclub during the evening of 17th December 2007;
   (ii) the allegation that the accused was in the vicinity of Connolley's nightclub in Chester city centre at or about 3.15 am on 18th December 2007;
   (iii) the allegation that the accused's vehicle registration number L251 CVM was in the vicinity of Connolley's nightclub in Chester city centre at or about 3.15 am on 18th December 2007;
   (iv) the allegation that the accused assaulted the complainant Vincent Lamb causing him actual bodily harm.
   (v) the truthfulness of the confession made by the accused when questioned by the police about the assault at Chester Police Station on 18th December 2007.

3. **The accused takes issue with the prosecution in relation to the matters of fact noted above for the following reasons:**
   (i) the complainant is incorrect in his allegation that the accused threatened the complainant at Connolley's nightclub during the evening of 17th December 2007;
   (ii) the prosecution witness John Barnard is mistaken both in his identification of accused as the individual who committed the assault, and in his identification of the accused's vehicle as the vehicle driven by the individual who committed the assault on 18th December 2007;
   (iii) the confession is untrue and was made by the accused only as a result of the police conducting the interview with the accused at the police station in an improper manner.

4. **The accused will give the following evidence of alibi**: that at 3.15 am on 18th December 2007 the accused was at his home address of 17 Marsh Street, Chester CH3 7LW. The accused will call a witness in support of this alibi. The name of the witness is Jill Summers (date of birth: 16/03/81). The address of the witness is 17 Marsh Street, Chester CH3 7LW.

5. **The accused will raise the following points of law at trial:**
   (i) the admissibility of the identification evidence of the complainant John Barnard will be challenged under s 78 of the Police and Criminal Evidence Act 1984 because the video identification was conducted in breach of Code D of the Codes Practice issued under s 66(1) of the Act;
   (ii) if the identification evidence of the complainant is held to be admissible, the credibility of this evidence will be challenged under the principles set out in *R v Turnbull* [1977] QB 224;
   (iii) the admissibility of the confession made by the accused when interviewed under caution at Chester Police Station will be challenged under ss 76(2) and 78 of the Police and Criminal Evidence Act 1984, on the basis that the accused was dissuaded from obtaining legal advice

prior to the interview commencing, and the conduct of the interview contravened Code C of the Codes of Practice issued under s 66(1) of the Act;

(iv) the prosecution have served notice that, pursuant to s 101(1)(d) of the Criminal Evidence Act 2003, they intend to adduce at trial evidence of the accused's convictions for the following offences in order to demonstrate that the accused has a propensity to commit offences of the kind charged:

- common assault – 29th November 2001;
- threatening behaviour – 10th September 2005 and 17th March 2006;
- assault occasioning actual bodily harm – 13th December 2006.

This notice is opposed because these offences do not demonstrate a propensity for the defendant to commit offences of this type because there is no factual similarity between such offences and the current offence (*R v Hanson, Gilmore and Pickstone* [2005] Crim LR 787). Also the evidential value of such convictions would be more prejudicial than probative in the eyes of the jury and it would therefore be unfair to the defendant for such convictions to be adduced in evidence (Criminal Justice Act 2003, s 101(3)). The admissibility of the conviction for common assault is also opposed under s 103(3) of the Criminal Justice Act 2003 because, as a result of the time which has elapsed since the conviction, it would be unjust for the conviction to be used in evidence.

6. **The accused requests the following disclosure of material which might undermine the prosecution case or which might assist the defence disclosed by this statement:**

(i) The first description given to the police by the prosecution witness John Barnard of the individual who committed the assault on Vincent Lamb on 18th December 2007.

(ii) The video identification record referred to at item 9 in the schedule of non-sensitive unused prosecution material.

[*The statement would list here any material the prosecution have not disclosed which the defence suspect the prosecution may have, any items mentioned on the schedule of non-sensitive unused material which have not actually been supplied to the defence, or any items mentioned in the schedule which should in fact have been disclosed as part of the prosecution case.*]

7. **Sensitive materials**

(i) Has a sensitive materials schedule been prepared?

(ii) Has the prosecutor been informed separately of the existence of material deemed to be too sensitive to be included in the schedule?

(iii) Has the prosecutor been informed separately of information about any prosecution witnesses' previous convictions (including spent convictions) or disciplinary issues involving police officers relating to this matter?

(iv) If the answer to (i), (ii) or (iii) above is yes, has the prosecutor decided that he is not under a duty to disclose:

(a) any material in (i) above?

(b) any material in (ii) above?

(c) any material in (iii) above?

(v) If the answer to (i), (ii) or (iii) above is yes, has an application been made to the court to order non-disclosure of any such material?

The defence reserves the right to amend the above statement on the receipt of further evidence.

Signed: *Gary Paul Dickson*

Dated: *8th March 2008*

### 10.8.7 Obtaining the defendant's approval of the defence statement

Section 6E of the CPIA 1996 provides that defence statements will be deemed to be given with the authority of the defendant unless the contrary is proved. A defendant's solicitor should therefore ensure that the defendant sees and approves a copy of the defence statement before this is served. As the defence statement will be drafted either by the defendant's solicitor or, if time permits, by counsel, the usual practice will be for the defendant's solicitor (or counsel) to sign the original statement which is served, and for the defendant to sign a copy of the statement which will be kept on the solicitor's file.

### 10.8.8 When may the court draw an adverse inference?

The reason why defence statements are effectively obligatory for defendants pleading not guilty in the Crown Court is that if there are any 'faults' in disclosure given by the defence, the court may draw an adverse inference from this when determining the defendant's guilt (CPIA 1996, s 11). These faults include:

(a) failing to provide a defence statement at all;

(b) late service of the defence statement;

(c) serving a defence statement that is incomplete;

(d) serving a defence statement which is not consistent with the defence put forward at trial; and

(e) failing to update a defence statement.

If any of these faults occurs the court or, with leave, any other party (such as the prosecution or any co-accused) may make such comments as appear appropriate, and the court or jury may draw such inferences as appear proper when deciding whether the defendant is guilty.

**Example 1**

Philippa is charged with theft. Her case is case is committed for trial at the Crown Court. She enters a not guilty plea at the PCMH. Philippa fails to serve a defence statement on the CPS. At her trial Philippa raises the defence of alibi, and claims that the prosecution witnesses who identified her as the person who committed the theft are mistaken. As Philippa failed to serve a defence statement setting out this defence, the trial judge or, with leave, the prosecution may comment on this and the jury may draw such inferences as appear proper.

**Example 2**

Javed is charged with unlawful wounding. His case is committed for trial at Crown Court. At the PCMH he enters a not guilty plea. In his defence statement, Javed claims that he was not present at the time of the alleged incident and raises the defence of alibi. At his trial, Javed accepts that he was present at the time of the incident and instead raises the defence of self-defence. As there is a disparity between what was said in his defence statement and the defence he is raising at trial, the judge or, with leave, the prosecution may comment on this and the jury may draw such inferences as appear proper.

In addition to the above, the trial judge has the power to order that a copy of the defence statement be disclosed to the jury to assist them in understanding the issues in the case (CPIA 1996, s 6E).

The judge may also order that a copy of the defence statement be supplied to any co-accused in a case where there are two or more defendants.

### 10.8.9 Other defence disclosure obligations

As in the magistrates' court, the defendant is not required to provide notice in advance that he will or will not be giving evidence on his own behalf at trial. However, under s 6C of the CPIA 1996, the defendant must serve a notice on the CPS and the court giving the names, addresses and dates of birth of any witnesses that he intends to call to give evidence on his behalf. Under s 6D of the CPIA 1996, the defendant must also serve details of the name and address of any expert witness he has consulted, even if that expert is not to be called to give evidence (see **8.4.2.3**).

### 10.8.10 Further disclosure obligations on the prosecution

The only 'reward' for a defendant who provides a defence statement is that the CPS must review its initial disclosure of unused material and determine if there is any further unused material in its possession which, in light of the matters contained in the defence statement, might now be deemed capable of undermining the case for the prosecution or of assisting the case for the defendant (CPIA 1996, s 7A – see **10.8.2** above).

#### Example

Gavin is jointly charged with Philip with the production of cannabis at premises owned by Philip. Gavin's defence is that he knows nothing about the production of cannabis at the premises and was employed by Philip at the premises solely to clean and valet cars. The CPS is not aware that this is the basis of Gavin's defence because he refused to answer any questions when interviewed at the police station. As part of their investigations, the police recover from the premises a number of documents, including receipts for various items of car-cleaning equipment. The CPS does not intend to use these receipts in evidence and is not under a duty to disclose such documents to Gavin's solicitor, because the documents neither undermine the prosecution case nor assist the case for the defence (because there has been no indication as to what the defence case is).

Gavin's solicitor subsequently serves a defence statement on the CPS stating that Gavin knew nothing about the premises being used for the production of cannabis and confirming that Gavin was employed at the premises solely to valet cars. The CPS is under a continuing duty of disclosure and so, in the light of the defence statement, it must now disclose the receipts to Gavin's solicitor, as the receipts assist Gavin's defence that he had an innocent explanation for being at the premises.

Section 8(2) of the CPIA 1996 enables a defendant who has provided a defence statement to make application to the court if the CPS has failed to comply with its continuing duty of disclosure in light of the matters contained in the defence statement. The defendant may ask the court for an order that the CPS disclose material provided the defendant has reasonable cause to believe that there is prosecution material which should have been, but has not been, disclosed. The defendant will only be permitted to make such an application if he has set out in detail in his defence statement the material which he considers the CPS has in its possession which it has not subsequently disclosed. The procedure to be followed when such an application is made is contained in Part 25 of the Criminal Procedure Rules.

A flowchart summarising the disclosure obligations imposed on both the CPS and the defendant in both the Crown Court and the magistrates' court is provided at **10.11** below.

## 10.9 Pre-trial hearings, preparatory hearings and further evidence

### 10.9.1 Pre-trial hearings

Section 40 of the CPIA 1996 allows a judge, prior to the trial starting, to rule on the admissibility of evidence and on any question of law relating to the case. The rulings can be made on the application of the prosecution or defence, or on the judge's own motion. During the course of a pre-trial hearing, a judge may use his case management powers to deal with issues (such as the admissibility of disputed points of evidence) by reference to written submissions rather than hearing oral argument.

### 10.9.2 Preparatory hearings (CrimPR, Part 15)

Part 3 of the CPIA 1996 created a statutory scheme for preparatory hearings in cases of fraud and other complex, serious or lengthy cases. A judge, acting either on his own motion or on the application of the prosecution or defence, can order such a hearing to take place if it is likely to bring substantial benefits because of the complexity or likely length of the case. The hearing can be use for any of the following purposes:

(a) to identify important issues for the jury;

(b) to help the jury's understanding of the issues;

(c) to speed up proceedings before the jury;

(d) to help the judge's management of the trial.

The judge conducting a preparatory hearing has the power to make rulings as to the admissibility of evidence, or on any point of law. Both the CPS and the defendant have the right to appeal to the Court of Appeal against any ruling made by the judge at a preparatory hearing (CrimPR, Part 65).

### 10.9.3 Notices of further evidence

A witness may be called to give evidence for the prosecution in the Crown Court even though his witness statement was not served on the defendant in accordance with the standard case management directions given by the magistrates when the case was sent to the Crown Court for trial. It may be, for example, that the witness came forward only after the PCMH had taken place. If the CPS wishes to call additional evidence from a 'new' witness at trial, a notice of intention to do so will be served on the defendant and the Crown Court. The notice will be accompanied by a copy of the relevant statement.

## 10.10 Trial procedure

### 10.10.1 Order of events

The procedure at a trial in the Crown Court is very similar to that in the magistrates' court (see **Chapter 9**). The order of events is as follows:

(a) The jury will be sworn in (commonly referred to as being 'empanelled'). The jury will comprise a randomly selected panel of 12 members of the public between the ages of 18 and 70, whose names are on the electoral roll for the local area and who have resided in the UK for at least five years. Certain persons are ineligible for jury service (for example, anyone suffering from a mental disorder), and certain classes of people are disqualified from being jurors (for example, anyone currently on bail in criminal proceedings).

(b) Prosecuting counsel will then give an opening speech to the jury, explaining what the case is about and what evidence he intends to call. The opening speech will usually contain the following elements:

(i) the legal elements of the offence(s) on the indictment;

(ii) an outline of the evidence the prosecutor intends to call;

(iii) an explanation of the operation of the burden and standard of proof in a criminal case (see **Chapter 16**);

Depending on the facts of the case, prosecuting counsel may highlight to the jury any points of law that he anticipates may arise during the case and possible defences open to the defendant.

(c) Each prosecution witness will then be called in turn to give evidence, starting with the 'victim' of the alleged crime. Each witness will be examined in chief by prosecuting counsel, cross-examined by defence counsel, and then (if necessary) re-examined by prosecuting counsel. Prosecuting counsel will read out the statements of any witness whose evidence has been accepted by the defendant under the s 9 procedure (see **8.4.4**) without the witness who gave the statement being required to attend court in person. He will also read out the statement of an witness whose evidence is to be admitted as hearsay evidence (see **Chapter 19**).

(d) If any disputes as to points of law or arguments as to the admissibility of evidence arise, a hearing known as a 'voire dire' (or a 'trial within a trial') will take place in the absence of the jury. Such hearings normally arise in the context of disputes as to the admissibility of a piece of evidence upon which the prosecution seek to rely (for example, a disputed confession). It is normal practice for defence counsel to notify prosecuting counsel prior to the trial of any items of prosecution evidence of which he will seek to challenge the admissibility at trial. Prosecuting counsel will not mention these items of evidence during his opening speech.

When the relevant point is reached during the presentation of the prosecution case, the judge will ask the jury to retire and he will then conduct the voire dire. The judge will hear evidence from witnesses, and then legal submissions from both prosecuting and defence counsel about the item of evidence in dispute. The judge will then make his ruling. If the judge rules that a particular piece of evidence is inadmissible, the jury will never hear about that piece of evidence. If the judge rules that the evidence is admissible, the party wishing to rely on that evidence (usually the prosecution) may then raise it during the trial. It will still be open to the other party (usually the defence) to attempt to undermine the reliability or cogency of that evidence either when cross-examining the witness giving the evidence, or when examining their own witnesses in chief.

(e) At the conclusion of the prosecution case, defence counsel may make a submission that there is no case for the defendant to answer. This submission will be made to the judge in the absence of the jury. The test which the judge will apply in deciding whether there is a case to answer is known as the '*Galbraith* test', following the case of *R v Galbraith* [1981] 2 All

ER 1060 in which it was first set out. The judge will ask himself if the prosecution evidence, taken at its highest, is such that a jury properly directed could not safely convict upon it. For the submission to succeed, defence counsel will need to show that the prosecution have failed to adduce evidence in support of an essential element of the offence, or that, even taking the best possible view of the prosecution evidence, the case against the defendant is so unreliable that a jury could not convict upon it. If the judge rejects a submission of no case to answer, he should give brief reasons for deciding that there is sufficient evidence to go before the jury (*R v Powell* [2006] All ER (D) 146 (Jan)).

(f) If the submission of no case to answer is successful, the jury will be asked to return and the judge will instruct them to return a verdict of not guilty. If the submission of no case to answer is unsuccessful, the judge may permit a defendant to change his plea from not guilty to guilty at this stage. A defendant may wish to do this if, for example, he has admitted his guilt to his solicitor but put the prosecution to proof of their case. A defendant may also wish to change his plea to guilty at the end of the prosecution case if the trial judge has made a ruling on a point of law, or on the admissibility of a piece of evidence, which deprives the defendant of a defence he had hoped to rely upon.

(g) If the submission of no case to answer is unsuccessful (and the defendant does not seek to change his plea), defence counsel will then present the defendant's case. If the defence intend calling a witness or witnesses in addition to the defendant, defence counsel is entitled to make an opening speech to the jury. He is not entitled to do this if only the defendant is to give evidence. If there is more than one defendant, each defendant will present his case in turn. The order in which this is done will follow the order in which the defendants' names appear on the indictment.

(h) Witnesses for the defence will then be called to give evidence. The defendant will be called first (assuming he is to give evidence). Should the defendant fail to give evidence, the judge will direct the jury that they may draw an adverse inference from such silence under s 35 of the CJPOA 1994 (see **9.6.1.2**). Each defence witness will be examined in chief by defence counsel, cross-examined by the prosecuting counsel and then (if necessary) re-examined by defence counsel.

(i) At the conclusion of the defence case, both prosecuting and defence counsel will deliver a closing speech to the jury. Prosecuting counsel will give his closing speech first, followed by defence counsel.

(j) Before the jury retire to consider their verdict, the judge will then give his 'summing up' to the jury. The summing up has two parts, namely directions on the law and a summary of the evidence.

When the judge directs the jury on the law he will cover three areas:

(i) the burden and standard of proof (see **Chapter 16**);

(ii) the legal requirements of the offence; and

(iii) any other issues of law and evidence that have arisen during the trial (for example, a *Turnbull* warning in the case of disputed identification evidence, or a direction as to the drawing of adverse inferences under ss 34 to 37 of the CJPOA 2004).

A very common ground of appeal raised by defendants following conviction at a trial in the Crown Court is that the judge has misdirected the jury on a point of law or evidence. To prevent judges misdirecting the jury, the Judicial Studies Board (JSB) has produced a set of specimen directions for judges to use. These directions cover most issues of law and evidence that are likely to arise during a trial. These directions may be found on the JSB website (www.jsboard.co.uk).

When the judge gives the jury a summary of the evidence, he will provide the following:

(i) a succinct summary of the issues of fact that the jury has to decide;

(ii) an accurate and concise summary of the evidence and arguments raised by both prosecution and defence; and

(iii) a correct statement of the inferences the jury are entitled to draw from their conclusions about the facts.

At the end of his summing up, the judge will tell the jury member to appoint a foreman, and will instruct them to retire to consider their verdict and to reach a unanimous conclusion.

(k) The jury will then retire to consider their verdict. The deliberations of the jury are in private and must remain completely secret. The jurors are permitted to consider only the evidence they have heard at trial when deciding their verdict, and are not permitted to discuss the case with anyone other than their fellow jurors. The jury must decide their verdict unanimously, although a majority verdict of 11:1 or 10:2 will be accepted if, after at least 2 hours and 10 minutes, unanimity is not possible (Juries Act 1974, s 17). If the case was lengthy or in any way complex, the judge is likely to wait much longer than this minimum period before telling the jury that he is prepared to accept a majority verdict.

(l) If the jury cannot reach a majority verdict within a reasonable time, the judge will discharge the jury. The CPS may then request a re-trial before a new jury.

(m) If the jury find the defendant not guilty, the defendant will be discharged by the judge and told that he is free to go. If the defendant's case was not funded by way of a representation order, the judge will usually order that his legal costs be paid from central funds (ie, by the State).

(n) If the jury find the defendant guilty, the judge will then proceed to sentence the defendant. The judge will either sentence the defendant immediately, or, if necessary, adjourn sentence so that pre-sentence reports can be obtained (see **Chapter 12**). If the judge adjourns sentence, he will remand the defendant either on bail or in custody. Although there is a presumption in favour of bail for a defendant who has been convicted but not yet sentenced, if the sentencing hearing has been adjourned so that pre-sentence reports may be prepared (see **Chapter 7**), a defendant who has been convicted of a serious offence is very unlikely to be granted bail before sentence. The judge is likely to refuse him bail on the grounds either that the defendant will fail to surrender to custody, or that it would be impractical to prepare the report unless the defendant is in custody. The procedure for sentencing a defendant is described in **Chapter 12**.

A flowchart summarising the above is set out at **10.11.2** below.

### 10.10.2 Role of the solicitor at trial

If counsel is representing the defendant at trial, it is rare for the solicitor who has been dealing with the matter in the magistrates' court to attend the whole trial. In a complex or lengthy case, the solicitor may attend the first day of the trial, but more commonly a paralegal or trainee solicitor will be sent to 'sit behind counsel'. The representative from the solicitor's firm who attends court will be present at any conference that take place between defence counsel and the defendant at court, and will assist counsel during the trial by taking notes of the evidence given by witnesses, and by making a note of any directions or evidential rulings made by the judge. Such notes will be important because counsel may wish to rely on them either when cross-examining a witness, or when giving his closing speech to the jury. Similarly, notes of comments made by the judge may be useful when a notice of appeal is being drafted based on a misdirection given by the judge (see **Chapter 13**).

The other important function played by the representative from the solicitor's firm who attends the trial is to meet any defence witnesses who are to attend court, and to ensure that such witnesses are ready to give evidence when called. As with witnesses called to give evidence on behalf of a defendant in the magistrates' court, a witness summons should have been obtained for any defence witness required to give evidence. The Crown Court will issue a summons for a witness to attend trial if that witness is likely to give evidence material to the case and it is in the interests of justice for a summons to be issued (Criminal Procedure (Attendance of Witnesses) Act 1965, s 2). The procedural requirements for obtaining a witness summons from the Crown Court are set out in Part 28 of the Criminal Procedure Rules.

At the end of the case, if the defendant has been convicted, counsel will have a further conference with the defendant to advise on the prospects of an appeal against conviction and/or sentence. Such a conference is likely to take place in the cells at the Crown Court. The representative from the solicitor's firm will attend this conference and again take a note of any advice given by counsel.

## 10.11 Procedural flowcharts

### 10.11.1 Disclosure (both magistrates' court and Crown Court)

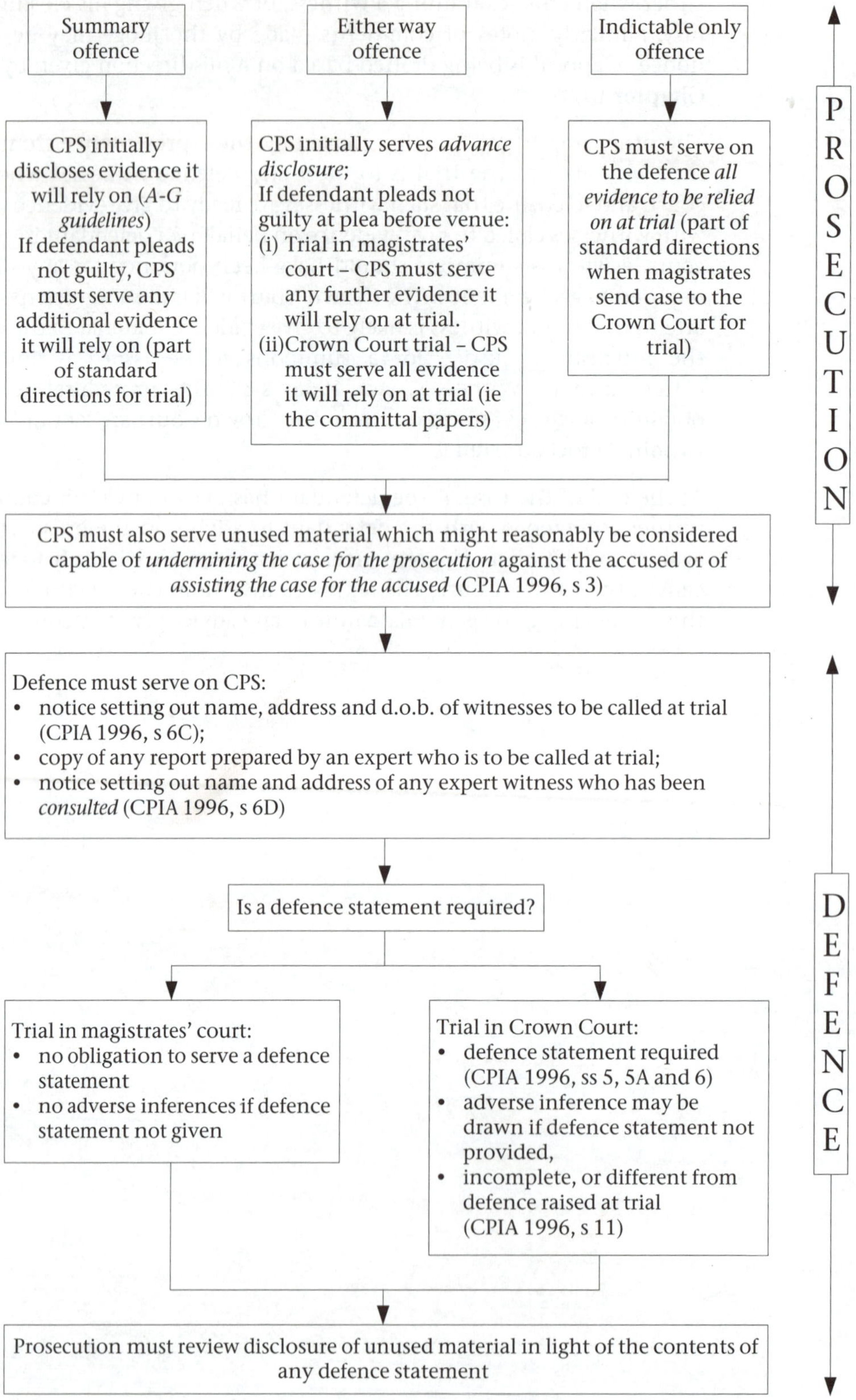

### 10.11.2 Trial procedure in the Crown Court

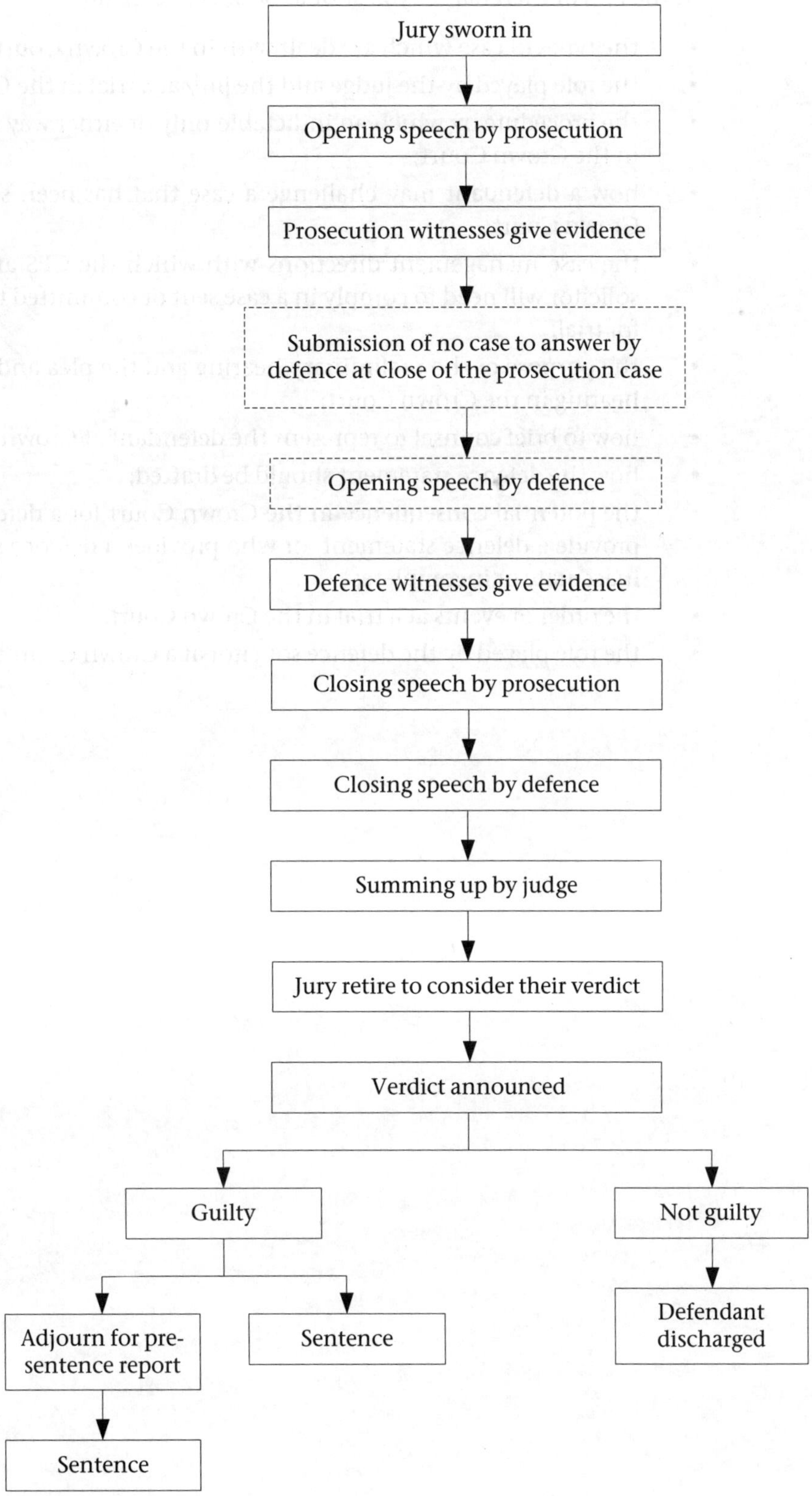

## 10.12 Checklist

At the end of this chapter you should be able to explain:

- the types of case which are dealt with in the Crown Court;
- the role played by the judge and the jury at a trial in the Crown Court;
- the procedure by which an indictable-only or either way offence gets to trial in the Crown Court;
- how a defendant may challenge a case that has been sent for trial to the Crown Court;
- the case management directions with which the CPS and the defendant's solicitor will need to comply in a case sent or committed to the Crown Court for trial;
- the purpose of the preliminary hearing and the plea and case management hearing in the Crown Court;
- how to brief counsel to represent the defendant at Crown Court;
- how the defence statement should be drafted;
- the potential consequence in the Crown Court for a defendant who fails to provide a defence statement, or who provides a defence statement which is inaccurate or incomplete;
- the order of events at a trial in the Crown Court.
- the role played by the defence solicitor at a Crown Court trial.

## 10.13 Key forms

### 10.13.1 Directions for case sent to the Crown Court

**MAGISTRATES' COURT**

**DIRECTIONS FOR CASE SENT TO THE CROWN COURT**

**.................................Magistrates' Court**
**Date sent: ...............................................**

**The Plea and Case Management Hearing will take place**

**on..................................at..........................................Crown Court**

| Name of defendant | Case no | Remand status | Youth jointly charged with adult? | Represented by: |
|---|---|---|---|---|
| D1 | | Bail/cust/COM | | |
| D2 | | Bail/cust/COM | | |
| D3 | | Bail/cust/COM | | |
| D4 | | Bail/cust/COM | | |

**COM= in custody on other matters**

Defence telephone numbers:
D1............................(home)..............................(mobile) D1 solicitor ..................................(office)
D2............................(home)..............................(mobile) D2 solicitor ..................................(office)
D3............................(home)..............................(mobile) D3 solicitor ..................................(office)
D4............................(home)..............................(mobile) D4 solicitor ..................................(office)

Prosecution telephone number....................................................

**CASE DETAILS**

1. Has the defendant been advised that the case may proceed in his or her absence?

D1: Y ☐ N ☐ D2: Y ☐ N ☐

D3: Y ☐ N ☐ D4: Y ☐ N ☐

2. Has the defendant been advised about credit for pleading guilty?

D1: Y ☐ N ☐ D2: Y ☐ N ☐

D3: Y ☐ N ☐ D4: Y ☐ N ☐

3. What pleas, if any, are indicated?
D1:..........................................................................................................................
D2:..........................................................................................................................
D3:..........................................................................................................................
D4:..........................................................................................................................

**NOTE: If the defendant decides to plead guilty after sending, the Crown Court must be notified immediately. The Crown Court will then list the case for a hearing as soon as possible.**

4. Does the defence intend to make an application under section 41 of the Youth Justice and Criminal Evidence Act 1999 to cross-examine the complainant about his or her sexual history?.......................................................(to be served within 28 days of primary/initial disclosure)

5. Please give details of any other matters which should be dealt with at the same time as these proceedings (e.g. other offences, offences to be taken into consideration)?

D1:.....................................................
.........................................................
D2:.....................................................
.........................................................
D3:.....................................................
.........................................................
D4:.....................................................
.........................................................

**Insert date by which Action 1 to be completed in blank box:**

| ACTION | TIME LIMITS | DIRECTIONS |
|---|---|---|
| 1 | **Cust:** 50 days after sent* <br> **Bail:** 70 days after sent* | • Prosecution to serve draft indictment, case papers and primary or initial disclosure. |
| 2 | **14 days after Action 1** | • Defence to notify prosecution of witness requirements <br> • Prosecution to serve any application for hearsay or defendant's bad character <br> • Defence to serve: <br> (i) Defence statement* (including any alibi details) OR notification of guilty plea <br> (ii) Any application for hearsay/bad character <br> (iii) Any notice of application to dismiss charges |
| 3 | **28 days after Action 1** | • Prosecution to serve final draft indictment and any special measures applications <br> • Defence to serve any application under section 41 of the Youth Justice and Criminal Evidence Act 1999 |
| 4 | **14 days after Action 2** | • Prosecution to serve responses to hearsay/bad character/dismissal of charges applications <br> • Defence to serve response to hearsay/bad character application by prosecution |
| 5 | **14 days after Action 3** | • Defence to serve response to any prosecution application for special measures <br> • Prosecution and defence to notify Crown Court of names of trial advocate and time estimate <br> • Defence to notify Crown Court of non-availability of expert witnesses, with reasons <br> • Witness Care Unit to notify Crown Court and prosecution of dates when witnesses required by defence are unavailable, with reasons |

**NOTE: if any party seeks a subsequent variation in the timetable or further direction, a written application must be made to the Crown Court within 14 days of date sent, and copies served on all other parties. A Crown Court judge may make directions as appropriate or fix a preliminary hearing. If at any time either party is unable to comply with any direction, it must notify the CPO immediately and apply to the Crown Court for a variation.**

*** indicates those time limits which cannot be varied by a magistrates' court.**

| |
|---|
| Please record any further directions here: |

**Received.....................................(defence signature) ................................(prosecution signature)**

## 10.13.2 Directions for case committed to the Crown Court

### MAGISTRATES' COURT

### DIRECTIONS FOR CASE COMMITTED TO THE CROWN COURT

**.................................................Magistrates' Court**
**Date committed.......................................................**

**The Plea and Case Management Hearing will take place**

**on...................................at...........................................Crown Court**

| Name of defendant | Case no | Remand status | Youth jointly charged with adult? | Represented by: |
|---|---|---|---|---|
| D1 | | Bail/cust/COM | | |
| D2 | | Bail/cust/COM | | |
| D3 | | Bail/cust/COM | | |
| D4 | | Bail/cust/COM | | |

**COM= in custody on other matters**

Defence telephone numbers:
D1..............................(home)................................(mobile) D1 solicitor ....................................(office)
D2..............................(home)................................(mobile) D2 solicitor ....................................(office)
D3..............................(home)................................(mobile) D3 solicitor ....................................(office)
D4..............................(home)................................(mobile) D4 solicitor ....................................(office)

Prosecution telephone number........................................................

**CASE DETAILS**

1. Has the defendant been advised that the case may proceed in his or her absence?

D1: Y ☐ N ☐ D2: Y ☐ N ☐

D3: Y ☐N ☐ D4: Y ☐ N ☐

2. Has the defendant been advised about credit for pleading guilty?

D1: Y ☐ N ☐ D2: Y ☐ N ☐

D3: Y ☐N ☐ D4: Y ☐ N ☐

3. What pleas, if any, are indicated?
D1:..........................................................................................................................
D2:..........................................................................................................................
D3:..........................................................................................................................
D4:..........................................................................................................................

**NOTE: If the defendant decides to plead guilty after committal, the Crown Court must be notified immediately. The Crown Court will then list the case for a hearing as soon as possible.**

4. Does the defence intend to make an application under section 41 of the Youth Justice and Criminal Evidence Act 1999 to cross-examine the complainant about his or her sexual history?..........................................................(to be served within 28 days of primary/initial disclosure)

5. Please give details of any other matters which should be dealt with at the same time as these proceedings (e.g. other offences, offences to be taken into consideration)?
D1:....................................................... D2:.......................................................
.......................................................... ..........................................................
D3:....................................................... D4:.......................................................
.......................................................... ..........................................................

**Insert committal date in blank box:**

| ACTION | TIME LIMITS | DIRECTIONS |
|---|---|---|
| 1 | Date committed | • Prosecution to serve provisional draft indictment, if not already done. |
| 2 | **14 days after Action 1** | • Prosecution to serve primary or initial disclosure<br>• Defence to notify prosecution of witness requirements<br>• Prosecution to serve any application for hearsay or defendant's bad character |
| 3 | **28 days after Action 1** | • Prosecution to serve final draft indictment and any special measures applications<br>• Defence to serve any application under section 41 of the Youth Justice and Criminal Evidence Act 1999 |
| 4 | **14 days after Action 2** | • Defence to serve:<br>• (i) Defence statement* (including any alibi details) OR notification of guilty plea<br>(ii) Any application for hearsay/bad character<br>(iii) Response to hearsay/bad character application by prosecution |
| 5 | **14 days after Action 3** | • Defence to serve response to any prosecution application for special measures<br>• Prosecution and defence to notify Crown Court of names of trial advocate and time estimate<br>• Defence to notify Crown Court of non-availability of expert witnesses, with reasons<br>• Witness Care Unit to notify Crown Court and prosecution of dates when witnesses required by defence are unavailable, with reasons. |
| 6 | **14 days after Action 4** | • Prosecution to serve responses to hearsay/bad character |

**NOTE: if any party seeks a subsequent variation in the timetable or further direction, a written application must be made to the Crown Court within 14 days of committal, and copies served on all other parties. A Crown Court judge may make directions as appropriate. If at any time either party is unable to comply with any direction, it must notify the case progression officer immediately and apply to the Crown Court for a variation.**

*** indicates those time limits which cannot be varied by a magistrates' court.**

Please record any further directions here:

**Received.....................................(defence signature) ................................(prosecution signature)**

# Part 3 Summary – Procedure from Charge to Trial

| *Topic* | *Summary* | *References* |
|---|---|---|
| Funding | To apply for a representation order, the defendant must submit an application form (CDS 14) and a statement of means (CDS 15) to the court. The defendant will receive an order only if it is in the interests of justice that he has legal representation *and* he satisfies a means test. | |
| Bail | Prior to conviction *all* defendants have a prima facie right to bail.<br>There are several exceptions to the right to bail when the defendant is charged with an imprisonable offence.<br>The exception most commonly relied upon by the prosecution is that there are *substantial* grounds for believing that, if released on bail, the defendant would:<br>• fail to surrender to custody;<br>• commit further offences on bail; or<br>• interfere with witnesses or subvert the course of justice.<br>In deciding whether such grounds exist, the court will consider the following factors:<br>• the nature and seriousness of the offence, and the probable sentence if the defendant is convicted;<br>• the defendant's character, antecedents, associations and community ties;<br>• the defendant's previous bail record; and<br>• the strength of the evidence.<br>The court may grant the defendant unconditional bail or bail subject to conditions (such as residence or reporting to a police station).<br>A defendant whose first application for bail is refused may make one further application using any argument as to fact or law. Thereafter the defendant may make a further application only if he can raise a *new* argument as to fact or law.<br>A defendant who is refused bail by the magistrates' court has a right of appeal to the Crown Court. | Bail Act 1976, s 4<br><br>Sch 1, Pt 1 |

| *Topic* | *Summary* | *References* |
|---|---|---|
| Summary offences | A summary offence may be dealt with only by the magistrates' court. The defendant will make his first appearance at an early first hearing or an early administrative hearing. If the defendant pleads not guilty, the magistrates will give the defendant and the prosecution case management directions to comply with prior to trial.<br>If the defendant pleads guilty, he may be sentenced immediately, or the magistrates may adjourn sentence in order to obtain a pre-sentence report from the Probation Service. | |
| Either way offences | An either way offence may be dealt with either by the magistrates' court, or by the Crown Court. The defendant will make his first appearance at an early first hearing or an early administrative hearing. This hearing will normally be adjourned for the prosecution to supply advance disclosure of its case to the defendant.<br>If the defendant indicates a not guilty plea at the plea before venue hearing, the mode of trial hearing will then take place. The magistrates will decide where the case should be dealt with and, if the magistrates retain jurisdiction, the defendant may elect trial at the Crown Court.<br>If the case remains before the magistrates' court, case management directions will be given for the parties to comply with prior to trial.<br>If the case is to be tried in the Crown Court, the case will be committed to the Crown Court for trial and a date for the plea and case management hearing at the Crown Court will be set. The magistrates will give case management directions for the parties to comply with.<br>If the defendant indicates a guilty plea at the plea before venue hearing, the magistrates will either sentence the defendant themselves, or will commit the defendant to the Crown Court if they consider their sentencing powers to be inadequate. | |
| Offences triable only on indictment | Offences triable only on indictment may be dealt with only by the Crown Court. The defendant will make an initial appearance before the magistrates' court. The case will then be sent to the Crown Court for trial under s 51 of the Crime and Disorder Act 1998 and a date for the plea and case management hearing at the Crown Court will be set. The magistrates will either give case management directions for the parties to comply with, or will have the case listed for a preliminary hearing at the Crown Court. | |

| *Topic* | *Summary* | *References* |
|---|---|---|
| Disclosure | The prosecution will disclose to the defendant the material upon which they intend to rely at trial.<br>The directions given by the court will include a requirement that the prosecution also disclose to the defendant any unused material in their possession which undermines the prosecution case or assists the defence case.<br>In the magistrates' court, the defendant may provide a defence statement to the court and the prosecution. It is rare for such a statement to be given.<br>In the Crown Court the defendant is effectively obliged to provide a defence statement because adverse inferences may be drawn should he fail to do so. The defence statement must set out the general nature of the defence, the facts upon which the defendant takes issue with the prosecution and any matters of law that may arise in the case. The defence statement should be given within 14 days of the prosecution disclosing any unused material they have. | <br><br>CPIA 1996, s 3 |
| Advocacy at trial | The trial will begin with the prosecution giving an opening speech setting out the facts of the case, the relevant law and the witnesses the prosecution will call.<br>Witnesses are examined in chief by the party that called them and then cross-examined. Examination-in-chief is about a witness telling his 'story'. Leading questions are not permitted. The purpose of cross-examination is to undermine the credibility of the witness and to put the 'other' party's case to the witness. Brief re-examination of the witness is permitted after cross-examination.<br>At the close of the prosecution case, the defendant's solicitor may make a submission of no case to answer which, if successful, will end the trial.<br>In a closing speech, the defendant's solicitor should sum up the case from the defendant's point of view and indicate the weaknesses in the prosecution case. | |

# Part 4

# SENTENCING AND APPEALS

# Chapter 11

# Sentencing – The Law



## 11.1 Introduction

The majority of defendants charged with having committed a criminal offence will either plead guilty, or be convicted after a trial in either the magistrates' court or the Crown Court. The final stage in the criminal litigation process (subject to any appeal the defendant may make – see **Chapter 13**) is for the defendant to be sentenced.

This chapter will examine the statutory provisions which are relevant to the sentencing of offenders aged 18 and over (the sentencing of juvenile offenders is described in **Chapter 14**). It will begin by explaining the purpose of sentencing, the types of sentence which the court may impose upon a defendant, and the factors which must be considered by the court when determining the type of sentence a defendant is to receive. The chapter will conclude by looking in more detail at the particular types of sentence which the court may impose.

## 11.2 Purpose of sentencing

Section 142(1) of the Criminal Justice Act (CJA) 2003 states that a court sentencing an offender aged 18 or over must have regard to the following five purposes of sentencing:

(a) the punishment of offenders;

(b) the reduction of crime (including its reduction by deterrence);

(c) the reform and rehabilitation of offenders;

(d) the protection of the public; and

(e) the making of reparation by offenders to persons affected by their offence.

The court need not have such regard if the sentence is fixed by law or subject to a statutory minimum (see **11.5.1**) or if the defendant is classed as a dangerous offender (see **11.5.3.2**).

Section 174 of the CJA 2003 imposes a duty on the court to give reasons for the particular sentence which is imposed on a defendant. When a defendant is being sentenced, the court must 'state in open court, in ordinary language and in general terms, its reasons for deciding on the sentence passed ...' (s 174(1)).

## 11.3 Types of sentence

### 11.3.1 The basic sentence

There are four basic types of sentence which a court may impose on an adult defendant (the types of sentence that may be imposed on a juvenile appearing before the Youth Court are detailed in **Chapter 14**). In descending order of severity, these sentences are as follows:

(a) *Custodial sentence* – this involves the defendant being deprived of his physical liberty by being detained in custody for a specified period of time (see **11.5** below). Defendants aged 21 and over will serve a custodial sentence in an adult prison. Defendants aged 18 to 20 will serve a custodial sentence in a young offenders' institution

(b) *Community sentence* – this involves the defendant being required to take part in one or more activities within the community whilst still retaining his liberty (see **11.6** below).

(c) *Fine* – this involves the defendant having to pay a financial penalty for his offending (see **11.7** below).

(d) *Discharge* – no immediate penalty is imposed on the defendant who receives a discharge, but if the discharge is conditional, the defendant may be sentenced for the original offence if he commits another offence within a period of time specified by the court (see **11.8** below).

The above list is sometimes referred to as the 'sentencing ladder', with the particular rung of the ladder upon which a defendant finds himself being determined by the seriousness of the offence. A flowchart depicting the sentencing ladder is to be found at **11.9** below.

### 11.3.2 Additional orders

#### 11.3.2.1 Introduction

In addition to the basic sentence which he receives, the court may also impose additional orders on a defendant convicted of a criminal offence. The most common types of additional order are set out below.

#### 11.3.2.2 Compensation

A defendant may be ordered to pay compensation to the victim of an offence for any injury or other loss suffered by the victim (Power of Criminal Courts (Sentencing) Act 2000, ss 130–133). An order to pay compensation is particularly common in cases of assault where the victim has suffered physical injury, but it can also be used in other cases (for example, a theft case where goods stolen by the defendant are destroyed or damaged). Magistrates may order a defendant to pay compensation up to a maximum figure of £5,000 per offence. There is no financial limit on the amount of compensation which may be ordered in the Crown Court, although the judge must have regard to the defendant's means when making an order.

#### 11.3.2.3 Prosecution costs

A defendant convicted of a criminal offence may be ordered by the court sentencing him to pay some or all of the costs incurred by the CPS in bringing the case against him. Such costs must be just and reasonable. The court must specify the exact amount to be paid by the defendant.

### 11.3.2.4 Defence costs

A defendant whose case is being funded by way of a representation order will not be required to make any contribution towards the costs of his case whilst the case is ongoing. However, in the Crown Court, following conviction the judge has the power to order a defendant who has the benefit of a representation order to pay some or all of the costs of his defence. This is referred to as a 'recovery of defence costs order' (RDCO).

The judge will consider whether to make an RDCO *after* he has taken into account any other financial orders and penalties that may be made. An RDCO should be made against every defendant who is convicted and has the financial means to pay towards the cost of his legal representation.

An RDCO may *not* be made against a defendant who:

(a) only appears in the magistrates' court;

(b) has been committed for sentence to the Crown Court having entered a guilty plea at the plea and directions hearing in the magistrates' court; or

(c) is appealing to the Crown Court against a sentence imposed by the magistrates' court.

### 11.3.2.5 Forfeiture orders

A court may order the forfeiture of any property which was in the defendant's possession or control at the time he was apprehended, if the property was:

(a) used for committing or facilitating any offence;

(b) intended to be used for committing or facilitating any offence; or

(c) unlawfully in his possession (Powers of Criminal Courts (Sentencing) Act 2000).

In addition, there are a number of specific statutory powers which provide for the forfeiture of drugs, firearms and offensive weapons.

Examples of items which may be the subject of a forfeiture order include:

(a) implements used in the production and/or distribution of drugs (for example, a set of scales);

(b) offensive weapons (such as guns, knives or a baseball bat);

(c) items used to gain unlawful access to premises (such as a jemmy or crowbar).

The court will normally order that any property subject to a forfeiture order should be destroyed (a 'destruction order').

An order for the forfeiture and destruction of a controlled drug will be made by the court under s 27 of the Misuse of Drugs Act 1971.

### 11.3.2.6 Confiscation and restitution orders

A defendant appearing in the Crown Court may be made the subject of a confiscation order in respect of the proceeds of his criminal activity (for example, a defendant who has made substantial profits from the supply of controlled drugs). Such orders were created by the Proceeds of Crime Act 2002. The detailed provisions of confiscation orders are beyond the scope of this book.

Section 28 of the Theft Act 1968 enables the court to make a restitution order. A restitution order is designed to restore to a person entitled to them goods which have been stolen or otherwise unlawfully removed from him, or to restore to him a sum of money representing the proceeds of the sale of the goods from money found in the defendant's possession.

### 11.3.2.7 Anti-social behaviour orders

A magistrates' court may make an anti-social behaviour order (ASBO) pursuant to s 1C of the Crime and Disorder Act 1998 if:

(a) the court considers that the defendant has acted in an anti-social manner (ie, a manner that caused, or was likely to cause, harassment, alarm or distress to one or more persons not of the same household as the defendant); *and*

(b) the court considers that an order is necessary to protect any person from further anti-social acts by the defendant (*R v Boness & Others* [2005] EWCA Crim 2395).

If these conditions are satisfied, the court may make an order under s 1C prohibiting the defendant from doing any act specified in the order. The most common types of order prohibit defendants from entering particular places or areas, or contacting particular individuals.

An ABSO can be made by the court only in addition to a sentence imposed for an offence, or in addition to a conditional discharge. The order will have effect for a period of time which will be specified by the court (subject to a minimum of two years and a maximum of five years). Breaching an ASBO is a criminal offence.

#### Example

Danny is a member of a gang which has been using a local housing estate as a place to race their cars in the early hours of the morning. Following an altercation with a local resident, Danny is charged with affray and subsequently convicted. In addition to the sentence for the affray, the court also makes an ASBO on the basis that Danny's behaviour (racing cars late at night) is anti-social, and an order is necessary to stop Danny committing further anti-social acts. The order prohibits Danny from entering the housing estate and is expressed to last for two years.

A court which makes an ASBO must ensure that the terms of the order are proportionate and commensurate with the risk to be guarded against. If not, the order may infringe the defendant's rights under the ECHR (*R v Boness & Others* – above).

The Court of Appeal has provided detailed guidance for courts to follow when considering the imposition of an ASBO (see, eg, *R v Wadmore & Foreman* [2006] EWCA Crim 686 and *M v DPP* [2007] All ER (D) 74 (Mar)).

If the defendant's anti-social behaviour is drug-related, at the same time as making an ASBO the court may impose an 'intervention order' requiring the defendant to comply with requirements designed to address the reasons for his drug-taking (Crime and Disorder Act 1998, ss 1G and 1H).

### 11.3.2.8 Binding over

A magistrates' court may make an order binding over anyone appearing before it. This includes not only a defendant, but also a witness or even a complainant. A binding over order is not a sentence as such, and is often used by magistrates in cases involving minor disturbances (typically disputes between neighbours which have resulted in proceedings for offences under ss 4, 4A and 5 of the Public Order Act 1986, or for common assault).

Before imposing a binding over order, the court must be satisfied that a breach of the peace involving violence or an imminent threat of violence has occurred, or that there is a real risk of violence in the future. Historically, a court making a binding over order would bind over an individual to 'be of good behaviour' or to 'keep the peace'. However, following judgments from the European Court of Human Rights (see, for example, *Steel v UK* (1999) 28 EHRR 603 and *Hashman & Harrup v UK* (2000) 30 EHRR 241), a court making a binding over order is now required to identify the specific conduct or activity which an individual should refrain from.

When making an order binding an individual over to refrain from specified types of conduct or activities, the court will require the individual to enter into a 'recognisance'. This is a sum of money which the individual will forfeit if he breaks the terms of the order. The order itself will usually last for no more than 12 months.

**Example**

Toyah and Leanne start a fight with each other at the pub after Toyah accuses Leanne of sleeping with her boyfriend. Toyah scratches Leanne's face and is subsequently charged with common assault. At her trial, Toyah is acquitted by the magistrates. The magistrates are concerned, however, that as Toyah and Leanne live near to each other and frequent the same pub, there is a risk that their future behaviour might lead to a breach of the peace. The magistrates therefore make a binding over order requiring them to refrain from using violent words or conduct towards the other for a period of 12 months. A recognisance of £50 is imposed. If either of them breaches the binding over order within the 12-month period, she will be ordered to forfeit the sum of £50.

#### 11.3.2.9 Sex offenders

The Sexual Offences Act 2003 requires a defendant convicted of or cautioned for a specified sexual offence to notify the police of his date of birth, National Insurance number, name, home address and any other address at which he regularly stays. Any change to these details must also be notified to the police. The police will retain this information on a database (the 'sex offenders register').

If a defendant has been convicted of a violent or sexual offence, the court may also make a sexual offences prevention order. An order lasts for at least five years and will prohibit the offender from doing anything specified in it thought necessary to protect the public or any particular members of the public from serious sexual harm (for example, preventing an offender from contacting his victims or from taking part in sporting activities that involve close contact with children).

#### 11.3.2.10 Drinking banning orders (DBOs)

Where a defendant has been convicted of an offence committed when under the influence of alcohol, the sentencing court must consider whether to make a DBO under ss 6 and 7 of the Violent Crime Reduction Act 2006. A DBO will prohibit the defendant from entering licensed premises. The order must be necessary to protect other persons from criminal or disorderly behaviour whilst the defendant is under influence of alcohol.

## 11.4 Principles of sentencing

### 11.4.1 The traditional approach to sentencing

Prior to the CJA 2003 coming into force, guidelines existed to ensure that a degree of consistency was achieved when courts were sentencing offenders for particular types of offence. For cases in the Crown Court, the Court of Appeal provided guidance in 'guideline' cases as to what the 'starting point' sentence should be for any given offence. In the magistrates' court, the Magistrates' Association published guidelines (the Magistrates' Court Sentencing Guidelines) indicating what the 'starting point' was for any given offence. The starting point sentence was based on a first-time offender who pleaded not guilty and was convicted following trial.

Once the judge or bench of magistrates had found the appropriate starting point, it would then be necessary to determine whether the facts of the specific offence being dealt with made the offence more or less serious than a 'standard' offence of that type. To determine this, the judge or magistrates would consider the existence of any aggravating or mitigating factors, and also whether the defendant had previous convictions for the same or for similar offences. Aggravating factors are factors which make an offence more serious than would otherwise be the case. Examples of aggravating factors included an offence being premeditated, the victim of the offence being chosen for his vulnerability (such as an elderly person) or, in the case of a violent offence, the use of a weapon. Mitigating factors are factors which make an offence less serious than would otherwise be the case. Examples of mitigating factors include a defendant committing an offence on impulse or out of desperation, the victim suffering only minor injuries (in the case of an assault) or an item stolen being of low value (in a theft case).

Finally the judge or magistrates would take into account whether the defendant had entered a guilty plea and, if he had, at what stage in the case the plea had been entered. The defendant would be entitled to a discount on his sentence for pleading guilty, although the size of this reduction would depend upon at which stage in the proceedings the plea had been entered. A defendant who entered a guilty plea at the first opportunity (ie, at his first court appearance) would be entitled to a discount of a maximum of one-third of the sentence he would have received had he pleaded not guilty and been convicted following a trial.

### 11.4.2 The Criminal Justice Act 2003

#### 11.4.2.1 Introduction

Although the system described in **11.4.1** above has not been completely removed, the CJA 2003 has made a number of significant changes to the way in which defendants are sentenced. In particular, the relative informality of the pre-CJA procedure has been replaced with statutory procedures designed to ensure a uniformity of approach to sentencing.

#### 11.4.2.2 The Sentencing Guidelines Council

One of the most important changes made by the CJA 2003 is the creation (by s 167) of the Sentencing Guidelines Council (SGC). The SGC is made up of the Lord Chief Justice (the senior criminal judge), seven judicial members and four non-judicial members. Its purpose is to encourage consistency in sentencing by producing definitive sentencing guidelines to which all courts (ie, the magistrates' court, the Crown Court, the Court of Appeal and the House of Lords) must have regard. In producing these guidelines, the SGC is assisted by a separate Sentencing Advisory Panel (SAP), which will produce reports and research papers for the SGC to consider.

In time, the guidelines produced by the SGC will replace the guidance given by the Court of Appeal in guideline cases and the Magistrates' Court Sentencing

Guidelines. So far the SGC has produced sentencing guidelines only for a limited range of offences (for example, robbery). It has not as yet issued guidance for most types of offence and, until it does, the previous guidelines – either from the Court of Appeal (for Crown Court cases) or contained in the Magistrates' Court Sentencing Guidelines (for cases in the magistrates' court) – will continue to be used by the courts. Indeed the SGC has produced a case compendium which comprises summaries of key current sentencing guideline cases from the Court of Appeal. This compendium can be found on the SGC website (www.sentencing-guidelines.gov.uk). Extracts from the Magistrates' Court Sentencing Guidelines, dealing with the most common cases dealt with in the magistrates' court, are set out in the **Appendix**. The full set of Guidelines can be found on the Judicial Studies Board website (www.jsboard.co.uk).

Section 172 of the CJA 2003 provides that a court, when sentencing a defendant, must have regard to any guidelines which are relevant to the defendant's case. If the sentencing court chooses to depart from the guideline sentence, it must give reasons for so doing (CJA 2003, s 174(2)).

### 11.4.2.3 The principle of seriousness

Prior to the CJA 2003 coming into force, the seriousness of an offence would determine the 'starting point' for the sentence the court would impose. The sentencing court would then take into account the presence of any aggravating or mitigating factors to arrive at its sentence.

The CJA 2003 does not change this. It does, however, list those matters which the sentencing court must consider when determining how serious an offence is. Section 143(1) of the Act provides that:

> In considering the seriousness of any offence, the court must consider the offender's *culpability* in committing the offence and any *harm* which the offence caused, was intended to cause or might foreseeably have caused. (emphasis added)

**Culpability**

The SGC has published a guideline, 'Overarching Principles: Seriousness'. In this guideline, the SGC identifies four levels of criminal culpability for sentencing purposes. In descending order of seriousness, the four levels are where the offender:

(a) has the *intention* to cause harm, with the highest culpability being when an offence is planned. The worse the harm intended, the greater the seriousness;

(b) is *reckless* as to whether harm is caused. This covers situations when the defendant appreciates that some harm would be caused but goes ahead, giving no thought to the consequences even though the extent of the risk would be obvious to most people;

(c) has *knowledge* of the specific risks entailed by his actions, even though he does not intend to cause the harm that results;

(d) is guilty of *negligence*.

The SGC guideline provides that the culpability of the defendant in the particular circumstances of the case should be the initial factor in determining the seriousness of an offence.

**Harm**

The SGC guideline on 'Seriousness' confirms that 'harm' not only includes harm which is actually caused, but also where there is a risk of harm even though no harm actually results.

Harm may be caused either to individuals, or to the community at large. The types of harm that may be caused include:

(a) physical injury;
(b) sexual violation;
(c) financial loss;
(d) damage to health; and
(e) psychological distress.

**Prevalence**

Although courts throughout the country should pass the same sentence for the same type of offence, in exceptional circumstances a court in a particular area may treat an offence more seriously than elsewhere. This may occur if the particular type of offence is prevalent in the area and the court has before it evidence that these offences are causing harm to the community at large. Common examples of offences which may be prevalent in a particular area are drugs-related offences and street robberies.

### 11.4.2.4 Aggravating and mitigating factors

**Statutory aggravating factors**

The concept of aggravating and mitigating factors has not been changed by the CJA 2003. There are, however, now four situations when the 2003 Act obliges the sentencing court to treat an offence as being more serious than it would otherwise have done (and so to impose a greater penalty):

(a) *Previous convictions* – under s 143(2), the court must treat any previous convictions as an aggravating factor if, having regard to the nature of the previous conviction and the time that has elapsed since the conviction, the court considers it reasonable to do so. In practice this means that previous convictions are likely to be regarded as aggravating factors if the offences have been committed recently and/or are for similar types of offence. For example, if a defendant convicted of a theft from a supermarket has several previous convictions for the same type of offence, these previous convictions will be seen by the sentencing court as an aggravating factor.

(b) *Offences committed whilst on bail* – under s 143(3), if the offender was on bail in respect of another offence at the time of the current offence, the court must treat this as an aggravating factor.

(c) *Racial or religious aggravation* – under s 145, any racial or religious motive for committing the offence must be treated as an aggravating factor.

(d) *Hostility based on sexual orientation or disability* – under s 146, any hostility towards the victim of an offence based on that victim's sexual orientation or any physical or mental disability, must be treated as an aggravating factor.

**Other aggravating and mitigating factors**

The SGC guideline on 'Seriousness' lists other factors which a sentencing court may consider to be aggravating or mitigating factors.

The list of *aggravating* factors includes:

(a) offences that are planned or premeditated;
(b) offenders operating in groups or gangs;

(c) the deliberate targeting of vulnerable groups (such as the elderly or disabled victims);
(d) offences committed whilst under the influence of drink or drugs;
(e) the use of a weapon;
(f) deliberate and gratuitous violence or damage to property, beyond that required to carry out the offence;
(g) offences involving the abuse of a position of trust;
(h) offences committed against those working in the public sector or providing a service to the public;
(i) in property offences, the high value (including sentimental value) of property to the victim.

The list of *mitigating* factors includes:

(a) offences where the defendant has acted on impulse;
(b) when the defendant has experienced a greater degree of provocation than normally expected;
(c) defendants who are suffering from mental illness or physical disability;
(d) if the defendant is particularly young or old (particularly in the case of young offenders who are immature and have been led astray by others);
(e) the fact that the defendant played only a minor role in the offending;
(f) defendants who were motivated by genuine fear;
(g) defendants who have made attempts to make reparation to their victim.

### 11.4.2.5 Reduction in sentence for a guilty plea

**Why is a reduction made?**

The sentencing guidelines provided by the SGC (for the Crown Court) and contained in the Magistrates' Court Sentencing Guidelines (for the magistrates' court) are based on a defendant who is convicted following a trial. Often, however, the court will be required to sentence a defendant who has pleaded guilty to the offence with which he has been charged.

Section 144 of the CJA 2003 provides that when sentencing a defendant who has entered a guilty plea, the court must 'take into account' the stage in the proceedings at which the defendant gave his indication of a guilty plea and the circumstances in which the indication was given. The rationale behind a reduction in sentence for defendants who pleads guilty is that a guilty plea avoids the need for a trial (and therefore enables other cases to be dealt with more quickly), saves money and, if made early in the case, saves victims and witnesses from stress and anxiety about having to attend court to give oral evidence.

The SGC guideline 'Reduction in Sentence for a Guilty Plea' confirms that the sentencing court should treat reductions in sentence for a guilty plea as being a separate issue from the presence of aggravating and mitigating factors. The court should first address the issue of the defendant's remorse, together with any mitigating features, when deciding the appropriate length of sentence, *before* calculating the reduction to be made for the guilty plea.

The SGC has also confirmed that where an offence crosses the threshold for the imposition of a community or custodial sentence (see **11.5** and **11.6** below), a sufficiently early guilty plea may allow the court to impose a fine or a discharge rather than a community sentence, or an alternative to an immediate custodial sentence.

**What level of reduction will be made?**

The level of the reduction in sentence will depend upon the stage in the proceedings at which the guilty plea was entered. The SGC has stated that the level of the reduction should be on a sliding scale, ranging from a maximum of *one-third* (where the guilty plea was entered at the first reasonable opportunity), reducing to a maximum of *one-quarter* (where the guilty plea is entered after a date for trial has been set), and to a maximum of *one-tenth* (for a guilty plea 'at the door of the court' or after the trial has begun). Set out below is a diagram reproduced from the SGC guideline which depicts this sliding scale.

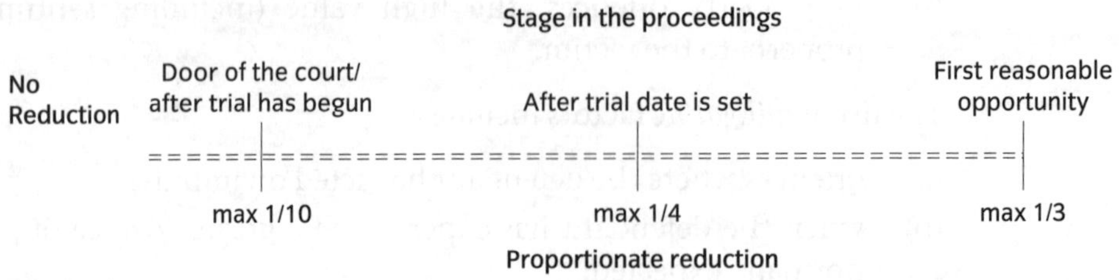


If the court considers that the evidence against the defendant was overwhelming and he had little alternative other than to plead guilty, the SGC has suggested that the court may depart from the above guidelines and make a reduction of only *one-fifth* where the defendant indicates a guilty plea at the first reasonable opportunity.

## 11.4.2.6 The totality principle

**Introduction**

When an offender is being sentenced, the court will take into account both the offence he is being sentenced for and any associated offences. An associated offence is an offence for which the defendant has been convicted in the same proceedings or for which he is to be sentenced at the same time, *or* an offence which the defendant has asked the court to take into consideration when passing sentence.

**Offences for which the defendant is convicted in the same proceedings or is to be sentenced at the same time**

It will often be the case that a defendant will be convicted of more than one offence in the same set of proceedings, or that a defendant who has been convicted of offences in different sets of proceedings will be sentenced for all of the offences at the same hearing. Whenever a court is sentencing a defendant who has been convicted of more than one offence, it must, when deciding on the appropriate sentence, look at the totality of the offending rather than considering each offence in isolation.

> **Example**
>
> Ruth is convicted of three separate offences of theft in the same proceedings. When Ruth is being sentenced, the court will not look at each offence separately, but will rather assess the total extent of Ruth's offending in determining the sentence that Ruth will be given. Only if the totality of Ruth's offending passes the appropriate thresholds (see **11.5** and **11.6** below) may a custodial or community sentence be imposed by the court.

### Offences taken into consideration

Defendants who are being sentenced for a particular offence may ask the court to take other offences into consideration (TIC) when considering the sentence to be imposed. This is particularly common with offenders convicted of property-related offences. In addition to the offence for which he was charged and convicted, a defendant may have committed several similar types of offence for which he has not yet been prosecuted but for which he may subsequently face prosecution. It is likely to be in the defendant's interests that all matters outstanding (or potentially outstanding) against him should be dealt with at the same time.

The usual practice is for the police to present the defendant with a list of additional offences for which he is under investigation and may subsequently be charged. The defendant may ask the court to take these other offences into consideration when deciding the sentence he is to receive for the offence(s) for which he is currently before the court. The offences to be taken into consideration should be of a similar nature to, or less serious than, the offence(s) for which the defendant has been convicted.

When sentencing the defendant, the court is entitled to take these additional offences into account. It may take other offences into consideration, however, only if the defendant expressly agrees to this (*R v Miles* [2006] EWCA Crim 256). The manner in which the court deals with offences taken into consideration depends on the context of such offences. Although in theory these additional offences should increase the severity of the sentence the defendant receives; in practice they might add nothing, or very little, to the sentence the court would otherwise have imposed. They are, however, capable of leading to a substantial increase in the sentence the defendant receives if the offences demonstrate a pattern of criminal activity which suggests careful planning, or if the offences were committed on bail after an earlier arrest.

The advantage to the defendant of having offences taken into consideration is that this 'wipes the slate clean', because he will not subsequently be prosecuted for such offences. The advantage to the police is that a large number of TICs improves their clear-up rates without the need to commence a fresh prosecution against the defendant.

#### Example

Sarfraz is convicted of one charge of burglary of commercial premises. Sarfraz asks the court to take into consideration three other burglaries of commercial premises which he admits to having carried out and which the police are currently investigating. If the court agrees to take these offences into consideration when deciding the sentence to be imposed on Sarfraz, he cannot subsequently be prosecuted for these offences. Sarfraz is, however, likely to receive a more severe sentence than if he had just been sentenced for the offence with which he was initially charged.

The procedure which takes place when a defendant asks that other offences be taken into consideration is that the defendant will be given a form by the police giving details of the other offences which the police suspect the defendant may have committed. The defendant may then sign the form and will be asked to admit before the court that he wishes the other offences to be taken into consideration on sentence.

## 11.5 Custodial sentences

### 11.5.1 Mandatory custodial sentences

Most offences which carry a custodial sentence allow the sentencing court discretion as to whether a custodial sentence should be imposed, and then as to the length of the sentence. There are a limited number of exceptions, where an offence carries either a mandatory sentence or a mandatory minimum term of imprisonment. For example, a defendant convicted of murder will receive a mandatory sentence of life imprisonment (Murder (Abolition of Death Penalty) Act 1965, s 1(1)).

### 11.5.2 Discretionary custodial sentences

Where the court has discretion as to whether to pass a custodial sentence, it must apply the test set out in s 152(2) of the CJA 2003:

> The court must not pass a custodial sentence unless it is of the opinion that the offence, or the combination of the offence and one or more offences associated with it, was so serious that neither a fine alone nor a community sentence can be justified for the offence.

This test is known as the custody threshold. Only if this threshold is passed may the court impose a custodial sentence. If the custody threshold has been passed, this does not necessarily mean that a custodial sentence should automatically be imposed. In *R v Seed; R v Stark* [2007] EWCA Crim 254, the Court of Appeal said that, where the custody threshold had only just been passed, a guilty plea or very strong personal mitigation might make it appropriate for a non-custodial sentence to be imposed.

The only circumstance in which this test will not be relevant is if the court considers that the defendant satisfies the definition of a 'dangerous offender' in ss 224–236 of the CJA 2003 (see **11.5.3** below). In such circumstances the court is obliged to impose a custodial sentence and so need not consider whether the custody threshold is satisfied.

If the custody threshold is passed and the court decides to impose a custodial sentence, the court must then consider the length of the custodial sentence. To determine the length of the sentence, the court must apply s 153(2) of the CJA 2003. This provides that a custodial sentence

> ... must be for the shortest term (not exceeding the permitted maximum) that in the opinion of the court is commensurate with the seriousness of the offence, or the combination of the offence and one or more other offences associated with it.

Separate sentences of imprisonment imposed on defendants convicted of two or more offences may be expressed by the sentencing court to be either concurrent or consecutive. A *concurrent* sentence means that the custodial terms are deemed to be served at the same time. A *consecutive* sentence means that one custodial sentence will start after the other one has finished.

**Example**

Alison is convicted in the Crown Court of unlawful wounding and theft. She is sentenced to three years' imprisonment for the unlawful wounding offence and one year's imprisonment for the theft. The judge tells Alison that the sentences are to run concurrently. This means that Alison has effectively received a total sentence of three years' imprisonment because the sentence for the theft will run at the same time as the first year of the sentence for the unlawful wounding.

Had the judge expressed the custodial terms to be consecutive, Alison's total sentence would amount to four years. The one-year sentence for the theft would take effect after Alison had served the three-year sentence for the unlawful wounding.

Consecutive sentences should not generally be imposed where matters of fact arise out of the same incident (*R v Lawrence* (1989) 11 Cr App R (S) 580).

### 11.5.3 Discretionary custodial sentences in the Crown Court

#### 11.5.3.1 The 'normal' approach to sentencing

Judges in the Crown Court have the power to sentence a defendant to a term of imprisonment up to the maximum permitted for that offence. Examples of the maximum prison sentences that may be imposed for some of the most common crimes dealt with in the Crown Court are:

(a) robbery – life imprisonment;
(b) wounding/causing gbh with intent (Offences Against the Person Act 1861, s 18) – life imprisonment;
(c) unlawful wounding/inflicting gbh (Offences Against the Person Act 1861, s 20) – five years;
(d) assault occasioning actual bodily harm (Offences Against the Person Act 1861, s 47) – five years;
(e) theft – seven years;
(f) burglary of domestic premises – 14 years;
(g) burglary of other premises – 10 years.

In practice, very few defendants receive the maximum sentence which the offence carries. In determining the length of the sentence, the judge will have regard to the guideline cases previously considered by the Court of Appeal. The SGC has put these cases together in a document entitled 'Guideline Judgments Case Compendium', which may be accessed from the SGC website (see **11.4.2.2** above).

#### 11.5.3.2 Dangerous offenders

**Introduction**

When the judge imposes a discretionary custodial sentence, he will normally impose such a sentence only if the test set out in s 152(2) of the CJA 2003 (see **11.5.2** above) is satisfied. Similarly, he will determine the actual length of the sentence by applying the test set out in s 153(2) above. These tests are modified, however, in the case of 'dangerous offenders', against whom it is considered the public require greater protection. Such offenders will receive longer sentences than they would were the court to apply the tests in ss 152(2) and 153(2).

If a defendant is classified as being 'dangerous', the court will impose one of the following forms of custodial sentence:

(a) imprisonment for life;
(b) imprisonment for public protection; or
(c) an extended sentence of imprisonment.

Each type of sentence will be examined below, after the new terminology employed by the CJA 2003 has been explained.

**Terminology**

The CJA 2003 has introduced the following terms:

(a) *Specified offence* – s 224(1) divides specified offences into:
   (i) specified violent offences – these offences include manslaughter, kidnapping, riot, affray, robbery, actual and grievous bodily harm and aggravated burglary; and
   (ii) specified sexual offences – these offences include rape, indecent assault, unlawful sexual intercourse and a range of offences known generically as 'paedophile offences'.

(b) *Serious offences* – s 224(2) defines a serious offence as being a specified offence (as described above) which is punishable by a maximum sentence of either life imprisonment, or a prison sentence of at least 10 years.

(c) *Serious harm* – this is defined in s 224(3) as meaning 'death or serious personal injury, whether physical or psychological'.

**Life sentences and sentences for public protection**

If a defendant is convicted of a serious offence *and* the court considers that there is a significant risk to members of the public of serious harm as a result of the defendant committing further specified offences, s 225 provides that the court must pass one of the following sentences:

(a) a discretionary life sentence (if the offence itself carries such a sentence as a maximum penalty and the seriousness of the offence justifies such a sentence). The judge will determine the minimum period the defendant must serve in custody before he becomes eligible for release on licence upon the recommendation of the Parole Board; or

(b) if a discretionary life sentence is not possible, a sentence of imprisonment for public protection. This will be a sentence of detention for an indeterminate period. The judge will set the minimum period of time that is to be served in custody for the purposes of punishment and deterrence, following which the defendant will become eligible for release on licence upon the recommendation of the Parole Board.

**Extended sentences**

A defendant will receive an extended sentence if he has been convicted of a specified violent or sexual offence (but which is not a serious offence), and the court considers that there is a significant risk to members of the public of serious harm occasioned by him committing further specified offences (CJA 2003, s 227(1)).

An extended sentence is made up of two parts:

(a) the appropriate custodial sentence (ie, the 'normal' sentence the court would impose, subject to a minimum sentence of 12 months); plus

(b) an additional period (referred to as the 'extension period') during which the defendant will be released subject to licence conditions. The extension period will be for as long as the court considers necessary for the purposes of protecting the public from serious harm caused by him committing further offences, subject to a maximum of five years for a specified violent offence and eight years for a specified sexual offence.

**The assessment of dangerousness**

Section 229 of the CJA 2003 lists the factors to be taken into account by the court when assessing whether there is a significant risk to members of the public of serious harm as a result of the defendant committing further specified offences. If a defendant has a previous conviction for one or more specified offences, the court must assume there to be a risk of significant harm by further offending unless it considers it unreasonable to find that there is such a risk (CJA 2003, s 229(3)). The Court of Appeal has also provided guidance on the assessment of 'dangerousness' (see, eg, *R v Lang* [2005] EWCA Crim 2864 and *R v Reynolds* [2007] EWCA Crim 538).

### 11.5.4 Discretionary custodial sentences in the magistrates' court

The maximum custodial sentence which a magistrates' court may impose on a defendant is six months' imprisonment, although magistrates may impose consecutive sentences up to a maximum of 12 months in aggregate when dealing with two or more either way offences (Magistrates' Courts Act 1980, ss 31 and 133(2)).

### 11.5.5 Suspended sentence of imprisonment

#### 11.5.5.1 When will a suspended sentence be imposed?

A custodial sentence of at least 14 days but no more than 12 months (or six months in the case of the magistrates' court) may be suspended for between six months and two years (CJA 2003, s 189(1)). The period during which the sentence is suspended is known as the 'operational period'.

The court will impose a suspended sentence only if it initially decides that the custody threshold in s 152(2) of the CJA 2003 has been passed (see **11.5.2** above), but then considers that particular circumstances exist which justify the suspension of the sentence.

**Example**

Jim is convicted of affray before the Crown Court. When sentencing Jim, the judge decides that the offence is so serious that the only appropriate sentence is custody. However, when giving his plea in mitigation, Jim's counsel told the judge that Jim is a single parent looking after a disabled child, and that a custodial sentence for Jim would mean the child needing to go into a care home. The trial judge considers that these particular circumstances justify the imposition of a suspended sentence. The judge therefore imposes a sentence of six months imprisonment, but suspends this for 12 months.

#### 11.5.5.2 Requirements which the court may impose

When a court imposes a suspended sentence, it must order the defendant to comply during a specified period (the 'supervision period') with one or more requirements falling within s 190(1) of the CJA 2003. The supervision period must end no later than the end of the operational period. The requirements that fall within s 190(1) are:

(a) an unpaid work requirement;
(b) an activity requirement;
(c) a programme requirement;
(d) a prohibited activity requirement;
(e) a curfew requirement;
(f) an exclusion requirement;
(g) a residence requirement;
(h) a mental health requirement;
(i) a drug rehabilitation requirement;

(j) an alcohol treatment requirement;

(k) a supervision requirement; and

(l) where the defendant is under 25, an attendance centre requirement.

These are the same type of requirements which the court may require a defendant to comply with when imposing a generic community order (see **11.6.2** below for details of what each requirement entails).

#### 11.5.5.3 Breach of a suspended sentence (CJA 2003, s 192 and Sch 12)

The sentence of imprisonment will not take effect unless either the defendant fails to comply with any requirements which have been imposed (see **11.5.5.2** above) or, during the operational period, the defendant commits a further offence and the court sentencing the defendant for the 'new' offence orders that the original sentence of imprisonment is to take effect.

A defendant will receive only a single warning about failure to comply with a requirement imposed under a suspended sentence. If there is a further failure to comply without reasonable excuse within the 12 months following such a warning, proceedings must be commenced.

If a defendant is found either to be in breach of a requirement or to have committed a further offence during the operational period, if the suspended sentence was imposed by the magistrates' court, he may be dealt with for the breach either by the magistrates' court or the Crown Court. If the suspended sentence was imposed by the Crown Court, any breach may be dealt with only by the Crown Court.

A court dealing with a defendant who has breached a suspended sentence must do one of the following:

(a) order the custodial sentence originally suspended to take effect unaltered;

(b) order the custodial sentence to take effect, but for a shorter period of time;

(c) amend the original order by imposing more onerous requirements on the defendant; or

(d) amend the original order by extending the operational period, or by extending the supervision period.

The court must make an order under (a) or (b) above unless it considers that it would be unjust to do so in view of all the circumstances (CJA 2003, Sch 12, para 8). The court may decide it would be unjust to make an order under (a) or (b) if the defendant is coming to the end of the supervision period (having complied with the requirements imposed) or if, in the case of a defendant convicted of a further offence, the new offence is a minor matter or is a completely different type of offence to the offence originally committed. The court will also take into account the time which has elapsed since the original offence was committed and any change in the defendant's circumstances.

If the court does make an order under (a) or (b), the term of imprisonment for the original offence will be consecutive to the sentence imposed for any new offence.

### 11.5.6 Deferred sentence

Section 278 of the CJA 2003 permits a court to defer sentencing a defendant for up to six months to enable the court to observe both the defendant's conduct during the deferment period and any changes in the defendant's circumstances during this period. Deferment of sentence may be used when a court is considering imposing an immediate custodial sentence, but a change (for the better) in the defendant's circumstances is imminent and the court wants to assess the effect of such change on the defendant before passing sentence. Typical examples of when a deferred sentence may be appropriate are when a defendant is just about to start a new job, or when a defendant has been given the opportunity to move away from the area where he committed his offences so that he may 'make a fresh start'.

The CJA 2003 permits a court, when deferring sentence, both to specify activities which the defendant should undertake during the deferment period and to assess the defendant's compliance with these activities when the case comes back before the court for sentence. Such activities will usually involve some form of reparation to the victim of the offence (for example, the court may require an offender convicted of causing criminal damage by covering premises with graffiti, to remove the graffiti). A defendant must consent to his sentence being deferred and must also undertake to comply with the requirements imposed by the court.

## 11.6 Community sentences

### 11.6.1 Threshold

The CJA 2003 has swept away various community-based penalties which a sentencing court previously had the power to impose on an defendant, and has replaced this with one type of community sentence – the generic community order.

Section 148 of the Act sets out the threshold which must be reached before a court can impose such an order:

> (1) A court must not pass a community sentence on an offender unless it is of the opinion that the offence, or the combination of the offence and one or more offences associated with it, was serious enough to warrant such a sentence.
>
> (2) Where a court passes a community sentence which consists of or includes a community order—
>
> (a) a particular requirement or requirements forming part of the community order must be such as, in the opinion of the court, is, or taken together are, the most suitable for the offender, and
>
> (b) the restrictions on liberty imposed by the order must be such as in the opinion of the court are commensurate with the seriousness of the offence, or the combination of the offence and one or more offences associated with it.

In addition to the threshold set out in s 148, s 151 of the CJA 2003 permits a court to impose a community sentence on persistent offenders who do not satisfy the s 148 test. 'Persistent offenders' are offenders who have three or more previous convictions, each of which was dealt with by the court by way of a fine only.

In *R v Seed* and *R v Stark* (see **11.5.2** above), the Court of Appeal held that if the defendant had sufficient means, the court should always consider imposing a heavy fine rather than a community sentence.

### 11.6.2 Contents of the generic community order

In making a generic community order the court may choose from a 'menu' of options and select those which are most appropriate for the defendant. Any limitations which the sentence imposes on the defendant must be proportionate to the seriousness of the offence and must reflect the principal aim of preventing the defendant from re-offending.

The order can last for up to three years, although certain requirements are subject to shorter time limits. For example, a requirement for the offender to carry out unpaid work within the community must be completed within 12 months of the order being made.

The options from which the court may choose are as follows:

(a) *Unpaid work requirement* – this requires the defendant to perform unpaid work in the community for between 40 and 300 hours. This work must be completed within a 12-month period.

(b) *Activity requirement* – this requires the defendant to take part in specified activities which may be designed to help the defendant overcome a particular problem (such as finding work), or which may be activities to make reparation to the victim (such as repairing damage caused).

(c) *Programme requirement* – this requires the defendant to take part in one or more courses to address the defendant's offending behaviour, such as courses in anger management, sex offending or substance misuse.

(d) *Prohibited activity requirement* – this requires the defendant to refrain from taking part in specified activities. This type of order is unlikely to be made in the case of adult defendants and is more appropriate for defendants in the Youth Court (see **Chapter 14**).

(e) *Curfew requirement* – this requires the defendant to remain at a particular location (normally the defendant's place of residence) specified by the court between specified times. The order can last for up to six months and the defendant will be electronically monitored.

(f) *Exclusion requirement* – this prohibits the defendant from entering a place or places (such as a city centre, or a particular type of establishment like a shop or a pub) for a period not exceeding two years. Again the defendant will be electronically monitored.

(g) *Residence requirement* – this requires the defendant to live at a particular place as specified in the court order.

(h) *Mental health treatment requirement* – this requires the defendant to submit to treatment from a mental health practitioner for a specified period of time.

(i) *Drug rehabilitation requirement* – this requires the defendant to submit to treatment to reduce or eliminate his dependency on drugs, and to submit to providing samples to determine whether he has drugs in his body. This will be for a period of time specified by the court, but it must be for at least six months.

(j) *Alcohol treatment requirement* – this requires the defendant to submit, during a period of time specified by the court, to treatment to reduce or eliminate his dependency on alcohol. The period must last for at least six months.

(k) *Supervision requirement* – this requires the defendant to attend appointments with a member of the Probation Service. The purpose of such meetings is to promote the defendant's rehabilitation, and the meetings will involve confronting the defendant's offending behaviour, discussing how the defendant might 'manage' his life and generally monitoring the defendant's progress. A supervision requirement may be imposed for up to three years.

(l) *Attendance centre requirement* – this requires the defendant to attend an attendance centre for a total of between 12 and 36 hours. Such an order can only be imposed on defendants who are under 25 years of age. Further details of the requirements of this type of order are provided in **Chapter 14**.

The sentencing court will choose one or more of these options to make up the overall community sentence to be imposed on the defendant.

The court may order that electronic monitoring be used to check the defendant's compliance with any of the specific requirements imposed under a generic community order (in the case of a curfew or exclusion requirement, such monitoring is mandatory).

### 11.6.3 Guidance from the SGC

Given the extremely wide scope of the potential requirements a court may impose as part of a generic community order, the SGC has provided guidelines as to how the court should approach the making of such an order.

In its guideline 'New Sentences: Criminal Justice Act 2003', the SGC stipulates that the court should initially decide (in consultation with the Probation Service if necessary) whether a community sentence is justified, and then, if it is justified, the court must decide which requirements should be included in the order. When deciding which requirements to include, the court must be satisfied as to three matters:

(a) that the restriction on liberty is commensurate with the seriousness of the offence;

(b) that the requirements are most suitable for the defendant; and

(c) that where two or more requirements are included, they are compatible with each other.

The guiding principles behind the making of a generic community order are said by the SGC to be 'proportionality and suitability'. The court should impose an order which has the maximum chance of successful completion. The SGC has identified three sentencing ranges (low, medium, and high) within the community sentence band, and a court considering the imposition of such a sentence must decide into which band the particular offence(s) with which it is dealing falls:

(a) *The low range* – this is for defendants whose offence was relatively minor and will include persistent petty offenders and those who have failed to respond to the previous imposition of fines. The types of offence this may cover are some public order offences, some thefts from shops and interference with a motor vehicle. Suitable requirements for defendants in the low range may include:
   (i) 40 to 80 hours of unpaid work; or
   (ii) a curfew requirement of up to 12 hours per day for a few weeks; or
   (iii) an exclusion requirement lasting a few months; or
   (iv) a prohibited activity requirement; or
   (v) an attendance centre requirement (where available).

(b) *The medium range* – this range is for offences which obviously fall within the community sentence band. The SGC guidelines suggest that the types of offence falling within this band will include handling stolen goods worth less than £1,000 acquired for resale, or somewhat more valuable goods acquired for the handler's own use, some cases of burglary in commercial premises, some cases of taking a motor vehicle without consent and some cases of obtaining property by deception. Suitable requirements for defendants in the medium range may include:
   (i) between 80 and 150 hours of unpaid work; or

(ii) an activity requirement in the middle range (20 to 30 days); or
(iii) a curfew requirement of up to 12 hours for two to three months; or
(iv) an exclusion requirement lasting approximately six months; or
(v) a prohibited activity requirement.

(c) *The high range* – this range is for offences that only just fall below the custody threshold, or where the custody threshold has been crossed but the court considers that a community sentences is appropriate in all the circumstances. The SGC suggests that an example of the latter type of offence might be a standard domestic burglary committed by a first-time offender. Suitable requirements for defendants in the high range may include two or more of the following requirements:
(i) between 150 and 300 hours of unpaid work;
(ii) an activity requirement up to the maximum 60 days;
(iii) an exclusion order lasting approximately 12 months;
(iv) a curfew requirement of up to 12 hours for four to six months.

### 11.6.4 Breach of a community sentence

The consequences for an offender who breaches the terms of a generic community order are dealt with by s 179 of the CJA 2003, which invokes Sch 8 to the Act.

The first thing that will happen when a defendant, without reasonable excuse, breaches a community order, is that defendant will receive a warning from a 'responsible officer'. This person is likely to be the member of the Probation Service who is supervising the defendant's compliance with his generic community order. The warning must:

(a) describe the circumstances of the failure;
(b) state that the failure is unacceptable; and
(c) inform the defendant that if, within the next 12 months, he again fails to comply with any of the requirements of the order, he will be liable to be brought before a court.

If, within the following 12 months, the defendant again fails without reasonable excuse to comply with the requirements of the order, the responsible officer will report this matter to the court which imposed the order in the first place and the defendant will be required to appear before that court.

If the court is satisfied that that the defendant has, without reasonable excuse, failed to comply with the requirements of the order, the court *must*:

(a) amend the order so as to impose requirements on the defendant which are more onerous (for example, by increasing the amount of unpaid work the defendant is required to complete); or
(b) revoke the order completely and re-sentence the defendant for the offence, but without taking into account the usual custody threshold (see **11.5.2** above); or
(c) where the defendant has wilfully and persistently failed to comply with the order, the court may revoke the order and impose a custodial sentence of up to 51 weeks (ie, custody plus). This can be done even if the original offence was not punishable by way of a custodial sentence.

**Example**

Gavin is convicted of assault occasioning actual bodily harm by the magistrates' court. He receives a generic community order which includes a requirement to complete 250 hours of unpaid work.

Gavin fails to attend his first unpaid work session. The probation officer supervising Gavin's sentence gives Gavin a warning. Gavin then fails to attend his second unpaid work session and is brought back before the magistrates' court. The magistrates must, if they are satisfied that Gavin had no reasonable excuse for failing to attend the unpaid work sessions, either amend the generic community order to add more onerous requirements or revoke the order and re-sentence Gavin. If the magistrates choose the latter course, the inevitable sentence will be custodial.

The options open to the court in the event that the defendant breaches his community sentence are incremental. Thus, in the above example, Gavin is likely to have his original order amended to impose more onerous requirements. Should Gavin fail to comply with these further requirements, the magistrates will then consider revoking the original order and re-sentencing Gavin.

### 11.6.5 Further offences committed during the currency of the generic community order

It will often be the case that a defendant who has received a generic community sentence is convicted of a further offence during the period when the generic community order is still in force. In such a situation, the magistrates may either allow the original generic community order to continue, or, if it is in the interests of justice having regard to the circumstances that have arisen since the original order was made, they may:

(a) revoke the order (this will be done if the magistrates are imposing a custodial sentence for the 'new' offence, since an offender in prison cannot comply with a community sentence); or

(b) revoke the order and re-sentence the defendant for the original offence as if he had just been convicted of it. If this is done, the court must have regard to the extent to which the defendant has complied with the original order.

It is likely that, in practice, the magistrates will take one of the steps in (a) or (b) above only if they are intending to impose a custodial sentence for the 'new' offence, or if they consider that it is appropriate to re-sentence the defendant for the original offence (perhaps because the defendant has re-offended only a short time after the original generic community order was imposed).

**Example 1**

Barry is convicted of common assault by the magistrates' court and receives a two-year generic community order with a supervision requirement, under which he must meet a probation officer once a fortnight. Barry complies with this requirement. Two months before the order is to come to an end, Barry is convicted of a minor public order offence. The magistrates are very unlikely to revoke the original order. Barry will not receive a custodial sentence for the public order offence and it would not be in the interests of justice to revoke the original order and re-sentence Barry, given that the order is almost at an end and Barry has complied with the terms of the order throughout its duration. The magistrates will allow the generic community order to continue, and sentence Barry separately for the public order offence.

**Example 2**

Miranda is convicted of assault occasioning actual bodily harm by the magistrates' court and receives a two-year generic community order. One year into the order

Miranda is convicted of two charges of unlawful wounding. It is likely that the court will want to impose a sentence of imprisonment for these offences. If so, the court will revoke the generic community order and impose a custodial sentence for the offences of unlawful wounding.

Example 3

Tarquin is convicted by the magistrates' court of the possession of a Class A drug and receives an 18-month generic community order, which includes a requirement that Tarquin complies with a drug rehabilitation requirement. Three months after the order is made, Tarquin is convicted of possession of a Class B drug. Whilst this offence would not in itself be likely to lead to a custodial sentence, the magistrates are likely to take the view that the generic community order has been unsuccessful because Tarquin is still taking drugs. The magistrates may therefore decide to revoke the generic community order and re-sentence Tarquin to a term of imprisonment for the original offence of possessing Class A drugs.

## 11.7 Fines

### 11.7.1 Introduction

Fines are the most common penalty imposed on those convicted of criminal offences. Approximately 70% of all offenders are dealt with by way of a fine. All fines which are imposed also carry an additional flat-rate 'victim's surcharge' of £15, which is paid into a fund aimed at helping improve services for victims of crime.

### 11.7.2 Fines in the magistrates' court

In the magistrates' court, the maximum level of fine which the magistrates can impose is set by the statute which creates the offence for which the offender has been convicted. The statute will usually stipulate the maximum fine to be one of five standard levels:

(a) Level 1 – £200;

(b) Level 2 – £500;

(c) Level 3 – £1,000;

(d) Level 4 – £2,500;

(e) Level 5 – £5,000.

By way of example, the maximum fine a magistrates' court may impose for the offence of theft is a level 5 fine (£5,000).

The actual size of the fine a defendant receives must reflect the seriousness of the offence, although the court must also take account of the defendant's financial circumstances (CJA 2003, s 164). The court will enquire into the defendant's financial circumstances (by asking him to complete a means form) before deciding upon the level of fine to be imposed.

To ensure consistency between different magistrates' courts, the Magistrates' Courts Sentencing Guidelines provide guideline fines based on the seriousness of the offence and the defendant's net weekly take-home pay or weekly state benefit payment. There are three levels of guideline fine – A, B and C. Fine level A represents 50% of the defendant's net weekly income; fine level B represents 100% of the defendant's net weekly income; and fine level C 150% of the defendant's net weekly income. The guidelines also provide that the magistrates should reduce the fine where a defendant has entered an early guilty plea (see **11.4.2.5**), and the presence of any aggravating or mitigating factors should be used to raise or lower the level of the fine as appropriate.

### 11.7.3 Fines in the Crown Court

For most offences, the Crown Court has the power to impose a fine instead of, or in addition to, any other sentence it imposes on the defendant (CJA 2003, s 163). There is no maximum limit to the size of fines in the Crown Court. However, as in the magistrates' court, the Crown Court will take into account the seriousness of the offence together with the financial circumstances of the defendant.

## 11.8 Conditional and absolute discharges

### 11.8.1 Introduction

Section 12(1) of the Powers of Criminal Courts (Sentencing) Act 2000 provides that:

> (1) Where a court by or before which a person is convicted of an offence . . . is of the opinion, having regard to the circumstances including the nature of the offence and the character of the offender, that it is inexpedient to inflict punishment, the court may make an order either—
>
> (a) discharging him absolutely; or
>
> (b) if the court thinks fit, discharging him subject to the condition that he commits no offence during such period, not exceeding three years from the date of the order, as may be specified in the order.

A discharge is not strictly a sentence as no penalty is imposed on the defendant.

### 11.8.2 Conditional discharge

If the court orders that the defendant be conditionally discharged, the defendant will not receive any immediate penalty for the offence he has committed. If, however, the defendant is convicted of a further offence committed during the period of the conditional discharge (this period will be specified by the court when making the order), the defendant will be in breach of the conditional discharge. The court may then revoke the conditional discharge and sentence the defendant for his original offence (in addition to any sentence which is imposed for the further offence). A conditional discharge may be imposed for a maximum period of three years. It is common for a sentencing court to impose a conditional discharge in situations where the offence is relatively minor, the defendant has no relevant previous convictions, and the court considers that a court appearance and the attendant publicity this attracts is sufficient punishment.

#### Example

Emily is 50 years of age. She pleads guilty to the theft of a tin of baked beans from her local supermarket. Emily has no previous convictions, and the court hears in mitigation that, at the time of the offence, Emily was taking anti-depressant medication which had been prescribed by her GP after her husband confessed to having an extra-martial affair. The magistrates decide that the loss of her good name and the publicity surrounding the case is sufficient punishment for Emily. The magistrates give Emily a two-year conditional discharge. The effect of this is that no immediate penalty will be imposed on Emily. However, were Emily to be convicted of a further offence committed within the specified two-year period, she would be liable to be sentenced for her original offence as well as for the further offence.

### 11.8.3 Absolute discharge

Absolute discharges are rare. A defendant who receives an absolute discharge will not be subject to any immediate penalty and, in contrast to a conditional discharge, cannot be later sentenced for the offence if he subsequently commits a further offence. An absolute discharge is likely to be imposed only when the court considers that the defendant, although technically guilty of an offence, is morally blameless (see, eg, *R v King* [1997] Crim LR 627).

## 11.9 Flowchart – the sentencing ladder

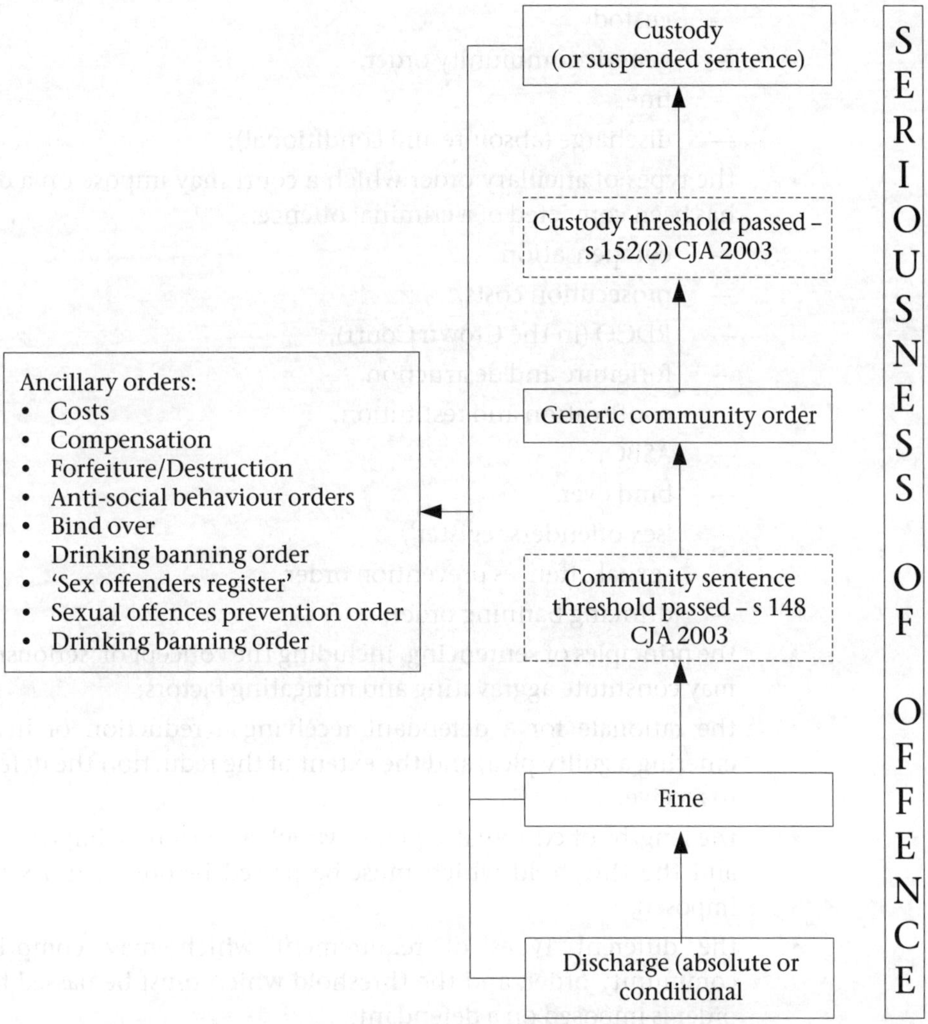

## 11.10 Checklist

At the end of this chapter you should be able to explain:

- the purposes of sentencing;
- the types of sentence which may be imposed on a defendant who has been convicted of a criminal offence:
  - custody,
  - generic community order,
  - fine,
  - discharge (absolute and conditional);
- the types of ancillary order which a court may impose on a defendant who has been convicted of a criminal offence:
  - compensation,
  - prosecution costs,
  - RDCO (in the Crown Court),
  - forfeiture and destruction,
  - confiscation and restitution,
  - ASBO,
  - bind over,
  - 'sex offenders register',
  - sexual offences prevention order,
  - drinking banning order;
- the principles of sentencing, including the concept of 'seriousness' and what may constitute aggravating and mitigating factors;
- the rationale for a defendant receiving a reduction of his sentence for entering a guilty plea, and the extent of the reduction the defendant is likely to receive;
- the lengths of custodial sentence which a court may impose on a defendant and the threshold which must be passed before such a sentence can be imposed;
- the different types of requirement which may comprise a generic community order, and the threshold which must be passed before such an order is imposed on a defendant;
- the level of any fine which a magistrates' court or Crown Court may impose on a defendant;
- the difference between a conditional and an absolute discharge, and the circumstances in which each type of order may be imposed on a defendant.

# Chapter 12
# Sentencing in Practice



## 12.1 Introduction

A defendant will be sentenced by the court either after entering a plea of guilty, or, if he pleaded not guilty, following his conviction at trial. In both situations the court may sentence the defendant immediately, or, if the court thinks it necessary, sentencing may be adjourned until the court has obtained one or more pre-sentence reports dealing with such matters as the defendant's personal history, his current family circumstances, his employment position and his attitude towards the offence for which he has been convicted.

This chapter will examine the practical aspects of sentencing. It will begin by looking at the types of pre-sentence reports that may be required by the court, and will then go on to examine the role played by the defendant's solicitor in the sentencing process. The procedure that is followed when a defendant is sentenced will be explained, and the chapter will conclude with some practical guidance on how the defendant's solicitor should deliver a plea in mitigation on his client's behalf.

## 12.2 Pre-sentence reports

### 12.2.1 Pre-sentence reports from the Probation Service

#### 12.2.1.1 Contents

The most common type of pre-sentence report which the court may require before sentencing a defendant is a pre-sentence report from the Probation Service. Such a report is prepared 'with a view to assisting the court in determining the most suitable method of dealing with an offender' (CJA 2003, s 158(1)). If the judge or magistrates require a report from the Probation Service, the sentencing of the defendant will be adjourned (usually for three weeks if the defendant is remanded in custody, or four weeks if the defendant is remanded on bail) to enable an officer from the Probation Service to meet the defendant and to prepare the report. Pre-sentence reports from the Probation Service follow a standard format and contain the following information:

(a) details of the offence and the defendant's attitude towards it – whether he now admit his guilt (if he had pleaded not guilty), or if he feels any genuine remorse for his crimes;

(b) information about the defendant's personal history and family situation, and any medical problems the defendant may have;
(c) the Probation Service officer's assessment of the risk of harm to the public from the defendant re-offending; and
(d) a conclusion incorporating the sentence which the officer preparing the report considers most appropriate for the defendant (and in particular a proposal in relation to what requirements could most appropriately be included in a generic community order).

#### 12.2.1.2 When will the court require a report?

Section 156(1) of the CJA 2003 provides that before deciding on whether a particular type of sentence is appropriate, the court must 'take into account all such information as is available to it about the circumstances of the offence or ... of the offence and the offence or offences associated with it, including any aggravating or mitigating factors'. Section 156(3) stipulates that the court must 'obtain and consider' a pre-sentence report before deciding the following:

(a) whether the custody threshold has been passed and, if it has, how long the custodial sentence should be (see **11.5.2**); and
(b) whether the threshold for imposing a community sentence has been passed and, if it has, the requirements that should be imposed on the defendant under a generic community order and the suitability of those requirements for that particular defendant (see **11.6.1**).

The court does not need to obtain such a report if it is of the opinion that a report is 'unnecessary' (s 154(1)). Such a situation is most likely to arise in the Crown Court where a defendant has been convicted of a serious offence and a lengthy custodial sentence is inevitable.

If the judge or magistrates adjourn sentence for the preparation of a pre-sentence report, the defendant will either be released on bail, or remanded in custody (see **12.5.1** and **12.5.2** below). If the defendant is remanded in custody pending the preparation of a report, he may be remanded for a maximum period of three weeks at any one hearing. Remands on bail may be for a maximum period of four weeks at any one time.

An example of a pre-sentence report in the Gary Dickson case study is set out below.

## <u>Key Document – Pre-sentence Report</u>

**PRE-SENTENCE REPORT ON GARY DICKSON**

**INTRODUCTION**

1. This report is based upon two interviews with Mr Dickson, both of which were carried out at 17 Marsh Street, Chester. Mr Dickson has pleaded guilty to one charge of assault occasioning actual bodily harm. I have read the prosecution papers and have seen the record of Mr Dickson's previous convictions.

**OFFENCE ANALYSIS**

2. I have discussed the circumstances of the offence with Mr Dickson. Mr Dickson pleaded not guilty initially but changed his plea to guilty on the

morning of the trial. Mr Dickson now accepts that he assaulted his victim in an unprovoked attack, punching Mr Lamb several times in the face. Mr Dickson's only explanation for his actions is that Mr Lamb had spent most of the evening taunting Mr Dickson because he was 'only' a bouncer and Mr Lamb had at one point during the evening tried to proposition Mr Dickson's girlfriend.

3. Mr Dickson has two previous convictions for offences of threatening behaviour, one previous conviction for the offence of assault occasioning actual bodily harm and one previous conviction for the offence of common assault. Mr Dickson informs me that all three offences occurred whilst he was working as a bouncer, when he was attempting to eject customers from nightclub premises.

**INFORMATION ABOUT THE OFFENDER**

4. Mr Dickson is 27 years old and was born and brought up in York. He lives with his girlfriend and her parents in Chester.
5. Mr Dickson left school at 16 with 4 GCSEs. He joined the army, and remained in the army until 2002.
6. Mr Dickson works full time as a scaffolder and steeplejack. He is self-employed and does contract work throughout the country. Mr Dickson has also had an evening and weekend job working as a bouncer at a nightclub in Chester. Mr Dickson informs me that he has recently been dismissed from this job as a result of the current proceedings. Mr Dickson has indicated that, as a result of being offered a well-paid, long-term contract to do some scaffolding work at a new building site in Chester, he will not be seeking to get another job as a bouncer.
7. Mr Dickson's partner has just found out that she is expecting his child. Mr Dickson is very excited at the prospect of becoming a father. He is anxious to fulfil his obligations as a father to his child, and is fearful of losing both his partner and his child should he receive a custodial sentence.

**RISK TO THE PUBLIC OF RE-OFFENDING**

8. Mr Dickson's history of offending appears to be tied closely to his employment as a bouncer. Mr Dickson tells me that when he was in the army he obeyed orders from senior officers without question. This made it hard for Mr Dickson to tolerate being abused by members of the public to whom he had given orders when he was working as a bouncer. All too often he would lose his temper and commit acts of violence.
9. If Mr Dickson were to return to work as a bouncer, I think Mr Dickson would present a significant risk to the public of re-offending. However, Mr Dickson has lost his job as a bouncer and will not be seeking another job in this area. As long as Mr Dickson stays away from this type of work, I would assess the risk of Mr Dickson re-offending as low. Mr Dickson does have anger management issues that he needs to address.

**CONCLUSION**

10. Mr Dickson's personal circumstances will change shortly with the birth of his child. He wants to do the best for his family and has the opportunity to take up a well-paid and long-term scaffolding contract.
11. Mr Dickson has pleaded guilty to a serious and unprovoked assault. I am aware that the court will be considering an immediate custodial sentence.

However, I believe that Mr Dickson has learned from his past mistakes and will not be returning to work as a bouncer.

12. To take account of the seriousness of the offence, the court may wish to impose a generic community order with significant limitations on Mr Dickson's free time. Mr Dickson would be suitable for such an order with the imposition of an unpaid work requirement and also a programme requirement under which he would have to attend an anger management course run by the Probation Service.

Signed: *Lucinda Smythe*
Probation Officer

#### 12.2.1.3 Specific sentence reports

If the court is minded to impose a generic community order (see **11.6** above) and wants to ensure that the defendant is suitable for such a sentence, rather than asking the Probation Service to prepare a full pre-sentence report the court may ask for a specific sentence report. This report will be shorter than a full pre-sentence report and will concentrate on the defendant's suitability for the terms of the order which the court is considering. The advantage of requesting such a report is that there will normally be a probation officer present in court who can see the defendant and prepare a report straight away, thus enabling the court to sentence the defendant immediately rather than having to adjourn the case for several weeks.

#### 12.2.1.4 Who sees the pre-sentence report?

Section 159 of the CJA 2003 provides that the court must supply a copy of the report to:

(a) the defendant or his legal representative; and

(b) the prosecutor.

The prosecutor has the right to make representations to the court if there is any information in the report about the offence which may be incorrect or misleading. The contents of the pre-sentence report are otherwise confidential, and the defendant's solicitor should not therefore disclose the contents of the report to anyone other than the defendant.

### 12.2.2 Medical reports

Under s 157 of the CJA 2003, the court is obliged to obtain and consider a medical report before it imposes a custodial sentence (other than a sentence fixed by law) if the defendant 'is or appears to be mentally disordered'.

Even if the defendant is not mentally disordered, the defendant's solicitor will often ask the court to adjourn sentence so that he can obtain a medical report to assist in the plea in mitigation he is to give on his client's behalf. Such a report may be useful if the defendant is suffering from some ongoing illness or injury, or if the defendant's medical condition at the time of his offending may go some way towards explaining the reason for his offending.

**Example**

Jenny has pleaded guilty in the magistrates' court to the offence of stealing from her employers. Jenny is 50 years of age and has no previous convictions. At the time she committed the offence, Jenny was in the middle of an acrimonious divorce and had been prescribed anti-depressant medication by her doctor. Jenny's solicitor will need to obtain a report from Jenny's doctor confirming this, to use in mitigation on Jenny's behalf.

## 12.3 Role of the defendant's solicitor

### 12.3.1 Introduction

The role of the solicitor whose client has either pleaded guilty or has been convicted following a trial, is to present to the court a plea in mitigation on the client's behalf before the client is sentenced. The purpose of the plea in mitigation is to reduce the severity of the sentence to be passed, and to seek to persuade the court to impose the most lenient penalty which might reasonably be given for the offence(s) the defendant has committed. Guidance on how to structure a plea in mitigation is provided at **12.7** below.

### 12.3.2 Preparation for the sentencing hearing

There are several steps which the defendant's solicitor needs to take prior to the sentencing hearing if he is going to be able to deliver an effective plea in mitigation on his client's behalf.

#### 12.3.2.1 Research the likely sentence

**Magistrates' court**

The first step is to carry out some research into the likely range of penalties to be imposed for the offence. In the magistrates' court the solicitor will need to consult the Magistrates' Court Sentencing Guidelines (or, in future, any guidelines issued by the SGC – see **Chapter 11**). The starting point for any plea in mitigation is to attempt to make a realistic assessment of the likely range of sentences that will be in the mind of the court.

For each offence which may be dealt with by the magistrates, the Magistrates' Court Sentencing Guidelines contain a chart which the magistrates must work through to arrive at their sentence. The chart begins by specifying both the maximum sentence for the offence and a 'guideline' sentence for a first-time offender who pleads not guilty and is then convicted following a trial. The chart then provides a list of potential aggravating and mitigating factors in respect of the offence, together with possible points of 'offender' mitigation which may be present (ie, factors personal to the defendant which may be relevant to mitigation). The chart also reminds the magistrates that the defendant is entitled to credit if he has entered a guilty plea and so removed the need for a trial to take place. Only when the magistrates have worked thought the chart should they decide upon the appropriate sentence.

Some extracts from the Guidelines have been included in the **Appendix** to illustrate how the Guidelines work.

**Crown Court**

In the Crown Court the plea in mitigation will be delivered by counsel rather than by the defendant's solicitor. The defence solicitor should still nevertheless find out the likely range of penalties to be imposed for the offence by checking either the guideline sentences given by the Court of Appeal and set out in the sentencing compendium prepared by the SGC (see **Chapter 11**), or any definitive guidelines the SGC has given for the relevant offence.

#### 12.3.2.2 See the client

The defendant's solicitor needs to take further instructions from his client before the sentencing hearing, covering the following matters:

(a) *The likely sentence* – the client will want to know 'what he is likely to get' for the offence.

(b) *The client's previous convictions* – if the client has previous convictions, the court may view these as an aggravating feature which will increase the severity of the sentence (see **11.4.2.4**). The defendant's solicitor needs to take full instructions on his client's previous convictions so that he may 'explain' to the court the circumstances behind such convictions and, if possible, attempt to distinguish them from the current offence. This is particularly important if the previous convictions are for the same type of offence as the offence for which the client is to be sentenced.

Example

George is to be sentenced for the offence of common assault following a drunken brawl in a pub. George has a previous conviction for common assault, which the magistrates may treat as an aggravating factor. George instructs his solicitor that the previous conviction occurred following a petty disagreement with a neighbour (which got out of hand) concerning the moving of a garden fence. George's solicitor will need to explain this in his plea in mitigation in order to distinguish this offence from the offence for which George is to be sentenced.

(c) *The client's financial circumstances* – it is likely that the defendant may be ordered to make some form of financial payment by the court. This may be a fine, an order to pay compensation to the victim, an order to pay prosecution costs, or, in the Crown Court, an order to pay or to contribute towards the defence costs. If the court makes such an order, it will expect the defendant's solicitor to put forward the defendant's proposals for payment. The defendant will normally instruct his solicitor that he can make payment within a specified number of days, or that he can make weekly payments of a certain amount until the amount due has been discharged. The court will expect the defendant's solicitor to have this information to hand when he is asked what the defendant's proposals for payment are.

(d) *Character references* – if the defendant is of previous good character (see **22.8**), the defendant's solicitor should discuss with his client whether there is anyone who occupies a position of respect or trust within the community (such as a teacher) who may be prepared to provide a character reference for the client, or to attend court to give such a reference in person at the sentencing hearing. If the client is in employment, it is particularly useful mitigation to obtain such a reference from the client's employer.

(d) *Medical reports* – as explained in **12.2.2** above, the defendant's solicitor may need to obtain a medical report from his client's doctor for use when delivering the plea in mitigation on the client's behalf. To obtain such a report, the defendant's solicitor will need to get a signed form of authority from his client to send to the doctor, authorising the doctor to release information about the client's medical situation.

#### 12.3.2.3 Obtain a copy of the pre-sentence report prepared by the Probation Service

As the pre-sentence report is prepared at the court's request, the Probation Service officer who prepared it is unlikely to disclose a copy of his report to the defendant's solicitor until the day of the sentencing hearing. The report may often be very detailed, and the solicitor needs to get to court sufficiently early to read the report and discuss its contents with the defendant. The solicitor needs to ensure that there is nothing in the report which is factually incorrect. He must also discuss with the defendant the sentencing recommendation set out in the report. The court will place great emphasis on the report's recommendations when deciding on the sentence to be imposed, and the solicitor needs to explain to the client exactly what the suggested sentence entails. This is particularly important when the report recommends that the defendant should comply with specific requirements as part of a generic community order (see **11.6**).

## 12.4 *Newton* hearings

Occasionally a defendant may plead guilty to the charge against him but dispute the specific factual version of events put forward by the CPS. If the dispute concerning the correct version of events is substantial (ie, if it may have a bearing on the type of sentence the court imposes), the court must either accept the defendant's version of events or allow both the CPS and the defendant to call evidence so that the court can determine the true factual circumstances of the offence on which the defendant's sentence will be based. If evidence is to be called, a hearing must be arranged so that witnesses can attend court to give evidence. This is referred to as a *Newton* hearing, following the case of *R v Newton* (1983) 77 Cr App R 13.

**Example**

Stanley pleads guilty to a charge of burglary of a dwelling. The CPS alleges that Stanley broke into the dwelling by smashing a window, ransacked several rooms in the property, soiled the carpets and took several items of high value. Stanley says that he got into the property through an open window (causing no damage to the window), denies ransacking the property or soiling the carpets, and says that he removed only a small transistor radio. The difference between the prosecution and the defence version of events is significant, and is likely to affect the type of sentence the court will impose. The court must therefore either hold a *Newton* hearing, or alternatively accept Stanley's account as being the correct version of events.

## 12.5 Sentencing procedure

### 12.5.1 Magistrates' court

The procedure that is followed at a sentencing hearing in the magistrates' court is as follows:

(a) The defendant will either enter a guilty plea, or will be convicted following a trial.

(b) If the defendant has entered a guilty plea, the court will be supplied with details of any offences which the defendant wishes to have taken into consideration (see **11.4.2.6**) and the prosecuting solicitor will outline the facts of the case to the magistrates (there will be no need to do this if the defendant is convicted following a trial because the magistrates will have heard the facts of the case during the course of the trial). The prosecutor may, as part of his submission, read out to the court a statement from the victim of the crime detailing the effect the crime has had on his or her life. This is known as a 'victim personal statement' or 'victim impact statement'. The court should take the statement into account prior to passing sentence (although the opinion of the victim as to what the sentence should be is not relevant). When making his submission, the prosecutor is under a duty to tell the court about any facts concerning the offence of which he is aware which may constitute mitigation on the defendant's behalf (see **1.6.3**).

(c) The prosecuting solicitor will then supply the court with a list of the defendant's previous convictions (if any). The court will check to make sure that a copy of this list has been supplied to the defendant's solicitor.

(d) The prosecuting solicitor will conclude his remarks by asking for any ancillary orders he wishes the magistrates to make (such as an application for the defendant to pay the prosecution costs). If required to do so, the prosecutor should be in a position to refer the court to any relevant sentencing guidelines.

(e) The defendant's solicitor will then address the magistrates. He may ask the magistrates to adjourn the case at his request (should he wish to obtain medical or other reports for use in mitigation), or he may ask the magistrates if they wish to adjourn the case so that a pre-sentence report may be obtained from the Probation Service.

(f) If the case is not adjourned, the defendant's solicitor will then give a plea in mitigation on his client's behalf. He may also call character witnesses to give evidence on the defendant's behalf.

(g) The magistrates will then sentence the defendant.

(h) If the magistrates decide to adjourn the case so that reports can be prepared, the case is likely to be adjourned for three or four weeks. During this period, the defendant will either be released on bail, or be remanded in custody (see **12.2.1.2** above). There is a presumption that a defendant whose case is adjourned for the preparation of reports will be granted bail (see **7.3**), although if the magistrates indicate that they are considering a custodial sentence, bail may be refused on the ground that there are substantial reasons for believing that the defendant will fail to surrender to custody.

(i) When the case comes back before the court for sentence, it is likely to be dealt with by a different bench of magistrates. The prosecuting solicitor will therefore need to repeat the facts of the case to the court (whether or not the defendant pleaded guilty), to check that the magistrates have before them details of the defendant's previous convictions, and to make an application for any ancillary orders he may require.

(j) The defendant's solicitor will then give a plea in mitigation on his client's behalf.

(k) The magistrates will then sentence the defendant. The court must explain to the defendant both the reasons for, and the effect of, the sentence which is imposed (CJA 2003, s 174(1)).

A flowchart summarising the above is set out at **12.8** below

### 12.5.2 Crown Court

The procedure which takes place when a judge sentences a defendant in the Crown Court is essentially the same as in the magistrates' court.

Unless the defendant has been convicted following a trial, prosecuting counsel will tell the judge what the facts of the case are. He will also provide the judge with details of the defendant's previous convictions and request any ancillary orders (such as an order for the payment of compensation or prosecution costs). Prosecuting counsel should also be in a position to draw to the attention of the court any sentencing guidelines given by the SGC or the Court of Appeal. If the judge considers that a pre-sentence report is necessary, he will adjourn sentencing for the preparation of reports and remand the defendant either on bail or in custody. When a judge who has presided over the defendant's trial adjourns sentencing for the preparation of pre-sentence reports, the judge will normally 'reserve' the case to himself to ensure that he will ultimately sentence the defendant once the necessary reports have been prepared. Although there is a presumption that a defendant whose case has been adjourned for the preparation of reports will be granted bail (see **7.3**), if the defendant has been convicted of a serious offence the judge is likely to refuse bail on the grounds either that there are substantial grounds for believing that the defendant will fail to surrender to custody, or that it would be impractical to prepare the report without keeping him in custody. Before the judge sentences the defendant, defence counsel will deliver a plea in mitigation on the defendant's behalf.

As in the magistrates' court, prosecuting counsel may read out to the judge a victim personal statement from the victim of the offence.

### 12.5.3 Reasons for and effect of sentence

When the judge or the magistrates sentence the defendant, the defendant must be told both the reasons for the sentence and the effect of the sentence (CJA 2003, s 174(1)). If guidelines (such as sentencing guidelines issued by the SGC - see **11.4.2.2**) indicate that a sentence of a particular kind, or in a particular range, would normally be appropriate for the offence, if the judge or magistrates impose a sentence of a different kind, or outside the particular range, the defendant must be told the reasons for this (CJA 2003, s 174(2)). Section 172 of the CJA 2003 requires the court to have regard to any guidelines that exist when sentencing an offender.

## 12.6 Professional conduct

Issues of professional conduct may arise for the defendant's solicitor when the list of his client's previous convictions (which the CPS produces to the court) is either inaccurate or incomplete. The defendant's solicitor should never be asked by the court clerk/legal adviser to confirm the accuracy of the list. If the solicitor is asked to do this, he should decline to comment. To confirm the list as being accurate would be a positive deception of the court, breaching the solicitor's duty not to mislead the court. However, the solicitor also owes a duty of confidentiality to his client, and disclosing to the court details of a client's previous convictions without the client's consent is a breach of this duty.

To prevent such problems occurring, the defendant's solicitor should obtain details of his client's previous convictions from the CPS in advance of the sentencing hearing. The solicitor should then discuss the accuracy of this list with his client. The client must be warned about the dangers of misleading the court. If the client insists that, if asked, he will pretend the list is accurate, or if the client asks the solicitor to pretend the list is accurate, the solicitor must cease to act for the client and withdraw from the case.

## 12.7 Plea in mitigation

### 12.7.1 Objective and structure

The objective of the plea in mitigation is to persuade the sentencing court to impose upon the defendant the most lenient sentence which the court could reasonably be expected to give for that offence. The structure of a plea in mitigation may be divided into four parts:

(a) *The 'starting point' sentence* – the defendant's solicitor should begin by identifying the 'starting point' sentence. This is the sentence which the court is likely to impose for a 'standard' offence of the type the defendant has committed, with no significant aggravating or mitigating features.

(b) *The offence* – the defendant's solicitor should then address the circumstances of the offence, minimising the impact of any aggravating factors and stressing the importance of any mitigating factors that are present.

(c) *The offender* – after dealing with the offence, the defendant's solicitor should then emphasise any personal mitigation which the defendant may have.

(d) *The suggested sentence* – the plea in mitigation should conclude with the defendant's solicitor suggesting to the court the type of sentence which he considers it would be most appropriate for the court to impose.

Each of these four parts will now be looked at in more detail. Although what is set out below concentrates on the delivery of a plea in mitigation in the magistrates' court, the same principles will apply when a plea in mitigation is being delivered in the Crown Court.

### 12.7.2 The 'starting point' sentence

If the defendant's solicitor has properly researched the likely range of sentences which will be in the mind of the court, he should be able to identify what the 'starting point' sentence is likely to be (see **12.3.2.1** above). The 'starting point' sentence is the sentence the magistrates are going to have at the back of their minds before they have heard any mitigation put forward on behalf of the defendant. The objective of the plea in mitigation is to persuade the magistrates to impose a sentence which is less severe than the 'starting point' sentence.

#### 12.7.2.1 Magistrates' court

The Magistrates' Court Sentencing Guidelines provides for each offence covered, a guideline sentence for a first-time offender who has pleaded not guilty and been convicted following a trial (this is before the magistrates have been told about the presence of any aggravating or mitigating factors).

For example, the guideline sentence for assault occasioning actual bodily harm is custody (see **Appendix**). The solicitor will acknowledge that this is the guideline sentence, and then tell the magistrates that he hopes to persuade them to deal with the offence other than by way of a custodial sentence (by imposing, for example, a generic community order). In contrast, the guideline sentence for theft is a community penalty (see **Appendix**). If there are a number of aggravating factors present (see **12.7.3** below), however, the magistrates may consider imposing a custodial sentence for this offence. In this situation the solicitor will tell the magistrates that he hopes to persuade them that the guideline penalty is in fact the appropriate penalty to impose on the defendant. Alternatively, if there are a number of mitigating factors present (see **12.7.3** and **12.7.4** below), the solicitor may tell the magistrates that he hopes to persuade them to deal with the offence by way of a fine or a conditional discharge.

Whatever offence the defendant has been convicted of, the solicitor must make an accurate assessment of the sentence the defendant is likely to receive and what alternative lesser sentence he may be able to persuade the court to impose.

If the defendant committed his current offence whilst he was subject to a suspended sentence or a conditional discharge imposed following a previous offence, the solicitor will also need to have as his objective persuading the court not to activate the sentence (in the case of a suspended sentence – see **11.5.5**) or not to revoke the discharge and then to sentence the defendant (in the case of a conditional discharge – see **11.8.2** above). Similarly, if the defendant is currently subject to a generic community order, the solicitor will seek to persuade the court not to revoke the order if the court indicates that it is considering revoking the order and re-sentencing the defendant to a term of imprisonment (see **11.6.5**).

#### 12.7.2.2 Crown Court

In the Crown Court, the 'starting point' sentence may be found either in the compendium of Court of Appeal sentencing guideline cases, or in any definitive sentencing guidelines given by the SGC, both of which may be found on the SGC website (www.sentencing-guidelines.gov.uk).

### 12.7.3 The offence

After identifying the 'starting point' sentence, the plea in mitigation should then focus on the offence itself. This requires the defendant's solicitor to:

- minimise the impact of any aggravating factors surrounding the offence; and
- emphasise the importance of any mitigating factors.

For each offence covered by the Magistrates' Courts Sentencing Guidelines, there is a list of possible aggravating and mitigating factors. For example, aggravating factors in a case involving the use of violence against another may include:

(a) the use of a weapon;
(b) extensive injuries to the victim;
(c) premeditation;
(d) a group action;
(e) the use of kicking;
(f) a victim who is particularly vulnerable (such as an elderly or disabled person, or a child).

Possible mitigating factors in such a case may include:

(a) minor injuries to the victim;
(b) an element of provocation;
(c) the use of a single blow;
(d) no weapon used;
(e) no element of premeditation.

Aggravating factors for a property-related offence such as the burglary of a dwelling house may include:

(a) the threat or use of force;
(b) stealing items of a high financial or sentimental value;
(c) an element of planning;
(d) significant damage to the property (eg, a house being ransacked, or significant damage caused when gaining entry);
(e) the presence of the victim at the time of the burglary (particularly if the burglary is at night).

Mitigating factors in such a case may include:

(a) no use of force or violence;

(b) only items of low value being stolen;
(c) an offence committed on impulse or an opportunistic crime;
(d) no damage caused to the property;
(e) the burglary being carried out when the property was vacant.

The defendant's solicitor should identify any aggravating factors which would normally lead the court to impose a sentence in excess of the 'starting point' sentence, and attempt (if possible) to disassociate the defendant's case from those factors. Similarly, the defendant's solicitor should emphasise to the court the presence of any mitigating factors.

### 12.7.4 The offender

After dealing with the facts of the offence, the plea in mitigation should move on to consider any personal mitigation the defendant may have. Factors which may be relevant here are set out below.

#### 12.7.4.1 The age of the defendant

The younger the defendant is, the more likely it will be that the court will want to pass a sentence designed to 'help' the defendant rather than to punish him. This is particularly the case if the court thinks that a young defendant who is immature and impressionable has been led astray by older co-defendants. The courts are also generally more likely to give sympathetic treatment to a defendant of advanced years, particularly if this is his first offence.

#### 12.7.4.2 The health of the defendant

It is unwise to suggest to the court in mitigation that the defendant committed an offence only because he was under the influence of drink or drugs at the time. The court is likely to regard this as an aggravating feature of the offence. If, however, there is evidence that the defendant is a drug addict or an alcoholic, this may be used to suggest to the court that a sentence designed to help the defendant overcome this addiction (for example, a generic community order that incorporates a drug rehabilitation requirement or an alcohol treatment requirement) may be more appropriate than a custodial sentence. Similarly, a defendant who is suffering from a long-term illness or injury is likely to receive some sympathy from the court, as is a defendant who may have been suffering from some form of mental illness (such as depression) at the time the offence was committed.

#### 12.7.4.3 Cooperation with the police/early guilty plea

The court will give the defendant credit for entering an early guilty plea to the offence (since the sentencing guidelines are based on the appropriate sentence for a defendant who is convicted following a trial). The amount of credit the defendant will receive depends upon the stage in the proceedings at which the defendant entered his guilty plea (see **11.4.2.5**). Such credit may amount to a maximum reduction of one-third of the sentence the defendant would have received had he pleaded not guilty (if the defendant has pleaded guilty at the first opportunity). The defendant's solicitor should (if appropriate) always remind the court of this. It would also be appropriate to tell the court if the defendant has positively assisted the police in their enquiries, for example by naming others involved in the crime or by revealing the whereabouts of stolen property. The fact that the defendant made a prompt confession when questioned by the police is also useful mitigation, showing that the defendant did not waste police time during the investigation process.

#### 12.7.4.4 Voluntary compensation

A defendant who voluntarily makes good the damage which he has caused, or who makes a voluntary payment of compensation to his victim, is likely to receive credit for this. This is particularly the case if the defendant is of limited means.

#### 12.7.4.5 Remorse

Evidence of *true* remorse is effective mitigation. A mere apology made by the defendant's solicitor to the court on behalf of his client is unlikely to have much effect, but the court will take into account any positive steps which the defendant has made to tackle the problems which led him to commit the offence. For example, the court is likely to give credit to a defendant who is to be sentenced for several public order offences committed whilst in a drunken state, if that defendant has begun to attend classes organised by Alcoholics Anonymous to combat his addiction. Similarly, the court will give credit to a defendant who has committed thefts to fund a drug habit, but who has voluntarily sought treatment for this.

#### 12.7.4.6 Character

If the defendant has previous convictions, the court may view these as aggravating factors (CJA 2003, s 143(2)). The court is likely to view a defendant's previous convictions as being aggravating factors if the relevant offences either were committed recently, or were the same type of offence as the offence for which the defendant is to be sentenced. If the defendant has any such convictions, the solicitor should attempt to distinguish such convictions from the facts of the current offence and 'explain' the circumstances of the defendant's previous offending. For example, a defendant convicted of theft may have several previous convictions for thefts which were committed in order to fund a drug habit. If the defendant is no longer taking drugs and the reason for the defendant having committed the current offence is different from his motive for committing the previous offences, his solicitor should explain this to the court.

Just as having previous convictions may be seen as an aggravating factor, so a defendant with no previous convictions (and so of previous good character) is entitled to have this taken into account. This is particularly important when there is a specific reason or explanation for a defendant of previous good character having committed an offence.

**Example**

Violet is 50 years of age and is of previous good character. She works on the check-out at her local supermarket and has been charged with stealing £500 in cash from her employers. The reason for Violet having committed the offence is that her husband has recently left her, taking all her savings and leaving her with insufficient funds to pay the rent on her house. Violet's solicitor can ask the court to take Violet's previous good character into account and suggest that there is a specific 'one-off' explanation for her committing a criminal offence.

In *R v Seed*; *R v Stark* [2007] EWCA Crim 254, the Court of Appeal held that the absence of previous convictions was important mitigation that might make a custodial sentence inappropriate, even if the custody threshold had been crossed (see **11.5.2**).

The defendant's solicitor may call character witnesses (see **12.3.2.2**) to give evidence as to the defendant's previous good character.

It is also appropriate to say in mitigation that, aside from any sentence imposed by the court, a defendant of hitherto good character will have lost his good name as a result of being convicted, and will suffer shame as a result. This will certainly be the case if the defendant has a respected position within the community (eg, is a doctor or a teacher).

#### 12.7.4.7 Family circumstances

If the court has requested a pre-sentence report from the Probation Service, this will look in depth at the defendant's personal background and family circumstances. The defendant's solicitor should also refer to the defendant's personal circumstances in the plea in mitigation, particularly if the defendant has a regular home and job, and has family who will be supportive in his attempts to stay out of trouble in the future. Although there is little to be gained from saying that the defendant's family will be caused upset or inconvenience if a custodial sentence is imposed, if exceptional circumstances exist, explaining to the magistrates the effect the defendant's imprisonment will have on his immediate family can be effective mitigation. For example, the defendant may have a partner who is dangerously ill or who is expecting a child, or the defendant may have a handicapped child. The defendant's solicitor should also tell the court if a custodial sentence will result in the defendant losing his job. This may persuade the court to impose a community penalty instead of imprisonment. It is often the case that defendants who are due to be sentenced may have received a recent offer of employment. This should be raised in mitigation, although the magistrates are likely to give this credence only if the defendant is able to produce a letter or other document confirming the offer.

If the defendant has had a troubled family background, it would also be appropriate to refer to this in mitigation, particularly if the defendant is still young. For example, a defendant may have come from a broken home, or have been physically or sexually abused as a child. Similarly, young defendants will often have become addicted to drugs or involved in prostitution at an early age. This will be particularly effective mitigation if the defendant's solicitor is able to say that the client has made a genuine attempt to overcome such a background.

#### 12.7.4.8 Other consequences of conviction

It is also appropriate to point out to the court any other adverse consequence suffered by the defendant as a result of the conviction. For example, a defendant convicted of a minor theft may have lost his job following his conviction if he worked in a professional capacity or in a position of trust. A defendant may also have had to relinquish other positions of responsibility following his conviction (for example, a defendant who was a local councillor or a school governor).

#### 12.7.4.9 Low risk of re-offending

The pre-sentence report from the Probation Service will address the risk of the defendant committing further offences. If this risk is assessed as being low, the defendant's solicitor should mention this in the plea in mitigation to support an argument that the defendant's offending was a one-off aberration for which the defendant has shown remorse and a willingness to change.

### 12.7.5 The suggested sentence

The plea in mitigation should conclude with the defendant's solicitor suggesting to the court the sentence which he thinks the court should impose upon his client. This should be lower than the 'starting point' sentence, and should reflect the all the mitigating factors which the defendant's solicitor has placed before the court. The sentence which the defendant's solicitor suggests to the court must be realistic, and so should be at the lower end of the range of possible sentences which will be in the mind of the court. If the sentence which the defendant's solicitor suggests as being appropriate is the same sentence as is recommended in the pre-sentence report, the solicitor should emphasise this point (given that the pre-sentence report is requested by the court to assist it in determining sentence).

In addition to suggesting to the court what an appropriate sentence would be for the current offence, the defendant's solicitor may also need to suggest to the court how to deal with any other matters for which the defendant may be dealt with at the sentencing hearing (if, for example, the defendant is currently subject to a suspended sentence, a conditional discharge or a generic community order). To prevent the court from activating a suspended sentence, the defendant's solicitor may suggest to the court that it would be unjust to activate the sentence because the defendant's current offence was committed towards the end of the suspension period, or because the defendant's current offence is of a different nature to the offence for which the suspended sentence was imposed. Similar arguments may be raised in order to persuade the court not to revoke a conditional discharge and then to sentence the defendant for his original offence. If the defendant has committed his current offence whilst still subject to a generic community order, the court may revoke the order and re-sentence the defendant for the original offence. Such a sentence is likely to be custodial. To persuade the court not to do this, the solicitor should emphasise the extent to which the defendant has complied with the requirements of the order, particularly if the order has been ongoing for some time and is nearing its conclusion.

An example of a plea in mitigation to be delivered to the court is set out below.

## Key Skill – Delivering a Plea in Mitigation

**PLEA IN MITIGATION**

Sir, before you pass sentence on Mr Dickson, it falls to me to give a plea in mitigation on his behalf. I understand from your legal adviser that you have already had the opportunity to read the pre-sentence report prepared by the Probation Service.

Clearly, sir, this is a serious matter, and you may be minded to consider imposing an immediate custodial sentence on Mr Dickson. I hope to persuade you that a more suitable method of disposing of this case would be for you to impose a community sentence as recommended in the pre-sentence report. I will begin by addressing the circumstances of the offence. I will then provide you with details of Mr Dickson's personal circumstances, before concluding by addressing the format of the generic community order which I hope to persuade you to impose.

Sir, my client accepts the version of events as outlined to you by the prosecution, save that there was an element of provocation in this matter. Whilst it is true to say that Mr Dickson assaulted Mr Lamb after Mr Lamb had left Connolley's nightclub, this incident must be placed in the context of events which occurred earlier in the evening. Mr Lamb had been working at Connolley's that evening as a disc jockey, with Mr Dickson working there as a bouncer. Throughout the evening Mr Lamb had taunted Mr Dickson about his status as a bouncer and, at one stage, had attempted to proposition Mr Dickson's partner. Whilst such conduct on the part of Mr Lamb should in no way condone Mr Dickson's later actions, it does help to explain why Mr Dickson acted in the way he did.

I would also ask you to note that Mr Dickson did to a certain extent act on impulse. As he was driving home from the nightclub, Mr Dickson saw Mr Lamb also leaving the nightclub. Mr Dickson saw his opportunity to get back at Mr Lamb for Mr Lamb's conduct earlier in the evening. Sir, this was not a planned or premeditated attack, nor was any weapon used by Mr Dickson in carrying out the attack. It was the impulsive act of a man who had been subjected to taunts throughout the evening.

Whilst it is correct that Mr Dickson initially entered a plea of not guilty to this offence, I would ask you to give such credit as you feel able for the fact that Mr Dickson did ultimately changed his plea to one of guilty.

Sir, Mr Dickson is 27 years of age. He has lived in the Chester area since 2002. Prior to moving to Chester, Mr Dickson served in the army for five years. Mr Dickson has been in full-time employment since leaving the army. In addition to working as a bouncer on a weekend and some weekday evenings, Mr Dickson also does contract work as a scaffolder and steeplejack.

Mr Dickson does have previous convictions for offences of violence, which you will have seen from the list of Mr Dickson's antecedents. These previous convictions arose from Mr Dickson's work as a bouncer at Connolley's, and followed altercations which Mr Dickson had with abusive customers at the nightclub. Mr Dickson would say that these convictions resulted from incidents where he had been provoked by such customers to the point at which he felt compelled to react in a violent manner. Mr Dickson's only other relevant conviction occurred some six years ago when he pleaded guilty to a charge of common assault following an incident in a pub when Mr Dickson pushed over a person who had been abusive towards him. Mr Dickson received a conditional discharge for this offence.

Sir, Mr Dickson's personal circumstances have recently changed. Mr Dickson has been living with his partner for 18 months. His partner has just been informed that she is expecting their first child, and Mr Dickson is acutely aware of the responsibilities impending fatherhood will impose on him. Mr Dickson has also recently been offered a long-term contract to do some scaffolding work in Chester. The financial value of this work is such that Mr Dickson will no longer need to continue with his part-time work as a bouncer. As you have read in the pre-sentence report, Mr Dickson has been dismissed from his job at Connolley's, but has no intention of seeking further work as a bouncer.

Sir, there is a theme running through Mr Dickson's offending. That theme is that Mr Dickson has difficulty in controlling his temper in situations where he is open to verbal provocation from others. As Mr Dickson will not be seeking further employment as a nightclub bouncer, Mr Dickson is effectively removing himself from the possibility of becoming involved in such situations. Indeed the pre-sentence report suggests that as long as Mr Dickson does not return to work as a bouncer, the risk of his re-offending is low, albeit that Mr Dickson needs to address those anger management issues which appear to be the root cause of his offending.

Sir, you will be aware that Mr Dickson has previously received a community sentence involving an unpaid work requirement. However, in my respectful submission, whilst that sentence served to punish Mr Dickson for his offending, the sentence failed to address the underlying reason for that offending.

As you will be aware, Sir, one of the five purposes of sentencing set out in section 142(1) of the Criminal Justice Act 2003 is the reform and rehabilitation of offenders. The sentence suggested by Ms Smythe in the pre-sentence report is a generic community order comprising an unpaid work requirement and, significantly, a programme requirement under which Mr Dickson would need to attend an anger management course. You may think that such a sentence is appropriate, Sir, as it would satisfy the need to punish Mr Dickson, but also the need to prevent him from offending again in the future. I would submit that the imposition of an immediate custodial sentence, whilst achieving the goal of punishing Mr Dickson, would not address this latter point. You will be aware, Sir, that many offenders who receive prison sentences offend again shortly after leaving prison.

You will also be aware, Sir, that another purpose of sentencing is the making of reparation by offenders to those affected by their offences. I would submit that such a purpose could be satisfied in this case by the making of an order that Mr Dickson pay compensation to Mr Lamb. Should you order compensation to be paid, or should you order that Mr Dickson pay the costs of the prosecution, I am instructed that such payment can be made by Mr Dickson within 14 days.

In conclusion, Sir, I would urge you to adopt the sentence recommended by Ms Smythe in the pre-sentence report, namely a generic community order incorporating an unpaid work requirement and a requirement that Mr Dickson take part in an anger management programme. In addition, Mr Dickson is in a position to make a payment of compensation to Mr Lamb should you deem this appropriate. In addition, Mr Dickson is in a position to make a payment of compensation to Mr Lamb should you deem this appropriate. Unless, Sir, you have any questions, that concludes my submissions on behalf of Mr Dickson.

## 12.8 Procedural flowcharts

### 12.8.1 Sentencing procedure

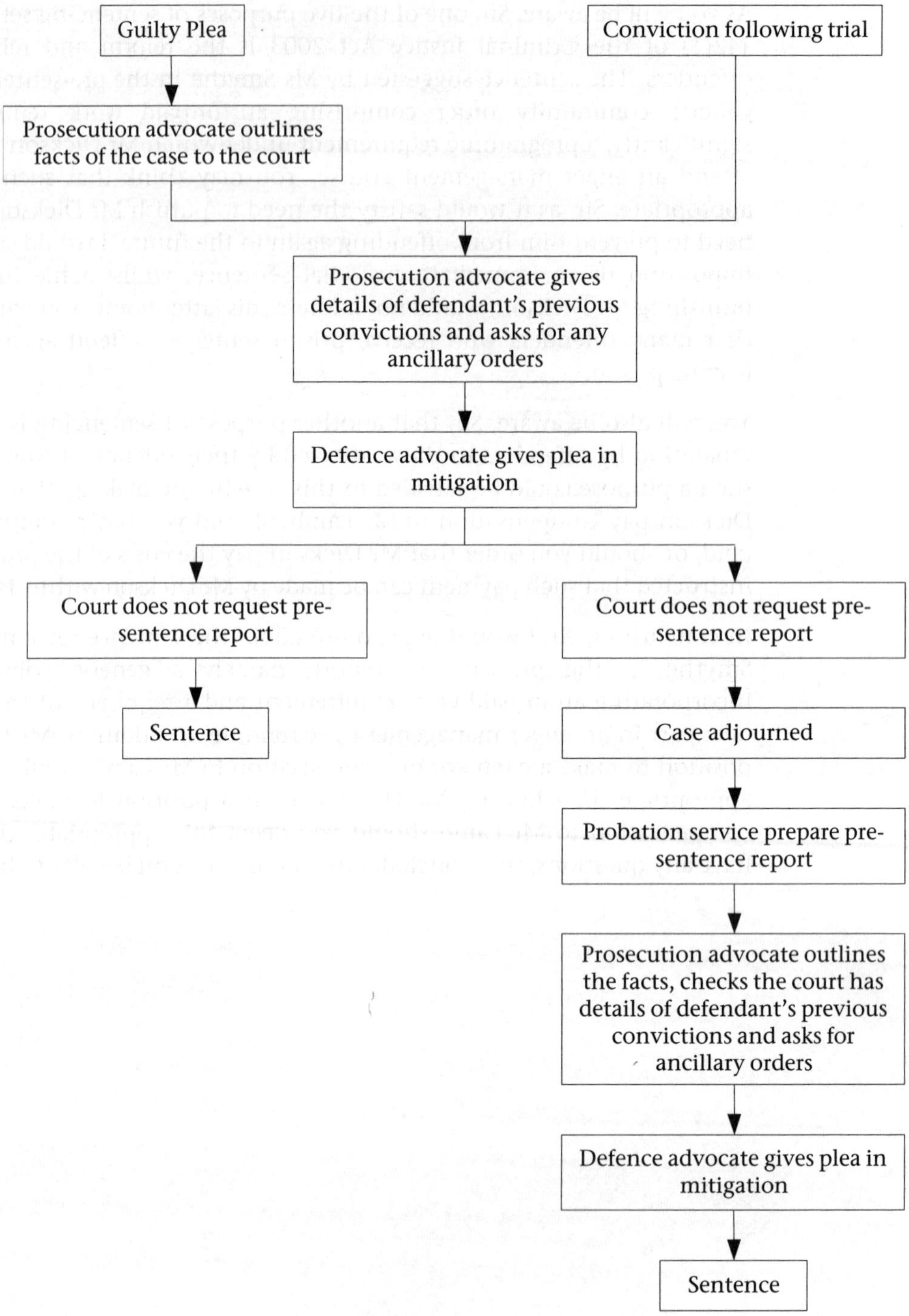

### 12.8.2 Structuring a plea in mitigation

1. *Identify the starting point sentence:*
   - Case in magistrates' court: Magistrates' Courts Sentencing Guidelines
   - Case in Crown Court: guideline sentence from Court of Appeal or definitive guidelines from SGC

↓

2. *Offence mitigation:*
   - Minimise impact of any aggravating factors
   - Emphasise importance of any mitigating factors, eg:

| *Assault* | *Property offence* |
|---|---|
| minor injuries | no use of force/violence |
| provocation | items of low value stolen |
| single blow | opportunistic |
| no weapon | no damage caused |
| provocation | property unoccupied |

↓

3. *Offender mitigation:*
   - age
   - health
   - co-operation with police/early guilty plea
   - voluntary compensation
   - remorse
   - character
   - family circumstances
   - other consequences of conviction
   - low risk of re-offending

↓

4. *Suggested sentence:*
   - Lower than starting point sentence
   - At bottom end of range of potential sentences
   - Incorporate recommendations in pre-sentence report (if appropriate)

## 12.9 Checklist

At the end of this chapter you should be able to explain:

- the purpose of a pre-sentence report and the types of pre-sentence report that may be prepared;
- the steps the defendant's solicitor must take in order to prepare for a sentencing hearing in the magistrates' court.
- the purpose of a *Newton* hearing and when such a hearing should take place;
- issues of professional conduct which may arise at or before a sentencing hearing;
- the procedure to be followed at a sentencing hearing in either the magistrates' court or the Crown Court;
- how to structure and deliver an effective plea in mitigation.

# Chapter 13
# Appeals



## 13.1 Introduction

Most criminal cases end either following the acquittal of the defendant at trial, or, if the defendant is convicted or pleads guilty, following sentence. This chapter will consider the options open to the defendant to appeal against his conviction or the sentence he has received. It will also examine the more limited rights of appeal that may be exercised by the CPS following the acquittal of the defendant or the imposition of a sentence which the CPS considers to be insufficient.

The rules which govern the procedure for the making of an appeal (either by the defendant, or by the CPS) are in Parts 63–74 of the Criminal Procedure Rules 2005.

## 13.2 Appeals from the magistrates' court (including the Youth Court)

### 13.2.1 Appeals to the Crown Court (CrimPR, Part 63)

#### 13.2.1.1 Who may appeal?

Section 108(1) of the Magistrates' Courts Act 1980 provides that a defendant convicted in the magistrates' court may appeal to the Crown Court in the following circumstances:

(a) if he pleaded guilty before the magistrates, he may appeal against the sentence he has received;

(b) if he pleaded not guilty before the magistrates, he may appeal against conviction and/or sentence he has received.

Appeals by juveniles against conviction and/or sentence in the Youth Court (see **Chapter 14**) are also covered by these provisions (since Youth Courts are deemed to be a particular type of magistrates' court).

The prosecution do not have the right to appeal to the Crown Court against either the acquittal of a defendant by the magistrates, or the sentence imposed on a defendant by the magistrates.

#### 13.2.1.2 Who hears the appeal?

The appeal (whether against conviction and/or sentence) will be heard by a circuit judge or recorder, who will sit with an even number of magistrates. This will normally be two magistrates, although up to four magistrates may sit on an appeal.

#### 13.2.1.3 Appeals against conviction

A defendant convicted following a trial in the magistrates' court may appeal against his conviction to the Crown Court on the basis that the magistrates made errors of fact and/or law.

The Crown Court will not consider an appeal against conviction from a defendant who pleaded guilty in the magistrates' court if the defendant subsequently regrets pleading guilty and thinks he has an arguable defence (*R v Marylebone Justices, ex p Westminster City Council* [1971] 1 WLR 567). The Crown Court will only consider an appeal against conviction from a defendant who pleaded guilty before the magistrates if either the defendant made an 'equivocal plea', or his plea of guilty was made under duress. An equivocal plea will occur when the defendant pleads guilty but subsequently makes a comment (often in mitigation) which suggests that his plea was a misunderstanding of the correct legal position.

**Example**

Anil is accused of the theft of a lawnmower from his neighbour Geoffrey. Anil decides not to seek legal representation. He enters a plea of guilty and the magistrates adjourn the case for a pre-sentence report. When Anil comes before the court for sentence, he says in mitigation that he took the lawnmower only because he thought it belonged to him. This would make his plea equivocal, because such a belief would have provided him with a possible defence to the charge.

In such cases, the Crown Court will remit the case back to the magistrates' court for trial, with a direction that the magistrates should treat the case as if a plea of not guilty had been entered. In *Revitt & Others v DPP* [2006] EWHC 2266 (Admin), the High Court held that where it became apparent to magistrates that the defendant did not appreciate the elements of the offence to which he was pleading guilty, it would be appropriate to allow the defendant to withdraw his plea if, after receiving legal advice, the defendant wished to change his plea (see also *R v Seymour* [2006] All ER (D) 220 (Nov)).

An appeal against conviction in the Crown Court is a full rehearing of the case (in effect another trial). Both the CPS and the defendant will need to call all those witnesses whose evidence they seek to rely on. The witnesses do not necessarily need to be the same witnesses who were called to give evidence at the original trial in the magistrates' court; new witnesses may be called, and new or different points of law may be relied on.

#### 13.2.1.4 Appeals against sentence

A defendant may appeal to the Crown Court against a sentence imposed by the magistrates' court on the basis that the sentence imposed by the magistrates is excessive. The Crown Court should carry out a full rehearing of the issues and take an independent view, based on the evidence, of what the correct sentence should be, rather than simply reviewing the sentence passed by the magistrates' court. The Crown Court is entitled to decide the appeal on a different factual basis to that determined by the magistrates' court, and the Crown Court is not bound by any findings of fact made by the magistrates.

#### 13.2.1.5 Procedure for appealing against conviction and/or sentence

A defendant wishing to appeal from the magistrates' court to the Crown Court must file a notice of appeal with both the magistrates' court and the CPS within 21 days of the magistrates passing sentence.

The clerk to the magistrates' court will send the notice of appeal to the relevant Crown Court, and the Crown Court will then arrange a date for the hearing of the appeal to take place. The Crown Court does not have any discretion to turn down an appeal at the notice stage. A defendant who has filed the notice in time is entitled to have his appeal heard.

If a defendant files his notice outside the 21 days, a Crown Court judge does have the discretionary power to extend this time limit if the defendant provides reasons (in writing) for the notice not being filed in time.

If the defendant's case before the magistrates' court was funded by way of a representation order, a separate representation order will be required to cover the hearing of the appeal by the Crown Court. Any advice and assistance given to the defendant in preparing the notice of appeal will be covered by the original representation order (see **6.4.3.5**).

An example of a completed notice of appeal to the Crown Court is set out below.

## Key skill – drafting a notice of appeal to the Crown Court

**TO**: the Justices' Clerk of the Magistrates' Court sitting at Chester

**AND TO**: the Branch Crown Prosecutor, Crown Prosecution Service, East Chambers, Saville Street, Chester CH1 4NJ

**On** 29th March 2007, I Gary Paul Dickson

of 17 Marsh Street, Chester CH3 7LW

was convicted by the above Magistrates' Court as follows

**Offence(s):** Assault Occasioning Actual Bodily Harm contrary to s 47 of the Offences Against the Person Act 1861

for which the court on the 19th April 2007 imposed a generic community order requiring me to complete 300 hours' unpaid work and to complete an anger management programme

I give notice that I intend to appeal to the Crown Court at Chester against my conviction and sentence.

The general grounds of appeal are that the magistrates erred in fact and law.

**Dated** *23rd April 2007*

**Signed** *Gary Paul Dickson*

### 13.2.1.6 Will the defendant be granted bail pending the hearing of the appeal?

When the magistrates impose a custodial sentence on a defendant, the magistrates may grant bail to the defendant pending an appeal to the Crown Court. There is, however, no presumption in favour of bail, as s 4 of the Bail Act 1976 does not apply to defendants appealing against conviction or sentence (see 7.3). If the magistrates do not grant bail, the defendant may apply to the Crown Court for bail pending the hearing of the appeal.

#### 13.2.1.7 Powers of the Crown Court

The powers which the Crown Court may exercise on hearing an appeal from the magistrates' court are set out in s 48 of the Supreme Court Act 1981. The Crown Court may:

(a) confirm, reverse or vary the decision of the magistrates;
(b) remit the case back to the magistrates' court with a direction (as in the case of an equivocal plea – see **13.2.1.3** above); or
(c) make any other orders that the court thinks are just, as long as such orders could have been made by the magistrates' court (for example, make an order for the payment of costs or compensation by the defendant).

The Crown Court has the power to impose on the defendant any sentence, as long as it is a sentence which the magistrates' court had the power to impose. This means that a defendant appealing against a sentence imposed by the magistrates may have that sentence increased if the Crown Court takes a more serious view of the case than did the magistrates. A solicitor instructed by a defendant who wishes to appeal should always point this out to the defendant before the appeal is made.

Example

Jonathan is convicted in the magistrates' court of careless driving. The magistrates disqualify Jonathan from driving for two months. Jonathan appeals against this sentence to the Crown Court. On hearing the appeal, the Crown Court takes a more serious view of the case and increases the sentence to one of four months' disqualification. The Crown Court is able to do this because this is a sentence which the magistrates' court had the power to pass.

A defendant who successfully appeals to the Crown Court against conviction and/or sentence, and whose case was not publicly funded, will have the reasonable costs of his appeal paid from central funds (ie by the State).

Both the CPS and the defendant are able to appeal to the High Court by way of case stated against any decision or order made by the Crown Court following an appeal from the magistrates' court. The appeal must be based either on a point of law, or on an argument that the Crown Court has exceeded its jurisdiction (see **13.2.2** below).

### 13.2.2 Appeal to the High Court by way of case stated (CrimPR, Part 64)

#### 13.2.2.1 Who may appeal?

Either the CPS or the defendant may appeal from a decision of the magistrates' court to the Queen's Bench Division of the High Court. Such a right of appeal exists when either:

(a) the decision which has been made by the magistrates is wrong in law; or
(b) the magistrates have acted outside their jurisdiction (Magistrates' Courts Act 1980, s 111).

Arguments often raised in an appeal by way of case stated are that:

(a) the magistrates misread, misunderstood or misapplied the law;
(b) the magistrates decided to hear a case when they did not have the jurisdiction to hear it;

(c) the magistrates made errors in deciding the admissibility or otherwise of evidence;

(d) the magistrates erred in their decision following a submission of no case to answer.

Example

Hugh is convicted by the magistrates of assault occasioning actual bodily harm. The key piece of evidence against him was a confession given in an audibly recorded interview at the police station. Hugh's solicitor argued before the magistrates that the confession should be excluded, because the interview was conducted without Hugh being allowed access to legal advice and the police conducted the interview in an oppressive manner. The magistrates refused to exclude the confession evidence and Hugh was subsequently convicted. Hugh may appeal to the High Court by way of case stated, raising the argument that the magistrates made an error in deciding that the confession was admissible in evidence.

Appeals by way of case stated should not be used to appeal against a finding of fact made by the magistrates (*Spillman v DPP* [2006] All ER (D) 78). Similarly, a defendant wanting to appeal against a sentence imposed by the magistrates which he considers to be excessive should appeal to the Crown Court (see **13.2.1** above) rather than by way of case stated.

#### 13.2.2.2 Procedure

The party wishing to appeal by way of case stated must apply to the magistrates' court within 21 days of the relevant decision being made by the magistrates. This is normally done by writing to the clerk to the magistrates' court. The application must identify the question of law on which the aggrieved party seeks the view of the High Court. Following receipt of this letter, the magistrates must then 'state a case' for the opinion of the High Court.

To do this, the clerk to the magistrates (in conjunction with the magistrates who heard the case) will prepare a 'statement of case' that will contain the following information:

(a) the facts which were in dispute in the case;

(b) any findings of fact made by the magistrates;

(c) the findings made by the magistrates on the point of law in question;

(d) details of any legal authorities the magistrates relied on; and

(e) the question of law the High Court is being asked to consider.

Once an initial draft of the 'statement of case' has been prepared, the clerk will send this out to the CPS and the defendant's solicitor to enable them to suggest any necessary amendments. Once a final version of the statement of case has been agreed, the clerk will send this to the party making the appeal. That party must then lodge this with the High Court in London, and give notice that this has been done to the other party.

#### 13.2.2.3 The hearing

The appeal is heard by the Divisional Court of the Queen's Bench Division, and will normally be heard by three judges. No evidence is given by witnesses (since the appeal is not concerned with matters of fact) and the hearing will be confined to legal argument based on the agreed facts set out in the statement of case.

The Divisional Court has the power to reverse, vary or affirm the decision made by the magistrates. It may also remit the case back to the same magistrates' court with a direction to acquit or convict the defendant, or to remit the case to a different bench of magistrates (if the case needs to be reheard). The Divisional Court may make an order that the costs of either party be paid from central funds (ie, by the state).

Both the CPS and the defendant are able to appeal to the House of Lords in respect of any decision or order made by the High Court following an appeal to the High Court by way of case stated. Any such appeal must be on a point of law only, and the High Court must certify it to be a point of law of general public importance. Further, either the High Court or the House of Lords must grant leave to appeal.

### 13.2.3 Judicial review

An application for judicial review is not strictly a form of appeal. It does, however, represent an alternative method of challenging a decision made by the magistrates' court. An application for judicial review may be made either by the CPS or the defendant if:

(a) the magistrates have made an order that they had no power to make (and so have acted 'ultra vires', or beyond their powers); or

(b) the magistrates have breached the rules of natural justice (either by contravening a party's right to a fair hearing, or by appearing to be biased).

An applicant for judicial review will seek an order from the Divisional Court either quashing the decision made the magistrates, or compelling the magistrates to act (or not act) in a certain way.

In *R (P) v Liverpool City Magistrates* (2006) 170 JP 453, QBD, the High Court held that judicial review was a more appropriate remedy where it was alleged that there had been unfairness in the way in which the magistrates had conducted the case. An appeal by way of case stated (see **13.2.2** above) would be more appropriate when it was alleged that the magistrates had made an error of law.

## 13.3 Appeals from the Crown Court

### 13.3.1 Rights of appeal open to the defendant (CrimPR, Part 68)

A defendant who is convicted in the Crown Court has the following rights of appeal to the Criminal Division of the Court of Appeal:

(a) *Appeal against conviction (Criminal Appeal Act 1968, s 1(1)).* The defendant may appeal against his conviction if either the Court of Appeal grants him leave to appeal, or the trial judge grants a certificate that the case is fit for appeal (Criminal Appeal Act 1968, s 1(2)). The appeal may be on a point of law or fact, or both (see **13.3.2** below).

(b) *Appeal against sentence (Criminal Appeal Act 1968, s 9).* The defendant may appeal against the sentence he has received if either the Court of Appeal grants him leave to appeal, or the judge who passes sentence has granted a certificate that the case is fit for appeal against sentence (Criminal Appeal Act 1968, s 11). The potential grounds of appeal against sentence are set out at **13.3.3** below.

If a Crown Court judge grants a certificate that a case is fit for appeal (whether against conviction or sentence), he may also grant bail to the defendant pending the hearing of the appeal, although this practice has been discouraged by the Court of Appeal (see *R v Harries* [2007] All ER (D) 224 (Mar)). There is, however, no presumption in favour of bail being granted (see 7.3). Alternatively, the defendant may ask the Court of Appeal to grant him bail pending the hearing of his appeal. This power to grant bail will be exercised by a single judge (see **13.3.2.2** below). It is rare for the Court of Appeal to grant bail pending the outcome of the appeal, unless the grounds of the appeal are very strong.

## 13.3.2 Appeals against conviction

### 13.3.2.1 When will an appeal against conviction be allowed?

If the Court of Appeal considers a conviction to be 'unsafe', it must allow the appeal (Criminal Appeal Act 1968, s 2). In all other cases, the Court of Appeal must dismiss the appeal.

This means that a conviction may be upheld if there was an error or mistake at the defendant's trial in the Crown Court, if the Court of Appeal considers that, even had the mistake not been made, the correct and only reasonable verdict would have been one of guilty.

**Example**

In *R v Boyle and Ford* [2006] EWCA Crim 2101, two co-defendants were convicted of murder. There was significant DNA and other forensic evidence against them. The trial judge misdirected the jury as to drawing of adverse inferences under s 34 of the Criminal Justice and Public Order Act 1994. The Court of Appeal held that the misdirection did not render the conviction unsafe because there was other compelling evidence against the defendants.

In a very small number of cases, however, the Court of Appeal may allow an appeal and quash a conviction even if the Court is satisfied that the defendant did commit the offence for which he was convicted. Such a situation is most likely to occur when there has been an abuse of process committed by the police or the prosecuting authorities, such as the 'bugging' of a privileged conversation between the defendant and his solicitor (see also *R v Randall* [2002] 1 WLR 2237).

Examples of the most common grounds of appeal raised by defendants to argue that their convictions are unsafe are:

(a) *a failure by the trial judge to direct the jury correctly* as to:
   (i) the burden and standard of proof (see **Chapter 16**),
   (ii) the substantive law concerning the offence(s),
   (iii) the fact that it is for the jury rather than the judge to determine what the facts of the case are (although it is the role of the judge to remind the jury of the prominent features of the evidence when summing up, it is the sole responsibility of the jury to judge the evidence and decide all the relevant facts of the case),
   (iv) the fact that the jury should try to return a unanimous verdict (and the judge will notify them when the time has arisen when he may be prepared to accept a majority verdict – see **10.10.1**),
   (v) the jury's power to convict the defendant of any lesser offence which there was evidence to support;

(b) *the trial judge wrongfully admitting or excluding evidence*, for example:
   (i) the judge wrongfully admitting in evidence a disputed confession or the defendant's previous convictions (see **Chapters 20** and **22**),
   (ii) the judge wrongfully excluding hearsay evidence which would have assisted the defendant's case (see **Chapter 19**);

(c) *the trial judge failing to administer the correct warnings to the jury*, for example:

(i) the judge failing to give a '*Turnbull*' warning in a case of disputed identification, or a corroboration warning where the defendant alleges that a witness has a purpose of his own to serve in giving evidence against the defendant (see **Chapter 17**),

(ii) the judge failing to give a proper direction to the jury as to the drawing of adverse inferences from the defendant's silence (see **Chapter 18**),

(iii) the judge failing to warn the jury that they should not find the defendant to be guilty merely because he has previous convictions either for offences of the kind with which he has been charged or for offences showing a propensity to be untruthful (see **Chapter 22**);

(d) *inappropriate interventions by the trial judge* – if, for example, the judge had constantly interrupted defence counsel during the cross-examination of a prosecution witness;

(e) *a failure by the trial judge when summing up the case to the jury to*:

(i) deal with the essential points of the defence case,

(ii) identify any inconsistencies in the prosecution case,

(iii) summarise the evidence on which the jury may properly rely in order to convict the defendant,

(iv) give a '*Vye*' direction where the defendant is of good character (see **22.8**) (when summing up, the judge should not usually tell the jury to place any evidential significance on a prosecution witness being of good character; this is 'oath-helping' and is not permitted – see **22.8.2**),

(v) tell the jury, when special measures have been used to enable a prosecution witness to give evidence, that they should not allow this to prejudice them against the defendant, nor assume that the use of special measures means the defendant has behaved improperly (see **16.5.4**),

(vi) explain to the jury the evidential significance of any previous sexual relationship between the defendant and the complainant where the defendant is charged with rape and raises the defence of consent (see **Chapter 9**);

(f) *fresh evidence* – even if a trial has been conducted properly, the defendant may argue his conviction is unsafe if fresh evidence comes to light which casts doubt upon his guilt. For example, a new witness may come forward to substantiate an alibi which was disbelieved by the jury, or expert evidence relied on by the prosecution at trial may be shown to be flawed. Fresh evidence will not in itself render a conviction unsafe. The issue for the Court of Appeal is whether the fresh evidence is such that, had it been placed before the jury, the verdict may have been different (*R v Boreman & others* (2006) WL 1635086; *R v Rogers* [2006] EWCA Crim 1371). When deciding whether to admit fresh evidence, the Court of Appeal must have regard to a number of factors, including whether there is a reasonable explanation for the failure to adduce the relevant evidence at the original trial (Criminal Appeal Act 1968, s 23(2)).

At the end of the trial, defence counsel will normally prepare a written advice on the merits of an appeal against conviction in accordance with the instructions contained in his brief (see **10.7.2**).

#### 13.3.2.2 Procedure for making the appeal (CrimPR, Part 68)

Only rarely will the defendant ask the trial judge to certify that the case is fit for appeal. In *R v Inskip* [2005] EWCA Crim 3372, the Court of Appeal said that such a certificate should be granted only in truly exceptional circumstances (such as where there was an unresolved point of law or where there were clear reasons for considering that an appeal would be allowed – see *R v Harries* [2007] All ER (D) 224 (Mar)), and that the normal rule is that it is for the Court of Appeal to consider whether a case is suitable for the granting of leave. This rule was established in *R v Bansal* [1999] Crim LR 484.

The usual method of commencing an appeal against conviction is for the defendant to seek leave to appeal from the Court of Appeal direct.

The procedure is as follows:

(a) Within 28 days of his *conviction* (not sentence), the defendant must send to the Registrar of Criminal Appeals a notice of application for leave to appeal together with draft grounds of appeal. The grounds are a separate document prepared by defence counsel, setting out the detailed arguments as to why the conviction is unsafe. The Court will grant the defendant leave to appeal out of time only where substantial injustice would otherwise be done to the defendant (*R v Ramzan and Others* [2006] All ER (D) 318 (July)).

(b) On receipt of these documents, the Registrar will obtain a transcript of the evidence that was given at trial and of the judge's summing up to the jury. The Registrar will then put the case papers before a single judge, who will determine whether leave to appeal ought to be granted. This is a filtering stage, designed to weed out appeals that are frivolous and have no chance of success. If leave to appeal is granted, the single judge will also grant the defendant public funding for the hearing of the appeal (any advice and assistance given to the defendant in connection with the preparation of the notice of application for leave to appeal will be covered by the representation order for the Crown Court proceedings). The single judge may grant the bail to the defendant pending the hearing of the appeal. He also has the power to order a witness to attend for examination at the appeal.

    In appeals that are completely without merit, the single judge may, when dismissing the appeal, make a direction as to loss of time under s 29 of the Criminal Appeals Act 1968. This means that any time spent by the defendant in custody awaiting the outcome of the appeal will not count towards the total time the defendant must serve for his sentence (as would normally be the case). This provision is designed to deter defendants from pursuing appeals that are without merit (see *R v Hart and others* [2006] EWCA Crim 3239).

(c) The hearing of the appeal will then take place before the full Court of Appeal, which will comprise a three-judge panel. The Court will hear oral arguments from the parties, and may also hear fresh evidence (including expert evidence) if that evidence:

    (i) appears to be credible;

    (ii) would have been admissible at the defendant's trial; and

    (iii) there is a reasonable explanation for the failure to adduce this evidence at the defendant's trial (Criminal Appeal Act 1968, s 23).

### 13.3.2.3 Powers of the Court of Appeal

Section 2 of the Criminal Appeal Act 1968 (as amended by the Criminal Appeal Act 1995) permits the Court of Appeal to do any of the following:

(a) quash the conviction and acquit the defendant – if, for example, new evidence has come to light which the Court considers would have led to the defendant's acquittal had such evidence been available at the defendant's trial;

(b) quash the conviction and order that a retrial take place – if, for example, the conviction is unsafe because the judge failed to direct the jury properly when summing up the case;

(c) allow part of the appeal and dismiss other parts of the appeal (if the defendant was appealing against conviction for more than one offence). In such a case the Court will probably then re-sentence the defendant in respect of the offences for which his conviction was upheld;

(d) find the defendant guilty of an alternative offence (in which case the Court will probably re-sentence the defendant); or

(e) dismiss the appeal.

The Court will dismiss the appeal unless it considers that the conviction is unsafe. If the conviction is unsafe, the Court must then decide whether to order a retrial. Section 7 of the Criminal Appeal Act 1968 enables the Court of Appeal to order a retrial where the Court allows an appeal against conviction and where it appears to the Court that 'the interests of justice so require'. If the Court is satisfied that the defendant would have been acquitted at trial (for example, had new evidence presented at the appeal been available at the original trial), the Court will not order a retrial. In other cases, the Court will normally order that a retrial take place unless a retrial would be unfair to the defendant or in some other way inappropriate. A retrial would, for example, be inappropriate where a significant amount of time has elapsed since the original trial, and the recollection of the witnesses is likely to be poor and unreliable (or where it would be impracticable or impossible to secure the attendance of the relevant witnesses).

### 13.3.3 Appeals against sentence

#### 13.3.3.1 Procedure (CrimPR, Part 68)

A defendant may also appeal to the Court of Appeal against the sentence imposed by the Crown Court (Criminal Appeal Act 1968, s 9). The procedure to be followed when an appeal against sentence is made to the Court of Appeal is essentially the same as for an appeal against conviction, with the defendant either requiring a certificate from the sentencing judge that the case is fit for appeal, or the defendant seeking leave from the Court of Appeal to proceed. It is rare for the sentencing judge to grant a certificate, and most defendants will seek leave of the Court of Appeal to proceed. If the defendant seeks leave from the Court of Appeal, a notice of application for leave to appeal together with draft grounds of appeal must be sent to the Registrar of Criminal Appeals within 28 days of *sentence* being passed in the Crown Court. The draft grounds of appeal will state why it is considered that the sentence passed in the Crown Court is either wrong or excessive. Assuming leave to appeal is granted by the single judge (see **13.3.2.2** above), the appeal will then be considered by a two- or three-judge panel. The appeal will usually be confined to legal submissions on what the appropriate sentence (or sentencing range) is in the particular case.

#### 13.3.3.2 When will an appeal be successful?

An appeal against sentence will be successful only if:

(a) the sentence passed by the trial judge is wrong in law (if, for example, the trial judge were to pass a sentence or make an order that he did not have the power to pass or make);

(b) the sentence passed by the trial judge is wrong in principle (if, for example, the trial judge passes a custodial sentence when the offence was not serious enough to merit such a sentence, or if the judge erroneously considered the defendant to be a dangerous offender and sentenced the defendant accordingly (see **11.5.3.2**);

(c) the judge adopted the wrong approach when sentencing. Examples of a judge adopting the wrong approach when sentencing are:

   (i) if the judge increased the sentence because the defendant had pleaded not guilty (since the 'guideline' sentencing cases from the Court of Appeal and any guidelines issued by the SGC start from the assumption that the defendant is convicted following a not guilty plea),

   (ii) if the judge failed to give the defendant an appropriate discount for entering a guilty plea (see **11.4.2.5**), or

   (iii) if the judge should have held a *Newton* hearing before determining the facts of the offence upon which the sentence was to be based (see **12.4** above), or

   (iv) if the judge failed to take into account (or failed to give sufficient credit for) any relevant offence or offender mitigation put forward by the defendant (see **12.7**);

(d) in the case of co-defendants, there is an unjustified disparity in the sentence each defendant receives, particularly where both defendants appear to have been equally culpable (although in *R v Tate* [2006] All ER (D) 07 (Sep), the Court of Appeal held that where a lenient sentence is passed on one co-defendant, this does not in itself mean that the other co-defendant's sentence must be reduced on appeal); or

(e) the sentence passed is manifestly excessive. This is the most common ground of appeal. A Crown Court judge sentencing a defendant will impose a sentence within a range of possible sentences which may be appropriate for the offence. The Court of Appeal will interfere only if the sentencing judge has gone beyond the upper limit of this range. The Court of Appeal will not reduce a sentence simply because it would have imposed a lower sentence within the appropriate range. For most offences, the Court of Appeal will have set out guidelines for appropriate sentences in previous cases before it and, if a judge in the Crown Court imposes a sentence which is within these guidelines, the Court of Appeal is unlikely to alter the sentence. In future, definitive sentencing guidelines will be given by the SGC established under the CJA 2003 (see **11.4.2.2**). Guideline sentences for all types of offence dealt with in the Crown Court can be found in a compendium on the SGC website (www.sentencing-guidelines.gov.uk).

After the defendant has been sentenced, defence counsel will normally provide a written advice on the prospects of a successful appeal against sentence in accordance with the instructions contained in his brief (see **10.7.2**).

#### 13.3.3.3 Powers of the Court of Appeal

The Court of Appeal may confirm a sentence passed by the Crown Court, or quash the sentence and replace it with an alternative sentence or order as it thinks appropriate. The Court of Appeal *cannot*, however, increase the sentence imposed by the judge in the Crown Court (Criminal Appeal Act 1968, s 11(3)). As with appeals against conviction, a loss of time direction may be made if the defendant makes an appeal against sentence that is deemed to be without merit (see **13.3.2.2** above).

A defendant whose case was not publicly funded and whose appeal to the Court of Appeal is successful will have his costs paid from central funds (see **13.2.1.7** above).

## 13.3.4 Prosecution appeals (CrimPR, Parts 66 and 70)

### 13.3.4.1 Termination and evidential rulings

**Introduction**

The CPS has no right of appeal in respect of a defendant who has been acquitted by a jury following a Crown Court trial. Sections 58–63 of the CJA 2003 do, however, give the CPS a right of appeal to the Court of Appeal in respect of rulings made by a trial judge either before or during the trial which:

(a) either effectively terminate the trial ('termination rulings'); or
(b) significantly weaken the prosecution case ('evidential rulings').

**Termination rulings**

Examples of termination rulings include:

(a) a ruling at the end of the prosecution case that the defendant has no case to answer (and that the case should be dismissed); or
(b) a ruling that a vital piece of prosecution evidence is inadmissible, leaving the CPS with no alternative than to offer no evidence against the defendant because it no longer has sufficient evidence to secure a conviction (for example, a ruling by the trial judge that evidence of a confession made by the defendant is inadmissible when this is the *only* evidence against the defendant).

If the CPS wishes to appeal against a termination ruling, it must inform the trial judge that it intends to appeal, or request an adjournment to consider whether to appeal. Leave to appeal must be obtained either from the trial judge, or from the Court of Appeal. Prosecuting counsel must agree with the trial judge that if leave to appeal is refused, or if the appeal is later abandoned, the defendant will be acquitted. If leave to appeal is granted, the appeal may be expedited (in which case the defendant's trial will be adjourned pending the outcome of the appeal) or non-expedited (in which case the jury will be discharged). In either case, the termination ruling and the subsequent acquittal of the defendant are placed 'on hold' until any appeal is heard or abandoned. The Court of Appeal may either uphold the trial judge's ruling and acquit the defendant, or reverse or vary the ruling and order either that the trial should continue or that a new trial should take place.

**Evidential rulings**

Examples of rulings which significantly weaken the prosecution case are:

(a) a confession being ruled inadmissible by the trial judge under ss 76 or 78 of PACE 1984 (see **Chapter 20**);
(b) identification evidence being ruled inadmissible by the trial judge under s 78 of PACE 1984 due to breaches of the Act or the Codes of Practice by the police (see **Chapter 17**); or
(c) the trial judge ruling that the defendant's previous convictions are inadmissible (see **Chapter 22**).

The CPS has a limited right of appeal to the Court of Appeal in respect of evidential rulings made by the trial judge which *significantly* weaken the prosecution case. This right is confined to more serious offences (for example, murder, manslaughter, rape and other serious sexual offences, robbery with a weapon and certain drugs offences). As with appeals against termination rulings, leave to appeal must be obtained either from the trial judge, or from the Court of Appeal. The trial judge must decide whether the appeal should be expedited (in which case the defendant's trial will be adjourned) or non-expedited (in which case the jury will be discharged). The Court of Appeal may confirm, vary or reverse the evidential ruling and, dependent on this, will order either that the defendant be acquitted, or that the trial be resumed or that a fresh trial take place.

### 13.3.4.2 Powers of the Attorney-General

The CPS has a right of appeal to the Court of Appeal if it considers that the Crown Court has passed a sentence which is 'unduly lenient'. Section 36 of Criminal Justice Act 1988 allows the Attorney-General to refer such a case to the Court of Appeal, which in turn has the power to increase the sentence. The Attorney-General may only refer a case to the Court of Appeal if the offence is indictable-only or is a specified either way offence. The list of specified either way offences includes a number of offences under the Misuse of Drugs Act 1971, cruelty to children, threats to kill, racially or religiously motivated assaults/criminal damage/harassment, and various offences under the Sexual Offences Act 2003.

The Attorney-General must obtain leave from the Court of Appeal before proceeding with the appeal. If the appeal is successful, the Court of Appeal will quash the sentence passed in the Crown Court and pass the sentence it considers appropriate. Any sentence imposed by the Court of Appeal must be a sentence that could have been passed in the Crown Court.

### 13.3.4.3 Applications for a retrial

**The rule against double jeopardy**

Prior to the enactment of the CJA 2003, a defendant could never be tried twice for the same offence. Legally this was known as 'autrefois acquit', although it was known more commonly as the rule against 'double jeopardy'.

The rule (traceable back to the Magna Carta) was based on the argument that a defendant was entitled to finality, and the further argument that, if the CPS was given a 'second chance', it might prepare the case less thoroughly and less fairly from the outset.

However, recent advances in technology (in particular DNA testing) mean that new evidence may now come to light that was unavailable at the time of trial, and which may conclusively prove guilt (or innocence). Such advances led to calls for the reform of the rule against double jeopardy. These calls for reform were given added impetus following the Stephen Lawrence case, in which four defendants were acquitted of an allegedly racist murder. After the case, a campaign developed for some of those accused of the murder to be retried after 'better' evidence emerged.

The result of this is the changes to the rule against double jeopardy contained in the CJA 2003.

**The new provisions**

Section 75 of the 2003 Act lists those offences for which a retrial is possible following the acquittal of a defendant. The list includes:

(a) murder and attempted murder;
(b) manslaughter;
(c) kidnapping;
(d) a number of sexual offences under the Sexual Offences Acts of 1956 and 2003, including rape, attempted rape and assault by penetration;
(e) various offences in relation to Class A drugs, such as unlawful importation and production; and
(f) arson endangering life or property.

A retrial may take place even if the defendant was acquitted before the passing of the CJA 2003.

**Procedure**

In order to prosecute a defendant for a second time for the same offence, the CPS must initially apply to the Court of Appeal for an order that:

(a) quashes the acquittal of the defendant; and
(b) provides for the defendant to be retried for that particular offence.

The Director of Public Prosecutions (who is the head of the CPS) must consent to such an application being made to the Court of Appeal. He may give such consent only if it is in the interests of justice for such an application to be made *and* the evidential requirements of s 78 of the Act (see below) are met.

The Court of Appeal must either make the order applied for or dismiss the application, depending on whether the evidential test and the interests of justice test (see below) are met (s 77(1)).

**The evidential test**

The evidential test is set out in s 78 of the CJA 2003. This requires that there be 'new and compelling' evidence of the defendant's guilt. 'New' evidence means evidence not adduced when the defendant was acquitted. To be 'compelling', this evidence must be reliable, substantial and highly probative of the case against the defendant.

**The interests of justice test**

This test is set out in s 79, which provides that the Court of Appeal should have particular (but not exclusive) regard to the following factors:

(a) whether existing circumstances make a fair trial unlikely;
(b) the length of time since the offence was allegedly committed;
(c) whether it is likely that the new evidence would have been adduced in the earlier proceedings, but for the failure of the police or the prosecution to act with due diligence and expedition; and
(d) whether, since the earlier proceedings, the police or prosecutor have failed to act with due diligence or expedition.

**Example**

In *R v Dunlop* [2006] EWCA Crim 1534, the defendant was acquitted of the murder of his lover in 1991. After his acquittal, and whilst in prison for other matters, he confessed to another prison inmate that he had committed the murder. He subsequently wrote letters to other people in which he admitted to the murder. When the reforms made by the CJA 2003 came into force, the CPS applied to the Court of Appeal for the defendant's acquittal on the murder charge to be quashed and for the defendant to be retried for this offence. The defendant argued that it would not be in the interests of justice for the court to quash his acquittal and order a retrial, because his later confession to the murder was made in the belief that he could not and would not be tried again for this crime. The Court of Appeal refused to accept these arguments, stating that the evidence of the confession was both new and compelling, and that it was clearly in the interests of justice for the acquittal to be quashed and a retrial ordered. At his retrial, the defendant entered a guilty plea to the murder charge.

**Additional provisions**

Section 80 of the 2003 Act gives details of the procedural steps required if the CPS wishes to make an application to the Court of Appeal for a defendant to be retried. Section 80 also amends the Criminal Appeal Act 1968, to allow for an appeal to the House of Lords against the decision of the Court of Appeal either to allow or disallow a retrial.

It is important that if a retrial may occur, reporting restrictions are put in place so as not to prejudice it. These are provided for in s 82, which allows the Court of Appeal to order that the proceedings before it must not be reported if such reporting would give rise to a substantial risk of prejudice to the fairness of a retrial. In *Re D (Acquitted Person Retrial)* (2006) *The Times*, 6 March, the Court of Appeal held that where an application was made to quash an acquittal and a new trial was ordered, publicity of the fact that the Court of Appeal had concluded that there was compelling evidence for making such an order might reasonably be regarded as prejudicial to the subsequent trial. In light of this judgment, it is likely that the Court of Appeal will make an order under s 82 in most cases when it is asked to quash a conviction and order a new trial. Orders made under s 82 may cover both the making of an application to quash a conviction and the judgment of the court if the application is successful and a new trial is ordered.

### 13.3.5 The Criminal Cases Review Commission

The Criminal Cases Review Commission was created under the provisions of the Criminal Appeal Act 1995. The purpose of the Commission is to investigate alleged miscarriages of justice and, where appropriate, to refer such cases to the Court of Appeal. The Commission may refer to the Court of Appeal either a conviction following a Crown Court trial, or a sentence imposed following a Crown Court trial (Criminal Appeal Act 1995, s 9). The Commission also has the power to refer to the Crown Court a conviction or sentence imposed in the magistrates' court (Criminal Appeal Act 1995, s 11).

The Commission will refer a case to the Court of Appeal (or the Crown Court) only if the test set out in s 13 of the 1995 Act is satisfied. Section 13 provides that a reference should not be made unless the Commission considers that there is a real possibility that the conviction or sentence would not be upheld were the reference to be made. The Court of Appeal may direct the Commission to carry out investigations in any particular case as the Commission sees fit (Criminal Appeal Act 1995, s 15). Other provisions of the 1995 Act empower the Commission to obtain documentary and other evidence.

## 13.4 Appeals to the House of Lords

Section 33 of the Criminal Appeal Act 1968 allows either the CPS or the defendant to appeal to the House of Lords from a decision made by the Court of Appeal if:

(a) the Court of Appeal certifies that the decision involves a point of law of general public importance; *and*

(b) either the Court of Appeal or the House of Lords gives leave to appeal.

The procedural requirements for appeals to the House of Lords are set out in Part 74 of the Criminal Procedure Rules 2005.

## 13.5 Procedural flowcharts

### 13.5.1 Appeals from the magistrates' court and the Youth Court

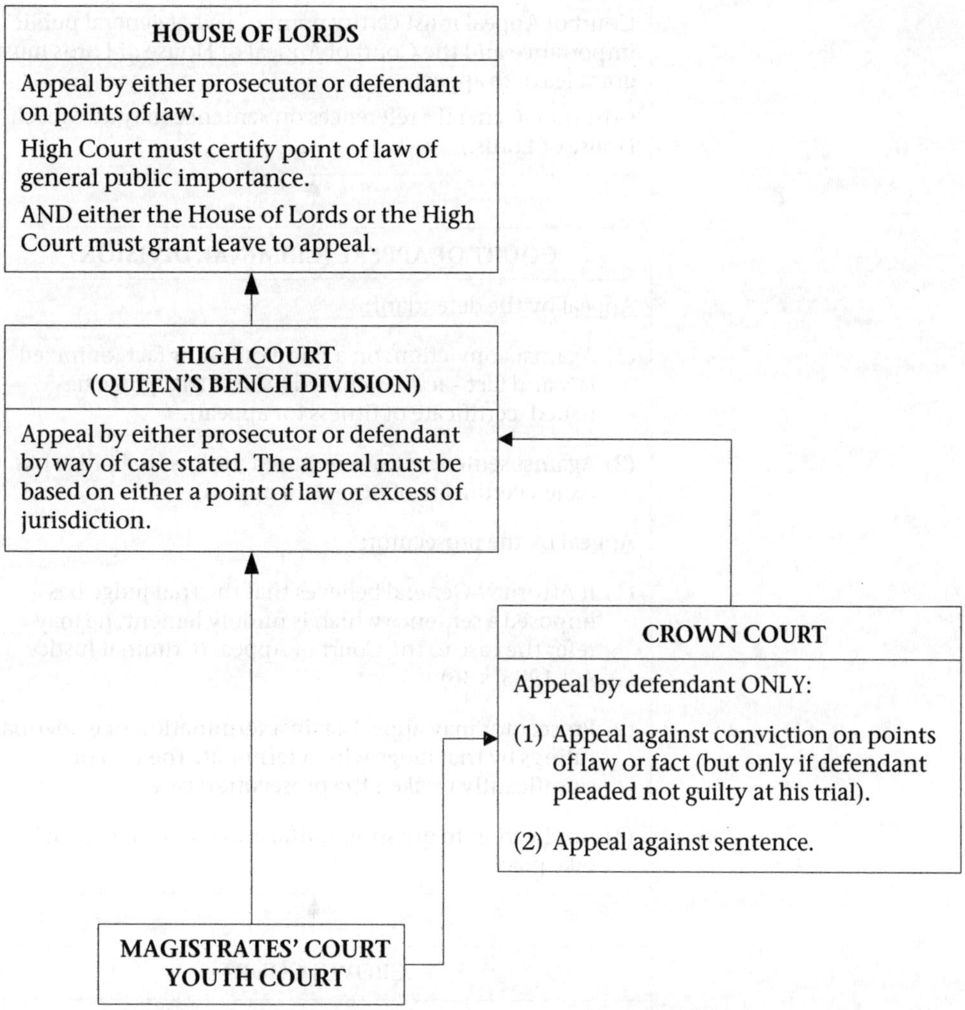

### 13.5.2 Appeals from the Crown Court

**HOUSE OF LORDS**

Appeal by prosecutor or defendant on points of law only.

Court of Appeal must certify point of law of general public importance and the Court of Appeal or House of Lords must grant leave to appeal.

(Attorney-General's references on sentence may also reach House of Lords.)

↑

**COURT OF APPEAL (CRIMINAL DIVISION)**

Appeal by the defendant:

(1) Against conviction: on a point of law or fact, or mixed law and fact – leave required (unless trial judge has issued certificate of fitness for appeal).

(2) Against sentence: leave required (unless trial judge has issued certificate of fitness for appeal).

Appeal by the prosecutor:

(1) If Attorney-General believes that the trial judge has imposed a sentence which is unduly lenient, he may refer the case to the Court of Appeal (Criminal Justice Act 1988, s 36).

(2) Prosecutor may appeal against termination or evidential rulings by trial judge which terminate the trial or significantly weaken the prosecution case.

(3) Application to quash acquittal and order that re-trial take place.

↑

**CROWN COURT**

## 13.6 Checklist

At the end of this chapter you should be able to explain:

- the rights of appeal to the Crown Court the defendant may exercise following conviction or sentence in the magistrates' court;
- the right, exercisable by either the defendant or the CPS, to appeal to the High Court by way of case stated against a decision made by the magistrates' court;
- the use of judicial review proceedings as an alternative to appealing against a decision made by the magistrates' court;
- the rights of appeal to the Court of Appeal the defendant may exercise following conviction or sentence in the Crown Court;
- the rights of appeal to the Court of Appeal the CPS may exercise in respect of a Crown Court matter:
  - — appeals against a termination or evidential ruling made by the trial judge,
  - — the Attorney-General's power to refer unduly lenient sentences to the Court of Appeal,
  - — applications for a conviction to be quashed and a retrial ordered;
- the right, exercisable by either the defendant or the CPS, to appeal to the House of Lords against a ruling on a point of law made by the Court of Appeal.

## Part 4 Summary – Sentencing and Appeals

| *Topic* | *Summary* | *References* |
|---|---|---|
| Purpose of sentencing | The five purposes of sentencing are to:<br>• punish offenders;<br>• reduce crime;<br>• reform and rehabilitate offenders;<br>• protect the public; and<br>• make reparation.<br>A court must always give reasons for the sentence it imposes on a defendant. | CJA 2003, s 142(1)<br><br><br><br><br><br>s 174 |
| Custodial sentences | Unless the offence carries a mandatory custodial sentence, a custodial sentence should be imposed only if the offence is so serious that neither a fine alone nor a community sentence is justified.<br>The length of the sentence should be for the shortest term the court considers commensurate with the seriousness of the offence.<br>Separate provisions exist if the court considers the defendant to be a 'dangerous offender'. | CJA 2003, s 152(2)<br><br>s 153(2)<br><br>ss 225–229 |
| Community sentences | A community sentence should be imposed only if the court considers the offence is serious enough to warrant such a sentence. The court will impose a generic community order by choosing from a menu of 'requirements' and selecting those most appropriate. | CJA 2003, s 148(1) |
| Fines | The court will normally enquire into the defendant's means before imposing a fine. In the magistrates' court, the maximum level of fine will be set by statute. In the Crown Court, there is no limit to the maximum size of fine. | |
| Discharges | A defendant who is given a conditional discharge receives no immediate penalty. He may, however, be re-sentenced for the offence if he re-offends during the period for which he is conditionally discharged (up to three years).<br>A defendant who is given an absolute discharge receives no immediate penalty and may not be re-sentenced should he re-offend. | |

| *Topic* | *Summary* | *References* |
|---|---|---|
| Ancillary orders | The ancillary orders which a court may make in addition to the 'main' sentence imposed on the defendant include:<br>• an order to pay prosecution costs;<br>• a recovery of defence costs order (in the Crown Court);<br>• forfeiture, restitution and confiscation orders;<br>• an anti-social behaviour order;<br>• a binding over order;<br>• entering the defendant's name on the 'sex offenders register';<br>• a sexual offences prevention order;<br>• a drinking banning order. | |
| Sentencing procedure | Unless the offence is very minor, the court will usually adjourn sentence so that it may obtain a pre-sentence report from the Probation Service.<br>The prosecution will begin the sentencing hearing by summarising the case and giving the court details of the defendant's previous convictions. If the defendant has pleaded guilty but disputes the prosecution version of events, a *Newton* hearing will take place to determine the factual basis upon which the defendant will be sentenced.<br>The defendant's solicitor will then give a plea in mitigation on his client's behalf. The plea in mitigation should deal both with the offence itself ('offence mitigation') and with the personal circumstances of the defendant ('offender mitigation'). The defendant's solicitor should identify the 'starting point' sentence the court will have in mind, and then persuade the magistrates to impose a lesser sentence.<br>When deciding on the sentence to be imposed, the court will take into account guidance from the Magistrates' Courts Sentencing Guidelines (in the magistrates' court) or the Sentencing Guidelines Council (in the Crown Court). The defendant will be given credit if he entered a guilty plea to the offence. The extent of such credit depends on at what stage in the case the guilty plea was entered. | |
| Appeals from the magistrates' court | The defendant may appeal as of right to the Crown Court against conviction and/or sentence.<br>The hearing at the Crown Court will take the form of a complete rehearing of the case.<br>Both the prosecution and defence may appeal to the High Court by way of case stated if the magistrates have exceeded their jurisdiction or made a decision that is wrong in law. | Magistrates' Courts Act 1980, s 108(1) |

| *Topic* | *Summary* | *References* |
|---|---|---|
| Appeals from the Crown Court | A defendant may appeal to the Court of Appeal against conviction and/or sentence. | Criminal Appeals Act 1968, s 1(1) and 9 |
| | The defendant will require either leave to appeal from the Court of Appeal, or a certificate from the trial judge that the case is fit for appeal. Appeals against conviction will succeed only if the Court of Appeal decides that the conviction is 'unsafe'. | s 2 |
| | Appeals against sentence will usually succeed only if the sentence passed in the Crown Court was 'manifestly excessive', or if the court imposed a sentence that it had no power to make. | |
| | The prosecution have the following rights of 'appeal': | |
| | • appeals against termination and evidential rulings made during the course of a trial; | CJA 2003, s 58–63 |
| | • the Attorney-General may refer a case to the Court of Appeal if he considers the sentence passed to be 'unduly lenient'; and | CJA 1988, s 36 |
| | • for certain offences, the prosecution may ask the Court of Appeal to quash an acquittal and order a retrial if 'new and compelling' evidence comes to light. | CJA 2003, s 75–82 |

# Part 5

# SPECIFIC TYPES OF PROCEEDINGS

# Chapter 14
# The Youth Court



## 14.1 Introduction

### 14.1.1 Overview

This chapter will examine the procedures which take place in the Youth Court, and how these differ from proceedings in the adult magistrates' court. The chapter will begin by describing which categories of defendant may be dealt with by the Youth Court, and describing the aims of the youth justice system. It will then consider the circumstances in which a defendant who would ordinarily appear in the Youth Court may have his case heard before either the magistrates' court or the Crown Court. The powers of the Youth Court in relation to the granting of bail will be examined, and the chapter will conclude by describing the sentencing powers which the Youth Court may exercise.

### 14.1.2 Which defendants appear before the Youth Court?

The Youth Court is part of the magistrates' court system. A hearing in the Youth Court will therefore take place before either a district judge or a bench of magistrates. The Youth Court deals with cases involving defendants aged between 10 and 17 inclusive. Children aged 10 and over are subject to the criminal law in the same way as adults. There is a conclusive presumption that children under the age of 10 cannot be guilty of committing a criminal offence (known as '*doli incapax*').

Defendants in the Youth Court are sometimes referred to as either 'children' or 'young people'. 'Children' are defendants aged between 10 and 13 inclusive. 'Young people' are defendants aged between 14 and 17 inclusive. This distinction is relevant in terms of the sentencing powers of the court (see **14.9** below).

Collectively defendants in the Youth Court are referred to as youths or 'juveniles'. There is a difference between the term 'juveniles' when applied to defendants in the Youth Court and 'juveniles' at the police station. A 'juvenile' at the police station is a suspect who is, or appears to be, under *17* years of age (see **3.6.1**). A 'juvenile' in the Youth Court is a defendant under *18* years of age.

Some defendants appearing before the Youth Court are classified by the court and the police as 'persistent young offenders' (PYOs). The Home Office categorises a

PYO as a defendant who has been sentenced on three separate occasions for one or more recordable offences (a recordable offence is any offence for which a defendant may receive a custodial sentence). A defendant who is a PYO will have his case expedited so the Youth Court may deal with him as quickly as possible.

### 14.1.3 Differences between the adult magistrates' court and the Youth Court

Procedures in the Youth Court are modified to take account of the age of the defendant. The layout of the courtroom is less formal than the magistrates' court, with all participants in the case sitting at the same level rather than there being a raised dock or bench. The defendant will usually sit on a chair in front of the CPS representative and his own solicitor, and in full view of the magistrates. The use of straightforward language rather than legal terminology is encouraged, and solicitors remain seated when addressing the court. Defendants (and any child witnesses) are usually spoken to and referred to by their first name. Witnesses 'promise' rather than 'swear' to tell the truth, and child witnesses under the age of 14 must give unsworn evidence (as, in fact, is the case in the adult magistrates' court). Emphasis is placed on there being as much communication as possible between the magistrates, the defendant and his parents or guardian.

Magistrates receive special training in youth justice matters before being allowed to sit in the Youth Court. If a case in the Youth Court is heard before a bench of magistrates (rather than a district judge), there must be three magistrates, one of whom must be female and one of whom must be male.

Some of the terminology in the Youth Court also differs from that in the adult magistrates' court. For example, there will be a 'finding of guilt' rather than a conviction, and the court will make an 'order upon a finding of guilt' rather than give a sentence.

Most of the procedural and evidential issues that may arise in the context of a case before the Youth Court are the same as for the case of an adult defendant before the magistrates' court. In particular, the magistrates will issue the same standard directions for the parties to comply with in advance of trial as would be issued were the case being tried before the adult magistrates' court (see **Chapter 8**). The only exception to this will be if the defendant is a PYO (see **14.1.1** above). If the defendant is a PYO, the magistrates will issue revised directions to ensure that an expedited trial takes place. Whether or not standard directions have been issued, a trial in the Youth Court will follow the same procedure as a trial before the adult magistrates' court (see **9.2**).

## 14.2 Aims of the youth justice system

The principal aim of the youth justice system is to prevent offending by children and young persons (Crime and Disorder Act 1998, s 37(1)). All those involved in the youth justice system (including solicitors representing defendants) must have regard to this aim. The Youth Court must also have regard to the welfare of the defendant (Children and Young Persons Act 1933, s 44(1)).

## 14.3 Youth offending teams

Youth offending teams (YOTs) are responsible for co-ordinating the provision of youth justice services in their particular local area. A member of the YOT will attend each sitting of the Youth Court. This is likely to be a member of the Probation Service who has received training in dealing with youth justice matters.

The YOT will assist the Youth Court with the following matters:

(a) investigating and confirming the personal circumstances and previous convictions of defendants;

(b) providing support for defendants who are granted bail;

(c) preparing pre-sentence reports; and

(d) administering any non-custodial sentence imposed by the Youth Court.

## 14.4 Role of parents and guardians

A defendant appearing before the Youth Court who is aged under 16 must be accompanied by his parents or guardian during each stage of the proceedings, unless the court is satisfied that it would be unreasonable to require such attendance (Children and Young Persons Act 1933, s 34A). For defendants aged 16 or 17, the court has a discretion as to whether to make an order requiring the attendance of the defendant's parents or guardian.

Parents or guardians who attend the Youth Court play an active role in the proceedings. The court will want to hear their views (particularly in relation to sentencing) and may direct questions to them.

## 14.5 Reporting restrictions

The only people who are usually allowed to attend a hearing in the Youth Court are:

(a) the magistrates;

(b) court staff (such as the court clerk and usher);

(c) the defendant and his parents or guardian;

(d) the CPS representative;

(e) the defendant's solicitor;

(f) a representative from the YOT;

(g) members of the press.

The press are restricted in what they are permitted to report about a hearing before the Youth Court. They cannot report the name, address or school, or any other details which are likely to lead to the identification of the defendant or any other child or young person (such as a witness) involved in the case.

Section 49 of the Children and Young Persons Act 1933 allows the court to lift these restrictions either to avoid injustice, or, following conviction, if the court is satisfied that it is in the public interest to reveal the defendant's identity. The courts should use this ability to 'name and shame' defendants only when doing so will provide some real benefit to the community, such as making the public aware of the identity of a prolific offender. This power should not be used as an 'extra' punishment imposed on the defendant.

## 14.6 Legal representation

Subject to having regard to s 37(1) of the Crime and Disorder Act 1998 (see **14.2** above), the solicitor representing a defendant in the Youth Court plays the same role as he would were he representing an adult defendant in the magistrates' court (see **6.3** above). Representation orders are applied for in the same manner as in the adult court and will be determined by the court applying the same interests of justice test.

The court must, however, take into account the age of the defendant when deciding whether a representation order should be granted.

## 14.7 Jurisdiction

### 14.7.1 Age

The Youth Court may only deal with defendants aged between 10 and 17 inclusive. Problems may arise when a defendant commits an offence when aged under 18, but reaches 18 before the proceedings in the Youth Court have been concluded.

If a defendant is charged with an offence when aged 17, but turns 18 prior to his *first* appearance in the Youth Court, the court does not have jurisdiction to deal with him and the case must be dealt with in the adult magistrates' court (*R v Uxbridge Youth Court, ex p H* (1998) 162 JP 327). If convicted, the defendant will be subject to the full range of sentencing powers which the magistrates' court may exercise.

If a defendant makes his first appearance in the Youth Court before his 18th birthday, but becomes 18 whilst the case is ongoing, the Youth Court may either remit the case to the adult magistrates' court, or retain the case (Children and Young Persons Act 1963, s 29). If the Youth Court retains the case, it will have the full range of sentencing powers that the adult magistrates' court would have were it dealing with the defendant (see **Chapter 11**).

### 14.7.2 Gravity of the offence

#### 14.7.2.1 Homicide (and certain firearms offences)

There is no plea before venue procedure in the Youth Court and defendants do not have the right to elect trial by jury. The Youth Court has jurisdiction to deal with all offences committed by juvenile offenders other than offences of homicide (such as murder and manslaughter) and some firearms offences. These offences may be dealt with only in the Crown Court (Magistrates' Courts Act 1980, s 24(1B)).

#### 14.7.2.2 Grave Crimes

The Youth Court may accept jurisdiction in a case involving a grave crime, or commit such a case to the Crown Court for trial. 'Grave' crimes are offences for which an offender aged 21 years or over may receive a custodial sentence of 14 years or more (such as robbery or rape), together with a number of specific sexual and firearms offences. Section 91 of the Powers of Criminal Courts (Sentencing) Act 2000 gives the Crown Court power to sentence a defendant aged between 10 and 17 to a period of long-term detention (ie, a sentence in excess of the maximum sentencing the Youth Court has the power to impose – see **14.9** below) if the defendant is convicted of a grave crime.

The Youth Court should commit for trial a case involving a grave crime only if it considers that its maximum sentencing powers (a 24-month detention and training order – see **14.9.2.6** below) will be insufficient in the event that the defendant is convicted, and that a sentence of long-term detention would be more appropriate (Magistrates' Courts Act 1980, s 24(1)(a); see also *R (H, A and O) v Southampton Youth Court* [2004] EWHC 2912 (Admin)).

Example

Vicky (aged 16) is charged with robbery and appears before the Youth Court. She has a previous conviction for the same offence. Vicky intends to plead not guilty to the charge. When they hear the facts of the case, the magistrates consider that, were Vicky to be convicted before them, their sentencing powers would be insufficient and that, were the case before the Crown Court, there is a real possibility that the judge would impose a sentence of long-term detention. The magistrates will commit Vicky to the Crown Court for trial.

#### 14.7.2.3 Dangerous offenders

The provisions set out in **Chapter 11** concerning the sentencing of adult offenders who are classified as 'dangerous' apply equally to juveniles. Sections 226 and 228 of the CJA 2003 permit a Crown Court, in an appropriate case, to impose upon a juvenile a sentence of detention for life, a sentence of detention for public protection or an extended sentence of detention. If the Youth Court considers that a defendant whom it has convicted is a 'dangerous offender', the court must commit the defendant to the Crown Court for sentence (Powers of Criminal Courts (Sentencing) Act 2000, s 3C).

### 14.7.3 Defendants jointly charged with adult offenders

#### 14.7.3.1 Magistrates' court

If a youth aged 17 or under is jointly charged with an adult and the offence is either summary only or an either way offence which is to be tried in the magistrates' court, both defendants will be tried together in the adult magistrates' court. If the youth is convicted, the magistrates may sentence him or remit his case to the Youth Court for sentence. If the juvenile is convicted, the magistrates will normally remit his case to the Youth Court for sentence unless they propose to deal with the matter by way of a fine or a discharge, in which case they will sentence the defendant themselves.

#### 14.7.3.2 Crown Court

If a youth aged 17 or under is jointly charged with an adult and the offence is either indictable-only or an either way offence which is to be tried in the Crown Court, there is a presumption that both defendants will be tried before the Crown Court if it is in the interests of justice (Magistrates' Courts Act 1980, s 24(1)(b)).

If a juvenile jointly charged with an adult is tried in the Crown Court, following conviction the judge may exercise any of the sentencing powers that would be open to the Youth Court had the defendant been convicted before the Youth Court (see **14.9** below).

## 14.8 Bail

### 14.8.1 Powers of the Youth Court

The Youth Court has the power to remand a defendant:

(a) on bail (with or without conditions);

(b) into local authority accommodation; or

(c) in the case of 17-year-olds, into custody.

The provisions of the Bail Act 1976 (see **Chapter 7**) apply to defendants in the Youth Court, although a defendant may be refused bail for his 'own welfare' rather than for his 'own protection' as is the case with adult offenders (Bail Act 1976,

Sch 1, Pt 1, para 3). This power is particularly important in situations when the court has concerns about the defendant's home environment. If a parent or guardian is required to act as a surety for a defendant, the court may require that person to ensure not only that the defendant answers his bail, but also that any other conditions imposed on bail are complied with by the defendant. If the defendant fails to comply with these conditions, the recognisance will become payable (see **7.5.1**).

Paragraphs 2A and 6 of the Bail Act 1976 (whereby a court will normally refuse bail to a defendant charged with an offence that carries a possible sentence of life imprisonment where the defendant is either alleged to have committed the offence whilst on bail for another matter, or has already absconded whilst on bail for the offence – see **7.4.1**) apply only to defendants aged 18 and over. However, when the court is considering whether there are substantial grounds for believing that a defendant aged 17 or under charged with an offence that carries a sentence of life imprisonment would commit further offences if released on bail, the court must give 'particular weight' to the fact that the defendant was on bail for another matter at the time he is alleged to have committed the current offence (Bail Act 1976, Sch 1, Pt 1, para 9AA(2)). Similarly, when the court is considering whether there are substantial grounds for believing that a defendant aged 17 or under charged with an offence that carries a sentence of life imprisonment may fail to surrender to custody if granted bail, 'particular weight' must be given to the fact that the defendant had previously been granted bail earlier in the proceedings and had then failed to surrender to custody (Bail Act 1976, Sch 1, Pt 1, para 9AB(3)).

In deciding whether to grant bail, the Youth Court will normally have before it a report from the YOT providing details of the defendant's antecedents and also his record in relation to previous grants of bail. In addition, the report will inform the court about the defendant's home situation and his attendance record at school, college or work. The YOT report will examine the viability of imposing conditions on any bail which is granted to the defendant and may prepare a 'bail support package' for the court to consider if bail is in issue. If the court is considering refusing bail, the report will comment on the availability of local authority accommodation into which the defendant may be remanded.

### 14.8.2 Refusal of bail

Defendants in the Youth Court will normally be granted bail, with or without conditions. If a defendant is granted conditional bail, electronic monitoring may be used on defendants aged between 12 and 17 inclusive to ensure that the defendant complies with such conditions. If, however, the defendant is aged under 17, electronic monitoring may be used only if:

(a) either (i) the defendant is charged with a violent or sexual offence, or an offence carrying at least 14 years' imprisonment, or (ii) the defendant is charged with an imprisonable offence and he has a recent history of repeatedly committing imprisonable offences while remanded on bail or to local authority accommodation; *and*

(b) a YOT has informed the court of its opinion that the imposition of electronic monitoring is suitable.

#### 14.8.2.1 Defendant aged between 10 and 16

Defendants aged between 10 and 16 who are refused bail will be remanded to the care of the local authority. This means that the defendant should stay in local authority accommodation. Often, however, no local authority accommodation will be available, in which case the defendant will return to live at home (although this will be under the care and supervision of the local authority).

In some circumstances the court may order that the defendant is to be remanded to secure local authority accommodation. For such a remand to be made, the defendant must be aged between 12 and 16 (inclusive), and the criteria set out in s 23(5) of the Children and Young Persons Act 1969 must be met. These criteria are that either:

(a) the defendant is charged with, or has been convicted of, a violent or sexual offence, or an offence punishable in the case of an adult offender with at least 14 years' imprisonment; or

(a) the defendant has a recent history of absconding whilst remanded to local authority accommodation, and is charged with, or has been convicted of, an imprisonable offence alleged or found to have been committed while he was so remanded;

*and*, in either case, the court is of the opinion that imposing a security requirement is the only way to protect the public from serious harm from the defendant, or to stop the defendant from committing imprisonable offences.

Although defendants aged between 12 and 16 may be remanded into secure accommodation, in practice shortages in such accommodation mean that the court is only ever likely to make such an order in respect of 15- or 16-year-olds.

#### 14.8.2.2 Male defendants aged 15 or 16

For defendants who are male and aged 15 or 16, if the court considers that the defendant satisfies the criteria set out in s 23(5) (see **14.8.2.1** above), the court will remand the defendant in custody rather than in secure local authority accommodation. The only restriction on this is that a remand in custody should not be made if there are concerns about the vulnerability of the defendant by reason of either his immaturity or his propensity to self-harm.

#### 14.8.2.3 Defendants aged 17

Defendants aged 17 who are refused bail will be remanded in custody. Such defendants will be remanded either to a remand centre, or to prison.

If bail is refused by the Youth Court, a defendant has the same right of appeal to the Crown Court as an adult offender in the magistrates' court (see **7.8.1** above).

## 14.9 Sentencing

### 14.9.1 Background and procedure

#### 14.9.1.1 Objective of sentencing

Before a defendant ever comes before a Youth Court, it is likely that he will have been through the formal system of reprimands and warnings created by ss 65 and 66 of the Crime and Disorder Act 1998 (see **Chapter 3**). When the Youth Court sentences a defendant, it must balance the seriousness of the offence (and the defendant's previous record) with the welfare requirements of the defendant. The court must at all times have regard to the principal aim of preventing offending.

#### 14.9.1.2 Sentencing procedure

Sentencing in the Youth Court follows a similar procedure to that in the adult magistrates' court (see **12.5.1**). The CPS representative will give the facts of the case to the magistrates (assuming the defendant has pleaded guilty rather than having been convicted following a trial), and the defendant's solicitor will then give a plea in mitigation. The court is also likely to want to hear from the defendant's parents or guardian before deciding the appropriate penalty.

A key document in the sentencing process is the pre-sentence report prepared by the YOT. The Youth Court must obtain this report before sentencing the defendant, unless the defendant has recently been sentenced by the Youth Court for another matter and the court is able to use the pre-sentence report prepared for that earlier matter (CJA 2003, s 156). The court is likely to indicate the type of sentence it has in mind when it orders a report, and the report will address the defendant's suitability for that type of sentence. The court will place great emphasis on the contents of the report when deciding the sentence to impose. The Youth Court may either adjourn the sentencing hearing to enable the YOT to prepare the pre-sentence report, or may ask the member of the YOT who is present in court to prepare a 'stand down' report (see **12.2.1.3**) so that sentencing can take place without the need for the case to be adjourned.

### 14.9.2 Types of sentence available

#### 14.9.2.1 Absolute and conditional discharges

The Youth Court has the power to order an absolute or a conditional discharge for a defendant in the same way as the magistrates' court may for an adult offender (see **11.8** above). If the defendant is convicted of a further offence committed during the period of the conditional discharge – which will be specified by the court when making the order – he may be sentenced for his original offence (in addition to any sentence imposed for the further offence). This period of the conditional discharge may be up to three years.

It is rare for such an order to be made in practice. A defendant coming before the Youth Court is likely to have been through the system of reprimands and final warnings at the police station (see **Chapter 3**), and the court is more likely impose a sentence which will actively help to prevent the defendant from re-offending than to give the defendant an absolute or conditional discharge. A conditional discharge is only likely to be given when the defendant has been convicted following a trial, the defendant has no previous convictions (and has not received any reprimands or final warnings from the police), and the court takes the view that immediate punishment of the defendant is unnecessary. A defendant who satisfies the above conditions but who pleaded guilty will receive a referral order rather than a conditional discharge (see **14.9.2.2** below).

#### 14.9.2.2 Referral orders

Referral orders were introduced by s 16 of the Powers of Criminal Courts (Sentencing) Act 2000. Referral orders can only be made in respect of a defendant who has not previously been convicted or bound over by a court.

A referral order *must* be made for a defendant who pleads guilty to an offence (which carries a possible custodial sentence) and who has never previously been convicted or bound over by a court, unless the court is proposing either to impose a custodial sentence or to make an absolute discharge. Referral orders *cannot* be made unless the defendant pleads guilty to the offence with which he is charged, although if the defendant has entered a mixed plea (ie, guilty to one or more offences but not guilty to others), the court has the power to make a referral order but is not obliged to do so.

If the court makes a referral order, the defendant will be referred to a 'youth offender panel'. The panel will speak with the defendant and his parents or guardian to help prevent any further offending. The referral order will require the defendant to attend meetings with the youth offender panel and specify the length of the youth offender contract (see below). The referral order will be 'spent' when the defendant has successfully complied with the terms of the youth offender contract.

The youth offender panel comprises a member of the YOT and two community volunteers. At the meetings the panel will speak to the defendant and his family with a view to:

(a) stopping any further offending;
(b) helping the defendant right the wrong he did to his victim; and
(c) helping the defendant with any problems he may have.

The panel will agree with the defendant a 'youth offender contract'. This is a programme of behaviour designed to prevent the defendant re-offending, and will last between three and 12 months. The terms of the contract are agreed between the defendant and the panel members, rather than by the Youth Court.

At the same time as making a referral order, the court may make an order for the payment of costs and/or compensation (see **14.9.2.3** below). A referral order may be combined with a parenting order (see **14.9.4** below).

#### 14.9.2.3 Fines, compensation and costs

**Fines**

The level of any fine imposed by a Youth Court must have regard to the seriousness of the offence and the defendant's financial circumstances. The maximum level of fine a Youth Court may impose is determined by the defendant's age. For defendants aged 10 to 13 inclusive, the maximum fine is £250. For defendants aged 14 to 17 inclusive, the maximum fine is £1,000.

If the court imposes a fine on a defendant aged under 16, it must order that the fine be paid by the parents or guardian of the defendant, although if the defendant has a source of income the court will often express its wish that the fine be paid from this. In the case of defendants aged 16 or 17, the court may order that the fine be paid either by the defendant, or by his parents or guardian.

**Compensation**

An order to pay compensation may be made against a defendant as a penalty in itself, or in addition to any other penalty which the court imposes. Such an order may be made by the Youth Court if it considers that the defendant's victim has suffered a loss which deserves to be compensated. For defendants aged under 16, any compensation ordered by the court will be payable by the defendant's parents or guardian. For defendants aged 16 or 17, the court may order that the compensation be paid either by the defendant, or by his parents or guardian.

**Costs**

The court may also order a defendant to make a contribution towards costs incurred by the CPS in bringing the case. This is not subject to any maximum figure. As with fines and compensation, for defendants aged under 16 the parents or guardian of the defendant will be ordered to pay this sum; and for defendants aged 16 or 17 the court may order that such costs be paid either by the defendant, or by his parents or guardian.

#### 14.9.2.4 Reparation orders

Reparation orders were introduced by s 73 of the Powers of Criminal Courts (Sentencing) Act 2000. These orders are based on the concept of 'restorative justice', in which the defendant is required to make reparation to his victim for the damage caused by his crime. Reparation orders are distinct from the community penalties described at **14.9.2.5** below.

Under the terms of the order, the defendant will be required to do some work to make reparation either to his victim, or to the community at large. This may, for example, include such tasks as cleaning off graffiti or tidying up damage caused to the victim's property. The order may require the defendant to do up to 24 hours' work. Before such an order is made, the court must obtain a report from the YOT confirming that the defendant is suitable to do such work, and also detailing the attitude of the victim to the making of such an order. The work required to be done under the reparation order will be supervised by the YOT and must be completed within a period of three months.

#### 14.9.2.5 Community penalties

**Introduction**

The CJA 2003 has made significant changes to the types of community penalty which the Youth Court may impose. The Act differentiates between offenders who are aged 15 and under, and offenders aged 16 or 17.

**Defendants aged 15 and under**

If the Youth Court decides to impose a community sentence on an offender who is aged 15 or under, the sentence will be a 'youth community order' (CJA 2003, s 147). A youth community order will be made up of one or more of the following:

(a) a curfew order;
(b) an exclusion order;
(c) an attendance centre order;
(d) a supervision order;
(e) an action plan order.

Each type of order is described below. A Youth Court should not make a youth community order unless it is of the opinion that the offence (or the combination of the offence and one or more offences associated with it) is serious enough to warrant such a sentence (CJA 2003, s 148(1)). A Youth Court making such an order must be satisfied that the component parts of the order are suitable for the defendant, and that the restrictions on the defendant's liberty imposed by the order are commensurate with the seriousness of the offending (CJA 2003, s 148(3)).

*Curfew orders*

The Youth Court may make such an order by virtue of ss 37 and 38 of the Powers of Criminal Courts (Sentencing) Act 2000. A curfew order may last for a maximum period of three months. The order will require the defendant to be indoors at a specified address between certain hours. The defendant may be electronically monitored to ensure that he complies with the order.

*Exclusion orders*

The Youth Court may make an exclusion order by virtue of s 40A(1) of the Powers of Criminal Courts (Sentencing) Act 2000. An exclusion order will prevent the defendant from entering a place or area as specified in the order. Orders may last for a maximum period of three months. Before making an order, the Youth Court must find out about the defendant's family circumstances and the likely effect of an order on those circumstances. A defendant may be electronically monitored to ensure that he complies with the order.

*Attendance centre orders*

A Youth Court may make such an order under s 60 of the Powers of Criminal Courts (Sentencing) Act 2000. An attendance centre order requires a defendant to attend a centre normally run either by the police, or by the YOT. This will usually take place on alternate Saturdays, when the defendant will be required to attend for up to three hours and take part in a planned series of activities.

The total number of hours a defendant can be ordered to complete is dependent on the defendant's age, although the total number of hours will usually between 12 and 24.

*Supervision orders*

This type of order was created by s 65 of the Powers of Criminal Courts (Sentencing) Act 2000. A supervision order enables the court to place a defendant under the supervision of the YOT for a minimum period of six months and a maximum period of three years. An officer from the YOT will 'advise, assist and befriend' the defendant, with a view to preventing him from re-offending. The court may impose conditions when making a supervision order, such as a requirement that the defendant live at a particular address, attend meetings with his supervisor, participate in certain activities, or make reparation to the victim of his offence.

*Action plan orders*

Action plan orders were created by s 69 of the Powers of Criminal Courts (Sentencing) Act 2000. An action plan order places a defendant under intense supervision for a fixed period of three months. The purpose of the order is to enable the YOT to 'take control' during this period, and ensure that the defendant attends regular meetings with the YOT. The court (or the officer from the YOT who provides the supervision) will also specify certain things the defendant must do during the three-month period, such as attending at an attendance centre, making reparation to the victim, attending school or some other form of training, meeting a drugs counsellor for advice or staying away from a particular location. The court will normally fix another hearing for some time during the course of the three-month period so that it can monitor the defendant's progress.

**Defendants aged 16 and 17**

If the youth court wishes to impose a community sentence on a defendant aged 16 or 17, the court may choose from one or more of the following options:

(a) a community rehabilitation order – this is similar to a supervision requirement for an adult defendant (see **11.6.2**);

(b) a community punishment order – this is similar to an unpaid work requirement for an adult defendant (see **11.6.2**);

(c) a drug treatment and testing order – this is similar to a drug rehabilitation requirement (see **11.6.2**);
(d) a curfew order (see above);
(e) an attendance centre order (see above);
(f) a supervision order (see above); and
(g) an action plan order (see above).

When relevant provisions in the CJA 2003 are brought into force, instead of imposing one of the above orders the court will be able to impose a generic community order (see **11.6**).

#### 14.9.2.6 Detention and training orders

The making of a detention and training order is provided for in ss 100 to 103 of the Power of Criminal Courts (Sentencing) Act 2000. A detention and training order is the only type of custodial sentence that the Youth Court has the power to impose. The Youth Court should not impose a detention and training order unless it is of the opinion that the offence (or the combination of the offence and one or more offences associated with it) is so serious that neither a fine alone nor a community sentence can be justified for the offence (CJA 2003, s 152(2)).

Detention and training orders cannot be imposed on defendants aged 10 or 11. If a defendant is aged between 12 and 14 inclusive, an order may only be made if the court considers that the defendant is a 'persistent young offender' (see **14.1.2** above). For defendants aged 15 or over, there is no restriction on the making of such an order, save that the threshold set out in s 152 above must be met.

An order may be imposed for fixed periods of 4, 6, 8, 10, 12, 18 or 24 months. The length of the order must be for the shortest period of time the court considers commensurate with the seriousness of the offence, or the offence and one or more offences associated with it (CJA 2003, s 153(2)). A detention and training order may be imposed only if the court has received from the YOT a pre-sentence report that specifically addresses custody as a possible sentencing option.

When the court makes such an order, the defendant will be held in detention in a young offenders' institution for one half of the period of the order. He will then be released into the community under the supervision of the YOT for the second half of the order. The degree of supervision is decided upon by the YOT (not the court), but is likely to include electronic monitoring and intensive supervision.

**Example**

Kevin appears before the Youth Court and is convicted of the burglary of domestic premises. The magistrates impose a detention and training order for a period of 12 months. Kevin will spend the first six months in detention at a young offenders institution. He will spend the second six months in the community under the supervision of the YOT.

Detention and training orders have become particularly common in recent years as a way of dealing with juveniles who commit street robberies to get mobile phones, or juveniles who commit other robberies against fellow school pupils.

### 14.9.3 Anti-social behaviour orders

A Youth Court can make an anti-social behaviour order (ASBO) where:

(a) a defendant has committed an offence;

(b) the court considers that the defendant has acted in a manner that was likely to cause harassment, alarm or distress to one or more people not in the same household as the defendant; and

(c) the court considers that such an order is necessary to protect persons from further anti-social acts committed by the defendant (see **11.3.2.7**).

The order will impose prohibitions on the defendant, such as a prohibition against entering a particular area or place, or not to engage in a particular type of behaviour. The order may last for a minimum of two years and a maximum of five years. If the defendant breaches the order, this will constitute a separate offence for which the defendant may be prosecuted.

A Youth Court that makes an ASBO may also make an individual support order (ISO). The idea behind such an order is that, at the same time as imposing restrictions on the defendant, the defendant is also given support by requiring him to participate in specified activities or follow directions given by a member of the YOT.

### 14.9.4 Parenting orders

Under ss 8 to 10 of the Crime and Disorder Act 1998, a Youth Court may make a parenting order when a defendant has been convicted of an offence. A parenting order can be imposed on the parents or guardian of a defendant. Such an order is mandatory where the defendant is aged under 16 and the court considers that such an order is necessary to prevent the defendant from re-offending. The order is discretionary when the defendant is 16 or over.

The order will require the defendant's parents or guardian to comply with any requirements that are specified in the order and to attend counselling or guidance sessions. The objective is to make parents accept responsibility for their children's offending and to prevent further offending.

The order may be imposed for a maximum period of 12 months, although the requirement to attend counselling or guidance sessions may last for a maximum period of three months only.

The Youth Court also has power to make an order binding over the parent or guardian of a defendant who is aged below 16, if the court is satisfied that to make such an order would be desirable in the interests of preventing the defendant committing further offences. The parent or guardian may be bound over in a sum not exceeding £1,000 to take proper care of the defendant and exercise proper control over him.

### 14.9.5 Sex offenders

The notification requirements imposed by the Sexual Offences Act 2003 apply to defendants convicted of a specified sexual offence before the Youth Court in just the same way as they do to defendants convicted of such an offence in the adult magistrates' court or Crown Court (see **11.3.2.9**).

## 14.10 Appeals

As the Youth Court is a type of magistrates' court, a defendant convicted or sentenced by the Youth Court has the same rights of appeal as a defendant who is convicted or sentenced by the adult magistrates' court (see **Chapter 13**).

## 14.11 Flowchart – the sentencing ladder in the Youth Court

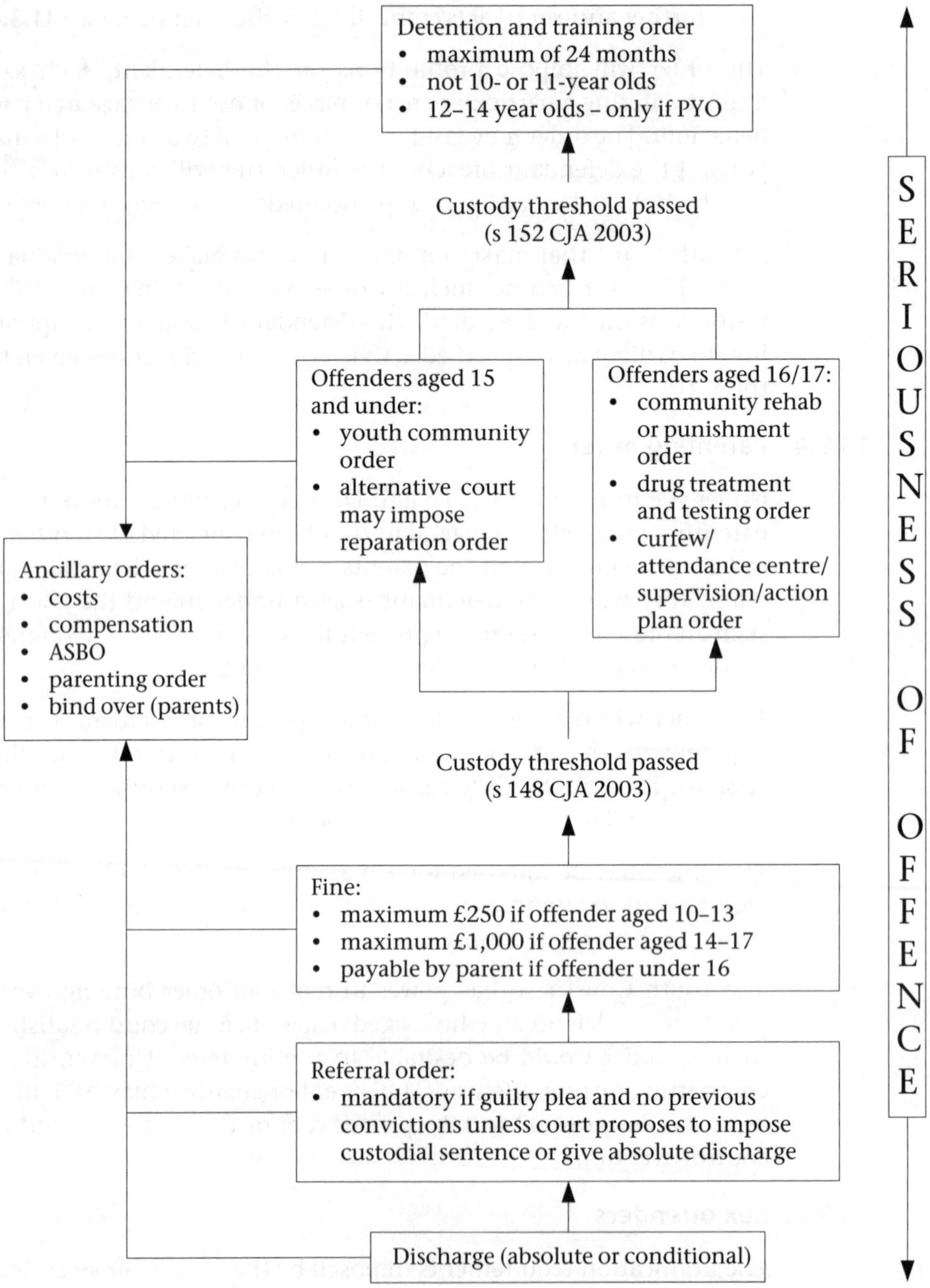

## 14.12 Checklist

At the end of this chapter you should be able to explain:

- the aims of the youth justice system;
- the role played by YOTs and the parents of defendants in the youth justice system;
- the differences between proceedings in the Youth Court and proceedings in the adult magistrates' court;
- the extent of the jurisdiction of the Youth Court and the circumstances in which a case involving a juvenile may be dealt with in the adult magistrates' court or the Crown Court;
- the powers of the Youth Court in relation to bail;
- the sentencing procedure in the Youth Court and the significance of the pre-sentence report prepared by the YOT;
- the types of sentence which the Youth Court may impose and the purpose behind such sentences.

# Chapter 15
# Road Traffic Offences



## 15.1 Introduction

This chapter will begin by listing the most common road traffic offences. It will then go on to consider what is meant by the 'endorsement' of a driving licence, to explain how the penalty points system works, and to look at when a defendant may be disqualified from driving. The chapter will conclude by examining the meaning of the terms 'mitigating factors', 'mitigating circumstances' and 'special reasons', and looking at the situations when these may be raised by a defendant.

For a more in-depth analysis of road traffic offences, the standard work of reference is *Wilkinson's Road Traffic Offences*. This two-volume publication is normally published every second year. It is accepted by the courts as an authoritative source of the law in road traffic matters, and should be consulted in all but the most straightforward of cases. The current, 22nd edition was published in 2005.

## 15.2 Specific offences

Prosecutions for road traffic offences will follow the same procedure at court as for any other type of offence. Road traffic offences may be summary only (eg, careless driving), either way (eg, dangerous driving) or indictable only (eg, causing death by dangerous driving). What sets road traffic offences apart from other offences is that, in addition to any other penalty which the offence may carry, most traffic offences will carry the following additional penalties:

(a) details of the conviction will be endorsed on the defendant's driving licence (see **15.3** below);

(b) the defendant may be subject to an obligatory or a discretionary disqualification from driving (see **15.5** below); and

(c) if the defendant is not disqualified from driving for the offence itself, a number of penalty points will be endorsed on the defendant's driving licence (see **15.4** below).

The table set out below gives examples of some of the most common 'endorsable' road traffic offences, the number of penalty points each offence carries, and whether, following conviction, disqualification for the offence is obligatory or discretionary. (Offences for which disqualification from driving is obligatory still carry penalty points. This is because, if the defendant is able to avoid obligatory disqualification by successfully arguing that 'special reasons' exist (see **15.6.3** below), the court may still impose penalty points.)

| *Offence* | *Number of penalty points* | *Disqualification* |
|---|---|---|
| Manslaughter by driver of a motor vehicle | 3–11 | Obligatory |
| *1988 Act* | | |
| Causing death by dangerous driving | 3–11 | Obligatory |
| Dangerous driving | 3–11 | Obligatory |
| Careless or inconsiderate driving | 3–9 | Discretionary |
| Causing death by careless driving when under influence of drink or drugs | 3–11 | Obligatory |
| Causing death by careless or inconsiderate driving | 3–11 | Obligatory |
| Causing death by driving when the driver was unlicensed, disqualified or uninsured | 3–11 | Obligatory |
| Driving or attempting to drive when unfit through drink or drugs | 3–11 | Obligatory |
| Being in charge when unfit through drink or drugs | 10 | Discretionary |
| Driving or attempting to drive with excess alcohol | 3–11 | Obligatory |
| In charge with excess alcohol | 10 | Discretionary |
| Failing or refusing to provide breath for preliminary test | 4 | Discretionary |
| Using vehicle in dangerous condition | 3 | Discretionary |
| Breach of requirements as to control of vehicle (including use of hand-held mobile telephone) | 3 | Discretionary |
| Breach of requirement as to brakes, steering gear or tyres | 3 | Discretionary |
| Driving otherwise than in accordance with a licence | 3–6 | Discretionary |
| Driving after refusal or revocation of licence | 3–6 | Discretionary |
| Driving while disqualified by court order | 6 | Discretionary |
| Using motor vehicle whilst uninsured | 6–8 | Discretionary |
| Failing to stop after accident | 5–10 | Discretionary |
| Failing to give particulars or report accident | 5–10 | Discretionary |
| *Theft Act 1968* | | |
| Stealing or attempting to steal a motor vehicle | | Discretionary |
| Taking or attempting to take etc, a motor vehicle without authority | | Discretionary |
| Aggravated vehicle-taking | 3–11 | Obligatory |
| Going equipped for stealing or for taking motor vehicles | | Discretionary |
| *RTR Act 1984* | | |
| Speeding offences | 3–6 or 3 (fixed penalty) | Discretionary |


*Wilkinson's Road Traffic Offences*, 22nd edn, 2005

For serious road traffic offences (such as dangerous driving), the court may impose a community penalty or custody in just the same way as for a non-road traffic offence. Similarly for minor road traffic offences (such as careless driving), the court may impose a fine. These penalties will be in addition to any order disqualifying the defendant from driving or imposing penalty points. The **Appendix** contains extracts from the Magistrates' Court Sentencing Guidelines for the most common road traffic offences dealt with in the magistrates' court.

## 15.3 Endorsement

Most road traffic offences are said to be 'endorsable'. This will result in two things if the defendant is convicted:

(a) details of the offence will be endorsed on the defendant's driving licence and the details sent to the Driver and Vehicle Licensing Authority (DVLA) in Swansea; and

(b) unless the defendant is disqualified from driving for the offence, a number of penalty points will also be endorsed on his licence (see **15.4** below).

Part 55 of the Criminal Procedure Rules provides that the following information must be recorded on a licence which is endorsed:

(a) the name of the magistrates' court which dealt with the offence;

(b) the date on which the offence was committed and details of the type of offence committed (this is recorded by means of a code; for example, CD is the code for careless driving and DR10 is the code for driving whilst over the prescribed alcohol limit);

(c) the date of conviction and the date of sentence (if different); and

(d) the penalty imposed, including the number of penalty points.

What happens in practice is that the defendant will surrender his licence to the court, which will then send this to the DVLA. The DVLA will enter the appropriate endorsement on the licence and then return this to the defendant. The DVLA will also retain details of the endorsement on its database, so that if in any subsequent proceedings there is a dispute about any endorsements on a licence, the court will be able to obtain a print out from the DVLA. Under provisions contained in s 8 of the Road Safety Act 2006, in future the Secretary of State will hold a 'driving' record for all road traffic offenders. This driving record will record all the endorsements an offender has received, and may be accessed by the courts and the police.

Endorsable offences may be divided into two separate categories: (i) offences where the court is obliged to disqualify the defendant (unless the defendant can establish the existence of 'special reasons – see **15.6.3** below); and (ii) offences where the court has a discretion as to whether to disqualify the defendant. Examples of the former type of offence are dangerous driving and driving whilst over the prescribed alcohol limit. Examples of the latter type of offence are careless driving and speeding.

## 15.4 Penalty points

### 15.4.1 How many points will the court impose?

The court will impose penalty points only if it does not disqualify the defendant from driving for the offence for which he has been convicted. A defendant *cannot* both be disqualified from driving and receive penalty points in respect of the same offence (see below).

The number of points to be endorsed is fixed in respect of some offences and variable in respect of others. Where the number of points is variable, the court will decide on the number of points to be imposed by reference to the seriousness of the offence. For example, a defendant convicted of careless driving may receive between 3 and 9 points. The actual number of points the court imposes will depend on the facts of the case and the view the court takes as to the seriousness of the offence.

If a defendant commits more than one endorsable offence on the same occasion, the number of penalty points he receives will usually be the number of points imposed for the offence that incurs the highest number of penalty points, although details of each offence will still be endorsed on the licence.

#### Example

John is convicted on the same occasion of careless driving (for which the court may impose 3 to 9 points – see above) and using a vehicle with defective tyres (which carries 3 points). The magistrates decide that 6 points are appropriate for the offence of careless driving. This is the total number of points that will be imposed (although details of *both* offences will be endorsed on John's licence).

The court does have the power to impose points for both offences if it thinks it fit to do so (Road Traffic Offenders Act 1988, s 28(4)). It is very rare for the court to exercise this power. In the above example, if there was evidence that John had been using his vehicle with defective tyres for some time, the court could in principle impose a further 3 points for this offence, making an overall total of 9 points.

If a defendant is convicted of an offence that carries penalty points, the court must endorse the defendant's licence with the appropriate number of penalty points unless either the court can find 'special reasons' for not doing so (see **15.6.3** below), or the court is proposing to disqualify the defendant for the offence itself.

If a court decides to disqualify a defendant for the offence itself, the defendant's licence will still be endorsed with the details of that offence but no penalty points will be endorsed on the licence.

#### Example

Michael is convicted of careless driving. The court may disqualify Michael from driving for this offence. If Michael is disqualified for this offence, his licence will be endorsed with details of the conviction but he will not receive any penalty points. If Michael is not disqualified for this offence, the court will impose between 3 and 9 penalty points on Michael's licence.

Under changes made by the Road Safety Act 2006, s 34, for certain specified offences (including speeding and careless and inconsiderate driving), where the court proposes to deal with the offence by way of penalty points rather than a disqualification, the court may offer the defendant the opportunity to take part in a driver rehabilitation course. The court may do this only if, after taking into account the number of points the court proposes to award for the current offence, the defendant will have between 7 and 11 points (inclusive) on his licence. If the defendant successfully completes the course, the court may order that 3 of the points imposed for the offence shall not be taken into account by a later court if, after 12 months have elapsed, the defendant is convicted of a further offence for which penalty points are imposed (and which may result in the defendant being disqualified from driving under the penalty points scheme).

### 15.4.2 When will a defendant be disqualified under the points system?

A defendant will be disqualified under the penalty points system if he collects 12 or more 'relevant points' on his licence (Road Traffic Offenders Act 1988, s 35). Relevant points are any penalty points imposed for any offences that are *committed* within a period of three years. This is often referred to as the 'totting up system'. When the number of points on a defendant's licence is being calculated, the court will start with the date the current offence was committed and then work back three years, adding together the points imposed for the current offence and any other offences committed within this three-year period (see **Example 1** below).

When adding up the number of points, the court will not need to go back the full three years if the defendant has an earlier penalty points disqualification during this period. The effect of such a disqualification is to 'wipe the slate clean' of any earlier penalty points, including any points awarded for the offence following which the defendant was disqualified under the penalty points scheme (see **Example 2** below).

If, however, a defendant is disqualified other than under the penalty points system during the three-year period prior to the commission of the current offence (ie, a disqualification for an offence carrying obligatory or discretionary disqualification), any penalty points already on the defendant's licence that were imposed prior to this disqualification will *not* be cleared away as a result of the disqualification (see **Example 3** below).

#### Example 1

Raj has convictions for offences committed on the following dates:

| | |
|---|---|
| 14 May 2005 | careless driving – licence endorsed with 7 points |
| 23 October 2006 | speeding – licence endorsed with 3 points |
| 11 January 2007 | defective tyres – licence endorsed with 3 points |

After conviction for the offence committed on 11 January 2007, Raj will be liable to disqualification under the penalty points system because he will have 12 or more points on his licence in respect of offences committed within a three-year period.

#### Example 2

Jane has convictions for offences committed on the following dates:

| | |
|---|---|
| 20 June 2004 | failing to stop – licence endorsed with 6 points |
| 12 February 2005 | careless driving – licence endorsed with 8 points (disqualified under the penalty points system for 6 months) |
| 3 March 2006 | defective brakes – licence endorsed with 3 points |
| 31 July 2006 | speeding – licence endorsed with 4 points |
| 2 February 2007 | careless driving – licence endorsed with 4 points |

Following the offence committed on 12 February 2005, Jane was disqualified under the points system for having 12 points or more on her licence in respect of offences committed within a three-year period. This disqualification 'wipes the slate clean', so that the points imposed for the offences on 20 June 2004 and 12 February 2005 will not be taken into account again. Therefore, following the offence committed on 2 February 2007 Jane will have only 11 points on her licence and so will not be liable to disqualification under the penalty points system.

Example 3

Seema has convictions for offences committed on the following dates:

| | |
|---|---|
| 11 November 2004 | speeding – licence endorsed with 6 points |
| 9 April 2005 | drink driving – disqualified from driving for 12 months (obligatory) |
| 13 August 2006 | careless driving – 5 points |
| 1 March 2007 | defective tyres – 3 points |

Following the conviction for the offence committed on 1 March 2007, Seema will be liable to disqualification under the penalty points system because she will have 12 points or more on her licence in respect of offences committed within a three-year period. The disqualification for drink driving on 9 April 2005 does not wipe the slate clean of the 6 points imposed for the speeding offence on 11 November 2004 because this was *not* a disqualification under the penalty points system.

### 15.4.3 How long is the period of disqualification?

If a defendant is disqualified under the penalty points system, the minimum period of disqualification is six months, unless the court finds there to be 'mitigating circumstances' either for not imposing a disqualification under the penalty points system, or for disqualifying the defendant for less than six months (see **15.6.2** below)

This minimum period is increased to one year for a defendant who has previously been disqualified for 56 days or more during the three-year period prior to the commission of the most recent offence in respect of which penalty points have been taken into account. If a defendant has more than one disqualification for 56 days or more within this three-year period, the minimum period is increased to two years.

When the minimum period is increased because of a previous disqualification of 56 days or more, the previous disqualification does not need to be under the penalty points scheme. It also includes offences where disqualification was obligatory, or where the magistrates exercised their discretion to disqualify the defendant. Thus in Example 3 at **15.4.2** above, Seema will receive a minimum disqualification of 12 months because she has one previous disqualification of 56 days or more in the three years prior to the commission of the most recent offence for which she received penalty points.

### 15.4.4 Newly-qualified drivers

The penalty points system operates differently for newly-qualified drivers, who must undergo a probationary period for two years after passing the driving test. If a newly-qualified driver receives 6 or more penalty points within this two-year period, his full driving licence will be revoked automatically and he will be required to pass a further driving test. However, he will not be disqualified from driving until he passes such a test; rather, he will revert to the status of a driver who has only a provisional licence (for which he will need to apply) and so, for example, he will not be allowed to drive unaccompanied or without displaying 'L' plates.

## 15.5 Disqualification from driving

### 15.5.1 Obligatory disqualification

A court has an obligation to disqualify a defendant in the following situations:

(a) A court must disqualify a defendant for at least 12 months if the defendant is convicted of an offence carrying obligatory disqualification (such as driving whilst over the prescribed alcohol limit or dangerous driving). The only exception to this is if the court finds that there are 'special reasons' for not disqualifying the defendant (see **15.6.3** below).

(b) The minimum period of disqualification in (a) is increased to two years if:
   (i) the defendant is convicted of causing death by dangerous driving, or causing death by careless driving whilst under the influence of drink or drugs; or
   (ii) in the three years prior to the current offence, the defendant has received more than one disqualification for a fixed period of at least 56 days.

(c) The minimum period of disqualification in (a) is increased to three years if the defendant is convicted of any offence involving 'drink driving' or driving whilst unfit through drugs, and the defendant has a conviction within the 10 years preceding the current offence for any similar type of offence.

(d) A court must disqualify a defendant for at least six months under the penalty points scheme when that defendant acquires 12 or more relevant points on his licence (see **15.4.3** above). The only exception to this is if the court finds that there are 'mitigating circumstances' for not disqualifying the defendant (see **15.6.2** below). If a defendant is disqualified under the penalty points scheme, the court *may* require him to undergo an extended driving test at the end of his period of disqualification before his licence is returned.

(e) A court must disqualify a defendant until he passes an extended driving test if the defendant is convicted of motor-related manslaughter, causing death by dangerous driving, dangerous driving or causing death by careless driving when under the influence of drink or drugs. The defendant will only be able to take such a test once the period of disqualification imposed for the offence has expired. For any other offence which carries an obligatory disqualification, the court *may* require the defendant to take an extended driving test at the end of his period of disqualification before his licence is returned.

Obligatory disqualification is merely part of the overall sentence the court may impose on a defendant, and in a serious case (such as dangerous driving) the court may impose a custodial or community penalty. If the court is considering such a sentence it will normally adjourn the case so that a pre-sentence report may be prepared by the Probation Service (see **12.2** above). In such circumstances the court has the power to impose an interim period of disqualification on the defendant until sentence is passed (Road Traffic Offenders Act 1988, s 26). It is important that a solicitor advises his client if an interim disqualification is likely, so that the client does not drive to court. The client should also be advised to have his driving licence with him at court if an interim disqualification is likely, as the licence will need to be handed in to the court.

The magistrates may also impose an interim disqualification if they commit the defendant to the Crown Court to be sentenced following a guilty plea because they consider their sentencing powers to be insufficient (see **6.9**).

## 15.5.2 'Drink drive' cases

### 15.5.2.1 Drink-Drive Rehabilitation Scheme

A defendant convicted of an offence involving 'drink driving' can obtain a reduction in the length of his disqualification by agreeing to take part in the 'Drink-Drive Rehabilitation Scheme'. A court sentencing such a defendant will usually offer the defendant the opportunity to attend a rehabilitation course, the purpose of which is to reduce the risk of further offending. The defendant will be required to pay to attend such a course. Following satisfactory completion of the course, the reduction in the length of the period of disqualification will be at least three months but not more than one-quarter of the period originally imposed (Road Traffic Offenders Act 1988, ss 34A–34C). For example, a defendant who receives a 12-month disqualification for driving whilst over the prescribed alcohol limit, would have this reduced to nine months upon successful completion of the course.

### 15.5.2.2 Alcohol ignition locks

Under changes made by s 15 of the Road Safety Act 2006, an experimental programme for the use of alcohol ignition locks has been introduced. This programme may be offered to a defendant who is convicted of a second drink driving offence within a period of two years and who is to be disqualified for no less than two years. Under the programme, the overall period of disqualification will be reduced if the offender complies with the conditions of the programme. The programme will last for at least at least 12 months, but must not exceed one-half of the original unreduced disqualification period. The conditions will include an element of education and counselling (in a similar way to the existing rehabilitation course), but the key feature of the programme is that, at the end of the reduced period of disqualification, the defendant agrees to drive only a vehicle fitted with an alcohol interlock device, which is designed to prevent the vehicle being driven until a specimen of breath has been given in which the proportion of alcohol does not exceed a specified amount. A driver who fails to comply with these conditions will have his full original disqualification period restored.

### 15.5.2.3 'High risk offenders'

Section 13 of the Road Safety Act 2006 provides that if a driver convicted of a drink drive offence is categorised as being a 'high risk offender', he will not be able to apply for the return of his licence at the end of the period of his disqualification until he has undergone a medical examination certifying that he is medically fit to drive. High risk offenders will be:

(a) offenders disqualified from driving whilst two and a half times (or more) over the prescribed limit;

(b) offenders disqualified on two or more occasions within 10 years for either exceeding the legal limit of alcohol in their breath, blood, or urine, or being unfit to drive through drink; and

(c) offenders disqualified for failure (without reasonable excuse) to provide a specimen for analysis.

## 15.5.3 Discretionary disqualification

A court has a discretion to disqualify a defendant in the following situations:

(a) A defendant convicted of an endorsable offence (such as careless driving or speeding) may be disqualified for that offence itself. There is no minimum or maximum period of disqualification, although in practice such disqualifications are generally between two weeks and six months. The only exception to this is if, as a result of committing the offence, the defendant is liable to disqualification under the penalty points system (because he has accumulated 12 or more relevant points on his licence). In such a case, any disqualification imposed on the defendant will be under the points system, and will be for a minimum period of six months (see **15.4** above).

(b) A defendant convicted of an endorsable offence may be disqualified until he passes a driving test.

(c) A defendant convicted of stealing or attempting to steal a motor vehicle, TWOC, or going equipped for stealing or taking motor vehicles may be disqualified.

(d) A defendant convicted of any form of assault may be disqualified if the assault was committed using a motor vehicle (Powers of Criminal Courts (Sentencing) Act 2000, s 147(1)).

(e) A Crown Court may disqualify a defendant where a motor vehicle has been used in the commission of any indictable offence for which the defendant could receive a custodial sentence of two years or more (Powers of Criminal Courts (Sentencing) Act 2000, s 147(2)). The Crown Court may exercise this power either where the defendant is convicted following a trial in the Crown Court, or where the defendant is committed to the Crown Court for sentence having entered a guilty plea in the magistrates' court.

In addition to the above, s 146 of the Powers of Criminal Courts (Sentencing) Act 2000 provides courts with a general power to disqualify a defendant from driving for such period as the court thinks fit in respect of any offence (whatever the nature of the offence) either in addition to or, in certain cases, instead of dealing with the defendant via an alternative type of sentence. Although this power appears remarkably wide, it is normally interpreted by the courts as giving them an additional power to disqualify a defendant who has not committed a driving-related offence and who has not used a vehicle in the commission of an offence. A court that chooses to disqualify a defendant convicted of a driving-related offence will use the other statutory powers at its disposal to impose the disqualification rather than the power under s 146.

### 15.5.4 Removal of disqualification

Section 42 of the Road Traffic Offenders Act 1988 gives the court power to make an order removing a disqualification, subject to the defendant having served part of the period of disqualification originally imposed. Applications under s 42 are normally made by defendants given a lengthy period of disqualification, who wish to show the court that they have reformed. The earliest date on which a defendant is permitted to make an application under s 42 is as follows:

(a) if the disqualification was for less than four years, *two years* after the disqualification was imposed;

(b) if the disqualification was for less than 10 years but not less than four years, after *one-half of the period of disqualification*;

(c) if the disqualification was for 10 years or more, *five years* after the disqualification was imposed (Road Traffic Offenders Act 1988, s 42(3)).

When the court is considering an application to remove a disqualification, it may have regard to the following factors:

(a) the character of the person disqualified and his conduct subsequent to the order;

(b) the nature of the offence;

(c) any other circumstances of the case (Road Traffic Offenders Act 1988, s 42(2)).

The court may either remove the disqualification from whichever date it sees fit, or refuse the application. Even if the applicant persuades the court to remove the disqualification, the court is likely to order him to pay the costs of the application. The court is only likely to exercise its powers under s 42 if the applicant has taken steps to reform (for example, by successfully completing a rehabilitation course – see **15.5.2** above) and there is a pressing need for him to be able to drive (for example, the nature of his employment requires him to be able to drive).

## 15.6 Mitigation

### 15.6.1 Mitigating factors

#### 15.6.1.1 Introduction

Unless the defendant is seeking to avoid either a mandatory disqualification from driving under the penalty points scheme (see **15.6.2** below), or an obligatory disqualification from driving or the obligatory endorsement of his licence with penalty points (see **15.6.3** below), the defendant's solicitor will give the normal plea in mitigation before the defendant is sentenced, just as he would for any other type of offence. In delivering such a plea, the defendant's solicitor may raise any mitigating factors which he considers relevant to his client's case.

Thus:

(a) if a defendant is convicted of an offence for which the court has a discretion to disqualify him (such as careless driving), mitigating factors may be raised to persuade the court:

(i) not to disqualify him, and

(ii) if the court decides not to disqualify him, to impose the lowest number of points the court feels able for the offence (where the court has a discretion as to the number of points that may be imposed), or

(iii) if the court decides to disqualify him, to reduce the period of disqualification to the shortest period of time the court feels able to impose, and

(iv) whether or not the defendant is disqualified, to limit the level of any other penalty that is imposed (such as a fine or an order to pay prosecution costs);

(b) if the defendant is convicted of an offence which carries obligatory disqualification (such as driving whilst over the prescribed alcohol limit), mitigating factors may be raised to persuade the court to limit the period of disqualification to the shortest period of time the court feels able to impose and to limit the level of any financial penalty;

(c) for serious offences (such as dangerous driving), where the court will be considering a custodial sentence in addition to disqualifying the defendant from driving, mitigating factors may be raised to persuade the court to deal with the matter other than by way of imprisonment. For example, a community sentence or a fine may be suggested as an alternative to custody.

#### 15.6.1.2 Examples of mitigating factors

Mitigating factors can relate to the circumstances of the offence itself, or to the personal circumstances of the defendant.

Some of the most common points that may be raised by way of 'offence mitigation' (particularly for offences such as careless driving when the defendant is seeking to avoid a discretionary disqualification, or to limit the number of penalty points to be imposed) are:

(a) the defendant's speed was not excessive;
(b) there was not much traffic on the road;
(c) the defendant was guilty only of a momentary lapse in concentration;
(d) only minor damage or injury was caused; and
(e) the defendant entered a timely guilty plea.

Examples of points commonly raised as 'offender mitigation' include:

(a) the defendant's age and the number of years he has been driving;
(b) the defendant having a 'clean' driving licence;
(c) the defendant's job requiring him to have a driving licence; and
(d) the fact that the defendant drives a large number of miles each year.

**Example 1**

Imran is convicted of careless driving. This is Imran's third conviction for careless driving, and the magistrates indicate that they are considering disqualifying Imran from driving for the current offence.

Imran is employed as a fork lift truck driver and has been told by his employer that if he is disqualified from driving he will lose his job. Imran's solicitor may raise this as a mitigating factor when seeking to persuade the court not to disqualify Imran from driving.

**Example 2**

Crystal is convicted of careless driving. Crystal has been driving for 25 years and this is her first conviction. The offence involved a momentary lapse in concentration when Crystal pulled out at a junction into the path of another vehicle. Very minor damage was caused to the vehicle, and Crystal pleaded guilty at the first opportunity. The magistrates indicate that they are not considering imposing a disqualification. They are, however, obliged to impose between 3 and 9 penalty points. Crystal's solicitor may raise the above matters as mitigating factors when seeking to persuade the court to impose the lowest number of points it feels able for the offence.

**Example 3**

Walter is convicted of driving whilst over the prescribed alcohol limit. Walter's breath/alcohol reading was only just over the limit. Walter was stopped by the police in the early hours of the morning when there were few other vehicles on the road. Walter pleaded guilty at the first opportunity. The offence carries obligatory disqualification from driving. Walter's solicitor will be able to use the above matters as mitigating factors to persuade the court to disqualify Walter from driving for as short a period as possible (the minimum period of disqualification being 12 months – see **15.5.1** above).

**Example 4**

Diane is convicted of driving whilst over the prescribed alcohol limit. Diane was three times the legal limit when stopped by the police, and the magistrates indicate that they are considering imposing a custodial sentence (in addition to a lengthy disqualification from driving). Diane has been driving for 30 years and has had no previous convictions. Diane drove on this occasion only after storming out of her house following a blazing row with her husband who had just disclosed that he had been having an affair with his secretary. Diane's solicitor will be able to raise these matters as mitigating factors to persuade the court not to impose a custodial sentence, and to consider an alternative penalty (such as a fine or a community penalty).

#### 15.6.1.3 Procedure

Where a defendant seeks to rely only on mitigating factors (and is not seeking to avoid a penalty points disqualification by raising mitigating circumstances, or an obligatory disqualification or endorsement by raising special reasons – see **15.6.2** and **15.6.3** below), the procedure at the sentencing hearing will be the same as for any other type of offence (see **12.7** above). The prosecutor will outline the facts of the case to the court (assuming the defendant entered a guilty plea) and the defendant's solicitor will then deliver a plea in mitigation, highlighting the mitigating factors that exist and arguing for the lowest possible penalty that the court feels able to impose. The magistrates will then retire to consider their sentence, before returning to court to announce the sentence.

### 15.6.2 Mitigating circumstances

#### 15.6.2.1 What are mitigating circumstances?

If a defendant accumulates 12 or more relevant penalty points on his driving licence, he will become liable to a mandatory disqualification under the penalty points system for at least six months (see **15.4.3** above). If, however, the defendant is able to prove on the balance of probabilities that mitigating circumstances exist, the magistrates have a discretion either not to disqualify him from driving under the penalty points scheme, or to disqualify him but for less than six months.

Mitigating circumstances may relate either to the offence itself, or to the personal circumstances of the defendant. They are, however, more limited in their scope than mitigating factors (see **15.6.1.2** above), because the following circumstances will *not* be taken into account by the court:

(a) the triviality of any of the offences for which points were imposed (since the penalty points system already takes into account differences in the seriousness of different offences, by allocating varying numbers of points to each offence depending on the seriousness of the offence);

(b) any hardship that will be suffered as a result of a disqualification, unless that hardship is *exceptional*. This may be hardship to the defendant or, more usually, someone other than the defendant, such as a family member or an employer. The fact that a defendant will lose his employment if he is disqualified will not normally be sufficient to constitute exceptional hardship. It is the knock-on effect of that loss of employment which may constitute exceptional hardship (if, for example, the defendant will no longer be able to pay his mortgage and his family are therefore at risk of having their home repossessed). The court will normally only find hardship to be exceptional if the disqualification would cause someone other than the defendant to suffer such hardship (for example, a sick or elderly relative whom the defendant takes to hospital by car on a regular basis; or an employer who relies on the defendant to drive in the course of his employment, and whose business will suffer badly if the defendant is no longer able to drive);

(c) any mitigating circumstances the defendant has previously raised in the three years prior to the current conviction in an attempt to avoid a disqualification under the penalty points system (this is because the defendant should not be allowed to escape disqualification by perpetually using the same argument).

In practice, a defendant seeking to avoid a disqualification under the penalty points system will normally need to persuade the court that such a disqualification would cause exceptional hardship (often to someone other than himself). The burden will be on the defendant to prove, on the balance of probabilities, that exceptional hardship will be caused, and the defendant will need to give evidence at court in support of this, and possibly call evidence from others (such as his employer).

### Example 1

Dwayne is convicted of careless driving following an incident when his car momentarily left the road and he collided with a bollard. The incident occurred in the early hours of the morning when no other drivers were using the road, and no damage was caused (other than to Dwayne's car). The magistrates impose 3 penalty points for this offence (the minimum number of points they could impose). Dwayne already has 9 relevant points on his licence, which means that he now has 12 relevant points and is liable to a disqualification under the penalty points scheme. Dwayne will not be permitted to raise the triviality of the current offence as a reason for not disqualifying him under the penalty points scheme.

### Example 2

Fred accumulates 12 relevant penalty points on his licence. He drives to work, which is 20 miles away from his home address. He claims that if he is disqualified from driving he will be unable to get to work, and so will lose his job and suffer exceptional hardship.

The magistrates will first want to be satisfied that Fred will actually lose his job – could he get to work by means of public transport, or could he get a lift to work? Would he lose his job if they imposed a period of disqualification that was under six months? Even if Fred would lose his job, how easily could he find another job? If he could find another job easily, this would not cause exceptional hardship. Even if Fred would lose his job and would find it difficult to get another job, the magistrates are unlikely to find that exceptional hardship will be caused if only Fred is affected as a result of the disqualification.

### Example 3

Albert accumulates 12 relevant points on his licence. Albert works as a sales representative for a publishing company, for which he receives a large salary. Albert usually drives over 1,000 miles per week in the course of his employment. Albert is told by his employer that he will lose his job if he is disqualified from driving. Albert and his wife Sue have a large mortgage. The monthly mortgage instalments are paid out of Albert's salary. Sue is not in employment. She stays at home to look after their two infant children. Albert argues that his family will suffer exceptional hardship if he is disqualified from driving because he will no longer be able to pay the mortgage from his salary and the family home will be repossessed.

The magistrates are likely to accept that, because of the nature of his job, Albert is likely to lose his employment if he is disqualified. However, before finding that exceptional hardship will be caused if Albert is disqualified, the magistrates will want to know how easy it would be for Albert to find alternative employment in order to fund the mortgage payments. Similarly, they would want to know if Sue could find employment to contribute towards the mortgage payments.

#### Example 4

Alan accumulates 12 relevant points on his licence. Alan works as a delivery driver for a small bakery in a rural area. The only other person who works at the bakery is Neville, the owner of the bakery. Neville does not have a driving licence and relies on Alan to make the deliveries. If Alan is disqualified from driving, the deliveries will not be made and the bakery will suffer large financial losses. Alan therefore argues that exceptional hardship will be suffered by Neville if he is disqualified from driving.

Before finding that exceptional hardship exists, the magistrates are likely to want to hear evidence from Neville. How easily could he find another delivery driver? What losses would he actually suffer if Alan was unavailable to drive? If Alan was disqualified for less than six months, would this still cause Neville exceptional hardship?

#### Example 5

Shabnam accumulates 12 relevant points on her licence. Her 6-year-old daughter suffers from leukaemia and Shabnam drives her to the local hospital on a weekly basis for medical treatment. The hospital is five miles away from their home address. Shabnam claims that if she is disqualified from driving she will be unable to drive her daughter to the hospital, which will cause her daughter exceptional hardship.

The magistrates will want to be satisfied that Shabnam is the only person who could drive her daughter to the hospital – is there anybody else who could take her, or is an ambulance service available? Given the proximity of the hospital, would it be possible to make the journey by public transport?

#### Example 6

Roger accumulates 12 relevant points on his licence. He avoided a disqualification under the points system two years ago by persuading the magistrates that disqualification would cause him exceptional hardship, because he lives in a rural area with no public transport and he suffers from arthritis which prevents him from being able to walk very far.

Roger will not be able to raise these circumstances again at the current hearing because he has already used such arguments within the previous three years to avoid a disqualification under the penalty points scheme.

The magistrates must find that mitigating circumstances exist before exercising their discretion not to disqualify the defendant for at least six months. If the magistrates do find that mitigating circumstances exist, they may choose either not to disqualify the defendant or to disqualify the defendant but for a reduced period (ie, for less than six months).

### 15.6.2.2 Procedure

A defendant who is liable to be disqualified under the penalty points system and wishes to raise mitigating circumstances, either to avoid such a disqualification or to reduce the period of the disqualification, has the burden of proving (on the balance of probabilities) that mitigating circumstances exist. The hearing at which the defendant will argue the existence of mitigating circumstances is first and foremost a sentencing hearing. The procedure that will take place at the hearing is as follows:

(a) The hearing will begin with the prosecutor outlining the facts of the case to the magistrates.

(b) The defendant will then give evidence in support of his argument that mitigating circumstances exist. The defendant will be examined in chief by his solicitor, cross-examined by the prosecutor (usually to put the defendant to proof that exceptional hardship would genuinely be caused were the defendant to be disqualified) and, if necessary, re-examined.

(c) Any other evidence which the defendant wishes to call will then be adduced. For example, the defendant's employer may attend court to confirm that the defendant will lose his job if he is disqualified, or a letter from the employer to this effect may be read out to the court. If the defendant argues that, as a result of losing his job, he will have his property repossessed because he will no longer be able to afford his mortgage, the magistrates will expect him to produce evidence to show what his monthly mortgage payments are.

(d) When all the evidence has been given, the defendant's solicitor will make submissions to the court in support of his argument that mitigating circumstances exist, and will also make a general plea in mitigation in respect of any other penalty the court may impose for the substantive offence (such as a fine or an order to pay the prosecution costs). In some magistrates' courts, the practice is for the defendant's solicitor to make his submissions *prior* to the defendant giving evidence.

(e) The prosecutor has the right to respond to the submissions made by the defendant's solicitor if there are any points of law in relation to mitigating circumstances which he wishes to bring to the attention of the court.

(f) The magistrates will then retire to consider whether the defendant has established, on the balance of probabilities, that mitigating circumstances exist.

(g) The magistrates will then return to court and announce whether such circumstances exist. They will then proceed to sentence the defendant. If the magistrates find that mitigating circumstances do exist, the defendant will either not be disqualified from driving under the penalty points scheme, or will be disqualified but for a period of less than six months. Whether or not the defendant is disqualified under the penalty points scheme, the court may impose other penalties (in addition to points) for the substantive offence which led to him having 12 (or more) points on his licence. This penalty is likely to be a fine together with an order to pay the prosecution costs.

If a defendant avoids a disqualification by raising mitigating circumstances, any points on his licence will remain. If he subsequently commits another offence for which he receives penalty points, the defendant will be liable once again to a disqualification under the penalty points scheme.

### Example

Sadie has convictions for offences on the following dates:

| | | |
|---|---|---|
| 12 March 2005 | speeding | licence endorsed with 3 points |
| 15 September 2006 | careless driving | licence endorsed with 7 points |
| 2 January 2007 | speeding | licence endorsed with 3 points |

Following the conviction for the offence on 2 January 2007, Sadie was liable to a disqualification under the penalty points scheme because she had accumulated 12 or more relevant points on her licence. However, Sadie was able to avoid a disqualification by raising as a mitigating circumstance the fact that an elderly relative whom she drove to a hospital appointment each week would suffer exceptional hardship were she to be disqualified.

On 5 April 2007 Sadie commits the offence of failing to stop after an accident, for which she receives 5 points. Sadie will now have a total of 18 points on her licence and will be liable to a disqualification under the penalty points scheme. Although Sadie may attempt to avoid such a disqualification by raising mitigating circumstances, she will not be able to raise the same argument as she did on the last occasion to avoid disqualification (see **15.6.2.1** above).

In some circumstances a solicitor may raise both mitigating factors and mitigating circumstances in the same submission.

Example

Lester pleads guilty to a charge of careless driving. Lester currently has 7 penalty points on his driving licence. Careless driving carries between 3 and 9 penalty points. If Lester receives 5 or more penalty points for this offence, he will have 12 (or more) penalty points on his licence and will be liable to a mandatory disqualification under the penalty points scheme. When giving his plea in mitigation, Lester's solicitor will raise mitigating factors as to the number of points the magistrates will impose for the offence itself (in an attempt to keep the number of points as low as possible), but will also raise mitigating circumstances in respect of any disqualification under the penalty points scheme which Lester will receive should the magistrates decide to impose 5 or more penalty points for the offence itself.

### 15.6.3 Special reasons

#### 15.6.3.1 When may special reasons apply?

If a defendant is convicted of an offence that carries either an obligatory disqualification from driving, or the obligatory endorsement of his licence with penalty points, he may avoid such penalties only if he is able to persuade a court that there are 'special reasons' why such a penalty should not be imposed.

Example 1

Erica is convicted of driving whilst over the prescribed alcohol limit, an offence which carries obligatory disqualification from driving for a minimum period of 12 months. Erica will be able to avoid such a penalty only if she is able to persuade the court that special reasons exist not to disqualify.

Example 2

Robin is convicted of careless driving. The magistrates decide not to disqualify Robin from driving for the offence, but they are obliged to impose between 3 and 9 penalty points. Robin will be able to avoid this penalty only if he is able to persuade the court that special reasons exist not to impose penalty points.

Special reasons are *not* a defence to the charge, and even if the existence of special reasons is established, the defendant will still be liable to any other penalty which the court may impose (such as a fine or the payment of costs). A defendant who argues the existence of special reasons bears the burden of proving (on the balance of probabilities) that such reasons exist.

#### 15.6.3.2 What are special reasons?

There is no statutory definition of what may amount to a special reason. The accepted definition of the term was given in the case of *R v Crossen* [1939] NI 106:

> A 'special reason' ... is one which is special to the facts of the particular case, that is special to the facts which constitute the offence. It is, in other words, a mitigating or extenuating circumstance, not amounting in law to a defence to the charge, yet directly connected with the commission of the offence and one which the court ought properly to take into consideration when imposing punishment. A circumstance peculiar to the offender as distinguished from the offence is not a 'special reason' within the exception.

In *R v Wickens* (1958) 42 Cr App R 236, the court said that four criteria had to be satisfied for a matter to amount to a special reason. The matter must:

(a) be a mitigating or an extenuating circumstance;

(b) not amount to a defence to the charge;

(c) be directly connected with the commission of the offence (and not the personal circumstances of the offender); and

(d) be a matter which the court ought properly to take into account when imposing a sentence.

As special reasons must be directly connected with the commission of the offence, factors that are relevant to the particular circumstances of an individual defendant *cannot* amount to special reasons. Thus a defendant cannot say that his previous good character is a special reason. Neither can a defendant argue that a special reason exists when he (or his family, his employers or anybody else) will suffer hardship, however severe this might be.

**Example**

Gordon, a doctor, is convicted of driving whilst over the prescribed alcohol limit. Gordon lives in a rural area and is the only doctor serving his community. Gordon cannot argue that there are special reasons not to disqualify him from driving because his job benefits the public and the public will suffer if he is disqualified. His particular circumstances are irrelevant, as they are not connected to the circumstances of the offence itself.

### 15.6.3.3 What may amount to special reasons?

Special reasons are most commonly raised by defendants convicted of 'drink drive' offences, particularly the offence of driving whilst over the prescribed limit. Defendants in such cases commonly argue that special reasons exist for one of the following reasons:

(a) their drinks were spiked;

(b) the distance driven was extremely short; or

(c) the only reason for driving was in response to an emergency.

**Spiked drinks**

Defendants often raise the argument that drinks they had consumed were spiked so that either the defendant did not realise that he was drinking alcohol at all, or the defendant knew he was drinking alcohol but was misled as to the alcoholic content of the drink.

In *Pugsley v Hunter* [1973] RTR 284, it was held that a court could find special reasons if a defendant was able to show that:

(a) his drink had been spiked by another person;

(b) he wasn't aware and didn't suspect that his drink had been spiked; and

(c) had his drink not been spiked, the level of any other alcohol in his blood would not have exceeded the prescribed limit.

In order to prove (c) above, it was held that the defendant would need to establish this by using medical or scientific evidence, unless it was obvious to a layman that the excess was explained by the added alcohol. In practice, a defendant will need to obtain expert evidence to show that, but for the spiking of his drinks, the amount of alcohol he says he consumed would not have put him above the prescribed limit.

In the *Pugsley* case, the court found that special reasons existed where the defendant was found to have an excessive amount of alcohol in his blood as a result of having taken cough medicine which he hadn't realised contained alcohol.

In *DPP v Younas* [1990] RTR 22, the defendant had been served with two pints of lager. Each pint had, without his knowledge, been spiked with a double Bacardi. The defendant drank one and three-quarter pints of the lager. The defendant was found to have an excessive amount of alcohol in his blood, and sought to persuade the court that special reasons existed. The magistrates, in the absence of any medical evidence, found that, but for drinking the Bacardi, the defendant would not have been over the limit, because it would have been obvious to the layman that one and three-quarter pints of lager would not have taken the defendant over the prescribed limit.

This case may be contrasted with *Smith v DPP* [1990] RTR 17. Here the Crown Court dismissed an appeal from the magistrates' court. The defendant had drunk one and a half pints of lager and had then consumed a fruit drink which, unknown to him, included one measure of vodka. The defendant failed to produce any medical evidence, and the court was not prepared to find that the additional alcohol in the fruit drink was the cause of his being over the prescribed limit.

In order to prove to the magistrates' court that special reasons exist, the defendant will need to place appropriate evidence before the court. Ideally, the defendant will need to find at least one witness to the spiking of the drink, and expert medical or scientific evidence should be sought to show that the defendant would not have exceeded the prescribed limit had the drink not been spiked.

Even if a defendant can persuade a court that special reasons exist, the court still has to determine whether or not to exercise its discretion not to disqualify the defendant from driving. Although the victim of a spiked drink may have an excuse for starting to drive, if the amount of alcohol in the defendant's blood is substantial, the court is likely to find that the defendant should have realised his faculties were impaired and to have then stopped driving immediately.

The courts have adopted a twofold approach in such cases. First, the court needs to determine if special reasons exist. If they do, the court should then determine whether the defendant should have realised that the amount of alcohol in his body made him unfit to drive (*R v Newton (David)* [1974] RTR 451).

In *Donahue v DPP* [1993] RTR 156, the court found that special reasons existed but nevertheless disqualified the defendant. The defendant had been served with alcoholic wine at a business function when he had asked for non-alcoholic wine. On leaving the function he crashed his car into a hedge and was found to be over the prescribed limit. A doctor told the court that the defendant might have attributed the effect of the alcohol mistakenly to tiredness, due to his having spent the previous evening looking after an ill relative. The magistrates found that the defendant was experienced enough to have realised that he had consumed alcohol which made him unfit to drive.

**Shortness of distance driven**

If a defendant has driven his vehicle only a very short distance (and particularly if this has been done at the request of another), this may amount to special reason as long as the distance driven was such that the defendant was unlikely to come into contact with other road users and danger would be unlikely to arise.

In *R v Agnew* [1969] Crim LR 152, special reasons were found when a passenger in a car was asked by the owner of the car to move it a distance of six feet. However, in *R v Mullarkey* [1970] Crim LR 406, special reasons were found not to exist in respect of a defendant who drove his vehicle some 400 yards in the early hours of the morning during the winter when there was very little traffic on the road.

In *Chatters v Burke* [1986] 3 All ER 168, the court considered the factors to be taken into account when a defendant convicted of driving whilst over the prescribed alcohol limit claimed special reasons existed on the basis of the shortness of the distance he had driven. The court said that the shortness of distance driven was only one of seven factors which the court needed to consider, as follows:

(a) the distance the vehicle was driven;

(b) the manner in which the vehicle was driven;

(c) the state of the vehicle;

(d) how much further (if at all) the defendant intended to drive;

(e) the road and traffic conditions at the time of the offence;

(f) if danger was a possibility as a result of the vehicle coming into contact with other vehicles or pedestrians; and

(g) the reason for the vehicle being driven.

In the *Chatters* case, the defendant was a passenger in a vehicle. The driver of the vehicle lost control, causing the vehicle to leave the road and roll over into an adjacent field. The defendant drove the vehicle back onto the road, but stopped it there and didn't intend driving it any further. The court found that special reasons did exist.

In *DPP v Bristow* [1998] RTR 100, the Divisional Court held that in such a case, the key question the magistrates should ask themselves in determining whether special reasons exist is this: would a sober, reasonable and responsible friend of the defendant who was present at the time of the incident (but a non-driver and so unable to assist himself) have advised the passenger to drive the vehicle or not to drive the vehicle? Thus in *DPP v Harrison* (2007), the Divisional Court held that magistrates had erred in finding that special reasons existed not to disqualify a driver following his conviction for driving whilst over the limit, where the driver had driven the vehicle for a distance of 446 yards on a major road in order to identify youths who had harassed him and damaged his property. The magistrates failed to have proper regard to the fact that the road driven upon was a major arterial road, which meant that there was real prospect of danger to other road users. Further, the 446 yards driven by the defendant was a significantly greater distance than those used to justify special circumstances in other cases, and there were alternative options open to the defendant other than driving his car. He could, for example, have asked a neighbour to drive him or pursued the youths on foot.

**Emergency**

Special reasons can arise when the only reason for the defendant having driven a vehicle was a genuine emergency. In *Brown v Dyerson* [1969] 1 QB 45, the court held that a sudden medical emergency, which was the only reason for the defendant driving, could amount to a special reason. However, a defendant seeking to raise this argument will need to prove that:

(a) there was a genuine emergency;

(b) there was no alternative other than for the defendant to drive; and

(c) the defendant had looked at all reasonable possible alternatives before driving.

In *R v Baines* [1970] Crim LR 590, the court refused to find special reasons when the defendant used his car to 'rescue' his partner's sick and elderly mother who had run out of petrol at night. The defendant had failed to look at any alternatives to driving, and the emergency had therefore not made it necessary for the defendant to drive.

In cases involving non-medical emergencies the courts have adopted a similar approach. For example, in *Jacobs v Reed* [1974] RTR 81, the defendant drove home from an airport whilst over the prescribed limit, after being telephoned by his wife following their daughter's failure to arrive at school. The court refused to find special reasons as the defendant had not considered any alternative method of getting home.

In *DPP v Cox* [1996] RTR 123, the Divisional Court upheld a finding of special reasons by magistrates in the case of a club steward who drove 300 yards from his home whilst over the prescribed limit in response to notification from the alarm company that the burglar alarm at the club had gone off. The defendant did not consider using alternative means of transport, or phoning another person who had a key to the club. The court took the view, however, that the shortness of the distance driven and the steward's responsibilities as a keyholder together constituted special reasons. The court gave particular emphasis to the fact that the club premises might have been the subject of vandalism, and the steward had no way of knowing how long it would be before the police arrived in response to the alarm.

#### 15.6.3.4 Procedure – what evidence will be placed before the court?

A defendant who argues the existence of special reasons must prove on the balance of probabilities that such reasons exist. The defendant is required to produce evidence to show the existence of special reasons. It is not enough for the defendant's solicitor simply to assert that special reasons exist. The usual procedure is for the defendant to enter a guilty plea to the offence and for the case then to be adjourned so that there can be a hearing to determine if special reasons exist before the court sentences the defendant.

As with a hearing at which the defendant seeks to argue the existence of mitigating circumstances, the hearing at which the defendant seeks to argue the existence of special reasons is still a sentencing hearing. The procedure that will take place at the hearing is as follows:

(a) The prosecutor will outline the facts of the case to the magistrates.

(b) The defendant will then adduce evidence in support of his argument that special reasons exist. The defendant will be required to give evidence himself. He will be examined in chief by his solicitor, cross-examined by the prosecutor (to test his version of events and put him to proof of what he says occurred) and, if necessary, re-examined.

(c) The defendant will then adduce any other evidence he wishes to call. If the defendant alleges that his drink was spiked, expert scientific or medical evidence will usually be required to show that, but for the alleged spiking of the drink, the defendant would have been below the prescribed alcohol limit (assuming the court accepts the defendant's account of what he thought he had drunk). Such expert evidence is normally accepted by the prosecution without the expert needing to attend court to give oral evidence. The defendant may also call any other witnesses whose evidence may be relevant (for example, a witness who saw the defendant's drink being spiked).

(d) The prosecutor may call witnesses to rebut anything the defendant has said (for example, if the defendant alleges that a particular person spiked his drink, the prosecutor may call that person to give evidence to deny having done this).

(e) After the witnesses have given evidence, the defendant's solicitor will make a submission to the court to argue that, on the basis of the evidence given, special reasons exist, and to persuade the court not to disqualify the defendant (or not to endorse his licence). The defendant's solicitor will also give a plea in mitigation in relation to the other sentencing powers the court may exercise (such as the level of any fine or an order to pay the prosecution costs).

(f) The prosecutor is entitled to reply to the submission made as to the existence of special reasons if there are any points of law which need to be brought to the court's attention.

(g) The magistrates will then retire to consider whether special reasons exist. When they return to court, the magistrates will announce whether or not they find that special reasons exist, and they will then proceed to sentence the defendant. Whether or not the defendant is able to establish the existence of special reasons for him not to be disqualified (or for penalty points not to be endorsed on his licence), he is still liable to receive any other penalty which the court may impose for the offence. This is likely to be a fine together with an order that the defendant pay the prosecution costs.

#### 15.6.3.5 What may the court do if it finds that special reasons exist?

**The court's discretion**

If a defendant can establish the existence of special reasons, the court has a discretion not to disqualify the defendant from driving for the minimum period, or to not endorse his licence with the appropriate number of penalty points. The court is not obliged to do this, however. Thus, in the examples at **15.6.3.1** above, even if Erica and Robin both established the existence of special reasons, the magistrates would still have the power:

(a) in Erica's case, to disqualify her from driving for a minimum period of 12 months; and

(b) in Robin's case, to endorse his licence with between 3 and 9 penalty points.

**Special reasons not to endorse the licence with penalty points**

If a court finds that special reasons exist for not endorsing the defendant's licence with the appropriate number of penalty points, the court cannot impose a lower number of points than the offence would normally carry. The court must either endorse the licence with the appropriate number of points (despite the existence of 'special reasons'), or not endorse the licence at all.

Example

Stuart pleads guilty to the offence of careless driving, but raises special reasons as to why his licence should not be endorsed with the appropriate number of penalty points. The magistrates find that special reasons exist. The magistrates must either endorse Stuart's licence with between 3 and 9 penalty points (despite the existence of special reasons), or not endorse the licence at all. The magistrates are not permitted to impose a lower number of penalty points than the offence would normally carry.

### Special reasons not to disqualify

In a case where disqualification is obligatory (such as driving whilst over the prescribed limit), even if the court finds that special reasons exist not to disqualify the defendant, the court will still be obliged to endorse the defendant's licence with the appropriate number of penalty points which the offence carries. The court need not do this, however, if it considers that the facts making up the special reasons for not disqualifying are also special reasons for not endorsing the licence with penalty points.

#### Example

Gregg is charged with driving whilst over the prescribed alcohol limit. He pleads guilty, but claims that he was over the prescribed limit only because his drinks had been spiked. The magistrates find that special reasons exist and exercise their discretion not to disqualify Gregg from driving. The magistrates must, however, endorse Gregg's licence with the appropriate number of penalty points (between 3 and 11 points for this offence), unless they find that the facts making up the special reasons for not disqualifying are also special reasons for not endorsing the licence with penalty points.

## 15.7 Flowchart – avoiding penalty points or disqualification from driving

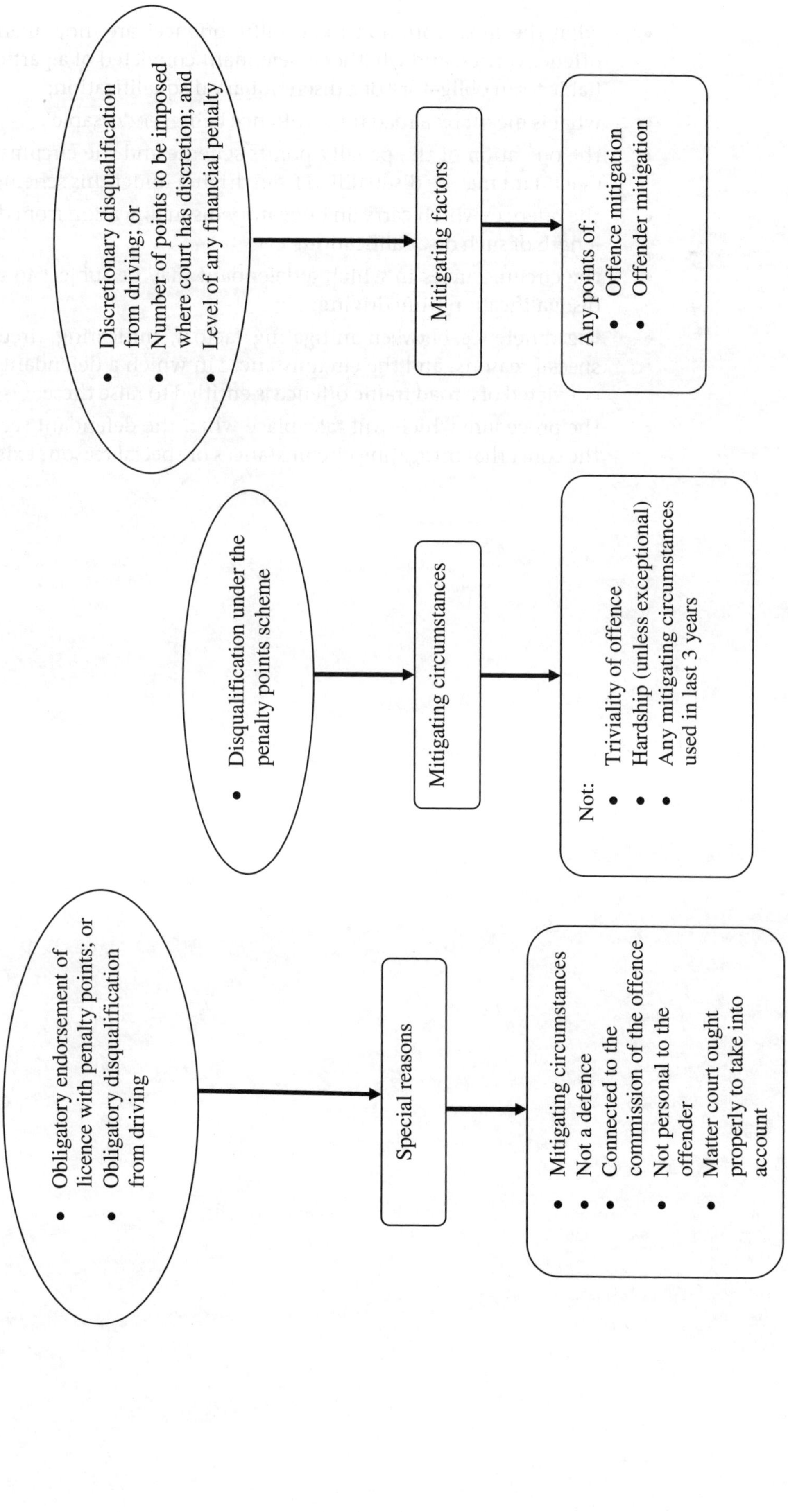

## 15.8 Checklist

At the end of this chapter you should be able to explain:

- what the most common road traffic offences are, how many points each offence carries, and whether a defendant convicted of a particular offence is liable to an obligatory or a discretionary disqualification;
- what is meant by a road traffic offence being 'endorsable';
- the operation of the penalty points scheme and the circumstances when a defendant may be disqualified from driving under this scheme;
- the offences which carry an obligatory disqualification from driving and the length of such disqualification;
- the circumstances in which a defendant may be subject to a discretionary disqualification from driving;
- the difference between mitigating factors, mitigating circumstances and special reasons, and the circumstances in which a defendant who has been convicted of a road traffic offence is entitled to raise these;
- the procedure which will take place when the defendant seeks to persuade the court that mitigating circumstances or special reasons exist.

# Part 6

# EVIDENCE

# Chapter 16

# Introduction to Evidence



## 16.1 Introduction

Whether a defendant who pleads not guilty to an offence is convicted or acquitted depends on the strengths and weaknesses of the evidence which is placed before the court by the prosecution and the defence. The next seven chapters will analyse the law concerning the admissibility of evidence in criminal proceedings. This chapter will provide a general introduction to the law of evidence, with subsequent chapters focusing on more specific areas.

This chapter will begin by examining the burdens and standards of proof which operate in a criminal case. It will then look at what is meant by 'evidence', before summarising the various types of evidence which may exist in criminal proceedings. The chapter will conclude by looking at particular rules relating to evidence from witnesses, including the use of special measures to enable a witness to give evidence and the admissibility of evidence from expert witnesses.

## 16.2 Burdens and standards of proof

### 16.2.1 The legal burden

In the overwhelming majority of criminal cases, the CPS will bear the legal burden of proving the defendant's guilt. The standard of proof that the CPS needs to satisfy in order to do this is to prove beyond a reasonable doubt that the defendant is guilty of the offence with which he has been charged. In other words, the magistrates or jury should convict the defendant only if they are *sure* of his guilt (*Woolmington v DPP* [1925] AC 462).

Occasionally the legal burden of proof will fall upon the defendant. An example of this is the defendant who pleads not guilty and raises the defence of insanity. A defendant pleading insanity is required to prove that fact. In cases where the defendant bears the legal burden of proof, the standard of proof that is required is proof on the balance of probabilities. This is a lower standard of proof than proof beyond a reasonable doubt, and simply means 'more probable than not'.

A defendant who raises a specific defence (for example, a defendant who asserts that he has an alibi, or that he was acting in self-defence), does *not* have the burden of proving that defence (see **16.2.2.2** below). The burden rests with the CPS (as part of the requirement that the prosecution prove the defendant's guilt beyond a reasonable doubt) to satisfy the magistrates or the jury that the defence is not true (see the example at **16.2.2.2** below).

### 16.2.2 The evidential burden

#### 16.2.2.1 The burden on the prosecution

As was explained in **Chapter 9**, the CPS will present its case first at trial. At the conclusion of its case, the CPS must have presented sufficient evidence to the court to justify a finding of guilt and to show that the defendant has a case to answer (this is before the defendant has adduced any evidence). If the CPS fails to do this, the defendant's solicitor (or counsel) will be entitled to make a submission of no case to answer, and to ask the court to dismiss the case (see **Chapters 9** and **10**).

#### 16.2.2.2 The burden on the defence

The defendant is not obliged to place any evidence before the court to show that he is innocent of the offence with which he has been charged. If the defendant does not adduce any evidence in his own defence, in his closing speech the defendant's solicitor or counsel may still ask the court to acquit the defendant on the basis that the evidence put forward by the CPS is not sufficient to prove the case against the defendant beyond a reasonable doubt (*DPP v Uddin* 2006 WL 1518702). However, a defendant who is raising a specific defence (ie alibi or reasonable self-defence) must place *some* evidence of that defence before the court if he wishes the magistrates or jury to consider that defence when deciding the verdict. This is the evidential burden that the defendant bears. It is relatively simple for the defendant to satisfy such a burden. All he need do is enter the witness box and give details of his defence. The onus will then fall on the CPS, as part of its legal burden (see **16.2.1**), to prove beyond a reasonable doubt that the defence which has been raised is not true.

**Example**

Alex is on trial for murder and raises the defence of alibi, claiming that at the time of the murder he was at home with his girlfriend. When presenting its case at court, the CPS must first satisfy its evidential burden by presenting sufficient evidence to the court to to show that Alex has a case to answer. Should the CPS fail to do this, Alex's counsel will make a submission of no case to answer and ask the judge to dismiss the case. If the CPS satisfies its evidential burden, Alex then bears the evidential burden of placing some evidence of his alibi defence before the court. Alex will satisfy this burden by entering the witness box and giving details of his alibi (he will probably also call his girlfriend to give evidence). In order to secure a conviction and to satisfy its legal burden, the CPS will then need to prove beyond a reasonable doubt both that Alex's alibi is untrue *and* that Alex did commit the murder.

## 16.3 What is evidence?

### 16.3.1 Introduction

In **Chapter 8** a case analysis model was described. The purpose of carrying out a case analysis is to determine the facts in issue in the case (ie, those areas where there is disagreement between the CPS and the defendant as to the facts). 'Evidence' is the information or material which the CPS and the defendant will then place before the court in order to persuade the court that their version of the facts which are in issue is the correct version.

### 16.3.2 Requirements of evidence

There are two basic requirements which need to be satisfied if the jury or the magistrates are to take a piece of evidence into account in deciding what the facts of the case are:

(a) Evidence must be *relevant* to the facts in issue in the case. If evidence is not relevant to a fact in issue, the court will not be concerned with it.

(b) Evidence must be *admissible*. This means that the rules which comprise the law of evidence must permit such evidence to be used in a criminal trial. If evidence is admissible, the magistrates or jury will then need to determine the reliability or cogency of such evidence (ie, how much weight should be attached to that piece of evidence).

Evidence that is both relevant and admissible may be either direct evidence of a defendant's guilt, or circumstantial evidence from which a defendant's guilt may be inferred.

> **Example**
>
> Janice is charged with the murder of Leslie. The CPS alleges that Janice stabbed Leslie with a knife whilst Leslie was drinking in a busy pub. The CPS has an eye-witness who identifies Janice as the assailant. The CPS also has a letter sent by Janice to Leslie shortly before the stabbing, in which Janice threatened to 'get even' with Leslie following an argument between them over some money. The evidence from the eye-witness will be direct evidence of Janice's guilt. The letter will be circumstantial evidence, since it is evidence that Janice had a motive for killing Leslie.

### 16.3.3 Matters that do not need to be proved by evidence

In deciding whether the CPS has proved its case against the defendant beyond a reasonable doubt, the jury or magistrates may only take into account a fact which has been proved by evidence. This rule is subject to some exceptions:

(a) Either the CPS or the defendant may formally admit certain facts either in advance of trial, or at trial itself (CJA 1967, s 10). There is no set procedure for doing this, although facts admitted in advance of trial will usually be admitted in writing, whereas facts admitted at trial will be admitted orally.

A common use for admissions under s 10 is when the court has ruled that the previous convictions of a defendant or other witness will be admissible in evidence at trial (see **Chapter 22**). Rather than making the party that seeks to rely on these convictions prove at trial that such convictions exist, the other party will often make an admission to this effect under s 10.

(b) If a court takes judicial notice of a fact, evidence of that fact will not then be required. For example, a court will take judicial notice of matters of law and so there is no requirement to prove the contents of a statute. A court will also take judicial notice of matters of common knowledge. For example, in a prosecution for dangerous driving where it is alleged the defendant drove at 80 miles per hour on the wrong side of the road, the CPS would not be required to prove that in Britain motorists should drive on the left hand side of the road, or that the standard national maximum speed limit is 60 miles per hour.

## 16.4 Forms of evidence

### 16.4.1 Introduction

There are three forms of evidence which may be used in criminal proceedings:

(a) oral testimony from witnesses;
(b) documentary evidence;
(c) real evidence.

Each of these forms of evidence will be examined in more detail below.

### 16.4.2 Oral testimony from witnesses

#### 16.4.2.1 Witnesses as to fact

The most common form of evidence given at a criminal trial is oral evidence from witnesses who attend trial to be examined on their evidence. The witness will be examined in chief by the party that has called the witness to give evidence, cross-examined by the other party, and then possibly re-examined (see **Chapter 9**). Most witnesses who attend court to give evidence are 'witnesses as to fact' (for example, the victim of an assault or an eye-witness to a theft). Such witnesses are entitled to give evidence as to factual matters but, subject to a limited number of exceptions, are not permitted to give evidence which amounts to an opinion. The most common exceptions to this rule allow witnesses as to fact to give opinion evidence based on their perceptions, such as an estimate as to the speed at which a vehicle was travelling or whether they considered a person to be in a drunken state.

Further rules concerning the admissibility of evidence from witnesses as to fact are examined at **16.5** below.

#### 16.4.2.2 Expert witnesses (CrimPR, Part 24)

The other type of witness that may be called in criminal proceedings is an expert witness. Unlike witnesses as to fact, expert witnesses are permitted to express opinion evidence (but only within the expert's particular sphere of expertise). The court will need the assistance of an expert when the matter on which the expert is to comment is a technical matter which is beyond the competence of the magistrates or jury (for example, whether a sample of paint found underneath the defendant's fingernails matches a sample of paint taken from the window sill of the house that the defendant is alleged to have burgled, or whether a particular type of knife found at the defendant's home could have caused the injuries inflicted on the person the defendant is alleged to have stabbed).

Examples of the types of expert who appear regularly in criminal proceedings include:

(a) forensic scientists (who may, for example, comment on DNA or other samples found at the scene of the crime and whether these match with samples taken from the defendant);
(b) fingerprint, handwriting or voice analysis experts;
(c) pathologists (to comment on the cause of death in a murder case); and
(d) forensic accountants (particularly in fraud cases).

Further rules concerning the admissibility of evidence from expert witnesses are examined at **16.6** below.

### 16.4.3 Documentary evidence

Documents may be placed before the court as pieces of evidence. Examples of documentary evidence include:

(a) the transcript of a defendant's audibly recorded interview at the police station;
(b) entries in a business ledger;
(c) invoices or receipts; and
(d) photographs or plans.

A document must be authenticated by a witness if it is to be admitted in evidence. This will usually involve the witness giving oral evidence to explain what the document is and how the document came into existence. For example, the police officer who interviewed the defendant at the police station will give a statement confirming that the interview took place and will attach as an exhibit to his statement the transcript of the interview record. When he gives evidence at trial, the officer will confirm that the interview took place and the transcript will then be read out to the court (unless the defence ask for the recording of the interview to be played).

The contents of a document may constitute hearsay evidence. The rules governing the admissibility of 'documentary hearsay' are discussed in **Chapter 19**.

### 16.4.4 Real evidence

Examples of items of real evidence include:

(a) stolen goods which have been recovered by the police;
(b) a weapon which it is alleged was used in an assault;
(c) drugs found by the police in a search of a suspect's premises;
(d) CCTV footage showing a crime being committed.

As with documentary evidence, in order for real evidence to be admissible it will normally be necessary for such evidence to be authenticated by a witness explaining the significance of the real evidence to the prosecution or defence case and how such evidence was obtained. For example, if the defendant is alleged to have attacked his victim with a baseball bat later found at the defendant's home, the police officer who found the bat will need to give evidence confirming where, when and in what circumstances the bat was found.

## 16.5 Witnesses as to fact

### 16.5.1 Competence and compellability

#### 16.5.1.1 Introduction

Rules exist to determine whether potential witnesses are both competent and compellable to give evidence at trial. The issue of 'competence' is concerned with whether the witness will be permitted to give evidence at all. 'Compellability' is concerned with whether a witness who is competent to give evidence may be compelled to attend court to give evidence (usually through the service of a witness summons).

#### 16.5.1.2 The defendant

A defendant is competent to give evidence on his own behalf at trial (Criminal Evidence Act 1898, s 1(1)). A defendant is not competent to be a witness for the prosecution.

A defendant cannot be compelled to give evidence on his own behalf at trial, although it is normal practice for a defendant to give such evidence. A defendant who chooses not to enter the witness box to give evidence is likely to have an adverse inference drawn from his silence at trial under s 35 of the CJPOA 1994 (see **Chapters** 9 and **18**).

#### 16.5.1.3 Co-defendants

Co-defendants who are tried together are not competent to be called as prosecution witnesses to give evidence against each other. However, if two defendants are jointly charged with the same offence, the CPS may call one defendant as a witness against the other if that defendant has either pleaded guilty at an earlier hearing, or is tried separately from the other defendant.

> **Example 1**
>
> David and Geoff are jointly charged with the production of a controlled drug. Both are pleading not guilty on the basis that they knew nothing about the production of the controlled drug and their co-defendant is solely responsible. The CPS will not be permitted to call David to give evidence against Geoff, or to call Geoff to give evidence against David. Neither is competent to be a prosecution witness.

> **Example 2**
>
> Amanda and Claire are jointly charged with assault. Amanda pleads guilty to the offence but Claire pleads not guilty. Amanda is now competent to give evidence for the CPS at Claire's trial to say that she and Claire committed the assault together.

If a defendant gives evidence in his own defence at trial, and in doing so implicates a co-defendant, this will be admissible in evidence against the co-defendant.

> **Example 1**
>
> Nick and Chris are jointly charged with assaulting Tina in a pub. Both plead not guilty on the basis that the assault was committed by the other. At trial, Nick gives evidence in his own defence and claims the assault was carried out by Chris. Chris then gives evidence in his own defence and claims the assault was carried out by Nick. The evidence given by each defendant will be admissible against his respective co-defendant.

> **Example 2**
>
> Pauline and Mary are jointly charged with the theft of goods from an electrical shop. Both plead not guilty and raise the defence of alibi, claiming that they were at home at the time of the alleged theft. When Pauline gives evidence in her own defence, however, she admits that both she and Mary were in the shop at the time of the theft, although she denies that either of them had anything to do with the theft. Pauline's admission that she and Mary were in fact in the shop will be admissible in evidence against Mary.

#### 16.5.1.4 The defendant's spouse

A defendant's spouse is competent to give evidence for the CPS. However, for most offences a spouse cannot be compelled to give evidence for the CPS (PACE 1984, s 80). The only exception to this is if the offence is one of a number of specified offences set out in s 80(3), the most common example being when the defendant is alleged to have assaulted his spouse and the spouse has provided the police with a statement to that effect.

#### Example

Stuart is charged with burglary. His defence is one of alibi. He complains that at the time of the burglary he was at home with his wife Anne. The police take a statement from Anne, who says that she was not at home at the relevant time because she was away visiting her sister. Anne is competent to give evidence for the CPS at Stuart's trial, but cannot be compelled to do so.

A defendant's spouse is always competent to give evidence on behalf of the defendant, and can be compelled (by means of a witness summons) to do so (PACE 1984, s 80(2)).

### 16.5.1.5 Other witnesses

The general rule is that all other witnesses are competent to give evidence. Only if a witness either cannot understand the questions that will be asked of him in court, or cannot answer them in a way that can be understood, will the witness not be competent to give evidence. The competence of a witness to give evidence maybe challenged by the CPS, the defendant or the court. In assessing whether a witness is competent to give evidence, the court must consider providing the witness with 'special measures' (see **16.5.6** below) to assist the witness in either understanding questions, or being able to answer questions. It is the responsibility of the party calling the witness to satisfy the court that the witness is competent to give evidence.

Before he gives evidence a witness will either swear on oath to tell the truth, or make an affirmation that he will do so. Children under the age of 14 are not permitted to swear on oath or make an affirmation. Such children are, however, permitted to give unsworn evidence. If the child is very young, questions may arise as to whether the child is too young to give evidence. In such a case the court must apply the test set out in s 53(3) of the Youth Justice and Criminal Evidence Act 1999, namely whether the child understands the questions being asked and whether the jury could understand the child's answers. The usual practice in such cases is for the child's evidence to be taken as soon as possible (usually by way of a video-recorded interview – see **16.5.4.1** below), and for the trial to be 'fast-tracked' so that the child may be cross-examined whilst he is still able to recall the relevant events (*R v Powell* [2006] EWCA Crim 3). If a defendant challenges the admissibility of such evidence under s 78 of PACE 1984 on the basis that the child was too young to give evidence and it would therefore be unfair for such evidence to be admitted (see **21.2**), the trial judge will allow such video-recorded evidence to be used only if he considers that a reasonable jury properly directed could be sure that the child had given a credible and accurate account on the video tape (*R v Hanton* [2005] EWCA Crim 2009; *R v K (Evidence: Child video interview)* [2006] EWCA Crim 472). If the judge allows the evidence to be placed before the jury, it is then a matter for the jury as to the weight they attach to it. The court should determine the competence of a very young child to give evidence as a preliminary issue to be dealt with at the start of the trial. The court will watch the videotaped interview with the child and/or ask the child questions to assess his competence (*R v MacPherson* [2005] EWCA Crim 3605).

In *R v H* [2006] EWCA Crim 853, the defendant was convicted of a series of rapes. The evidence against him came from children, including the 6-year-old victim.

There were numerous inconsistencies in the evidence given and, on appeal, the defendant argued that the trial judge should have found there to be no case to answer on the basis of such inconsistencies. The Court of Appeal rejected this argument, finding that the judge was in a much better position than an appellate court to decide whether the inconsistencies were such that the trial ought to be stopped.

Children over the age of 14 are eligible to give sworn evidence only if they understand the solemnity of a criminal trial and that taking an oath places a particular responsibility on them to tell the truth. There is a presumption that, unless evidence is offered to the contrary, such witnesses will give sworn evidence.

### 16.5.2 Self-made evidence

A witness is not permitted to back up the oral evidence he gives at trial by referring to a statement he made on a previous occasion. For example, a defendant who is charged with assault and claims at trial that he was acting in self-defence will not be permitted to tell the court that, when he was detained at the police station, he gave a 'no comment' interview to the police but also provided a statement to his solicitor (which was not given to the police) saying that he had acted in self-defence. Similarly, his solicitor would not be able to give evidence as to what he had been told. This is known as the rule against self-made evidence. There are, however, several exceptions to this rule:

(a) *Rebutting a suggestion of recent fabrication.* If during cross-examination it is put to a witness that he has recently concocted his evidence, evidence of a previous statement made by the witness may be admitted to rebut this allegation. In the above example, if it was put to the defendant that he had fabricated his defence of self-defence just before trial, both he and his solicitor would be permitted to give evidence confirming that he had provided the solicitor with a written statement whilst at the police station, stating that he had been acting in self-defence in order to show that the allegation of recent fabrication was incorrect. In addition, if the written statement of a witness is admitted as evidence to rebut the suggestion that his oral evidence at trial has been fabricated, that statement is admissible as evidence of any matter stated of which oral evidence by the witness would be admissible (CJA 2003, s 120(2)). Thus, in the above example, as well as being admissible to refute the allegation of recent fabrication, the written statement given by the defendant to his solicitor would be admissible in evidence to support his claim that he had been acting in self-defence.

(b) *Statements forming part of the* res gestae. The *res gestae* principle applies to a statement made so spontaneously that there is no possibility of its having been concocted (*Ratten v The Queen* [1972] AC 378). The principle permits the court to hear about a statement made at the time of an event, since the statement may help to explain the event. The *res gestae* principle is an exception to the rule excluding hearsay evidence and is explained more fully in **Chapter 19**.

(c) *Exculpatory statements made to the police.* When a defendant is questioned at the police station about his alleged involvement in an offence, he may put forward an explanation which, if later accepted by the court at trial, would lead to his acquittal. Such statements are admissible in evidence to show consistency between the account given by the defendant at the police station and the evidence he later gives at trial.

Example

Nicholas is charged with common assault. When interviewed at the police station, he claims to have been acting in self-defence. If, when giving evidence at his trial, Nicholas repeats this defence, the comments made at the police station will be admissible to show that Nicholas has given a consistent account since first being arrested.

As a matter of practice, although such statements in interview will not assist the prosecution case, when giving evidence at the defendant's trial the interviewing officer will give evidence of what was said in the interview at the police station, and the court will accept such evidence as an exception to the rule against self-made evidence.

(d) *Documents used to refresh the memory of the witness.* A witness attending court to give oral evidence is not generally permitted to have a copy of his statement before him when giving evidence. The witness may, however, ask the court for leave to refresh his memory from a document which was made or verified by him at an earlier time (CJA 2003, s 139(1)). If the court permits a witness to use a document for this purpose and the witness is then cross-examined on the contents of the document, the document will become a piece of evidence and will be admissible as evidence of any matter of which oral evidence by the witness would have been admissible. Some examples of the operation of s 139 are set out at **9.8.2.4**.

(e) *Previous consistent statements.* Section 120(4) of the CJA 2003 permits a previous consistent statement made by a witness to be admissible as evidence of any matter stated of which oral evidence by the witness would be admissible, provided certain conditions are satisfied. These conditions are explained at **9.8.2.5**.

### 16.5.3 Do witnesses need to attend court to give evidence?

Most witnesses will attend court to give oral evidence and be cross-examined on such evidence. If the evidence to be given by the witness is not disputed by the other party, the witness's statement will normally be read out to the court pursuant to s 9 of the CJA 1967 rather than the witness attending court to give oral evidence (see **8.4.4**). In certain circumstances, if a witness is not available to attend court, his written statement may be read out to the court as hearsay evidence under s 116 or 117 of the CJA 2003, even if that statement has not been accepted under the s 9 procedure. This will be considered more fully in **Chapter 19**.

### 16.5.4 Special measures (CrimPR, Part 29)

#### 16.5.4.1 The Youth Justice and Criminal Evidence Act 1999

Sections 16 to 33 of the Youth Justice and Criminal Evidence Act (YJCEA)1999 introduced a number of 'special measures' which are available to assist witnesses (other than the defendant) who might otherwise have difficulty in giving evidence in criminal proceedings, or who might be reluctant to do so. The following categories of witness may apply to the court for the assistance of special measures to help them give evidence in court:

(a) children aged under 17;

(b) those suffering from a mental or physical disorder, or having a disability or impairment that is likely to affect their evidence;

(c) those whose evidence is likely to be affected by their fear or distress at giving evidence in the proceedings (YJCEA 1999, ss 16 and 17).

Witnesses who are alleged to be the victims of a sexual offence will automatically be considered eligible for special measures under (c) above when giving evidence, unless the witness tells the court that he or she does not want such assistance. In all other cases, it is for the court to determine whether a witness falls into any of these categories.

Under s 116(2)(e) of the CJA 2003, a witness who is fearful about having to give evidence at trial may, with the leave of the court, have his written statement read out to the court rather than having to attend court in person to give oral evidence (see **19.5.1.2**). If leave is granted, the defendant will be deprived of the opportunity to cross-examine the witness on his account. Thus, before giving leave, the trial judge should assess whether the fears of the witness may be allayed by the employment of special measures to enable the witness to give evidence. If special measures are used, the defendant will not be deprived of the opportunity to cross-examine the witness.

The types of special measure which may be used are:

(a) screens, to ensure that the witness does not see the defendant (YJCEA 1999, s 23);

(b) allowing a witness to give evidence from outside the court by live television link (s 24);

(c) clearing people from the court so evidence can be given in private (s 25);

(d) in a Crown Court case, the judge and barristers removing their wigs and gowns (s 26);

(e) allowing a witness to be examined in chief before the trial and a video-recording of that examination-in-chief to be shown at trial, instead of the witness being examined in chief at trial (s 27);

(f) allowing a witness to be cross-examined (and re-examined) before the trial and a video-recording of that cross-examination (and re-examination) to be shown at trial, instead of the witness being cross-examined (or re-examined) at trial (s 28);

(g) allowing an approved intermediary (such as an interpreter or speech therapist) to help a witness communicate when giving evidence at the court (s 29);

(h) allowing a witness to use communication aids, such as sign language or a hearing loop (s 30).

If a witness is eligible for the use of special measures, the court must then:

(a) determine whether any of the special measures available in relation to the witness (or any combination of them) would, in its opinion, be likely to improve the quality of evidence given by the witness; and

(b) if so–

  (i) determine which of those measures (or combination of them) would, in its opinion, be likely to maximise so far as practicable the quality of such evidence, and

  (ii) give a direction providing for the measure or measures so determined to apply to evidence given by the witness (YJCEA 1999, s 19(2)).

In determining whether any special measure(s) would or would not be likely to improve, or to maximise so far as practicable, the quality of evidence given by the witness, the court must consider all the circumstances of the case, including:

(a) any views expressed by the witness; and

(b) whether the measures or measures must tend to inhibit such evidence being effectively tested by a party to the proceedings (YJCEA 1999, s 19(3)).

Where special measures are employed, s 32 of the 1999 Act contains an important evidential safeguard. Section 32 obliges the trial judge to warn the jury that the fact that special measures have been used should *not* in any way prejudice them against the defendant or give rise to any suggestion that the defendant has behaved in any way improperly towards the witness.

A defendant is unlikely to succeed in raising an argument that the use of special measures for prosecution witnesses contravenes his right to fair trial under Article 6 of the ECHR (see, for example, *R v H* at **16.5.1.5** above).

### 16.5.4.2 The Criminal Justice Act 2003

**Section 51**

Section 51 of the CJA 2003 allows the court to make an order that *any* witness other than the defendant (ie, not just those special categories of witness listed at **16.5.4.1** above) be permitted to give evidence by live link if it is in the interests of the efficient or effective administration of justice for the person concerned to give evidence in this way. This will enable witnesses to give evidence from a part of the country other than where the trial is taking place (and even from overseas). In considering whether to use a live link, the court must consider all the circumstances of the case, and in particular:

(a) the availability of witnesses;
(b) the need for a witness to attend in person;
(c) the importance to the case of the witness's evidence;
(d) the views of the witness;
(e) the suitability of the facilities at the place where the witness would give evidence via a live link; and
(f) whether allowing a witness to give evidence in this way might tend to inhibit any party from effectively testing the witness's evidence in cross-examination (s 51(7)).

**Section 137**

Section 137 of the 2003 Act allows a video-recording of the account of an eye-witness other than the defendant, given whilst events were still fresh in the mind of the witness, to amount to the evidence-in-chief of that witness. The witness must claim to have seen events alleged by the prosecution to include conduct constituting the offence or part of the offence, or events closely connected with such events. Section 137 applies to all indictable-only offences and some prescribed either way offences. Leave of the court will be required to admit evidence under s 137. The court may grant leave only if the witness's recollection of the events in question is likely to have been significantly better when he gave the recorded account than it will be when he gives oral evidence in the proceedings, *and* it is in the interests of justice for the recording to be admitted (s 137(3)(b)). In deciding whether it is in the interests of justice, the court must consider:

(a) the time interval between the events and the making of the video;
(b) factors affecting the reliability of what is said in the video (for example, if made shortly after the event, the comments may be tainted by anger or grief);

(c) the quality of the recording itself;

(d) any view of the witness as to whether his account should be given orally or by way of video (s 137(4)).

### 16.5.4.3 Procedure

Parts 29 and 30 of the Criminal Procedure Rules contain the procedural rules which must be followed when a party seeks a special measures directions, or when evidence is to be given by live television link.

Both the CPS and the defendant may make a pre-trial application to the court for a direction authorising the use of special measures for a particular witness who is to be called. The standard directions that will normally be given for not guilty cases in both the Crown Court (see **Chapter 10**) and the magistrates' court (see **Chapter 8**) provide time limits for the making of such an application.

An application for a special measures direction must be made in writing, using a prescribed form (CrimPR, r 29.1(1)). A party opposing the use of special measures at trial must notify both the court and the party that made the application (CrimPR, r 29.1(6)). This notification must be in writing and must set out the reasons for the objection.

In the Crown Court, a party seeking a special measures direction from the court must make an application for such a direction within 28 days of the service of the prosecution case papers in the case of an indictable-only offence (CrimPR, r 29.1(4)(c)(iv), or within 28 days of committal in the case of an either way offence (CrimPR, r 29.4(4)(c)(i)). Any party opposing the application then has 14 days in which to respond (CrimPR, r 29.1(6)).

In the magistrates' court, an application for a special measures direction must be made within 14 days of the defendant indicating his intention to plead not guilty (CrimPR, r 29.1(4)(b)). Any party opposing the application will then have 14 days in which to respond (CrimPR, r 29.1(6)).

### 16.5.4.4 Witness anonymity

In addition to the special measures introduced by statute, the court has always had an inherent jurisdiction at common law to control its own proceedings. This power has on occasions been used to enable a witness to give evidence anonymously (ie from behind a screen and with his voice disguised), with the defendant and his legal representatives being unaware of the true identity of the witness. The court is likely to exercise this power only where the witness would genuinely be in fear of his life if the defendant became aware of his identity. In *R v Davis & Others* [2006] EWCA Crim 1155, the defendants were convicted of murder after key prosecution witnesses had given evidence anonymously. The defendants appealed against conviction, arguing that the preservation of the witnesses' anonymity had prevented them from properly cross-examining the witnesses and so had infringed their rights under Article 6(3)(d) of the ECHR 'to examine or have examined witnesses against [them]'. Rejecting the appeals, the Court of Appeal considered that the concealment of the identity of witnesses was not inconsistent with the right to a fair trial, provided that the following conditions were met:

(a) the need to preserve the anonymity of the witness was clearly established;

(b) defence counsel was permitted to cross-examine the witness; and

(c) other forms of protection had been considered; and

(d) ultimately the trial was fair.

## 16.6 Expert evidence

### 16.6.1 Introduction

Any witness who is designated as an expert is allowed to give opinion evidence to the court on any matter within his particular field of expertise.

> **Example**
>
> Laurie is charged with murdering Steve by stabbing him with a particular type of kitchen knife that was one of a set of knives found by the police in Laurie's kitchen. The CPS wishes to adduce evidence from a pathologist who has examined Steve's body and who will say that the wound on the body is consistent with the type of wound that would be caused by that particular type of knife. This is opinion evidence on the part of the pathologist, but will be permitted by the court because this matter is within the pathologist's field of expertise.

### 16.6.2 Disclosure of experts' reports

#### 16.6.2.1 The requirements of the Criminal Procedure Rules, Part 24

Both the CPS and the defendant may call expert evidence at trial, and it will often be the case that experts called by the prosecution and defence will differ in the opinions they put forward. Any party seeking to rely on expert evidence at trial must serve a copy of the expert's report on the other party in advance of trial. Detailed rules concerning the disclosure of expert evidence are set out in Part 24 of the Criminal Procedure Rules. Rule 24.1 provides that a party seeking to adduce evidence from an expert at trial must supply the other parties in the case (and the court) with a copy of the expert's report 'as soon as practicable' after either:

(a) the defendant has entered a not guilty plea (in a case to be tried in the magistrates' court); or

(b) the case has been committed or sent for trial under s 51 of the Crime and Disorder Act 1998 (in a case to be tried in the Crown Court).

#### 16.6.2.2 Standard directions

Directions for the service of experts' reports form part of the case management directions that the court will give in both the magistrates' court (see **Chapter 8**) and the Crown Court (see **Chapter 10**). In addition to serving on the CPS the report of any expert on whose evidence he seeks to rely at trial, the defendant must also supply the CPS with the name and address of any expert who has been *consulted* but on whose evidence he does not seek to rely (Criminal Procedure and Investigations Act 1996, s 6D; see **8.4.3.2**).

**Magistrates' court**

In the magistrates' court, the standard directions to be given in a not guilty case provide that:

(a) if either the CPS or the defendant seeks to rely on evidence from an expert, they must serve a copy of that expert's report within *28 days* of the directions being given;

(b) the party served with the expert's report must indicate whether the expert is required to attend at the trial, and either serve its own expert evidence in response or indicate that it is not intending to rely on expert evidence, within *28 days* of receipt of the other party's expert evidence;

(c) a meeting of experts to agree non-contentious matters and identify issues, if appropriate and the parties agree, must take place within *28 days* of service of both parties' expert evidence;

(d) the parties must notify the court within *14 days* of an experts' meeting whether the length of the trial is affected by the outcome of the meeting.

**Crown Court**

In the Crown Court, the standard directions given by the magistrates when a case is sent or committed for trial do not contain any specific reference to the disclosure of expert evidence. However, the CPS will include the report of any expert on whose evidence it seeks to rely at trial in the prosecution case papers which must be served on the defendant. The judge will give further directions as to the disclosure of expert evidence at the preliminary hearing (if such a hearing is necessary), or at the plea and case management hearing (see **Chapter 10**).

### 16.6.3 Role of the expert witness in criminal proceedings (CrimPR, Part 33)

Part 33 of the Criminal Procedure Rules provides that the role of an expert witness in criminal proceedings is to help the court to achieve the overriding objective by giving objective, unbiased opinion on matters within his expertise. This duty overrides any obligation to the person from whom the expert receives instructions or by whom he is paid (CrimPR, r 33.2).

Rule 33.3 of the Criminal Procedure Rules states that an expert's report must:

(a) give details of the expert's qualifications, relevant experience and accreditation;

(b) give details of any literature or other information which the expert has relied on in making the report;

(c) contain a statement setting out the substance of all facts given to the expert which are material to the opinions expressed in the report or upon which those opinions are based;

(d) make clear which of the facts stated in the report are within the expert's own knowledge;

(e) say who carried out any examination, measurement, test or experiment which the expert has used for the report and–
  (i) give the qualifications, relevant experience and accreditation of that person,
  (ii) say whether or not the examination, measurement, test or experiment was carried out under the expert's supervision, and
  (iii) summarise the findings on which the expert relies;

(f) where there is a range of opinion on the matters dealt with in the report–
  (i) summarise the range of opinion, and
  (ii) give reasons for his own opinion;

(g) if the expert is not able to give his opinion without qualification, state the qualification;

(h) contain a summary of the conclusions reached;

(i) contain a statement that the expert understands his duty to the court, and has complied and will continue to comply with that duty; and

(j) contain the same declaration of truth as a witness statement.

If more than one party wants to introduce expert evidence at trial, the court may direct that the experts discuss the issues upon which evidence from them is required, and prepare a statement for the court of the matters on which they agree and disagree, giving their reasons (CrimPR, r 33.5). A party may not introduce expert evidence without the court's permission if the expert has not complied with a direction under r 33.5 (CrimPR, r 33.6). In cases where more than one defendant wants to introduce expert evidence on an issue at trial, the court may direct that the evidence on that issue is to be given by a single joint expert (CrimPR, r 33.7).

### 16.6.4 Does the expert need to give oral evidence at trial?

Although it is normal practice for an expert witness to attend trial to give oral evidence, s 30 of the CJA 1988 enables the court to give leave for an expert's report to be admissible as an item of hearsay evidence (see **16.6.5** below) without the expert needing to attend court to give oral evidence. Before giving such leave, the court needs to consider a number of criteria, including:

(a) the contents of the report;

(b) the reasons for the non-attendance of the expert; and

(c) the risk of unfairness to the defendant, particularly if the contents of the report are controversial and the defendant will be deprived of the opportunity to cross-examine the expert on his report.

It is unlikely that a court will grant leave when the expert's evidence is of any real importance to the prosecution case and the defendant wishes to take issue with the contents of his report.

### 16.6.5 The contents of an expert's report and the rule excluding hearsay evidence

#### 16.6.5.1 Criminal Justice Act 2003, s 118(1)

Hearsay evidence is an out-of-court statement that is repeated at court in order to prove the truth of the matter stated out of court. Such evidence is inadmissible in criminal proceedings unless it falls within one of four exceptions set out in s 114(1) of the CJA 2003 (see **19.4.2**). One of these exceptions comprises a list of common law rules of evidence set out in s 118 of the same Act. This list includes 'any rule of law under which in criminal proceedings an expert witness may draw on the body of expertise relevant to his field' (CJA 2003, s 118(1)).

Example

Terry is charged with burglary of shop premises. A forensic expert in glass analysis gives evidence for the CPS that glass found embedded in Terry's shoe is identical to glass from a window that was smashed during the burglary, and that such glass is extremely rare. To reach his opinion about the rarity of the glass, the expert had to draw on the published findings of others within his field of expertise. This is hearsay evidence, but will nevertheless be admissible by virtue of s 118(1).

#### 16.6.5.2 Criminal Justice Act 2003, s 127

Section 127 of the CJA 2003 permits a court to admit in evidence a statement on which an expert bases his opinion, even if the maker of the statement does not attend court to give evidence (thus making the statement hearsay evidence). This provision is designed to allow an expert to give an opinion based on information gathered by anyone assisting him in the preparation of his report, without that person needing to attend court to give evidence. It may also be used in more controversial circumstances, however, as set out in the example below.

**Example**

Nancy is charged with dangerous driving following a serious road traffic accident. The CPS intends to call an accident reconstruction expert to give his opinion on the likely cause of the accident. The expert will say that the accident was caused by Nancy driving her vehicle at an excessive speed. The expert's opinion is in part based on eye-witness accounts of the accident. The eye-witnesses will not be attending court to give evidence. The prosecution will seek to have the expert's opinion evidence admitted under s 127.

The court may refuse to admit evidence under s 127 if another party to the case opposes this and the court considers that it is not in the interests of justice for the evidence to be admitted (CJA 2003, s 127(4)). In deciding whether it is in the interests of justice for the evidence to be admitted, the court must consider:

(a) the expense of calling as a witness the person who prepared the statement;
(b) whether relevant evidence could be given by that person which could not be given by the expert; and
(c) whether that person can reasonably be expected to remember the matters stated well enough to give oral evidence of them (CJA 2003, s 127(5)).

## 16.7 Flowchart – admissibility of evidence

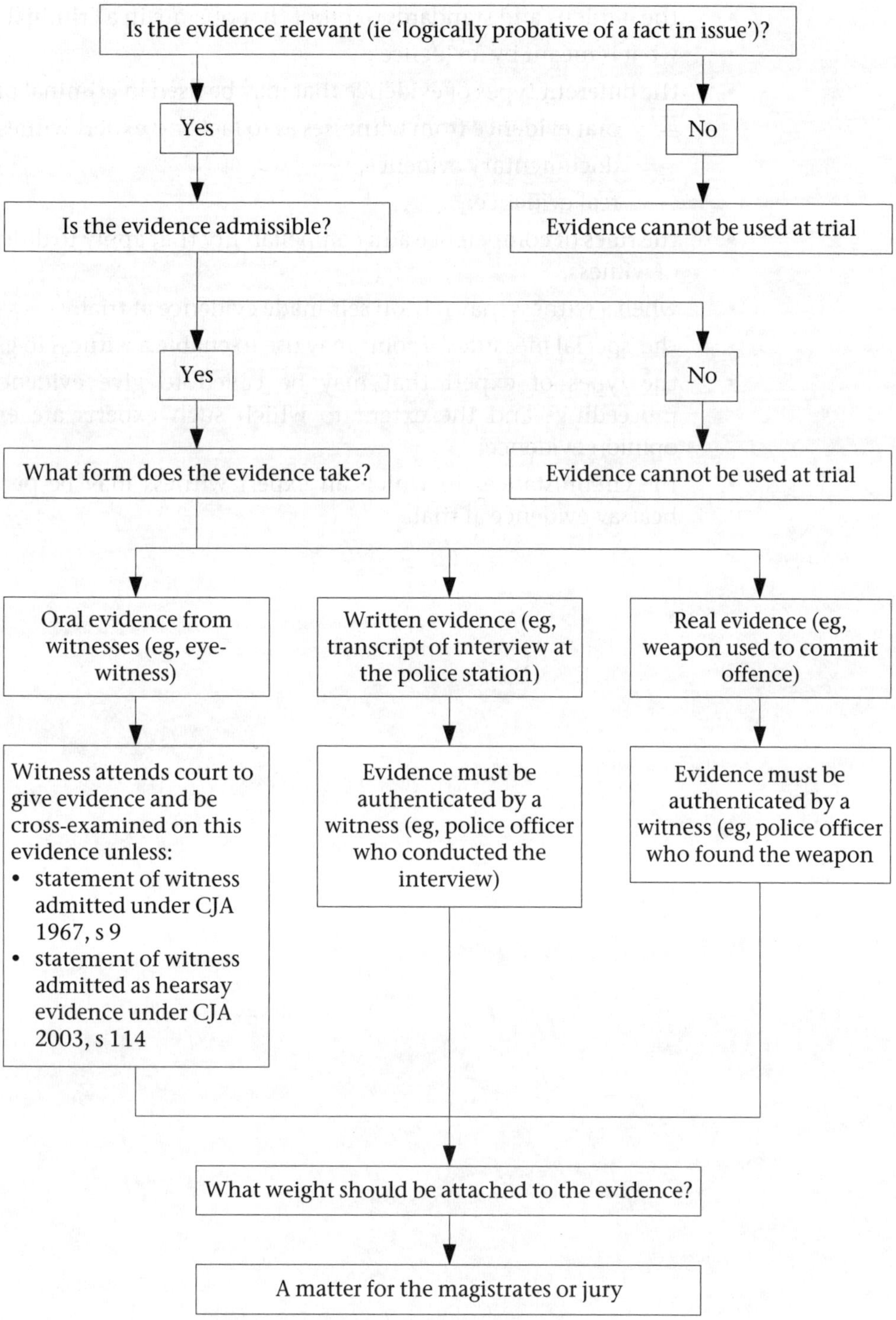

## 16.8 Checklist

At the end of this chapter you should be able to explain:

- the burdens and standards of proof that operate in a criminal case;
- what is meant by 'evidence';
- the different types of evidence that may be used in criminal proceedings:
  - oral evidence from witnesses as to fact and expert witnesses,
  - documentary evidence,
  - real evidence;
- the rules of competence and compellability that apply to different categories of witness;
- when a witness may rely on self-made evidence at trial;
- the 'special measures' a court may use to enable a witness to give evidence;
- the types of expert that may be called to give evidence in criminal proceedings and the extent to which such experts are entitled to give opinion evidence;
- the circumstances in which an expert witness may be permitted to give hearsay evidence at trial.

# Chapter 17

# Visual Identification Evidence and Corroboration



## 17.1 Introduction

One of the most common forms of evidence relied upon by the CPS in a criminal trial is visual identification evidence from a witness who claims to have seen the defendant committing the crime with which he has been charged. Evidence from eye-witnesses is, however, notoriously unreliable, and the defendant will often dispute the visual identification which the eye-witness claims to have made. This chapter will examine the guidelines which apply in such cases and will look at the factors the court will take into account in deciding whether disputed visual identification evidence is admissible and, if it is, how the quality of that evidence should be assessed. The chapter will also look at what is meant by the term 'corroboration' and when corroboration of evidence given by a witness is either essential or desirable.

## 17.2 The *Turnbull* guidelines

Special guidelines apply when a witness who gives evidence for the CPS visually identifies the defendant as the person who committed the crime, *and* the defendant disputes that identification. The guidelines were laid down in the case of *R v Turnbull* [1977] QB 224.

A witness will identify the defendant as the person who committed the offence if:

(a) the witness picks out the defendant informally (if, for example, a witness points out to a police officer in the street an individual whom the witness recognises as the person he saw committing an offence at an earlier time); or

(b) the witness identifies the defendant at a formal identification procedure at the police station (ie, a video identification, identification parade, group identification or confrontation – see **Chapter 3**); or

(c) the witness claims to recognise the defendant as someone previously known to him.

Such a witness is known as a '*Turnbull* witness'. In all three cases, the *Turnbull* guidelines will apply *only* if the defendant disputes the visual identification made by the witness.

**Example 1**

Joe is on trial for theft. A witness called by the CPS tells the court that he saw a man committing the theft and later identified Joe as that man at a video identification held at the police station.

(a) If Joe denies being at the scene of the theft, the *Turnbull* guidelines will apply.

(b) If Joe admits to being at the scene of the theft but denies that he was the person who committed the theft, and suggests that it was somebody else who was present at the time who committed the theft, the *Turnbull* guidelines will apply.

(c) If Joe admits taking the item but denies acting dishonestly because he claims to have had the right to take the item, the *Turnbull* guidelines will not apply. In this case Joe will not be disputing the identification evidence given by the witness.

**Example 2**

Jane is on trial for assault. A witness tells the court that he saw Jane commit the offence. He says that he knows Jane because he has occasionally seen her walking past his house.

(a) If Jane denies being at the scene of the assault, the *Turnbull* guidelines will apply.

(b) If Jane admits to being at the scene of the assault but denies that she was the person who committed the assault, and states that it was somebody else who was present at the time who committed the assault, the *Turnbull* guidelines will apply.

(c) If Jane admits striking the victim but claims that she was acting only in self-defence, the *Turnbull* guidelines will not apply because Jane does not dispute the identification evidence given by the witness.

If a witness simply gives a description to the court of the person who committed the crime, but there is no direct evidence that it was the defendant (other than the fact that the defendant's physical appearance matches the description given), the *Turnbull* guidelines will not apply.

**Example**

Peter is on trial for burglary. A witness who saw the burglary tells the court that it was committed by a man who was 'approximately 6ft tall, with brown, spiky hair and a moustache'. Peter matches this description, but the witness failed to pick Peter out at a video identification at the police station.

The *Turnbull* guidelines will not apply in this case, because there is no direct evidence from the witness identifying Peter as the person responsible for the burglary.

## 17.3 The *Turnbull* guidelines in the Crown Court

### 17.3.1 Role of the trial judge

In the Crown Court the trial judge is responsible for assessing the quality of the identification evidence given by a witness called by the CPS. The judge must look at the circumstances of the *original* sighting of the defendant by the witness, and determine how strong this evidence is. The *original* sighting is the sighting of the defendant made by the eye-witness at the time the offence was committed.

In assessing the quality of this evidence, the trial judge will take into account a number of factors, including the following:

(a) *The length of the observation* – did the witness see the defendant for a lengthy period of time, or did he just get a fleeting glimpse?

(b) *Distance* – was the witness close to the defendant, or did he see the defendant only from a long distance away?

(c) *Lighting* – did the observation happen in daylight or at night? If at night, was there any street lighting? If the observation occurred inside a building, was the building well lit or was it dark?

(d) *Conditions* – if the sighting was outside, what were the weather conditions at the time? Was it a clear day, or was it raining or foggy? How many other people were present at the time and did they obstruct the witness's view? Did anything else obstruct the view? If the sighting was in a building such as a pub, was there a smoky atmosphere, or did any part of the building (such as a pillar) obstruct the view?

(e) *How much of the suspect's face did the witness actually see* – did the witness see all of the suspect's face, or merely part of it? Can the witness give a clear description of the suspect's face, or is the description vague and lacking detail?

(f) *Whether the person identified was someone who was already known to the witness (a recognition case), or someone the witness had never seen before.*

(g) *Whether the person identified may have been seen by the witness at an earlier time in innocent circumstances, with the witness then mistakenly believing that he had in fact seen the person committing the offence.*

(h) *How closely does the original description given by the witness to the police match the actual physical appearance of the defendant?* Are there any discrepancies in height, build, hair colour/length or age?

The judge will base his assessment of the strength of the identification evidence on what the witness who gives this evidence has said both in examination-in-chief and in cross-examination. It is therefore important for the defendant's solicitor or counsel to seek to undermine the credibility of the identification evidence when cross-examining the *Turnbull* witness. The mnemonic 'ADVOKATE' may be used as a reminder to ensure that the necessary issues are raised in the cross-examination of a *Turnbull* witness:

Amount of time the person was under observation.
Distance between the witness and the person observed.
Visibility.
Obstructions blocking the witness's view.
Known or seen before (ie, did the witness know the person observed, or had he seen that person before)?
Any reason to remember (ie, was there any particular reason why the witness should remember the person he saw)?
Time lapses (ie, between the sighting of the person by the witness and the witness giving a statement describing that person to the police, or identifying that person at an identification procedure).
Errors or discrepancies between the first description of the person seen given by the witness to the police and the actual appearance of the defendant.

### 17.3.2 Identification good

If the judge considers the quality of the original sighting made by the eye-witness to be good, when he sums up the case to the jury before they retire to consider their verdict he will point out to them the dangers of relying on identification evidence, and the special need for caution when such evidence is relied on. He will tell the jury that it is very easy for an honest witness to be mistaken as to identity, and he will direct the jury to examine closely the circumstances of the original sighting and take into account the factors listed at **17.3.1** above when considering the quality of the identification evidence. This is usually referred to as a '*Turnbull* warning'.

**Example**

Nigel is charged with assault occasioning actual bodily harm. The CPS seeks to rely on evidence from an eye-witness to the assault who later picked out Nigel at a video identification at the police station. When giving evidence at court, the witness states that he saw the assault take place over a period of 40 seconds. He also says that he had an unobstructed view of the assault from only 5 metres away, and that the assault occurred in daylight when the weather conditions were bright and clear. The judge considers that the quality of the initial sighting by the eye-witness is good. When summing up the case at the end of the trial he will give a '*Turnbull* warning' to the jury. He will warn the jury about relying on identification evidence and will direct them to take into account the factors listed in **17.3.1** above when considering the quality of the identification evidence.

If the prosecution case is based solely on identification evidence by a single witness which the judge considers to be of good quality, the judge must exercise particular care when summing up to the jury. In particular, the judge must set out fully the strengths and weaknesses of the identification evidence given by the witness (*R v Garnett Edwards* [2006] UKPC 23).

In *R v Capron* [2006] UKPC 34, the Privy Council held that a *Turnbull* warning should be given even in a case where the witness claims to have recognised the defendant as someone already known to him (ie, a recognition case).

### 17.3.3 Identification poor but supported

If the judge considers the quality of the initial sighting by the eye-witness to be poor, but this identification evidence is supported by other evidence, a '*Turnbull* warning' similar to that described at **17.3.2** should be given to the jury. The judge will point out the dangers of relying on identification evidence and the special need for caution when the jury are considering such evidence. The judge will also draw to the specific attention of the jury the weaknesses in the identification evidence which has been given.

Supporting evidence means some other independent evidence which suggests that the identification made by the witness is reliable. The judge will normally warn the jury about the dangers of convicting on the basis of the identification evidence alone, and tell the jury to look for other supporting evidence. He will direct the jury as to what other evidence may amount to supporting evidence. Examples of supporting evidence include:

(a) a confession made by the defendant;
(b) other evidence placing the defendant at the scene of the offence (such as fingerprints);
(c) in a theft case, stolen property being found in the defendant's possession;
(d) adverse inferences being drawn from the defendant's silence when questioned at the police station.

**Example**

Frank is charged with unlawful wounding. The CPS has two items of evidence: (i) Frank's fingerprints, found on a knife which it is alleged he used as a weapon; and (ii) evidence from an eye-witness to the wounding who picked Frank out in a video identification at the police station. When giving evidence at Frank's trial, the eye-witness concedes that the incident occurred at night in an alley where there was no lighting. The eye-witness also says that he observed the incident only for a moment and saw only part of the attacker's face.

At the end of the prosecution case, the judge assesses the identification evidence given by the eye-witness as being of poor quality. However, this evidence is supported by Frank's fingerprints on the knife. When summing up the case, the judge will give a '*Turnbull* warning' to the jury. He will warn the jury about the dangers of relying on identification evidence and the special need for caution when such evidence is being considered. He will also point out all the weaknesses in the identification evidence that has been given. The judge will tell the jury about the dangers of convicting on the basis of the identification alone and to look for other supporting evidence. Finally he will explain to the jury what other evidence is capable of amounting to supporting evidence (ie, the fingerprints on the knife).

### 17.3.4 Identification poor and unsupported

If the judge considers the identification evidence to be of poor quality, and it is not supported by any other prosecution evidence, the judge should stop the trial at the end of the prosecution case and direct the jury to acquit the defendant. This will normally follow a submission of no case to answer being made by the defendant's counsel (see **10.10.1**).

#### Example

Rebecca is charged with theft. The only evidence called by the CPS is from an eye-witness who picked Rebecca out at a video identification at the police station. When cross- examined at court, the witness concedes that she got only a fleeting glimpse of the person who committed the theft, and that this was from a long distance away at a time when it was raining heavily and a lot of other people were present to obstruct her view. At the end of the prosecution case, Rebecca's counsel will make a submission of no case to answer. If the judge assesses the identification evidence which has been given to be of poor quality and unsupported, he will stop the trial and direct the jury to acquit Rebecca.

## 17.4 The *Turnbull* guidelines in the magistrates' court

In the magistrates' court, the magistrates decide matters of both fact and law, and it will therefore be necessary for the defendant's solicitor to address the magistrates on the *Turnbull* guidelines during the course of the trial.

If the defendant's solicitor considers that the quality of the identification evidence given by an eye-witness is poor, and the CPS has no other supporting evidence, he should make a submission of no case to answer at the end of the prosecution case (see **9.5** above). The submission will be on the basis that the evidence called by the prosecution is manifestly unreliable. In making his submission the defence solicitor should list the relevant factors mentioned at **17.3.1** above, and point out to the magistrates why he considers the identification evidence to be of poor quality.

If the identification evidence given by the eye-witness is either good or is poor but supported by other evidence called by the CPS, the defendant's solicitor is unlikely to make a submission of no case to answer. He will instead address the *Turnbull* guidelines in his closing speech to the magistrates, and will point out that, however strong it might appear, identification evidence from an eye-witness is notoriously unreliable and the magistrates should exercise caution when considering such evidence. The defendant's solicitor will also point out any weaknesses in the identification evidence that has been given. The ADVOKATE mnemonic is useful here as a checklist for areas of potential weakness in the quality of the identification evidence (see **17.3.1** above). The defendant's solicitor may also use his closing speech to undermine the significance or credibility of any other evidence adduced by the CPS which supports the disputed identification evidence. For example, if the supporting evidence consists of the defendant's fingerprints being found on a stolen item, the defendant's solicitor may suggest an innocent explanation for this.

## 17.5 Disputed identification evidence and PACE, s 78

Section 78 of PACE 1984 provides the court with the discretion to exclude evidence upon which the prosecution seek to rely if 'the admission of such evidence would have such an adverse effect on the fairness of proceedings that the court ought not to admit it'. Section 78 is examined more fully in **Chapter 21**; in summary, however, it is commonly raised by the defendant's solicitor when the methods employed by the police to obtain evidence constitute a serious and substantial breach either of PACE 1984, or of the Codes of Practice (see **Chapters 2** and **3**).

In the context of disputed visual identification evidence, such a situation may occur if the police breach the rules for holding an identification procedure contained in Code D of the Codes of Practice (see **3.5** above). For example:

(a) at a video identification the police may breach the requirement that the other images shown to the witness must resemble the suspect in age, general appearance and position in life (Code D, Annex A, para 2);

(b) at an identification parade the police may breach the requirement that the witnesses attending the parade are segregated both from each other and from the suspect before and after the parade (Code D, Annex B, para 14);

(c) a breach of the Codes of Practice will occur if, whilst the defendant was detained at the police station, the police failed to hold an identification procedure when such a procedure should have been held pursuant to para 3.12 of Code D (see **3.5.3.7**).

If the defendant's solicitor considers that disputed identification evidence upon which the prosecution seek to rely has been obtained following a serious and substantial breach of Code D, he should initially challenge the admissibility of this evidence, and ask the court to exercise its discretion to exclude the evidence under s 78 of PACE 1984. Only if the court declines to exercise its discretion under s 78 should the solicitor then consider how, in cross-examination, to undermine the quality of the evidence of the *original* sighting of the defendant which the witness claims to have made, and what representations to make to the court in respect of the *Turnbull* guidelines.

### Example

George is charged with robbery. Mildred, the victim of the robbery, gives a statement to the police describing her attacker. She comments that she got only a brief glimpse of her attacker's face, and there are several dissimilarities between the description she gives and the actual appearance of George. Mildred is nevertheless able to pick George out at an identification parade carried out at the police station. The identification parade was carried out in breach of Code D because four of the other participants in the parade did not resemble George and the officers investigating the robbery were present during the parade. George denies taking part in the robbery and claims that Mildred is mistaken.

At trial, George's solicitor will make an application to the court under PACE 1984, s 78, for the identification evidence given by Mildred to be excluded, on the basis of the breaches of Code D which occurred when the identification parade took place. Only if this application is unsuccessful will George's solicitor then need to consider how in cross-examination he may undermine the quality of Mildred's original sighting of her attacker at the time of the robbery, and what representations he should make to the court in respect of the *Turnbull* guidelines.

## 17.6 Other forms of visual identification

In addition to visual identification evidence from a witness, the CPS may adduce evidence from CCTV footage or photographic stills to identify the defendant as the person who committed the offence. This is particularly common in the case of assaults or public order offences committed late at night in city centres covered by CCTV, or thefts from shops fitted with security cameras. If the prosecution attempt to adduce such evidence, a statement will be required from a witness verifying how such evidence was obtained (see **16.4.4**). If the video footage or still is of poor quality, the CPS may still adduce it in evidence, but the trial judge must warn the jury not to attempt to identify the suspect from that evidence but rather merely to observe the nature of the incident and its location.

## 17.7 Corroboration

### 17.7.1 What is corroboration?

When a jury or bench of magistrates are deciding their verdict, they will assess the strength of the evidence which has been placed before them. Although the law does not say that one particular form of evidence is 'better' than another, rules do exist as to when evidence which has been given by a witness should be corroborated.

Corroboration is other, independent evidence which supports the evidence to be corroborated and which implicates the defendant in the crime with which he has been charged.

### 17.7.2 Examples of corroboration

The following is a non-exhaustive list of examples of evidence which may corroborate evidence given by a witness called by the CPS:

(a) The evidence of another witness.

#### Example

Lisa is accused of theft. A witness called by the CPS visually identifies Lisa as the person he saw committing the theft. Lisa disputes this identification evidence. The CPS has evidence from another eye-witness who saw Lisa running away from the scene of the theft at the time the theft was alleged to have taken place. This will corroborate the account given by the eye-witness who identified Lisa as the thief.

(b) A confession which has been made by the defendant.

#### Example

Daniel is accused of murder. An eye-witness has identified Daniel as the person who committed the murder. Daniel disputes this identification but confessed to the murder when interviewed at the police station. The confession corroborates the identification made by the eye-witness.

(c) Circumstantial evidence such as possession of stolen property, or forensic evidence.

**Example**

Scott is charged with theft. An eye-witness has visually identified Scott as the person who committed the theft. Scott disputes this identification. When the police arrested Scott on suspicion of theft, his flat was searched and a number of items of property that were stolen when the theft took place were recovered. The stolen items corroborate the account given by the eye-witness.

(d) The refusal of a defendant to take part in an identification procedure.

**Example**

Fiona is charged with theft. The CPS has obtained a statement from an eye-witness who visually identifies Fiona as the person who committed the theft. Fiona denies committing the theft, and claims that she was elsewhere at the time. However, Fiona refuses to take part in an identification procedure at the police station. Her refusal corroborates the evidence given by the eye-witness.

In the Crown Court, the judge will direct the jury as to evidence which is capable of amounting to corroboration. It will then be for the jury to decide whether to accept or reject such evidence. In the magistrates' court, the magistrates will decide what evidence is capable of amounting to corroboration, and then whether to accept or reject such evidence.

### 17.7.3 When is corroboration essential?

For a limited number of offences, the defendant cannot be convicted solely on the evidence of a single witness. For such offences some form of corroboration is required. These offences include treason, perjury and driving in excess of the speed limit (unless the evidence is from a roadside camera). If the CPS fails to produce evidence which is capable of amounting to corroboration, a submission of no case to answer made by the defendant's solicitor or counsel at the end of the prosecution case will be successful. If there is evidence which is capable of amounting to corroboration, it will then be left to the jury or the magistrates to decide whether or not to accept that evidence as corroboration.

### 17.7.4 When is corroboration desirable?

In some cases, corroboration may be desirable because the evidence given by a witness is in some way 'suspect'. Examples include:

(a) witnesses with a purpose of their own to serve in giving false evidence; and

(b) where the prosecution witness is a mental patient.

Category (a) above may include evidence from a co-defendant, evidence from a witness with a grudge against the defendant, or evidence from a witness whom the defendant alleges committed the offence. Corroboration is particularly important in a situation where a co-defendant has entered a guilty plea on an earlier occasion and is now giving evidence for the CPS against his fellow defendant who has pleaded not guilty.

**Example**

Steven and John are jointly charged with common assault. Steven pleads not guilty. John pleads guilty and the court adjourns sentencing in his case until the end of Steven's trial. Having pleaded guilty, John now gives evidence for the CPS at Steven's trial, stating that Steven played a more significant role in the assault than he did.

> John may be giving evidence against Steven in the hope of minimising his role in the offence and so getting a lighter sentence. It is therefore desirable that the evidence given by John be corroborated.

In the Crown Court, if the judge considers that evidence given by a witness is in any way unreliable, or that the witness has a purpose of his own to serve in giving evidence, he will direct the jury that there is a special need for caution to be exercised by them when considering this evidence, and that it would be dangerous to convict the defendant on the basis of this evidence alone (*R v Makanjuola* [1995] 1 WLR 1348).

In the magistrates' court, when making his closing speech, the defendant's solicitor should warn the magistrates about the dangers of convicting solely on the evidence of a witness who is either unreliable, or who has a purpose of his own to serve in giving evidence against the defendant.

## 17.8 Flowchart – visual identification evidence

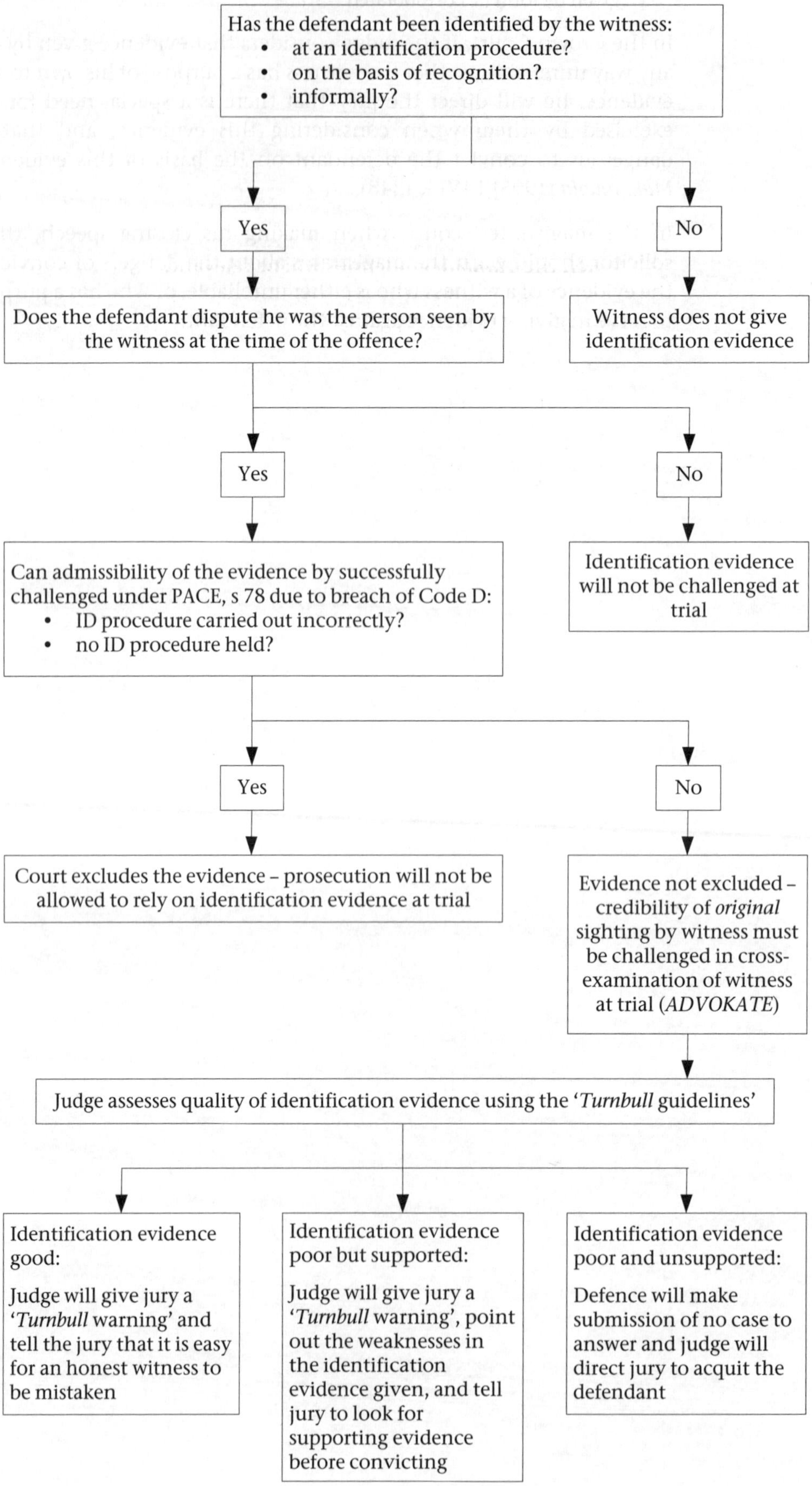

## 17.9 Checklist

At the end of this chapter you should be able to explain:

- the circumstances in which a witness called by the CPS may give visual identification evidence at trial;
- when the court may exclude disputed visual identification evidence under PACE 1984, s 78;
- the matters that should be raised in cross-examination of a witness who gives disputed identification evidence at trial;
- what the *Turnbull* guidelines are;
- when the *Turnbull* guidelines will be relevant;
- how the *Turnbull* guidelines will be applied in the Crown Court;
- how the *Turnbull* guidelines will be applied in the magistrates' court;
- what is meant by 'corroboration';
- the types of evidence which may amount to corroboration;
- when corroborative evidence is necessary at trial;
- when corroborative evidence is desirable at trial.

# Chapter 18
# Inferences from Silence



## 18.1 Introduction

### 18.1.1 The 'right to silence'

Anyone who is arrested on suspicion of having committed a criminal offence is entitled to remain silent when interviewed at the police station. However, under the provisions of the Criminal Justice and Public Order Act (CJPOA) 1994, when a defendant's case comes to trial, the court may be permitted to draw what are termed 'adverse inferences' from his earlier silence when being questioned about the offence. This chapter will examine when a court is permitted to draw such inferences, and the potential evidential consequences which may arise at trial when a solicitor advises a client not to answer questions when interviewed at the police station. This chapter must be read in conjunction with **Chapter 4**, which looks, inter alia, at the advice a solicitor may give to a suspect at the police station as to whether to answer questions in interview.

### 18.1.2 What is an adverse inference?

The term 'adverse inference' means that the court is permitted to draw a negative conclusion from the defendant's silence when interviewed at the police station. In other words, the court may hold a defendant's silence against him. The usual inference that the jury or magistrates will draw is one of recent fabrication, namely that the defendant remained silent when interviewed by the police because he had no adequate explanation for his conduct, and that he fabricated the facts which make up his defence at trial after being charged by the police. Alternatively, the court may draw an inference that, even though the defendant did not fabricate his defence after leaving the police station, the defendant did not put his defence forward when interviewed by the police because he did not believe that defence would stand up to further investigation by the police.

A defendant may not be convicted of an offence if the only evidence against him is an adverse inference under ss 34, 36, or 37 of the CJPOA 1994, because a defendant's silence when interviewed by the police cannot on its own prove guilt (CJPOA 1994, s 38(3)). Before the prosecution may ask the court to draw an adverse inference from a defendant's silence when interviewed by the police, the prosecution must have adduced other evidence of the defendant's guilt. Such evidence must establish that the defendant has a case to answer, and must call for an explanation from the defendant (see **18.2.2** below).

The court is not permitted to draw an adverse inference from a defendant's silence if that silence occurred at a time when the defendant had not been allowed the opportunity to consult a solicitor to obtain independent legal advice (Youth Justice and Criminal Evidence Act 1999, s 58, see below). Inferences may be drawn only when a defendant has been given the opportunity to take independent legal advice. In cases where the police are allowed to delay a suspect receiving legal advice (see **Chapter 3**), no inferences may be drawn from the defendant's silence in any interview which takes place before the defendant is permitted to obtain legal advice.

## 18.2 Criminal Justice and Public Order Act 1994, s 34

### 18.2.1 Introduction

Section 34 permits the court or jury to draw an adverse inference from a defendant's silence when the defendant was being questioned or charged at the police station. Section 34 provides:

> (1) Where in any proceedings against a person for an offence, evidence is given that the accused—
>
> (a) at any time before he was charged with the offence, on being questioned under caution by a constable trying to discover whether or by whom the offence had been committed, failed to mention any fact relied on in his defence in those proceedings; or
>
> (b) on being charged with the offence or officially informed that he might be prosecuted for it, failed to mention any such fact,
>
> being a fact which in the circumstances existing at the time the accused could reasonably have been expected to mention ... the court or jury ... may draw such inferences from the failure as appear proper.

Example

Erica is arrested on suspicion of theft. Erica refuses to answer questions put to her by the police when interviewed at the police station. Erica is subsequently charged with the theft. At her trial, Erica raises the defence of alibi, claiming that she was at a friend's house at the time the alleged theft took place. Section 34 allows the court to draw an adverse inference from Erica's failure to mention her alibi defence when being questioned by the police.

Adverse inferences may not be drawn under s 34(1) if, when questioned at the police station, the defendant had not been allowed an opportunity to consult a solicitor prior to such questioning taking place (CJPOA 1994, s 34(2A)).

### 18.2.2 When will s 34 apply?

#### 18.2.2.1 Pre-conditions

In *R v Argent* [1997] 2 Cr App R 27, the Court of Appeal said that certain conditions had to be satisfied before adverse inferences could be drawn from a defendant's silence in police interview under s 34(1)(a) above:

(a) the interview had to be an interview under caution;

(b) the defendant had to fail to mention any fact later relied on in his defence at trial;

(c) the failure to mention this fact had to occur *before* the defendant was charged;

(d) the questioning of the defendant at the interview in which the defendant failed to mention the fact had to be directed to trying to discover whether or by whom the alleged offence had been committed; and

(e) the fact which the defendant failed to mention had to be a fact which, in the circumstances existing at the time, the defendant could reasonably have been expected to mention when questioned.

In *Condron v UK* (2001) 31 EHRR 1, the European Court of Human Rights held that a jury should be directed that an adverse inference from a defendant's silence could be drawn only if the court was satisfied that the real reason for the defendant's silence was that he had no answer to the questions that were being put to him, or no answer that would stand up to scrutiny.

In *R v Betts and Hall* [2001] 2 Cr App R 257, the Court of Appeal stated that if a defendant remained silent during his initial interview at the police station and then answered questions during a subsequent interview, inferences from his failure to answer questions in the first interview might still be drawn at trial.

It is unlikely that, in practice, a court will seek to draw an inference under s 34(1)(b). If a defendant places his factual defence on record when interviewed by the police, a court will not draw an adverse inference if he says nothing when he is subsequently charged. If, conversely, the defendant remains silent in interview and then raises a defence at trial, the court will draw an adverse inference under s 34(1)(a). The only occasion when the court is likely to draw an adverse inference under s 34(1)(b) is if the defendant was not actually interviewed by the police (so there is no possibility of an inference under s 34(1)(a)), but was simply told that he was to be charged with an offence (see, for example, *R v Goodsir* [2006] All ER (D) 326).

#### 18.2.2.2 Directions to the jury

In the current specimen direction which the Judicial Studies Board (JSB) supplies to judges for use when giving directions to juries in cases where s 34 applies, the jury must be told that they may draw an adverse inference from a defendant's silence when interviewed only if they think it is a fair and proper conclusion, *and* they are satisfied that:

(a) when he was interviewed, the defendant could reasonably have been expected to mention the facts on which he now relies in his defence at trial;

(b) the only sensible explanation for his failure to mention these facts is that, at the time he was interviewed, he had no answer at the time or none that would stand up to scrutiny; and

(c) apart from his failure to mention those facts, the prosecution's case against him is so strong that it clearly calls for an answer by him (in other words, the jury may draw an adverse inference from the defendant's silence only if the prosecution have *other* evidence which establishes that the defendant has a case to answer and which in turn calls for an explanation from the defendant).

The full guideline may be found on the JSB website (www.jsboard.co.uk).

### 18.2.3 Use of a written statement

A solicitor advising a client at a police station will often suggest to a client that rather than answering questions in interview, the client should instead hand to the police a written statement, which the solicitor will prepare on the client's behalf (see **4.4.5**). The advantage of this is that it allows the client's version of events to be set out in a clear and logical way. This is particularly useful for a client whom the solicitor feels may not come across well in interview (for example, a client who is distressed, emotional or tired).

In *R v Knight* [2003] EWCA Crim 1977, the Court of Appeal held that the purpose of s 34 was to encourage defendants to make an early disclosure of their defence to the police, not to permit the police to scrutinise and test that defence *in interview* (although of course the police would be able to investigate the facts of the defence *outside* of the interview by, for example, speaking to witnesses who the defendant said would support his case). Therefore, as long as a written statement which is handed to the police contains all the facts which a defendant later relies on in his defence at court, the court will not be able to draw an adverse inference under s 34 if, having handed in the statement, the defendant then refuses to answer questions from the police based on the contents of that written statement.

In the rare situations when a defence solicitor prepares a written statement for his client but does not hand this in to the police (see **4.4.5.3**), whilst this will prevent the court at trial from drawing the inference of recent fabrication, it will not prevent the court from drawing an inference that the defendant was not sufficiently confident about his defence to expose this to investigation by the police following the interview.

### 18.2.4 When may a solicitor advise a suspect to remain silent?

Much of the case law surrounding s 34 comes from cases where a defendant remained silent at the police station on the basis of legal advice from his solicitor. The courts have said that in a number of situations it may be appropriate for a solicitor to advise his client to remain silent when interviewed by the police, as follows:

(a) *Level of disclosure given by the police* – although the police are not under a general duty to disclose to the suspect's solicitor details of the evidence which they have obtained against the suspect, the courts have held that if the absence of meaningful disclosure means that a solicitor is unable properly to advise his client, this may amount to a good reason for advising the client to remain silent (*R v Argent* (see **18.2.2** above); *R v Roble* [1997] Crim LR 449).

(b) *Nature of the case* – if the material the police have is particularly complex, or relates to events which occurred a long time ago, the solicitor may advise his client to remain silent when it would not be sensible to give an immediate response to the police (*R v Roble* (see above); *R v Howell* [2003] Crim LR 405).

(c) *Personal circumstances of the suspect* – if the solicitor considers the suspect to be suffering from some form of ill health, the suspect is mentally disordered or vulnerable, is excessively tired or is otherwise confused, shocked or intoxicated, the solicitor would be justified in advising the suspect to remain silent (*R v Howell*, above).

### 18.2.5 Can a defendant avoid an adverse inference by claiming his refusal to answer questions was based on legal advice?

A defendant who at trial claims that the only reason for his silence when interviewed by the police was as a result of legal advice he received from his solicitor will *not* automatically prevent the court from drawing an adverse inference if he subsequently raises in his defence a fact which he failed to mention at the police station. The European Court of Human Rights has accepted that this does not breach a defendant's right to a fair trial under Article 6 of the ECHR (see

**1.8** above), although the Court has pointed out that legal advice is a fundamental part of the right to a fair trial and, as such, the fact that a defendant was advised by his solicitor to not answer questions in the police station must be given appropriate weight at trial (*Condron v UK* [2000] Crim LR 679).

Following the *Condron* case, two conflicting lines of authority emerged concerning the position when a suspect refused to answer questions at the police station as a result of legal advice received from his solicitor. In *R v Betts and Hall* [2001] Crim LR 754, it was held that adverse inferences could not be drawn from a defendant's silence in the police station where that silence was based on legal advice the defendant had received, if the court or jury were satisfied that this was a genuine reason for the defendant's failure to mention at the police station facts which he later relied on in his defence at trial. In *R v Howell* [2003] Crim LR 405, however, it was held that even if the court or jury were satisfied that the legal advice he had received was a genuine reason for the defendant's silence, it would still be permissible for the court draw adverse inferences from that silence.

The situation was resolved by the Court of Appeal in *R v Beckles* [2004] EWCA Crim 2766. The Court held that where a defendant explained his reason for silence as being his reliance on legal advice, the ultimate question for the court or jury under s 34 was whether the facts relied on trial were facts which the defendant could *reasonably* have been expected to mention in police interview. If they were not then no adverse inference could be drawn. If the court or jury considered that the defendant *genuinely* relied on the advice he had received from his solicitor, that would not necessarily be the end of the matter because it still might not have been reasonable for him to rely on the advice, or the advice might not have been the true explanation for his silence. Lord Justice Kay commented that 'a person who is anxious not to answer questions because he has no adequate explanation to offer, gains no protection from his lawyer's advice because that advice is no more than a convenient way of disguising his true motivation for not mentioning facts'.

Following the *Beckles* case, the jury will now be directed by the trial judge that adverse inferences should not be drawn under s 34 if the jury believe that the defendant *genuinely and reasonably* relied on the legal advice to remain silent.

### 18.2.6 Legal privilege

Conversations between a suspect and his solicitor at the police station, and the details of any advice given by the solicitor to the suspect, are protected by legal privilege. In an interview the police are not permitted to ask a suspect what advice he has received from his solicitor (or, if the police were to ask, the solicitor would instruct the suspect not to answer). At trial, however, a defendant may give evidence which has the effect of waiving privilege and allowing the prosecution to cross-examine him about reasons for the legal advice that he was given.

If at trial, in order to prevent an adverse inference being drawn by the court, a defendant gives evidence that he remained silent in interview only following advice from his solicitor, this will not in itself waive privilege (*R v Beckles* – see **18.2.5** above; *R v Wishart* [2005] EWCA Crim 1337). However, if a defendant simply states that he remained silent following legal advice, this is unlikely to prevent the court from drawing an adverse inference from such silence. If an adverse inference is to be avoided, the court is likely to want to know the reasons for the solicitor's advice. Once a defendant gives this information, privilege is waived (*R v Bowden* [1999] 1 WLR 823). This means that if a defendant, when giving evidence-in-chief, gives reasons for the legal advice he received, he (and conceivably his solicitor should the solicitor give evidence on the defendant's behalf) may then be cross-examined as to any other reason for the solicitor's decision to advise him to remain silent. Similarly, the prosecution will be entitled to cross-examine the defendant (and his solicitor) on the instructions which the defendant gave to his solicitor whilst at the police station which led to the solicitor advising him to remain silent in interview.

**Example**

Nick is on trial for theft. When interviewed at the police station, Nick gave a 'no comment' interview following legal advice from his solicitor. The solicitor advised Nick to remain silent because the solicitor considered the police had made insufficient disclosure of their case against Nick. Another reason for the solicitor advising Nick to remain silent was because Nick was unable to recall his whereabouts at the time the alleged theft took place. At trial Nick raises an alibi defence, claiming that he was elsewhere at the time the theft was committed. In order to avoid the inference being drawn that he fabricated his defence after he had left the police station, Nick gives evidence that he remained silent in interview on the basis of the legal advice he received. Nick tells the court that his solicitor advised him to remain silent because the police had failed to make proper disclosure of their case against him. Nick (and his solicitor should the solicitor give evidence on Nick's behalf) may then be cross-examined on whether there was any other reason for the solicitor advising Nick to remain silent in interview.

The only circumstance in which privilege will not be lost is if, when giving evidence-in-chief, the defendant says nothing about the reason(s) for his silence when interviewed, but then in cross-examination the prosecution allege that the defendant fabricated his defence after leaving the police station. If the defendant did in fact disclose his defence to his solicitor whilst at the police station (but the solicitor advised him to remain silent for other reasons), the defendant will not waive privilege by stating this to the court in order to rebut the allegation of recent fabrication made by the prosecution (*R v Loizou* [2006] EWCA Crim 1719).

To counter potential problems with legal privilege being waived at trial and the defendant and/or his solicitor then being cross-examined about the legal advice given to the defendant whilst he was at the police station, many solicitors who advise a client to remain silent in interview now give such advice on tape at the start of the interview. The following form of words is normally used:

> I *now* advise you to remain silent because ... [the disclosure given by the police is so limited that I cannot properly advise you/I do not consider you to be in a fit state to be interviewed/the offences you are alleged to have committed occurred so long ago or are so complex that you cannot be expected to give an immediate response, etc].

This does not amount to a waiver of privilege because the advice is being given to the client there and then, and the solicitor is not merely confirming advice given to the client before the interview took place. Further, by putting his advice on record at the start of the interview, the solicitor should prevent there being any need for the client to give evidence at trial as to the reason for his silence in the interview, which should in turn remove the risk of the client waiving privilege when giving evidence.

## 18.3 Criminal Justice and Public Order Act 1994, s 36

Section 36 permits the court or jury to draw an adverse inference if, when interviewed by the police, the defendant failed to account for the presence of an object, substance or mark. Section 36 provides:

(1) Where—

(a) a person is arrested by a constable, and there is:

(i) on his person; or

(ii) in or on his clothing or footwear; or

(iii) otherwise in his possession; or

(iv) in any place in which he is at the time of his arrest,

any object, substance or mark, or there is any mark on any such object; and

(b) that or another constable investigating the case reasonably believes that the presence of the object, substance or mark may be attributable to the participation of the person arrested in the commission of an offence specified by the constable; and

(c) the constable informs the person arrested that he so believes, and requests him to account for the presence of the object, substance or mark; and

(d) the person fails or refuses to do so,

then ... the court or jury ... may draw such inferences from the failure or refusal as appear proper.

**Example 1**

Joe is arrested on suspicion of assaulting Fred. In an interview at the police station, Joe is asked to account for the fact that when he was arrested there was blood on his shirt and his knuckles were grazed. Joe does not reply to this question. Section 36 permits a court to draw an adverse inference from Joe's failure to account for his bloodstained shirt and grazed knuckles.

**Example 2**

Ronald is arrested on suspicion of the burglary of commercial premises. Entry to the premises was gained by the use of a crowbar to open a window. In an interview at the police station, Ronald is asked to account for the fact that when he was arrested he had in his possession a crowbar. Ronald does not reply to this question. Section 36 permits a court to draw an adverse inference from Ronald's failure to account for his possession of the crowbar.

Adverse inferences may not be drawn under s 36(1) if, when questioned at the police station, the defendant had not been allowed an opportunity to consult a solicitor prior to the request being made for the defendant to account for the presence of the object, substance or mark (CJPOA 1994, s 36(4A)).

Although there is a degree of overlap between ss 34 and 36, whilst s 34 will apply only if a defendant raises a fact, which he failed to mention at the police station, in his defence at trial, s 36 will operate irrespective of any defence put forward. It may apply even if no defence is raised at trial, because the inference arises from the defendant's failure to account for the object, substance, or mark *at the time he is interviewed*. The inference which is likely to arise in such a case is that the defendant had no explanation for the presence of the object, substance or mark, or no explanation that would have stood up to police questioning.

**Example**

An assault occurs in the street. The police are called and they arrest Keith nearby. Keith's shirt is bloodstained. In an interview at the police station, Keith is asked to account for the fact that his shirt is bloodstained. Keith refuses to answer this question.

Were Keith to give evidence at his trial that he was walking home from a night club, tripped up and as a result injured his arm and got blood on his shirt, s 34 will apply (as Keith did not mention this fact in interview). Whether or not Keith puts forward an explanation for his bloodstained shirt, s 36 will apply because Keith failed to explain the reason for his shirt being bloodstained when he was interviewed at the police station.

Inferences may only be drawn under s 36 if the police officer requesting the explanation for the object, substance or mark has told the suspect certain specified matters before requesting the explanation (the 'special caution'). The suspect must be told:

(a) what the offence under investigation is;
(b) what fact the suspect is being asked to account for;
(c) that the officer believes this fact may be due to the suspect taking part in the commission of the offence in question;
(d) that a court may draw an adverse inference from failure to comply with the request; and
(e) that a record is being made of the interview and that it may be given in evidence if the suspect is brought to trial (PACE Code C, para 10.11).

## 18.4 Criminal Justice and Public Order Act 1994, s 37

Section 37 allows the court to draw an adverse inference if, when questioned at the police station, the defendant failed to account for his presence at a particular place. Section 37 provides:

> (1) Where—
> (a) a person arrested by a constable was found by him at a place at or about the time the offence for which he was arrested is alleged to have been committed; and
> (b) that or another constable investigating the offence reasonably believes that the presence of the person at that place and at that time may be attributed to his participation in the commission of the offence; and
> (c) the constable informs the person that he so believes, and requests him to account for that presence; and
> (d) the person fails or refuses to do so,
>
> then ... the court or jury ... may draw such inferences from the failure or refusal as appear proper.

**Example**

Leonard is arrested on suspicion of the burglary of a jewellery shop. Leonard is arrested by the police whilst standing outside the jewellery shop, only two minutes after the shop's burglar alarm went off. When interviewed at the police station, Leonard is asked to account for his presence near the shop at or about the time of the burglary. Leonard does not reply to this question. Section 37 permits the court to draw an adverse inference from Leonard's failure to account for his presence near the shop at or about the time of the burglary.

Adverse inferences may not be drawn under s 37(1) if, when questioned at the police station, the defendant had not been allowed an opportunity to consult a solicitor prior to the request being made for the defendant to account for his presence at the particular place and at that particular time (CJPOA 1994, s 37(3A)).

There is some overlap between ss 34 and 37, but whilst s 34 will apply only if a defendant raises a fact, which he failed to mention at the police station, in his defence at trial, s 37 will operate irrespective of any defence put forward. It may apply even if no defence is raised at trial, because the inference arises from the defendant's failure to account for his presence at a particular place at or about the time of the offence *at the time he is interviewed*. The inference which is likely to be drawn in such circumstances is that the defendant has no explanation for his presence at that particular place at or about the time the offence was committed, or no explanation that would have stood up to police questioning.

**Example**

Sophie is arrested whilst walking late at night along an alley behind a house which has just been burgled. Sophie is interviewed at the police station and is asked to account for her presence in the alley at or about the time of the burglary. Sophie refuses to answer this question.

If, at her trial, Sophie states that she was walking along the alley because she was taking a short cut home, s 34 will apply because Sophie did not mention this fact when interviewed at the police station. Whether or not at trial Sophie puts forward an explanation for her presence in the alley, s 37 will apply because Sophie failed to explain the reason for her presence in the alley when she was interviewed at the police station.

As with s 36, inferences may be drawn under s 37 only if a suspect has been given the 'special caution' (see **18.3** above).

## 18.5 Silence at trial

Unless at his trial a defendant makes a successful submission of no case to answer at the end of the prosecution case, the defendant will then have the opportunity to put his case before the court. A defendant is not obliged to give evidence on his own behalf at trial. Neither is a defendant obliged to raise any facts in his own defence. The defendant is entitled to remain silent at trial (Criminal Evidence Act 1898, s 1(1)) and rely on an argument that the CPS has failed to prove his guilt beyond a reasonable doubt. In this situation, since the defendant will not be raising any facts in his defence at trial which he did not mention in the police station, no adverse inferences may be drawn under s 34.

However, a defendant who fails to give evidence on his own behalf at trial may be subject to an adverse inference being drawn by the court or jury under s 35 of the CJPOA 1994 (see **9.6.1.2**). In particular, if the defendant raises a specific defence, such as self-defence or alibi, his failure to enter the witness box to substantiate this defence may lead the court to draw an adverse inference. The inference in such a case will be that the defendant has no plausible explanation, or that any explanation he does have is too weak to stand up to cross-examination by the prosecution. Similarly, if the CPS has adduced evidence of a confession made by the defendant, and the defendant denies that the confession is true, the defendant will need to give evidence to explain why he made a false confession. Should he fail to do so, the court will draw an adverse inference that the defendant has no satisfactory explanation for giving the confession other than the fact that the confession is in fact true.

A defendant may not be convicted of an offence if the only evidence against him is an adverse inference from his failure to give evidence in his defence at trial (CJPOA 1994, s 38(3)).

## 18.6 Procedural flowcharts

### 18.6.1 Adverse inferences under s 34

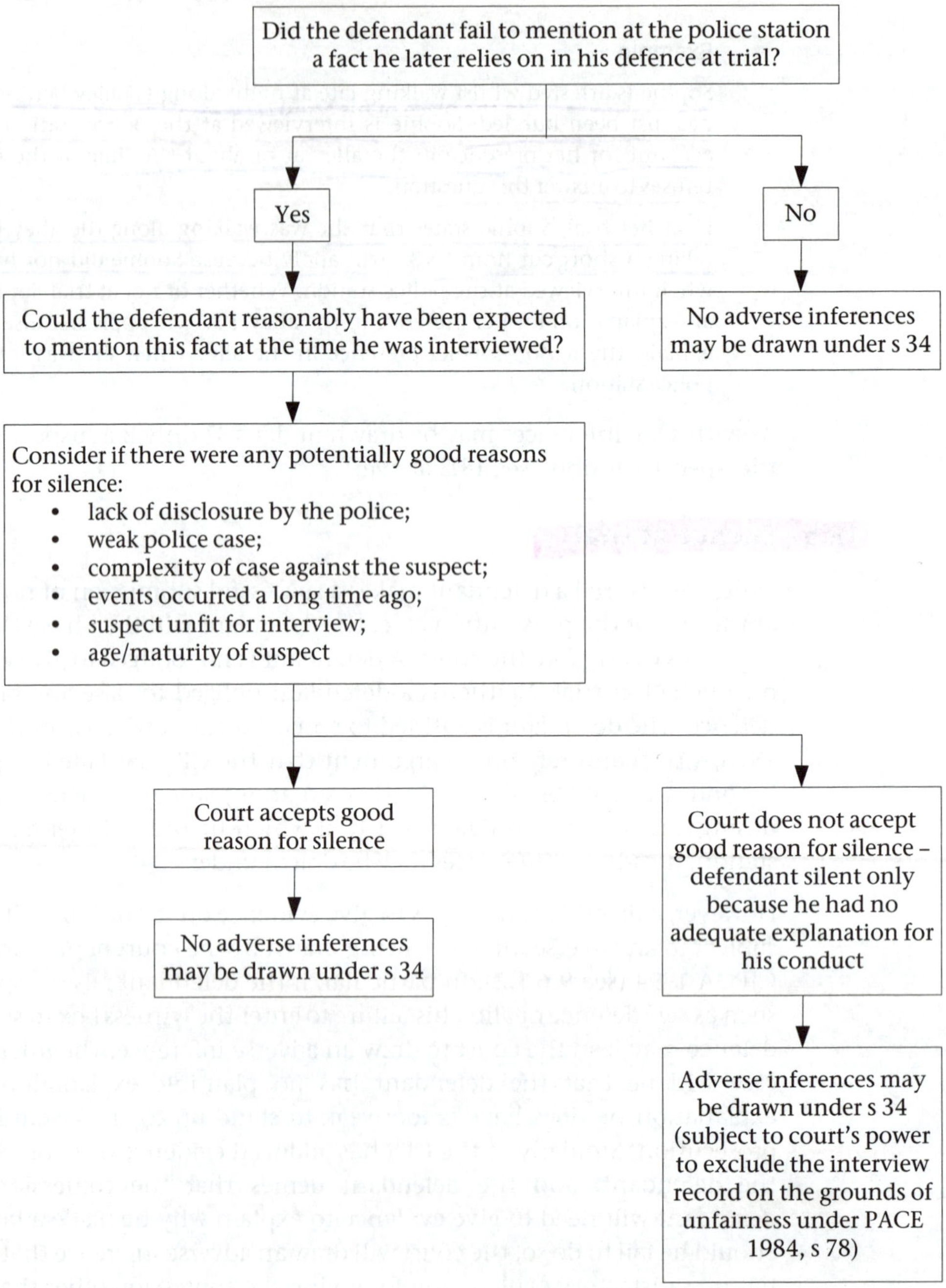

## 18.6.2 Adverse inferences under s 36

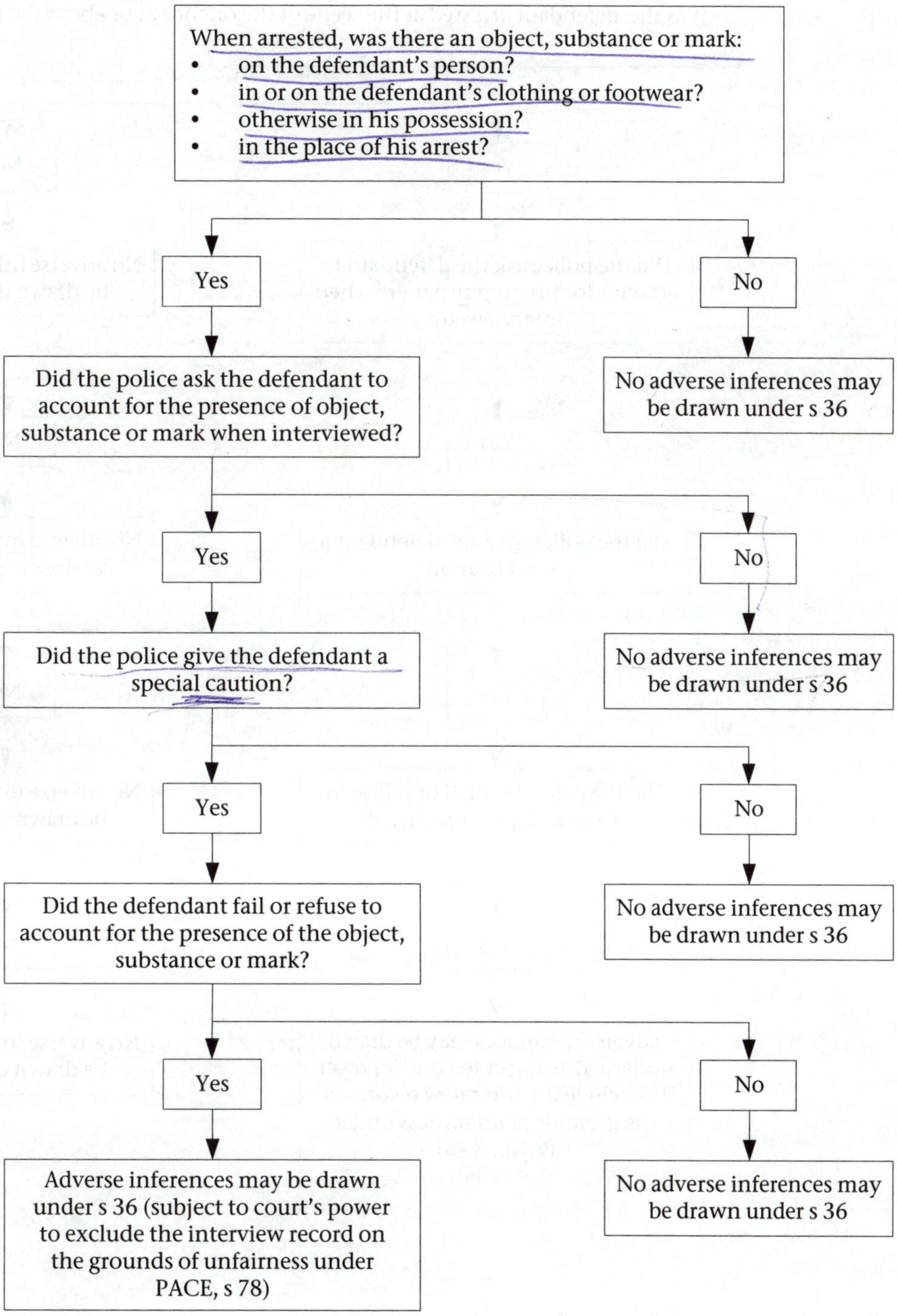

### 18.6.3 Adverse inferences under s 37

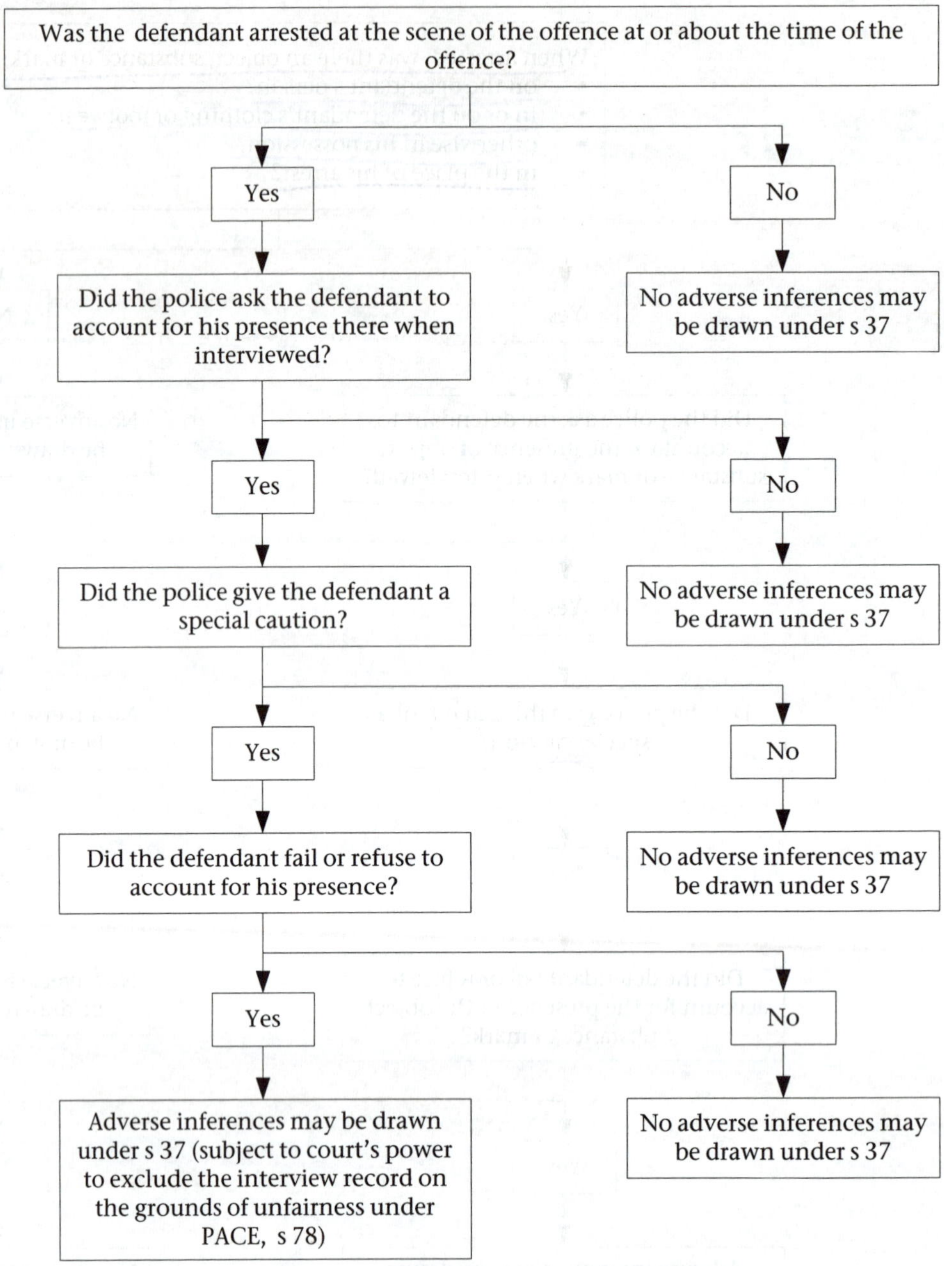

## 18.7 Checklist

At the end of this chapter you should be able to explain:

- the meaning of an 'adverse inference';
- the types of adverse inference which a court may draw from a defendant's silence;
- the significance of a defendant:
  - failing to mention when questioned by the police any fact he later relies on as part of his defence (CJPOA 1994, s 34),
  - failing to account for the presence of an object, substance or mark when interviewed by the police (CJPOA 1994, s 36),
  - failing to account for his presence at a particular place when interviewed by the police (CJPOA 1994, s 37),
  - failing to give evidence in his own defence at trial (CJPOA 1994, s 35).

# Chapter 19

# Hearsay Evidence



## 19.1 Introduction

This chapter will begin by explaining what has historically constituted hearsay evidence and the general common law rule that excluded such evidence from being used in criminal proceedings. It will then examine the statutory definition of hearsay evidence provided by the Criminal Justice Act (CJA) 2003, and the various forms of hearsay evidence that are made admissible in criminal proceedings by virtue of the Act. The chapter will examine how hearsay evidence made admissible under the 2003 Act may be excluded at trial, before concluding with an examination of the procedural requirements that must be complied with should either the CPS or the defendant seek to adduce hearsay evidence at trial.

## 19.2 What is hearsay evidence?

Historically, hearsay evidence could be broken down into four parts:

(a) an oral or written statement;

(b) made out of court;

(c) repeated in court;

(d) to prove the truth of the matter stated out of court.

Examples of such hearsay evidence include a witness repeating at court what he had been told by another person, a witness statement being read out in evidence at court rather than the witness attending court to give oral evidence, or a business document containing factual information (such as an entry in a ledger or a handwritten receipt) being produced in evidence.

## 19.3 The rule against hearsay evidence

Prior to the CJA 2003 coming into effect, there was a general common law rule that hearsay evidence was inadmissible in criminal proceedings. The rationale behind this rule was the inherent unreliability of such evidence. Hearsay evidence was deemed to be 'second-hand' evidence because it was repeating something that had been said elsewhere, and the maker of the original statement could not therefore be directly cross-examined on its contents. This general rule was subject to a number of exceptions, contained both in the common law and in a number of statutes. Dissatisfaction with this variety of exceptions led to the CJA 2003 abolishing the common law rule and putting in place a new statutory framework under which hearsay evidence may be admissible only if it satisfies certain requirements.

## 19.4 The statutory definition of hearsay evidence

### 19.4.1 How is hearsay evidence defined?

#### 19.4.1.1 The statutory definition

The CJA 2003 provides a statutory definition of hearsay evidence and stipulates that such evidence will be admissible in only four situations (see **19.4.2** below).

A 'hearsay statement' is defined in s 121(2) as 'a statement, not made in oral evidence, that is relied on as evidence of a matter in it'.

**Example 1**

Garth is charged with handling a stolen bike. At Garth's trial, the CPS calls Adam to give evidence. Adam tells the court: 'Garth showed me a bike. He told me he had just been given it by a mate of his who had nicked it from somewhere else.' This will be hearsay evidence because the CPS will rely on the statement made by Garth to Adam to show that he was in possession of a bike which he knew to be stolen. The statement by Garth is being relied on as evidence of a matter stated in it.

**Example 2**

Mark is charged with assaulting Janine. The CPS alleges that Mark went round to Janine's house and punched her in the face. Mark accepts that he went round to Janine's house, but denies punching her. When giving evidence at his trial, Mark says: 'I went round to Janine's house because my son told me that she had used abusive language towards him.'

This will not be hearsay. Although the statement from Mark's son is not made in oral evidence, Mark is not seeking to rely on the statement to show that Janine did in fact use abusive language towards his son. Rather, he is using his son's statement to explain why he went round to Janine's house. The statement made by Mark's son is not being relied on as evidence of a matter stated in it.

A 'statement' is defined in s 115(2) as 'any representation of fact or opinion made by a person by whatever means; and it includes a representation made in a sketch, photofit or other pictorial form'. This definition means that a statement does not necessarily need to be in writing. An oral statement (such as that made by the store detective in the example in (a) at **19.4.1.2** below) will satisfy the definition. Similarly, a statement could be made by way of a gesture, such as someone nodding or shaking his head in answer to a question. A sketch or photofit of a person alleged to have committed an offence, which is put together by the police in conjunction with a victim or a witness, will also be a statement, as will a diagram prepared by a witness (for example, a plan of the layout of a building or shop). A piece of video or CCTV footage will not satisfy this definition, however, since neither would be a statement of fact or opinion made by a *person*. Computerised records may constitute hearsay evidence (see **19.4.1.3** below).

The purpose, or one of the purposes, of the person making the statement must appear to the court to have been to cause another person to believe that the matter, or to cause another person to act (or a machine to operate) on the basis that the matter, is as stated (CJA 2003, s 115(3)). Thus in *R v N* [2006] EWCA

Crim 3309, entries in a diary were held not to be hearsay evidence because the diary was never intended to be read by or to influence others.

### 19.4.1.2 Examples of hearsay evidence in criminal proceedings

Examples of hearsay evidence that commonly arise in criminal proceedings are:

(a) a witness repeating at trial what he has been told by another person;

**Example**

PC Smith gives evidence for the CPS in a shoplifting case. He says to the court: 'When I arrived at the shop I was told by the store detective that the defendant had left the store without paying for the goods.'

This will be hearsay evidence because the statement by the store detective was not made by him in oral evidence and the statement is being relied upon to show that the defendant left the shop without paying for the goods.

(b) a statement from a witness being read out at trial instead of the witness attending court to give oral evidence;

**Example**

Suzanne is charged with common assault. Marie witnesses the assault and gives a statement to the police confirming what she saw. Marie is subsequently unavailable to attend Suzanne's trial to give oral evidence. If the CPS seeks to read out Marie's written statement at Suzanne's trial, this will be hearsay evidence, because the statement by Marie was not made by her in oral evidence and the statement is being relied upon to show that Suzanne committed the assault.

(c) a police officer repeating at trial a confession made to him by the defendant at or before the time of the defendant's arrest;

**Example**

Sean is charged with assault occasioning actual bodily harm. At Sean's trial, the arresting officer tells the court: 'When I arrested the defendant, he told me that he punched the complainant because the complainant had been rude to his girlfriend.'

This will be hearsay evidence because the statement by Sean was not made by him in oral evidence and the statement is being relied upon to show that Sean committed the assault.

(d) a transcript of the defendant's interview at the police station being read out at trial;

**Example**

Michael is arrested on suspicion of theft and is interviewed at the police station. During the interview, Michael admits to having carried out the theft and is charged with this offence. Michael subsequently pleads not guilty to the charge. The police prepare a written transcript of the interview to be read out at Michael's trial. The written transcript will be hearsay evidence. The statement made by Michael (ie, the admission that he carried out the theft) was not made by him in oral evidence and the statement is being relied upon to show that Michael committed the theft.

(e) a business document (such as an entry in a ledger, a receipt or an invoice) being introduced in evidence at trial.

**Example**

Rupert is charged with stealing £500 in cash from the safe at the bank where he works. The CPS seeks to adduce in evidence a ledger entry compiled by a clerk at the bank showing that, on the day of the alleged offence, £500 was deposited in the safe.

The ledger entry will be hearsay evidence because the statement by the clerk (ie, the entry in the ledger) was not made by him in oral evidence and the statement is being relied upon to show that the £500 was deposited in the safe.

#### 19.4.1.3 Do computer records constitute hearsay evidence?

Records produced by a computer or other machine may constitute hearsay evidence. If a computer is used to store information supplied by a person, and a party then seeks to rely on this information at trial by producing a printout from the computer, this will be hearsay evidence. If, however, a computer is used merely to perform a calculation (for example, an automated ticket machine), any printout which records this calculation this will not be hearsay evidence because the court is not being asked to accept the truth of a matter stated by *a person*. In such a case, a record generated by the computer will be admissible as long as it is proved that any information supplied to the computer to enable it to perform the calculation was correct (CJA 2003, s 129(1)).

#### 19.4.1.4 First-hand and multiple hearsay

Hearsay evidence may be either 'first-hand' hearsay, or 'multiple' hearsay.

**Example 1**

Jason is on trial for theft. The arresting officer (PC Blake) gives evidence that when he arrested Jason, Jason made the following confession: 'Okay, fair enough, it was me. I only did it for drug money.'

This is first-hand hearsay evidence, because PC Blake is repeating a statement that he heard Jason make. Details of the contents of Jason's statement did not pass through anyone else before getting to PC Blake.

**Example 2**

Bill sees a burglary take place and recognises Roger as the person committing the burglary. Bill tells Susan that he saw Roger commit the burglary. Susan in turn tells Anthea what she has been told by Bill. Anthea then gives a statement to the police repeating this. If Anthea gives evidence at court in accordance with the contents of her statement, her evidence will be multiple hearsay. She is repeating what she heard from Susan, who had in turn repeated to Anthea what she (Susan) had heard from Bill.

**Example 3**

Andrea is a bank clerk. She receives a cash deposit of £5,000 from a customer and places this in the bank's safe. She tells Brian, the senior cashier, who in turn tells Fred, the manager. Fred makes a record of the deposit in a ledger. An armed robbery subsequently takes place and the £5,000 is stolen. At the robber's trial, the CPS seeks to use the entry in the ledger to show how much money was in the safe. The entry in the ledger will be multiple hearsay. The details of the amount of money placed in the safe have passed from Andrea to Brian, then from Brian to Fred, and then from Fred into the ledger itself.

The circumstances in which a statement containing multiple hearsay is admissible in evidence are more limited than when a statement contains only first hand hearsay (see **19.5.5** below).

### 19.4.2 When will hearsay evidence be admissible?

Hearsay evidence will be admissible if it falls within one of four categories. Section 114 of the CJA 2003 states:

(1) In criminal proceedings a statement not made in oral evidence in the proceedings is admissible as evidence of any matter stated if, but only if—
(a) any provision of this Chapter or any other statutory provision makes it admissible,
(b) any rule of law preserved by section 118 makes it admissible,
(c) all parties to the proceedings agree to it being admissible, or
(d) the court is satisfied that it is in the interests of justice for it to be admissible.

Each of the four circumstances in which hearsay evidence is admissible in criminal proceedings by virtue of s 114 is examined in detail at **19.5** below. A flowchart summarising the admissibility of hearsay evidence in criminal proceedings is provided at **19.10.1** below.

## 19.5 Exceptions to the rule excluding hearsay evidence

### 19.5.1 Hearsay admissible under a statutory provision – s 114(1)(a)

#### 19.5.1.1 Introduction

The first category of hearsay evidence which is admissible by virtue of s 114 is hearsay made admissible by virtue of any statutory provision. Hearsay evidence is made admissible as a result of a statutory provision in the following situations:

(a) cases where a witness in unavailable – CJA 2003, s 116 (see **19.5.1.2** below);
(b) business and other documents – CJA 2003, s 117 (see **19.5.1.3** below);
(c) previous inconsistent statements of a witness – CJA 2003, s 119 (see **9.8.3.5**);
(d) previous consistent statements by a witness – CJA 2003, s 120 (see **9.8.2.5**);
(e) reports prepared by experts (if leave of the court is obtained) – CJA 1988, s 30 (see **16.6.4**);
(f) evidence of a confession made by the defendant – PACE 1984, s 76(1) (see **19.5.2.2** below and **20.3.1**);
(g) evidence raised by a defendant of a confession made by a co-accused – PACE 1984, s 76A(1) (see **20.3.3.2**);
(h) statements from a witness which are not in dispute – CJA 1967, s 9 (see **8.4.4**); and
(i) formal admissions – CJA 1967, s 10 (see **16.3.3**).

#### 19.5.1.2 Cases where a witness is unavailable to attend court

Section 116 of the CJA 2003 provides:

(1) In criminal proceedings a statement not made in oral evidence in the proceedings is admissible as evidence of any matter stated if—
(a) oral evidence given in the proceedings by the person who made the statement would be admissible as evidence of that matter [ie, the statement must be 'first-hand hearsay', see **19.4.1.4** above],
(b) the person who made the statement (the relevant person) is identified to the court's satisfaction, and
(c) any of the five conditions mentioned in subsection (2) is satisfied.

The conditions referred to in s 116(2)(a)–(e) are that:

(a) the relevant person is dead;
(b) the relevant person is unfit to be a witness because of his bodily or mental condition;

(c) the relevant person is outside the United Kingdom and it is not reasonably practicable to secure his attendance;
(d) the relevant person cannot be found, although such steps as it is reasonably practicable to take to find him have been taken;
(e) through fear the relevant person does not give oral evidence in the proceedings, either at all or in connection with the subject matter of the statement, *and* the court gives leave for the statement to be given in evidence.

For s 116(2)(b) to be satisfied, the party seeking to rely on the hearsay evidence must prove beyond a reasonable doubt that the witness is unfit to attend trial because of his bodily or mental condition (*R (on the application of Meredith) v Harwich Magistrates' Court* [2006] All ER (D) 45 (Dec)).

Before s 116(2)(c) is satisfied, the court will want to know what steps have been taken to secure the attendance of the witness at trial. In *R v C and K* [2006] EWCA Crim 197, the Court of Appeal held that the court should be reluctant to admit a witness statement under s 116(2)(c) if the prosecution, by making greater efforts, could have secured the attendance of the witness at trial.

'Fear' in s 116(2)(e) is 'to be widely construed and includes, for example, fear of the death or injury of another person or of financial loss' (CJA 2003, s 116(3); see also *R v Davies* [2006] EWCA Crim 2643). The court will give leave under s 116(2)(e) only if it considers that the statement 'ought to be admitted in the interests of justice', having regard to:

(a) the contents of the statement (ie, how important the statement is in the context of the case as a whole);
(b) any risk that its admission or exclusion will result in unfairness to any party to the proceedings (and in particular to how difficult it will be to challenge the statement if the relevant person does not give oral evidence and so cannot be cross-examined on his evidence);
(c) the court's power in appropriate cases to use special measures for the giving of evidence by fearful witnesses (such as the witness giving evidence from behind a screen, or by a live TV link away from the court – see **16.5.4.1**); and
(d) any other relevant circumstances (s 116(4)).

If at all possible, the court should seek to use special measures to enable the prosecution witness to give evidence rather than allow the statement of the witness to be read out at court, particularly if the evidence to be given by the witness forms a significant part of the case.

Leave of the court will be required only in the case of an application made under s 116(2)(e). If any of the conditions in s 116(2)(a)–(d) is relied upon, as long as the relevant condition is satisfied, leave of the court will not be required.

#### Example 1

Zoë witnesses an assault and gives a signed statement to the police describing what she saw. Before the case comes to trial, Zoë is killed in a road traffic accident. Zoë's written statement will be admissible in evidence because she satisfies the condition in s 116(2)(a) and oral evidence given by her of what she saw when the assault occurred would have been admissible at trial.

**Example 2**

Anne witnesses an armed robbery at the bank where she works, and provides a witness statement describing what happened and identifying the robbers. Before the case comes to trial, Anne is involved in a serious road traffic accident and is placed on a life support machine. Anne's witness statement will be admissible in evidence because she satisfies the condition in s 116(2(b) and oral evidence given by her of what she saw when the robbery occurred and her identification of the robbers would have been admissible at trial.

**Example 3**

Arthur, a serving soldier, witnesses a theft and gives a signed statement to the police describing what he saw. Before the case comes to trial, Arthur is posted abroad. Arthur's written statement will be admissible in evidence because he satisfies the condition in s 116(2)(c) (assuming it is not reasonably practicable to secure his attendance at trial) and oral evidence given by him of what he saw when the theft occurred would have been admissible at trial.

**Example 4**

Iqbal lives in a shelter for the homeless. He witnesses a road traffic accident in which a young child is seriously injured. Iqbal gives a witness statement to the police, and the driver involved in the accident is subsequently charged with dangerous driving. Before the trial takes place, Iqbal leaves the shelter. Despite making extensive enquiries, the police are unable to locate Iqbal's current whereabouts. Iqbal's written statement will be admissible in evidence because the condition in s 116(2)(d) appears to be satisfied and oral evidence given by Iqbal of what he saw when the accident occurred would have been admissible at trial.

**Example 5**

Emily witnesses a murder. She gives a signed statement to the police describing what she saw. Before the case comes to trial, Emily receives several anonymous letters telling her that if she gives evidence at court her baby son will be killed. Emily refuses to attend court to give oral evidence of what she saw. Emily's written statement may be admissible in evidence. She appears to satisfy the condition in s 116(2)(e) and oral evidence given by her of what she saw when the murder occurred would have been admissible at trial. However, the trial judge will still need to give leave for her written statement to be admitted in evidence, having regard to the matters listed in s 116(4) above.

**Example 6**

Fred owns an off-licence. At the end of each day's trading, Fred makes a record in a ledger detailing how much money he has taken that day. He then places the money in a safe at the back of his shop premises. One evening, after making a record in the ledger, but before putting the money in the safe, two robbers enter Fred's shop. Fred is knocked unconscious and the robbers steal the takings. Fred is traumatised by these events and suffers a mental breakdown, which renders him incapable of attending court to give evidence. Fred's entry in the ledger may be admissible in evidence. He appears to satisfy the condition in s 116(2)(b) and oral evidence given by him as to the amount of the day's takings that were stolen in the robbery would have been admissible. (Fred's entry in the ledger will also be admissible under s 117 – see **19.5.1.3** below.)

In all of the above examples it will be necessary for the party wanting to adduce the hearsay evidence to demonstrate that the appropriate condition in s 116(2) is satisfied. By way of illustration, in **Examples 2 and 6** above the court will require medical reports to show that Anne and Fred are unable to give evidence; and in **Example 4** the court will require evidence to show what steps have been taken to attempt to locate Iqbal.

Section 116 applies only to 'first-hand' hearsay. In other words, a statement can be admissible under this section only if the person who made that statement would have been permitted to give oral evidence at trial of the matters contained in the statement. In the six examples given above, the statement of each witness who was unable to come to court to give oral evidence would constitute 'first-hand' hearsay because their evidence had not passed through any other hands and was direct evidence of what they either saw (in the cases of Zoe, Arthur, Emily and Iqbal) or did (in the case of Anne and Fred). Below is an example of 'second-hand' or multiple hearsay. Such evidence is not admissible under s 116.

**Example**

Lydia witnesses an assault. She tells Jenny what she saw when the assault occurred. Jenny then gives a signed statement to the police repeating what she had been told by Lydia. Before the case comes to trial, Jenny is killed in a road traffic accident. Jenny's statement will *not* be admissible under s 116. Although Jenny satisfies the condition in s 116(2)(a)) above, she would not have been permitted to give oral evidence at court as to the contents of her statement because her statement merely repeated what she had been told by Lydia and was itself hearsay. Any evidence given by Jenny would be multiple hearsay and therefore not admissible under s 116 (Jenny's statement may, however, be admissible under s 114(1)(d) – see **19.5.4** below).

A flowchart summarising the operation of s 116 is set out at **19.10.1** below.

### 19.5.1.3 Business and other documents

**Introduction**

Section 117 of the CJA 2003 provides:

> (1) In criminal proceedings a statement contained in a document is admissible as evidence of any matter stated if—
> (a) oral evidence given in the proceedings would be evidence of that matter,
> (b) the requirements of subsection (2) are satisfied, and
> (c) the requirements of subsection (5) are satisfied, in a case where subsection (4) requires them to be.

The requirements of s 117(2) are that:

(a) the document (or the part of it containing the statement) must have been created or received by a person in the course of a trade, business, profession or other occupation, or as the holder of a paid or unpaid office;

(b) the person who supplied the information contained in the statement (the relevant person) had, or may reasonably be supposed to have had, personal knowledge of the matters dealt with; and

(c) each person (if any) through whom the information was supplied from the relevant person to the person mentioned in paragraph (a) received the information in the course of a trade, business, profession or other occupation, or as the holder of a paid or unpaid office.

The practical effect of s 117 is to make both 'first-hand' and 'multiple' hearsay in certain documents admissible in evidence.

**Business records**

Section 117 will commonly be used to ensure the admissibility in evidence of business ledgers or records.

### Example 1

Robin is charged with armed robbery. The CPS alleges that Robin bought the shotgun used in the robbery from a local gun shop two weeks prior to the robbery taking place. The CPS seeks to adduce in evidence a handwritten receipt given to Robin at the time the shotgun was purchased. The receipt was prepared by Neville, the owner of the gun shop.

Neville → the receipt prepared by Neville → 'first-hand hearsay'

The receipt will be first-hand hearsay evidence and will be admissible under s 117. The receipt is a statement in a document and was prepared by Neville in the course of his business from information about which he had first-hand knowledge, namely Robin's purchase of the shotgun.

### Example 2

Paul deposits £500 in a safe at the bank where he works. He tells Geoffrey, a clerk at the bank, who records the deposit in a ledger.

Paul → Geoffrey → Geoffrey's entry in the ledger → 'multiple hearsay'

The ledger is multiple hearsay, but it will be admissible under s 117. The entry in the ledger is a statement in a document and was created by Geoffrey in the course of business. The person who supplied the information contained in the ledger (Paul) had personal knowledge of the making of the deposit.

### Example 3

Anthony deposits £1,000 in a safe at the betting shop where he works. He tells Shona, one of his colleagues. Shona passes this information on to Gavin, the owner of the shop, who records the deposit in a ledger.

Anthony → Shona → Gavin → Gavin's entry in the ledger → 'multiple hearsay'

The entry in the ledger is multiple hearsay, but it will be admissible under s 117. The entry in the ledger is a statement in a document which was created by Gavin in the course of business. The person who supplied the information contained in the ledger (Anthony) had personal knowledge of the making of the deposit, and the person through whom the information was passed (Shona) received the information in the course of business.

### Example 4

Quentin is charged with theft of £5,000 in cash after the police find this money in a suitcase at Quentin's flat. Quentin's defence is that he won the money following a successful bet on the horses which he placed two days earlier at a local bookmakers. Quentin produces a betting slip to support this. The betting slip is a statement in a document. It is therefore hearsay evidence, but will be admissible by virtue of s 117 if Quentin can show that the betting slip was created by a person at the bookmakers' shop where Quentin placed the bet. If the person who created the betting slip was not the person to whom Quentin actually spoke when the bet was made, Quentin will need to show that the information on the betting slip was supplied by the person he dealt with, and that anyone through whom this information passed before the slip was actually created also worked for the bookmakers.

### Example 5

Younis is charged with the theft of a car from Shoaib. Younis claims to have bought the car from a local garage. Younis produces a sales receipt for the car to support this defence. The sales receipt is a statement in a document and is therefore hearsay evidence. It will be admissible by virtue of s 117 if Younis can show that the sales receipt was created by a person at the garage from which he purchased the car. If the person who created the sales receipt was not the same person with whom Younis actually dealt when he purchased the car, Younis will need to show that the information on the sales receipt was supplied by the person with whom he dealt, and that anyone through whom this information passed before the receipt was created also worked at the garage.

### Statements prepared for use in criminal proceedings

If the statement was prepared for 'the purposes of pending or contemplated criminal proceedings, or for a criminal investigation' (s 117(4)), the requirements of s 117(5) must be satisfied. The requirements of s 117(5) will be satisfied if:

(a) any of the five conditions mentioned in s 116(2) is satisfied (see **19.5.2** above); or

(b) the relevant person cannot reasonably be expected to have any recollection of the matters dealt with in the statement (having regard to the length of time since he supplied the information and all other circumstances).

#### Example 1

Roberta witnesses an assault. She tells PC Smith what she saw. PC Smith prepares a statement for Roberta to sign, setting out what Roberta told him. Before Roberta has the opportunity to check and sign the statement, she is killed in a road traffic accident (had she been able to sign the statement before her death, it would have been admissible under s 116(2)(a) – see **19.5.1.2** above). The written statement prepared by PC Smith will be multiple hearsay, but will be admissible in evidence under s 117. The written statement is a statement in a document. PC Smith created the statement in the course of his profession as a police officer and the person who supplied the information contained in the statement (Roberta) had personal knowledge of the matters dealt with in the statement. As the statement was prepared for the purpose of criminal proceedings, the requirements of s 117(5) must be satisfied. These requirements are satisfied because Roberta is dead and so satisfies s 116(2)(a).

#### Example 2

A burglary occurs at a shop. The police ask Charles, the owner of the shop, to prepare a list of all the items taken in the burglary. Charles tells PC Briggs what he thinks was taken in the burglary and PC Briggs writes out a list. Two years later the police arrest Robert and charge him with the burglary. At Robert's trial, the CPS seeks to use the list to prove what was taken in the burglary. Charles is able to attend trial to give evidence but, given the time which has elapsed since the time of the burglary, he is unable to recall what he told PC Briggs should go in the list. The list of stolen items compiled by PC Briggs is multiple hearsay but should nevertheless be admissible in evidence under s 117. The list of stolen items is a statement in a document. PC Briggs created the list in the course of his job as a police officer and the person who supplied the information contained in the list (Charles) had personal knowledge of the matters dealt with in the list. As the list was complied for use in contemplated criminal proceedings, one of the requirements in s 117(5) must be satisfied. These requirements are satisfied because, although Charles can attend court to give oral evidence, due to the time which has elapsed since the list was complied, he cannot reasonably be expected to have any recollection of the matters dealt with in the statement.

### Can the court refuse to admit a statement under s 117?

The court retains a discretionary power to make a direction that a statement shall not be admitted under s 117 (CJA 2003, s 117(6)). The court may make such a direction if it is satisfied that the statement's reliability as evidence for the purpose for which it is tendered is doubtful in view of:

(a) its contents;

(b) the source of the information contained in it;

(c) the way in which or the circumstances in which the information was supplied or received; or

(d) the way in which or the circumstances in which the document concerned was created or received (CJA 2003, s 117(7)).

A flowchart summarising the operation of s 117 is set out at **19.10.3** below.

### 19.5.1.4 Human rights considerations

Article 6(3)(d) of the ECHR provides that a defendant has the right 'to examine or have examined witnesses against him'. Sections 116 and 117 of the CJA 2003 (see **19.5.1.2 and 19.5.1.3 above**) allow the CPS to adduce evidence given by witnesses who will not attend court to give oral evidence upon which they may be cross-examined. Do these sections breach Article 6(3)(d)?

In *R v Trivedi* [1997] EHRLR 521, the European Court of Human Rights held that the statutory provisions which ss 116 and 117 replaced (and which were worded in a very similar way) were compatible with Article 6. The same conclusion was reached by the Court of Appeal in *R v Xhabri* [2005] EWCA Crim 3135. The Court held that Article 6(3)(d) did not give a defendant an absolute right to examine every witness whose testimony was adduced against him. Rather, Article 6(3)(d) would be breached only if the fairness of the trial required that a witness be available for cross-examination, and this could be determined only by looking at the facts of each individual case.

In *R v Sellick* [2005] EWCA Crim 651, the Court of Appeal held that it was proper for a court to convict on the basis of a witness statement given to the police by a witness who is then unavailable to give evidence at trial, where the evidence given by the witness is compelling and the jury are instructed to exercise caution.

In *R v Campbell* [2005] EWCA Crim 2078, the Court of Appeal found that there was no breach of a defendant's right to a fair trial even when the sole substantial evidence against the defendant was hearsay evidence, provided that it was in the interests of justice for such evidence to be admitted.

The Court took the same approach in *R v Khawaja* [2005] EWCA Crim 2697. In this case, the defendant was convicted on two counts of indecent assault. The sole witness to one of the assaults was the victim of the assault, who had since died. The trial judge permitted her statement to be read in evidence by virtue of s 116(2)(a). The defendant argued that this breached his right to a fair trial under Article 6(3)(d). The Court of Appeal held that where a witness who was the sole witness to a crime had made a statement to be used in the prosecution of that crime and had since died, there would be a strong public interest in the admission of the statement in evidence so that the prosecution might proceed. Whilst that public interest should not be permitted to override the requirement for the defendant to have a fair trial, the provision in Article 6(3)(d) stipulating that the defendant should be able to cross-examine the witness against him was merely one part of a fair trial. If, as in this case, such a witness could not be cross-examined, it was necessary to examine whether the proceedings as a whole were fair. The Court of Appeal concluded that the proceedings as a whole were fair, and the defendant had received a fair trial, because the defendant had been given the opportunity at trial to attack the credibility of the victim's statement both through expert evidence and by exposing the inconsistencies between the victim's account and evidence given by other witnesses.

There are provisions in the CJA 2003 which permit a party to challenge the credibility of evidence adduced under ss 116 and 117 (see **19.6** below), and in the Crown Court a judge has the power in certain circumstances to stop a case based largely on unconvincing hearsay evidence (see **19.7** below). A court will also have the power to exclude hearsay evidence under s 126 of the Act if the hearsay evidence is of limited importance and its admission would take up an inordinate amount of time (see **19.8** below). In addition, the court will always have a general discretion to exclude any prosecution evidence under s 78 of PACE 1984, if the admission of the evidence would have such an adverse effect on the fairness of proceedings that the court ought not to admit it (see **Chapter 21**).

### 19.5.2 Common law exceptions to the rule against hearsay evidence – s 114(1)(b)

#### 19.5.2.1 Introduction

Section 118(1) of the CJA 2003 preserves several common law exceptions to the rule excluding hearsay evidence. The most important exceptions preserved by s 118(1) are:

(a) evidence of a confession made by the defendant (see **19.5.2.2** below);

(b) evidence admitted as part of the *res gestae* (see **19.5.2.3** below);

(c) opinion evidence from an expert based on previously published works (see **19.5.2.4** below); and

(d) statements made by a party to a common enterprise being admissible against another party to the enterprise (see **19.5.2.5** below).

Other common law exceptions which are preserved include matters of general public information, evidence concerning a family's reputation or tradition, and public documents.

Section 118(2) provides that, with the exception of the rules preserved by s 118(1), the common law rules governing the admissibility of hearsay evidence are abolished.

#### 19.5.2.2 Confessions

Prior to the enactment of the CJA 2003, evidence that the defendant had made a confession was admissible at common law as an exception to the rule excluding hearsay evidence. This rule was subsequently codified by s 76(1) of PACE 1984, which provides:

> (1) In any proceedings a confession made by an accused person may be given in evidence against him insofar as it is relevant to any matter in issue in the proceedings and is not excluded by the court in pursuance of this section.

A confession which is prima facie admissible under s 76(1) may be inadmissible as a result either of s 76(2), or of the court exercising its power to exclude unlawfully obtained evidence under s 78 (see **20.4** and **20.5**).

Section 118(1) preserves the common law rule that a confession made by a defendant will be admissible in evidence against him, even if the confession is hearsay evidence.

#### 19.5.2.3 Evidence admitted as part of the *res gestae*

The common law principle of evidence being admitted as part of the *res gestae* provided that a statement made contemporaneously with an event would be admissible as an exception to the hearsay rule because the spontaneity of the statement meant that any possibility of concoction could be disregarded.

**Example**

Gerry is charged with murder. The CPS alleges that Gerry shot his victim with a rifle. Gerry's defence is that the rifle went off by accident as he was examining it. Gerry wants to call a witness to give evidence on his behalf who will say that, just after the gun went off, Gerry said: 'Oh God, my hand just slipped!' This would be hearsay evidence, but would be admissible as part of the *res gestae*.

Section 118(1) of the CJA 2003 preserves the common law rule admitting evidence that forms part of the *res gestae*. Such statements will now be admissible if one of the following conditions is satisfied:

(a) the statement was made by a person so emotionally overpowered by an event that the possibility of concoction or distortion can be disregarded;
(b) the statement accompanied an act which can properly be evaluated as evidence only if considered in conjunction with the statement; or
(c) the statement relates to a physical sensation or a mental state (such as intention or emotion) (CJA 2003, s 118(1)).

### 19.5.2.4 Expert evidence

Section 118(1) permits an expert to give opinion evidence at trial which is based on other published works within that expert's body of expertise. For example, a pathologist giving evidence in a murder case as to the cause of death may state that, in his opinion, the cause of death was due to the deceased suffocating after being exposed to excessive quantities of a particular noxious gas. The expert will be permitted to draw on the findings of research by others (which will therefore be hearsay) to explain to the court what would constitute an excessive quantity of such gas. This rule is examine more fully in **Chapter 16** (which looks more generally at the admissibility of expert evidence in criminal proceedings).

### 19.5.2.5 Statements made by a party to a common enterprise being admissible against another party to the enterprise

Section 118(1) of the CJA 2003 preserves the common law rule whereby a statement made by a party to a common enterprise is admissible against another party to the enterprise as evidence of any matter stated. This rule allows the actions or comments of one party to be used in evidence against the other, and usually arises in cases of alleged conspiracy.

**Example**

In *R v Singh* [2006] EWCA Crim 660, the defendant was convicted of conspiracy to kidnap. The CPS alleged that the defendant was at the time of the kidnapping the user of two mobile phones, which he used to make and receive a number of calls from his co-conspirators at or around the time the kidnapping took place. The Court of Appeal held that the trial judge had properly allowed the CPS to adduce in evidence against him the entries in mobile phone records belonging to other conspirators which showed the calls that been made between these phones and the phones owned by the defendant. The entries were hearsay evidence, but were admissible by virtue of s 118(1) because they constituted a statement made by a co-conspirator which implicated the defendant.

### 19.5.3 Hearsay admissible by agreement – s 114(1)(c)

This is largely self-explanatory. If all the parties in the case agree, any form of hearsay evidence can be admissible in evidence.

Example

Brian is charged with unlawful wounding. The CPS alleges that Brian punched someone who pushed in front of him whilst he was waiting to get off a bus. Brian accepts that he punched the other person, but says that he was only acting in self-defence after this person had attacked him. Trevor, the bus driver, is to give evidence for the prosecution. Trevor will say that, after Brain had got off the bus, one of the other passengers approached Trevor and identified Brian by name as one of the people involved in the incident. Although Trevor's evidence will be hearsay (because he will be repeating what he was told by the other passenger), Brian will not object to such evidence being adduced. Brian does not dispute being identified as one of the people involved in the incident. His defence will be that, although he was involved, he was only acting in self-defence.

### 19.5.4 Hearsay admissible in the interests of justice – s 114(1)(d)

The most significant change made to the admissibility of hearsay evidence by the CJA 2003 has been to introduce a 'catch-all' provision, allowing the court to admit hearsay evidence that would not otherwise be admissible if it is in the interests of justice to do so. The objective of this provision is to give the courts a very wide discretion to admit hearsay evidence which is cogent and reliable, and then to allow the magistrates or jury to determine the weight to be attached to such evidence.

In deciding whether to admit hearsay evidence under s 114(1)(d), the court must have regard to the following factors:

(a) how much probative value the statement has (assuming it to be true) in relation to a matter in issue in the proceedings, or how valuable it is for the understanding of other evidence in the case;

(b) what other evidence has been, or can be, given on the matter or evidence mentioned in para (a);

(c) how important the matter or evidence mentioned in para (a) is in the context of the case as a whole;

(d) the circumstances in which the statement was made;

(e) how reliable the maker of the statement appears to be;

(f) how reliable the evidence of the making of the statement appears to be;

(g) whether oral evidence of the matter stated can be given and, if not, why not;

(h) the amount of difficulty involved in challenging the statement; and

(i) the extent to which that difficulty would be likely to prejudice the party facing it (CJA 2003, s 114(2)).

In assessing these factors, the court will need to have regard to the defendant's right to a fair trial enshrined in Article 6 of the ECHR (see **1.8.3**).

The Court of Appeal considered the application of s 114(1)(d) and s 114(2) in *R v Taylor* [2006] EWCA Crim 260. The Court held that to reach a proper conclusion on whether the evidence should be admitted under s 114(1)(d), the trial judge was required to exercise his judgment in the light of the factors in s 114(2), give consideration to them and to any other factors he considered relevant, and then to assess their significance and the weight that in his judgment they carried.

In *R v Xhabri* (see **19.5.1.4** above), the prosecution alleged that the defendant had kidnapped the complainant and forced her to work against her will as a prostitute. The trial judge permitted the prosecution to adduce evidence from various witnesses of calls the complainant had made to them on borrowed mobile telephones, explaining what had happened and asking for help. Such evidence was hearsay, but the Court of Appeal held that the evidence was admissible under s 114(1)(d).

In *Maher v DPP* [2006] EWHC 1271 (Admin), the High Court gave further guidance on the circumstances in which s 114(1)(d) might be used to introduce hearsay evidence at trial. The appellant (M) appealed by way of case stated against her convictions for careless driving, failing to stop at the scene of an accident and failing to report an accident to the police. The DPP had alleged that, whilst reversing her car in a car park, M had struck a parked car owned by a third party (X), causing damage to that car. The DPP further alleged that M then left the scene of the accident without leaving her contact details. An individual claimed to have seen the accident as it occurred and left a note on X's car with the registration number of the car that allegedly struck X's car. X's girlfriend saw the note and immediately rang the police, who made a record of the contents of the note on their incident log. Thereafter M was traced through the registration given in the note, and she admitted in a police interview that she had driven her car in the car park on the day that the alleged accident occurred. She claimed, however, that she did not hit X's car. At the date of trial the original note was lost and the DPP sought to adduce the police log as hearsay evidence pursuant to s 117 (see **19.5.1.3** above). M challenged the admissibility of the log and contended that the requirements under s 117(2)(c) for the person supplying the information to have been acting in the course of a trade or business were not met. The magistrates' court rejected M's submission and convicted her.

The High Court held that the magistrates' court erred in admitting the log as hearsay evidence pursuant to s 117. The log was based upon the information supplied by X's girlfriend. She was not acting in the course of her business when she informed the police of the information that she received via the note. However, the court went on to say that the evidence contained in the log fell within the magistrates' court's discretion under s 114(1)(d), and it would therefore have been appropriate to admit the police log as hearsay evidence in the interests of justice. There was no basis to suggest that the admission of the evidence was not in the interests of justice, and the evidence was substantial and reliable. Further, the fact that the contents of the log was multiple hearsay (see **19.4.1.4** above) would not affect its admissibility under s 114(1)(d) because of the provisions of s 121 concerning the admissibility of multiple hearsay evidence (see **19.5.5** below).

In *R v Isechei* [2006] EWCA Crim 1815, one of the pieces of evidence used to identify the defendant as a robber was the fact that the victim recalled another person referring to her attacker as 'Marvin', which was the defendant's first name. The defendant argued that the trial judge should not have allowed the prosecution to rely on this evidence because it was inadmissible hearsay evidence. The Court of Appeal rejected this argument, stating that the evidence was admissible in the interests of justice under s 114(1)(d) because it was relevant to the question of the identification of the defendant.

In *McEwan v DPP* [2007] EWHC 740 (Admin), the defendant appealed against his conviction for criminal damage. The prosecution case relied on the evidence of a minor, who had stated in a witness statement that he had seen the defendant scratch the complainant's vehicle with a beer can. A medical report was submitted in relation to the witness that stated that he suffered from a serious bowel condition that might worsen through the stress of giving evidence. The prosecution sought an adjournment so that it could ascertain whether the witness was so ill that he could not attend court. The magistrates' court refused that application but agreed to an application by the prosecution to have the witness's evidence admitted under s 114(1)(d) and (2). The magistrates' court held that it was in the interests of justice for the witness statement to be admitted. The High Court held that the magistrates' court failed to give any, or any sufficient, weight to the prejudicial effect that the inability to challenge the witness's evidence would have on M's defence, and the conviction was quashed.

### 19.5.5 Additional requirements for the admissibility of multiple hearsay evidence

If a statement upon which a party seeks to rely contains 'multiple hearsay' (see **19.4.1.4** above), such a statement will be admissible in evidence only if:

(a) it is admissible under s 117 – a statement in a business document (see **19.5.1.3** above);

(b) it is admissible under s 119 – a previous inconsistent statement by a witness (see **Chapter 9**);

(c) it is admissible under s 120 – a previous consistent statement by a witness (see **Chapter 9**);

(d) all the parties agree to the statement being admitted (see **19.5.3** above); or

(e) the court is satisfied that the value of the evidence in question, taking into account how reliable the statements appear to be, is so high that the interests of justice require the later statement to be admissible (CJA 2003, s 121).

## 19.6 Challenging the credibility of hearsay evidence

If hearsay evidence is admitted by the court, the maker of the statement will not be in attendance at court to give oral evidence. This will deprive the other party of the opportunity to cross-examine the maker of the statement in an attempt to undermine that person's credibility as a witness. In such a case, however, s 124 of the CJA 2003 permits the following evidence to be admissible:

(a) any evidence which (if the witness had given oral evidence) would have been admissible as relevant to his credibility as a witness; and

(b) with the leave of the court, any evidence which (if the witness had given oral evidence) could have been put to him in cross-examination as relevant to his credibility as a witness (for example, evidence that the witness had previous convictions for offences where he had been untruthful, such as perjury).

#### Example

Peter is on trial in the Crown Court for theft. Part of the prosecution case consists of a witness statement from Julia, Peter's ex-girlfriend, who claims to have witnessed Peter committing the theft. Julia's witness statement has been admitted as hearsay evidence under s 116(2)(b) because Julia had a serious accident just prior to the trial and is in a critical condition in hospital. Peter alleges that Julia fabricated her statement to get revenge on him after he broke off their relationship. Julia also has two previous convictions for offences of perjury. As Julia will not be attending trial to give oral evidence, Peter will be unable to put to her in cross-examination that she has a grudge against him and so has a reason for giving a false statement. Neither will he be able to cross-examine her about her previous convictions (assuming the judge would have given him leave to do so – see **Chapter 22**). Peter will, however, be able to place before the jury evidence of his breaking off the relationship to show that Julia might have had a grudge against him, as this is a matter relevant to Julia's credibility as a witness. Peter will also seek leave to place before the jury evidence of Julia's previous convictions, as again these are matters relevant to her credibility as a witness and are matters which could, with the leave of the court, have been put to her in cross-examination.

## 19.7 Stopping the case where evidence is unconvincing

In a Crown Court trial, if the judge is satisfied at any time after the close of the prosecution case that:

(a) the case against the defendant is based wholly or partly on hearsay evidence; and

(b) the hearsay evidence is so unconvincing that, considering its importance to the case against the defendant, his conviction of the offence would be unsafe,

the judge must direct the jury to acquit the defendant (or discharge the jury if the judge considers there ought to be a retrial) (CJA 2003, s 125).

### Example

Erica is charged with unlawful wounding. The only evidence against Erica is from two witnesses who claim to have seen Erica commit the alleged assault. Both witnesses gave statements to the police but have since disappeared, despite the police having taken steps to find them. The statements are admissible as hearsay evidence under s 116(2)(d), as the makers of the statements cannot be found although such steps as it is reasonably practical to take to find them have been taken. However, the quality of the identification evidence given in the statements is weak and, at trial, Erica adduces evidence under s 124 (see **19.6** above) that both witnesses have previous convictions for offences involving deception. If the trial judge considers that the evidence provided by the statements is so unconvincing that it would render any conviction unsafe, he must direct the jury to acquit Erica.

## 19.8 The general discretion to exclude evidence

Section 126(1) of the CJA 2003 gives the court a general discretion to refuse to admit a statement that constitutes hearsay evidence if 'the court is satisfied that the case for excluding the statement, taking account of the danger that to admit it would result in undue waste of time, substantially outweighs the case for admitting it, taking account of the value of the evidence'.

This provision allows a court to exclude a piece of hearsay evidence if the evidence is of limited importance to the case and an inordinate amount of time would be spent in the evidence actually being given. In *R v Xhabri* (see **19.5.1.4** above), however, the Court of Appeal said that s 126 could be used more generally to exclude hearsay evidence where the court considered that the admission of such evidence would have an adverse effect on the fairness of the trial. This much wider interpretation of s 126 was upheld by the Court of Appeal in *R v C and K* (see **19.5.1.2** above). The Court interpreted s 126 as giving the court 'a general discretion to exclude evidence in criminal proceedings'.

Section 126(2) provides that nothing in the CJA 2003 concerning the admissibility of hearsay evidence prejudices the court's overriding general power to exclude evidence under s 78 of PACE 1984 (see **Chapter 21**).

## 19.9 Procedure for admitting hearsay evidence

### 19.9.1 Introduction

The procedural rules to be followed should a party seek to rely on hearsay evidence at trial (or to challenge the admissibility of hearsay evidence on which another party seeks to rely) are contained in Part 34 of the Criminal Procedure Rules (CrimPR). These rules do not, however, apply in all cases when a party wishes to use hearsay evidence at trial. The rules in Part 34 only apply to cases where:

(a) it is in the interests of justice for the hearsay evidence to be admissible (s 114(1)(d));

(b) the witness is unavailable to attend court (s 116);

(c) the evidence is contained in a business or other document (s 117); or

(d) the evidence is multiple hearsay (s 121) (CrimPR, r 34.1).

For hearsay evidence which is admissible on any other grounds, the procedural rules contained in Part 34 do not apply. If, for example, the defendant made a confession at the time of his arrest, the rules in Part 34 will not apply should the CPS seek to rely on the arresting officer repeating details of that confession when he gives evidence at the defendant's trial. Similarly, the rules in Part 34 will not apply if the hearsay evidence is admissible under any of the preserved common law exceptions to the rule excluding hearsay evidence. The significance of this is that, if the hearsay evidence to be adduced at trial does not fall within one or more of the four sections noted at (a) to (d) above, the party seeking to rely on that evidence will not need to serve on the other party notice of its intention to rely on such evidence (see below).

A party wishing to adduce hearsay evidence to which Part 34 applies, or to oppose another party's application to introduce such evidence, must give notice of its intention to do this both to the court and to the other parties in the case (CrimPR, r 34.2). Notice must be given using a set of prescribed forms which are set out at **19.12** below. As part of the standard directions that will be given in both the magistrates' court (see **Chapter 8**) and the Crown Court (see **Chapter 10**), the court will impose time limits for the CPS and the defendant to give notice of their intention to adduce hearsay evidence at trial. The relevant time limits are set out in r 34.3 (for the CPS to give notice of its intention to introduce hearsay evidence) and r 34.4 (for the defendant to give notice of his intention to introduce hearsay evidence). The time limits for either the CPS or the defendant to send a notice opposing another party's intention to introduce hearsay evidence are set out in r 34.5.

### 19.9.2 Magistrates' court

If the CPS wishes to adduce at trial hearsay evidence to which Part 34 applies, it must send a notice of intention to introduce hearsay evidence at trial both to the court and to the other parties in the case (CrimPR, r 34.2). This notice must be sent at the same time as the CPS complies or purports to comply with its initial duty to disclose to the defendant any unused material it has (CrimPR, r 34.3(a)). If the defendant opposes this, he must send a notice to this effect to both the court and the other parties in the case within *14 days* of receiving the notice from the CPS.

If the defendant seeks at trial to rely on hearsay evidence to which Part 34 applies, he must send a notice of intention to introduce hearsay evidence both to the court and to the other parties in the case (CrimPR, r 34.2). This notice must be sent within *14 days* of the date on which the CPS complies or purports to comply with its initial duty to disclose to the defendant any unused material it has (CrimPR, r 34.4). If the CPS opposes this, it must send a notice to this effect both to the court and to the other parties in the case within *14 days* of receiving the notice from the defendant (CrimPR, r 34.5).

### 19.9.3 Crown Court

If the CPS seeks to adduce at trial hearsay evidence to which Part 34 applies, it must send both to the court and to the other parties in the case a notice of its intention to introduce hearsay evidence at trial (CrimPR, r 34.2). For an either way offence, this notice must be sent within *14 days* of committal (CrimPR, r 34.3(b)(i)). For an indictable only offence, the notice must be sent within *14 days* of the date on which the CPS serves the prosecution case papers on the defendant (CrimPR, r 34.3(b)(iv)). The defendant has *14 days* from receiving this notice in which to send a notice to the court and to the other parties in the case opposing this (CrimPR, r 34.5).

If the defendant seeks at trial to rely on hearsay evidence to which Part 34 applies, he must send a notice of intention to introduce hearsay evidence both to the court and to the other parties in the case (CrimPR, r 34.2). This notice must be given within *14 days* of the date on which the CPS complies or purports to comply with its initial duty to disclose to the defendant any unused material it has (CrimPR, r 34.4). If the CPS opposes this, it must send a notice to this effect both to the court and to the other parties in the case within *14 days* of receiving the notice from the defendant (CrimPR, r 34.5).

### 19.9.4 Must the parties comply with the above time limits?

Rule 34.7 of the Criminal Procedure Rules permits the court to dispense with the requirement to give notice of hearsay evidence, to allow notice to be given orally rather than in writing, and to shorten or extend the time limits for giving notice. In *R (Robinson) v Sutton Coldfield Magistrates' Court* [2006] EWHC 307 (Admin), the Divisional Court upheld permission given by the magistrates to allow the CPS to adduce a witness statement from the complainant as hearsay evidence when the application was made the day before trial.

### 19.9.5 Determining the admissibility of hearsay evidence

When either the CPS or the defendant has made an application to adduce hearsay evidence at trial, and this application is opposed by the other party, the court will usually determine the admissibility of such evidence at a pre-trial hearing. In the magistrates' court, this is likely to be at the case management hearing/pre-trial review, or at a specific pre-trial hearing to resolve disputes about the admissibility of evidence (see **Chapter 8**). In the Crown Court, this is likely to be at the plea and case management hearing, or at a specific pre-trial hearing (see **Chapter 10**).

Completed examples of the forms used in both the magistrates' court and the Crown Court to apply to give notice of an intention to introduce hearsay evidence or to oppose the introduction of such evidence are set out at **19.12** below.

## 19.10 Procedural flowcharts

### 19.10.1 Criminal Justice Act 2003, s 114

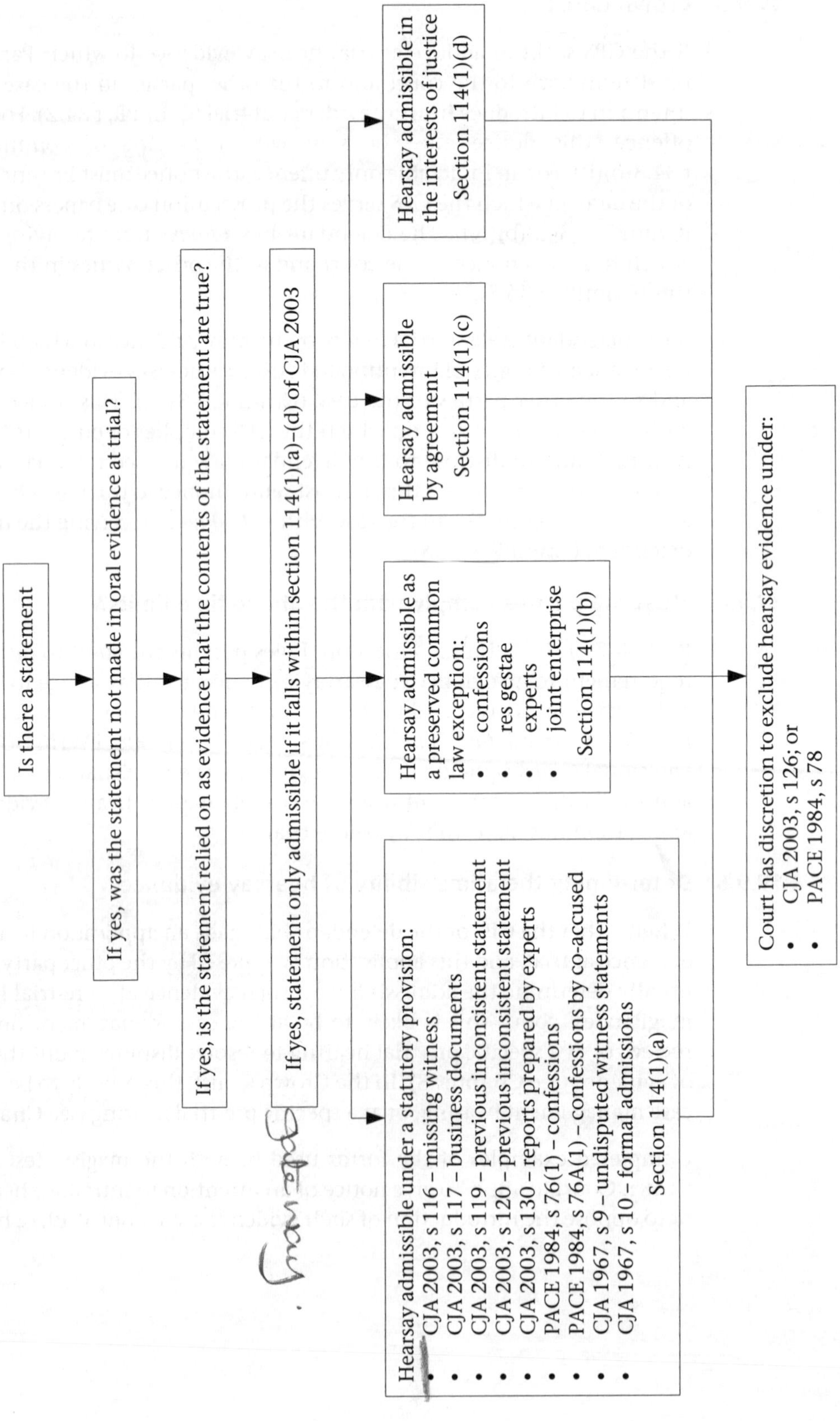

### 19.10.2 Criminal Justice Act 2003, s 116 – the 'missing witness'

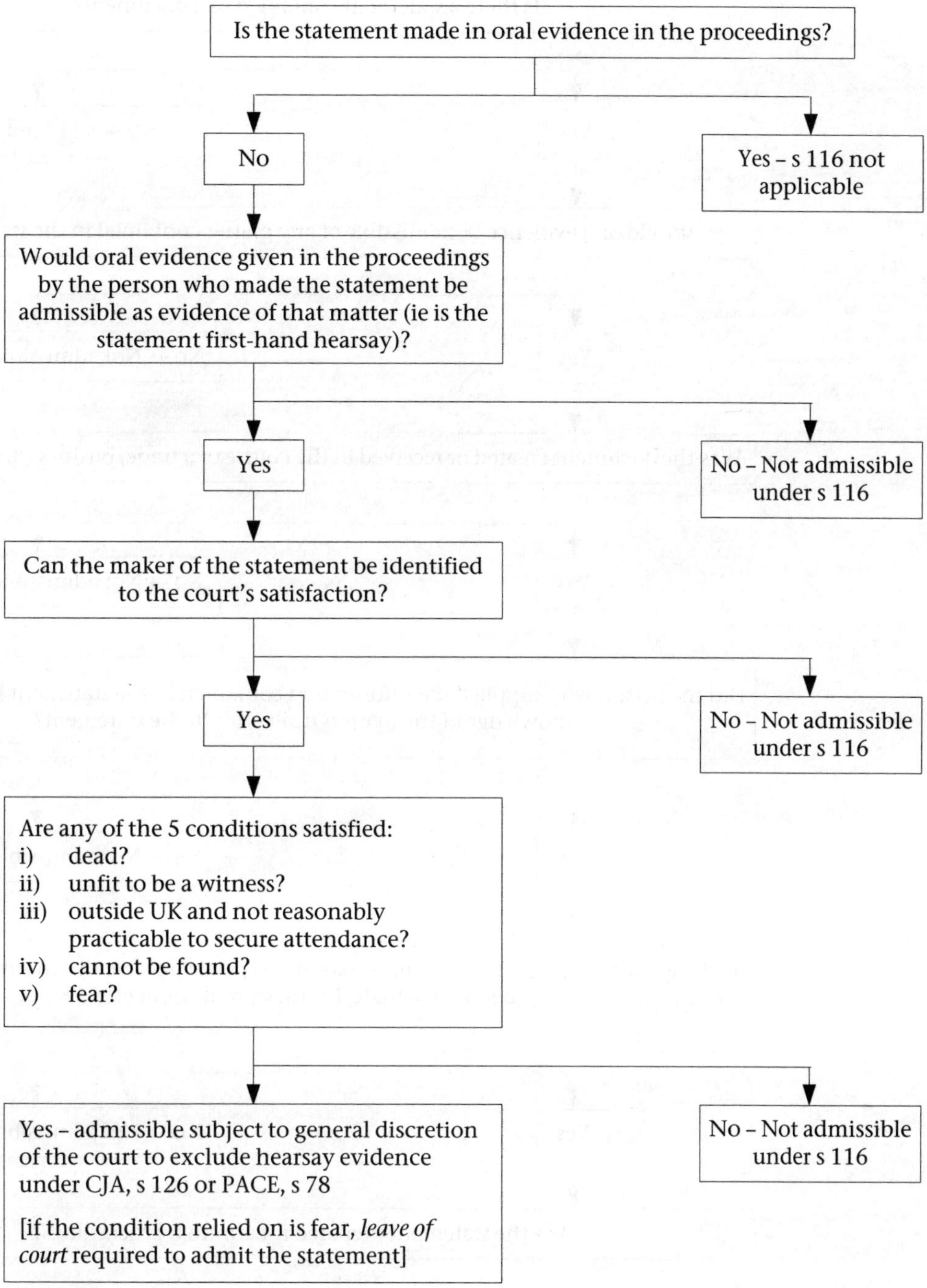

### 19.10.3 Criminal Justice Act 2003, s 117

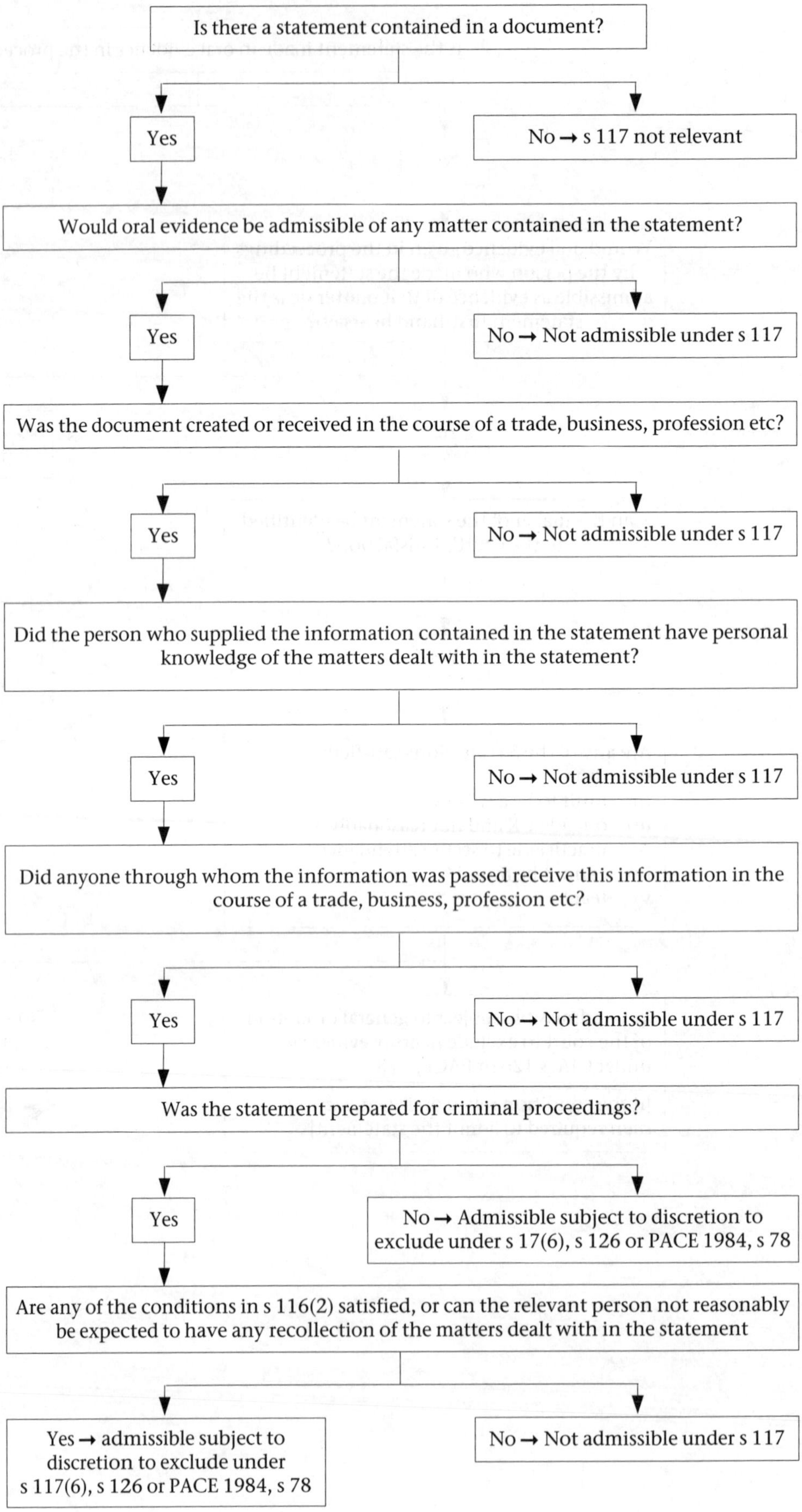

## 19.11 Checklist

At the end of this chapter you should be able to explain:

- the statutory definition of hearsay evidence in the CJA 2003;
- the four circumstances in which hearsay evidence is admissible in criminal proceedings:
  - evidence admissible by virtue of a statutory provision (s 114(1)(a));
  - common law exceptions to the rule excluding hearsay evidence preserved by the CJA 2003 (s 114(1)(b));
  - evidence which all the parties agree shall be admissible (s 114(1)(c)); and
  - evidence which it is in the interests of justice to admit (s 114(1)(d)).
- the power of the court to exclude hearsay evidence that would otherwise be admissible at trial;
- the way in which the credibility of hearsay evidence may be challenged at trial;
- the procedural rules to be followed if a party wishes to rely upon hearsay evidence at trial, or to challenge hearsay evidence that another party seeks to rely upon at trial (CrimPR, Part 34).

## 19.12 Key forms

### 19.12.1 Introduction

Two forms are set out below:

(a) notice of intention to introduce hearsay evidence (see **19.12.2**); and

(b) notice of opposition to the introduction of hearsay evidence (see **19.12.3**).

### 19.12.2 Notice of intention to introduce hearsay evidence

| | |
|---|---|
| **Notice of intention to introduce hearsay evidence**<br>**Under s 114, Criminal Justice Act 2003**<br>(Criminal Procedure Rules, rr 34.2, 68.20(1)) | |
| This form must be used to give notice of intention to introduce hearsay evidence on one or more of the grounds set out in s 114(1)(d), s 116, s 117 and s 121, Criminal Justice Act 2003. | |
| **Details of party giving notice**<br>Surname: *Crown Prosecution Service*<br>Forename(s): *N/A*<br>Address: *East Chambers, Saville Street, Chester* | State the name and address of the party giving notice of hearsay evidence. (If in custody give address where detained) |
| **Case Details**<br>The *Crown* Court at Chester<br>Case Reference Number *CH/080248*<br>Name of Judge: *HHJ Hutton*<br>Date the trial or proceedings is due to start/started: *PCMH – 16/04/08*<br>Name the prosecuting agency (if relevant): *CPS*<br>Name of defendant(s): *Gary Paul Dickson* | Enter the name of the Court and the case no. |
| **Charges:**<br>*Assault occasioning actual bodily harm on Vincent Lamb on 18th December 2007* | Give brief details of the charges to which this notice applies. |
| **To the named recipient(s) of this notice:** *Gary Paul Dickson*<br>I give you notice of my intention to introduce hearsay evidence, details of which are set out below, in these proceedings. | |

**Grounds for introducing the hearsay evidence**

On which of the following grounds do you intend to introduce the hearsay evidence?

(a) ☐ It is in the interests of justice for it to be admissible.

(b) ☑ The witness is unavailable to attend.

(c) ☐ It is in the interests of justice for it to be admissible.

(d) ☐ The evidence is multiple hearsay.

Tick as appropriate to show which of ss 114(1)(d), 116, 117 or 121 of the CJA 2003 you rely on to introduce the evidence.

Where box (a) is ticked you must specify below which of the factors set out in s 114(2), CJA 2003 are relevant and explain how they are relevant.

**Further details of grounds:**

*Criminal Justice Act 2003, s 116(2)(c) – that the relevant person is outside the UK and it is not reasonably practicable to secure her attendance. The witness in question has returned to live and work in Australia, and will not be returning to the UK in the foreseeable future.*

**Details of hearsay evidence**

The details of the hearsay evidence are as follows:

*Written witness statement from Kate Ramsey who worked as a barperson at Connolley's Nightclub and who witnessed the defendant threaten the complainant Vincent Lamb by shaking his fist in Mr Lamb's face.*

*A copy of Miss Ramsey's witness statement is attached and has been served on the defendant Gary Paul Dickson through her solicitors Messrs Collaws.*

Give brief details of the evidence that you want to introduce as hearsay evidence

A complete copy of that evidence must be attached to this notice, if it has not already been served on the other parties.

**Extension of time**

Are you applying for an extension of time within which to give this notice? Yes/No – *NO*

If yes, state your reasons:

**Signed:** *J Boothroyd*

**Dated:** *2nd March*

### 19.12.3 Notice of opposition to the introduction of hearsay evidence

| | |
|---|---|
| **Notice of opposition to the introduction of hearsay evidence**<br>**Under s 114, Criminal Justice Act 2003**<br><br>(Criminal Procedure Rules, rr 34.3, 34.5, 68.20(1)) | |
| This form shall be used to give notice of opposition to the introduction of hearsay evidence given under rule 34(2) | |
| **Details of party opposing the introduction of hearsay evidence**<br><br>Surname: *Dickson*<br><br>Forename(s): *Gary Paul*<br><br>Address: *17 Marsh Street, Chester CH3 7LW*<br><br>Date that you were given notice that hearsay evidence will be introduced in these proceedings: *3rd March 2007* | State the name and address of the party giving notice of their opposition to the introduction of hearsay evidence. (If in custody give address where detained) |
| **Case Details**<br><br>The *Crown* Court at *Chester*<br>Case Reference Number *CH 080248*<br><br>Name of Judge: *HHJ Hutton*<br><br>Date the trial or proceedings is due to start/started:<br>*PCMH – 16/04/08*<br><br>Name the prosecuting agency (if relevant): *CPS*<br>Name of defendant(s): *Gary Paul Dickson*<br><br>Charges:<br><br>*Assault occasioning actual bodily harm on Vincent Lamb on 18th December 2007* | Enter the name of the Court and the case no.<br><br>Give brief details of the charges to which this notice applies. |
| **Details of the hearsay evidence that you want to exclude**<br><br>*Written witness statement from Kate Ramsay dated 20th December 2007. Objection to the entire witness statement.* | Give brief description of the hearsay evidence that you want to exclude from the proceedings. Specify whether you object to all or part of that evidence. |

| **Grounds for excluding the evidence** | |
|---|---|
| *The evidence given by the witness is an account of an incident alleged to have taken place on the evening of 17th December 2007 at Connolley's Nightclub when the defendant is alleged to have threatened the complainant by shaking his fist in the face of the complainant. The defendant denies having done this and further asserts that the witness has a purpose of her own to serve by giving this evidence against him. If the witness does not attend court to give evidence, the defendant will be deprived of the opportunity of putting these matters to the witness in cross-examination.*<br><br>*The court is asked to exercise its discretion under s 126(1) of the Criminal Justice Act 2003 and s 78 of PACE 1984 to exclude the statement on the grounds that its admission would have an adverse effect on the fairness of the trial.* | Set out the grounds for excluding the hearsay evidence that you object to.<br><br>Any relevant skeleton argument or case law that might bear on the issue may be attached to this notice. |
| **Extension of time** | |
| Are you applying for an extension of time within which to give this notice? *NO*<br><br>If yes, state your reasons: | Yes/No |
| **Signed:** *Collaws*<br><br>**Dated:** *12th March 2008* | |

# Chapter 20

## Confession Evidence



### 20.1 Introduction

This chapter will examine what constitutes a confession and when confession evidence is admissible in evidence at trial. The chapter will also look at the circumstances in which confession evidence may be excluded and the procedure to be followed when the defendant challenges the admissibility of confession evidence upon which the CPS seeks to rely.

### 20.2 What is a confession?

#### 20.2.1 PACE 1984, s 82(1)

A confession is 'any statement wholly or partly adverse to the person who made it, whether made to a person in authority or not and whether made in words or otherwise' (PACE 1984, s 82(1)).

Confessions will usually be made by a defendant when interviewed at the police station, although a defendant may also make a confession outside the police station, either to the police or to someone else. If, for example, a defendant admits to a friend that he committed a theft, this would be a confession. Confessions do not need to amount to a full admission of guilt. Anything said by a defendant that constitutes an admission of any element of the offence with which he is subsequently charged, or that is in any way detrimental to his case, will satisfy the definition of a confession in s 82(1).

**Example 1**

Julian is arrested on suspicion of theft from a supermarket. When interviewed at the police station, Julian tells the police: 'Yeah, it was me who nicked the stuff. I wanted to sell it to get money for drugs.' Julian's comments satisfy the definition of a confession in s 82(1) because he has admitted to carrying out the theft.

**Example 2**

Claudia, a juvenile, is charged with the theft of an MP3 player. The prosecution allege that Claudia took the MP3 player from the desk of Kate, a pupil in Claudia's class at school. The prosecution have obtained a witness statement from Naomi, another pupil in the class. Naomi overheard Claudia telling one of her friends that the MP3 player was hidden inside her locker. Claudia's remark will satisfy the definition of a confession in s 82(1). Although Naomi has not heard Claudia admitting to stealing the MP3 player, Claudia's remarks are adverse to her case – she has admitted to being in possession of the stolen MP3 player, and to having hidden this in her locker.

#### Example 3

PC Jones is called to a pub where an assault has taken place. On arriving at the pub, PC Jones obtains a description of the person alleged to have committed the assault. Shortly after leaving the pub, PC Jones sees Michael in the street. Michael matches the description of the person who committed the assault. PC Jones asks Michael if he has been at the pub that evening. Michael replies: 'I was at the pub but it wasn't me that hit him.' Although Michael has not said that he committed the assault, his comments still satisfy the definition of a confession in s 82(1) above. This is because, in the event that Michael is later charged with the assault, the comments he made will be adverse to his case. Michael admits to having being at the pub, and also admits to knowing that an assault has taken place (for which he may be a suspect).

#### Example 4

PC Graham is searching a warehouse owned by Roger, after receiving a tip-off that the premises are being used to cultivate cannabis. Roger tells PC Graham: 'I'm the only person who has a key to the warehouse. Nobody else can gain access.' PC Graham subsequently finds a number of cannabis plants. Roger is subsequently charged with various offences under the Misuse of Drugs Act 1971. Although Roger has not admitted to cultivating the cannabis plants, his comments will still satisfy the definition of a confession in s 82(1) above because his comments are adverse to his case. Roger has told PC Graham that he is the only person who can gain access to the premises where the cannabis plants were found.

### 20.2.2 Can silence amount to a confession?

The general rule is that an accused's silence in the face of an allegation made against him that would normally call for some kind of denial or allegation from him, is not admissible as evidence to show that he admits the allegation.

#### Example

In *R v Christie* [1914] AC 545, the defendant was charged with indecently assaulting a young boy. Shortly after the alleged assault occurred, and in the presence of the boy's mother and a police officer, the boy confronted the defendant with the words, 'That is the man', and then went on to give details of the alleged assault. The defendant replied with the comment: 'I am innocent.' The Court of Appeal held that, had the defendant remained silent in the face of the allegation made by the boy, this could not be evidence to show that he admitted the allegation made, even though the making of such an allegation would reasonably call for some kind of explanation from the defendant.

The situation is the same if the police put to a suspect an allegation which has been made against him by a co-accused. The suspect's silence in the face of such an allegation is not evidence that the suspect accepts the truth of the allegation. The position is different, however, if a suspect remains silent when, *in his presence*, a co-accused makes a confession in which he is implicated (see **20.3.3.1** below).

## 20.3 Admissibility of confession evidence

### 20.3.1 Confessions

A confession made by a defendant prior to his trial will be admissible in evidence at trial by virtue of s 76(1) of PACE 1984:

> In any proceedings a confession made by an accused person may be given in evidence against him insofar as it is relevant to any matter in issue in the proceedings and is not excluded by the court in pursuance of this section.

This means that a pre-trial confession will be admissible at trial to prove the truth of its contents (ie, to prove the defendant's guilt).

A confession made by the defendant before trial which is then repeated in evidence at his trial will be hearsay evidence (see **Chapter 19**). Hearsay evidence is generally inadmissible in criminal proceedings unless it falls within one of the exceptions contained in s 114(1) of the CJA 2003 (see **19.5.1**). A confession made by the defendant will fall within the exception created by s 114(1)(a), which provides that hearsay evidence will be admissible at trial if it is made admissible by virtue of any statutory provision. As confession evidence is made admissible by s 76(1) of PACE 1984, it is covered by s 114(1)(a).

**Example 1**

James is charged with theft. He admits the theft in an audibly recorded interview at the police station. A transcript of the interview is subsequently read out at James's trial. The transcript is hearsay evidence, but it will be admissible in evidence by virtue of s 76(1) to prove his guilt.

**Example 2**

James is arrested on suspicion of theft. As he is being arrested, James tells the arresting officer: 'Okay I did it. You know I only steal because I have no money.'

When he is later interviewed at the police station, James denies having made this confession. At James's trial, the arresting officer repeats the comment made by James at the time of his arrest. This will be hearsay evidence, but it will be admissible in evidence by virtue of s 76(1) to prove his guilt.

**Example 3**

James is charged with theft. He denied the theft when interviewed at the police station, but later admits to his friend Margaret that he committed the theft. Margaret has provided the CPS with a statement in which she repeats the confession which James has made. If Margaret repeats this at court when giving oral evidence, this will be hearsay evidence, but it will be admissible in evidence by virtue of s 76(1) to prove his guilt.

### 20.3.2 Mixed statements

A confession may sometimes also include a statement which is favourable to the defendant. These are referred to as 'mixed statements'. The whole statement will be admissible under s 76(1) as an exception to the rule excluding hearsay evidence.

**Example**

Cedric is charged with assault. When interviewed at the police station, he says: 'I hit the victim in the face but I only did this in self-defence.' This is a mixed statement, because Cedric makes a confession (admitting he hit the victim in the face) but he also makes a statement favourable to his defence (saying that he was acting in self-defence). The entire statement will be admissible under s 76(1).

### 20.3.3 Confessions and a co-accused

#### 20.3.3.1 Is a confession made by one defendant admissible in evidence against his co-defendant?

**Pre-trial confessions**

Confessions made out of court are admissible in evidence only against the person making the confession (PACE 1984, s 76(1)). A confession made to the police by one defendant is therefore not admissible in evidence against a co-defendant who may be implicated in that confession (see 'Confessions made at trial', below, for the position if the confession is repeated in oral evidence at trial).

**Example 1**

Violet and Jason are jointly charged with arson. Both are pleading not guilty. When interviewed by the police, Violet made a confession, stating that she and Jason committed the offence together. Violet now claims that this confession was untrue. If, at trial, the CPS adduces evidence of Violet's confession, the confession will only be admissible in evidence against Violet as the person who made the confession. The confession will not be admissible in evidence against Jason.

**Example 2**

Sunita and Deepak are jointly charged with burglary. Both are pleading not guilty. Ravi alleges that, a few days after the burglary occurred, Sunita confessed to him that she and Deepak carried out the burglary together. Ravi gives a statement to this effect to the police. If Ravi repeats the details of the confession allegedly made to him by Sunita when he gives oral evidence at court, the confession will be admissible in evidence against Sunita (as the person who made the confession). The confession will not be admissible in evidence against Deepak.

In *R v Hayter* [2005] UKHL 6, the House of Lords held that a confession by one defendant could not be used directly as evidence against another. The Lords found that when in a joint trial the case against a defendant depended on the prosecution proving the guilt of a co-defendant, and the evidence against the co-defendant consisted solely of his own out of court confession, then that confession would be admissible as against the defendant only in so far as it went to proving the co-defendant's guilt. The confession of the co-defendant could not be used as direct evidence of the defendant's guilt.

The only exception to this is that, at common law, a confession made by a defendant which also implicates a co-defendant may be admissible in evidence against the co-defendant if the confession was made *in the co-defendant's presence* and the co-defendant does nothing at that time to challenge what the defendant has said about his involvement in the offence (*R v Coll* [2005] All ER (D) 82).

**Example**

Gary and Eric are jointly charged with criminal damage, the allegation being that they smashed the windows on a car. They were seen doing this by an eye-witness who gave their descriptions to the police. The police found them together at a local pub and, when asked about their involvement, Gary said (in the presence and hearing of Eric): 'Okay, it was us that did it. I smashed the wing mirrors and Eric did the windscreen.'

This confession will be admissible to prove Gary's guilt. It will also be admissible in evidence against Eric, if Eric says nothing at the time of Gary's comment to challenge what Gary has said about his involvement in the offence. It will then be a matter for the magistrates or jury to decide whether Eric's failure to respond to Gary's incriminating remark could amount to an admission of guilt on his part.

**Confessions made at trial**

Any evidence given by a co-defendant at trial which implicates the defendant (including a confession or an admission made by the co-defendant) will be admissible in evidence against the defendant. Also, if the co-defendant has pleaded guilty at an earlier hearing and is giving evidence for the prosecution at the trial of the defendant, any evidence he gives implicating the defendant in the commission of the offence will be admissible in evidence against the defendant.

**Example 1**

Trisha and Marlon are jointly charged with theft. Tricia is to plead guilty and Marlon will plead not guilty. Tricia enters her guilty plea on her first appearance before the court. She then gives a statement to the CPS stating that she and Marlon committed the theft together. As Tricia is no longer being tried with Marlon (because she has pleaded guilty), she will be able to give evidence as a prosecution witness at Marlon's trial. If, when giving evidence, Tricia states that she and Marlon committed the theft together, this will be admissible in evidence against Marlon.

**Example 2**

Nicola and Jessica are jointly charged with the theft of cosmetics from a supermarket. Both plead not guilty and claim to have bought the items allegedly stolen. However, when being cross-examined by the prosecution at trial, Jessica says: 'Okay we both nicked the stuff, but I only took part because Nicola said she would beat me up if I didn't.' Jessica's confession will be admissible in evidence against both her and Nicola.

#### 20.3.3.2 Can one defendant adduce evidence of a confession made by another defendant?

Where two (or more) co-defendants are pleading not guilty and are tried jointly, s 76A(1) of PACE 1984 allows one defendant to adduce in evidence the fact that a co-defendant has made a confession. Evidence of the confession may be adduced either by cross-examining the co-defendant on the alleged confession, or, adducing evidence of the confession if the co-defendant declines to give evidence (*R v Finch* [2007] EWCA Crim 36). Evidence of the confession is admissible both to show the guilt of the co-defendant and also to undermine the credibility of any evidence given by the co-defendant.

**Example 1**

Robert and Patrick are jointly charged with common assault. Both are pleading not guilty. When interviewed by the police, Patrick confessed to having carried out the assault. At their joint trial, Robert will be entitled to cross-examine Patrick about this confession or, if Patrick declines to give evidence, Robert will be permitted to adduce evidence of the confession having been made.

**Example 2**

Sarah and Rachel are jointly charged with theft. Both are pleading not guilty. After being charged, Sarah told Diane, a friend of Rachel, that she committed the theft. At their joint trial, Rachel will be entitled to cross-examine Sarah about this confession and, if Sarah declines to give evidence or denies having made the confession, will be permitted to call Diane to give evidence to confirm what Sarah said.

## 20.4 Challenging the admissibility of a confession: PACE 1984, s 76

### 20.4.1 Introduction

A defendant who is alleged to have made a confession may challenge the admissibility of this confession at his trial by arguing either:

(a) that he did not make the confession at all, and that the person (usually a police officer) to whom he made the alleged confession was either mistaken as to what he heard or has fabricated evidence of the confession; or

(b) that he did make the confession, but only for reasons other than the fact that he was actually guilty of having committed the offence. In this case, the defendant will say that the confession is untrue.

If the defendant accepts that he made a confession but denies that the confession is true, he will usually challenge the admissibility of the confession under s 76(2) of PACE 1984:

> If, in any proceedings where the prosecution proposes to give in evidence a confession made by an accused person, it is represented to the court that the confession was or may have been obtained—
>
> (a) by *oppression* of the person who made it; or
>
> (b) in consequence of anything said or done which was likely, in the circumstances existing at the time, to render *unreliable* any confession which might be made by him in consequence thereof,
>
> the court shall not allow the confession to be given in evidence against him except in so far as the prosecution proves to the court beyond reasonable doubt that the confession (notwithstanding that it may be true) was not obtained as aforesaid. (emphasis added)

This means that if a defendant argues that a confession was obtained in the manner or circumstances detailed under paras (a) or (b) above, the court must not allow that confession to be used as evidence by the prosecution, unless the prosecution prove beyond a reasonable doubt that the confession was not so obtained. Even if the court thinks that the confession is true, the court must still rule that the prosecution cannot use the confession in evidence unless the prosecution can prove that the confession was not obtained by oppression or in circumstances which render it unreliable.

**Example**

Jeff is charged with murder. When interviewed at the police station he confessed to having committed the murder. At his trial, Jeff argues that the confession was obtained by oppression and should be ruled inadmissible by the trial judge. The CPS must prove beyond a reasonable doubt that the confession was not obtained by oppression, even if the judge believes the confession to be true. If the prosecution fail to do this, the judge must not allow evidence of the confession to be placed before the jury.

### 20.4.2 Oppression

The Police and Criminal Evidence Act 1984 provides a partial definition of the term 'oppression'. Section 76(8) states that 'oppression' includes 'torture, inhuman or degrading treatment, and the use or threat of violence (whether or not amounting to torture)'. This was not intended to be a full definition of the meaning of the term, and it will be very rare for a defendant to argue that he confessed only because the police subjected him to this kind of treatment. In *R v Fulling* [1987] 2 WLR 923, the Court of Appeal said that the word 'oppression' was to be given its ordinary meaning. The Court said that oppression consisted of 'the exercise of authority or power in a burdensome, harsh or wrongful manner; unjust or cruel treatment of subjects, inferiors, etc; the imposition of unreasonable or unjust burdens'.

An argument that a confession should be excluded under s 76(2)(a) on the grounds of oppression is likely to arise only where there has been deliberate and serious misconduct on the part of the police. Examples of when the court has found oppression are:

(a) *R v Davison* [1998] Crim LR 442 – the defendant confessed after being unlawfully held at the police station, unlawfully denied access to legal advice and questioned about an offence for which he had not been arrested.

(b) *R v Paris* (1993) 97 Cr App R 1999 – in an audibly recorded interview at the police station, the defendant was bullied and hectored into making a confession. The Court of Appeal said that, other than actual physical violence, it would find it hard to think of a more hostile and intimidating approach adopted by interviewing officers.

Paragraph 11.5 of Code C of PACE 1984 (the Code of Practice for the Detention, Treatment and Questioning of Persons by Police Officers) specifically states that no police officer may try to obtain answers or elicit a statement from a suspect by the use of oppression (see **3.5.2.4**).

### 20.4.3 Unreliability

Findings of oppression are rare, and it is more likely that a defendant will argue that his confession should be excluded under s 76(2)(b) because it is unreliable.

For the court to exclude a confession under s 76(2)(b), something must be said or done which, in the circumstances that existed at the time, would render any confession which the defendant made unreliable. In other words, something must have been said or done (usually by the police) which might have caused the defendant to make a confession for reasons other than the fact that he had actually committed the offence and wanted to admit his guilt. Although s 76(2)(b) does not require deliberate misconduct on the part of the police, the thing which is said or done will usually involve an alleged breach of Code C (see **20.4.2** above). Examples of the types of breach of Code C which may lead to a confession being excluded on the grounds of unreliability include:

(a) *denying a suspect refreshments or appropriate periods of rest between interviews*, so that the suspect either is not in a fit state to answer questions properly, or makes admissions in interview simply to get out of the police station as soon as possible or to obtain rest or refreshments (this may be particularly relevant if the suspect is suffering from some form of illness or ailment, even if the police are not aware of this condition);

(b) *offering a suspect an inducement to confess*, for example, telling a suspect that if he confesses he will receive a lesser sentence, suggesting to the suspect that he will be able to leave the police station much more quickly if he admits his guilt, or telling the suspect that he will only be granted police bail if he makes a confession;

(c) *misrepresenting the strength of the prosecution case*, for example by telling a suspect that the prosecution case is much stronger than it actually is and that there is no point in denying his guilt;

(d) *questioning a suspect in an inappropriate way*, for example by repeatedly asking a suspect the same question, or badgering a suspect until he gives the answer which the officer wants;

(e) *questioning a suspect who the police should have known was not in a fit state to be interviewed* either because the suspect had consumed drink or drugs, or because the suspect was suffering from some form of medical condition or ailment. The answers given by such a suspect in interview may be unreliable;

(f) *threatening a suspect*, for example by telling him that he will be kept at the police station until he makes a confession, so that that the suspect thinks he has no option other than to confess if he wants to get out of the police station.

A very common example of an argument used to exclude a confession on the unreliability ground under s 76(2)(b) is for a defendant to argue that his confession is unreliable because he was denied access to legal advice at the police station in breach of Code C and s 58 of PACE 1984 (see **3.4.2**). A breach of s 58 and Code C will not, however, in itself lead to the exclusion of the confession. In order for the confession to be excluded, there must be a causal link between the breach and the unreliability of the confession that was subsequently made. The defendant will need to show that had he been allowed access to legal advice, he would not have made a confession. Therefore, if denial of access to legal advice is relied upon as an argument to exclude a confession under s 76(2)(b), a defendant will find it hard to establish a causal link if he is an experienced criminal who was fully aware of his rights when detained at the police station. In contrast, a suspect who has never previously been arrested and has no experience of police detention or knowledge of his rights when at the police station, may find it easier to have a confession excluded under s 76(2)(b) if he raises the same argument.

Example 1

In *R v Trussler* [1998] Crim LR 446, the defendant was a drug addict who was kept in custody for 18 hours. He was interviewed several times without being given any rest and was denied access to legal advice. His confession was excluded under s 76(2)(b).

Example 2

In *R v Alladice* (1998) 87 Cr App R 380, the defendant was denied access to legal advice and confessed to a robbery. When giving evidence at trial, the defendant stated that he knew of his rights and that he understood the police caution. The defendant's application to exclude his confession was rejected by the trial judge. Although denying access to legal advice was a serious breach of Code C, there was nothing to suggest that this might render any confession he had made unreliable, because he was fully aware of what his rights were.

### 20.4.4 Challenging the admissibility of a confession adduced in evidence by a co-defendant

Section 76A(1) of PACE 1984 permits a defendant to adduce evidence that a co-defendant has made a confession where both defendants plead not guilty and are tried jointly (see **20.3.3.2** above).

Under s 76A(2), however, if the co-defendant who made the confession represents to the court that his confession was obtained as a result of oppression, or in circumstances rendering it unreliable (as described in **20.4.3** above), the court must exclude the evidence of the confession (even if the court believes the confession to be true), unless the court is satisfied that the confession was not obtained in such a way. The court need only be satisfied on the balance of probabilities that the confession was not obtained either by oppression or in circumstances rendering it unreliable in order for the confession to be admissible.

Example

Richard and Paul are jointly charged with common assault. Both are pleading not guilty. When Paul was interviewed by the police he confessed to having committed the crime. Under s 76A(1), Richard is entitled to raise Paul's confession in evidence at trial to show that it was Paul rather than he who committed the assault. However, Paul argues at trial that the confession he made when interviewed was obtained only as a result of threats made by the police to keep him in custody indefinitely until he confessed, and so is unreliable. If Richard attempts to adduce evidence of Paul's confession and Paul challenges the admissibility of this, the court must exclude the evidence of Paul's confession under s 76A(2) (even if the court believes the confession to be true) unless the court is satisfied on the balance of probabilities that the confession was not obtained in circumstances making it unreliable.

## 20.5 Challenging the admissibility of a confession: PACE 1984, s 78

### 20.5.1 Introduction

Section 76 of PACE 1984 deals exclusively with the court's power to exclude evidence of a confession made by the defendant (see **20.4** above). Under s 78, the court has a more general discretion to exclude prosecution evidence (see **Chapter 21**). This includes evidence of a confession made by a defendant. Section 78 provides the court with the *discretion* to exclude confession evidence on which the CPS seeks to rely if the court considers that the admission of the confession would have such an adverse effect on the fairness of proceedings that it ought not to be admitted. Section 78 may be relied on either when the defendant admits making a confession but claims that the confession is untrue, or when the defendant denies making the confession at all.

### 20.5.2 Confessions the defendant accepts having made

When a defendant alleges that the police breached the provisions of PACE 1984 and/or the Codes of Practice in obtaining a confession from him, the court is likely to exercise its discretion under s 78 to exclude such evidence only if these breaches are both significant and substantial (*R v Walsh* (1989) 91 Cr App R 161; *R v Keenan* [1990] 2 QB 54).

For example, if the police fail to caution a suspect at the start of an interview at the police station and the suspect then makes a confession during the interview, the failure to caution the suspect will be a significant and substantial breach of Code C. Paragraph 10.1 of Code C provides that a suspect must be cautioned before he is questioned about an offence (see **3.5.2.3**). If the police failed to caution the suspect, the suspect might not have appreciated that he was under no obligation to answer questions in the interview. In such circumstances, it would be unfair at trial to allow the CPS to rely on a confession made in the interview because, had he been properly cautioned, the suspect might have chosen to stay silent in interview.

There is a significant degree of overlap between the court's discretion to exclude a confession (which the defendant admits to having made) under s 78, and the duty of the court to exclude a confession under the 'unreliability' ground in s 76(2)(b). The examples of breaches of Code C at **20.4.3** above, which would lead the court to exclude a confession on the grounds of unreliability under s 76(2)(b), could also be raised to support an argument under s 78 that it would be unfair to allow the prosecution to rely on confession evidence. If, for example, the defendant made a confession only after being told by the police that he would be able to leave the police station much sooner if he admitted his guilt, an argument could be made under s 78 that it would be unfair to allow the prosecution to rely on the confession because the defendant might have confessed as a means of ensuring his prompt release from police custody, rather than because he was actually guilty of the offence.

Many of the cases in which the court has exercised its discretion to exclude evidence of a confession made by the defendant under s 78 are concerned with suspects who have been denied access to legal advice. In *R v Walsh* (1989) 91 Cr App R 161, the Court of Appeal said that in most cases where a defendant had been denied access to legal advice in breach of s 58 of PACE 1984 or the provisions of Code C, this would lead to the court exercising its discretion to exclude any confession that the defendant subsequently made, since allowing the CPS to rely on such evidence would have an adverse effect on the fairness of the proceedings.

Another example of when the court has used s 78 to exclude evidence of a confession made by the defendant is when the police have deliberately misled the defendant as to the strength of the evidence they have obtained, in order to make the defendant think that he has no option other than to confess. In *R v Mason* [1998] 1 WLR 139, a police officer told the defendant's solicitor that fingerprint evidence existed, tying the defendant in to the crime he was suspected of having committed. The defendant then made a confession. In fact there was no such fingerprint evidence, and this was a deliberate lie on the part of the police officer. The Court of Appeal held that the trial judge should have exercised his discretion under s 78 to exclude the confession.

A confession which the defendant accepts having made may be excluded under s 78 even when nothing has been said or done (either by the defendant, or by the police), and where there is no suggestion that the police have acted improperly or in breach of the Codes of Practice. This may occur when:

(a) the physical condition of the defendant renders the confession unreliable. This may be the case if the defendant was tired, emotional, or suffering from the effects of illness or medication (about which he had not told the police) at the time the confession was made;

**Example**

Ruth is arrested on suspicion of theft. Ruth is a diabetic but fails to disclose this to the custody officer or interviewing officer. Whilst at the police station Ruth's blood sugar level falls, and as a consequence Ruth becomes light-headed and is unaware of what she is saying. In interview, Ruth admits to having committing the offence. At her subsequent trial, she denies the theft. In such circumstances the court is likely to exclude the confession under s 78 because Ruth was not aware of what she was saying.

(b) the defendant has an ulterior motive for making a confession, such as needing to get out of the police station as soon as possible for reasons unconnected to the police investigation, or wanting to protect another person.

**Example**

Emma is arrested at a supermarket on suspicion of shoplifting. She is subsequently taken to the police station. Emma has two young children whom she has left at home while shopping. Emma does not disclose this fact to the police, because she is worried that the police might inform the social services department at the local council that she has left her children at home unattended. When interviewed about the offence, even though she was not in fact shoplifting, Emma makes an immediate confession so that she can leave the police station as soon as possible and return to her children. Again, the court is likely to exclude such a confession under s 78, as the reason for the confession was not Emma's guilt but rather her concern about getting into trouble with social services.

### 20.5.3 Confessions the defendant denies having made

A defendant will often be alleged to have made a confession 'outside' the police station when first approached by the police. If the defendant subsequently denies having made such a confession, he may challenge the admissibility of this confession under s 78.

A confession allegedly made by the defendant when questioned by the police in an interview 'outside' the police station is likely to be excluded under s 78 if the police breached the provisions of Code C of PACE 1984 by:

(a) failing to caution the defendant before conducting the interview (Code C, para 10.1), as the defendant would not then appreciate the legal significance and consequences of any comments he might make;
(b) failing to make an accurate record of the defendant's comments (Code C, para 11.7(a)), as the police would not then be able to substantiate that such comments were in fact made by the defendant;
(c) failing to give the defendant an opportunity to view the record of his comments and to sign this record as being accurate, or to dispute the accuracy of the record (Code C, para 11.11), as the defendant would then be deprived of the opportunity to challenge the accuracy of the police record; or
(d) failing to put this admission or confession to the defendant at the start of his subsequent interview at the police station (Code C, para 11.4), as the whole point of putting the confession to the defendant at the start of the audibly recorded interview is to ensure that the defendant has the opportunity to confirm or deny 'on the record' what he is alleged to have said.

In *R v Canale* [1990] 2 All ER 187, the police alleged that the defendant had made certain admissions to them. The defendant denied making these admissions. The interviewing officer to whom these admissions had allegedly been made failed to make a contemporaneous note of the interviews as required by Code C (see **2.3.3.3**), and the defendant was therefore denied the opportunity to comment on the accuracy of the record of these interviews. The evidence was excluded by the court under s 78 because its admission would have been unfair to the defendant.

This case may be contrasted with *Watson v DPP* [2003] EWHC 1466. The magistrates' court convicted the defendant of drink driving. The police officer who attended the road traffic accident in which the defendant had been involved spoke to the defendant, who admitted being the driver of the vehicle. The officer was unable to make a contemporaneous note of the interview, or to invite the defendant to sign such a note, because he was called away to attend another emergency. The defence raised by the defendant at his trial was that he had not been the driver of the vehicle. He argued that the police officer's breaches of the Codes of Practice meant that his alleged admission that he had been the driver should have been excluded at his trial under s 78. His appeal was dismissed. Whilst it was accepted that there had been a breach of Code C, the court had nevertheless been entitled to admit evidence of the alleged admission because the defendant had ample opportunity at the police station to deny that he had been the driver of the vehicle, and the only reason the officer had failed to make a contemporaneous note was because he had been called away in an emergency. In those circumstances, there was nothing unfair about the evidence of the admission being used at trial. This case illustrates the limitations of s 78, and in particular the fact that excluding evidence under s 78 is very much within the *discretion* of the court.

## 20.6 Procedure for challenging the admissibility of a confession

### 20.6.1 Crown Court

In the Crown Court, the admissibility of disputed confession evidence will be determined by the trial judge in the absence of the jury at a voire dire (see **10.10.1**). If the confession was made by the defendant in an interview at the police station, the interviewing officer will give evidence as to how the confession was obtained and the defendant will then give his version of events. The record of the interview will also be played. If the confession was made 'outside' the police station, the officer to who the confession was made will give evidence, as again will the defendant. Prosecuting and defence counsel will then make submissions to the judge on whether the confession should be excluded in the light of the evidence given. The judge will then make his ruling.

If the judge rules the confession to be inadmissible, the jury will hear nothing about the confession. If the judge rules the confession to be admissible, the interviewing officer will then give evidence of the confession when giving his evidence to the jury. The defendant will still be able to attack the cogency of the confession (either when giving evidence himself, or when the police officer is being questioned) in an attempt to persuade the jury to attach little or no weight to it. In his summing up to the jury, the trial judge must direct the jury that, if they consider the confession to have been obtained by oppression or other improper conduct, they should disregard it (*R v Mushtaq* [2005] 1 WLR 1513).

### 20.6.2 Magistrates' court

In the magistrates' court, a ruling as to the admissibility of the disputed confession will normally be sought when the interviewing officer gives evidence. If the defendant seeks to exclude evidence of the confession under s 76 of PACE 1984, the magistrates must hold a voire dire (see **9.4.3**). If the defendant raises submissions under s 76 and s 78, both arguments should be dealt with at the same voire dire. If the defendant seeks to rely only on s 78, there is no obligation to hold a voire dire. In such cases, a challenge to the admissibility of the confession may be left either to the close of the prosecution case (if the defendant's solicitor wishes to make a submission of no case to answer), or to the end of the trial when the defendant's solicitor makes his closing speech.

### 20.6.3 Challenging the credibility of a disputed confession not excluded by the court

If the trial judge or the magistrates rule that a confession is not to be excluded under s 76 or s 78, the defendant may still challenge the credibility or reliability of the confession during the trial. For example, the defendant may give evidence-in-chief that he made the confession for reasons other than the fact that he was guilty, or that he never actually made the confession and evidence of the confession has been fabricated. Similarly, the defendant's solicitor or counsel may cross-examine the police officers to whom the confession was made to suggest either that the confession was obtained only after breaches of PACE 1984 or the Codes of Practice had occurred, or that evidence of the confession has been fabricated. It will then be a matter for the jury or magistrates (when considering their verdict) as to what weight should be attached to the confession as an item of prosecution evidence.

## 20.7 Evidence obtained as the result of an inadmissible confession

The fact that the court excludes evidence of a confession made by a defendant will not affect the admissibility in evidence of any facts discovered as a result of the confession, although the CPS will not be able to tell the court that such facts were discovered as a result of a confession made by the defendant.

**Example**

Martin is charged with murder. As a result of a confession made by Martin, the police are able to recover both the murder weapon and the body of his victim. The trial judge rules that the confession made by Martin is inadmissible under s 76(2)(b). The CPS will be able to adduce evidence as to where and when the murder weapon and the body were discovered, but it will not be able to raise in evidence that these items were discovered as a result of a confession made by Martin.

## 20.8 Procedural flowchart – confession evidence

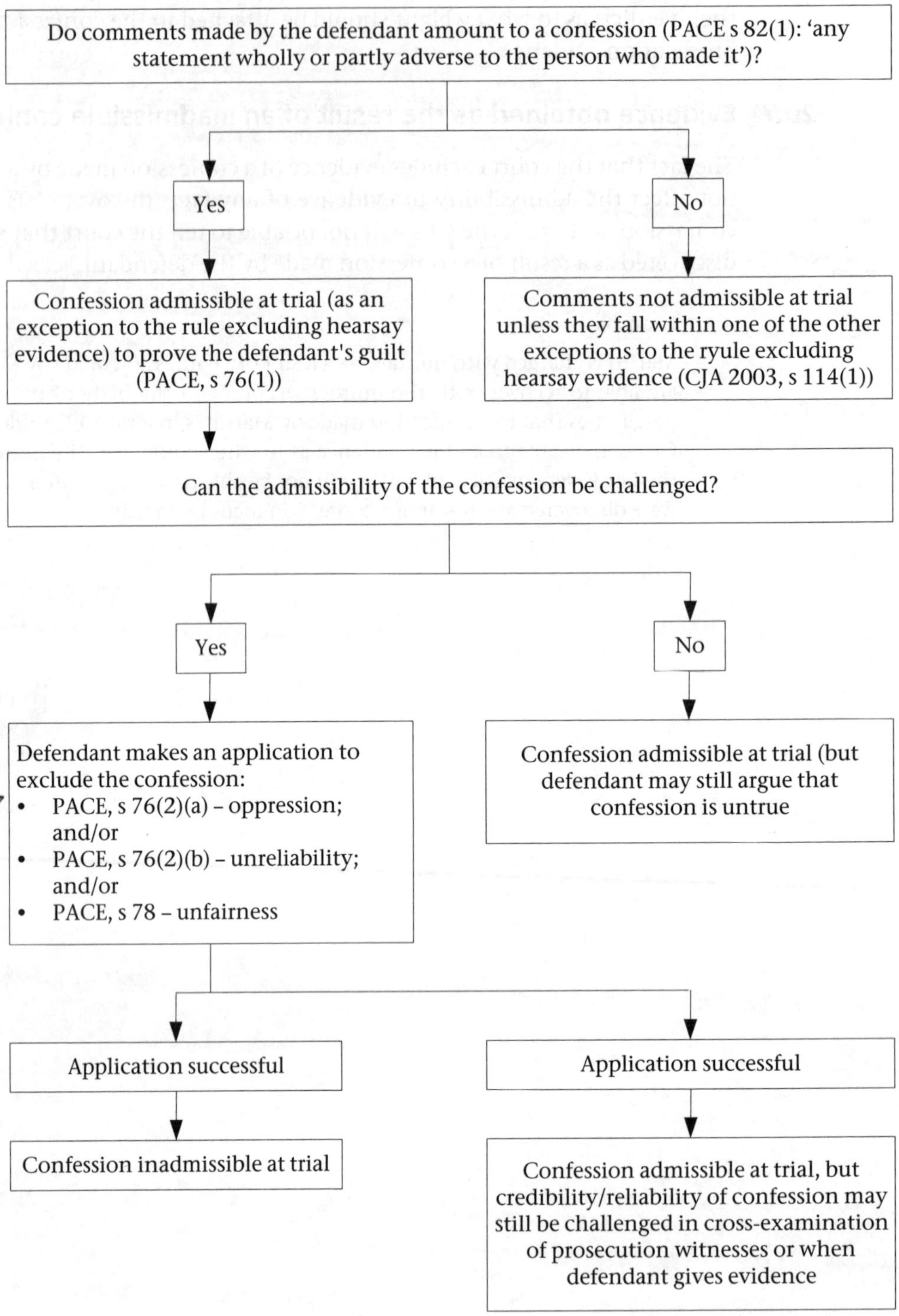

## 20.9 Checklist

At the end of this chapter you should be able to explain:

- the statutory definition of a confession (PACE 1984, s 82(1));
- the basic rule as to the admissibility of confession evidence at trial (PACE 1984, s 76(1));
- the circumstances in which a confession made by a defendant is admissible in evidence against a co-defendant;
- the circumstances in which a defendant may adduce evidence of a confession made by a co-defendant;
- how to challenge the admissibility of a confession using PACE 1984, s 76(2)(a) – confession obtained by *oppression*;
- how to challenge the admissibility of a confession using PACE 1984, s 76(2)(b) – *unreliability* of the confession;
- how to challenge the admissibility of a confession using PACE 1984, s 78 – *unfair* to admit the confession in evidence;
- the procedure by which a defendant may challenge the admissibility of a disputed confession in either the Crown Court, or the magistrates' court;
- the admissibility of evidence obtained as the result of a confession which the court has ruled to be inadmissible.

# Chapter 21
# Exclusion of Evidence



## 21.1 Introduction

There are occasions when the CPS may seek to rely on evidence which has been obtained by the police in an illegal or unfair manner. This chapter will examine the principles which the court will apply in deciding whether or not such evidence is admissible at trial. It will begin with an explanation of the power the court has to exclude such evidence under s 78 of PACE 1984. It will then examine how this power is exercised in relation to particular types of evidence. The chapter will conclude by examining situations when the court may stop a case entirely for 'abuse of process' by the police.

## 21.2 Police and Criminal Evidence Act 1984, s 78

Prior to PACE 1984 coming into force, the position at common law was that evidence which had been obtained by the police illegally or unfairly was still admissible in evidence at the defendant's trial if it was relevant to the case. For example, in *Jeffrey v Black* [1978] QB 490, drugs were seized from the defendant's property following an illegal search. At his trial for the illegal possession of these drugs, the defendant argued that the court should rule this evidence to be inadmissible. The court declined to do so. The court said that the key issue in deciding the admissibility of the evidence was not whether it had been obtained unfairly, but rather whether it was *relevant* to the charge which the defendant faced. Finding the drugs at the defendant's premises was clearly relevant to a charge of illegal possession drugs, and the evidence was therefore admissible. The court said that an irregularity in obtaining evidence did not render such evidence inadmissible.

Following the enactment of PACE 1984, the courts were given a statutory power to exclude prosecution evidence by virtue of s 78(1):

> In any proceedings a court may refuse to allow evidence on which the prosecution proposes to rely to be given if it appears to the court that, having regard to all of the circumstances, including the circumstances in which the evidence was obtained, the admission of the evidence would have such an adverse effect on the fairness of the proceedings that the court ought not to admit it.

Case law on s 78 suggests that this section has been interpreted broadly in line with the pre-existing common law position. The power in s 78 is *discretionary*, and the court is likely to exercise its discretion to exclude prosecution evidence under s 78 only if there is something unreliable about the evidence which the police have obtained, which in turn means that it would be unfair to allow the CPS to rely on such evidence. If the evidence is relevant to the charge faced by the defendant, and there is nothing in the way in which it has been obtained which casts doubt on its reliability, the evidence is unlikely to be excluded under s 78, even if the police have breached the provisions of PACE 1984 and/or the Codes of Practice when obtaining it.

The courts have said repeatedly that applications by defendants to exclude prosecution evidence under s 78 on the ground that the police have breached PACE 1984 or the Codes of Practice in the obtaining of such evidence, should be granted only if the breaches are 'significant and substantial' (*R v Walsh* (1989) 91 Cr App R 161; *R v Keenan* [1990] 2 QB 54; *R v Rehman* [2006] EWCA Crim 1900).

Common examples of prosecution evidence which a defendant may seek to persuade a court to exclude under s 78 are:

(a) evidence obtained following an illegal search;

(b) identification evidence;

(c) confession evidence (including confessions made on arrest, as well as in interview at the police station);

(d) evidence obtained from the use of covert listening and surveillance devices; and

(e) evidence obtained in 'undercover' police operations.

## 21.3 Illegal searches

The pre-PACE position, as set out in *Jeffrey v Black* (see **21.2** above), remains unchanged. In *R v Stewart* [1995] Crim LR 500, the CPS was allowed to rely on evidence obtained following an illegal search where there had been a number of breaches of Code B. The court reiterated that if items found following an illegal search are relevant to the charge the defendant faces, the fact that such items were found only as a result of an illegal search does not affect the fairness of the trial because such evidence is relevant to the defendant's guilt. There was also nothing in the case to suggest that there were any doubts as to the reliability of the items found as genuine pieces of evidence.

The only occasion on which evidence obtained following an illegal search should be excluded is if a court considers there to be a real risk that the way in which the evidence has been obtained has affected the reliability of such evidence and, in consequence, the fairness of the trial. An example of such a situation is where police officers conducting a search have ignored Code B completely, and the defendant alleges that the officers in fact planted the evidence which they claimed to have found. In this case, although the items recovered following a search may be relevant to the charge faced by the defendant, doubts as to the authenticity of the items found may lead a court to exercise its discretion under s 78 in favour of the defendant, and to exclude the evidence.

## 21.4 Identification evidence

### 21.4.1 Identification procedures

The court may exclude identification evidence on which the CPS wishes to rely if the defendant can establish a significant breach of Code D. A breach of Code D will not automatically render such evidence inadmissible, but the court will exclude this evidence under s 78 if the defendant can show that it would be unfair to admit it. To do this, the defendant will need to satisfy the court that the breach of Code D cast doubts upon the reliability of the identification evidence on which the CPS seeks to rely.

The court may exclude identification evidence obtained in breach of Code D if either:

(a) *the police have not used the appropriate identification procedure*. For example, if:
   (i) the police arrange a group identification after making an insufficient effort to arrange an identification parade or video identification, or
   (ii) the police arrange a confrontation after the defendant has requested an identification parade and it is practicable to hold such a parade; or

(b) *there is a defect in the conduct of the identification procedure chosen*. This is most likely to arise in the case of an identification parade or video identification. Arguments casting doubt on the reliability of identification evidence obtained at an identification parade or video identification may be raised if, for example:
   (i) the other participants in the identification parade or video identification did not resemble the defendant (in age, general appearance and position in life), with the resulting possibility that the witness identified the defendant only because there were insufficient volunteers who resembled him,
   (ii) there is a breach of the rule that the investigating officer should take no part in an identification procedure (since there would then be a suspicion that the officer may have 'contaminated' the procedure by indicating to a witness, inadvertently or otherwise, the person whom the witness should pick out),
   (iii) the police had not properly segregated witnesses before and/or after the procedure, so that the witnesses had either been brought into contact with each other or, in the case of an identification parade, had seen the defendant separately from the other volunteers taking part in the parade. In particular, if there is more than one witness and the witnesses are kept together in the same room, there would be a possibility that the first witness attending the identification procedure might, on returning to the room, tell the other witnesses the number of the person he picked out.

The court will exercise its discretion to exclude identification evidence under s 78 only if it considers that evidence to be unreliable as a result of breaches of Code D.

**Example 1**

Sebastian is arrested on suspicion of theft. He agrees to take part in a video identification. Sebastian has a slim build, is clean shaven and has short blond hair. The other volunteers whose images are taken for use in the video identification are of medium or large build, and none of them has short blond hair. Some of them have a moustache. Sebastian is picked out by the witness. At trial, Sebastian's solicitor will ask the court to exclude the identification evidence under s 78. The basis of the application will be that the video identification has been carried out in breach of Code D (see **3.5.3.2**), and it would be unfair to allow the CPS to rely on such evidence because the reason for Sebastian having been picked out by the witness might have been not that the witness actually recognised Sebastian, but that Sebastian was the only participant in the video identification who in any way resembled the person the witness saw carrying out the theft.

(Had this been an identification parade instead of a video identification, and the volunteers who attended the parade did not resemble Sebastian, the same type of application would be made to the court to exclude the identification evidence under s 78.)

**Example 2**

Ronald is arrested on suspicion of causing criminal damage and agrees to take part in identification parade. When the parade takes place, the investigating officer (PC Roberts) is present and is given the responsibility of escorting the witness from a waiting room to the room where the parade is to take place. Ronald is picked out at the parade. At his trial, Ronald's solicitor will ask the court to exclude this identification evidence under s 78. The basis of the application will be that the identification parade has been carried out in breach of Code D (see **3.5.3.3**), and it would be unfair to allow the CPS to rely on the identification evidence because PC Roberts might have contaminated the parade by indicating to the witness the person on the parade whom the witness should pick out.

The court may also exclude disputed identification evidence if, whilst the defendant was detained at the police station, the police failed to hold an identification procedure when such a procedure should have been held pursuant to para 3.12 of Code D (see **3.5.3.7**). The purpose of holding an identification procedure at the police station is to test the ability of the witness to identify the person he saw on a previous occasion and to provide a safeguard against mistaken identification. If the police fail to carry out an identification procedure, the defendant has lost the benefit of these safeguards.

**Example**

Tariq is arrested on suspicion of theft. A witness who saw the theft take place identifies Tariq as the thief . The witness claims to know Tariq, because he and Tariq had worked together at the same factory for six months several years beforehand. Tariq raises the defence of alibi. Tariq vaguely recalls the witness, but he says that he never worked in the same department as the witness and that he is not well known to the witness. The police decide not to hold an identification procedure. This is a breach of Code D, para 3.12. Tariq disputes the identification made by the witness, and he disputes that he is well known to the witness. In these circumstances an identification procedure should have been held at the police station, both to test the ability of the witness to identify the person he saw committing the theft and to provide a safeguard against mistaken identification. Tariq has lost the benefit of this, and his solicitor should therefore ask the court to exclude the disputed identification evidence under s 78.

### 21.4.2 Samples

If the police obtain a sample from a suspect in breach of PACE 1984 and the Codes of Practice, such evidence is unlikely to be excluded by the courts if it is relevant to the charge which the defendant faces. In *R v Cooke* [1995] 1 Cr App R 318, a sample of hair was obtained from a suspect at the police station in breach of the 1984 Act. This sample was then used to prepare a DNA profile which implicated the suspect in the crime. The court refused to exclude such evidence under s 78. It said that the method used to obtain the sample, whilst illegal, did not cast any doubt on the relevance or reliability of the evidence subsequently obtained.

## 21.5 Confessions and police interviews

The ability of the court to exclude confession evidence under s 78 is explained in **Chapter 20**, which deals with the admissibility of confession evidence.

Even if a defendant does not make an admission or a confession in an interview at the police station, it may still be in his interests to have the record of his interview at the police station ruled inadmissible by the court. Examples of when a defendant may not wish to have his interview record used as part of the prosecution case are:

(a) if the defendant failed to mention in the interview a fact which he now wants to raise as part of his defence (because the court may draw an inference under s 34 of the CJPOA 1994 if the interview record is used as part of the prosecution case – see **18.2**);

(b) if, after being given a 'special caution', the defendant failed in the interview to account for the presence of an object, substance or mark, or failed to account for his presence at a particular place (because the court may draw an inference under ss 36 or 37 of the CJPOA 1994 if the interview record is used as part of the prosecution case – see **18.3** and **18.4**); or

(c) if the defendant gave the facts of his defence during the interview (and so avoided the risk of adverse inferences being drawn), but the answers he gave were muddled or confusing, and might lead the jury or magistrates to doubt the credibility of his evidence at trial.

To persuade the court that the record of his interview at the police station should be ruled inadmissible, the defendant will need to show why it would be unfair for the CPS to be allowed to use this record in evidence. An application to exclude an interview record is likely to succeed only if the police carried out the interview in an inappropriate manner (for example, by breaching PACE 1984 or the Codes of Practice), or if there are factors personal to the defendant (whilst he was detained at the police station) which would make it unfair to allow the interview record to be admitted in evidence.

Examples of inappropriate behaviour by the police in the conduct of an interview would include asking a suspect several questions at the same time (with the result that the suspect does not know which question to answer so that his answers are unclear), or interrupting a suspect when he is replying to questions (so that he is unable to answer properly the questions that have been put to him).

Example of factors personal to a suspect which may lead to the exclusion of the interview record are the suspect being unduly tired or emotional when being interviewed, or suffering from the effects of an illness or medication, such that he was unable to answer properly the questions which were being put to him, or was unable to appreciate the evidential significance of such questions.

## 21.6 Covert listening and surveillance devices

The police often attempt to obtain evidence by secretly recording the words of a suspect. The normal method by which this is done is to place a covert listening or surveillance device (such as a bug or a hidden camera) inside a suspect's home, business premises or vehicle. Following *R v Khan* [1997] AC 558, the courts are unlikely to exclude evidence obtained by such means under s 78. Khan was charged with the importation of heroin. The only evidence against him was from a recording the police had made (using a covert listening device) of a conversation Khan had with another person concerning the importation of heroin. Khan's application to have this evidence excluded under s 78 was rejected on the basis that such a recording did not affect the fairness of the proceedings against Khan. The court said that such evidence should not be excluded because it was relevant to the charge Khan faced, and there was nothing in the way in which the evidence had been obtained which cast any doubt on its reliability or credibility as a piece of evidence.

This case subsequently went to the European Court of Human Rights (*Khan v United Kingdom* [2000] Crim LR 684). Khan alleged that the obtaining of the evidence against him using a covert listening device was in breach of his rights under Article 6 (the right to a fair trial) and Article 8 (the right to respect for private and family life) of the ECHR (see **1.8.3**).

The European Court of Human Rights held that there had been a violation of Article 8 because, at the time of Khan's conviction, domestic law in the United Kingdom did not regulate the use of covert listening devices. However, the Court did not find there to have been a breach of Article 6. The Court said that the recording of Khan's conversation, whilst in breach of Article 8, had not been unlawful in the sense of being contrary to domestic criminal law. The Court was satisfied that the ability of the trial judge to exclude evidence under s 78 was sufficient to guarantee Khan's right to a fair trial, and thus there had been no breach of Article 6. (For more on the right to a fair trial and s 78, see **21.8** below.)

In *R v Bailey* [1993] 3 All ER 513, two co-accused who had refused to answer questions in police interview were charged and then placed together in a cell which the police had bugged. Whilst in the cell the co-accused had an incriminating conversation, which the trial judge subsequently refused to declare inadmissible under s 78. Although the conversation had taken place only as a result of some deception on the part of the police, it was held that there was nothing in either PACE 1984 or the Codes of Practice to prevent a cell from being bugged. The conversation was therefore admissible in evidence.

Although evidence obtained from covert listening and surveillance devices is admissible, s 17 of the Regulation of Investigatory Powers Act 2000 prevents the details of any intercepted telephone calls (often referred to as 'wiretapping') from being used in evidence.

## 21.7 Police undercover operations

Sometimes the police will employ 'entrapment' techniques in order to induce the committing of a criminal offence. Evidence obtained as a result of such entrapment may be excluded by the court under s 78. The test which the courts employ is to decide whether the police did nothing more than give the defendant an opportunity to commit a crime. For example, in *Williams v DPP* [1993] 3 All ER 365, the police were investigating a spate of thefts from vehicles. Plain-clothed police officers parked an unlocked van, containing a substantial quantity of cigarettes, in a busy area. The defendant was subsequently observed by the officers taking the cigarettes from the van. It was held on appeal that the trial court had been correct in refusing to exercise its discretion under s 78 to rule that the evidence from the police officers should be inadmissible. The Court said that the officers had done nothing more than give the defendant an opportunity to commit a crime. The defendant had not been actively encouraged by police officers to commit the crime.

In *R v Loosely* [2001] 1 WLR 2060, the House of Lords said that the courts should be more willing to exercise their discretion to exclude evidence under s 78 if it could be shown that the police have caused the commission of the offence, as opposed to simply providing the defendant with the chance to commit an offence.

Thus, in *R v Moon* [2004] EWCA Crim 2872, the Court of Appeal held that proceedings against a drug addict for supplying an undercover police officer with a small quantity of drugs should have been stayed as an abuse of process (see **21.9** below) where:

(a) the addict was approached by the officer;

(b) the officer had persistently asked the addict for drugs;

(c) the officer pretended that she was an addict suffering from withdrawal symptoms; and

(d) the addict told the officer never to approach her again for drugs.

The Court considered that the undercover officer had caused crime and had lured the defendant into committing crime.

## 21.8 Section 78 and the right to a fair trial

Article 6 of the ECHR (see **1.8.3**) provides that anyone charged with a criminal offence is entitled to a 'fair' hearing. The appellate courts have held, on several occasions, that the discretion given to a trial judge to exclude evidence under s 78 where the admission of that evidence would otherwise lead to unfairness, ensures that a defendant will receive a fair trial. Similarly, in cases such as *Khan* (see **21.6** above), the European Court of Human Rights has stated repeatedly that the key question to be answered when determining whether the defendant's rights under Article 6 have been breached is whether the proceedings as a whole were fair. The width of the discretion given to the trial judge by s 78 should ensure that proceedings are conducted in a manner which is fair to the defendant.

## 21.9 Abuse of process

In cases where misconduct by the police or the prosecuting authorities is so grave as to threaten the rule of law, the court will not simply exclude evidence obtained as a result of that misconduct but rather will stay the proceedings against the defendant as an abuse of process. This means that the proceedings against the defendant will not be permitted to go any further.

An example of this is *R v Grant* [2005] EWCA Crim 1089. The defendant was arrested on suspicion of conspiracy to murder. The police deliberately eavesdropped upon and tape-recorded privileged conversations between the defendant and his solicitor in the exercise yard at the police station. The trial judge refused to stay the proceedings as an abuse of process. On appeal, the Court of Appeal said that the proceedings should have been stayed. Although the defendant suffered no prejudice as a result of the eavesdropping (because no information gained as a result of the eavesdropping was used against him at trial), the Court said that such unlawful acts were an affront to the integrity of the justice system and consequently the rule of law. The duty of a court in such a situation was to stop the case from proceeding any further.

In *A v Secretary of State for the Home Department* [2005] UKHL 71, the House of Lords held that evidence obtained by torture carried out by officials of a foreign state was not admissible under UK law. Needless to say, if evidence against a defendant was obtained as a result of torture carried out by the police, the court would stay any proceedings against the defendant as an abuse of process.

Defendants often argue that proceedings should be stayed as an abuse of process when there is a significant difference of time between the date of the offences allegedly committed by the defendant and his later prosecution for these offences. Proceedings will be stayed as an abuse of process on the grounds of delay only when the extent of the delay makes it impossible for the defendant to challenge properly the allegations against him, such that he cannot receive a fair trial (see, eg, *R v J* [2006] All ER (D) 321 (Oct) and *(1) Ali (2) Altaf v Crown Prosecution Service* [2007] EWCA Crim 691).

## 21.10 Procedure for excluding prosecution evidence

### 21.10.1 Crown Court

In the Crown Court, the admissibility of the evidence which the defendant seeks to persuade the trial judge to exclude under s 78 will usually be determined at a voire dire in the absence of the jury (see **10.10.1**). The judge will ask the jury to retire and he will then hear evidence from witnesses about the disputed piece of evidence and legal submissions from prosecuting and defence counsel. If the judge rules the item of evidence to be inadmissible, the jury will hear no evidence about it. If the judge rules that the evidence is admissible, it may then be raised during the trial. The defendant will still be able to attempt to undermine the reliability or cogency of that evidence, however, either when cross-examining the prosecution witnesses or when giving evidence in chief. It will then be a matter for the jury as to the weight to be attached to the evidence when considering their verdict.

As an alternative to holding a voire dire during the course of the trial, the judge may determine the admissiblity of a piece of prosecution evidence which the defendant seeks to persuade him to exclude under s 78 at a pre-trial hearing (see **10.9**).

### 21.10.2 Magistrates' court

In the magistrates' court, a voire dire may be held to decide upon the admissibility of the piece of evidence. Alternatively, the defendant's solicitor may make a submission to the magistrates that the item of evidence should be excluded either as part of a submission of no case to answer made at the conclusion of the prosecution case, or in his closing speech before the magistrates retire to consider their verdict. If the magistrates rule that the item of evidence is inadmissible, they will disregard it when considering their verdict. If the magistrates decide not to exclude the evidence under s 78, the defendant may still challenge the reliability or cogency of that evidence either when cross-examining the prosecution witnesses, or when giving evidence in chief. It will then be a matter for the magistrates as to the weight to be attached to the evidence when considering their verdict.

As an alternative to the above, the magistrates may determine the admissibility of a piece of prosecution evidence which the defendant seeks to exclude under s 78 at a pre-trial review (see **8.2.2**).

## 21.11 Flowchart – the operation of s 78

Although the court may exercise its discretion to exclude prosecution evidence in situations where the police have not acted inappropriately but there are factors personal to the defendant which would make it unfair for the evidence to be admitted at trial (see **21.5** above), most occasions when the court excludes evidence under s 78 will involve the police having breached either PACE 1984 or the Codes of Practice. The flowchart below sets out how the court will approach an application by the defendant to exclude evidence in such circumstances.

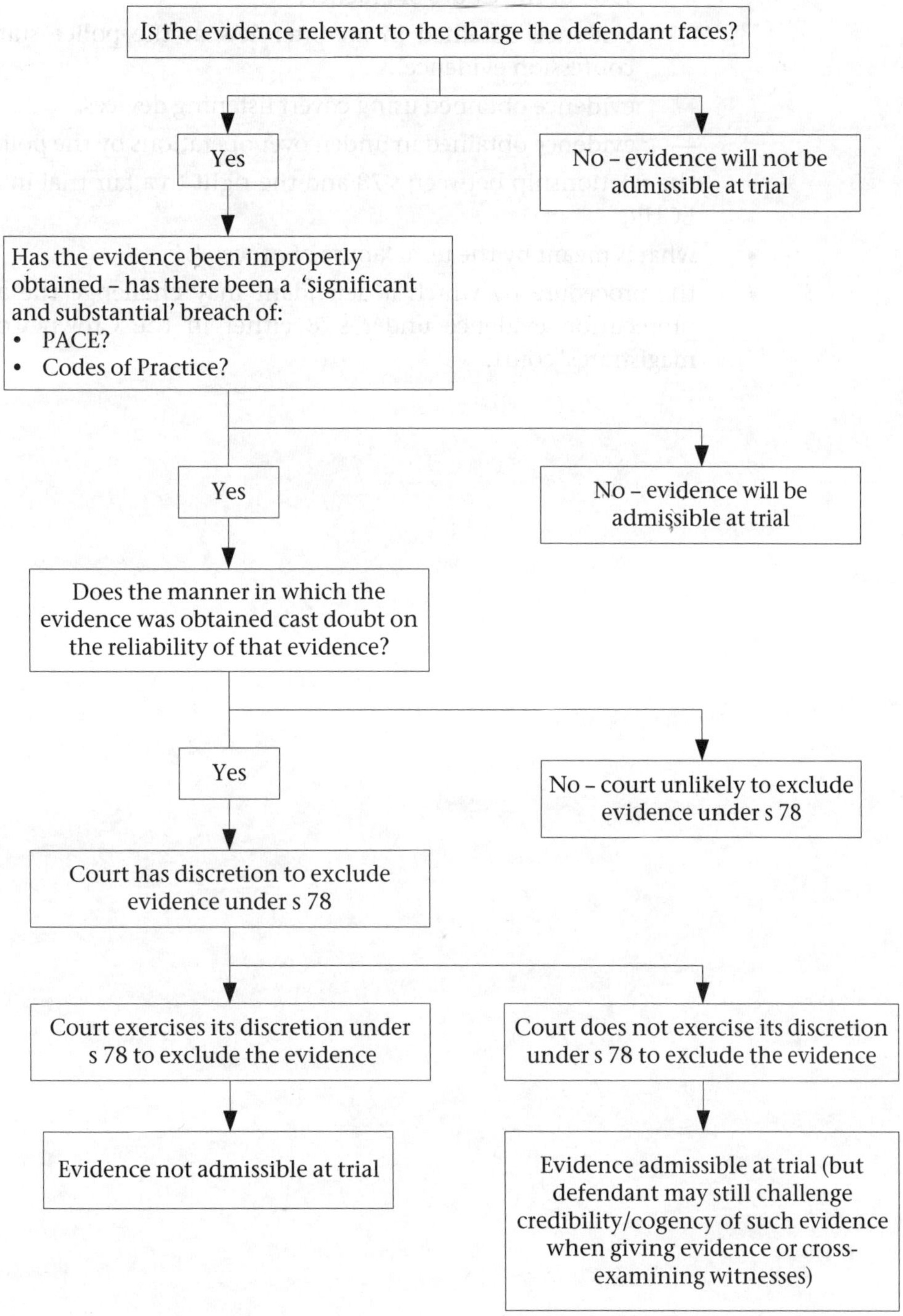

## 21.12 Checklist

At the end of this chapter you should be able to explain:

- the meaning of PACE 1984, s 78;
- the circumstances in which s 78 may be used by the defendant to persuade the court to exclude evidence on which the CPS seeks to rely at trial;
- the relationship between s 78 and the following types of prosecution evidence:
  - evidence obtained following an illegal search,
  - visual identification evidence or samples obtained in breach of PACE 1984 or the Codes of Practice,
  - evidence obtained in an interview at the police station (including confession evidence),
  - evidence obtained using covert listening devices,
  - evidence obtained in undercover operations by the police;
- the relationship between s 78 and the right to a fair trial in Article 6 of the ECHR;
- what is meant by the term 'abuse of process';
- the procedure by which a defendant may challenge the admissibility of prosecution evidence under s 78 either in the Crown Court, or in the magistrates' court.

# Chapter 22

# Character Evidence



## 22.1 Introduction

Defendants in a criminal case will often have previous convictions for offences they have committed in the past. Similarly, persons other than the defendant who are involved in the case (such as witnesses for the prosecution or the defence) may have such convictions. This chapter will examine the circumstances in which such previous convictions may be admitted in evidence at trial and the evidential significance of such convictions. It will begin by explaining the law regarding the admissibility of previous convictions prior to the enactment of the Criminal Justice Act (CJA) 2003. The 2003 Act made significant changes to the law in this area, but it is important to understand the pre-CJA position in order to place these changes in context. The chapter will then examine the law as it now stands in relation to the admissibility of a defendant's previous convictions, before looking at when the previous convictions of persons other than the defendant may be raised at trial. It will conclude by examining the evidential significance of a defendant having no previous convictions and so being of good character.

## 22.2 Admissibility of previous convictions pre-Criminal Justice Act 2003

### 22.2.1 Previous convictions of the defendant

Prior to the CJA 2003 coming into effect, an *exclusionary* approach was adopted in relation to a defendant's previous convictions. In other words, evidence that a defendant had previous convictions was not admissible at trial except in very limited circumstances. The rationale behind this was that if the magistrates or the jury heard about a defendant's previous convictions, they would decide upon his guilt or innocence of the offence with which he was currently charged not on the basis of the evidence they heard about that offence, but on the basis of his previous convictions. Evidence of the defendan's bad character was considered to be more prejudicial than probative.

The CPS could raise as part of the its case evidence that a defendant had previous convictions only if those convictions amounted to 'similar fact' evidence. Similar fact evidence was evidence that the defendant had previously committed offences that were so strikingly similar to the current offence in the manner in which they were carried out as to be positively probative of the defendant's guilt, rather than just showing that the defendant had a tendency to commit the offence charged.

**Example**

In *R v Straffen* [1952] 2 QB 911, the defendant, who had escaped from Broadmoor psychiatric hospital, was accused of strangling a girl a short distance away from the hospital. Evidence was admitted of the fact that the defendant had previous convictions for strangling two other girls, and that the features of the two previous crimes were strikingly similar to the offence charged. This similar fact evidence was admitted not to show that the defendant had a disposition to commit murder, but because the features of the case provided a strong indication that the defendant was guilty of the offence charged.

The only other way in which a defendant's previous convictions could be raised in evidence was if the defendant entered the witness box to give evidence as part of his defence case. The general rule was that if the defendant entered the witness box, he had a shield against being cross-examined by the prosecution (or by a co-accused) as to his previous convictions. This shield could be lost, however, if:

(a) the defendant had previous convictions which amounted to similar fact evidence (see above);

(b) the defendant gave evidence to suggest that he was of good character;

(c) the defendant attacked the character of a prosecution witness; or

(d) the defendant gave evidence implicating a co-accused.

Even if the defendant lost his shield against cross-examination as to his previous convictions, any cross-examination on such convictions was relevant only to the defendant's credibility as a witness (ie, whether the defendant's account of events should be believed) rather than to his propensity to commit the crime with which he had been charged.

### 22.2.2 Previous convictions of other witnesses

Prior to the CJA 2003 being enacted, an *inclusionary* approach was adopted towards evidence that any witness in the case other than the defendant (whether giving evidence for the prosecution or defence) had previous convictions. Such a witness could always be cross-examined as to his previous convictions. This cross-examination was relevant to the credibility of the evidence given by the witness (ie, whether the evidence given by the witness should be believed).

## 22.3 Criminal Justice Act 2003 – what is meant by bad character?

The provisions of the CJA 2003 concern the admissibility in evidence of a person's 'bad character'. 'Bad character' is defined in s 98 as being 'evidence of, or a disposition towards, misconduct', other than evidence connected with the offence for which the defendant has been charged. 'Misconduct' is defined in s 112 as 'the commission of an offence or other reprehensible behaviour'. 'Other reprehensible behaviour' may include evidence that a person:

(a) was charged for an offence that was not subsequently prosecuted;

(b) was prosecuted for an offence but was acquitted at trial – if, for example, the acquittal was in any way tainted or was on a legal technicality (it has also been argued that any acquittal should be admissible on the basis that an acquittal does not mean that a defendant is innocent of the offence charged, merely that a court or jury have not found him guilty beyond a reasonable doubt);

(c) has received a warning, caution or a conditional caution in respect of a previous matter, or, in the case of a juvenile, a reprimand or final warning;

(d) has behaved in a blameworthy manner which was not the subject of criminal proceedings (for example, if a person is alleged to have used violence, or told lies on a previous occasion);

(e) is the subject of an anti-social behaviour order, a bind over or has been made the subject of an injunction in civil or family law proceedings;

(f) was dismissed from a previous job for misconduct;

(g) has been involved in a sexual, financial or other type of scandal;

(h) is, or was, a member of an organisation that most people find objectionable; or

(i) has done anything else which might be considered to be objectionable (eg, downloading pornographic images from the Internet).

In *R v Osbourne* [2007] EWCA Crim 481, the Court of Appeal held that, where the defendant had been charged with the murder by stabbing of a close friend, the fact that the defendant was liable to shout at his partner (but not use violence) over the care of their infant son was not reprehensible behaviour within the meaning of s 112 and did not therefore amount to evidence of bad character.

If the alleged misconduct by the defendant is connected to the offence with which he has been charged, this will not fall within the definition of bad character in s 98, and will therefore be admissible in evidence *without* needing to consider whether it satisfies the test for admissibility of bad character evidence set out in the CJA 2003 (*R v Edwards & Rowlands* [2005] EWCA Crim 3244).

**Example**

Adrian is charged with the murder of Frank, his father. The CPS alleges that Adrian fabricated a will in Frank's name, leaving all Frank's assets to Adrian, and that Adrian then murdered Frank so that he could take these assets. The allegation that Adrian fabricated Frank's will is an allegation of misconduct on the part of Adrian. It will not fall within s 98 of the CJA 2003, however, because it is connected to the subsequent murder of Frank. Evidence of the fabrication of the will is therefore admissible without needing to consider whether it satisfies the test for admissibility of bad character evidence set out in the CJA 2003.

This distinction between evidence of bad character within the meaning of s 98 and evidence concerning the facts of the alleged offence also applies to persons other than the defendant. In *R v Machado* [2006] All ER (D) 28 (Mar), the Court of Appeal held that the trial judge had been wrong to exclude evidence that the victim of an alleged robbery was under the influence of an ecstasy tablet at the time of the alleged offence. The judge had excluded this evidence on the basis that this was evidence of the victim's bad character and did not satisfy any of the potential grounds for admissibility under s 100 (see **22.6** below). The Court said evidence that the victim may have been taking drugs at the time of the offence was evidence in connection with the circumstances of the offence rather than evidence of bad character.

## 22.4 Bad character of the defendant – the seven 'gateways'

### 22.4.1 Introduction

Evidence of a defendant's bad character may be raised at trial through one or more of seven 'gateways' which are set out in s 101(1) of the CJA 2003. Section 101(1) provides that:

(1) In criminal proceedings evidence of a defendant's bad character is admissible if, but only if:

(a) all parties to the proceedings agree to the evidence being admissible,

(b) the evidence is adduced by the defendant himself or is given in answer to a question asked by him in cross-examination and intended to elicit it,

(c) it is important explanatory evidence,

(d) it is relevant to an important matter in issue between the defendant and the prosecution,

(e) it has substantial probative value in relation to an important matter in issue between the defendant and a co-defendant,

(f) it is evidence to correct a false impression given by the defendant, or

(g) the defendant has made an attack on another person's character.

If the defendant is aged 21 or over, evidence of his conviction for an offence when under the age of 14 will not be admissible unless *both* offences (ie, the offence for which the defendant was convicted previously and the offence with which the defendant is currently charged) are triable only on indictment, and the court is satisfied that it is in the interests of justice for the evidence to be admissible (s 108(2)).

A defendant's bad character cannot of itself prove guilt. The prosecution must adduce other evidence to substantiate their case before the jury or magistrates are permitted to take his bad character into account.

Each of these seven gateways will now be examined in more detail. A flowchart summarising the operation of s 101(1)(a)–(g) is set out at 22.9.1 below.

### 22.4.2 Gateway (a) – all parties to the proceedings agree to the evidence being admissible

This gateway is self-explanatory. If the CPS and the defendant are in agreement that the evidence is admissible, it may be admitted under this gateway.

### 22.4.3 Gateway (b) – the evidence is adduced by the defendant himself or is given in answer to a question asked by him in cross-examination and intended to elicit it

This gateway allows a defendant to introduce evidence of his own bad character either by telling the court about this when he gives evidence-in-chief, or by asking a prosecution witness (such as a police officer) to confirm that he has previous convictions. A defendant may seek to do this if he has only very minor previous convictions and does not want the jury or magistrates to think that, because he is not adducing evidence of his own good character, he may have extensive previous convictions. Another example of when a defendant may do this is if he has pleaded guilty on previous occasions but is pleading not guilty to the current matter. The defendant may use such convictions to say to the jury that he accepts his guilt when he has committed an offence, but on this occasion he is pleading not guilty because he genuinely has not committed the offence charged.

### 22.4.4 Gateway (c) – it is important explanatory evidence

Only the prosecution may adduce evidence of the defendant's bad character under gateway (c). The gateway is, however, likely to be used only in limited circumstances. Evidence is important explanatory evidence if:

(a) without it, the magistrates or jury would find it impossible or difficult properly to understand the case; and

(b) the value of the evidence for understanding the case as a whole is substantial (CJA 2003, s102) ('substantial' in this context is likely to mean more than merely trivial or marginal – see **22.4.5.1** below).

**Example 1**

In *R v Edwards* [2005] EWCA Crim 1813, the defendant was charged with robbery. The prosecution relied on identification evidence from an eye-witness who claimed to have recognised the defendant as he was running away from the scene. The defendant raised the defence of alibi, claiming that he was elsewhere at the time the robbery occurred. The trial judge permitted the eye-witness to give evidence that she recognised the defendant because she had regularly bought drugs from him in the past. The Court of Appeal held that the trial judge had correctly allowed this evidence to be admitted under gateway (c), since it was necessary to explain the basis on which she had recognised the defendant.

**Example 2**

In *R v Campbell* [2005] EWCA Crim 248, the defendant was convicted of the kidnapping and murder of his 15-year-old niece. The prosecution alleged that the defendant was infatuated with his niece and that his infatuation was partly sexual. The Court of Appeal held that the trial judge had correctly allowed the prosecution to adduce evidence that the defendant had downloaded material from teenage sex sites, because such evidence was necessary to explain the defendant's motive for committing the offence.

**Example 3**

In *R v S* [2006] EWCA Crim 756, the defendant was convicted of various sexual offences against his sisters committed 30 years previously. The sisters reported the matter to the police only after hearing that the defendant had recently received a caution for indecently assaulting a child, this in turn triggering their recollection of events. The Court of Appeal held that evidence of this caution had been properly admitted at the defendant's trial since this explained why the sisters had not made their complaint at the time of the offences and why the defendant was being prosecuted some 30 years after the offences occurred.

Unlike gateways (d) and (g), if the prosecution can establish that the test for admitting evidence of the defendant's bad character through this gateway is satisfied, the court has no power under the CJA 2003 to prevent the admission of this evidence. The court does, however, retain the discretionary power to exclude such evidence under s 78 of PACE 1984 (see **22.4.9** below).

### 22.4.5 Gateway (d) – it is relevant to an important matter in issue between the defendant and the prosecution

#### 22.4.5.1 Introduction

'An important matter' is defined as 'a matter of substantial importance in the context of the case as a whole' (CJA 2003, s 112(1)). Although the word 'substantial' is not defined in the Act, the 'Explanatory Notes' accompanying it suggest that 'substantial' should be taken to mean something that is more than merely trivial or marginal.

Important matters in issue between the defendant and prosecution include:

(a) the question whether the defendant has a *propensity to commit offences of the kind with which he is charged* (except where his having such propensity makes it no more likely that he is guilty of the offence); and

(b) the question whether the defendant has a *propensity to be untruthful* (except where it is not suggested that the defendant's case is untruthful in any respect) (CJA 2003, s 103(1)).

Only the prosecution may adduce evidence of a defendant's bad character under gateway (d).

### 22.4.5.2 Propensity to commit offences of the kind with which he is charged

**Introduction**

The CPS is now permitted to place before the court evidence that a defendant has previous convictions in order to suggest that the defendant has a propensity to commit offences of the kind with which he is currently charged. To place such evidence before the court, the CPS must first satisfy the court that establishing such propensity makes it more likely that the defendant committed the offence.

Section 103(2) of the CJA 2003 states that

> a defendant's propensity to commit offences of the kind with which he is charged may (without prejudice to any other way of doing so) be established by evidence that he has been convicted of:
>
> (a) an offence of the same *description* as the one with which he is charged, or
>
> (b) an offence of the same *category* as the one with which he is charged. (emphasis added)

This subsection does not apply in the case of a particular defendant if the court is satisfied that, as a result of the time which has passed since the conviction (or for any other reason), it would be unjust for it to be applied (CJA 2003, s 103(3)). This is most likely to arise in situations where a defendant's previous convictions are 'spent' (see **22.4.5.4** below).

**Example**

Peter is on trial for common assault. Peter has a previous conviction for common assault. This conviction occurred 10 years ago. Peter's solicitor will argue that this previous conviction should not be admitted in evidence at Peter's trial to show that Peter has a propensity to commit this type of offence. Given the amount of time that has elapsed since Peter's previous conviction, he will argue under s 103(3) that it would be unjust for this conviction to be used in the present case.

Similarly, the CPS may not raise a defendant's previous convictions to show propensity to commit offences of the kind with which he is charged if such a propensity makes it no more likely that he is guilty of the offence (s 103(1)(a)). This covers situations where there is no dispute about the facts of a case and the question is whether those facts constitute an offence.

**Example**

Jeremy is charged with the possession of a controlled drug under the Misuse of Drugs Act 1971. Jeremy has several previous convictions for such offences. Jeremy's defence to the current charge is that whilst he admits to having possession of the drug, he denies that it is a controlled drug as defined in s 2 of the Act. The question for the court to decide is not whether Jeremy had the drugs, but whether the drugs he had satisfied the legal definition of a controlled drug. Jeremy's previous convictions for the same offence will not be admissible, since they do not make it more likely that he is guilty of the offence.

### Offences of the same description

Two offences will be of the same *description* as each other if the statement of the offence in a written charge or an indictment would, in each case, be in the same terms (CJA 2003, s103(4)(a)).

**Example**

Stephen is charged with assault occasioning actual bodily harm. He pleads not guilty on the basis that he was acting in reasonable self-defence. He has two previous convictions for the same offence. These will be offences of the same description because they would be described in the same way in a written charge or an indictment. The CPS may therefore attempt to raise these convictions at trial to show that Stephen has a propensity to commit offences of this type.

It is not necessary for the earlier conviction to be described in identical terms. What matters is whether the facts of the earlier conviction would be sufficient to support an offence charged in the same terms. For example, on a charge of burglary, a previous conviction for theft committed on premises whilst the defendant was a trespasser, would be in the same terms as the burglary.

### Offences of the same category

Two offences will be of the same *category* as each other if they belong to the same category of offences prescribed by the Secretary of State (CJA 2003, s 103(4)(b)). The Secretary of State has so far prescribed two categories of offences which are in the same category:

(a) the *sexual offences category*, which specifies a number of sexual offences committed against children under 16 years of age; and

(b) the *theft category*, which includes the following offences:

- (i) theft;
- (ii) robbery;
- (iii) burglary;
- (iv) aggravated burglary;
- (v) taking a motor vehicle or conveyance without authority;
- (vi) aggravated vehicle taking;
- (vii) handling stolen goods;
- (viii) going equipped for stealing;
- (ix) making off without payment;
- (x) any attempt to commit any of the above substantive offences;
- (xi) aiding, abetting, counselling, procuring or inciting the commission of any of the above offences.

**Example**

Felicity pleads not guilty to a charge of theft. She has two previous convictions for the offence of burglary and one previous conviction for the offence of handling stolen goods. These will be offences of the same category because they fall within the 'theft category' prescribed by the Secretary of State. The CPS may therefore seek to raise these convictions in evidence to show that Felicity has a propensity to commit offences of this type.

### May other offences be used to demonstrate a propensity to commit offences of the same kind?

Even if an earlier offence is not of the same description or in the same category as the offence charged, evidence of the defendant's conviction for the earlier offence may still be admissible under this gateway if there are significant factual similarities between the offences, since this would fall within the definition of having a propensity to commit offences of the kind with which the defendant is charged. This is much wider than the old 'similar fact' evidence provisions referred to at 22.2.1 above.

**Example 1**

In *R v Brima* [2006] EWCA Crim 408, the Court of Appeal held that previous convictions for assault and robbery which both involved the use of a knife were admissible in the defendant's trial for murder where the defendant was alleged to have stabbed his victim. The convictions demonstrated that the defendant had a propensity to commit violent offences using a knife.

**Example 2**

In *R v Eastlake* [2007] EWCA Crim 603, the Court of Appeal held that a previous conviction for street violence was admissible to show a propensity to act violently where the defendant was charged with offences under ss 20 and 47 of the Offences Against the Person Act 1861.

**Example 3**

In *R v Leaver* [2006] EWCA Crim 2988, the Court of Appeal held that the trial judge had erred in allowing the prosecution to adduce evidence of the defendant's previous conviction for indecent exposure where he was charged with grievous bodily harm. The previous conviction demonstrated a propensity to degrade women for sexual purposes, not a propensity for violence.

### May a propensity to commit offences of the kind charged be demonstrated other than through evidence of a defendant's previous convictions?

Although in most cases, propensity under s 101(1)(d) will be established by the CPS adducing evidence of the defendant's previous convictions, s 103(2) provides that this is 'without prejudice' to any other way of proving propensity to commit offences of the kind with which the defendant has been charged. This means that the CPS may attempt to show propensity other than through a defendant's previous convictions.

**Example 1**

Clive pleads not guilty to a charge of unlawful wounding. Shortly before the events giving rise to this charge, Clive was acquitted at trial on another charge of unlawful wounding. Clive was acquitted only after the victim of the assault failed to attend the trial to give evidence against him. The CPS may attempt to adduce in evidence the fact that Clive was previously tried for the same offence (and acquitted only after his victim failed to attend court) to show a propensity to commit this type of offence.

**Example 2**

Wayne is charged with criminal damage. It is alleged that he was part of a gang that sprayed graffiti on a wall. Wayne pleads not guilty, claiming that although he was present at the time, he had nothing to do with the graffiti. Twelve months earlier Wayne received a caution from the police for spraying graffiti on another wall. The CPS may attempt to adduce evidence of the fact that Wayne has previously received a caution for the same offence to show a propensity to commit this type of offence.

### *R v Hanson, Gilmore & Pickstone*

In *R v Hanson, Gilmore & Pickstone* [2005] Crim LR 787, the Court of Appeal set out guidelines for judges or magistrates to consider when the CPS seeks to adduce evidence of a defendant's previous convictions in order to demonstrate his propensity to commit offences of the kind with which he is charged. The Court stated as follows:

(a) Three questions need to be considered should the CPS seek to adduce evidence of the defendant's bad character under this part of gateway (d):
   (i) Does the defendant's history of offending show a propensity to commit offences?
   (ii) If so, does that propensity make it more likely that the defendant committed the current offence?
   (iii) If so, is it just to rely on convictions of the same description or category, having in mind the overriding principle that proceedings must be fair?

   Only if the answer to each of these questions is in the affirmative should the convictions be allowed in evidence.
(b) Offences which can be relied upon by the CPS to show this propensity may go beyond offences of the same description or of the same category.
(c) The fewer the number of previous convictions the defendant has, the less likely it is that propensity will be established. If the defendant has only one previous conviction of the same description or category, this is unlikely to show propensity unless there are distinguishing circumstances or a tendency towards unusual behaviour. The Court gave examples of unusual behaviour as including fire starting and the sexual abuse of children.

   **Example**

   In *R v Heffernan* [2006] EWCA Crim 2033 the Court of Appeal held that the trial judge had correctly permitted the prosecution to adduce evidence that the defendant, who was charged with burglary, had a single previous conviction for the same offence some eight years previously, as there were a number of significant similarities between the facts of the previous offence and the current offence.
(d) The manner in which the previous and current offences were carried out may be highly relevant to propensity and the probative value of a defendant's previous convictions. The Court said that it was the factual circumstances of previous convictions that were important, rather than the simple fact that the defendant had been convicted.

**Example 1**

Norma is on trial for unlawful wounding involving the use of a knife. She is alleged to have stabbed her husband after she found out he had been having an affair. She has previous convictions for assaulting a police officer in the execution of his duty and common assault. These convictions arose after Norma got drunk in a pub and refused the landlord's request that she leave the pub premises. Norma punched the landlord and then punched a policeman who tried to arrest her. It is likely that these convictions would not be admissible through this gateway. They are not offences of the same description, neither are they offences of the same category (as they do not fall within the two categories prescribed by the Secretary of State). Nor are they admissible generally to show 'propensity'. They would be admissible only if there were significant factual similarities between them and the current offence with which Norma is charged. Such similarities do not exist here because there is a marked difference between punching a stranger when drunk and attacking a spouse with a knife.

Example 2

Sharon, a juvenile, is on trial for the theft of a mobile phone from the school locker of a fellow pupil. Sharon is pleading not guilty. Sharon has three previous convictions for offences of theft. On each occasion Sharon entered shop premises and stole cosmetic items. The prosecution will seek to adduce evidence of these convictions under gateway (d) to show that Sharon has a propensity to commit offences of the same description as the offence she is currently charged with. Sharon's solicitor may, however, argue that her previous convictions do not show a propensity to commit this type of offence because of the significant factual differences between the circumstances of these offences (thefts from a shop) and the facts of the current offence (theft from the locker of another pupil). It would then be for the court to determine whether the factual differences were such that the previous convictions could not be said to demonstrate a propensity to commit offences of theft.

Example 3

Max is on trial for threatening behaviour (Public Order Act 1986, s 4) after he threatened some children who had thrown stones at his front door. Max has two previous convictions for the same offence. These convictions arose out of incidents at a local nightclub where Max works as a bouncer. On both occasions Max used threatening behaviour towards people in a drunken state who were attempting to gain entry to the nightclub. Max has committed offences of the same description as the offence he is currently charged with, and at his trial the prosecution will seek to adduce evidence of these convictions under gateway (d). Max's solicitor may, however, argue that Max's previous convictions do not show a propensity to commit this type of offence because of the significant factual differences between the circumstances of these offences and the facts of the current offence. It would then be for the court to determine whether the factual differences were such that the previous convictions could not be said to demonstrate a propensity to commit the offence of threatening behaviour.

### 22.4.5.3 Propensity to be untruthful

**When may the CPS suggest that the defendant has a propensity to be untruthful?**

The CPS may place before the court evidence of a defendant's previous convictions to show that the defendant has a propensity to be untruthful (and therefore that evidence given by the defendant at trial may lack credibility). The CPS will be permitted to do this only if it is suggested that the defendant's case is in any way untruthful (s 103(1)(b)).

**Which offences will demonstrate a propensity to be untruthful?**

In *R v Hanson, Gilmore & Pickstone* (see **22.4.5.2** above), the Court of Appeal held that a defendant's previous convictions will not be admissible to show that the defendant has a propensity to be untruthful unless:

(a) the manner in which the previous offence was committed demonstrates that the defendant has such a propensity (because he had made false representations), or

(b) the defendant pleaded not guilty to the earlier offence, but was convicted following a trial at which his account was disbelieved.

*Manner in which previous offence was committed*

The Court drew a distinction between a propensity to be dishonest and a propensity to be untruthful. Only if a defendant's previous convictions demonstrated a propensity to be *untruthful* will they become admissible under this gateway. The Court stressed that the only types of offence that would demonstrate a propensity to be untruthful were offences where the defendant had actively sought to deceive or mislead another person by the making of false representations. This includes previous convictions for perjury and offences involving an active deception of another (such as fraud), but not other offences where dishonesty forms part of the mental element of the offence but where the defendant has not actually been untruthful and has not actively deceived anyone. For example, a previous conviction for theft is unlikely to demonstrate a propensity to be untruthful because, unless the defendant had actually sought to mislead or had lied to another person as part of the commission of the theft, although the defendant had acted dishonestly, he had not been untruthful. In practical terms this means that if the CPS seeks to rely on offences such as theft to demonstrate the defendant's propensity to be untruthful, it will need to investigate the actual circumstances of the offence to find out if the defendant made false representations during its commission.

#### Example 1

Duleep is charged with common assault. The CPS alleges that he punched his victim in the face for no reason. Duleep denies the charge, claiming that he was initially attacked by his victim and that he was acting only in self-defence. Duleep's alleged victim refutes this. Duleep has previous convictions for perjury and fraud. These are offences which the CPS may attempt to raise in evidence to demonstrate that Duleep has a propensity to be untruthful.

#### Example 2

Miranda is charged with burglary. She denies the charge, raising the defence of alibi. Miranda has two previous convictions for fraud and a previous conviction for theft from a shop. The CPS may seek to use the convictions for the deception to demonstrate that Miranda has a propensity to be untruthful, because such offences involve actively misleading another person. The CPS will not be allowed to use the conviction for theft for the same purpose. Although this conviction shows that Miranda acted dishonestly, it does not show that she was untruthful.

(The only exception to this would be if Miranda had actively misled or lied to someone during the commission of the theft.)

*Convictions following a not guilty plea*

Offences of *any* description may also fall within this part of gateway (d) if the defendant pleaded not guilty but was convicted following a trial at which the magistrates or jury disbelieved his version of events, since this will demonstrate that the defendant has been found by a court to have been untruthful on a previous occasion. This will be particularly significant when, on a prior occasion, the defendant employed the same defence as he is raising in the current proceedings, and was disbelieved by the jury or magistrates.

#### Example 1

Kathy is charged with common assault. She is pleading not guilty and will raise the defence of alibi at trial. Kathy has several previous convictions for various offences. On each occasion she pleaded not guilty and raised the defence of alibi, but was convicted following a trial in which her alibi was disbelieved. The CPS may attempt to raise these previous convictions in evidence to show that Kathy has a propensity to be untruthful.

**Example 2**

Indira is charged with theft of goods from a shop. She pleads not guilty on the basis that she forgot to pay for the items. Indira has two previous convictions for theft from a shop. On both occasions she raised as her defence the fact that she had merely forgotten to pay for the items, but was convicted following a trial at which her version of events was disbelieved. The prosecution will attempt to raise these previous convictions to show that Indira has a propensity to be untruthful.

**Example 3**

Tim is charged with affray after a fight between two groups of men which was caught on a CCTV camera. Tim denies the charge and raises an alibi defence. He claims that the image caught on the camera is that of someone else and that he was at home at the time of the alleged affray. Tim has two previous convictions for assault occasioning actual bodily harm. On both occasions Tim pleaded not guilty on the basis that he was acting in reasonable self-defence. He was convicted, however, following a trial before the magistrates. Although Tim's defence to the charge of affray is not the same defence which he raised when accused of assault (and which was disbelieved by the magistrates), the CPS may nevertheless attempt to use the convictions for assault to show that Tim has a propensity to be untruthful.

Although it is not necessary for the CPS to show that when he was convicted of the previous offence(s), the defendant raised the same defence as he is raising in the current proceedings, it will be of huge evidential significance for the CPS to demonstrate that a defendant has a 'stock' defence which a previous jury or bench of magistrates have disbelieved.

In his commentary on the *Hanson* case, Professor J R Spencer QC stated:

> ... s 103(1)(b) does not make potentially admissible evidence of previous convictions generally, or even previous offences of dishonesty. It does, however, make admissible evidence for convictions of offences that involve telling lies – and also previous convictions in fought cases where the defendant gave evidence, and his word was plainly disbelieved. (*New Law Journal*, 28 April 2005)

**May a propensity to be untruthful be shown other than through previous convictions?**

The CPS may attempt to show that a defendant has a propensity to be untruthful other than by reference to his previous convictions. For example, in *R v Malone* [2006] EWCA Crim 1860, the Court of Appeal held that evidence that the defendant had forged a private detective's report was admissible to show a propensity to be untruthful.

### 22.4.5.4 Excluding evidence admitted under gateway (d)

Only the prosecution may adduce evidence of a defendant's previous convictions under gateway (d). Under s 101(3) of the CJA 2003, the court *must* not admit this evidence if:

> ... on an application by the defendant to exclude it, it appears to the court that the admission of the evidence would have such an adverse effect on the fairness of the proceedings that the court ought not to admit it.

This is the same test that that the court must apply when deciding whether to exclude unfairly obtained evidence under s 78 of PACE 1984 (see **21.21** above), save that under s 78 the court has a *discretion* to exclude the evidence if the test is satisfied, whereas under s 101(3) the court *must* exclude the evidence if the test is satisfied. The courts are most likely to use their powers under s 101(3) in three situations:

(a) When the nature of a defendant's previous convictions is such that the jury are likely to convict a defendant on the basis of these convictions alone, rather than examining the other evidence placed before them, or where the evidence of the previous convictions is more prejudicial than probative.

(b) When the CPS seeks to adduce previous convictions to support a case which is otherwise weak (*R v Hanson, Gilmore & Pickstone* [2005] Crim LR 787 – see **22.4.10** below).

(c) When the defendant's previous convictions are 'spent'. The Rehabilitation of Offenders Act 1974 provides that after a prescribed period of time, certain convictions are spent. This means that, for most purposes (such as completing an application form for a job), the convicted person is to be treated as never having been convicted of the spent offence. The rehabilitation period varies with the sentence, as follows:

| | |
|---|---|
| absolute discharge | 6 months |
| conditional discharge | 1 year or period of order |
| fine/community sentence | 5 years |
| custodial sentence up to 6 months | 7 years |
| custodial sentence between 6 and 30 months | 10 years |

A conviction for an offence which was punished by a custodial sentence exceeding 30 months cannot become spent.

Although the Act specifically does not prevent 'spent' convictions from being admissible in evidence in subsequent criminal proceedings, it is likely that the court will consider exercising its power under s 101(3) in such cases. In particular, s 101(4) provides that when an application to exclude evidence is made under s 101(3), the court must have regard to the length of time between the matters to which that evidence relates and the matters which form the subject of the offence charged.

(In addition to the court's power to exclude evidence of a defendant's previous convictions under s 101(3), the court must not allow the prosecution to adduce evidence of a previous conviction of a defendant in order to show that the defendant has a propensity to commit offences of the kind charged if the court is satisfied that, as a result of the time which has passed since the conviction, it would be unjust for it to be applied (CJA 2003, s 103(3)) – see **22.4.5.2** above. As with its power under s 101(3), the court is likely to consider it unjust to rely on a previous conviction to demonstrate a propensity to commit offences of the kind charged when that previous conviction is spent.)

### 22.4.5.5 Gateway (d) – summary

The prosecution will seek to adduce evidence of a defendant's previous convictions under gateway (d) to demonstrate that:

(a) the defendant has a propensity to commit offences of the kind charged; or
(b) the defendant has a propensity to be untruthful.

Previous convictions showing a propensity to commit offences of the kind charged will be convictions for offences of the same description or category, or convictions for offences where there is a significant factual similarity between the previous conviction and the current offence.

Previous convictions showing a propensity to be untruthful will be convictions for specific offences where a lie has been told (eg, fraud or perjury), or offences where the defendant pleaded not guilty but was convicted following a trial.

Offences of dishonesty (such as theft) will not generally show a propensity to be untruthful.

The defendant's solicitor may seek to challenge the admissibility of previous convictions which the prosecution seek to admit under gateway (d) in two ways:

(a) He may argue that the previous convictions do not actually demonstrate the relevant propensity and so do not satisfy gateway (d). For example:
   (i) How many convictions does the defendant have? One conviction is unlikely to show a propensity.
   (ii) If the previous convictions are being adduced to show a propensity to commit offences of the same kind:
      — do the factual circumstances of the previous convictions differ from the facts of the current offence;
      — would it be unjust to rely on them given the time which has elapsed since they occurred (s 103(3)); or
      — does the propensity make it no more likely that the defendant is guilty of the offence?
   (iii) If the previous convictions are being adduced to show a propensity to be untruthful, is it not suggested that the defendant's case is in any way untruthful?
(b) If the previous convictions do show the relevant propensity, can the court be persuaded to exercise its power under s 101(3) to exclude the convictions? Arguments that may be raised include:
   (i) Would the convictions be more prejudicial than probative? Is there a danger that the defendant would be convicted on the basis of his previous convictions alone, due either to the extent or to the nature of such convictions?
   (ii) Are the convictions being used to support a prosecution case that is otherwise weak?
   (iii) Are the previous convictions spent?

A flowchart to illustrate the operation of gateway (d) is set out at **22.9.3** below.

### 22.4.6 Gateway (e) – it has substantial probative value in relation to an important matter in issue between the defendant and a co-defendant

#### 22.4.6.1 Introduction

This gateway may be used by one defendant to admit evidence of another defendant's bad character. It cannot be used by the CPS. Section 104(2) of the CJA 2003 provides that only evidence which is adduced by a co-defendant, or which a witness gives in cross-examination by a co-defendant, is admissible under s 101(1)(e). The Explanatory Notes to the CJA 2003 suggest that the term 'substantial probative value' is to be widely construed, and that a court should exclude evidence only where its value is no more than 'marginal or trivial'. 'An important matter' is defined as 'a matter of substantial importance in the context of the case as a whole' (CJA 2003, s 112(1)).

A co-defendant is likely to want to admit evidence of defendant's bad character to demonstrate that the defendant has a propensity to be untruthful (and thus to undermine the credibility of the evidence given by the defendant), or to show that the defendant has a propensity to commit the kind of offence with which they have both been charged (thereby suggesting that it is the defendant, rather than the co-defendant, who committed the offence).

### 22.4.6.2 Propensity to be untruthful

Section 104(1) of the CJA 2003 states:

> (1) Evidence which is relevant to the question whether the defendant has a propensity to be untruthful is admissible on that basis under section 101(1)(e) only if the nature or conduct of his defence is such as to *undermine* the co-defendant's defence (emphasis added)

This preserves the pre-CJA 2003 position in relation to 'cut-throat' defence situations. A 'cut-throat' defence situation occurs when there are two (or more) defendants jointly charged with an offence, and each defendant pleads guilty and accuses the other(s) of having committed the offence. In such a situation, it will be an advantage for a co-defendant to be able to adduce evidence of his fellow defendant's previous convictions, in order to undermine the credibility of that defendant's evidence and to suggest that the co-defendant's version of events is the more credible.

The most relevant previous convictions of a defendant which a co-defendant will seek to adduce in evidence in order to demonstrate that the defendant has a propensity to be untruthful will be convictions for specific offences which involve the making of a false statement or representation (for example, perjury or fraud), or convictions for any offence where the defendant was convicted at trial after entering a not guilty plea but having his defence disbelieved by the court (although in *R v Lawson* [2006] All ER (D) 116 (Aug), the Court of Appeal held that a previous conviction for an offence that does not in itself involve untruthfulness may nevertheless be raised by a co-defendant under gateway (e) to demonstrate that a defendant has propensity to be untruthful).

Whilst gateway (e) will most commonly be used by a co-defendant in a 'cut-throat' defence situation, it may also be used if the defendant's defence is merely inconsistent with that of the co-defendant rather than contradicting it completely (since this will still undermine the co-defendant's defence).

#### Example 1

Albert and Harold are jointly charged with the burglary of a warehouse. Each pleads not guilty, alleging that the other was solely responsible for carrying out the burglary (ie, a 'cut-throat' defence situation). Albert has several previous convictions for offences of obtaining property by deception. As Albert's defence (that Harold carried out the burglary) will clearly undermine Harold's defence, at trial Harold will adduce evidence of Albert's previous convictions to show that Albert has a propensity to be untruthful, and to undermine the credibility of the evidence that Albert gives.

#### Example 2

Albert and Harold are jointly charged with the burglary of a warehouse. The CPS case is that they forced open a window with a crowbar and then stole the contents of the warehouse. Both plead not guilty. Albert raises an alibi defence, and claims that he does not know Harold. Harold raises a separate alibi defence. He does, however, admit to knowing Albert and to selling Albert a crowbar shortly before the burglary took place. Harold has previous convictions for perjury and conspiracy to pervert the course of justice. Although Harold is not raising a cut-throat defence (because he is not alleging that Albert committed the burglary), his defence is inconsistent with Albert's defence because he claims to know Albert and to have sold him a crowbar. To this extent, his defence undermines Albert's defence. At trial, Albert will adduce evidence of Harold's previous convictions to show that Harold has a propensity to be untruthful, and to undermine the credibility of the evidence that Harold gives.

A co-defendant may not use gateway (e) to adduce a defendant's previous conviction's in order to undermine the credibility of that defendant's evidence if the defendant merely denies participating in the offence and does not say anything to undermine the defence put forward by the co-defendant (*R v Edwards & Rowlands* – see **22.3** above).

**Example**

Graham and Arthur are jointly charged with assaulting Brian. Both enter not guilty pleas. Graham has several previous convictions for offences of deception. Graham raises the defence of alibi, claiming that he was elsewhere at the time of the assault and that he has been mistakenly identified as one of the assailants. Arthur claims that he was acting in self-defence after he had been attacked by Brian. Arthur says that a third person pulled Brian off him, but the incident happened so quickly that he cannot recall what that person looked like. If Graham raises the defence of alibi at trial, Arthur will not be able to raise Graham's previous convictions under s 101(1)(e) to demonstrate that Graham has a propensity to be untruthful. Graham's defence does not contradict the defence put forward by Arthur: Graham is not saying that Arthur carried out the assault; neither is Arthur saying that Graham was the other person involved in the assault.

#### 22.4.6.3 Propensity to commit offences of the same kind

A co-defendant may also want to introduce in evidence the fact that a defendant has previous convictions for offences of the kind with which they have both been charged, in order to show that the defendant has a propensity to commit such offences and is therefore the more likely of the two to have committed the current offence.

A co-defendant who seeks to introduce evidence of a defendant's previous convictions for this purpose does *not* need to show that the nature or conduct of the defendant's defence undermines his own defence. He will, however, need to demonstrate that such convictions are relevant to an important matter in issue between himself and the defendant, and that the relevance of such convictions is more than merely marginal or trivial (see **22.4.6.1** above).

**Example**

*R v Edwards and Others* [2005] EWCA Crim 3244 – two defendants (M and S) were jointly charged with wounding with intent to cause GBH. Both defendants entered not guilty pleas, on the basis that they were not involved in the attack on the victim. Neither defendant sought to blame the other for the attack. M had previous convictions for offences of wounding, assault and affray. S made an application under gateway (e) to adduce evidence of these convictions on the basis that they demonstrated a propensity to act in a violent manner. The trial judge granted this application, and M was subsequently convicted. The Court of Appeal upheld the conviction. The Court's reasoning was that each defendant's defence was that he was not involved in the violence, and if one defendant has previous convictions for offences of violence, this has a substantial probative value to the issue between them, namely, which of them was in fact responsible for the offence.

Unlike gateways (d) and (g), if the co-defendant can establish that the test for admitting evidence of the defendant's bad character through this gateway is satisfied, the court has no power under the CJA 2003 to prevent the admission of this evidence.

### 22.4.7 Gateway (f) – it is evidence to correct a false impression given by the defendant

Only the prosecution may adduce evidence of a defendant's bad character under gateway (f).

A defendant will give a false impression 'if he is responsible for the making of an express or implied assertion which is apt to give the court or jury a false or misleading impression about the defendant' (CJA 2003, s 105(1)(a)).

A defendant will be treated as being responsible for making such an assertion if the assertion is:

(a) made by the defendant in the proceedings (for example, when giving evidence in the witness box, or in a defence statement served on the CPS);

(b) made by the defendant when being questioned under caution by the police before charge, or on being charged;

(c) made by a witness called by the defendant;

(d) made by any witness in cross-examination in response to a question asked by the defendant that is intended to elicit it; or

(e) made by any person out of court, and the defendant adduces evidence of it in the proceedings (CJA 2003, s 105(2)).

**Example 1**

Alan is on trial for theft. He has several previous convictions for various offences. When giving evidence-in-chief, Alan says that he is of previous good character and has no previous convictions. The CPS will be permitted to correct the false impression given by Alan by by adducing evidence of his previous convictions.

**Example 2**

Phillip is on trial for common assault. Phillip has several previous convictions for offences involving violence. When the allegation of assault was put to Phillip in interview at the police station, Phillip said: 'I would never do such a thing. I'm a good Christian and I go to church every Sunday.' The CPS will be permitted to correct the false impression given by Phillip in the police interview by adducing evidence of his previous convictions (see also *R v Ullah* [2006] EWCA Crim 2003).

**Example 3**

Frances is on trial for theft. She has two previous convictions for theft. Frances calls her mother Doreen as an alibi witness. When giving evidence Doreen says: 'My daughter would never steal anything. I've brought her up better than that.' The CPS will be permitted to correct the false impression Doreen has given about her daughter by adducing evidence of Frances' previous convictions.

Section 105(4) of the CJA 2003 widens the manner in which a defendant may create a false impression by providing that:

> (4) Where it appears to the Court that a defendant, by means of his conduct (other than the giving of evidence) in the proceedings, is seeking to give the Court or jury an impression about himself that is false or misleading, the Court may if it appears just to do so treat the defendant as being responsible for the making of an assertion which is apt to give that impression.

'Conduct' here includes appearance or dress. This subsection is designed to cover situations where a defendant changes his appearance, or dresses in a manner which is intended to create a false or misleading impression about him.

Example

William is on trial for armed robbery. He appears before the jury wearing an army uniform and several medals for gallantry. William has never served in the army. He does, however, have previous convictions for offences of violence. The CPS will be permitted to correct the false impression given by William by adducing evidence of his previous convictions.

Evidence may be admitted under gateway (f) 'only if it goes no further than is necessary to correct the false impression' (CJA 2003, s 105(6)). Further, the defendant's bad character cannot be admitted under this gateway if, having made a false impression, the defendant 'withdraws or disassociates himself from it'. This provision is intended to cover the situation where the defendant says or does something to create a false impression, but subsequently (and prior to trial) makes some form of retraction.

Unlike gateways (d) and (g), if the prosecution can establish that the test for admitting evidence of the defendant's bad character through this gateway is satisfied, the court has no power under the CJA 2003 to prevent the admission of this evidence. The court does, however, retain the discretionary power to exclude such evidence under s 78 of PACE 1984 (see **22.4.9** below).

### 22.4.8 Gateway (g) – the defendant has made an attack on another person's character

#### 22.4.8.1 What constitutes an attack on another person's character?

Under the law prior to the CJA 2003 coming into force, a defendant was given some latitude in what he was permitted to say about prosecution witnesses before he lost his shield against cross-examination as to his bad character (see **22.2.1** above). In particular, a defendant was permitted to make an emphatic denial of guilt (which often by implication meant an accusation that a prosecution witness was lying) without losing his shield. The defendant's shield would be lost only if he:

(a) alleged that a prosecution witness had committed the offence with which he (the defendant) was charged;

(b) alleged that a witness for the prosecution had a specific reason for telling lies (such as an allegation that the witness was biased or had a grudge against him);

(c) alleged that the police had acted improperly either by purposely breaching PACE 1984 or the Codes of Practice, or by fabricating evidence; or

(d) cross-examined a witness for the prosecution about that witness's previous convictions.

Gateway (g) widens considerably the way in which a defendant may now have his bad character raised at trial. Under this gateway, a defendant's bad character will become admissible against him (even if he does not himself give evidence at trial) if he makes an attack on *any* person's character. The attack does not necessarily need to be on the character of a witness for the prosecution who is attending court to give evidence. It may be an attack on the character of a person who is dead, or a person whom the CPS does not intend to call to give evidence. Furthermore, the attack on the character of the other person does not necessarily need to take place at trial. The attack may be made when the defendant is being questioned at the police station, or in a defence statement which is served on the CPS.

Only the prosecution may adduce evidence of a defendant's previous convictions under gateway (g).

Section 106(1) of the CJA 2003 provides that:

> (1) For the purposes of section 101(1)(g) a defendant makes an attack on another person's character if—
>
> (a) he adduces evidence attacking the other person's character,
>
> (b) he [or his legal representative] asks questions in cross-examination that are intended to elicit such evidence, or are likely to do so, or
>
> (c) evidence is given of an imputation about the other person made by the defendant—
>
> (i) on being questioned under caution, before charge, about the offence for which he is charged, or
>
> (ii) on being charged with the offence or officially informed that he might be prosecuted for it.

Evidence attacking another person's character is evidence to the effect that the other person has:

(a) committed an offence (whether a different offence from the one with which the defendant is charged or the same one); or

(b) behaved, or is disposed to behave, in a reprehensible way (CJA 2003, s 106(2)).

In *R v Hanson, Gilmore & Pickstone* [2005] Crim LR 787 (see **22.4.5.2** above), the Court of Appeal said that when considering this gateway, authorities preceding the CJA 2003 will remain relevant. This will be particularly important if there is a dispute as to whether comments made by the defendant (or questions asked of a witness for the prosecution in cross-examination) constitute an attack on the character of that witness. Although the courts are likely to find that a defendant who makes an emphatic denial of guilt has not attacked the character of another (even if this denial suggests that a prosecution witness has fabricated his account), it is likely that the courts will give a very wide interpretation to s 106(2). For example, in *R v Ball* [2005] EWCA Crim 2826, the defendant was charged with rape and raised the defence of consent. When interviewed at the police station, the defendant emphatically denied the complainant's version of what had taken place, but then went further and made a disparaging remark about the complainant's sexual promiscuity, referring to her as a 'slag'. This imputation was held to be sufficient to enable the CPS to raise at trial evidence of the defendant's previous convictions. The Court of Appeal did say, however, that the defendant's claim that the complainant had fabricated the allegation of rape would not have been sufficient in itself to invoke s 101(1)(g). Gateway (g) came into play only because the defendant had gone further and cast an imputation on the complainant's character.

**Example 1**

John is on trial for murder. John has previous convictions for perjury and attempting to pervert the course of justice. Part of the evidence relied upon by the CPS is an alleged confession that John made to PC Smith when he was initially arrested for the offence. When John gives evidence at trial he tells the jury: 'The confession is a pack of lies. I never said anything and PC Smith is as bent as they come.' Accusing PC Smith of being corrupt is an attack on PC Smith's character. At trial the CPS will seek to adduce evidence of John's previous convictions because John has attacked the character of PC Smith.

#### Example 2

Jim is on trial for the burglary of factory premises where he had worked until recently. Jim has a number of previous convictions for similar offences. One of the witnesses for the prosecution is PC Gray, who claims to have found the items stolen in the burglary at Jim's flat. In cross-examination, Jim's solicitor puts to PC Gray the allegation that he (PC Gray) planted the stolen items in Jim's flat in order to frame him for the crime. Suggesting that PC Gray planted evidence in this way is an attack on the character of PC Gray. At trial the CPS will seek to adduce evidence of Jim's previous convictions because Jim has attacked the character of PC Gray.

#### Example 3

Trudy is on trial for common assault. She has several previous convictions for offences involving the use of violence, and also convictions for various offences of deception. Her defence is one of mistaken identity. She claims the assault was in fact carried out by Carrie, a witness for the prosecution. When giving evidence, Trudy tells the magistrates: 'It wasn't me that did it, it was Carrie. It wouldn't be the first time she's smacked someone. She's got a real temper on her.' This is an attack on the character of Carrie. At trial the CPS will seek to adduce evidence of Trudy's previous convictions because she has made an attack on the character of Carrie.

#### Example 4

Veronica is on trial for theft of items from a jewellery shop. Veronica has several previous convictions for offences of theft and deception. When she was questioned under caution at the police station, Veronica told the police: 'I had nothing to do with the theft. The owner of the shop is just trying to swindle his insurance company.' This is an attack on the character of the owner of the shop. At trial, the CPS will seek to adduce evidence of Veronica's previous convictions because Veronica has attacked the character of the owner of the shop.

#### Example 5

Henry is on trial for rape. He has previous convictions for various sexual offences. In his defence statement, Henry raises the defence of alibi and accuses Vincent of having committed the rape. This is an attack on Vincent's character. Vincent has not been charged with any offence and will not be giving evidence at Henry's trial. Even though Vincent will not be attending court to give evidence, at trial the CPS will seek to adduce evidence of Henry's previous convictions because Henry has attacked the character of Vincent.

### 22.4.8.2 Excluding evidence admitted under gateway (g)

As with gateway (d), the court must exclude evidence that would otherwise be admitted under this gateway if, on an application by the defendant, the admission of the evidence would have such an adverse effect on the fairness of the proceedings that the court ought not to admit it (CJA 2003, s 101(3)) (see **22.4.5.4** above).

The court is likely to exercise its power here when the effect of allowing the CPS to bring forward evidence of the defendant's previous convictions would be out of proportion to the significance of the defendant's attack on the character of another person (ie, where the evidence would be more prejudicial than probative). In such a situation, admitting evidence of previous convictions would have an adverse effect on the fairness of the trial because there would be a danger that the jury would convict the defendant on the basis of his previous convictions alone, rather than considering all the evidence in the case.

### Example

Fergus is charged with assault occasioning actual bodily harm following a fight in a pub when he is alleged to have pushed a fellow customer (John) to the ground, causing a gash to John's cheek. Fergus pleads not guilty and elects trial at the Crown Court. In his interview at the police station, Fergus said to the police: 'John's had it in for me ever since I moved in. He's a troublemaker and a bully'

This is an attack on John's character which would then permit the prosecution to adduce evidence of Fergus's previous convictions at his trial. Fergus has previous convictions for a number of sexual offences, including sexual assault and gross indecency with children. Although these convictions would be admissible under gateway (g), the trial judge may exercise his power under s 101(3) to prevent the prosecution adducing evidence of these convictions at trial. It is likely that the prejudicial effect of the jury finding out about such convictions would outweigh the probative value of such convictions in determining Fergus's guilt.

In *R v Nelson* [2006] All ER (D) 290 (Dec), the defendant was convicted of assault and affray. When interviewed by the police, he suggested that his neighbour, who may have observed the incident but did not give evidence at trial, was a user of Class A drugs and had colluded with the complainant to fabricate the allegations against him. The defendant did not persist in these allegations at trial. The prosecution successfully applied for evidence of the defendant's previous convictions for drug offences to be admitted, pursuant to s 101(1)(g), on the basis that the defendant had, when interviewed, made an attack on another person's character. The Court of Appeal held that evidence of a defendant's bad character ought not to be admitted when the only basis for it is an attack on the character of a person who was neither a witness nor an alleged victim, since this would damage the fairness of the proceedings. It was also held to be improper for the prosecution to adduce evidence of comments made by the defendant in interview (but not repeated by him at trial) merely for the purpose of satisfying s 101(1)(g).

The court may also exercise its power to exclude a defendant's previous convictions which the CPS seeks to adduce under s 101(1)(g) if those convictions are 'spent' (see **22.4.5.4** above), or if the CPS is attempting to raise such convictions to support a case which is otherwise weak.

If the defendant has attacked the character of another person during the course of an interview at the police station, the court may exercise its power under s 101(3) to prevent the prosecution from adducing evidence at trial of the defendant's previous convictions if the defendant can argue that he made an attack on the character of that other person only because of the nature of the questioning techniques employed by the police (if, for example, the defendant was goaded into attacking the character of a prosecution witness, or the interviewing officer specifically asked the defendant what his opinion of a particular person was).

If the court rules that because of the manner in which the police conducted the interview, the entire interview record is inadmissible, any attack which the defendant made on the character of another person during the course of the interview will not entitle the prosecution to adduce evidence of the defendant's bad character under gateway (g), since details of the defendant's attack on the character of that other person will not be adduced in evidence. The court will not need to exercise its power under s 101(3) in such a situation, since the prosecution will be unable to argue that the test for admitting evidence of the defendant's bad character under gateway (g) is satisfied.

#### 22.4.8.3 Gateway (g) – summary

The prosecution will seek to adduce evidence of a defendant's previous convictions under gateway (g) if the defendant has attacked the character of another person. The defendant may do this by:

(a) attacking the character of the person when he is interviewed at the police station;
(b) attacking the character of the person in his defence statement;
(c) asking a witness about his previous convictions in cross-examination; or
(d) adducing evidence of a witness's previous convictions.

If this gateway is satisfied, the prosecution will be entitled to adduce evidence of *all* the previous convictions which the defendant has.

The defendant's solicitor may seek to challenge the admissibility of previous convictions which the prosecution seek to admit under gateway (g) in two ways:

(a) He may argue that the test for admitting evidence of the defendant's bad character under gateway (g) has not been satisfied. For example:
  (i) If the defendant has merely accused the witness of fabricating his story, this is unlikely to satisfy gateway (g) (*R v Ball* – see **22.4.8.1** above).
  (ii) If the attack on the character of the person was made during an interview at the police station, can the interview record be excluded because of breaches of PACE 1984 or the Codes of Conduct by the police?
(b) If (a) is unsuccessful, can the court be persuaded to exercise its power under s 101(3) to exclude the convictions? Arguments that may be raised include:
  (i) Would the convictions be more prejudicial than probative? Is there a danger that the defendant would be convicted on the basis of his previous convictions alone, due to the extent or the nature of such convictions?
  (ii) Are the convictions being used to support a prosecution case that is otherwise weak?
  (iii) Are the previous convictions spent?
  (iv) If the attack on the character of the witness was made during an interview at the police station, did the defendant make the attack only because of the questioning techniques adopted by the police? Was he goaded into making the attack?

A flowchart summarising the operation of s 101(1)(a)–(g) is set out at **22.9.1** below.

### 22.4.9 Does the court have any other power to exclude bad character evidence?

The court has no power under the provisions of the CJA 2003 to exclude bad character evidence admitted under any gateway other than (d) and (g). Bad character evidence under gateways (a), (b), (c), (e) and (f) is automatically admissible if the requirements for each of these gateways are satisfied.

The court does, however, retain a discretionary power under s 78 of PACE 1984 to exclude evidence on which the prosecution propose to rely if the admission of the evidence would have such an adverse effect on the fairness of the proceedings that it ought not to be admitted (see **Chapter 21**). In *R v Highton & Others* [2005] EWCA Crim 1985, the Court of Appeal held that judges should apply the provisions of s 78 when making rulings as to the use of evidence of bad character, and exclude evidence where it would be appropriate to do so under s 78 (this will apply to bad character evidence which the prosecution seek to adduce under gateways (c) and (f)).

## 22.4.10 General guidance about the bad character provisions of the Criminal Justice Act 2003

### 22.4.10.1 General principles

In *R v Hanson, Gilmore & Pickstone* [2005] Crim LR 787 (see **22.4.5.2** above), the Court of Appeal took the opportunity to lay down general guidelines for dealing with evidence of a defendant's bad character under the CJA 2003:

(a) Prosecution applications to adduce evidence of the defendant's bad character should *not* be made as a matter of routine. Such applications should be carefully balanced, depending on the facts of the case.

(b) Where the evidence against the defendant is otherwise weak, it may be unfair to admit evidence of the defendant's previous convictions to bolster this evidence or to prejudice the minds of the jury against the defendant. Courts should also have regard to the amount of time which has elapsed between the earlier conviction(s) and the commission of the offence for which the defendant is charged. Old convictions may affect the fairness of current proceedings.

Example

In *R v Gyima* [2007] All ER (D) 101, two defendants were jointly convicted of theft and assault occasioning actual bodily harm. The only evidence against them was videotaped testimony from the victim's cousin (who had not been able to identify the defendants at an identification procedure), which was admitted as hearsay evidence under s 116(2)(c) because the cousin resided in the USA and it was not practicable to bring him back for trial. The CPS successfully applied to the trial judge for permission to adduce the defendant's previous convictions in evidence under gateway (d). One defendant had a single previous conviction for attempted robbery and the other a single previous conviction for robbery. The Court of Appeal held that neither previous conviction should have been admitted because they served to bolster what was an otherwise weak prosecution case.

(c) Each individual previous conviction needs to be examined separately, rather than the court simply applying a broad-brush approach and deciding that all previous convictions should be admissible.

(d) Details of the sentence passed in relation to the earlier offence are unlikely to be probative or admissible, even if the offence itself is admissible.

(e) The Court of Appeal will be slow to interfere with a trial judge's discretion to admit evidence of a defendant's bad character, and will interfere only if such discretion has been exercised in an irrational manner.

(f) When the CPS makes an application to adduce evidence of the defendant's bad character, it should decide at that point whether it seeks to rely on the fact of the conviction alone or on the factual circumstances of the offence as well.

### 22.4.10.2 Role of the trial judge

In addition to providing general guidelines about the new rules, the Court of Appeal also said in *Hanson* that a judge, when directing a jury in a case where the jury had been told about the defendant's previous convictions, should tell the jury that:

(a) they should not conclude that a defendant is guilty or untruthful merely because he has previous convictions;

(b) although previous convictions may show a propensity either to commit offences or to be untruthful, this does not mean that the defendant has committed the current offence or has been untruthful in the current case;

(c) whether the previous convictions do show a propensity is for them to decide;

(d) they must take into account what (if anything) a defendant has said about his previous convictions; and

(e) although they are entitled, if they find propensity is shown, to take this into account when determining guilt, propensity is only one relevant factor and they must assess its significance in the light of all the other evidence in the case.

The Court of Appeal stressed that the judge should warn the jury against placing undue reliance on previous convictions and should direct the jury that evidence of bad character cannot be used to bolster a weak case or to prejudice the minds of the jury against a defendant.

In the subsequent case of *R v Chohan* [2005] EWCA Crim 1813, the Court of Appeal held that a trial judge, when allowing evidence of a defendant's bad character to be placed before the jury, had to give a clear warning that reliance on previous convictions could not by itself prove guilt.

In *R v Renda & Others* [2005] EWCA Crim 2826, which involved several conjoined appeals concerning the practical application by trial judges of the bad character provisions in the 2003 Act, the Court of Appeal held that, having provided general guidance in the *Hanson* case as to how these provisions were to be interpreted, the detailed application of these principles was a matter for the judge at trial rather than an appellate court. The Court said that the trial judge's 'feel' for the case (and whether it would be unfair to admit evidence of the defendant's bad character) was important. This was confirmed in *R v Edwards & Rowlands* (see **22.3** above), when the Court of Appeal said that it would interfere with the decision of a trial judge only if it considered a conviction to be unsafe.

## 22.4.11 May bad character evidence admitted under one gateway be used for another purpose?

The CJA 2003 does not expressly identify the purpose for which bad character evidence may be used if it passes through one of the seven gateways created by s 101(1). However, in *R v Highton & Others* [2005] EWCA Crim 1985 (see **22.4.9** above), the Court of Appeal held that evidence of a defendant's bad character which is adduced under one gateway may then be used for any purpose for which bad character evidence was relevant in the particular case. Thus, for example, evidence of a defendant's previous convictions adduced as important explanatory evidence under gateway (c) may, once admitted in evidence, be used to show that the defendant has a propensity to commit the type of offence charged (under gateway (d)).

In the *Highton* case, the Court of Appeal held that a distinction had to be drawn between the admissibility of evidence of bad character (which depended on that evidence getting through one of the seven gateways) and the use to which that evidence could be put when admitted. Once bad character became admissible through one of gateways, it could then be used for any purpose for which bad character evidence was relevant in the particular case.

## 22.5 Stopping contaminated cases

Section 107 of the CJA 2003 permits a judge in the Crown Court either to direct the jury to acquit the defendant, or to order a retrial in circumstances where evidence of the defendant's bad character is 'contaminated'. Contamination may occur if witnesses have colluded in order to fabricate evidence of the defendant's bad character. Section 107 does not apply to trials in the magistrates' court.

## 22.6 Bad character of persons other than the defendant

### 22.6.1 Introduction

In contrast to the numerous ways in which a defendant's bad character may now be admissible in evidence at trial, the bad character of *persons other than the defendant* (ie, not just other witnesses in the case) is now admissible only on very limited grounds. These grounds are set out in s 100(1) of the CJA 2003:

> (1) ... evidence of the bad character of a person other than the defendant is admissible if and only if—
> (a) it is important explanatory evidence,
> (b) it has substantial probative value in relation to a matter which—
> (i) is a matter in issue in the proceedings, and
> (ii) is of substantial importance in the context of the case as a whole, or
> (c) all parties agree to the evidence being admissible.

### 22.6.2 Section 100(1)(a) – it is important explanatory evidence

This is very similar to gateway (c) for evidence of a defendant's previous convictions (see **22.4.4** above). The evidence will be important explanatory evidence only if:

(a) without it, the court or jury would find it impossible or difficult properly to understand other evidence in the case; and
(b) its value for understanding the case as a whole is substantial (s 100(2)).

'Substantial' in this context is likely to mean more than merely trivial or marginal (see **22.4.5.1** above).

#### Example 1

Michael is the former manager of a care home for children. He is on trial for sexually abusing the children in his care. The offences are alleged to have taken place over a number of years and the CPS needs to explain why the victims of the abuse did not seek help from another person. The only other person to whom the victims could have spoken was Laura, the matron at the home. The reason why the victims did not report the abuse to Laura was because she also participated in the abuse. Laura has already been prosecuted (and convicted) for her role in the abuse. The CPS will be able to raise Laura's convictions for abuse to explain why Michael's victims did not go to her for help.

#### Example 2

Derrick is charged with assaulting Tracey, his partner. The CPS alleges that Derrick grabbed Tracey by the hair as she was attempting to put Matthew, their baby son, to bed. Tracey has a previous conviction for assaulting Matthew after she punched him when he wouldn't stop crying. Derrick's defence is that he grabbed Tracey by the hair because he thought she was going to assault Matthew. As Tracey went to put Matthew to bed, he heard her say: 'For God's sake, will he never shut up!' On hearing this,

Derrick thought that Tracey might assault Matthew again. To explain why he grabbed Tracey by the hair, Derrick may seek to adduce evidence of Tracey's previous conviction for assaulting Matthew.

Under s 100(4), leave of the court will be required if a party wishes to adduce evidence of the bad character of a person other than the defendant under s 100(1)(a).

### 22.6.3 Section 100(1)(b) – it has substantial probative value in relation to a matter in issue in the proceedings

#### 22.6.3.1 Introduction

Although this ground may apply to any person other than the defendant (and so may apply to a witness for the defence as well as to a witness for the prosecution), it is most likely to arise when the defendant seeks to adduce evidence of the previous convictions of a witness for the prosecution in order to support an allegation that the witness is either:

(a) lying or has fabricated evidence against the defendant; or

(b) is himself either guilty of the offence with which the defendant has been charged, or has engaged in misconduct in connection with the alleged offence.

In *R v Weir and Others* [2005] EWCA Crim 2866, the Court of Appeal held that evidence of the bad character of a witness which is adduced under s 100(1)(b) may be used either to show that witness engaged in misconduct in connection with the offence (see **22.6.3.3** below), or to show that that the evidence given by the witness lacks credibility because the witness has a propensity to be untruthful (see **22.6.3.2** below).

In assessing the probative value of the evidence of another person's previous convictions, the court must have regard to:

(a) the nature and number of the events, or other things, to which the evidence relates; and

(b) when those events or things are alleged to have happened or to have existed (s 100(3)).

The term 'substantial' is likely to be construed by the courts as meaning more than merely marginal or trivial (see **22.4.5.1** above).

#### 22.6.3.2 Credibility as a witness

Previous convictions of a witness for the prosecution which may be used to suggest that the evidence given by the witness lacks credibility may be:

(a) convictions for offences where the witness has made a false statement or representation (such as perjury, fraud, or theft, where the witness has lied to or deceived another person as part of the commission of the theft). In *R v Stephenson* [2006] EWCA Crim 2325, the Court of Appeal suggested that previous convictions of a witness which demonstrated a propensity to be dishonest (as opposed to a propensity to be untruthful) may nevertheless be admissible under s 100(1)(b) to undermine the credibility of the witness; or

(b) convictions when the witness has been found guilty of an offence to which he pleaded not guilty but was convicted following a trial at which his version of events was disbelieved; or

(c) other convictions which may cast doubt on the credibility of the evidence given by the witness.

**Example 1**

George is on trial for theft of a gold watch from a jewellery shop. Peter, the owner of the shop, is a witness for the prosecution, and will say that he saw George place the watch in his pocket and walk out of the shop without paying for it. George denies this and claims that Peter has made up the allegation as part of an insurance swindle. Peter has two previous convictions for fraud. George will seek to use Peter's previous convictions to undermine Peter's credibility as a witness when he gives evidence at George's trial by showing that twice previously Peter has been convicted of an offence involving untruthfulness.

**Example 2**

Kathryn is on trial for assault occasioning actual bodily harm, following an incident outside a pizza shop when she is alleged to have punched Michelle. The CPS alleges that Kathryn punched Michelle after Michelle accidentally knocked Kathryn's pizza to the floor. Kathryn accepts that Michelle knocked her pizza to the floor, but denies punching her. She claims that Michelle has made up the allegation because she (Kathryn) has just started going out with Michelle's ex-boyfriend. Michelle has previous convictions for offences of theft and criminal damage. Michelle pleaded not guilty to both of these offences, but on both occasions was convicted following a trial. Kathryn will seek to use Michelle's previous convictions to undermine Michelle's credibility as a witness when she gives evidence at Kathryn's trial, by showing that Michelle has twice previously given evidence in criminal proceedings which has been disbelieved.

#### 22.6.3.3 Misconduct in connection with the current offence or guilty of that offence

The other reason for a defendant wanting to raise the bad character of a person other than himself is to use such evidence to suggest either that:

(a) the other person has committed some form of misconduct in connection with the current offence (for example, a defendant charged with assault may claim that he was acting merely in self-defence, and that he was in fact attacked by his alleged victim); or

(b) the other person is in fact guilty of the offence with which the defendant has been charged.

Although this ground applies equally to witnesses called either by the defence or by the prosecution, it is likely to be used most regularly by a defendant to suggest that a witness for the prosecution either committed the offence with which the defendant is charged, or is guilty of some other form of misconduct in connection with that offence.

**Misconduct in connection with the current offence**

If it is alleged that evidence of another person's misconduct has probative value because there is a similarity between that misconduct and alleged misconduct in connection with the current offence, the court will have regard to the nature and extent of the similarities and dissimilarities between each of the alleged instances of misconduct (s 100(3)(c)).

**Example**

Michael is on trial for assaulting Brian at a pub. The CPS alleges that Michael punched Brian in the face. Michael denies the offence, claiming that he was in fact attacked by Brian (who was in a drunken state) after Michael had made a provocative remark about Brian's girlfriend. Brian has previous convictions for offences of common assault and threatening behaviour. Michael will seek to use evidence of Brian's previous convictions to show that Brian is more likely to have been the aggressor on this occasion.

In deciding whether evidence of Brian's previous convictions is admissible, the court will have regard to the nature and extent of the similarities and dissimilarities between his previous convictions and the facts of the current offence. The court will want to know if Brian's previous convictions arose in similar circumstances, and in particular if Brian committed these offences after any provocation and/or whilst in a drunken state.

In *R v Bovell* [2005] EWCA Crim 1091, the Court of Appeal held that a judge could admit evidence of previous convictions relied upon to show the propensity of a prosecution witness to commit a particular type of offence, if the defendant could show sufficient factual similarities between the earlier offence and the current incident.

**Guilty of committing the current offence**

If it is alleged that evidence of another person's misconduct has probative value because it is suggested that the person is responsible for having committed the offence with which the defendant has been charged, the court will have regard to the extent to which the evidence shows or tends to show that the same person was responsible each time (s 100(3)(d)).

Example

Terry is on trial for the theft of items from a warehouse. One of the witnesses for the prosecution is Gordon, the night watchman at the warehouse. Gordon claims to have seen Terry committing the theft. Terry denies the offence and alleges that Gordon has fabricated evidence against him because he (Gordon) was in fact responsible for the theft. Gordon has two previous convictions for offences of theft. Terry will seek to use evidence of Gordon's previous convictions to show Gordon to have been the more likely of the two to have been responsible for the theft. In deciding whether the evidence of Gordon's previous convictions is admissible, the court will have regard to the nature and extent of the similarities and dissimilarities between Gordon's previous convictions and the facts of the current offence. If the facts of the previous conviction are markedly different, it is highly unlikely that the court will permit the defendant to raise this conviction at trial (see, eg, *R v Gadsby* [2005] EWCA Crim 3206).

### 22.6.3.4 Witnesses who are not giving evidence

Although the defendant will usually rely upon s 100(1)(b) in respect of a witness for the prosecution who has previous convictions, it may also be used in relation to persons who are not giving evidence in the case.

Example

Oscar is on trial for the murder of Claude. It is alleged that Oscar stabbed Claude with a knife. Oscar raises the defence of self-defence. He alleges that Claude attacked him with a knife and that Claude was stabbed after he (Oscar) managed to turn the knife against him. Claude had a previous conviction for carrying a knife as an offensive weapon. Oscar will want to use this previous conviction to support his defence of self-defence. In deciding whether the evidence of Claude's previous conviction is admissible, the court will have regard to the nature and extent of the similarities and dissimilarities between the facts of Claude's previous conviction and the facts of the current case.

#### 22.6.3.5 Leave of the court

Under s 100(4), leave of the court will be required if a party wishes to adduce evidence of the bad character of a person other than the defendant under s 100(1)(b).

### 22.6.4 Section 100(1)(c) – all parties to the proceedings agree to the evidence being admissible

This ground is self-explanatory. If all parties to the case are in agreement, evidence of the bad character of a person other than the defendant will always be admissible.

If s 100(1)(c) applies, leave of the court is not required to admit evidence of the bad character of a person other than the defendant.

A flowchart summarising the operation of s 100(1) is set out at **22.9.2** below.

## 22.7 Procedure for admitting bad character evidence

### 22.7.1 Introduction

If the CPS wishes to adduce at trial evidence of the defendant's bad character, notice of this intention must be given both to the court and to the other parties in the case (CrimPR, r 35.4(1)). If either the CPS or the defendant wishes to adduce at trial evidence of the bad character of a non-defendant (usually a witness), an application must be made to the court for permission to do this, with the application also being sent to the other parties (CrimPR, r 35.2). In both of the above cases a prescribed form must be used, with a written record of the previous convictions the party giving the notice or making the application is seeking to adduce being attached to the form. The relevant forms are reproduced at **22.11.2** and **22.11.4** below.

As part of the standard directions that will be given in both the magistrates' court (see **8.2.3**) and the Crown Court (see **10.5.1**), the court will impose time limits for the parties to serve any notice or make any application to adduce bad character evidence at trial. The relevant time limits are set out in r 35.4 (for the CPS to give notice of its intention to introduce evidence of the defendant's bad character) and r 35.2 (for either the CPS or the defendant to apply for permission to introduce evidence of the bad character of a non-defendant).

If a defendant opposes the introduction of evidence of his bad character at trial, he must apply to the court for such evidence to be excluded. The application must be sent both to the court and to the other parties in the case. The time limit for making this application is set out in r 35.6. A copy of the prescribed form which the defendant must use to make this application is reproduced at **22.11.3** below. If either the CPS or the defendant opposes an application to introduce the bad character of a non-defendant at trial, notice to this effect must be given both to the court and to the other parties in the case. The time limit for giving this notice is set out in r 35.3.

### 22.7.2 Magistrates' court

If the CPS wishes to adduce at trial evidence of the defendant's bad character, it must give notice of intention to do this both to the court and to the other parties in the case (CrimPR, r 35.4(1)). The notice must be given at the same time as it complies or purports to comply with its initial duty to disclose to the defendant any unused material it has (CrimPR, r 35.4(2)(a)). The defendant must make any application to exclude evidence of his bad character at trial within *14 days* of receiving the notice from the CPS (CrimPR, r 35.6). Any such application by the defendant must be sent both to the court and to the other parties in the case.

If the defendant wishes to introduce the bad character of a prosecution witness at trial, r 35.2(a) provides that he must make an application for permission to do this within *14 days* of the date on which the CPS either complies or purports to comply with its initial duty to disclose to the defendant any unused material it has, or within *14 days* of the date on which the CPS discloses to the defendant details of the previous convictions of any of its witnesses (details of such convictions will normally fall within the disclosure obligations on the CPS in respect of unused material in its possession, since such convictions are likely to be material capable of undermining the prosecution case or assisting the defence case – see **8.4.6.2**). This application must be sent both to the court and to the other parties in the case. If the CPS opposes the defendant's application, it must send a notice to this effect both to the court and to the other parties in the case within *14 days* of receiving the defendant's application.

If the CPS wishes to adduce at trial evidence of the bad character of a witness (other than the defendant) who is to give evidence for the defence, r 35.2(b) provides that it must make an application to do this 'as soon as reasonably practicable'. The application must be sent to the court and to the other parties in the case. If the defendant opposes this application, he must give a notice to this effect within *14 days* of receiving the application from the CPS (CrimPR, r 35.3). The notice must be sent to the court and to the other parties in the case.

### 22.7.3 Crown Court

If the CPS wishes to adduce at trial evidence of the defendant's bad character, it must send a notice of its intention to do this both to the court and to the other parties in the case (CrimPR, r 35.4(1)). For an either way offence, the notice must be sent within *14 days* of committal (CrimPR, r 35.4(2)(b)(i)). For an indictable-only offence, the notice must be sent within *14* days of the service of the prosecution case papers on the defendant (CrimPR, r 35.4(2)(b)(iv)). If the defendant opposes this, he has *14 days* from receipt of the notice to make an application to exclude evidence of his bad character at trial (CrimPR, r 35.6). This appplication must be sent to the court and to the other parties in the case.

The defendant must make an application for permission to introduce the bad character of a prosecution witness at trial within *14 days* of the date on which the CPS complies or purports to comply with its initial duty of disclosure in respect of any unused material in its possession, or within *14 days* of the date on which the CPS discloses to the defendant details of the previous convictions of any of its witnesses (CrimPR, r 35.2(a)). As with cases before the magistrates' court, details of any such convictions should form part of the unused material which the CPS must disclose to the defence, as such convictions are likely to be material capable of undermining the prosecution case or assisting the defence case (see **Chapter 10**). This application must be sent both to the court and to the other parties in the case. If the CPS opposes this application, it has *14 days* from receipt of the application in which to serve a notice opposing this (CrimPR, r 35.3). The notice must be sent to the court and to the other parties in the case.

If the CPS wishes to adduce evidence of the bad character of a witness (other than the defendant) who is to give evidence for the defence at trial, it must make an application for permission to do this 'as soon as reasonably practicable' (CrimPR, r 35.2(b)). This application must be sent both to the court and to the other parties in the case. If this application is opposed by the defendant, a notice to this effect must be sent to the court and to the other parties in the case. This notice must be sent within *14 days* of the defendant receiving the application from the CPS (CrimPR, r 35.3).

### 22.7.4 Co-defendants

In either the magistrates' court or the Crown Court, a defendant who wants to introduce at trial evidence of a co-defendant's bad character, or who wants to cross-examine a witness to elicit such evidence, must give notice of this both to the court and to the other parties in the case within *14 days* of the CPS complying with its initial duty to disclose any unused material in its possession (CrimPR, r 35.5). If the co-defendant wishes to oppose this notice, he must make an application to exclude evidence of his own bad character at trial within *14 days* of receiving the defendant's application (CrimPR, r 35.6). The application must be sent to the court and to the other parties in the case.

### 22.7.5 Must the parties comply with the above time limits?

The court may allow oral notice to be given at trial and extend or shorten any time limit for the giving of any notice or the making of any application under Part 35 if it is in the interests of justice to do so (CrimPR, r 35.8). This would, for example, allow the CPS to apply to adduce evidence of a defendant's bad character when at trial the defendant gives a false impression about himself when giving evidence.

In *R (Robinson) v Sutton Coldfield Magistrates' Court* [2006] EWHC 307 (Admin), the CPS served a notice to adduce evidence of the defendant's bad character at trial three days prior to the date of the trial. The Court of Appeal held that it was the duty of all parties to comply with the Criminal Procedure Rules 2005 and that all necessary time limits should be adhered to. The Court went on to say, however, that there was a discretionary power under r 35.8 to extend the time limit for service of the notice, and that it was unnecessary for the court to find 'exceptional' reasons before allowing an extension. What the court should take into account in such a situation was the overriding objective under r 1.1 of the Criminal Procedure Rules (see **1.4.2**), whether there were justifiable reasons for the failure to comply with the Rules, and whether the defendant had been prejudiced by the late service of the notice (see also *R v Lawson* [2006] All ER (D) 116 (Aug) and *R v M* [2006] All ER (D) 164 (May)).

### 22.7.6 Procedure for adducing bad character evidence at trial

Where either the CPS or the defendant has made an application to adduce bad character evidence at trial, and this application is opposed by the other party, the court will usually determine the admissibility of such evidence at a pre-trial hearing. In the magistrates' court, this is likely to be at the case management hearing/pre-trial review, or at a specific pre-trial hearing to resolve disputes about the admissibility of evidence. In the Crown Court, this is likely to be at the plea and case management hearing, or at a specific pre-trial hearing as in the magistrates' court.

The method by which the previous convictions of either the defendant or any other witness are proved at trial is by the party seeking to adduce this evidence producing a certificate or memorandum of conviction to the court (PACE 1984, s 73(1); *DPP v Parker* [2006] EWHC 1270). If the CPS is seeking to adduce the previous convictions of the defendant, the certificate will usually be produced by the police officer in the case when he gives evidence-in-chief. If either the CPS or the defence are seeking to adduce the previous convictions of a witness (or a defendant is seeking to adduce the previous convictions of a co-defendant), such convictions will usually be put to the witness (or co-defendant) in cross-examination. A certificate of conviction will be required only if the defendant or witness denies having the previous conviction(s). In practice, if the court has ruled that a previous conviction of a defendant or other person is admissible, the party against whom the evidence is to be adduced will often make a formal admission as to the existence of the conviction under s 10 of the CJA 1967 (see 16.3.3).

If, in order to demonstrate a defendant's propensity to commit a particular type of offence, the CPS wants to adduce evidence of the *details* of what the defendant was alleged to have done when committing previous offences (rather than just the fact that the defendant was convicted of a particular offence), it must call witnesses at trial who can give first-hand evidence of what happened, such as the victims of the previous offences (*R v Humphries* (2005) *The Times*, 19 September). Merely having a police officer repeat details of what is alleged to have happened when the previous offences were committed is not sufficient.

Similarly, if there is a dispute between the CPS and the defendant as to the facts supporting any previous conviction, oral evidence from witnesses will be required to enable the court to establish what the facts actually were (*R v Ainscough* [2006] EWCA Crim 694).

## 22.8 Evidence of good character

### 22.8.1 Good character of the defendant

A defendant who is of good character (in other words, a defendant who has no previous convictions and who has not otherwise engaged in any 'reprehensible behaviour') is entitled to have this taken into account by the magistrates or jury at his trial. The accepted method of confirming the defendant's good character at trial is for the defendant's solicitor or counsel to ask the police officer who gives evidence verifying the record of the interview in the police station, to confirm that the defendant is of good character. The defendant may also be allowed to give brief details of his good character when he starts to give evidence in the witness box (for example, details of any charitable works he has done). He may also call witnesses as to his good character. Such witnesses are likely to be either persons in a position of respect or trust within the community (for example, a teacher or doctor), or the defendant's current or former employer.

If a defendant is of good character, this will be relevant both to his credibility as a witness (provided he has put his defence 'on record') and to show the absence of a propensity to commit the offence with which he has been charged (*R v Vye, Wise & Stephenson* (1993) 97 Cr App R 134). In the Crown Court, if a defendant of previous good character gives evidence in his own defence at his trial, the judge will give a direction to the jury that this is relevant both to matters of credibility and propensity (a '*Vye* direction'). If the defendant does not give evidence at his trial, the judge will give a direction as to propensity only, unless the defendant has put his defence on record elsewhere (if, for example, the defendant does not give evidence at trial, but did give details of his defence when interviewed at the police station). In the magistrates' court, the defendant's solicitor will remind the magistrates of the significance of the defendant's good character as to matters of propensity and credibility when giving his closing speech to the court.

Example

Charles in on trial for possession of Class A drugs with intent to supply. Charles has no previous convictions. When being cross-examined by Charles's counsel, the officer in the case confirms that Charles is of good character. Charles subsequently gives evidence in his own defence. When he is summing up the case to the jury before they retire to consider their verdict, the judge will give the jury a '*Vye*' direction. He will direct the jury that they should take Charles's good character into account when deciding whether the prosecution have satisfied them as to Charles's guilt. The jury are entitled to conclude that Charles's good character enhances the credibility of the evidence he has given, *and* that his good character means that he is less likely to have committed the offence for which he is on trial.

In *R v Barrington Payton* [2006] EWCA Crim 1226, the Court of Appeal held that a trial judge's failure to give a '*Vye*' direction where appropriate was a misdirection which would render any subsequent conviction unsafe.

If two co-defendants are tried together, with one being of good character and the other having previous convictions, the defendant who is of previous good character is entitled to have the judge give a '*Vye* direction'. If the bad character of the co-defendant has not come out during the course of the trial, the trial judge may either say nothing about his character when summing up to the jury, or may tell the jury that they have heard nothing about his character but should not speculate as to the reason for this (*R v Aziz* [1995] 3 All ER 149).

### 22.8.2 Good character of other witnesses

Evidence of the good character of a witness other than the defendant is inadmissible at common law and should not be raised at trial. Such evidence is said to be 'oath helping' (ie, adduced to bolster the credibility of the evidence given by the witness) and is not permitted. In *R v Beard* [1998] Crim LR 585, the defendant was charged with robbery. It was alleged that his victim was vulnerable as he had learning difficulties. When giving evidence, the victim stated that he had been threatened with a 'kicking' by the defendant if he did not give him money. In his defence, the defendant claimed that the victim was a compulsive liar. The prosecution were granted leave to call a social worker to rebut this assertion, saying that the victim was an honest and truthful person. The defendant's subsequent conviction was quashed by the Court of Appeal. The Court held that the trial judge had been wrong to allow the prosecution to adduce such evidence since it amounted to 'oath helping' and served no useful purpose.

In *R v Tinsley* [2006] EWCA Crim 2006, the defendant was convicted of indecently assaulting his niece. The Court of Appeal held that the trial judge had wrongly allowed the prosecution to bolster the credibility of the niece's evidence by allowing them to adduce evidence that other members of the defendant's family had been convicted of various sexual offences against her after she had made allegations against them. Such evidence was 'oath helping' because it was not relevant to the allegations made against the defendant and was admitted solely to bolster the credibility of the evidence given by the niece.

In some cases involving sexual conduct, however, differences between questions that go to the credibility of a complainant and questions going to an issue in the case (eg, consent in a rape case) are sometimes impossible to separate, and the court may allow some evidence to be given as to the character of the complainant (*R v Tobin* [2003] Crim LR 408).

## 22.9 Procedural flowcharts

### 22.9.1 Bad character of the defendant

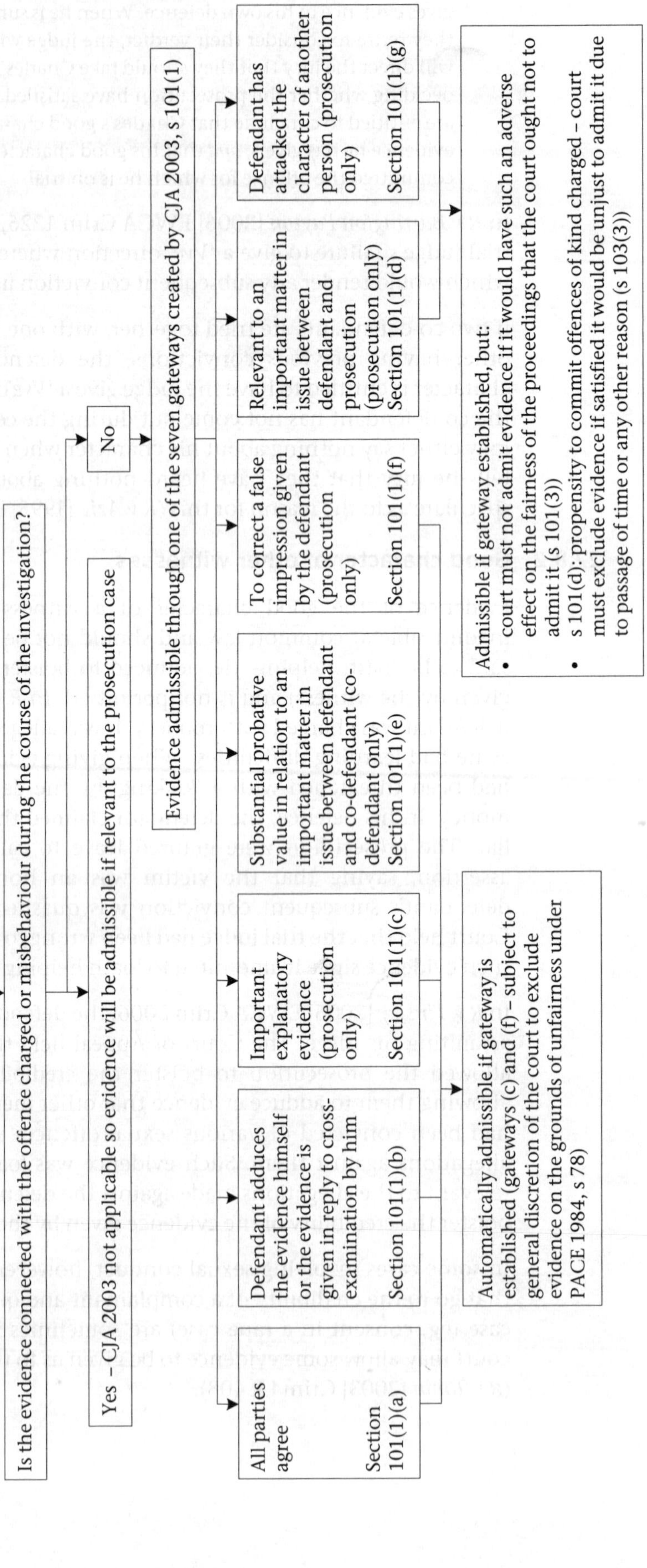

### 22.9.2 Bad character of persons other than the defendant

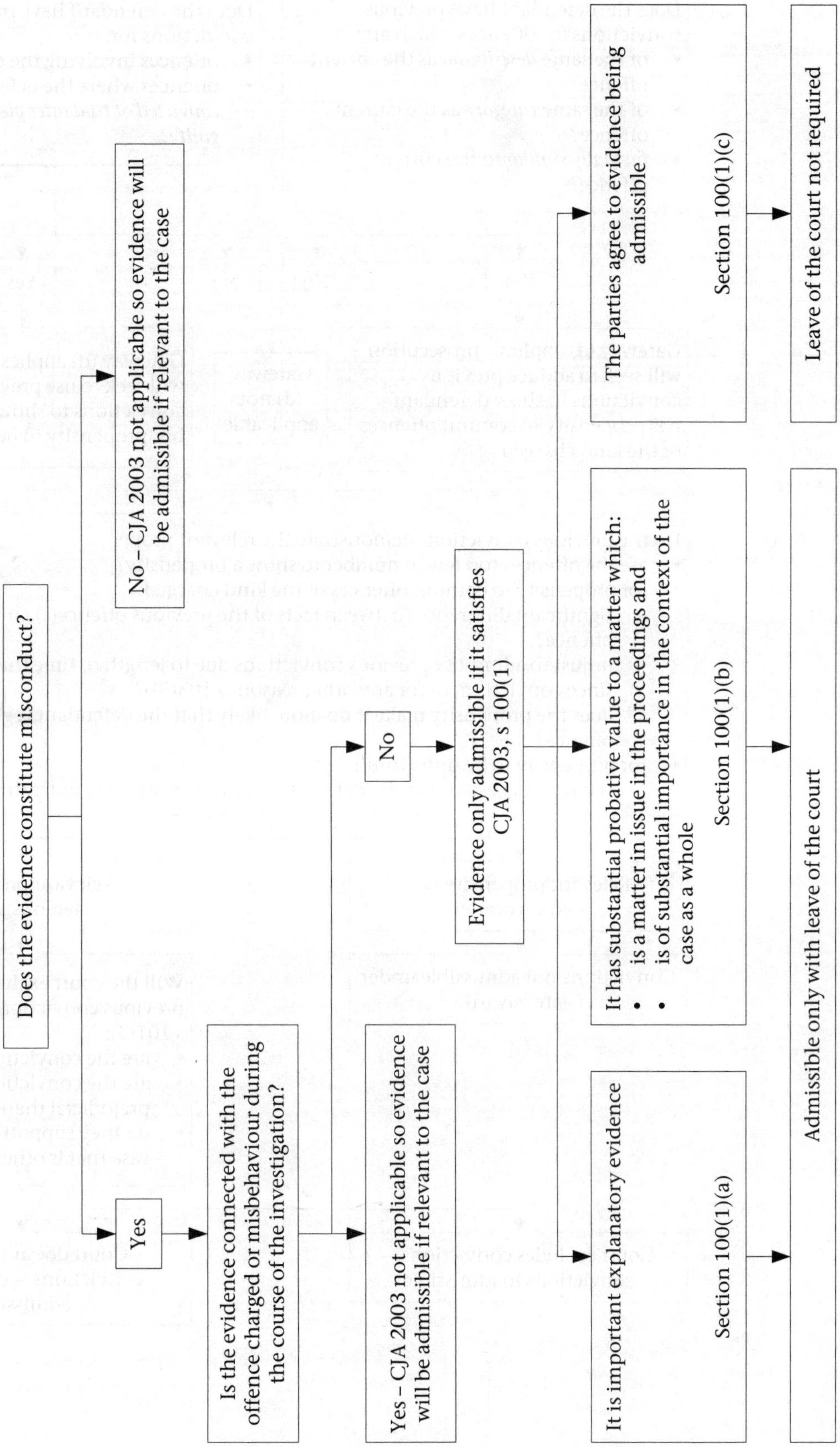

### 22.9.3 The operation of gateway (d)

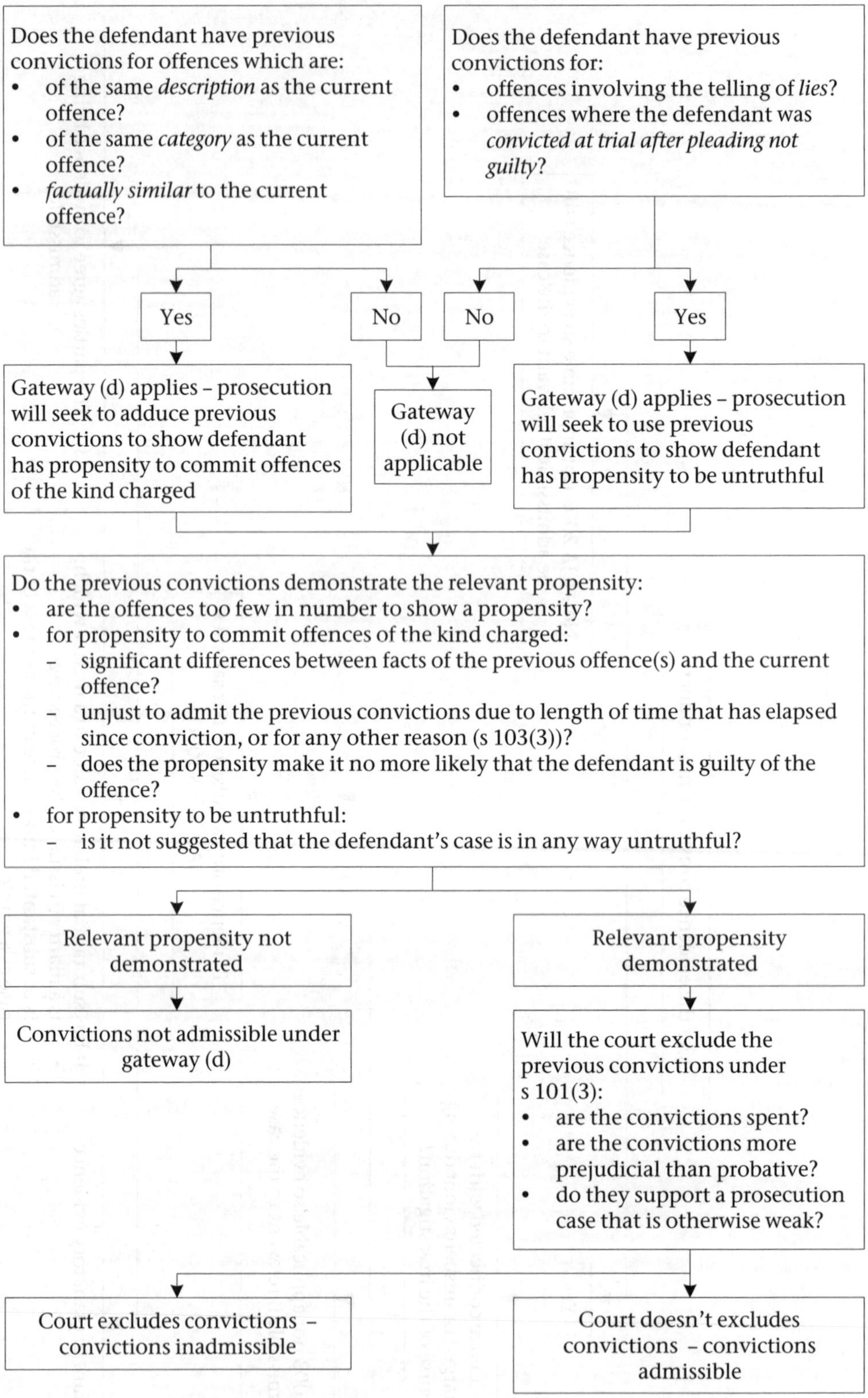

## 22.9.4 The operation of gateway (g)

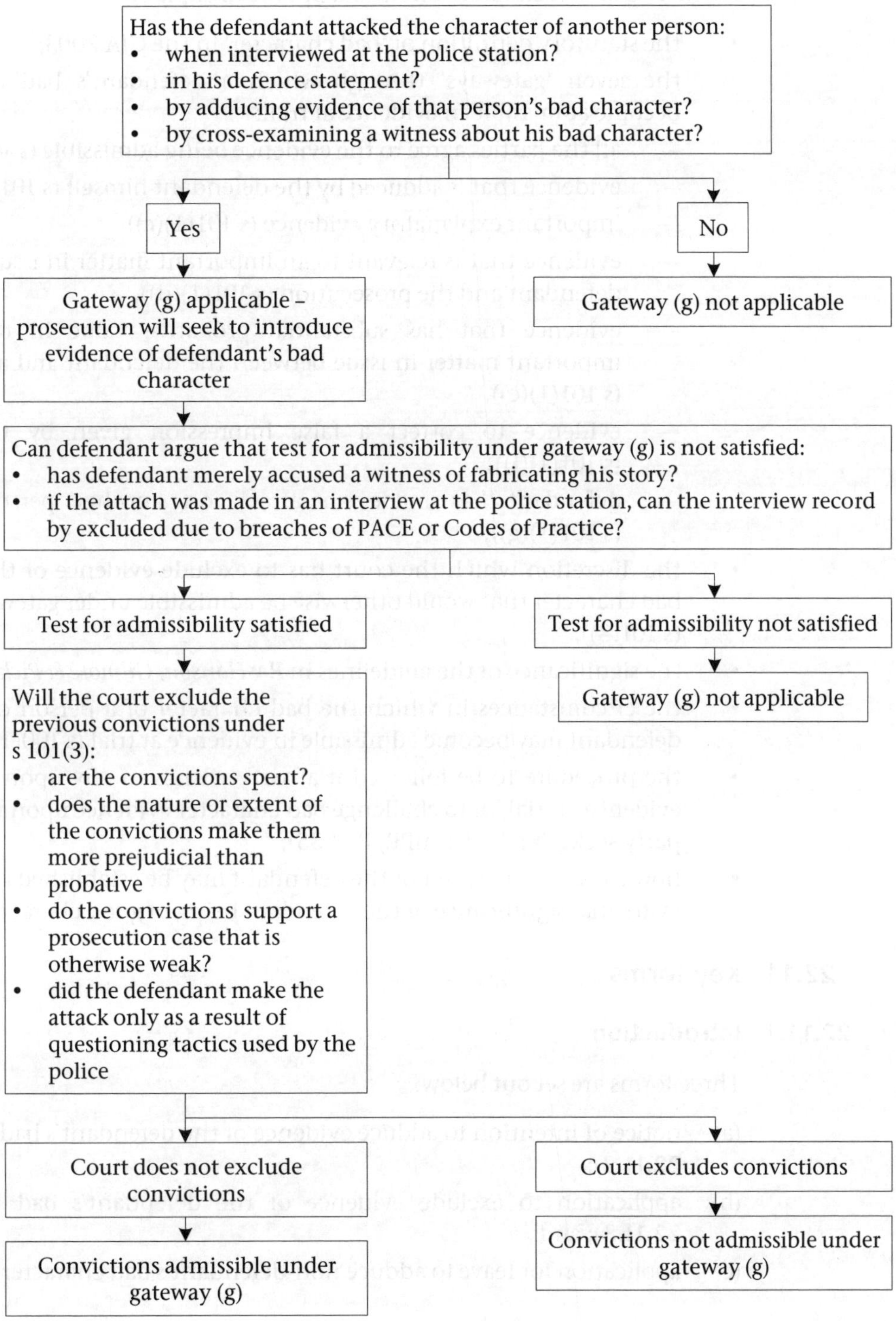

## 22.10 Checklist

At the end of this chapter you should be able to explain:

- the statutory definition of 'bad character' in the CJA 2003;
- the seven 'gateways' through which a defendant's bad character may become admissible in evidence at trial:
  - — all the parties agree to the evidence being admissible (s 101(1)(a)),
  - — evidence that is adduced by the defendant himself (s 101(1)(b)),
  - — important explanatory evidence (s 101(1)(c)),
  - — evidence that is relevant to an important matter in issue between the defendant and the prosecution (s 101(1)(d)),
  - — evidence that has substantial probative value in relation to an important matter in issue between the defendant and a co-defendant (s 101(1)(e)),
  - — evidence to correct a false impression given by the defendant (s 101(1)(f)),
  - — defendant has made an attack on another person's character (s 101(1)(g));
- the discretion which the court has to exclude evidence of the defendant's bad character that would otherwise be admissible under gateways (d) and (g) (s 101(3));
- the significance of the guidelines in *R v Hanson, Gilmore & Pickstone*;
- the circumstances in which the bad character of a person other than the defendant may become admissible in evidence at trial (s 100(1)(a)–(c));
- the procedure to be followed if a party wishes to rely upon bad character evidence at trial, or to challenge bad character evidence upon which another party seeks to rely (CrimPR, Part 35);
- how the good character of the defendant may be established at trial, and the evidential significance of the defendant being of good character.

## 22.11 Key forms

### 22.11.1 Introduction

Three forms are set out below:

(a) notice of intention to adduce evidence of the defendant's bad character (see **22.11.2**);

(b) application to exclude evidence of the defendant's bad character (see **22.11.3**); and

(c) application for leave to adduce non-defendant's bad character (see **22.11.4**).

### 22.11.2 Notice of intention to adduce evidence of the defendant's bad character

| **Notice of intention to adduce bad character evidence under s 101 Criminal Justice Act 2003** (Criminal Procedure Rules, IT 35.4(1), 68.21) | |
|---|---|
| *Details Required* | *Notes* |
| **1. Details of applicant**<br><br>Name: *Crown Prosecution Service*<br>Address: *East Chambers, Saville Street, Chester*<br>Name of prosecuting agency (if relevant) | |
| **2. Case details**<br><br>Case reference numbers: *CH 060248*<br>Date of trial or proceedings is due to start/or started: *PCMH – 16/04/08*<br>Name of defendant(s): *Gary Paul Dickson*<br>Charges:<br>*Assault occasioning actual bodily harm on Vincent Lamb on 18th December 2007* | *Give brief details of those charges to which this application applies.* |
| **3. Details of this Notice**<br><br>To the named defendant:<br>You are hereby given notice that bad character evidence, particulars of which are detailed below, is to be adduced or elicited in these proceedings.<br>The particulars of that bad character evidence are as follows:<br>*(a) Evidence of the accused's record of previous convictions (record attached). The officer in charge of the case, PC 911 Chambers, will be called to give this evidence.*<br>*(b) Grounds:*<br>*s 101(1)(d) CJA 2003 – relevant to an important matter in issue between the prosecution and defence as to propensity to commit offences of the type charged [convictions for common assault on 29/11/01, threatening behaviour on 10/09/05 and 17/03/06, and conviction for ABH on 13/12/06] and to truthfulness [conviction for theft on 18/05/03]*<br>*s 101(1)(g) CJA 2003 – defendant made an attack on another person's character when interviewed at the police station [interview record attached]. All convictions on attached list are relevant.* | *In this section include:*<br>*(a) a description of the bad character evidence and how it is to be adduced or elicited in the proceedings (including the names of any relevant witnesses); and*<br>*(b) the grounds for the admission of evidence of the defendant's bad character under section 101 of the Criminal Justice Act 2003.*<br>*Please attach any relevant documentation.* |
| **4. Extension of time**<br><br>Are you applying for an extension of time for service? (yes/no) NO<br><br>If yes, state your reasons. | |
| Signed: *J. Boothroyd*<br><br>Dated: *2nd March 2008* | |

[Note: Formerly set out in the Schedule to the Magistrates' Courts (Amendment) Rules 2004 (SI 2004/2993) relating to rule 72A of the Magistrates' Court Rules 1981 and form BC2 of the Crown Court (Amendment No 3) Rules 2004 (SI 2004/2991) relating to rule 23D of the Crown Court Rules 1982 and form 22 of the Criminal Appeal (Amendment No 2) Rules 2004 (SI 2004/2992) relating to rule 9D of the Criminal Appeal Rules 1968.]

### 22.11.3 Application to exclude evidence of the defendant's bad character

| **Application to exclude evidence of the defendant's bad character under ss 101, 108(2) Criminal Justice Act 2003**<br>*(Criminal Procedure Rules, IT 35.6, 68.21)* | |
|---|---|
| *Details Required* | *Notes* |
| **1. Details of applicant**<br><br>Name: *Gary Paul Dickson*<br>Address: *17 Marsh Street, Chester CH3 7LW*<br>Date of Birth: *28/10/80*<br><br>If you are in custody, please give your Prison Index No and address where detained: | |
| **2. Case details**<br><br>Case reference numbers: *CH 060248*<br>Date of trial or proceedings is due to start/or started: *PCMH – 16/04/08*<br>Charges:<br>*Assault occasioning actual bodily harm on Vincent Lamb on 18th December 2007*<br>Date that you were served with the notice of the intention to adduce bad character evidence in these proceedings: *9th March 2008* | |
| **3. Details of this Notice**<br><br>This section must include the following information:<br><br>(a) why the admission of the bad character evidence would have such an adverse effect on the fairness of the proceedings that the court should not admit it.<br><br>*Convictions for common assault on 29/11/01, threatening behaviour on 10/09/05 and 17/03/06, and ABH on 13/12/06 do not demonstrate a propensity to commit offences of the kind charged since the factual circumstances of these offences are different to the facts of the current offence – it would therefore be more prejudicial to the defendant than probative of the defendant's guilt for the jury to learn about these convictions*<br><br>*Also conviction for common assault on 29/11/01 occurred too long ago to be relevant to demonstrate propensity.*<br><br>*Conviction for theft on 18/05/03 not relevant to issue of truthfulness since not committed in a way that would reflect on propensity to be untruthful [R v Hanson] and defendant pleaded guilty to charge. Evidential value of the conviction would be more prejudicial than probative of the defendant's guilt.*<br><br>*Admissibility of interview record will be challenged at trial. Alternatively attack on character of prosecution witness made only as result of officer's style of questioning and it would therefore be unfair to admit evidence of the defendant's previous convictions in such circumstances.* | *Note that an application to exclude this evidence under section 101(3) of the Criminal Justice Act 2003 can only be made if you have been notified of a party's intentions to adduce this evidence under subsection 101(1)(d) (it is relevant to an important matter in issue between the defendant and the prosecution) or subsection 101(1)(g) (that the defendant has made an attack on another person's character)*<br><br>*Section 101(4) of the 2003 Act.* |

| | |
|---|---|
| (b) details as to the length of time between the matters to which the bad character evidence relates and the matters which form the subject of the offence charged.<br><br>*Conviction for common assault on 29/11/01 is too long ago to be of any evidential value – over 6 years prior to date of alleged offence (18/12/07).*<br><br>(c) if you are applying for the exclusion of this evidence on grounds other than section 101(3) of CJA 2003, please set out such objections.<br><br>*Section 103(3) – by reason of the length of time which has elapsed since the conviction for common assault on 29/11/01, it would be unjust for it to apply in this case.*<br><br>*Section 101(d) – test for admissibility of previous convictions in s 101(d) is not satisfied as previous offences of violence occurred in different factual circumstances to the current offence and therefore do not show the relevant propensity.* | |
| **4. Extension of time**<br><br>Are you applying for an extension of time for service? (yes/no) NO<br><br>If yes, state your reasons. | |
| Signed: *G Dickson*<br><br>Dated: *12th March 2008* | |

### 22.11.4 Application for leave to adduce non-defendant's bad character

**EVIDENCE OF BAD CHARACTER**
(CRIMINAL PROCEDURE RULES, PART 35)

| **Application for leave to adduce non-defendant's bad character under s 100 Criminal Justice Act 2003** (Criminal Procedure Rules, IT 35.2, 68.21) | |
|---|---|
| *Details Required* | *Notes* |
| **1. Details of applicant**<br><br>Name: *Gary Paul Dickson*<br>Address: *17 Marsh Street, Chester CH3 7LW*<br>Name of prosecuting agency (if relevant) | |
| **2. Case details**<br><br>Case reference numbers: *CH 060248*<br>Date of trial or proceedings is due to start/or started: *PCMH – 16/04/08*<br>Name of defendant(s): *Gary Paul Dickson*<br>Charges:<br>*Assault occasioning actual bodily harm on Vincent Lamb on 18th December 2007* | *Give brief details of those charges to which this application applies.* |
| **3. Details of this application**<br><br>Please provide the following details<br>(a) the particulars of the bad character evidence including how it is to be adduced or elicited in the proceedings (including the name of the relevant non-defendant and all other relevant witnesses)<br><br>*Previous convictions of the complainant Vincent Lamb for perjury on 10/05/05 and common assault on 21/09/06 (latter conviction was following a trial at which the complainant had entered a not guilty plea)*<br><br>(b) the grounds for the admission of evidence of a non-defendant's bad character under section 100 of CJA 2003.<br><br>*Section 100(1)(b) – convictions have substantial probative value in relation to a matter in issue in the proceedings. The matter in issue is whether the defendant threatened the complainant in Connolley's Nightclub on the evening of 17/12/07. The defendant alleges that he did not threaten the complainant. The previous convictions of the complainant are relevant to show that the complainant has a propensity to be untruthful.* | *s 100 Criminal Justice Act 2003*<br><br>*Please attach any relevant documentation.* |
| **4. Extension of time**<br><br>Are you applying for an extension of time for service? (yes/no) NO<br><br>If so provide details. | |
| Signed: *Gary Paul Dickson*<br><br>Dated: *8th March 2008* | |

# Part 6 Summary – Evidence

| *Topic* | *Summary* | *References* |
|---|---|---|
| Burdens and standard of proof | The prosecution bear the legal burden of proving beyond a reasonable doubt that the defendant is guilty of the offence with which he is charged. When presenting their evidence, the prosecution also have the evidential burden of showing that the defendant has a case to answer. A defendant who raises a specific defence must place some evidence of this before the court. The prosecution must then disprove the defence in order to prove the defendant's guilt. | |
| Forms of evidence | Evidence must be relevant and admissible. Evidence may come from witnesses (either witnesses as to fact or experts), from documents, or may be in the form of real evidence. Expert witnesses may give opinion evidence. Witnesses as to fact are generally not permitted to give opinion evidence. | |
| Witnesses – competence and compellability | A defendant is competent to give evidence on his own behalf but cannot be compelled to do so. A defendant will usually give evidence in his defence to prevent the drawing of adverse inferences under CJPOA 1994, s 35. A defendant is not competent to be a prosecution witness. Co-defendants tried together are not competent to be called as prosecution witnesses against each other. A defendant's spouse is competent to be a prosecution witness but cannot be compelled to give evidence for the prosecution. | CJPOA 1994, s 35 |
| Disputed visual identification evidence | A witness identifies a defendant if he picks him out informally, identifies him at a formal identification procedure or claims to recognise the defendant as someone previously known to him. The admissibility of this evidence may be disputed by the defendant if the evidence has been obtained improperly. The court may exclude improperly obtained identification evidence under PACE 1984, s 78. If the evidence is admissible, the credibility of the *original* sighting by the witness may be undermined in cross-examination of the witness at trial. The judge will assess the quality of the identification evidence using the '*Turnbull* guidelines' and, in appropriate cases, will give a '*Turnbull* warning' to the jury. | PACE 1984, s 78 |

| *Topic* | *Summary* | *References* |
|---|---|---|
| Inferences from silence | The court may draw an adverse inference from the defendant's silence when questioned at the police station if, at trial, the defendant raises facts in his defence which it would have been reasonable for him to mention at the police station. | CJPOA 1994, s 34 |
| | The court may draw an adverse inference if, when questioned at the police station, the defendant failed to account for the presence of an object, substance or mark. | s 36 |
| | The court may draw an adverse inference if, when questioned at the police station, the defendant failed to account for having been arrested at the scene of the offence at or about the time of the offence. | s 37 |
| Hearsay evidence | A hearsay statement is 'a statement, not made in oral evidence that is relied on as evidence of a matter in it'. | CJA 2003, s 121(2) |
| | Hearsay evidence is admissible in criminal proceedings only if: | |
| | it is made admissible by statute; | s 114(1)(a) |
| | it is a preserved common law exception; | s 114(1)(b) |
| | the parties agree; or | s 114(1)(c) |
| | it is admissible in the interests of justice. | s 114(1)(d) |
| | In some situations the party seeking to adduce hearsay evidence at trial must give notice of this. This notice may be opposed. | CrimPR, Part 34 |
| | The court has a general discretion to exclude hearsay evidence at trial. | CJA 2003, s 126(1) |
| Confessions | A confession is 'any statement wholly or partly adverse to the person who made it ...'. | PACE 1984, s 82(1) |
| | Evidence of a confession made by a defendant is admissible at trial to prove the truth of the confession. | s 76(1) |
| | A defendant may challenge the admissibility of disputed confession evidence by arguing that the confession was obtained by oppression, or that the confession is unreliable. | s 76(2)(a) or s 76(2)(b) |
| | The defendant may also challenge the admissibility of disputed confession evidence by asking the court to exercise its discretion to exclude the evidence if it has been obtained unfairly. | s 78 |

| *Topic* | *Summary* | *References* |
|---|---|---|
| Unfairly obtained evidence | The court has an overriding discretion to exclude prosecution evidence if it considers that 'the admission of the evidence would have such an adverse effect on the fairness of the proceedings that the court ought not to admit it'.<br>Applications under s 78 usually involve allegations that the police have breached PACE and the Codes of Practice. The defendant will need to show a significant and substantial breach, and there must be a causal link between the breach and the evidence that was obtained as a result of it. | PACE 1984, s 78 |
| Character evidence | Bad character is defined as 'evidence of, or a disposition towards, misconduct on [a person's] part'. | CJA 2003, s 98 |
| | 'Misconduct' is 'the commission of an offence or other reprehensible behaviour'. | s 112 |
| | A defendant's bad character will be admissible at trial if comes within any of the seven gateways created by CJA 2003. | s 101(1)(a)–(g) |
| | The court has a discretion to exclude evidence of the defendant's bad character which would otherwise be admissible through gateways (d) and (g) if admitting the evidence 'would have such an adverse effect on the fairness of the proceedings that the court ought not to admit it'. | s 101(3) |
| | Evidence of the bad character of any other person is admissible only on limited grounds. | s 100(1)(a)–(c) |
| | A party seeking to adduce bad character evidence at trial must give notice of this. Such notice may be opposed. | CrimPR, Part 35 |

# Appendix
# Magistrates' Court Sentencing Guidelines

| Assault – actual bodily harm | Offences Against the Person Act 1861 s.47<br>Triable either way – see Mode of Trial Guidelines<br>Penalty: Level 5 and/or 6 months |
|---|---|

## CONSIDER THE SERIOUSNESS OF THE OFFENCE
*(INCLUDING THE IMPACT ON THE VICTIM)*

*IS DISCHARGE OR FINE APPROPRIATE?*

*IS IT SERIOUS ENOUGH FOR A COMMUNITY PENALTY?*

***GUIDELINE: → IS IT SO SERIOUS THAT ONLY CUSTODY IS APPROPRIATE?***

*ARE YOUR SENTENCING POWERS SUFFICIENT?*

*THIS IS A GUIDELINE FOR A FIRST-TIME OFFENDER PLEADING NOT GUILTY*

## CONSIDER AGGRAVATING AND MITIGATING FACTORS AND THE WEIGHT TO ATTACH TO EACH

| + | − |
|---|---|
| **for example**<br>Abuse of trust (domestic setting)<br>Deliberate kicking or biting<br>Extensive injuries (may be psychological)<br>Headbutting<br>Group action<br>Offender in position of authority<br>On hospital/medical or school premises<br>Premeditated<br>Victim particularly vulnerable<br>Victim serving the public<br>Weapon<br>*This list is not exhaustive* | **for example**<br>Minor injury<br>Provocation<br>Single blow<br>*This list is not exhaustive* |

***If offender is on bail, this offence is more serious***

***If offender has previous convictions, their relevance and any failure to respond to previous sentences should be considered – they may increase the seriousness. The court should make it clear, when passing sentence, that this was the approach adopted.***

## TAKE A PRELIMINARY VIEW OF SERIOUSNESS, THEN CONSIDER OFFENDER MITIGATION

**for example**
- Age, health (physical or mental)
- Co-operation with police
- Evidence of genuine remorse
- Voluntary compensation

## CONSIDER YOUR SENTENCE

***Compare it with the suggested guideline level of sentence and reconsider your reasons carefully if you have chosen a sentence at a different level. Consider a reduction for a timely guilty plea.***

## DECIDE YOUR SENTENCE
***NB. COMPENSATION – Give reasons if not awarding compensation***

| **Burglary (dwelling)** | **Theft Act 1968 s.9**<br>**Triable either way – see Mode of Trial Guidelines**<br>**Penalty: Level 5 and/or 6 months** |
|---|---|

## CONSIDER THE SERIOUSNESS OF THE OFFENCE
***(INCLUDING THE IMPACT ON THE VICTIM)***

*IS DISCHARGE OR FINE APPROPRIATE?*
*IS IT SERIOUS ENOUGH FOR A COMMUNITY PENALTY?*
*IS IT SO SERIOUS THAT ONLY CUSTODY IS APPROPRIATE?*
***GUIDELINE: →*** ***ARE YOUR SENTENCING POWERS SUFFICIENT?***

*THIS IS A GUIDELINE FOR A FIRST-TIME OFFENDER PLEADING NOT GUILTY*

## ⊕ CONSIDER AGGRAVATING AND MITIGATING FACTORS AND THE WEIGHT TO ATTACH TO EACH ⊖

| + | − |
|---|---|
| **for example**<br>Force used or threatened<br>Group enterprise<br>High value (in economic or sentimental terms) property stolen<br>More than minor trauma caused<br>Professional planning/organisation/ execution<br>Significant damage or vandalism<br>Victim injured<br>Victim present at the time<br>Vulnerable victim<br>*IF ANY of the above factors are present you should commit for sentence.* | **for example**<br>First offence of its type AND low value property stolen AND no significant damage or disturbance AND no injury or violence<br>Minor part played<br>Theft from attached garage<br>Vacant property<br>*ONLY if one or more of the above factors are present AND none of the aggravating factors listed are present should you consider NOT committing for sentence.* |

***If racially or religiously aggravated, or offender is on bail, this offence is more serious***
***If offender has previous convictions, their relevance and any failure to respond to previous sentences should be considered – they may increase the seriousness. The court should make it clear, when passing sentence, that this was the approach adopted.***

## TAKE A PRELIMINARY VIEW OF SERIOUSNESS, THEN CONSIDER WHETHER THE CASE SHOULD BE COMMITTED FOR SENTENCE, THEN CONSIDER OFFENDER MITIGATION

**for example**
- Age, health (physical or mental)
- Co-operation with police
- Evidence of genuine remorse
- Voluntary compensation

## CONSIDER COMMITTAL OR YOUR SENTENCE

***Compare it with the suggested guideline level of sentence and reconsider your reasons carefully if you have chosen a sentence at a different level. Consider a reduction for a timely guilty plea.***

## DECIDE YOUR SENTENCE
***NB. COMPENSATION – Give reasons if not awarding compensation***

Theft Act 1968 s.9
Triable either way – see Mode of Trial Guidelines
Penalty: Level 5 and/or 6 months

## Burglary (non-dwelling)

## CONSIDER THE SERIOUSNESS OF THE OFFENCE
***(INCLUDING THE IMPACT ON THE VICTIM)***

*IS DISCHARGE OR FINE APPROPRIATE?*
***GUIDELINE: → IS IT SERIOUS ENOUGH FOR A COMMUNITY PENALTY?***
*IS IT SO SERIOUS THAT ONLY CUSTODY IS APPROPRIATE?*
*ARE YOUR SENTENCING POWERS SUFFICIENT?*

*THIS IS A GUIDELINE FOR A FIRST-TIME OFFENDER PLEADING NOT GUILTY*

## + CONSIDER AGGRAVATING AND MITIGATING FACTORS AND THE WEIGHT TO ATTACH TO EACH −

| + | − |
|---|---|
| **for example** | **for example** |
| Forcible entry | Low value |
| Group offence | Nobody frightened |
| Harm to business | No damage or disturbance |
| Occupants frightened | *This list is not exhaustive* |
| Professional operation | |
| Repeat victimisation | |
| School or medical premises | |
| Soiling, ransacking, damage | |
| *This list is not exhaustive* | |

***If racially or religiously aggravated, or offender is on bail, this offence is more serious***
***If offender has previous convictions, their relevance and any failure to respond to previous sentences should be considered – they may increase the seriousness. The court should make it clear, when passing sentence, that this was the approach adopted.***

## TAKE A PRELIMINARY VIEW OF SERIOUSNESS, THEN CONSIDER OFFENDER MITIGATION

**for example**
- Age, health (physical or mental)
- Co-operation with police
- Evidence of genuine remorse
- Voluntary compensation

## CONSIDER YOUR SENTENCE

***Compare it with the suggested guideline level of sentence and reconsider your reasons carefully if you have chosen a sentence at a different level. Consider a reduction for a timely guilty plea.***

## DECIDE YOUR SENTENCE
***NB. COMPENSATION – Give reasons if not awarding compensation***

| Common assault | Criminal Justice Act 1988 s.39<br>Triable only summarily<br>Penalty: Level 5 and/or 6 months |
|---|---|

**CONSIDER THE SERIOUSNESS OF THE OFFENCE**
***(INCLUDING THE IMPACT ON THE VICTIM)***

*IS DISCHARGE OR FINE APPROPRIATE?*
***GUIDELINE: → IS IT SERIOUS ENOUGH FOR A COMMUNITY PENALTY?***
*IS IT SO SERIOUS THAT ONLY CUSTODY IS APPROPRIATE?*

*THIS IS A GUIDELINE FOR A FIRST-TIME OFFENDER PLEADING NOT GUILTY*

**+ CONSIDER AGGRAVATING AND MITIGATING FACTORS AND THE WEIGHT TO ATTACH TO EACH −**

| for example | for example |
|---|---|
| Abuse of trust (domestic setting)<br>Group action<br>Injury<br>Offender in position of authority<br>On hospital/medical or school premises<br>Premeditated<br>Spitting<br>Victim particularly vulnerable<br>Victim serving the public<br>Weapon<br>*This list is not exhaustive* | Impulsive<br>Minor injury<br>Provocation<br>Single blow<br>*This list is not exhaustive* |

***If offender is on bail, this offence is more serious***
***If offender has previous convictions, their relevance and any failure to respond to previous sentences should be considered – they may increase the seriousness. The court should make it clear, when passing sentence, that this was the approach adopted.***

**TAKE A PRELIMINARY VIEW OF SERIOUSNESS, THEN CONSIDER OFFENDER MITIGATION**

**for example**
Age, health (physical or mental)
Co-operation with police
Evidence of genuine remorse
Voluntary compensation

**CONSIDER YOUR SENTENCE**

***Compare it with the suggested guideline level of sentence and reconsider your reasons carefully if you have chosen a sentence at a different level. Consider a reduction for a timely guilty plea.***

**DECIDE YOUR SENTENCE**
***NB. COMPENSATION – Give reasons if not awarding compensation***

| | |
|---|---|
| **Bail Act 1976 s.6**<br>**Triable only summarily**<br>**Penalty: Level 5 and/or 3 months** | **Failure to surrender to bail** |

## CONSIDER THE SERIOUSNESS OF THE OFFENCE

*IS DISCHARGE OR FINE APPROPRIATE?*

***GUIDELINE: → IS IT SERIOUS ENOUGH FOR A COMMUNITY PENALTY?***

*IS IT SO SERIOUS THAT ONLY CUSTODY IS APPROPRIATE?*

*THIS IS A GUIDELINE FOR A FIRST-TIME OFFENDER PLEADING NOT GUILTY*

## CONSIDER AGGRAVATING AND MITIGATING FACTORS AND THE WEIGHT TO ATTACH TO EACH

| + | − |
|---|---|
| **for example**<br>Leaves jurisdiction<br>Long term evasion<br>Results in ineffective trial date<br>Wilful evasion<br>*This list is not exhaustive* | **for example**<br>Appears late on day of hearing<br>Genuine misunderstanding<br>Voluntary surrender<br>*This list is not exhaustive* |

***A curfew order may be particularly suitable***

***Previous convictions for this offence increase the seriousness – consider custody***

## TAKE A PRELIMINARY VIEW OF SERIOUSNESS, THEN CONSIDER OFFENDER MITIGATION

**for example**

Age, health (physical or mental)
Co-operation with police
Evidence of genuine remorse

## CONSIDER YOUR SENTENCE

***Compare it with the suggested guideline level of sentence and reconsider your reasons carefully if you have chosen a sentence at a different level.***

***Consider a reduction for a timely guilty plea.***

## DECIDE YOUR SENTENCE

| Handling stolen goods | Theft Act 1968 s.22<br>Triable either way – see Mode of Trial Guidelines<br>**Penalty: Level 5 and/or 6 months** |
|---|---|

## CONSIDER THE SERIOUSNESS OF THE OFFENCE
***(INCLUDING THE IMPACT ON THE VICTIM)***

*IS DISCHARGE OR FINE APPROPRIATE?*

***GUIDELINE: → IS IT SERIOUS ENOUGH FOR A COMMUNITY PENALTY?***

*IS IT SO SERIOUS THAT ONLY CUSTODY IS APPROPRIATE?*

*ARE YOUR SENTENCING POWERS SUFFICIENT?*

*THIS IS A GUIDELINE FOR A FIRST-TIME OFFENDER PLEADING NOT GUILTY*

## ⊕ CONSIDER AGGRAVATING AND MITIGATING FACTORS AND THE WEIGHT TO ATTACH TO EACH ⊖

| + | − |
|---|---|
| **for example**<br>High level of profit accruing to handler<br>High value (including sentimental) of goods<br>Provision by handler of regular outlet for stolen goods<br>Proximity of the handler to the primary offence<br>Seriousness of the primary offence<br>Sophistication<br>The particular facts, eg the goods handled were the proceeds of a domestic burglary<br>Threats of violence or abuse of power by handler in order to obtain goods<br>*This list is not exhaustive* | **for example**<br>Isolated offence<br>Little or no benefit accruing to handler<br>Low monetary value of goods<br>*This list is not exhaustive* |

***If offender is on bail, this offence is more serious***

***If offender has previous convictions, their relevance and any failure to respond to previous sentences should be considered – they may increase the seriousness. The court should make it clear, when passing sentence, that this was the approach adopted.***

## TAKE A PRELIMINARY VIEW OF SERIOUSNESS, THEN CONSIDER OFFENDER MITIGATION

**for example**
- Age, health (physical or mental)
- Co-operation with police
- Evidence of genuine remorse
- Voluntary compensation

## CONSIDER YOUR SENTENCE

***Compare it with the suggested guideline level of sentence and reconsider your reasons carefully if you have chosen a sentence at a different level. Consider a reduction for a timely guilty plea.***

## DECIDE YOUR SENTENCE

***NB. COMPENSATION – Give reasons if not awarding compensation***

Theft Act 1968 s.15
Triable either way – see Mode of Trial Guidelines
Penalty: Level 5 and/or 6 months

# Obtaining by deception

## CONSIDER THE SERIOUSNESS OF THE OFFENCE
*(INCLUDING THE IMPACT ON THE VICTIM)*

*IS DISCHARGE OR FINE APPROPRIATE?*
***GUIDELINE: → IS IT SERIOUS ENOUGH FOR A COMMUNITY PENALTY?***
*IS IT SO SERIOUS THAT ONLY CUSTODY IS APPROPRIATE?*
*ARE YOUR SENTENCING POWERS SUFFICIENT?*

*THIS IS A GUIDELINE FOR A FIRST-TIME OFFENDER PLEADING NOT GUILTY*

## + CONSIDER AGGRAVATING AND MITIGATING FACTORS AND THE WEIGHT TO ATTACH TO EACH −

**for example** (+)
- Committed over lengthy period
- Large sums or valuable goods
- Two or more involved
- Use of stolen credit/debit card, cheque books, or giros
- Victim particularly vulnerable

*This list is not exhaustive*

**for example** (−)
- Impulsive action
- Short period
- Small sum

*This list is not exhaustive*

***If offender is on bail, this offence is more serious***
***If offender has previous convictions, their relevance and any failure to respond to previous sentences should be considered – they may increase the seriousness. The court should make it clear, when passing sentence, that this was the approach adopted.***

## TAKE A PRELIMINARY VIEW OF SERIOUSNESS, THEN CONSIDER OFFENDER MITIGATION

**for example**
- Age, health (physical or mental)
- Co-operation with police
- Evidence of genuine remorse
- Voluntary compensation

## CONSIDER YOUR SENTENCE

***Compare it with the suggested guideline level of sentence and reconsider your reasons carefully if you have chosen a sentence at a different level. Consider a reduction for a timely guilty plea.***

## DECIDE YOUR SENTENCE
***NB. COMPENSATION – Give reasons if not awarding compensation***

| Theft | Theft Act 1968 s.1<br>Triable either way – see Mode of Trial Guidelines<br>Penalty: Level 5 and/or 6 months<br>May disqualify where committed with reference to the theft or taking of a vehicle |
|---|---|

## CONSIDER THE SERIOUSNESS OF THE OFFENCE
***(INCLUDING THE IMPACT ON THE VICTIM)***

*IS DISCHARGE OR FINE APPROPRIATE?*

***GUIDELINE: → IS IT SERIOUS ENOUGH FOR A COMMUNITY PENALTY?***

*IS IT SO SERIOUS THAT ONLY CUSTODY IS APPROPRIATE?*

*ARE YOUR SENTENCING POWERS SUFFICIENT?*

*THIS IS A GUIDELINE FOR A FIRST-TIME OFFENDER PLEADING NOT GUILTY*

## ⊕ CONSIDER AGGRAVATING AND MITIGATING FACTORS AND THE WEIGHT TO ATTACH TO EACH ⊖

| for example | for example |
|---|---|
| High value<br>Planned<br>Sophisticated<br>Adult involving children<br>Organised team<br>Related damage<br>Vulnerable victim<br>*This list is not exhaustive* | Impulsive action<br>Low value<br>*This list is not exhaustive* |

***If racially or religiously aggravated, or offender is on bail, this offence is more serious***

***If offender has previous convictions, their relevance and any failure to respond to previous sentences should be considered – they may increase the seriousness. The court should make it clear, when passing sentence, that this was the approach adopted.***

## TAKE A PRELIMINARY VIEW OF SERIOUSNESS, THEN CONSIDER OFFENDER MITIGATION

**for example**

- Age, health (physical or mental)
- Co-operation with police
- Evidence of genuine remorse
- Voluntary compensation

## CONSIDER YOUR SENTENCE

***Compare it with the suggested guideline level of sentence and reconsider your reasons carefully if you have chosen a sentence at a different level. Consider a reduction for a timely guilty plea.***

## DECIDE YOUR SENTENCE
***NB. COMPENSATION – Give reasons if not awarding compensation***

| Theft Act 1968 s.1<br>Triable either way – see Mode of Trial Guidelines<br>Penalty: Level 5 and/or 6 months | **Theft in breach of trust** |
|---|---|

## CONSIDER THE SERIOUSNESS OF THE OFFENCE
### *(INCLUDING THE IMPACT ON THE VICTIM)*

*IS DISCHARGE OR FINE APPROPRIATE?*

*IS IT SERIOUS ENOUGH FOR A COMMUNITY PENALTY?*

**GUIDELINE: → *IS IT SO SERIOUS THAT ONLY CUSTODY IS APPROPRIATE?***

*ARE YOUR SENTENCING POWERS SUFFICIENT?*

*THIS IS A GUIDELINE FOR A FIRST-TIME OFFENDER PLEADING NOT GUILTY*

## CONSIDER AGGRAVATING AND MITIGATING FACTORS AND THE WEIGHT TO ATTACH TO EACH

| + | − |
|---|---|
| **for example**<br>Casting suspicion on others<br>Committed over a period<br>High value<br>Organised team<br>Planned<br>Senior employee<br>Sophisticated<br>Vulnerable victim<br>*This list is not exhaustive* | **for example**<br>Impulsive action<br>Low value<br>Previous inconsistent attitude by employer<br>Single item<br>Unsupported junior<br>*This list is not exhaustive* |

***If racially or religiously aggravated, or offender is on bail, this offence is more serious***

***If offender has previous convictions, their relevance and any failure to respond to previous sentences should be considered – they may increase the seriousness. The court should make it clear, when passing sentence, that this was the approach adopted.***

## TAKE A PRELIMINARY VIEW OF SERIOUSNESS, THEN CONSIDER OFFENDER MITIGATION

**for example**
- Age, health (physical or mental)
- Co-operation with police
- Evidence of genuine remorse
- Voluntary compensation

## CONSIDER YOUR SENTENCE

***Compare it with the suggested guideline level of sentence and reconsider your reasons carefully if you have chosen a sentence at a different level. Consider a reduction for a timely guilty plea.***

## DECIDE YOUR SENTENCE

***NB. COMPENSATION – Give reasons if not awarding compensation***



*Issued October 2003 for implementation 1 January 2004*

## Wounding – grievous bodily harm

**Offences Against the Person Act 1861 s.20**
**Triable either way – see Mode of Trial Guidelines**
**Penalty: Level 5 and/or 6 months**

### CONSIDER THE SERIOUSNESS OF THE OFFENCE
***(INCLUDING THE IMPACT ON THE VICTIM)***

***IS DISCHARGE OR FINE APPROPRIATE?***
***IS IT SERIOUS ENOUGH FOR A COMMUNITY PENALTY?***
***IS IT SO SERIOUS THAT ONLY CUSTODY IS APPROPRIATE?***
***GUIDELINE: → ARE YOUR SENTENCING POWERS SUFFICIENT?***

***THIS IS A GUIDELINE FOR A FIRST-TIME OFFENDER PLEADING NOT GUILTY***

### CONSIDER AGGRAVATING AND MITIGATING FACTORS AND THE WEIGHT TO ATTACH TO EACH

| + | − |
| --- | --- |
| **for example**<br>Abuse of trust (domestic setting)<br>Deliberate kicking/biting<br>Extensive injuries<br>Group action<br>Offender in position of authority<br>On hospital/medical or school premises<br>Premeditated<br>Prolonged assault<br>Victim particularly vulnerable<br>Victim serving the public<br>Weapon<br>*This list is not exhaustive* | **for example**<br>Minor wound<br>Provocation<br>*This list is not exhaustive* |

***If offender is on bail, this offence is more serious***
***If offender has previous convictions, their relevance and any failure to respond to previous sentences should be considered – they may increase the seriousness. The court should make it clear, when passing sentence, that this was the approach adopted.***

### TAKE A PRELIMINARY VIEW OF SERIOUSNESS, THEN CONSIDER WHETHER THE CASE SHOULD BE COMMITTED FOR SENTENCE, THEN CONSIDER OFFENDER MITIGATION

**for example**
- Age, health (physical or mental)
- Co-operation with police
- Evidence of genuine remorse
- Voluntary compensation

### CONSIDER COMMITTAL OR YOUR SENTENCE

***Compare it with the suggested guideline level of sentence and reconsider your reasons carefully if you have chosen a sentence at a different level. Consider a reduction for a timely guilty plea.***

### DECIDE YOUR SENTENCE
***NB. COMPENSATION – Give reasons if not awarding compensation***

| Road Traffic Act 1988 s.3<br>Triable only summarily<br>Penalty: Level 4<br>Must endorse (3-9 points OR may disqualify) | **Careless driving** |
|---|---|

## CONSIDER THE SERIOUSNESS OF THE OFFENCE

***GUIDELINE: →*** ***IS DISCHARGE OR FINE APPROPRIATE?***

***IS IT SERIOUS ENOUGH FOR A COMMUNITY PENALTY?***

***(COMMUNITY REHABILITATION AND CURFEW ORDERS ARE THE ONLY AVAILABLE COMMUNITY PENALTIES FOR THIS OFFENCE)***

*THIS IS A GUIDELINE FOR A FIRST-TIME OFFENDER PLEADING NOT GUILTY*

## *GUIDELINE FINE – STARTING POINT B*

## CONSIDER AGGRAVATING AND MITIGATING FACTORS AND THE WEIGHT TO ATTACH TO EACH

| + | − |
|---|---|
| **for example**<br>Excessive speed<br>High degree of carelessness<br>Serious risk<br>Using a hand-held mobile telephone<br>*This list is not exhaustive* | **for example**<br>Minor risk<br>Momentary lapse<br>Negligible/parking damage<br>Sudden change in weather conditions<br>*This list is not exhaustive* |

***Death, serious injury or damage is capable of being aggravation***

***If offender is on bail, this offence is more serious***

***If offender has previous convictions, their relevance and any failure to respond to previous sentences should be considered – they may increase the seriousness. The court should make it clear, when passing sentence, that this was the approach adopted.***

## TAKE A PRELIMINARY VIEW OF SERIOUSNESS, THEN CONSIDER OFFENDER MITIGATION

**for example**

Co-operation with police
Evidence of genuine remorse
Voluntary compensation

## CONSIDER YOUR SENTENCE

***Endorse (3-9 points OR period of disqualification)***

***Consider other measures (including disqualification until test passed if appropriate – for example, age, infirmity or medical condition)***

***Compare it with the suggested guideline level of sentence and reconsider your reasons carefully if you have chosen a sentence at a different level.***

***Consider a reduction for a timely guilty plea.***

## DECIDE YOUR SENTENCE

  *Issued October 2003 for implementation 1 January 2004*

## Dangerous driving

**Road Traffic Act 1988 s.2**
**Triable either way – see Mode of Trial Guidelines**
**Penalty: Level 5 and/or 6 months**
**Must endorse and disqualify at least 12 months**
**Must endorse (3-11 points) if not disqualified**
**MUST ORDER EXTENDED RE-TEST**

### CONSIDER THE SERIOUSNESS OF THE OFFENCE
***(INCLUDING THE IMPACT ON THE VICTIM)***

*IS DISCHARGE OR FINE APPROPRIATE?*
*IS IT SERIOUS ENOUGH FOR A COMMUNITY PENALTY?*
**GUIDELINE: → *IS IT SO SERIOUS THAT ONLY CUSTODY IS APPROPRIATE?***
*ARE YOUR SENTENCING POWERS SUFFICIENT?*

*THIS IS A GUIDELINE FOR A FIRST-TIME OFFENDER PLEADING NOT GUILTY*

### ⊕ CONSIDER AGGRAVATING AND MITIGATING FACTORS AND THE WEIGHT TO ATTACH TO EACH ⊖

| + | − |
|---|---|
| **for example**<br>Avoiding detection or apprehension<br>Competitive driving, racing, showing off<br>Disregard of warnings, eg from passengers or others in vicinity<br>Evidence of alcohol or drugs<br>Excessive speed<br>Police pursuit<br>Prolonged, persistent, deliberate bad driving<br>Serious risk<br>Using a mobile telephone<br>*This list is not exhaustive* | **for example**<br>Emergency<br>Speed not excessive<br>*This list is not exhaustive* |

***Serious injury or damage is capable of being aggravation***

***If offender is on bail, this offence is more serious***
***If offender has previous convictions, their relevance and any failure to respond to previous sentences should be considered – they may increase the seriousness. The court should make it clear, when passing sentence, that this was the approach adopted.***

### TAKE A PRELIMINARY VIEW OF SERIOUSNESS, THEN CONSIDER OFFENDER MITIGATION

**for example**
- Co-operation with police
- Evidence of genuine remorse
- Voluntary compensation

### CONSIDER YOUR SENTENCE

***Endorse licence and disqualify at least 12 months unless special reasons apply.***
***MUST ORDER EXTENDED RE-TEST.***
***Compare it with the suggested guideline level of sentence and reconsider your reasons carefully if you have chosen a sentence at a different level.***
***Consider a reduction for a timely guilty plea.***

### DECIDE YOUR SENTENCE



*Issued October 2003 for implementation 1 January 2004*

## Excess alcohol (drive or attempt to drive)

**Road Traffic Act 1988 s.5(1)(a)**
**Penalty: Level 5 and/or 6 months**
**Triable only summarily**
**Must endorse and disqualify *at least* 12 months: disqualify at least 36 months for a further offence within 10 years**

### CONSIDER THE SERIOUSNESS OF THE OFFENCE

***THE LEVEL OF SERIOUSNESS AND GUIDELINE SENTENCE ARE RELATED TO THE BREATH/BLOOD/URINE LEVEL***

### CONSIDER AGGRAVATING AND MITIGATING FACTORS AND THE WEIGHT TO ATTACH TO EACH

| + | − |
|---|---|
| **for example**<br>Ability to drive seriously impaired<br>Caused injury/fear/damage<br>Police pursuit<br>Evidence of nature of the driving<br>Type of vehicle, eg carrying passengers for reward/large goods vehicle<br>High reading (and in combination with above)<br>*This list is not exhaustive* | **for example**<br>Emergency<br>Moving a vehicle a very short distance<br>Spiked drinks<br>*This list is not exhaustive* |

***If offender is on bail, this offence is more serious***
***If offender has previous convictions, their relevance and any failure to respond to previous sentences should be considered – they may increase the seriousness. The court should make it clear, when passing sentence, that this was the approach adopted.***

### TAKE A PRELIMINARY VIEW OF SERIOUSNESS, THEN CONSIDER OFFENDER MITIGATION

**for example**
Co-operation with police

### CONSIDER YOUR SENTENCE

***Offer a rehabilitation course.***
***Compare your decision with the suggested guideline level of sentence and reconsider your reasons carefully if you have chosen a sentence at a different level.***
***Consider a reduction for a timely guilty plea.***

### DECIDE YOUR SENTENCE

| BREATH | BLOOD | URINE | DISQUALIFY NOT LESS THAN | GUIDELINE |
|---|---|---|---|---|
| 36-55 | 80-125 | 107-170 | 12 months | B |
| 56-70 | 126-160 | 171-214 | 16 months | C |
| 71-85 | 161-195 | 215-260 | 20 months | C |
| 86-100 | 196-229 | 261-308 | 24 months | CONSIDER COMMUNITY PENALTY |
| 101-115 | 230-264 | 309-354 | 28 months | |
| 116-130 | 265-300 | 355-400 | 32 months | CONSIDER CUSTODY |
| 131+ | 301+ | 401+ | 36 months | |

Road Traffic Act 1984 s.89(10)
Triable only summarily
Penalty: Level 3 (Level 4 if motorway)
Must endorse (3-6 points OR may disqualify)

## Speeding

### CONSIDER THE SERIOUSNESS OF THE OFFENCE

***GUIDELINE: →*** ***IS DISCHARGE OR FINE APPROPRIATE?***

*(COMMUNITY REHABILITATION AND CURFEW ORDERS ARE THE ONLY AVAILABLE COMMUNITY PENALTIES FOR THIS OFFENCE)*

*THIS IS A GUIDELINE FOR A FIRST-TIME OFFENDER PLEADING NOT GUILTY*

### CONSIDER AGGRAVATING AND MITIGATING FACTORS AND THE WEIGHT TO ATTACH TO EACH

| + | − |
|---|---|
| **for example**<br>LGV, HGV, PCV or taxi or private-hire vehicles<br>Location/time of day/visibility<br>Serious risk<br>Towing caravan/trailer<br>*This list is not exhaustive* | **for example**<br>Emergency established<br>*This list is not exhaustive* |

***If offender is on bail, this offence is more serious***

***If offender has previous convictions, their relevance and any failure to respond to previous sentences should be considered – they may increase the seriousness. The court should make it clear, when passing sentence, that this was the approach adopted.***

| GUIDELINE PENALTY POINTS | LEGAL SPEED LIMITS | EXCESS SPEED – MPH | FINE |
|---|---|---|---|
| 3 | 20-30 mph<br>40-50 mph<br>60-70 mph | Up to 10 mph<br>Up to 15 mph<br>Up to 20 mph | A |
| 4 or 5<br>OR<br>disqualify up to 42 days | 20-30 mph<br>40-50 mph<br>60-70 mph | From 11-20 mph<br>From 16-25 mph<br>From 21-30 mph | B |
| 6<br>OR<br>disqualify up to 56 days | 20-30 mph<br>40-50 mph<br>60-70 mph | From 21-30 mph<br>From 26-35 mph<br>From 31-40 mph | B |

### TAKE A PRELIMINARY VIEW OF SERIOUSNESS, THEN CONSIDER OFFENDER MITIGATION

**for example**
- Co-operation with police
- Fixed penalty not taken up for valid reason

### CONSIDER YOUR SENTENCE

***Endorse (3-6 points OR period of disqualification. If a new driver accumulates 6 points this will result in automatic revocation of the licence by the DVLA, see note on page 100.)***
***Consider other measures (including disqualification until test passed if appropriate).***
***Compare it with the suggested guideline level of sentence and reconsider your reasons carefully if you have chosen a sentence at a different level.***
***Consider a reduction for a timely guilty plea.***

### DECIDE YOUR SENTENCE

## Road traffic offences

### *Disqualification*

Some offences carry mandatory disqualification. This mandatory disqualification period may be automatically lengthened by the existence of certain previous convictions and disqualifications.

Sentencers should not disqualify defendants in their absence although there is provision in statute to do so provided that an offender is given adequate notice of the hearing at which the court will consider disqualification. This discretionary power should only be exercised in out of the ordinary circumstances. As with all decisions of this type, account should be taken of human rights legislation. The court must give cogent and explicit reasons for any decision to disqualify in absence.

### *Penalty points and disqualification*

All endorsable offences carry also as an alternative discretionary power to disqualify instead of imposing penalty points.

Dangerous driving carries an obligatory minimum disqualification of one year and a mandatory extended re-test.

For any offence which carries penalty points the courts have a discretion to order a re-test provided there is evidence of inexperience, incompetence or infirmity. It would be an ordinary test except where disqualification is obligatory when an extended test would be required.

The number of variable penalty points or the period of disqualification is targeted strictly at the seriousness of the offence and in either case must not be reduced below the statutory minimum, where applicable.

Offences committed on different occasions may carry points, even where they are dealt with on the same occasion.

### *Disqualification until a test is passed*

A magistrates' court **must** disqualify an offender until he passes an *extended driving test* where he is convicted of an offence of dangerous driving.

The court has a **discretion** to disqualify until a test is passed where the offender has been convicted of an offence involving obligatory disqualification. In this case it is the ordinary driving test that must be undertaken.

An offender disqualified as a 'totter' under the penalty points provisions **may** also be ordered to re-take a driving test, in which case it will be the *extended test.*

The discretion is likely to be exercised where there is evidence of inexperience, incompetence or infirmity; or the disqualification period imposed is lengthy (ie the offender is going to be 'off the road' for a considerable time).

### *Disqualifications for less than 56 days*

A disqualification for less than 56 days is also more lenient in that it does not revoke the licence and cannot increase subsequent mandatory periods even if it is imposed under the points provisions.

***Reduction for guilty plea***

The precise amount of credit for a timely guilty plea will depend on the facts of each case. It should be given in respect of the fine or periods of community sentence or custody. An early guilty plea may also affect the length of a disqualification or the number of penalty points but cannot apply so as to reduce minimum mandatory periods of disqualification.

***The multiple offender***

Where an offender is convicted of several offences committed on one occasion, it is suggested that the court should concentrate on the most serious offence, carrying the greatest number of penalty points or period of disqualification.

The application of the totality principle may then result in the court deciding to impose no separate penalty for the lesser offences, or to reduce fines for these offences below the level which might normally be imposed.

***Totting***

Repeat offenders who reach 12 points or more within a period of three years become liable to a minimum disqualification for 6 months, and in some instances 12 months or 2 years – but must be given an opportunity to address the court and/or bring evidence to show why such disqualification should not be ordered or should be reduced. Totting disqualifications, unlike other disqualifications, erase all penalty points.

Totting disqualifications can be reduced or avoided for exceptional hardship or other circumstances. No account is to be taken of non-exceptional hardship or circumstances alleged to make the offence(s) not serious. No such ground can be used again to mitigate totting, if previously taken into account in totting mitigation within the three years preceding the conviction.

***New drivers***

Newly qualified drivers who incur 6 points or more during a two-year probationary period from the date of passing the driving test will automatically have their licence revoked by the Secretary of State and will have to apply for a provisional licence until they pass a repeat test. This total must include any points imposed prior to passing the test provided they are within three years.

***Fixed penalties***

If a fixed penalty was offered, the court should consider any reasons for not taking it up and, if valid, fine the amount of the appropriate fixed penalty (provided the amount is within the means of the offender), endorse if required, waive costs and allow a maximum of 28 days to pay. If a fixed penalty was refused or not offered, the court should consider whether there are aggravating factors which merit increasing the fine or there should be any credit for a guilty plea.

# Index